The Writer's Handbook

Edited by

SYLVIA K. BURACK

Editor, The Writer

Publishers   THE WRITER, INC.   Boston

CONTENTS

PART I—BACKGROUND FOR WRITERS

CHAPTER

v

THE WRITER'S HANDBOOK

1

THE WRITER'S COMPASS

By William Stafford

WE WRITERS try to help each other, sometimes. But there is a catch in this generosity: if you begin to rely only on what others say about your work, you may become like a compass that listens to the hunches of the pilot. You may be good company, but you are useless as a compass.

So, when we meet, say at a conference or workshop, we look each other in the eye with an estimate hovering between us. We know that our kind of activity has some complexities not evident to others, and we wonder if those complexities will be recognized in any interchanges about our craft.

For instance, we know that our work is insufficiently judged if much time is given over to assessing the topics of our work. We know that a critic who discusses whether we talk enough about Nicaragua or not, or human rights or not, or the general topic of enlightenment or not, is missing the mark.

We know that there is something supremely important in the creating of a story or poem that all too often will escape the attention of an outsider trying to assess it. And for those outsiders, general readers, even critics, it may not be devastating if they talk at large: the main point is that such readers be affected, no matter what they ascribe our influence to. But for us writers it would be fatal to be misled by superficial assessments; and in fact one of the main hazards for a "successful" writer may be the insidious intrusion of those outer assessments on the inner process that allows us writers to find our way.

We must have an inner guide that allows us to rove forward through the most immediate impulses that come our way. For us, our whole lives are our research; and caught up by our best subjects we become not just an expert, but the only expert there is. We have to be the sole authority for what comes toward us, where we are, with our unique angle of seeing.

Though this inner guide is difficult to talk about, it is supremely important; and it is different from that urge for money, publication, recognition, that is glibly identified as the bait for a writer. You can get lost, following the whims of the public. And the public can give you recognition, or withhold it; but afterward you must set forth again, alone.

If the most significant writing comes from this inner guidance, who will help you find it? Would it be someone who interposes the considerations of the marketplace while the delicate time of discovery is going on? Would it be the person who puts primary emphasis on your imitation of forms and strategies?

Let me plead, not for ignoring advice from wherever it comes, but for allowing in your own life the freedom to pay attention to your feelings while finding your way through language. Besides that audience out there in the world, there is some kind of ideal audience that you have accumulated within your individual consciousness—within your conscience!; and abiding guidance is your compass, one that constitutes what you have to contribute to discourse with others.

Moving back and forth from the inner to the outer world might be the way to your best writing.

Into the unknown you must plunge, carrying your compass. It points at something more distant than any local guidance. You must make "mistakes"; that is, you must explore what has not been mapped out for you. Those mistakes come from somewhere; they are disguised reports from a country so real that no one has found it. When you study that country, shivers run down your back—what a wilderness out there! What splendid stories flicker among those shadows! You could wander forever.

Odd words keep occurring to you—pauses, side glances—mysterious signals. What hidden prejudice brought that next word into your mind? If you hastily retreat to an expected progression, what shadowy terrain might you be neglecting? What revelations might you miss by any "expert" weaving of another well-crafted poem or story?

Like Don Quixote on his unorthodox steed you must loosen the reins and go blundering into adventures that await any traveler in this multilevel world that we too often make familiar by our careful threading of its marked routes between accustomed places.

And like Don Quixote you must expect some disasters. You must

4

write your bad poems and stories; for to write carefully as you rove forward is to guarantee that you will not find the unknown, the risky, the surprising.

Art is an activity in which the actual feel of doing it must be your guide; hence the need for confidence, courage, independence. And hence the need for guardedness about learning too well the craft of doing it.

By following after money, publication, and recognition, you might risk what happened to the John Cheever character who in like manner "damaged, you might say, the ear's innermost chamber where we hear the heavy noise of the dragon's tail moving over the dead leaves."

2

CONSISTENT VERSUS VENTURESOME WRITERS

By Joanne Greenberg

DOES A WRITER deliberately decide to be consistent or venturesome in his work, or is the decision part of his personality that reflects itself in his writing? I would like to explore both sides.

A consistent writer stakes out a subject or approach and stays with it from book to book. Readers know what they are getting when they pick up one of his works. There is comfort in this for readers; near surprises will come in plot twist but not in subject matter or approach. Louis Auchincloss is consistent; so is Louis L'Amour, although he has written books on other subjects in other styles. Kurt Vonnegut is consistent. So is Flannery O'Connor. Since *The Drifters,* so is Michener. Hemingway for all his changes in background was more consistent than Steinbeck, who wrote historical novels, comedies, romances, epics, in many different emotional climates and on different intellectual planes.

Like Steinbeck, venturesome writers become restless when faced with limits. They won't or can't stay on subject or style or point of vantage, consistent in pace or stance. John Williams has written a classic "western" *(Butcher's Crossing),* an academic novel in traditional style, but he won the National Book Award for a historical novel in the form of letters to and from Octavius, Augustus Caesar. Ray Bradbury is venturesome. So are Gore Vidal and Norman Mailer and Truman Capote. So am I.

You can see by the writers I listed in both categories that I am not comparing talent or style. My favorite writers come from both camps. There are advantages to each and drawbacks, strengths with each and weaknesses, glory and besetting sin.

For consistent writers, the commercial questions are easier. There is a readership, a "market," to which they address themselves and with which, from book to book, they can become more comfortable. Classification may limit them somewhat, but it is greatly to their advantage because they become associated with a mood, a flavor, which is identifiable. Readers will go to those writers when they want that mood. [This, of course, occasionally backfires. I was once very ill, and my husband, thinking to give me the healing laughter of a fine comic writer, got me one of Peter DeVries' books. Unfortunately, it was *Blood of the Lamb,* a shattering account of his child's death from leukemia. It nearly did me in.] Publishers and agents are comfortable with consistent writers. Their own competence in marketing can be displayed and readers respond with increased sales. Sure things.

The besetting sin for the consistent writer is, of course, repetition. Zane Grey, the ultimate in consistency, ended by writing the same book again and again. His Swedish translator, whom I met in 1976, spoke feelingly of *Riders of the Purple Sage.* Having read this book on his own, he was so enthusiastic that he contracted to do Grey's complete corpus. "It was two books later when I realized what I had done—twenty-six more translations, and all of them minute variations on *Riders of the Purple Sage!* I suffered for the next three years for my mistake."

But study Grey: He endures as few of us will. Lasting fame seems more likely to be granted to the consistent than the venturesome writer. There seems to be a need for a critical mass, a certain volume of work to assure reputation, even if only one or two books continue to be read. The books that are read only by scholars need to be neatly classifiable—in a word, consistent.

Venturesome writers pay for their courage (perhaps it is only restlessness), but they have more fun. "I never know what you are going to come up with next!" my agent complains. "I never know what you are going to come up with next!" a reader exults.

Relatively few readers do exult, however, and critics often seem to be comparing any new work with the one before, to its detriment. "If only she'd write another book like *I Never Promised You a Rose Garden,* or *In This Sign,* or *The King's Persons.*" Sometimes readers feel a sense of betrayal because the writer's switch in subject or approach has been into an area they cannot follow. "I liked you until all of a sudden you went religious on me." Two of my cousins protested that about my story collection *High Crimes and Misdemeanors.* My religious subject matter did not come all of a sudden; the writing about it did. They felt deceived in some way; I let them down. Except out of personal love, I

7

suspect they would not read my work thereafter. Once bitten . . . I have often felt the same way. I love Mary Renault, but only as a historical novelist. I read her World War II novel yearning for the first person account of high adventure in Homeric Greece or in Alexander's Macedonia.

Venturesome writers seem less likely to endure over time, and we are a present drag to our agents and publishers. Our besetting sin is that in covering all the bases, we may be sacrificing depth for novelty. Our strength is that we keep our careers interesting longer. I think we also provide something valuable to literature in general. Avant-garde writers are usually consistent—radical in style, but consistent. So, venturesome writers provide a link between what is avant-garde and what is seen as conventional. Their work bridges what few people presently read and what many will read in ten or fifteen years. They also test and extend the limits of the forms they work in. Because they are not wedded to one form or approach, they are often the ones whose work readies the public for the avant-garde writer. More people saw and loved Thornton Wilder's *The Skin of Our Teeth* than read James Joyce's *Ulysses*. Wilder was venturesome, Joyce avant-garde and consistent (after his more conventional warm-up—*Dubliners* and *Portrait of the Artist*). I believe that Wilder helped people to approach Joyce and appreciate him.

If a writer looks at his style—his way of approaching a story, his stance (the distance he stands from the characters and events he is portraying), and his subject (who and what he cares about) as part of himself, he is more likely to be consistent: My style is me, my writing is me. If a writer looks at himself as the teller of the story, and his style as being at the service of the characters or the plot, he is more likely to be venturesome. Each of these ways is valid, but if you are a consistent writer who is in trouble with a piece of work, perhaps your character or plot is calling for a change, a night out, some new approach. If you are venturesome and your work seems to have lost some of its flavor, you may need to go back and deepen the mine a little.

3

FIVE-FINGER EXERCISES, OR WHAT TO DO TILL THE MUSE COMES BACK

By B. J. Chute

I WAS BORN WITH A WRITER'S BLOCK, and more than five decades of writing fiction have not resigned me to those depressing times when story ideas do not exist at all or wilt instantly on contact with my typewriter.

At some time or another, almost every writer goes through this experience, and almost every writer seems to have a different remedy. Kite flying, mountain climbing, a change of shoelaces, a change of scenery, a new job/husband/wife/typewriter—you name it, some frantic author will have tried it, with or without results.

As for myself, experience tells me that, eventually, my faithless Muse will return, wearing that Oh-were-you-looking-for-me? expression of hers. Steam will start to come out of my ears and out of my typewriter. Peace (or, rather, action—who wants peace at the typewriter?) will reign.

However, *eventually* is a sometime word, and experience is small comfort to a writer hunched over his desk and producing sentences composed of old marshmallows. Despair sets in. You are convinced that all is lost, but you know that baying at the moon will get you nowhere and that hibernation is for the bears. What to do?

Well, I have found one method that helped me out of more than one creative pothole, and it may help you. I speculate.

This does not mean that you should run to the nearest stockbroker and invest in Brussels sprouts futures. No, my brand of speculation is a different way of playing games, and the stricken writer can play it anywhere, making up rules along the way and not risking a penny. All that's needed are open eyes, something to look at, and that peculiar gift for weaving imagination around people and things without which one cannot write fiction.

9

I happen to live in New York City, the Baghdad of everyone and everything. A constantly changing extravaganza, a seesaw of hope and despair, a roller coaster of sensation, grist to any writer's mill. . . .

I know, I know. But your Muse has fled from you, and the city streets are dirty and the crowds push and the rain falls or the sun is hot. The last story idea you had collapsed weeks ago. Your head is full of nothing, your writing career is over, and you are sunk without a trace.

Perhaps tomorrow morning you will feel fresher? No, tomorrow morning you will feel the same, only swampier. At this point, grasping at straws, you mutter to yourself the nine-letter word that I have recommended: SPECULATE.

But on what? you ask. You have been speculating, endlessly, numbly. Your story line has turned to cold spaghetti. Your characters lie lifeless in your head, all of them as dead as that famous doornail in *A Christmas Carol,* as dead as Scrooge's partner Marley. Deader, in fact, because you can picture Marley as clearly as you can picture all Dickens's people—Oliver Twist and David Copperfield, Mrs. Gummidge and Mr. Micawber, Little Nell and Tiny Tim, bad and good, funny and tragic, ruthlessly real and as ruthlessly sentimental. Did Dickens ever have a writer's block? No, of course not. Dickens was a genius.

For a moment, you hate Charles Dickens, sitting there with his paper and quill pen, inventing people who still walk around inside your head, while your own characters in your own story will not even speak to you. When did Ebenezer Scrooge start to come alive? Did Dickens, one day, see a sour old man, walking along, not speaking to anyone? Did Dickens wonder about him idly—the people he knew, the nightcap he wore to bed, the knocker on his door? Did he say to himself, "I wonder where that old man lives, what he eats for supper, what his name is," and did he then say suddenly, with the conviction of the inevitable, "Ebenezer! His name is Ebenezer Scrooge!"

Who really knows what goes on inside a writer's head? Often, not even the writer knows—and I am taking liberties with Charles Dickens who was a genius. Geniuses are rare, so let me turn my attention to taking liberties with you.

Suppose, instead of walking a London street in the 1840's, you are sitting in a New York subway in the 1980's. Your writing mind is a complete blank, and you stare numbly into space. Space is occupied by the man across from you. He is small, gray, and very neat in his neat

10

gray suit. Next to him is a hard-faced woman, rather stout, with touched-up blonde hair. They, like you, are staring into space, and after a moment you dismiss them with a shrug. They are dull clichés, just like the characters in your story, and you sit and brood on your own dullness. You feel sorry for yourself.

But self-pity is a dead-end street. It may be tempting but it is also a bore. The word *speculate* drifts subliminally across your mind, and you pull yourself together enough to wonder what their names are; they need identification tags. Margaret? Richard? Safe names, because they have so many nicknames—Peg, Peggy, Dick, Dicky . . . No, this one is Richard. Even as a child he was Richard, a sober little boy who named his dog Spot. *Her* dog was a cat, and it was named Fluffy, but sometimes she called it Fluffy-Wuffy. In spite of the hardness in her face now, she still talks baby talk. "Men like baby talk, you know, it makes them feel big and strong." Richard wouldn't like it.

Or would he? That's unexpected. Maybe he would. Maybe he would like a fortyish blonde who calls him Dicky-bird. Oh, for Pete's sake—! But why not? After all, he's only human.

Hang on to him. He is the first human character who has visited your mind in many a moon. You feel a faint stirring of curiosity. Suppose these two met each other, shared a table in a crowded coffee shop. He orders corned beef on rye; she orders tuna salad and fudge cake. Is she stout or merely plump? Is he scrawny or thin? In the interest of research, you glance once more across the aisle, and it is a shock to find they have both left the train, their places taken by strangers.

No matter. You can do your five-finger exercises without them. Where does the blonde live? (Answer quickly.) Brooklyn walk-up. Got a boy friend? Sure, probably several. Where does the little gray man live? West Side, two rooms. What does he do? Works in an accounting office, he's good at it, he likes numbers. Got a girl friend? Nope.

But all this is too obvious, too easy. They're turning into clichés again. You thought for a moment that the Muse had come back, wings and all, but now she's vanished, not even a feather dropped on the ground. Your mind and your body slump. Back to Square One, and you're sorrier for yourself than ever. "Speculate!" you tell yourself sardonically. It takes more than speculating to pull a writer's head together. Five-finger exercises do not a symphony make, and there's more to writing a story than daydreaming on a subway. . . .

11

And there's more to Ebenezer Scrooge than an old man on a London street. Certainly Scrooge walks off the pages, but there must have been a time when he existed only in a writer's speculation. What did it take to make him come alive?

Words, just words. Not "just words," of course, but the right ones. They may have come easily or have been rewritten a dozen times; we don't know, and it doesn't matter. Ebenezer Scrooge is words on paper.

Dickens saw an old man—on the street or in the camera of his mind's eye. He could have described him as an old miser who had white hair and stubble on his chin, ate his meals alone in a dark room, was wholly indifferent to his fellow man, and was feared. A catalogue of simple facts, leaving the reader to draw the picture.

But, of course, Dickens did nothing of the kind. The "old miser" becomes that "covetous old sinner, hard and sharp as flint," who takes his gruel (not "meals," you notice) in a dark room; instead of "dark room," Dickens tell us that "Darkness is cheap, and Scrooge liked it," describing not only the darkness but the man himself. Nor does Dickens comment philosophically on Scrooge's uncaring attitude toward the needy; he lets Scrooge say it—"If they would rather die, they had better do it, and decrease the surplus population"—and the reader feels a cold shiver of revulsion.

The white hair and stubble become "A frosty rime was on his head, and on his eyebrows, and his wiry chin," conjuring up the miser's perpetual winter. And, as to his being feared, are we merely told that people were afraid of him? No, we are told that even the blind men's dogs, when they saw him coming, "would tug their owners into doorways and up courts."

All this and much more turns Scrooge into someone alive? If Dickens were sitting beside you now, what would he make of Richard and Fluffy-Wuffy? Would he merely speculate as you have been doing—give them names, jobs, somewhere to live? Or would he, by genius, magic or craft, record them on paper and turn them into real people?

But, I hear you shriek, that is exactly what *you* yearn to do, and you cannot even begin. You know that, the moment you sit down at your desk, everything will go flat and you will stare blankly at blank paper. You are, in fact, defeated before you start, and if *you* saw an old man in a London street . . .

"Frosty rime," you remember, "wiry chin." Richard is gray all over, but will that make the reader picture him as a real person? His suit is gray. Banker's gray? No, that image is totally wrong, and you reject it instantly. Grim-gray, gray-grim? No, he is sad, not grim. Ledger-gray? Definitely better. A neat man in a ledger-gray suit. Not just neat. Excruciatingly neat. The picture becomes a little sharper, the words are more precise. Thinking about Richard's grayness, you recall the false blondness of Fluffy-Wuffy's hair. Brassy? Fake-gilt?

Dickens would do it better, but Dickens was a genius. So what? You use the same tools, you use words. Do you use those tools only when you are sitting at your desk? Are you just a part-time writer?

"Shrill," you think suddenly. "Shrill-blonde hair." Does it work? Can you get away with it? It's certainly closer to what you want to say, closer to what you want the reader to see. Ledger-gray. Shrill-blonde. Right or wrong, these are a writer's words, a writer's choice. You feel a faint hopefulness, and you try another tack. "Hard-faced" you called her when you first saw her, but that was before she became Fluffy-Wuffy. What gave her away—her eyes? her mouth? You decide that it was her mouth, which was . . . You grope for the right word. *Vulnerable*. Not a colorful word, but a very touching one, a word that carries a lot of emotion to the reader.

Oh, so you have a reader again, although you are not yet putting words down on paper. You are not totally blocked then, are you? Perhaps that writer's block is made of plaster, not granite. Something is beginning to move in your writer's mind.

Perhaps, if you were at your desk now, you would not sit and stare so numbly. If your characters still lay on the pages like flounders, you could defy them (and defy yourself at the same time). Flat as a founder is a cliché, but once it must have a been a fine new simile. Flat as a— You spin possibilities in your mind, play with them. Flat as Marley's ghost?

You almost smile, thinking of what a man named Charles Dickens made of a ghost and a door knocker. Dickens must have used his tools all the time, kept them sharp, rejoiced in their brightness and gleam. Or did even Dickens sometimes suffer his own writer's blocks? If he did, he must always have come out of them, whole and lively, time after time.

The word *time* rouses you. You leap to your feet. You have missed your stop. Rushing to the door as it opens (as it *sighs* open, you think

13

triumphantly), you brush shoulders with a tall young man whose workman's cap is on the back of his head. "Jaunty," you think, "Rakish. No, cocksure!"

Suddenly, you are a writer again. You are using and choosing words, even if they are only in your head. (What do you mean—*only?* Where else does a writer live?) Speculation; and the right words. At least, you have made a start, and you have chipped away a fragment of that writer's block.

But what will you do if, back at your desk, the black granite looms up again? What will you do if the paper in front of you stays as frighteningly blank as ever?

You will go on speculating and choosing words, that's what you will do. But you will not speculate idly, dimly, and you will not choose words that are second best. Second best is never good enough. You can and you should and you must use your tools all the time and use them properly. If, for the time being, you still can't get your story and its people down on paper, keep doing the five-finger exercises. Don't pamper yourself. Work at your craft where you are.

And stop being afraid. The Muse will come back. The Muse likes writers.

4

EVERYTHING YOU NEED TO KNOW ABOUT WRITING SUCCESSFULLY—IN TEN MINUTES

By Stephen King

I. *The First Introduction*

THAT'S RIGHT. I know it sounds like an ad for some sleazy writers' school, but I really am going to tell you everything you need to pursue a successful and financially rewarding career writing fiction, and I really am going to do it in ten minutes, which is exactly how long it took me to learn. It will actually take you twenty minutes or so to read this essay, however, because I have to tell you a story, and then I have to write a *second* introduction. But these, I argue, should not count in the ten minutes.

II. *The Story, or, How Stephen King Learned to Write*

When I was a sophomore in high school, I did a sophomoric thing which got me in a pot of fairly hot water, as sophomoric didoes often do. I wrote and published a small satiric newspaper called *The Village Vomit*. In this little paper I lampooned a number of teachers at Lisbon (Maine) High School, where I was under instruction. These were not very gentle lampoons; they ranged from the scatological to the downright cruel.

Eventually, a copy of this little newspaper found its way into the hands of a faculty member, and since I had been unwise enough to put my name on it (a fault, some critics would argue, of which I have still not been entirely cured), I was brought into the office. The sophisticated satirist had by that time reverted to what he really was: a fourteen-year-old kid who was shaking in his boots and wondering if he was going to get a suspension . . . what we called "a three-day vacation" in those dim days of 1964.

I wasn't suspended. I was forced to make a number of apologies—they were warranted, but they still tasted like dog-dirt in my mouth—

15

and spent a week in detention hall. And the guidance counselor arranged what he no doubt thought of as a more constructive channel for my talents. This was a job—contingent upon the editor's approval—writing sports for the Lisbon *Enterprise,* a twelve-page weekly of the sort with which any small-town resident will be familiar. This editor was the man who taught me everything I know about writing in ten minutes. His name was John Gould—not the famed New England humorist or the novelist who wrote *The Greenleaf Fires,* but a relative of both, I believe.

He told me he needed a sports writer and we could "try each other out," if I wanted.

I told him I knew more about advanced algebra than I did sports.

Gould nodded and said, "You'll learn."

I said I would at least try to learn. Gould gave me a huge roll of yellow paper and promised me a wage of ½¢ per word. The first two pieces I wrote had to do with a high school basketball game in which a member of my school team broke the Lisbon High scoring record. One of these pieces was straight reportage. The second was a feature article.

I brought them to Gould the day after the game, so he'd have them for the paper, which came out Fridays. He read the straight piece, made two minor corrections, and spiked it. Then he started in on the feature piece with a large black pen and taught me all I ever needed to know about my craft. I wish I still had the piece—it deserves to be framed, editorial corrections and all—but I can remember pretty well how it looked when he had finished with it. Here's an example:

Last night, in the ~~well-loved~~
~~gymnasium of~~ [Lisbon High School], partisans
and Jay Hills fans alike were stunned by
an athletic performance unequalled in school
history: Bob Ransom~~, known as "Bullet" Bob~~
~~for both his size and accuracy~~, scored
thirty-seven points. He did it with grace
and speed...and he did it with an odd courtesy
as well, committing only two personal fouls
in his ~~knight-like~~ quest for a record which
                         is basketball team
has eluded Lisbon ~~thinclads~~ since 1953...

16

When Gould finished marking up my copy in the manner I have indicated above, he looked up and must have seen something on my face. I think *he* must have thought it was horror, but it was not: it was revelation.

"I only took out the bad parts, you know," he said. "Most of it's pretty good."

"I know," I said, meaning both things: yes, most of it was good, and yes, he had only taken out the bad parts. "I won't do it again."

"If that's true," he said, "you'll never have to work again. You can do *this* for a living." Then he threw back his head and laughed.

And he was right: I *am* doing this for a living, and as long as I can keep on, I don't expect ever to have to work again.

III. *The Second Introduction*

All of what follows has been said before. If you are interested enough in writing to be a purchaser of this magazine, you will have either heard or read all (or almost all) of it before. Thousands of writing courses are taught across the United States each year; seminars are convened; guest lecturers talk, then answer questions, then drink as many gin and tonics as their expense-fees will allow, and it all boils down to what follows.

I am going to tell you these things again because often people will only listen—really *listen*—to someone who makes a lot of money doing the thing he's talking about. This is sad but true. And I told you the story above not to make myself sound like a character out of a Horatio Alger novel but to make a point: I saw, I listened, and *I learned*. Until that day in John Gould's little office, I had been writing first drafts of stories which might run 2,500 words. The second drafts were apt to run 3,300 words. Following that day, my 2,500-word first drafts became 2,200-word second drafts. And two years after that, I sold the first one.

So here it is, with all the bark stripped off. It'll take ten minutes to read, and you can apply it right away . . . if you *listen*.

IV. *Everything You Need to Know About Writing Successfully*
1. *Be talented*

This, of course, is the killer. What is talent? I can hear someone shouting, and here we are, ready to get into a discussion right up there

17

with "What is the meaning of life?" for weighty pronouncements and total uselessness. For the purposes of the beginning writer, talent may as well be defined as eventual success—publication and money. If you wrote something for which someone sent you a check, if you cashed the check and it didn't bounce, and if you then paid the light bill with the money, I consider you talented.

Now some of you are really hollering. Some of you are calling me one crass money-fixated creep. And some of you are calling me *bad* names. *Are you calling Harold Robbins talented?* someone in one of the Great English Departments of America is screeching. *V. C. Andrews? Theodore Dreiser? Or what about you, you dyslexic moron?*

Nonsense. Worse than nonsense, off the subject. We're not talking about good or bad here. I'm interested in telling you how to get your stuff published, not in critical judgments of who's good or bad. As a rule the critical judgments come after the check's been spent, anyway. I have my own opinions, but most times I keep them to myself. People who are published steadily and are paid for what they are writing may be either saints or trollops, but they are clearly reaching a great many someones who want what they have. Ergo, they are communicating. Ergo, they are talented. The biggest part of writing successfully is being talented, and in the context of marketing, the only bad writer is one who doesn't get paid. If you're not talented, you won't succeed. And if you're not succeeding, you should know when to quit.

When is that? I don't know. It's different for each writer. Not after six rejection slips, certainly, nor after sixty. But after six hundred? Maybe. After six thousand? My friend, after six thousand pinks, it's time you tried painting or possibly computer programming.

Further, almost every aspiring writer knows when he is getting warmer—you start getting little jotted notes on your rejection slips, or personal letters . . . maybe a commiserating phone call. It's lonely out there in the cold, but there *are* encouraging voices . . . unless there is nothing in your words which warrants encouragement. I think you owe it to yourself to skip as much of the self-illusion as possible. If your eyes are open, you'll know which way to go . . . or when to turn back.

2. *Be neat.*

Type. Double-space. Use a nice heavy white paper, never that erasable onion-skin stuff. If you've marked up your manuscript a lot, do another draft.

3. *Be self-critical*

If you *haven't* marked up your manuscript a lot, you did a lazy job. Only God gets things right the first time. Don't be a slob.

4. *Remove every extraneous word*

You want to get up on a soapbox and preach? Fine. Get one and try your local park. You want to write for money? Get to the point. And if you remove all the excess garbage and discover you can't find the point, tear up what you wrote and start all over again . . . or try something new.

5. *Never look at a reference book while doing a first draft*

You want to write a story? Fine. Put away your dictionary, your encyclopedias, your World Almanac, and your thesaurus. Better yet, throw your thesaurus into the wastebasket. The only things creepier than a thesaurus are those little paperbacks college students too lazy to read the assigned novels buy around exam time. Any word you have to hunt for in a thesaurus is the wrong word. There are no exceptions to this rule. You think you might have misspelled a word? O.K., so here is your choice: either look it up in the dictionary, thereby making sure you have it right—and breaking your train of thought and the writer's trance in the bargain—or just spell it phonetically and correct it later. Why not? Did you think it was going to go somewhere? And if you need to know the largest city in Brazil and you find you don't have it in your head, why not write in Miami, or Cleveland? You can check it . . . but *later*. When you sit down to write, *write*. Don't do anything else except go to the bathroom, and only do that if it absolutely cannot be put off.

6. *Know the markets*

Only a dimwit would send a story about giant vampire bats surrounding a high school to *McCall's*. Only a dimwit would send a tender story about a mother and daughter making up their differences on Christmas Eve to *Playboy* . . . but people do it all the time. I'm not exaggerating; I have seen such stories in the slush piles of the actual magazines. If you write a good story, why send it out in an ignorant fashion? Would you send your kid out in a snowstorm dressed in Bermuda shorts and a tank top? If you like science fiction, read the magazines. If you want to write confessions stories, read the magazines. And so on. It isn't just a matter

19

of knowing what's right for the present story; you can begin to catch on, after awhile, to overall rhythms, editorial likes and dislikes, a magazine's entire slant. Sometimes your reading can influence the *next story,* and create a sale.

7. *Write to entertain*

Does this mean you can't write "serious fiction"? It does not. Somewhere along the line pernicious critics have invested the American reading and writing public with the idea that entertaining fiction and serious ideas do not overlap. This would have surprised Charles Dickens, not to mention Jane Austen, John Steinbeck, William Faulkner, Bernard Malamud, and hundreds of others. But your serious ideas must always serve your story, not the other way around. I repeat: if you want to preach, get a soapbox.

8. *Ask yourself frequently, "Am I having fun?"*

The answer needn't always be yes. But if it's always no, it's time for a new project or a new career.

9. *How to evaluate criticism*

Show your piece to a number of people—ten, let us say. Listen carefully to what they tell you. Smile and nod a lot. Then review what was said very carefully. If your critics are all telling you the same thing about some facet of your story—a plot twist that doesn't work, a character who rings false, stilted narrative, or half a dozen other possibles—change that facet. It doesn't matter if you really liked that twist or that character; if a lot of people are telling you something is wrong with your piece, it *is.* If seven or eight of them are hitting on that same thing, I'd still suggest changing it. But if everyone—or even most everyone—is criticizing something different, you can safely disregard what all of them say.

10. *Observe all rules for proper submission*

Return postage, self-addressed envelope, all of that.

11. *An agent? Forget it. For now*

Agents get 10% of monies earned by their clients. 10% of nothing is nothing. Agents also have to pay the rent. Beginning writers do not

20

contribute to that or any other necessity of life. Flog your stories around yourself. If you've done a novel, send around query letters to publishers, one by one, and follow up with sample chapters and/or the manuscript complete. And remember Stephen King's First Rule of Writers and Agents, learned by bitter personal experience: You don't need one until you're making enough for someone to steal . . . and if you're making that much, you'll be able to take your pick of good agents.

12. *If it's bad, kill it*

When it comes to people, mercy killing is against the law. When it comes to fiction, it *is* the law.

That's everything you need to know. And if you listened, you can write everything and anything you want. Now I believe I will wish you a pleasant day and sign off.

My ten minutes are up.

5

TO BE A WRITER: WHAT DOES IT TAKE?

By John Jakes

You can answer the question two ways.

If you're an aspiring fiction writer, you might say something like, "It takes the ability to sense, imagine, and tell a strong story. It also takes talent for writing efficient dialogue that gives the illusion of reality and carries a lot of plot or characterization freight at the same time. Besides that, it takes good powers of description. . . ." You could spin out your answer to cover all the basic tools and techniques of the fiction writer's craft, and you would be right.

If you're an aspiring poet, you might mention meter and form first. A dramatist would think of structure and exposition. Those answers, too, would be right.

There's a second answer, though, equally correct but more fundamental. An answer that actually precedes the learning of technique, no matter what sort of writing you prefer.

By way of illustration, think about golf. I think about it a lot, because I love it, and I play badly. Obviously, good golf calls for certain skills. Strong, straight drives based on a good swing. Dependable putting. A keen eye for reading greens. Expert chipping to rescue your ball from a trap. But you can achieve none of that without certain broader fundamentals. Excellent hand-eye coordination and muscle memory (I don't have either one). Ability to concentrate. A liking for the game itself. All these underlie technique.

So, too, do certain attitudes underlie all the skills a writer must have. I call those attitudes states of being. During a professional career that spans thirty-seven years, I've thought about these states of being a lot. Added some, subtracted others. Finally distilled and described seven. I believe a writer must "be" all seven, even before taking the first steps toward technical mastery. Indeed, so crucial are these seven states of

22

being, I believe that if you lack them, you will never be a professional, only an eternal novice.

Each of the seven is simple to describe, but profound in its impact on your life. Here they are, then . . . the seven "states of being" that support a writing career.

1. BE SURE. Do you really want to pay the price? It isn't small. Are you willing to isolate yourself day after day, session after session, year after year, in order to learn your craft the only way you can—by writing?

There are much easier, more pleasant ways to pass the time, though few so rewarding intellectually and spiritually. But it's no sin to be honest and admit it if you'd rather garden, fish, or socialize with friends than go it alone as a writer, with no guarantee of success. If you aren't sure you're up to all that writing demands of a person, go no further.

2. BE DETERMINED. This is a re-statement of one of my "three P's" of a writing career—practice. You must have guessed by now that I believe many parts of the writing process (though not all) can be learned, just as golf can be learned. It's true. You may never be a Fuzzy Zoeller or a Nancy Lopez—there are few out-and-out champions in any field—but, with determination and practice, you can probably become at least a part-time professional. To do it, however, you must write and keep on writing, trying to improve all the time.

3. BE PATIENT. This equates with the second of my "three P's," persistence. The writing profession is not, thank God, the record business. Idols are neither born nor made on the strength of a single three-minute album cut. A more substantial body of work is required. Nor do many stars emerge in the writing field at eighteen (only to be forgotten six months later). Except for a very few, a solid writing career usually arrives later in life.

Also, you must remember that publishing, like any other art that is part industry, changes constantly. Editorial people change jobs. A house or publication that rejects you this year may, under a new editor, say yes the next. Failure to realize this can increase your impatience to the danger point . . . the point at which you say, "What's the use?"

We live in an age of instant gratification. You won't get it writing . . . except for the joy in the work itself.

23

4. BE OPEN. This is the last of my "three P's"—professionalism. By being open, I mean being willing and eager to have all the flaws in your work exposed, so that you can fix them. I mean being anxious to have a working partnership with an editor who admires your strengths but won't spare you criticism of your weaknesses.

Don't let the editor do all the work, though. You must want to find the weak places for yourself, before the editor sees them. It is this rather cold-blooded attitude that sets most money-earning writers apart from dabblers and those who would rather talk about being a writer than do what it takes to be one. "No pain, no gain," runners say. It's the same with writing. Unless you're open to tough criticism and willing to do something about it, you'll never go the distance.

5. BE CURIOUS. Read everything you can read. Read widely, not merely in your chosen field of writing. Spend as much time as you can with your mouth shut and your eyes and ears open. Don't strive for attention . . . strive to go unseen in a crowd, on the beach, at a party. Watch people. Watch the sky. Watch a baby's repertoire of expressions. Watch the way sun puts shadow on a wrinkled garment. Nothing should escape your notice. Everything eventually contributes to what you write, even though the way it contributes is totally unknown to anyone, including you.

6. BE SERIOUS. Give unstintingly of yourself when you write. The kind of effort NFL players casually refer to as "110 percent." There's something to it.

Once again, if you dabble . . . withhold part of your energy . . . refuse to commit your whole mind and heart to the work . . . that will be reflected in a lackluster creative product. Give your work the best you have to offer at the moment you do it. Give it a clear head, and a body that's fit and rested.

On the other hand, while you're taking the work seriously, don't take yourself seriously. I abhor the kind of writer who can't laugh at himself . . . who can't avoid pretentious pronouncements (probably to cover a raging insecurity) . . . who carries "the gift" like a royal scepter and never stops waving it about for others to see.

Too many writers unwittingly play what I call Immortality Roulette. They get involved in worrying about their own reputations. How will they be remembered in a hundred years? They grow desperate, some-

24

times almost maniacal about it. They write nasty letters to harsh critics—or at least talk about doing it. They are happy or sad depending on a few words from a total unknown (most reviewers). The result of all this is often compensation in the form of overweening self-importance.

The saddest cases are the most marginal . . . those very competent popular writers who probably will be largely forgotten, except by a few trivia scholars or aficionados, as time goes by. Since most of us can't answer questions about posterity—a Hemingway, acknowledged a genius in his own lifetime, is a rarity—just do the best you can. No one can ask more, and what more can you logically ask of yourself? Posterity will take care of itself, with or without you.

7. BE YOURSELF. Above all, let who you are, what you are, what you believe shine through every sentence you write, every piece you finish. I don't mean preach. Just be natural. The originality and power of Tolstoy's *War and Peace* do not lie in the fact that he was the first to write a mammoth novel about Imperial Russia facing Napoleon. I don't know whether he was first or not. I suspect so; it doesn't matter. What matters is that he was unique, a singular person, and his great novel emerged from what *he* had to say about his homeland and its people in wartime. One of my favorite statements about writing, encountered so long ago I can't even acknowledge the source, is this:

"True originality lies not in saying what has never been said, but in saying what you have to say."

So there you are. Seven "states of being" you must achieve before you start your work in order to master the specific tools of your craft. Again, if you honestly feel these requirements are too tough—simply not for you—no one will blame or criticize you. But if you say, "Yes, I will be a writer because I can be all of those things . . . I am all of those things . . . or I'm willing to try to become them," then I predict eventual success for you.

Not enormous wealth, mind you. Not a best seller every year. Not immortality—just the solid satisfaction of being a *writer*. It's a proud and ancient profession . . . and it's a great feeling to achieve even a little success in the business of entertaining and enlightening millions with your own words. It's a calling very much worth the price.

25

6

DON'T THINK: WRITE!

By Madeleine L'Engle

WHEN we write, for whom do we write? Or, as we would be more likely to ask, whom do we write for?

It sounds like an easy question to answer, and in some ways it is. But when it is applied to the matter of fiction, the logical answer—that we write for a specific audience—does not work. At least not for me.

Each year I teach at one or more writers workshops. I enjoy them for many reasons, not the least of which is the opportunity to meet other workshop leaders, often writers whose work I have long admired. Writing is a solitary profession, and a writers conference gives us a chance to get together. Another reason I enjoy the workshops is that I am forced to articulate what I have learned about the techniques of the craft of fiction writing; it is easy to get forgetful and sloppy. Having to explain imagery, simile, metaphor, point of view, is a way to continue to teach myself as well as the people who have come to the workshop.

At one workshop, I talked, as usual, about all the hard work that precedes the writing of fiction. Often there is research to be done. For my Time Trilogy I had to immerse myself in the new physics: first, Einstein's theories of relativity and Planck's quantum theory for *A Wrinkle in Time;* then cellular biology and particle physics for *A Wind in the Door;* and astrophysics and non-linear theories of time for *A Swiftly Tilting Planet.* For *The Love Letters* I had to learn a great deal more about seventeenth-century Portuguese history than I needed or wanted to know, so that the small amount needed for the book would be accurate. Before, during, and after research, the writer needs to be thinking constantly about the characters, and the direction in which the novel seems to be moving.

Does the story have the Aristotelian beginning, middle, and end? How do the events of the novel relate to me, personally, in my own

26

journey through life? What are my own particular concerns at the time of writing, and how should they affect—or not affect—the story? When I actually sit down to write, I stop thinking. While I am writing, I am listening to the story; I am not listening to myself.

"But," a young woman in the class said in a horrified tone of voice, "my creative writing teacher says that we must keep the audience in mind at all times."

That is undoubtedly true for the scientist writing an article that is expected to be understood by people who have little or no scientific background. The writer will have to keep simplifying scientific language, explaining technical terms. Keeping the audience in mind is probably valuable for reporting in newspapers and magazines. The reporter is writing for the average reader; language should be neither so bland as to be insulting, nor so technical as to demand special knowledge.

As for lawyers, I assume they have each other in mind at all times as they write. Certainly they don't have most of us in mind. Their grandiosity appalls me. In a movie contract, I was asked to grant the right to my book to the producers, in perpetuity, throughout the universe. When I wrote in, "With the exception of Sagittarius and the Andromeda galaxy," it was accepted. Evidently the lawyers, who are writing to avoid litigation in a litigious world, did not anticipate a lawsuit from Sagittarius.

Of course I am being grossly unfair to many lawyers; I come from a family of fine lawyers. But the language used in a will or a contract is indeed a special language, and it is not aimed at the reader who enjoys stories, the reader of fiction.

Whom, then, does the writer of fiction write for? It is only a partial truth to say that I write for myself, out of my own need, asking, whether I realize it or not, the questions I am asking in my own life.

A truer answer is that I write for the book.

"But why do you write for children?" I am often asked.

And I answer truthfully that I don't. I haven't been a child for a long time, and if what I write doesn't appeal to me, at my age, it isn't likely to appeal to a child. I hope I will never lose the child within me, who has not lost her sense of wonder, of awe, of laughter. But I am not a child; I am a grown woman, learning about maturity as I move on in chronology.

A teacher, in introducing me to a class of seventh graders, said,

27

"Miss L'Engle has made it in the children's field, and she is now trying to break into the adult market."

I felt that I had better not explain to this teacher that I had no desire to break into the adult market and see my fiction in "adult bookstores." I am not interested in writing pornography. I did explain that my first several books were regular trade novels, which means that they were marketed for a general audience, not for children. And I explained that when I have a book that I think will be too difficult for a general audience, then we will market it as a juvenile book. It is a great mistake to think that children are not capable of understanding difficult concepts in science or philosophy.

A book that has a young protagonist will likely be marketed as a children's book, regardless of content. Since adolescents are usually more willing than their elders to ask difficult questions, and to accept the fact that the questions don't have nice, tidy answers but lead on to more difficult questions, approximately half of my books have young protagonists. But while I am writing, I am not thinking of any audience at all. I am not even thinking about myself. I am thinking about the book.

This does not imply anything esoteric. I do not pick up the pen and expect it to guide my hand, or put my fingers on the keyboard of the typewriter and expect the work to be done automatically. It is work. But it is focused work, and the focus is on the story, not on anything else.

An example of the kind of focus I mean is a good doctor. The good doctor listens to the patient, truly listens, to what the patient says, does not say, is afraid to say, to body language, to everything that may give a clue as to what is wrong. The good doctor is so fully focused on the patient that personal self-consciousness has vanished. Such focused listening does not make the doctor—or any of the rest of us—less ourselves. In fact, such focused listening makes us more ourselves.

The same thing is true in listening to a story as we write it. It does not make us any less writers, this strange fact that we do not think about writing as we are writing; it makes us more writers.

Then, of course, there is all the revising to be done. We do not always listen well. We do not always have our full attention on the story. Some scenes will need to be written and rewritten a dozen or more times before they work. We do have to revise with attention to infelicities of rhythm, flaw of syntax; there is, indeed, a great deal of conscious work

28

to be done. But still, the writer is paying attention to the work itself, not the potential audience. I have, it is true, toned down scenes when the decision has been made to market a book as a "young adult" novel, because I know that young adult novels are read as often by nine- and ten-year-olds as by young adults. But such revisions are done long after the story has been listened to as attentively as possible, and cannot mutilate or betray the intent or integrity of the story.

It would be very inhibiting for me to have to keep an audience in mind. It would take a large piece of my mind off the story as it is unfolding, and I want all of my mind to be where it belongs: on the writing.

Have I had an audience in mind while I have been writing this piece? Not particularly. I'm telling myself things I need to remember. Nobody but someone interested in the writing of fiction is going to want to read this, so I am also writing for people who share my own concerns.

So, gentle reader (the Victorians seems to assume that all readers are gentle), give yourself the pleasure of forgetting earnestly to remember your audience at all times, and give yourself the fun of plunging deeply into your story, and having your mind focused on that, and nothing else. If the story that comes from this way of writing is a better story than the forcedly audience-centered story (and I am convinced it will be), it will have a wider audience. And isn't that what we hope for?—to reach as many people as possible, because we believe that what the story has to say is worth saying.

29

7

THE KING'S LESSON

By John McCollister

Once upon a time lived a king whose every wish was a command. To his servants he issued orders that were carried out with haste. Even the queen responded with such urgency that on more than one occasion she accidentally knocked her jar of honey from the table onto the parlor floor. People on street corners doffed their caps and bowed when he rode by in his horse-drawn carriage, for it was the king who had absolute power, and no one dared to disobey.

But after a while, absolute obedience not only becomes boring but disturbing as well. The king thought he had some good ideas to share with others, but he wasn't quite sure. The influence of a king is limited by geographic boundaries. Only his subjects heard his royal pronouncements. Although they nodded their heads in agreement with everything he said, the king wasn't fooled. He knew they were little more than puppets responding to tugs on a string.

How could he be certain that others would listen to him for what he had to say, not because of his title?

"I've got it," said the king. "I'll become a writer. I'll use a pen name, of course, so no one will know who wrote the words. When my thoughts become published, I can see what people think of them."

The king marched swiftly to his den and sat in front of his word processor. For one full hour, he did nothing but stare at a blank screen. He had so much to say, but had such a difficult time determining how to begin. "Blah! Why should I worry?" he muttered to himself. "After all, I am the king."

With a royal measure of chutzpah, the king pecked away. One draft, that's all he would need. He stuffed the pages into an envelope and shipped off the 2,000 words to a selected magazine editor.

Two weeks later, when he returned to his castle after a hard day of counting money, the king eagerly opened the envelope from the editor that had been placed on top of the pile of personal mail. His heart sank when he read the form letter that began: "We are sorry, but your manuscript does not meet our current editorial needs. . . ."

"Ye gods!" cried the king. "The magazine does not respond as I command."

The king blinked his eyes twice—once with shock at the thought of anyone saying no to him, and again with awareness that something had to be done. He summoned the most respected writing instructor in his kingdom and, behind closed doors, confided his desire to be a writer. He shoved the rejected manuscript into the instructor's hands. "See what they did to me?" asked the king with a deep sigh that showed his state of frustration. "Why don't they understand what I'm trying to say? After all, look who I am."

The patient instructor merely shook his head. "Your Majesty," he said, "in writing everyone is equal. Your commands, I'm afraid, are useless. You must obey the rules."

"The rules, indeed," snapped the king. "*I* make my own rules."

"Not in writing, you don't," cautioned the instructor as he reached for a blue pencil. "Here you must learn them and obey them. For example, there are certain items called grammar, style, syntax. . . ."

"Then I simply order you to make me a writer," the king demanded.

"That's not one of the rules," answered the instructor. "I only advise; everyone must learn for himself the best way to string words together."

At first the king rebelled against this challenge to his authority. Yet every time he deviated from those prescribed rules, his writing suffered; his only rewards were more rejection slips.

Gradually, however, the king suppressed his royal ego and yielded to the rules about which his instructor spoke. To his amazement, it was not demeaning; it was rewarding. He was not *subservient* to the rules as much as he was in *harmony* with them.

It happened so unexpectedly. A messenger approached the throne, delivering another envelope, this time sans manuscript. In its place was a check along with a hand-written note from the magazine's editor asking for more material.

For the first time in his life, the king knew what it meant to be a success. Through his own efforts, he shared the joys and thrills of influencing others through the written word.

31

Later that afternoon, without any fanfare, the monarch removed his crown, then slipped the purple mantle from his shoulders. They were necessary no longer. His instructor was right. In writing, everyone is equal.

Everyone is a king.

8

HOW TO FIND TIME TO WRITE WHEN YOU DON'T HAVE TIME TO WRITE

By Sue Grafton

EARLY in my writing career, I managed to turn out three novels, one right after another, while I was married, raising two children, keeping house, and working full time as a medical secretary. Those novels were never published and netted me not one red cent, but the work was essential. Writing those three books prepared the way for the fourth book, which *was* published and got me launched as a professional writer. Ironically, now that I'm a "full-time" writer with the entire work day at my disposal, I'm often guilty of getting less work done. Even after twenty-five years at it, there are days when I find myself feeling overwhelmed . . . far less effective and efficient than I know I could be. Lately, I've been scrutinizing my own practices, trying to determine the techniques I use to help me produce more consistently. The underlying challenge, always, is finding the time to write and sticking to it.

Extracting writing time from the fabric of everyday life is a struggle for many of us. Even people who are technically free to write during an eight-hour day often can't "get around" to it. Each day seems to bring some crisis that requires our immediate attention. Always, there's the sense that tomorrow, for sure, we'll get down to work. We're uncomfortably aware that time is passing and the job isn't getting done, but it's hard to know where to start. How can you fit writing into a schedule that already *feels* as if it's filled to capacity? If you find yourself lamenting that you "never have time to write," here are some suggestions about how to view the problem and, better yet, how to go about solving it.

First of all, accept the fact that you may never have the "leisure" (real or imaginary) to sit down and complete your novel without interruption. Chances are you won't be able to quit your job, abandon your family, and retire to a writers' colony for six weeks of uninterrupted writing

33

every year. And even if you could, that six weeks probably wouldn't get the job done. To be productive, we have to make writing part of our daily lives. The problem is that we view writing as a luxury, something special to allow ourselves as soon as we've taken care of the countless nagging duties that seem to come first. Well, I've got news for you. It really works the other way. Once you put writing first, the rest of your life will fall into place.

Successful writers disagree about how much time is needed per stint—ranging anywhere from one to ten hours. I feel that two hours is ideal and not impossible to find in your own busy day. One of the first tricks is to make sure you use precious writing time for *writing* and not for the myriad other chores associated with the work.

"Writing" is made up of a number of sub-categories, each of which needs tending to. A professional doesn't just sit down and magically begin to create prose. The process is more complex than that, and each phase requires our attention. Analyzing the process and breaking it down into its components will help you understand which jobs can be tucked into the corners and crevices of your day. In addition to actual composition, writing encompasses the following:

Planning—initiating projects and setting up a working strategy for each.

Research—which includes clipping and filing.

Outlining—once the material has been gathered.

Marketing—which includes query letters, manuscript typing, Xeroxing, trips to the post office.

And finally, *follow-up* for manuscripts in submission.

All of these things take time, but they won't take *all* of your time, and they shouldn't take your best time. These are clerical details that can be dispatched in odd moments during the day. Delegate as much as possible. Hire someone for these jobs if you can. Have a teen-ager come in one day a week to clip and file. Ask your spouse to drop off a manuscript at the post office on his or her way to work. Check research books out of the library while the kids are at story hour. Use time waiting for a dental appointment or dead time at the laundromat to jot down ideas and get them organized. Take index cards with you every place.

Now take a good look at your day. Feel as if you're already swamped from dawn to dark? Here are some options:

34

1. *Stay up an hour later each night.* At night, the phone doesn't ring and the family is asleep. You'll have fewer distractions and no excuses. You won't drop dead if you cut your sleep by an hour. The time spent creatively on projects important to you will *give* you energy. Eventually, you can think about stretching that one hour to two, but initially, stick to a manageable change and incorporate it thoroughly into your new schedule before tackling more. I used to write from ten at night until midnight or one a.m., and I still find those hours best for certain kinds of work.

2. *Get up an hour earlier,* before the family wakes. Again, shaving an hour from your sleep will do you no harm, and it will give you the necessary time to establish the habit of daily writing. Anthony Trollope, one of my favorite writers, worked for most of his adult life as a postal clerk, on the job from eight until five every day. His solution was to get up at five a.m. and write 250 words every fifteen minutes till eight— three hours. If he finished a book before the time to go to work, he started a new project at once. In his lifetime, he turned out forty-six full-length books, most of them while he earned a living in another capacity.

3. *If you're employed outside your home, try working en route.* British crime writer Michael Gilbert wrote 23 novels . . . all while riding the train to his work as a solicitor. He used the 50-minute transit time to produce 2 to 2½ pages a day, 12 to 15 pages a week. Buses, trains, commuter flights can all represent productive time for you. Use those periods for writing, while you're inaccessible to the rest of the world.

4. *What about your lunch hour?* Do you go out to lunch every day to "escape" the tensions and pressures of the job? Why not stay at your desk, creating a temporary haven in your own head? Pack a brown bag lunch. It's cheaper, among other things, and if you limit yourself to fruit and raw vegetables, you can get thin while you pile up the pages!

5. *Look at your week nights.* See if there's a way to snag one for yourself. You'd make the time if you decided to take an adult education class. Invent a course for yourself, called "Writing My Novel At Long Last" and spend three hours a week in the public library. I heard about a writer who finished a book just this way, working only on Tuesday nights.

6. *Weekends generally have free time tucked into them.* Try Saturday afternoons when the kids are off at the movies, or Sunday mornings when everyone else sleeps late.

7. *Revamp your current leisure time.* Your schedule probably contains hidden hours that you could easily convert to writing time. Television is the biggest time-waster, but I've also realized that reading the daily paper from front to back takes ninety minutes out of my day! For a while, I convinced myself that I needed to be informed on "current events," but the truth is that I was avoiding my desk, squandering an hour and a half that I desperately needed to complete a manuscript. I was feeling pressured, when all the while, the time was sitting right there in front of me . . . literally. Recently, too, I took a good look at my social calendar. I realized that a dinner party for six was requiring, in effect, two full days of activity . . . time I now devote to my work. I still have friends. I just cut my entertainment plans by a third.

Now.

Once you identify and set aside those newly found hours, it's a matter of tailoring the work to suit the time available. This can be done in four simple steps:

1. Make a list of everything you'd like to write . . . a novel, a short story, a film script, a book review for the local paper, that travel article you outlined during your last trip.

2. Choose three. If you only have one item on your agenda, how lucky you are! If you have more than three projects on your list, keep the remaining projects on a subsidiary list to draw on as you complete the items on your primary list and send them out into the marketplace. I generally like to have one book-length project (my long-term goal) and two smaller projects (an article, a short story . . . short-term goals) on my list.

3. Arrange items on the list in the order of their true priority. Be tough about this. For instance, you might have a short story possibility, an idea you've been toying with for years, but when you come right down to it, it might not seem important enough (or fully developed enough) to place among the top three on your list. My first priority is

36

always the detective novel I'm writing currently. I work on that when I'm at my freshest, saving the smaller projects for the period after my first energy peaks. Having several projects in the works simultaneously is good for you psychologically. If you get stuck on one, you can try the next. As you finish each project, the feeling of accomplishment will spur you to renewed effort on those that remain. In addition, by supplying yourself with a steady stream of new projects, you'll keep your interest level high.

4. Once you select the three projects you want to work on, break the writing down into small, manageable units. A novel isn't completed at one sitting. Mine are written two pages at a time over a period of six to eight months. Assign yourself a set number of pages . . . 1 or 2 . . . and then meet your own quota from day to day. Once you've completed two pages, you can let yourself off the hook, moving on to the next task. By doing a limited amount of work on a number of projects, you're more likely to keep all three moving forward. Don't burden yourself with more than you can really handle. Assigning yourself ten pages a day sounds good on the surface, but you'll soon feel so overwhelmed that you'll start avoiding the work and won't get *anything* done. Remember, it's persistence that counts, the steady hammering away at the writing from day to day, day *after* day, that produces the most consistent work and the greatest quantity of it.

Essentially, then, all you need to do is this:

> Analyze the task.
> Scrutinize your schedule.
> Tailor the work to fit.

I have one final suggestion, a practice that's boosted my productivity by 50%. Start each day with a brief meditation . . . five minutes of mental quiet in which you visualize yourself actually sitting at your desk, accomplishing the writing you've assigned yourself. Affirm to yourself that you'll have a good, productive day, that you'll have high energy, solid concentration, imagination, and enthusiasm for the work coming up. Use these positive messages to block out your anxieties, the self-doubt, the fear of failure that in fact comprise procrastination. Five minutes of quiet will reinforce your new determination and will help you make the dream of writing real.

37

9

HOOKED ON BOOKS

By Michael Dirda

BOOK COLLECTING, it must be confessed, resembles a kind of madness. In its highest form this passion for print may approach literary or historical scholarship, yet at its most degenerate it calls to mind those *National Enquirier* stories about spinsters buried alive in tiny apartments beneath 30 tons of once-carefully stacked newspapers. For most people though collecting is simply reading and saving the books of favorite writers. Nothing pathological about that. Things get dangerous only when a person starts to buy books without necessarily intending to read them right away, or at all.

The key to book collecting is design. No mere accumulation of books—regardless of their rarity or cost—makes a collection, only a well-stocked library. What matters is the carrying through of a plan, the completing of a pattern. A real collector buys a book because he needs it for his imagined edifice: To own, for instance, everything by or about Stephen King; all the printings of Whitman's *Leaves of Grass*; every book published by the Hogarth Press; the early Anchor paperbacks designed by Edward Gorey; the high spots in the history of Modernism; books and dust jackets illustrated by Leo and Diane Dillon; all the black autobiographies ever written in this country; anything in hardcovers by anyone named Smith.

A collector needs camaraderie. One of the pleasures of booking is talking to dealers and other collectors, trading gossip, learning what's come on the market, finding out how much your books have increased in value.

What should a person collect? The best answer to this is the simplest: Collect what you like. Or at least collect for a project you like, regardless of the merit of individual books. A lawyer might pursue mysteries with courtroom scenes; doctors often create personal libraries devoted to the history of medicine. Someone in publishing may keep

38

the best sellers since World War II, not for themselves, but to understand better the evolution of dust jacket illustration. A Washington book dealer I know collects author's first books; a local rare book librarian seeks out works of prose by poets. Many younger collectors go after early softcovers (in part because they are cheap)—Dell Mapbacks, Gold Medal originals, Armed Services Editions. Fascinating collections no doubt have been made of novels set on college campuses; works by our friend Anon; or all the translations of Dante into English.

Once settled on an idea, the new collector needs a plan of attack. Suppose, for instance, a mother decides to gather the complete Viking Portable Library as a present for her son. She can simply pick up these books whenever they turn up in shops or at book sales, which they do with some frequency. But if she's more serious or in a hurry, there are other methods that require a few simple decisions. Does she want first editions? In dust jackets? In fine condition? Or will clean reading copies do? A next step might be to make a list of the books wanted; as it happens the Viking Portables often describe the other titles in the series, during the early years typically on the inside of the dust jacket. With "wants" in hand, the collector can then visit stores in a systematic fashion, never worrying whether she already owns a certain title or not. What's more, she can enlist the aid of a dealer.

Many antiquarian book dealers like nothing better than to work with a customer who is actively building a collection. Everyone benefits from such an arrangement. The dealer knows he has an immediate buyer for a particular item, and the customer gains full-time professional help in scanning the marketplace for his needs.

Generally a collector is advised to purchase the best copies he can afford. Books in fine or mint condition increase in value, while those without dust jackets or of a shabby appearance do well just to maintain their original purchase price. Moreover, few collectors are ever happy for long with inferior examples of books they prize. A copy in dust jacket of John Gardner's first novel *The Resurrection* has sold for as much as $600; without the dj, it might be worth $50. No one collecting Gardner wants the keystone of his library in anything but fine condition. *The Resurrection* without a jacket is just an expensive reading copy.

For collectors who pursue exceptionally scarce items—such material as manuscripts, advance proofs, and the like—only a real bookshop will do. Still, a good deal of fun, and the occasional serendipitous treasure, can be found in more casual venues. Thrift shops, junk stores, church bazaars, Saturday morning garage sales, farmer's markets—all these usually boast a shelf or table full of books. Libraries sell off volumes no longer wanted; usually these look pretty shelf worn, but not always, and occasionally they are rare enough to be desirable even as ex-library copies. Sometimes you can even acquire pristine dust jackets because libraries wrap everything in plastic or mylar covers. You can then hope to find a cheap jacketless copy that can be instantly transformed into a desirable book. (I should point out that purists frown on this practice.) Of course, paperback collectors do especially well in such out of the way places: Indeed since many antiquarian bookshops downplay paperbacks, thrift shops are still among the best places to find early softcovers, especially of science fiction and tough guy thrillers.

Ultimately, the best way to get started as a collector is simply to visit as many secondhand bookshops as possible, chat with book people, study catalogues, read *AB Bookman's Weekly* (the trade's professional journal), and buy books. You'll make mistakes, but as your judgment grows, there will be fewer white elephants and more treasures on your shelves. Every collector knows the esthetic and egotistic pleasure of surveying his bookcases, of casting his eyes across rows of titles, noting lacunae, enjoying the sight of a hard-to-find book finally in its proper place.

When I was in fifth grade I was elected King of the Book Fair. In the course of the pageant, I had to wear a paper crown and hold up a sign, a sign that it now seems to me marked out the course of my life: "Who hath a book hath but to read/And he will be a king indeed." All collectors know this oddly regal feeling even when they are reminded that no one truly owns a book until he's actually read it.

10

GIVE THEM WHAT THEY WANT

By Roger Caras

WHEN YOU ENCOUNTER A TWENTY-FIVE-YEAR-OLD WRITER who has sold thirty major magazine pieces and is working on a book and then you meet a thirty-eight-year-old writer who has yet to sell anything over ten lines long, the difference may have less to do with writing talent than you might expect. (I confess, I am not exactly certain what writing talent is besides battered finger tips and the ability to be alone for extended periods of time.) What might the difference be between the working writer and the would-be writer? A sense of the marketplace in a buyer's market.

There is an apocryphal story of the press agent who sold a re-frigerator to an eskimo, but I never knew of a writer who sold a piece on hand-loading shotgun shells to a needlepoint magazine or a needlepoint story to a computer software magazine.

There really is no excuse for not knowing what article should be submitted where. You can't afford the money or time to subcribe to all of the magazines now on the market (your mailman would surely sue you after his first coronary), but libraries have many of them, and there are usually broad-spectrum magazine stands in most major cities. If you buy something, they won't mind your browsing as you stand in the checkout line. It would be difficult today not to find a specialty maga-zine on any subject of interest to you and your typewriter.

I can't do the full litany, but just consider the specialty magazines you have seen: hunting, fishing, backpacking, camping, canoeing, boating, needlework, skiing, antiques, stamp collecting, interior decorating, kitchen design, wine, food, money management, investing, home eco-nomics, Black interests, the Civil War, soldier of fortune interests, pistols, guns in general, dogs, cats, horses, rabbits, cage birds, con-servation, oceanography, women's styles, men's styles, autographs and other paper collectibles, computers, word processors, religion, philosophy, secretarial interests, foreign affairs, American regional interests and an endless number of journals on medicine, dentistry, psychiatry, psychology, behavioral disorders, art in general, law, linguistics, archaeology, western art, oriental studies, aquarium fish, reptiles, and amphibians. I doubt that list covers even twenty percent of the special-interest magazines published. If you can come up with a subject that doesn't seem to have an appropriate outlet, you are really into something so arcane that you may be better off not telling the world of your interest in it. There are even magazines that offer instruction in criminal activity under the guise of patriotism and "real manhood."

If a subject interests you and offers you an exciting research opportunity (field or library or both), find the right magazine and read several issues. If it is published regularly, you will know that the editors are satisfying their readers. Your chance to sell an article to those editors depends on two things: You must come up with an idea that hasn't just been exhausted by an earlier piece, and you must fit into the editors' concept of what they have to offer to their readers. They have conducted polls, and they have seen the mail. Take their word for it; don't argue if you want to get a second chance. (I limit the pegs on which your success might hang to two, assuming that you will have the skill to research and write and, if necessary, supply photos to illustrate your own article.)

What do you look for when you read a magazine as a potential market for your work? There are a few critical points that can make or break your chances with the editor. First, subject matter, of course. Next, I believe, is personal involvement of the writer. Many of the outdoor magazines thrive on "I heard a twig snap and turned slowly" kind of writing, and others will be turned off immediately by any personal narrative intruding on the subject matter. Be sure you are on firm footing there, or the editor will not get beyond the first couple of paragraphs. (Many magazines will offer advice or even have printed submission guidelines for writers new to them. Check that out first.)

After you have the subject matter and the degree, if any, of personal narrative sorted out, check for vocabulary and intellectual level. There is no sense dodging this point; some magazines are written for people who didn't make it into or at least out of high school. Hit them with words like ambiance, ambidextrous and ambergris, and you will think the editorial halls have rubber walls, so fast will your manuscript come bouncing back. If you are writing for this kind of magazine (they pay, too!), admit it. On the other hand, if you are proposing an article for *Foreign Affairs* or *Natural History,* you had better have a good solid grasp on the appropriate jargon.

A very important point: No matter what magazine or journal you are approaching, be certain you know what you are talking about. If your article is the four millionth piece on "trout fishing secrets," you might not have to enthrall Carl Sagan, or Henry Kissinger, but you had better know more about trout fishing (or enough at least to be reinforcing) to interest someone who has been fishing for thirty years. To a brain surgeon you may be a trout fisherman, but to a trout fisherman are you a trout fisherman? Seemingly unsophisticated people can be the toughest to fool. They are often single-minded. (None of the above is to suggest that trout fisherman are not intellects, but I had to pick on someone to make the point.)

So, then, you have the right magazine for your idea; you know how much, if any, personal involvement they want; and you know pretty well what level of vocabulary to employ and how intellectual you should be. Again, we assume you can write. We assume, too, you know enough about your subject to warrant someone's reading your thoughts on the matter. What is left? I would suggest the word *novelty* except it sounds like something in a Cracker Jack box. In fact, though, a *novel* approach (read that as *fresh* approach) can be the maker or breaker. Find a way to tell your story and convey your knowledge so that it doesn't sound as if every other writer in the country picked the same subject. The hard part is to be fresh, original, and perhaps even unique.

Balance these things out. When you have them all in a row you are doing a thing called writing. And only people who write deserve to be paid for being printed. Give them (editors and readers) what they want, and they will give you what you most earnestly desire—money, exposure, experience, and that not-to-be-defined pleasure of being in print.

11

THE WRITER'S EYE

BY RANDALL SILVIS

A PART of every successful writer is, and must be, amoral. Detached. Unfeeling. As nonjudgmental as a tape recorder or camera. It is this capacity to stare at pain or ugliness without flinching, at beauty without swooning, at flattery and truth without succumbing to the lure of either, which provides the mortar, the observable details, to strengthen a story and make it a cohesive unit. This capacity I call the writer's eye.

As a child, I was and still am fascinated by the peaks and valleys of people's lives. I was blessed—or cursed—with what was often referred to as "morbid curiosity." At the scene of a funeral, I would be the one trying to inch a bit closer to the coffin, one ear turned to the dry intonations droning from the minister; the other to the papery rustle of leaves overhead. I would take note of how the mourners were standing, where they held their hands, if there were any clouds in the sky, who wept and who did not even pretend to weep, which shoes were most brilliantly shined, the color of the casket, the scent of smoke from someone's backyard barbecue, a killdeer whistling in the distance.

This is how I would remember and record the day, the event. In the details themselves, unbiased, unvarnished and pure, was every nuance of emotion such a tragedy produced. The same held true for weddings and baptisms, for joyous moments as well as sad. Almost instinctively I seemed to know that every abstraction had an observable form: To remark that my neighbor, a tired and lonely man, was drunk again, said nothing; to say that he was standing by the side of the road, motionless but for his gentle, oblivious swaying even as the cars zipped by and blasted their horns at him, his head down, eyes half-closed, hands shoved deep in his pockets as he sang a mumbled "Meet Me Tonight in Dreamland," said it all.

The writer's eye discriminates. It does not and cannot record every detail in a particular scene, only the most telling ones. It is microscopic in focus, telescopic in intent. If, for example, you wish to depict a woman who is trying to look poised despite her nervousness, does it deepen the depiction to say that she wears a two-carat diamond ring on her left hand? Probably not. But if she is shown sitting very straight, knees and feet together, a pleasant smile on her lips as her right hand unconsciously and repeatedly pulls at and twists the diamond ring on her left? These details are in and of themselves emotionally pallid, but in sum, they add to a colorful, revealing whole. In such a description, the word *nervous* need never be uttered. Yet the conclusion is inescapable, and all the more acute because the reader has not been informed of the woman's uneasiness but has witnessed it for himself.

In my novel *Excelsior* (Henry Holt, October, 1987), one of the most important scenes is a moment of closeness between an inept father and his six-year-old son. The scene takes place in a YMCA locker room minutes after the father accidentally knocked the terrified boy, who cannot swim, into the pool. Bloomhardt, the father, despises himself for his own incompetence, and believes that his son does, too. But during a rare moment of openness, six-year-old Timmy admits *his* feelings of frustration and failure. At this point, it would have been quick and easy to state simply that Bloomhardt was relieved, grateful that his son did not despise him, and was filled with a fervent, though awkward, desire to reassure the boy. Instead, I chose to show his state of mind as evidenced in observable details:

> Bloomhardt blinked, his eyes warm with tears. He leaned sideways and kissed his son's damp head. . . . He faced his open locker again, reached for a sock and pulled it on. He smiled to himself.

Bloomhardt's actions are elemental and, on their own, nearly empty of emotional value. But in the context of this passage and in relation to the man's and boy's characters as defined prior to this scene, these details are all that are needed to show the beginnings of a mutual tenderness, trust, and love.

The writer's eye is not merely one sense, but every power of observation the writer possesses. It not only sees, but also smells, tastes, feels, and hears. It also senses which details will paint the brightest picture, which will hint at an unseen quality, which will allow the reader to see beneath the surface of a character to the ice and fire of emotion within.

45

Think of each phrase of description, each detail, as a dot of color on a Seurat landscape. Individually, each dot is meaningless, it reveals nothing, neither laughter nor sorrow. But if you choose your dots carefully and arrange them on the canvas in their proper places, you might, with luck and practice, compose a scene to take the breath away.

12

STOP WHEN YOU'RE THROUGH

By Phyllis A. Whitney

Openings of stories and novels are fun to write. Everything is fresh, and you are eager to plunge in, meet the characters, and bring to life what has been teeming in your imagination. You may do an opening over several times, but this is never a grim task. Endings, on the other hand, are difficult and dangerous. Fortunately, you can mitigate the dangers. You can conclude a piece of fiction less painfully if you are aware of the pitfalls and learn to use various "tools" that will help you write a satisfactory ending.

Some writers prefer to think of the climax first. They may have the solution, the conclusion, in mind, and then work back to find their characters and story line. This method would be impossible for me, since I start with a character faced by a problem, and build ahead one step at a time. I can't think about a story any other way. However, if you are one of those who work "backwards," the points I want to talk about will still be useful.

All parts of the story are important. If you don't pull the readers into your opening, they will never read to the end. If you don't hold their interest along the way, they can easily put your novel aside. When it comes to the ending, your purpose is to leave the reader satisfied. Even an unhappy ending can be right for a particular kind of plot. No matter how good your novel or story may be, if the reader is disappointed in its resolution, you've failed. One way or another, heroes or heroines must achieve what they set out to do, *or* they must receive their comeuppance.

There can be a difference between reader-satisfaction and author-satisfaction, and writers need to be aware of this. Our satisfaction as writers may simply grow out of relief to have the long stint of writing a novel over; there's a sense of triumph because we've filled all those pages. Readers, on the other hand, are involved with an emotion that has to do entirely with the characters and the story they've just finished.

47

As a writer, you may be permitted your moment of satisfaction at finishing the book, but then you must start rereading objectively to discover if you've really done what you set out to do. There are measuring sticks to help you at this stage.

Presumably, you have given the main character an important problem, one that is difficult to solve. If you are to satisfy your readers, your main character must *deserve* to solve his or her difficulties. He must prove his mettle through conflict, setbacks, seeming defeat—ultimately winning out through courage against great odds. The climax scene is the big test that hero or heroine faces, and you must be careful to play it through fully.

Once, when I was a very young writer and had to approach a climax scene that I was afraid to write (didn't know how to write), I thought I would be clever and let myself off the hook. So, I skipped the actual scene, went on to a time after the climax, and then looking back, told what had happened. Fiasco! Readers want the satisfaction of living through a climax to the full. Both your main character and your reader must be rewarded with a dramatic climax that is important and is satisfying.

All through any novel, there must be threats and conflicts. These culminate in the climax scene, and you must make them seem *real*. This isn't as obvious as it seems. Again, it's so easy to fool yourself. You may think you're dealing with a real problem, when the difficulty is really something that could be explained in a few words at any point along the way, ending the story. So of course you drag it on. Your characters must never be in tight spots just by chance. Let's say Mary believes that Bill has done something she can never forgive; she is mistaken, and an explanation would clear everything up. But there is no real story, and consequently, no reader satisfaction. The threats you provide must be real, and the disaster disastrous. If the main character is to win out, the rewards at the end should be worthwhile. Failure should mean loss of life, or certainly loss of happiness. Never a balloon that collapses at a prick!

I prefer happy endings for my novels. I am an entertainer, and I know readers like to step into my make-believe world to follow someone who will pull through in the end. A disappointing ending will not bring a reader back for more—and most editors are quite aware of this. Real life is filled with confusion, and the orderly pattern of fiction can counteract the chaos around us. I don't belittle "escape." Escape can be the playtime that all human beings need to help them heal, and to give them relief at least for a little while.

In the climax scene, the main character must prove what she or he is made of. When readers like and admire your main characters, they're with them right to the end. When these characters win out in some unexpected and surprising way, there is sure to be reader-satisfaction, since readers love to be surprised. So it's important to do the unexpected as often as possible.

When a character is forced to take action (whatever the reason), the scene is bound to be interesting. This action needn't always be physical. A scene in dialogue can be packed with psychological "action" while tension is building up and the outcome is uncertain. In the climax, however, there is apt to be danger of both a physical and psychological kind. By this time you will have created a state of anxiety in the reader. Anxiety is one of your most important tools. Real anxiety on the part of the main character—for good cause—will result in anxiety in the reader. Anxiety results in suspense and will keep your readers turning pages to culminate in the climax scene that you are, of course, going to provide.

You can test the strength of this anxiety by asking yourselves about rewards and punishments. What terrible consequences will befall your main characters if they fail in their quest? What wonderful rewards will success bring? When you set this all down on paper, weaknesses will show up, and you can strengthen where necessary.

Tied into all this is what you are trying to say to the reader at the end of the novel. Something called "theme"—the meaning we give to our fiction. If you haven't said anything, you haven't gone anywhere. At the end of the story, the theme must be evident, though you must handle it subtly. Show, don't tell, and never sound preachy.

I don't always know what I want to say until I'm well into the writing of a novel. My characters will reveal meaning to me in the course of a story, as they learn and grow. The main character must change in some way. We must look for meaning in a story, just as we do in life, and when we find the point we want to make, its significance will strengthen the story.

The climax scene does just what it implies—it brings all elements of a novel together and leads to a logical solution. This need for logic can often make a writer stumble. The author's purpose and logic may not always be the same as the character's. Perhaps you want Mary to take some foolish action that would further the plot. But you'd better trust Mary, who will surely behave in a more sensible way. She doesn't care about plot twists, and you should listen and make sure that your surprises follow the logic of the characters. You need to hear what they try to tell you.

Books on writing fiction used to deal with the come-to-realize ending. This term is seldom used now, but the concept is still sound and needs to be examined. This type of ending is often required, but it can fall flat if you're not aware of what you're doing.

Let's say your main character needs to learn something in the course of the novel if she is to carry out its theme. Perhaps she is trying to avoid facing something she fears or is wrong about. She needs to learn a better way. That is, she must *come-to-realize*. By the end of the story she must change. If this change comes about because someone points out that she is wrong, and she listens, decides to change—and you leave if there—the story will be weak and unsatisfying. There are three steps to observe in this type of ending.

1. Character is doing the wrong thing.

2. Something dramatic *happens* to show her the error of her ways. She may also have been told, but has paid no attention.

3. She then *takes action*—she does something dramatic to *prove* that she has changed. This should be tied up with the climax, but it is an important step the writer can easily forget. It's not enough for the character to say, "Now I understand, and I'll change." She must prove through action that she really has changed.

In my newest novel, *Rainbow in the Mist,* Christy, my main character, has psychic talent that frightens her, and from which she tries to escape. Of course, she can't and she finally learns that she must take a stand and use her gift. In the climax scene, she accepts her talent and decides to use it to good effect, so the readers know she has changed.

Your ending should come as soon after the climax as possible, and every loose end must have been satisfactorily tied up. I use "have been" advisedly. Tie up as many loose ends as you can *before* you get to the final scene. This is especially important in a mystery novel, in which red herrings have been tossed about as the story progresses, and had better be explained by the end. It's very easy during the writing for the writer to use some confusing event that has an explanation other than the one

50

the reader expects—and then to forget all about it, so it's left hanging. Later, the reader may in annoyance go back to ask the question you haven't answered.

So make lists. Whenever I read back through my pages, I watch for these questions that need to be picked up and explained later, and I make sure in revising that each one is answered. Sometimes I can even remove the difficulty and drop it altogether. More often it is something I need, and I must work out a resolution, an explanation. This is best done before the climax scene, if at all possible.

In *Rainbow in the Mist,* I use a llama farm in several scenes. One of the characters buries something in the llama pen—a nice mystery at the time. Later, I wished I'd never thought of it, because the explanation was hard to make logical. But by that time it was needed in the story, and I had to figure it out.

It used to be customary in a mystery novel to have the characters sit around *after* the big climax scene while everything was explained. But these long explanations became so tiresome and anticlimatic that few writers do this any more. They have to work harder to get all the explanations in ahead of time, but it pays off in reader satisfaction. However, if you tell all too soon, you may give away the story's surprise, and you must guard against this mistake as well. To avoid such an anticlimax, make sure that something important is left hanging till the very end, something the reader still wants to know and is *anxious* about. Not just an explanation, but some unfinished business. If you can hold this off until the last page—even the last paragraph—the reader will stay with you.

The most important thing to remember about endings is to *stop when you're through.* Never go on and on for pages after you've given the reader all the answers. Watch endings of novels and stories as you read, and learn from writers who manage to conclude their novels successfully.

Last paragraphs and closing lines are important, and I am seldom happy with mine. Life doesn't end until it ends, but fiction must. I always do these lines over and over. When they won't come out right, I go back for my final rereading, and when I read the ending again, the right phrases may then come to mind more easily.

Whatever you do—leave your reader satisfied and stop when you're through!

13

INVOLVE YOUR READER

By Richard Martin Stern

How much does a fiction writer have a legitimate right to expect from his readers? The question is, I think, a proper one, and the answers can frequently be vexing.

Obviously, if writing for a general audience, the writer has a legitimate expectation that his reader will have a command of the language as it is spoken and generally appears in print.

But has he the right to expect that words or phrases in foreign tongues will also be readily understood, even standard foreign phrases such as, *Cui bono? C'est ça? Manana por la manana? Wie geht's?*

And how about the jargon that seems to be a part of almost every line of work—lawyerese? medical gobbledegook? accounting terms, or scientific language which seems to exist in a world of its own with words such as parameters, vector forces, neurons or DNA; or, for that matter, kilotons versus megatons, words we hear all too frequently these days?

Can the reader be expected to understand the technical workings of a power generating plant? A jet aircraft? Or even the inner secrets of his or her own automobile engine?

To narrow the question: Are foreign words, phrases, technical terms or esoteric references ever necessary in a story or novel?

The answer is that they sometimes are; the problem is how to deal with them.

Let's take the first statement first. Why are they ever necessary? There are several reasons. In Tony Hillerman's fine mystery novels, for example, all of them set in the Southwest and featuring a Navajo detective inevitably involved in matters connected with the Navajo culture, the author *has* to explain to his readers something of the way the Navajo people think and how they view matters most of us take for granted such as clouds, rock formations, formal dances or healing, lore that has been handed down for generations. He also introduces certain words in the Navajo tongue, and explains their meanings. If he does not fill the reader in as he goes along, *the plot would become meaningless.*

In *The Milagro Beanfield War* (now a motion picture), John Nichols has to explain about irrigation ditches, the vital importance of water in the arid New Mexico land and the feelings that exist between the local Hispanic and Anglo cultures—or the entire story makes little sense.

The first reason for esoterica, then, is to help explain the workings of the plot. Not always easy, but frequently necessary.

Another reason is to give the story authenticity, to instill in the reader the feeling that the writer does indeed know what he is talking about and that the matters described are in real life what the story depicts them to be. Then and only then will the reader follow happily along with the story.

In *Presumed Innocent,* high on the best-seller lists for over a year, Scott Turow, the author, relies heavily on legal detail in the office of the Public Prosecutor of a large midwestern city. As you read the book, you *know* that Scott Turow has *been* there, and you as a reader are content that you are in good hands.

The importance of this sense of authenticity cannot be over-emphasized. It is vital in order to lend credibility to the story itself because frequently characters in works of fiction do not behave as people you know do, and the actions of these fictional characters *depend* on their surroundings, which the writer *must* make you accept.

The sense of authenticity comes, too, from the way the characters talk, frequently using words you would not normally use, frequently words with which you are not familiar, such as those technical terms I mentioned earlier. Without these unfamiliar words and patterns and rhythms of speech you, as the reader, may well resist what in fiction *has* to be achieved: that you are reading about real people in real situations, and that the story as it unfolds is *credible*.

You cannot, for example, have an automobile mechanic refer to, "the gadget that turns the what's it," in your automobile engine.

Instead, he will refer to the *crankshaft,* and if the writer is not sure that you know what a crankshaft is, then it is up to him to instruct you. Which brings us to the second part of that proposition that foreign words, phrases, technical terms or esoteric references *are* sometimes necessary. Or almost.

Here, let me throw in a no, no: there is absolutely no excuse for a writer to throw in esoterica merely to show the reader what a knowledgeable fellow he is, as, I am afraid, is done all too often. For every reader who might be impressed, it is my guess that 100 will be annoyed if not downright antagonized by an unnecessary display of erudition. If you as a writer are going to use a word, phrase or reference that will not be readily understood, it must be *because the story demands it*. There is no other justification.

Now let's get to the problem of *how* you make your reader *understand* the words, phrases, technical workings, or other matters he cannot be expected to be totally familiar with. That can be a tough one.

In *Presumed Innocent,* however, the writer's task is easy. When he is explaining the workings of the Public Prosecutor's office, Turow is writing in the first person and, therefore, is presumed to be speaking directly to you, the reader, as if he were sitting in your living room. So all he has to do is tell you that, for example, LNU means "last name unknown" in the special jargon of the Public Prosecutor's world. No problem.

This is not to say that writing in the first person is easy *per se*. It may appear to be, but it is not for a number of reasons, not the least of which is that the narrator must always be on the scene witnessing what is happening, and that can lead to near-impossibilities in the plot.

So what if you are writing in the third person, which most of us prefer, if only because you, the writer, can then move around freely from scene to scene witnessing them through the eyes of whichever character you choose? Then the task of explaining unfamiliar terms or facts to your reader becomes somewhat more difficult, but it *still must be done*.

The usual device is to have your principal character explain to another character how something works, or what it means, or, perhaps, even what it is. Sherlock Holmes always had Dr. Watson handy for that purpose if for no other. In the earlier Hercule Poirot stories, Captain Hastings was always around to ask stupid questions and absorb the answers along with the reader.

In my novel *Tsunami!* I deal with a phenomenon usually, but incorrectly called "tidal wave." Actually, the scientific, oceanographic definition of *tsunami* is a huge wave generated by an earthquake or volcanic eruption on the floor of the ocean. When explained, it is easy for the reader to understand—and frightening in the extreme. In order to tell my tale, I *had* to have two protagonists, not one, because explanations were mandatory, and I decided they could best be accomplished in dialogue between my two main characters without diminishing the stature of either. I hope I have been successful.

Another way of getting the unfamiliar across to the reader is to have your main character discover the fact and figure it out for himself, right along with the reader. This can work well because it tends to forge a bond between the character and the reader, the bond of mutual and simultaneous discovery, which involves the reader emotionally in the events of the novel.

The purpose of all this, of course, is to bring your reader *into* your story so that he may be carried along by it, instead of standing off and looking at it critically. The trick is to do it without disrupting the narrative flow, and that entails caution in another direction—bringing in information that may be fascinating but is also irrelevant.

I return to Scott Turow's *Presumed Innocent*. It is filled with explanations of the unfamiliar, but all of them have a definite bearing either by providing a sense of authenticity or by aiding the reader in understanding the twists and turns of the plot. It is a neat tightrope walk between the germaine and the extraneous, and the result is a taut and dramatic tale.

I have said it before, and I will say it again and again: Fiction writing is largely a process of *selection*, of choosing only what is necessary and steadfastly refusing to include what is not. Almost inevitably you are going to have to bring into your story *something* that may be unfamiliar to *some* of your readers. The trick is not to lecture and not to overexplain, but nevertheless to make sure that you are carrying your reader along with you and not leaving him at the last plot turning, wondering what is going on because he hasn't understood some words or terms.

But here let me throw in a warning: In the process of making everything clear to the reader, *do not talk down to him*. All that will produce is resentment. Your reader is not a dolt merely because he may not understand or be familiar with some matters that are quite plain to you. Consider him an interested friend, and treat him accordingly. There is no other way.

14

THE READER AS PARTNER

By Tony Hillerman

SOMETIME VERY EARLY in my efforts to make a living as a writer, I noticed an odd little fact, trivial but useful: People just back from seeing the Rocky Mountains didn't describe the Front Range. They told me about the clump of mountain iris they'd seen blooming through the edge of a dwindling snowbank. Witnesses of a train wreck I interviewed when I was a reporter would describe the women's clothing scattered along the right-of-way and ignore the big picture. The fellow drinking beer after watching the rodeo would talk about the sounds the bulls made coming out the gate—not the derring-do of the champion rider.

I noticed my own brain worked that way, too: It would store a scattering of details in full color and with every stitch showing, but the general scene would be vague and ill-defined. I presumed that this was the way run-of-the-mill men and women remembered things, and thus, it would be useful for writers in the process of converting a scene that exists in our minds into words that would recreate it in the imagination of those who read what we write.

I doubt if there is anything new or original about this thinking or this tactic. Selecting significant details to cause the reader to focus attention exactly where it's wanted was being done with quill pen on papyrus and probably before. Except for those dilettantes of the "art for art's sake" school, every writer is engaged in a joint venture every time he writes. He looks at what's behind his own forehead and translates it into words. At the other end of the crosscut saw, the reader drinks in those words and tries to transmute them back into images.

It's a partnership. We work at it. So does the reader.

But we're getting paid for it, in money, fame (if we're lucky), and in the fun of controlling the process. The reader expects a different reward for the cash and time he or she invests. Even so, that reader is a working member of the team.

I always write with some clear notions about those for whom I write. They are, for example, a little more intelligent than I am and have a bit better education. They have good imaginations. They enjoy suspense. They are impatient. They are middle-aged. They are busy. They know very little about the specific subject I'm writing about. They are interested in it only if I can provoke that interest.

Given that, how should I go about my business? For example, how should I describe in physical terms this benign character I am about to introduce in chapter three? Not much, probably, if that character is to be important to the plot, and the reader is to come to know him from repeated meetings. But quite a bit if said character takes the stage only briefly.

Why this odd inversion? Because my intelligent, well-educated, middle-aged, imaginative reader knows from personal experience what various sorts of people look like. Therefore, if you use a character a lot, the reader paints his own portrait. For example, as far as I can remember, I have never given more than the vaguest descriptions of either Joe Leaphorn or Jim Chee, the two Navajo tribal policemen who are often the protagonists in my mystery novels. Yet scores of readers have described them to me. Tall and short, big and little, plump and lean, handsome and homely. The reader's imagination creates the character from his or her own experience, making the policeman look exactly the way he should look. Why should the writer argue with that? Why should the person who is investing money and time in reading my story be denied his role in the creative process?

Minor characters, I think, need more description. The reader is likely to see them only briefly through the eyes of the protagonist. He should be as curious about minor characters as is the viewpoint character— looking for the spot of gravy on the necktie, the nervous twitch at the corner of the eye, the dark roots of the bleached blonde hair, the scar tissue on the left cheek. Our reader won't see this minor actor enough to fit him into any personal mold.

Sometimes, of course, the writer must exercise more control over the image the reader would create. The story line may demand that the reader know the character is burly, has an artificial hand, and that his eyes tend to water if he stands too long reading the sympathy cards in the Hallmark shop. Otherwise, I count on the reader to perform his half of the task with no interference from me. I think he enjoys it more.

This notion of the reader as partner in a game of imagination affects how I write in many other ways. For example, there's that hard-to-define something that I think of as "mood." It exists in my mind as I write a scene. Sometimes it is merely the mental state of the viewpoint character through whose eyes whatever is happening is seen. But it can be more than that, or even different from that. For example, I may need to send signals to the reader that it is time for nervous anxiety, while the protagonist is still happily remembering that there's nothing left to worry about.

I tend to take on the mood of the scene—writing with lower lip gripped between my teeth when doom is impending, writing with a grin when all is well in chapter nine. I want the reader to join me in this mood. And here I'm on shaky ground. I simply have no way of knowing if my tactics work.

They involve engaging the reader's senses. I interrupt the dialogue or the action to show the reader through the eyes of the protagonist the dust on the windowsill, the grime on the windowpane, the tumbleweeds blowing across the yard, the broken gate creaking in the wind, the spider scurrying toward the center of its web, the stuffed weasel in its frozen leap toward the cowering quail in the taxidermy display. I have the reader notice the odors of old age, of decay, and of air breathed too often in a closed and claustrophobic room. I have him hear the sort of vague sounds that intrude into tired, tense silences. These are the sorts of signals my senses are open to when I am in this certain mood. If they don't contribute to causing it, at least they reflect it. Perhaps the same will be true for the reader.

Another mood. Another set of sensory signals. Take satisfaction-contentment-happiness (what my Navajo characters might call "hozro"). There's the smell of rain in the air (remember, I write mostly about a landscape where rain is all rare and a joyful blessing), the aroma of brewing coffee, the promising voice of distant thunder, the sound of birds, the long view through slanting sunlight of sage and buffalo grass, and the mountains on the horizon, a sense of beauty with room enough and time enough to enjoy it, and the good feeling of fresh-baked bread under the fingertips.

Unless some psychologist can come up with a universal catalogue of which objects/smells/sounds are connected in the mind of Average

Human with which mood, neither you nor I will ever know how effective this technique is. My conversations with those who have read my work suggest that sometimes I can make it work, and sometimes I fail. But I am working at it, using my only laboratory animal—myself—as guinea pig.

Someone I meet pleases me. I think I would like them. Why? Well, you know . . . there was just something about him. But specifically, exactly what was it? Go back, you sluggard, and remember. What was it, specifically and exactly, that first caused you to start looking at and listening to this stranger? It was the body language, the expression, that told you he was really and intently listening when you talked to him. Interested in you and in what you were saying. So how can that be described most effectively? And what else was there? The way he said things? The turn of phrase. To defer. Not to interrupt. The tendency not to overdescribe, to presume his listener was intelligent and informed. Whatever it was, isolate it. Remember it. Have it handy the next time you want to introduce this sort of person to the reader.

A scene depresses me, leaves me out of sorts and angry. Why? The coldness of the room, the dim, yellow light, the tarnish on the gold tassel on the rope, the arrogant stare of the hostess, the slick, clammy coolness of the surface of this table. . . . What else?

I awake at night from a bad dream, tense and anxious. Quick. Dissect the mood before it evaporates. Nightmares are rare these days for me. For a man who deals in suspense, fear, and tension, they are too valuable to waste. What was in it and in the darkness around the bed that provokes this uneasiness and anxiety? Specifically, what do you hear, or smell, or feel or see that causes this painful tension?

I have been doing this for years: stripping down people and places, dissecting their looks and their mannerisms, filling the storage bins of imagination with useful parts; doing the same with street scenes, with landscapes, with the weather. When I wrote only nonfiction, such stuff was jotted in my notebook—the telltale details I trained my mind to isolate and collect. The anthropologist squatted on a grassy slope beside an anthill, his callused fingers sifting through those tiny grains ants bring to the surface, frowning in his fierce hope of finding a chip from a Stone Age artifact. The same fingers sorting through the residue left on the sifter-frame over his wheelbarrow, eliminating the gravel, roots, and rabbit droppings, saving the tiny chips flaked from a flint lance point; finding a twig to fish out the angry scorpion and return him to the grass. And that final detail, I hope my reader will agree, does more than put him on the scene with me. It gives him insight into the character of the man who owns the callused fingers.

15

THE ROAD TO ROMANCE

By Rosamunde Pilcher

A FEW YEARS AGO, when I had already established myself as a writer of romantic stories and novels, a close friend, of whom I was very fond, moved into the business. She asked me for advice, and I helped her as much as I could, with useful tips and practical advice. Since that day, she has become quite successful in the romantic short story field.

Some of the advice I gave her, she had not expected. I had long since learned to ignore the instinctive reaction of acquaintances when they learned the type of writing I turned out. So, I said, don't expect anybody, least of all your immediate family, to be either impressed or even interested. "She writes romantic stories for magazines" seems to be an euphemism for, "Poor soul, she must have a thousand sexual hang-ups and frustrations."

And then, there is the maddening friend's comment: "Darling, I read your little story in *Woman's Weekly* last week at the hairdresser's, when I was under the dryer. Thought you'd like to know. So clever. Such fun. I've often thought I could do that. I'm full of marvelous ideas. But, of course, there's never time. . . ."

You give a big swallow and smile. It takes effort, but it's not worth either justifying yourself, or trying to explain. To begin with, there are the sheer mechanics of the business. To write a bad novel takes just as much time and physical effort as writing a good novel, the only difference being that probably nobody is ever going to give you any money for the bad one. Producing romantic stories and novels that actually sell—i.e., that are professionally crafted and peopled with believable characters—is as demanding and time-consuming as any other form of writing. The essentials are similar. You have a story to tell, a point to make, a moral to push. You must be able to raise a belly-laugh, or bring a tear to the reader's eye. This isn't easy, but you do it to the very best of your ability, and to hell with the scorners.

The collected letters and diaries of James Pope-Hennessy, the eminent British biographer (his biography of Queen Mary was a model of its kind), were published under the title *A Lonely Business*. Writing, he had said, like living, was a lonely business.

It is no good imagining that one is going to be a writer—be it of romance, history, biography, stream-of-consciousness novel, or whatever—unless one can deal with this inherent loneliness and the self-discipline that has to go with it. Your finished product comes from the inside of your own head, and no person but you has the ability to set it down and so, set it free.

I have been turning out romantic fiction for nearly forty-five years, and looking back, I realize that my method of working has changed remarkably little. With a tenuous idea drifting around at the back of my mind, I suddenly turn upon it, when it isn't looking, and grab it. Then, swiftly, before the delicate, captured creature dies, I briefly note the sequence and form that the story is to take. If it is to be a short story, I try to keep it within the time span of a single day. Working thus, I find it easier to dispense with the necessity of complicated flashbacks, which I think make a true short story top-heavy, and destroy proportion and balance. Working to such a narrow specification ensures that no single word is wasted. Each phase of dialogue, description, and narrative either establishes character or develops plot. At the end of the first draft, banged out on an old steam typewriter, I prune. Pruned, the story is retyped. And, on principle, never touched again. The system seems to work for me.

My novels are simply an extenuation of this process, though, of course, they take longer to conceive and considerably longer to write. But in both cases I live with and know my characters well, long before I have put pen to paper. In the case of a novel, these characters are carefully plotted and charted, with ages and backgrounds carefully detailed and filled in.

My recently published long novel, *The Shell Seekers*, was submitted to the publishers before it was completed: six chapters and a detailed resumé of the remaining ten chapters. When I finally completed the book, I read through the resumé once more and discovered that I had followed it word for word.

Writing light fiction over such a long time span has produced its own crop of problems. Times change, and in order to keep up with them and not to find ourselves dated or left behind in the modern literary worlds, we must keep pace with social developments, maintaining liberal attitudes and open, listening minds. There is no point, any longer, in pretending that young people don't live together before marriage, change their partners, and generally take their time before deciding to settle down for good.

There is, however, still one romantic novelist in England—Barbara Cartland—who insists, indeed, boasts, that all her heroines remain pure and unsullied until the wedding ring is slipped upon their fingers. But she can keep up this remarkable record only by setting all her novels (and she is a prolific author, so there are hundreds of them) in some bygone era: Early Victorian, perhaps, or Regency days. As far as I can see, there is no other possible way she could get away with such marvelously outmoded attitudes.

Rosamond Lehmann, a writer who made her name in the 1930s (and is lately enjoying a new reappraisal and popularity), was asked in an interview a couple of years ago why, in the light of her great success, she had not written more novels, for her output, though brilliant, was sparing. Her reply was that there were other facets to her life: home, children, grandchildren, friends, travel, dogs, a garden. She did not mean that these made unwanted demands upon her time, but rather that they were her pleasures, bestowing not impatience, but joy and satisfaction.

While in the thick of writing a novel, treading upstairs after lunch to settle down to work again, glancing from the window at a sun-filled garden, seeing my grandchildren by the swimming pool, I sometimes broodily wish that I were a man. A man could choose his time to work, while his wife, or some other obliging female, shopped, cooked, washed clothes, ironed them, mowed the grass, pushed the vacuum cleaner around, and entertained the weekend guests.

But only *sometimes* do I broodily wish this, because most of the time I am in control, and able to keep my life on an even balance. Besides, if I worked all day long at my typewriter, I shouldn't be living, and if I didn't live, I should run out of fuel to keep my mental boiler fired.

I should miss the conversation of the two Scottish ladies, waiting for their haddock in the Dundee fishmonger's queue:

"Yer affly broon, hen," ("Hen," in Scotland, is a common term of endearment.)
"Aye. I've been on ma holidays."

63

"Where'd yer go?"

"Casablanca."

"Where the hell's that?"

"I don't know. We flew."

I should miss the winter beauty of a walk, with dogs, on the foreshore of my son's farm. The hills of Fife, rose-stained in the sunset, lie across the deep blue waters of the Firth of Tay. Here, at low tide, the mudflats are loud with the cry of wild geese and shellduck and the piping curlews, which the local country people call "Whaups."

But mostly, I should miss out on my children and their children and their many friends. To them I owe so much, because it has always been through their young eyes that I have observed the changing mores of this world, as they really happen, and so I can express them in my stories authentically and convincingly.

Living and writing go hand in hand. Sometimes fact and fiction become weirdly intertwined. Some years ago I wrote a story called "Toby," about a small boy whose great friend was the local farmer. The old man dies, and for the first time in his life, the boy comes to terms with death. My own grandson Oliver also had a great friend, Bert Dewar, the cattleman on his father's farm. Oliver spent much of his time with Bert, but Bert became ill and after a long and painful struggle, during which Oliver visited him every day, Bert also died. The day of Bert's funeral, my story "Toby" was published in a British magazine. I gave it to Oliver's mother, and I think she read it aloud to him. I hope it afforded him some comfort.

In my novel *Wild Mountain Thyme,* I based Jock Dunbeath's house, Benchoile, on a house called Gordonbushe, which I had glimpsed in the distance, across the wide reaches of Loch Brora in Sutherland. It was a huge house, hidden in a stand of Scotch pines, and all that could be seen of it was a gable or two and some tall chimneys. But it caught my imagination. After *Wild Mountain Thyme* was finished and had been accepted by St. Martin's Press, I went north again, on a visit, and the people with whom I stayed took me to Gordonbushe. We turned off the main road onto the bumpy track that led through the heather and along the north shore of the loch, and I was visited with the strangest sense of recognition, because it was all exactly as I had described it. At last we came to the open gate, set in a drystone wall, the cattle-grid, the tall soughing pines. We drove up the winding lane, and the trees fell away, and the house revealed itself at last. Not Gordonbushe, but my house. Benchoile. As we got out of the car, the front door opened and our hostess appeared and came to welcome us. I was astonished and almost resentful, because she was herself and not my Jock Dunbeath.

16

A NOVELIST ANSWERS QUESTIONS ON WRITING

By Sidney Sheldon

Q. *What are some of the devices you have found most successful in getting your readers to ask breathlessly, "What next?"*

A. The secret is simple: Take a group of interesting characters and put them in harrowing situations. I try to end each chapter with a cliff-hanger, so that the reader must turn just one more page to find out what happens next. Another thing I do is to cut out everything that is extraneous to the story I am telling.

Q. *What is the hardest part of a novel for you to write?*

A. The hardest part of a book is the beginning. When I begin a book, I have no plot in mind, only a character. I start dictating to my secretary, and as I talk, the character comes to life and gets involved with the other characters. I have no idea where the story is going to lead me.

I want to emphasize that I do not recommend this way of working for any but the most experienced writers, since writing without an outline can lead to a lot of blind alleys. For a beginning writer, I think an outline is very important. Novels should have a beginning, a middle, and an end, and it is a good idea to have a road map to tell you where you are going. Without an outline, it's very easy to wander all over the place. At best, you can get lost; at worst you can go over a cliff and find out you do not have a novel.

Q. *Describe for us a typical day's writing session.*

A. When I begin writing in the morning, I will read the last few pages from the day before and go on from there. A helpful trick in writing is that at the end of the day when you finish a scene, begin a new scene and then stop. In the morning when you are ready to go to work, you have already begun the new scene.

Q. *You've said that your novels go through many stages of revision. How extensive are these revisions? Does the shape of the novel ever change?*

A. I usually do up to a dozen rewrites of a manuscript. The first rewrite will be very extensive. I will discard a hundred or two hundred pages at a time, tightening the book and clarifying the characters. As the rewrites progress, there is less work to do, since it becomes a matter of polishing the script.

Q. *Have you ever started on a novel, written well into the middle of it, only to find that you don't like the direction it is taking or that you cannot resolve the plot in a way to satisfy you or the reader?*

A. I usually want to give up in the middle of all my novels. I try to create great problems for my characters, because that makes it more interesting for the reader. But sometimes I find it almost impossible to resolve the problems I have created, and that makes it very difficult for the writer. As an example, when I was researching pharmaceutical companies for *Bloodline,* I came across so many horrendous examples of the ruthlessness and callousness of the large pharmaceutical firms that I almost gave up the idea of writing the book. How could I make my heroine, who was running a large pharmaceutical firm, a sympathetic character? I resolved that by attributing most of the chicanery that went on to other firms and having my heroine fight against using those tactics.

Another example is that in writing *Bloodline,* I apparently got carried away with the character of Old Samuel. He should have been a minor character, and I found that I had devoted 300 pages to him. I resolved that by throwing away 250 of those pages. If I had plotted out that book in advance, I would have been spared that editorial job.

Q. *Do you believe that there are any really unbreakable rules in writing fiction?*

A. The only unbreakable rule in writing fiction is that there are no unbreakable rules. Unlike the dramatic forms of writing, where you are limited by a time framework and a budget, when you write a novel the only limits are the perimeters of your imagination. You can go back and forth in time and space, create other planets, play God. Make your own rules!

Q. *How do you get the reader emotionally involved in your characters, or make them share the characters' emotions and reactions?*

A. You get your readers emotionally involved in your characters by being emotionally involved yourself. Your characters must come alive for you. When you are writing about them, you have to feel all the emotions they are going through—hunger, pain, joy, despair. If you suffer along with them and care what happens to them, so will the reader.

Q. *What roles can minor characters play in a novel, and how are they best used to highlight the actions and goals of the main characters?*

A. Someone once said that in movies there are no small parts—only small actors. In a sense, there are no minor characters in novels, meaning that every character should be as distinctive and colorful as possible. Make that character physically unusual, or give him an exotic background or philosophy. The reader should remember the minor characters as well as the protagonists.

Q. *What is the relative importance of plot in a novel? Can it be considered separate from theme and character?*

A. Years ago when I was writing movies, I learned the difference between an "A" picture and a "B" picture: Characterization. Of course plot is important, but if you do not have characters that hold your reader, the plot does not matter. The trick is to create live people so that your reader gets deeply involved and cares what happens to those characters. The plot is the engine that drives the book. In essence, both are extremely important. *Rebecca* is a perfect example of wonderful characterization and an exciting plot.

Q. *How did you develop the discipline to write on a regular schedule?*

A. Writing *is* discipline. It is planting the seat of your pants—or your skirt—in a chair and hanging in there through all the pain and loneliness of creation.

A number of years ago I was living in New York and in desperate

68

need of money. I had to write something that I could sell quickly, but unfortunately I did not have an idea. I remember planting myself in a chair and resolving not to get up until I had a premise for a story. I sat there for hours until I got an idea, then I continued to sit and develop it in my mind. It was sold to David Selznick, who hired me to write the screenplay for it. He re-titled it *The Bachelor and the Bobby Soxer,* and I got an Oscar for it.

Q. *Do you think diaries or journals are useful?*

A. I wish I had kept a diary over the years. I think it is very useful for any writer. The memory sometimes plays tricks or is forgetful, and we miss a lot of the past that could be helpful in our present.

Q. *You do most of the research for a book before you start writing. How do you organize your material? How do you decide when to stop searching and start writing?*

A. Once I know where the locale of my next novel is going to be, I go there and research the atmosphere, customs, etc., and look for specific things that I will be using in the book. I will sometimes prepare in advance a list of all the things I need to find out. When I have completed my research, I begin writing the novel.

Q. *Do you have any favorite resources (Almanac, librarian, daily newspaper, etc.)?*

A. Public libraries are treasure troves of information and in their files you will find almost anything you need to know.

Q. *Should slang be used sparingly?*

A. All dialogue should come out of character. It should never come from the author. If a character speaks in slang, then it is perfectly proper to let him do so. It would obviously be out of place to put slang in the mouth of a character to whom such language would be alien. If you want dialogue to be strong and vivid, make it *real.* Elmore Leonard is a master at this. He writes taut, lean dialogue. Hammett was another example, along with Hemingway. If you really know your characters, you will know exactly how they should speak.

Q. *How has your experience in television and film influenced your novel writing? Do you "see" scenes in your mind before (or while) you create them?*

A. My experience in writing for the dramatic form (motion pictures, plays and television shows) has strongly affected my approach to the narrative form. Because I have been trained to write scenes to be played by actors and dialogue to be read by actors, I have learned to write visually so that in writing a novel, I "see" scenes in my mind. It helps to make my novels more visual and realistic.

Q. *How difficult was it for you to make the transition from screenwriter to novelist, having to depend less on dialogue and more on a descriptive narrative to carry the scene?*

A. It was extremely difficult for me to make the transition from screenwriter to novelist. Descriptions in a screenplay are sparse, at best. You do not describe your leading man as tall and lanky, because if Clint Eastwood turns down your script, you are going to be in trouble when you give it to Dustin Hoffman. Screenwriters do not describe in any detail rooms or clothes, because the best set decorators and couturiers are going to take care of those. In a novel obviously the writer must visualize every single detail and convey it to the reader.

Q. *How do you decide whether to use the first-person or third-person viewpoint? When is one preferable over the other, or can there be any generalizations about this?*

A. I have never tried to write a book in the first person. I suppose the primary reason is that I would find it very limiting. If you are writing in the first person, you can't describe what is happening elsewhere or what other characters are thinking. There are, however, authors who do write in the first person and manage it very successfully. I would suggest that you use the technique that is most comfortable for you.

Q. *How can you guard against having some of your strong beliefs and feelings spill over into your novel?*

A. We come back to that old question of reality again. If your characters are real, then everything they do and say will feel and sound

70

right to the reader. If unsuitable points of view are superimposed on your characters, then you have created a false note that the reader most certainly will be aware of.

Q. *Is there any special checklist that you use to determine that your manuscript is right, satisfies you, and is ready to send off to the publisher?*

A. Every artist has to have his own sense of when his work is ready. My own personal checklist is rewriting. I rewrite my manuscripts up to a dozen times and I will spend from a year to a year and a half rewriting. The manuscript is not sent to the publisher until I am satisfied that it is as good as I know how to make it.

Q. *Should writers at the outset of a novel believe they are going to write "the great American novel," or, as one writer once said, "I'm going to write a classic"?*

A. If the question is "Should one aim high?" the answer is "Yes." Not every writer has it in him to write "the great American novel." The trick is to do your best. It is an unfortunate fact of life that too many writers—like too many people in other fields—are satisfied with less than their best.

Q. *Is there any single ingredient which you believe led to your success as a writer?*

A. I think the single ingredient that makes my novels work is believable characterization. If your readers care about your characters, they will be affected by what happens to them.

17

THE USES OF AUTOBIOGRAPHY

By Gail Godwin

THE FIRST story I ever wrote was about a henpecked husband named Ollie McGonnigle. Leaving the house one morning, Ollie is so happy to be "escaping" that he forgets to look where he is walking and falls into an open manhole. As he is climbing out, a man comes along and says: "Why didn't you watch where you were going!" Ollie hits the man over the head with his umbrella. That night, Ollie comes home to find that his wife has invited company for dinner. The dinner guest turns out to be the man Ollie hit over the head with his umbrella. And, moreover, this man is also . . . THE MAYOR OF THE TOWN.

Now, when I wrote this story (I was eight or nine at the time), there was no man living at our house. I was being brought up by my mother and grandmother. I doubt that I had even met a henpecked husband, except for Dagwood Bumstead, or Jiggs, in the comic strips. But the reason I wanted to write that story, and the reason Ollie was my sympathetic character, was because Ollie McGonnigle was myself.

That slapstick little man, full of eagerness to be out on his own in the morning, so eager that he ignores that voice of authority whose favorite expression is, "Watch where you are going," was I. Ollie McGonnigle, who wanted to make his own mistakes, without anyone saying, "I told you so!" was I. And how gleefully I let him wield his umbrella against complacent authority, even though I knew it was his denouement to knuckle under by suppertime. And how did I know that? Because that was my fate, each evening, when I washed off what little dirt I had been allowed to pick up outdoors and sat down at the table with the authorities. And, on those few occasions when I didn't knuckle under, my grandmother always won by threatening to call her cousin Bill—who really *was* the mayor of our town.

It is revealing to me, to leaf through that file of childhood stories. Ollie the henpecked husband; the one about the rich and lonely little boy who lived behind a high ornate fence and waited each day for the perfect friend to come to play with him; the one about the dog on holiday—from the dog's point of view. What did I know about husbands, about being rich, about being a dog, about being a boy? Yet, behind each disguise, the protagonist was the young author, working out a problem in her life: how to coexist with the authorities; how to put up with solitude until you found the right friend who could get through that fence of perfectionism you'd built around yourself; how it would feel if you could take a vacation from civilization altogether, and get down on your four legs, and run off snarling and panting, to raise hell— even though you get smacked with a rolled newspaper at the end of your outing.

In adolescence, I came out from behind my male/animal disguise and began to write about women. There was a story called "A Sunday in Early New England," which began:

It was the year 1663 and the day was Sunday. All over the New World, people were getting ready to go to church. Prudence Purity was quite upset, however, as she prepared for the long walk with her father and mother and six brothers to the meeting house. The reason for her frustration was that she could not seem to tuck into her hat one bright curl which made her look like a Jezebel.

Looking back, I see clearly that the pressing theme behind all my teen-age stories with female protagonists was how to make peace with the social structure into which I was born—and yet salvage that one bright curl that refuses to tuck itself into the contemporary bonnet. I tried historical distance. In another story, I tried humor. I tried pathos in still another entitled, "I Broke the Code" (rejected by *True Confessions*). The bright curl led me on . . . and still does.

Another theme that surfaced, around high school time, was the theme of choices. The most unsubtle and badly executed of these stories was called "The Choice." It was about a girl who had to decide whether to spend her money to attend a gala where she would be able to shake hands with the world's most beautiful woman, or on a jar of a certain face cream that the beautiful woman used. My heroine chose the face cream.

My first published story, while I was in college, was about an old newspaper vendor who had gone without lunch for a week so he could pay the admission fee to a traveling Rembrandt show at the local art museum. But when he arrives at the museum, he discovers the fee has been raised for that particular show.

I try to recall the impetus for writing that story, over twenty years ago. I believe I wanted to write about how it feels to aspire to art and not know whether you'll have the price of admission when you get to the gates—a theme that has continued to haunt me, in life, as well as art. I was to confront this theme again, years later, in my novel about an artist called *Violet Clay*.

It is easy to look back through your juvenilia and say, "Oh, that's what I was doing. Those were my pet themes. Of course!" What is interesting is that, though the writing has improved, the old themes haven't changed very much. I'm still writing about the importance of salvaging and showing that bright curl, while coexisting with society at the same time; I'm still fascinated by the choices one has to make. And the aspiration theme continues to attract me, as does its dark counterpart: the thwarted aspiration theme! I combined the two of them in my novel, *The Finishing School*.

All of which is to say: I believe our lives shape our fiction just as much as our fiction gives shape to our lives. I'm most comfortable speaking for myself, but I'm convinced that I'm speaking for my favorite writers, as well. They wrote what they wrote, not "out of the blue," but because their lives made it necessary that they write just exactly what they wrote at that particular time. They wrote to discover, to work out, to test their ideas in the process of writing. As they worked on their novels, they worked on their lives: on their vision of life. They tested it, revised it, expanded it. They found—as Tolstoy found, as he worked on *Anna Karenina*—that they often began with one set of attitudes and gradually discovered, draft by draft; that there was quite another attitude beneath that one. They revised their judgments as they became more implicated with their characters, they stumbled on new connections, they watched new insights, and, as their characters grew and changed, they found themselves growing and changing, too.

"Let there be no question about it," writes Dickens's biographer, Edgar Johnson, "what a writer has not experienced in his heart, he can do no more than coldly image from without. Only what he has proved within emerges from those depths with irresistible power, and when new figures lighted in strong emotion force themselves into his imaginative world, they are a projection of that inward reality, no matter how thoroughly the mere surface details may have been changed and disguised."

I write what I write because I am attracted to a certain subject, a certain theme, a certain character I wish to send off on a mission for myself. I write because I need to re-examine some memory that just won't go away, because I need to re-imagine something until I can discover the real truth that lay behind the literal happening. I write because I want to know how it feels to be another kind of person who will do things I can't or won't do. I write to explore alternative choices, life patterns that may run parallel to mine for awhile, then deviate, on a track I cannot follow—except in my fiction.

I'm dubious when anyone tells me, "I never write autobiographical fiction," just as I'm dubious when someone says, "I've got to hurry and finish this story, because I'm afraid someone else will steal the idea." I want to respond, "How can anyone steal something that only you can write?" And if anybody else can write it, what's the point?

When I'm working best, I feel I'm writing something I have to write, something nobody else in the world can write. I feel everything in my life contributing to the destination of this work, determining even the shapes of the sentences. I am always afraid I'm going to die before I finish it.

When a story or novel dies on *me,* and, with a feeling of nausea and sadness, I put it away in a folder (I can't stand throwing out months of effort), I have come to know that the reason it died was that it didn't belong to me in the first place. People begin stories or novels for many reasons. "Wouldn't that make a good story?" someone says. Or someone hands you a clipping ("I cut this out of a newspaper just for you. It's *your* kind of story"), and when you read the clipping, you either catch fire or you don't. Or sometimes you catch fire and start to write and then realize that the anecdote *was* the story; you don't want to know any more. Sometimes I know as soon as I read a clipping that it just does not call out to me in any shape or form. It has no place in my mythology. If I were forced to write it, I suppose I could come up with a workmanlike story, but it would be, to quote Edgar Johnson, *"coldly imaged from without."* And that's not how I write.

I write because I'm looking for answers as well as the right questions.

75

Because I'm seeking consolation, but also revenge. Because it makes me feel better every time I come up with the precise sentence and the vivid image that expresses an aspect of life that attracts me or haunts me. Everything I have written since that long ago story about Ollie McGonnigle and the mayor of the town was written because I needed to find out what my characters knew, and because I was the only person in the world who could write their stories. All my protagonists—slapstick, allegorical, disguised by gender or species, occupation or social class, or hardly disguised at all—are parts of myself.

18

THE LONG AND SHORT OF IT

By John Lutz

SHORT STORY or novel? Which should I write and why? What are the differences? Not just in word length—what are the *real* differences? These are questions that cross the fertile minds of a great many writers, novices and veterans, but especially those at the beginning of their careers.

First of all, let's see the short story as it really is. Since the demise of a number of high-paying markets for this form of fiction, the short story seems to have suffered an accompanying diminution in status in the minds of many who read, and write, popular fiction. There's a common misconception that a writer begins with short stories and, after gaining enough proficiency, moves on to the more demanding task of writing novels. Ain't so. Not any more than it's true that an Olympic gold medalist in the hundred-yard dash is merely in the process of working his or her way up to running a mile, and then the 26-mile marathon. The old saw that the shorter the piece the more difficult it is to write applies here, as it does in most instances.

While the novel is a somewhat forgiving form, the short story is a high-wire act: One slip can be fatal, as far as creating an effective work of fiction is concerned. If the illusion is punctured, the writer has lost the reader. The writer's miscalculation isn't diluted by many paragraphs and pages done right, as in the novel; one drop of acid in the relatively small vessel of the short story, and you have potent poison.

It is true that many writers begin by writing short stories and then move on to careers as novelists, but the reasons have more to do with economics than with levels of skill. It's also true that there are more short story writers who go on to write novels than there are novelists who later write short stories. Again, economics. Primarily. No getting around it, there's a greater return of money for effort in novels than in short stories. That, regrettably, is the state of the market.

But there's something else involved here. It's more likely that a short story writer will also be able to write novels, than it is that a novelist will also be able to write short stories. The skills involved in short story writing are somewhat different, generally more intense, and not within every writer's capabilities.

An editor once said of a short story writer known for his tightly written stories that he could write *War and Peace* on the back of an envelope. A good short story writer is able to pack maximum meaning and emotion into the fewest possible words, and that's a skill that can be extremely useful in novel writing. As a novelist, the writer of short stories is able to draw character, create situation, and set scene and mood in a few sentences or paragraphs, an ability many novelists don't possess. This isn't to be confused with the ability to condense; the short story writer actually tells it differently. The ability to write incisively and directly to the nerve is a skill, acquired by writing short stories and more short stories—and a skill worth cultivating. The art of economy might not be essential to a career as a novelist, but it sure helps.

No novel maintains constant mood and pace and climbs in a straight line to crisis, climax, and anti-climax. If novels were reduced to lines on graphs, they would appear as a series of peaks and valleys. It's how the valleys are handled that often determines the readability and success of novels. At those inevitable points at which lengthy explanation is necessary, or scenes must be set in detail, or clues must be planted, the novelist who can also write short fiction is able to use the short story writer's unique abilities to keep the novel moving with technique rather than situation, and to hold reader interest. Again, it's not the art of condensing, but that of knowing, of sensing, the essence of what needs to be related, and then penetrating to the core of it with the least possible digression and the greatest possible deftness. A slightly different skill from that usually employed in novels, and one learned only through writing short stories. I don't think it's inaccurate to say that a novelist's education isn't complete without some experience in writing short fiction.

But what are the really practical reasons for writing short stories as opposed to novels, aside from honing separate skills and laying the groundwork for a wider range of techniques as a novelist? While there isn't as much potential monetary gain in the writing of short stories, there also isn't as much time invested as in writing novels. Not as much bulk work. And a short story is more likely than a novel not only to sell more than once—to foreign markets and anthologies—but to keep on selling years, often decades, after the initial sale and publication. My agent recently sold Italian radio rights to a story I'd written over ten years ago. And at the same time sold to the same market a short story he'd had published when he was writing professionally in 1946, over *forty* years ago. Checks tend to turn up unexpectedly in the mailboxes of short story writers, and of course they're always welcome. So over a period of years, even decades, the time and effort involved in writing a short story can sometimes be very profitable. In fact, one writer I know makes a good living writing short stories almost exclusively, though this is something of a rarity these days and is probably going the way of the snail darter. The author established himself as a top-flight writer of short fiction in the years when there was a larger number of magazines publishing short stories. And while the market for short fiction has changed (and not for the better), it does seem to be improving lately. Or at least it is trying to improve. New magazines that print short fiction are born and most of them die, but there are survivors, and they seem to be hardy enough to withstand the rigors of the marketplace. The public never left the short story; with the elimination of most of the general magazines that published short fiction, the short story left the public. There is still, among people who read for entertainment and enlightenment, an appetite for short fiction.

More important than the above reasons for writing short stories, there are some short stories that *should* be told, and that simply aren't suitable for novel form. Narrow but powerful themes present themselves, as do intriguing situations and fictional characters who are best suited for direct and vivid tales without subplot or elaboration. At its best, the short story can attain the power of parable, something almost impossible for the novel. And, as we know, writers are at the mercy of their muse; they have some control over what they write, but not over what they *want* to write. In every writer there are tales that demand to be written.

For the novice writer, one of the advantages in the creation of short stories is that it is, I think, still easier to break into professional writing with a short story than with a novel. A few years ago I was on an award committee choosing the best mystery short story by a beginning writer. Several of the mystery magazines revealed to committee members which stories were first-publication authors, and I was surprised by the large number and by the quality of the stories. There's a wealth of talent out there; and it's producing quality fiction.

Once the beginning writer has a short story or two published, whether they're award winners or not, he or she has established professionalism and a track record. This can make it easier to sell that first novel, if that's what the writer has in mind. And that seems to be what most writers *do* have in mind.

One successful and well-known short story writer often says that he prefers writing short stories because "when I'm finished I'm the same person I was when I started." I know what he means. A novel's a lengthy proposition. It nags. Sometimes writing it is like keeping a dozen plates spinning at the same time, rushing from one end of the table to the other. That can be invigorating, even exciting. Also wearing. And a novel *does* simply take a long time to write; the author would grow and become a different person even if those months were spent watching television or reading instead of writing. Well, maybe not watching television.

Another analogy might be that of a painter working in oils, standing a few feet from the canvas, deciding on a dab here, a swipe there, a color blend here, not quite sure *precisely* what's been created until he or she moves well back and gains perspective. Not so unlike a novelist. No matter how much control you exercise over your material, there's always that distorting passage of time and experience between the first word and the last. Only when the first draft is finished does the novelist gain clearer perspective and *really* know what he or she has wrought.

But a short story is something you as a writer, after enough experience, will see whole within a relatively brief time after the first glimmer of idea. It's something over which you have much influence because early in the writing process you can catch it in your mind in its entirety. You can almost hold it in your hand as if it were a gem of your creation and turn it this way and that and polish it to your idea of perfection.

There's a mode, a mind-set, for writing short stories, and one for writing novels, and the rewards of each should be sampled in order to be a complete writer.

It pays in a number of ways for the novelist to work also in short story form—not to develop novelists' skills before moving on to longer fiction, but to develop different, *additional* skills that can prove valuable in writing novels and provide an advantage over writers who throughout their careers stick to working in one length.

Shifting back and forth between short fiction and long can be difficult at first. It requires developing a sort of dual professional personality, and many writers seem unable to do this. But it's wise to find out if you're one of the people who can make this mental shift and see, think, and write in short story as well as novel form.

Novels can be a joy to create, but if you think you'd like watchmaking, diamond cutting, or building ships in bottles, and if you're willing to apply yourself with the necessary intensity for any of those tasks, short stories can offer their own keen and unique satisfaction—and give you specialized writing skills that will widen your scope as a novelist.

19

SO YOU WANT TO WRITE A BESTSELLER?

By Barbara Taylor Bradford

When I'm on tour to promote a new novel, I meet many people in bookstores, TV audiences, and lecture halls, who tell me they want to be a bestselling novelist. They seek my advice. Generally, I tell them to sit down and do it, because that is the only way a book is ever written. However, I usually make a point of asking each one the same question: Why do you want to be a novelist?

Invariably they tell me that they want to make a lot of money and become a famous celebrity.

These are the wrong reasons.

There is only one reason to write a novel and that is because writing fiction is absolutely essential to one's well-being. It is to mine and it always has been. In other words, it is the work that really counts, the sense of creation that is the important thing to me.

Don't misunderstand me. Of course I want readers, every author does. But I have never sat down at a typewriter and told myself that I'm about to write a great bestseller. I have no idea if a book of mine is going to sell in the millions when I actually start it. How could I know, since I don't have a secret recipe? All I have is a story to tell about a number of characters who are very real people to me. I knew I wanted to be a novelist when I was a child in Yorkshire. I had no brothers or sisters so I invented playmates and told them stories. When I was ten, my father bought me a second-hand typewriter and I typed out these little tales and stitched them in a folder with a hand-painted title.

When I was 12 I submitted one—about a little horse, I think—to something called *The Children's Magazine* and it was actually published. I got ten and six for it. I have never stopped writing since.

The first novel I attempted was about a ballet dancer named Vivienne Ramage who lived in a garret in Paris! By this time I had managed to get a job on the *Yorkshire Evening Post* and had been to the Paris fashion shows with the women's page editor.

Paris totally overwhelmed me. I came back, and began this story. My ballet dancer was desperately poor and it was all terribly dramatic and suspiciously reminiscent of Dumas' *La Dame aux Camélias*! Anyway, I got to about page ten and suddenly thought: I've a feeling I've read this somewhere before.

I kept experimenting like that all though my girlhood. Being on a newspaper, doing the police beat, covering the coroners' courts, exposed me to life in the raw and taught me that you can't just write about the landscape or a room setting—a story is only interesting if it's about people. Their tragedies, their dramas, their joys.

That's what I'm dealing in now, human emotions. The hope is that I can get them down on paper in such a way as to touch a nerve in the reader so that he or she identifies and is moved. At 17 I was very much in love with being a newspaperwoman—a newspaper*man* I should say—even down to wanting a dirty trench coat. My mother accused me of having dragged it round in the street to make it grubby.

But my newspaper career didn't begin as a reporter. The only job I could get at the start was in the typist pool. First day I was still typing away long after everybody had gone home. As I was leaving I saw the wastepaper basket overflowing with the company's crumpled, vellum-like notepaper and I thought, I'm going to get fired for wasting their stationery. So I took a handful into the ladies' room, lit a match to it and threw it down the toilet.

Well, the blaze was so enormous I then thought: this way I'll be fired for being an arsonist! So I collected up the rest, smoothed it out and hid it in the bottom drawer of my desk.

For a week after that I took one of my mother's shopping bags to work with me and brought the telltale paper home in batches. I think I eventually got a job as a cub reporter because I was such an awful typist.

But I worked at getting moved, too—I did little stories and handed them in to my editor, who finally put me in the newsroom.

At 18, I became women's editor. When I was 20 I left Upper Armley, Yorkshire, for London and a job on *Woman's Own* as a fashion editor, followed by a stint as a reporter and feature writer on the *Evening News*.

Naturally, that was a job in which I met actors, film stars, novelists, screenwriters, politicians—people who were "achievers"—but I never expected to find success or be rich and famous myself. However, when I look back, I realize my mother always instilled in me a desire to do my best. I wanted to please her. She loved the theatre, movies, music and art and she got me my first two library tickets when I was still very small. When she died in 1981—only 5 weeks after I lost my father—I found those tickets in her purse.

I continued writing after I moved to the United States, where I have lived since my marriage in 1963 to a Hollywood film producer, Robert Bradford. I wrote non-fiction books between 1963 and 1974, mostly on interior design, and two books for children.

Between 1968 and 1974, when I was writing a syndicated column for American newspapers, I started four novels but discarded them all after a few hundred pages. One was set in Paris and North Africa. It was called *Florabelle*. I liked strong heroines from the start. That one was an actress.

Yet another novel was set in North Africa—I was smitten with Morocco at that time—and that tale was about a woman photo-journalist. My next was sited in the South of France. But the one I was writing when I thought of *A Woman of Substance* was called *The Jasper Cypher*. It was a Helen MacInnes-type suspense novel starting in New York and moving to Spain.

But obviously I was wrong, wasn't I? I should have been writing about Yorkshire, not Morocco. I got to chapter four and I thought, this is boring. I asked myself a lot of questions that day. It was like a dialogue with myself. I said: Well, what *do* you want to write about? What *sort* of book do you want to write? Where do you want to set it? And of course I knew, suddenly, that I really wanted to set it in England, specifically Yorkshire. Then I said: And I want to write about a strong woman.

So, having decided to write about a Yorkshire girl who emancipates herself and creates a big business empire, I could see it would be more effective if she were born poor and in an age when women were not doing these things, and to have her working for a rich family who falls as she rises.

After a couple of hours of thinking along these lines I had the nucleus of my plot and started to jot down a few notes and I thought, yes, she becomes a woman of substance. And I looked at that on my pad and thought, that's a marvelous title.

At a point like this I put paper in typewriter and tap out a few details. I might take two days experimenting with a name for the character. It has to have just the right ring. Then I create the other protagonists, maybe draw a family tree, listing names and ages, their relationships.

All the time I'm asking myself questions and answering them on paper. When is it going to start, how old is she, what is her background, what motivates her, why did this woman do what she did, become what she became? All my characters are totally analyzed, as if I were a psychiatrist.

I then transpose these notes onto index cards, and I maintain these character cards as if I'm dealing with real people—and they become very real to me. As I develop them, somehow the plot falls into place almost automatically.

Once I have title, characters and story line in note form, I divide the book into parts. It's a way to organize the material. In *A Woman of Substance* I got titles for the sections from the land—the valley, the abyss, the plateau, the pinnacle, the slope. It was a method of tracing the rise and fall of a life. In *Voice of the Heart,* I used the stage— overture, wings, Act 1, downstage right and so on. In *Hold the Dream,* the phases are entitled "Matriarch"—that's Emma Harte in old age— and "Heiress and Tycoon," which is the ascent of her granddaughter, Paula.

At this stage I write a piece like the copy on a novel's dust jacket, the bare bones of the story. Then I finish the outline, which is ten to 20 pages. That takes me about a week to ten days.

Once I get going on a novel, a good day is when I've written five finished pages. I usually start in longhand, using a fine nibbed pen (Sanford's Expresso, if you like to know that sort of thing) and then move to the typewriter.

Someone once asked me what a novel is and I said: It's a monumental lie that has to have the absolute ring of truth if it is to succeed.

It's easy to know when something is good and, in a way, it's easy to know when something is bad. But to know *why* it's bad, that's the thing. And how do you change it?

I've gone back and looked at my first attempts at fiction, and there wasn't too much wrong with them, except that I wanted basically to write about Yorkshire and didn't know it. So I wouldn't say to the would-be novelist: press on with *anything* you start. You could be on the wrong subject matter, as I was.

However, I now realize that as I labored, I was in effect honing my craft, teaching myself how to write a novel. I truly believe that learning the craft of fiction writing is vital and that you can't do that at classes. You can perhaps learn techniques—I borrowed library books on journalism when I was trying to become a reporter—but no one can teach you to write a novel. You have to teach yourself.

Basic writing ability is still not enough. A would-be novelist must also observe what I call the five Ds:

D for desire—the desire to want to write that novel more than do anything else.

D for drive—the drive to get started.

D for determination—the will to continue whatever the stumbling blocks and difficulties encountered on the way.

D for discipline—the discipline to write every day, whatever your mood.

D for dedication to the project until the very last page is finished.

Finally, there is a sixth D—to avoid! This is for distractions—perhaps the most important D of all, the enemy of all writers, whether would-be or proven.

Writing novels is the hardest work I've ever done, the salt mines, really. I sit long hours at my desk, starting out at six in the morning and finishing around six or seven in the evening. And I do this six and a half days a week, till my neck and shoulders seize up. I make tremendous social and personal sacrifices for my writing, but after all, I chose to be a novelist. Nobody held a gun to my head.

But in all truth, it's not possible to be a full-time novelist and a social butterfly, living the so-called glamorous existence of the bestselling novelist.

There's nothing which faintly resembles glamour about the work I do. I spend all of my working hours alone, facing a blank sheet of paper, and myself. For I have to dredge through my soul and my memories every day of my life.

When a book is finished I have to go on promotion tours. This may sound exciting. But it isn't. Taking a different plane or train every day and heading for another city is hardly my idea of fun; neither are crowded airports, poor hotels or bad food eaten on the run.

Then there are the fairytales. When reporters come to interview me they sometimes have a preconception. It's nothing to do with what they've learned about me, it's what they've decided without knowing me. They want to make me into Emma Harte. They want a rags-to-riches story. Somebody asked me the other day about my enormous change of lifestyle since I wrote a bestseller. Well, I started off simply enough but, to be truthful, my lifestyle changed when I married 22 years ago and went to live in Manhattan and also had an apartment in Beverly Hills.

But whatever I say, they're determined to write the story they want to tell. So the only thing I can do when I read a misleading story is smile and say, well at least they spelled my name right! But I'm not Cinderella, and never was.

Still, I admit that a bit of fiction about oneself is not much to put up with. I've been accused of dressing my Bichon Frisé puppy, Gemmy, in a diamond-studded collar and of wearing a £25,000 dress. I was due to go and stay with an old friend in Ripon and she roared with laughter when she read that. "Do I have to get a burglar alarm installed?" she kidded me. She knew a Yorkshire girl would never spend £25,000 on a dress, that she'd be doing something extraordinary if she paid £250!

So why do I go on? The answer is easy. I can't *not* do it. Writing is a means of self-expression for me, and it gives me great gratification. Especially when I know that a novel I have striven over truly works, not only for me, but for readers all over the world . . . readers who have derived enjoyment from my work, who have seen life through my angle of vision . . . who have been touched, enlightened and entertained. That is the greatest satisfaction of all.

And if you are a would-be novelist, hellbent on pursuing this career, then what better inspiration is there?

Ten Questions for Would-Be Novelists

Let us assume that the would-be novelist has both ability and a talent for using words. What else is required in the writing of fiction? I think I would have to ask you these questions.

1. Are you imaginative?

If you create characters in your imagination that are interesting and different and yet with whom the reader can identify, then you have a good start. If you can picture scenes between characters you create and can also feel caught up in their emotions, that's what I call imagination.

2. Have you got insight?

A novelist must be able to understand what makes people tick. Insight is being able to weigh someone up, to understand why they do the things they do. You must have compassion, and be willing to understand all points of view.

3. Can you get under the skin of a character, express his or her nature?

You have to be able to put the feeling and thought processes of your characters on paper effectively. I think writing up character studies is helpful. It teaches you how to develop a *whole* person on paper, remembering that nobody is all good, nobody is all bad; we are all made up with many complexities in our nature.

4. Can you make readers care about your characters?

That depends on whether you can flesh them out so that the reader believes they truly exist. I've found reading biographies very useful since they are about real people.

5. Can you really tell a story?

If it's to be compelling, make the reader want to turn the page to find what happens next, a novel has to combine structure, plot and action in a way that produces narrative drive. I have what I call my "loving ears"—two girlfriends I can ring and say: May I read you these few pages? That's what I sometimes do if I'm trying to say something complex, and their reaction helps me know if I've refined it enough. Do they want to "hear on"? Some feedback is helpful if you're feeling unconfident.

Structure is very important. Studying favorite books is good homework here. The structure of *Tai Pan* by James Clavell, who also wrote *Shogun,* is marvelous. And Wilbur Smith did a trilogy, *Flight of the Falcon, Men of Men* and *The Angels Weep,* which are all well-constructed novels. And the classics of course. There's nothing better than studying Dickens. And Colette. Colette, by the way, said: Two things are important in life. Love and work. I like that. Yorkshire people have the work ethic. My mother was always polishing a chair or making a stew and I still feel I must work all day, every day, or God will strike me dead.

6. Have you a talent for plots?

Working out story lines and getting them down in, say, ten pages is the best way of finding out. For myself, an event will trigger a plot. For instance, a former friend who was dying and wanted to make peace with me and other friends she had once hurt led to my plot for *Voice of the Heart.* The story line may "unreel" in the bath or on a bus in anything from ten minutes to an hour.

I never use anything exactly as it has befallen me or my friends, but I've seen so much of what happens to people that I know my plots are not too far-fetched, not larger than life. Nothing is larger than life.

7. Can you create a sense of time and place, mood and atmosphere?

I rely on memory for scenes from nature but I have occasionally taken snapshots for interiors. For *Voice of the Heart,* I photographed a *schloss* in Germany, to help me keep the mood of the place in my mind. Note-taking is another helpful tool, and sensible for people who don't have photographic memories.

I can't explain how you create atmosphere. I mean, Stephen King, the "horror" writer who wrote *Carrie* and *The Shining,* among many others, is brilliant when he creates an atmosphere of horror, and I think he does it with his choice of words. Atmosphere is not something visual, it's a feeling, and it's conveyed by particular words, so I too feel I must find the *exact* word and I'll spend hours sometimes to arrive at it. But, having said that, it's hard for a writer to analyze how he or she writes: I always fear I might analyze it away!

8. Do you have the knack of writing dialogue?

Dialogue has to do several things. It has to move the plot along and provide information of some kind. It has to delineate the character of the person speaking—or somehow reflect his personality. It should add to the flavor of the book, convey emotion or feeling. So it has to be very structured, even though it must sound natural.

Ask yourself if the dialogue you have written does all of these things, and if in all honesty you have to answer "no" you will almost certainly find that you can throw it out without loss—indeed it will be an improvement—to your book.

Written dialogue is totally different from spoken dialogue—write down a taped conversation and you'll see it's unreadable.

9. Are you organized enough?

If you want your novel to have a feeling of authenticity, then you must write from strength, from knowledge—and that means research. But the important thing about research is to be able to throw it away! Put it all in and it slows down the narrative drive. I might do a day's research just for a few lines of dialogue but it has to be integrated so it's not apparent.

An efficient filing system is vital, as are good reference books and address books that record sources—or you will waste precious time and work in a muddle. I have a table next to my desk where I keep handy a large dictionary and the *Columbus Encyclopaedia,* along with a thesaurus, *Bartlett's Familiar Quotations,* a world atlas, and maps of England.

10. Do you have a sense of drama?

There's so much drama every day in the newspapers, surely everyone has. Reading plays, watching movies helps to sharpen a dramatic sense, teach you what makes a "story." A book I go back to time and again is *Wuthering Heights.* Every time I read it I find something I hadn't noticed before. It is extremely emotional to me, a very Yorkshire book—though structurally it's said *not* to be good.

20

"WHERE DO YOU GET YOUR IDEAS?"

By Elizabeth Peters

ONE OF THE QUESTIONS most often asked of writers by readers and interviewers is, "Where do you get your ideas?" I used to sputter and roll my eyes when this query was put to me; there was in it the implication that ideas were physical objects, like avocados, and all one had to do was go to the proper store in order to pick up a supply.

However, my prejudice began to diminish when I started thinking seriously about the question. It is not a silly question. I thought it was silly only because I didn't know the answer. I still don't know the answer, but I have arrived at some answers—the sources from which I derive many of my ideas. I can't answer for other writers, but perhaps some of these will work for you.

First, let's define the term: An idea is not a plot. This distinction may seem so obvious that it isn't worth mentioning, but many of the earnest souls who offer me "plots" or "ideas" ("You write the book, and we'll split the royalties") don't know the difference. What I call an idea is not a plot. An idea is the germ from which a plot may one day develop if it is properly nurtured and tended. For me, the "idea" has two distinct stages.

It begins with a "one-liner"—a single sentence or a visual image, characterized by brevity and vividness. Since an idea is not an avocado, you can't simply go out and get one. In fact, the technique of finding a usable idea is more akin to birdwatching than to chasing butterflies: There are ideas all over the place, the trick is to recognize one of the elusive creatures when it flits past. I'm not being whimsical. It is certainly possible to search actively for an idea, but unless you know one when you see one, there is no point in looking.

The most obvious source of inspiration is your own hobby or profession or job specialty. My training is in archaeology and history, so I derive a good many plot ideas from those fields. The archaeology themes have been particularly prominent in my Elizabeth Peabody novels.

My hobbies—cats, needlework and gardening—have also provided me with ideas. Once when I was absorbed with collecting and embroidering samplers, I thought vaguely, "I wonder if I could use a sampler as a clue in a book?" This idea ended up as *House of Many Shadows*. I usually have an animal, or three or four, in my books, but cats have played seminal roles in the inspiration of ideas. "How about a ghost cat, who shows up in the nick of time to save the heroine?" That one turned out to be *Witch*.

Ideas don't always come from nonfiction reading. Sometimes irritation spawns a plot idea—when I read a book with a smashing twist that doesn't quite come off, prompting me to mutter, "I would have done that differently. . . ." And I do. Sometimes admiration of a particular book prompts not imitation so much as emulation. *Sons of the Wolf,* one of my early Gothics, was inspired by Wilkie Collins's *The Woman in White*. I took his two heroines, one dark and homely and competent, the other beautiful and blond and fragile. . . . Or so she seemed. It surprised me as much as it did some of my readers when the fragile blond came to the rescue in a moment of crisis, but her development was probably the result of my unconscious resentment of Victorian assumptions about women, which affected even so sensitive and gifted a writer as Collins. I turned his stereotype around to produce different characters and a different plot.

When you are looking for a plot idea, it is helpful, therefore, to read as widely as possible. I got one idea from the *Smithsonian Magazine,* not from an article but from a reader's letter that described a black rainbow. I had never heard of such a thing, but the image was so evocative I knew I had to use it.

Since I am by nature and by training a reader, I derive most of my ideas from books. However, visual images can also be useful. The most obvious visual image is physical—a handsome old house, a quaint village, a medieval town. The dark closes of old Edinburgh, the triple-layered church of San Clemente in Rome, a country inn in Western Maryland—these and other locations have inspired books of mine.

Other images from which I have derived ideas are also physical, but they are one step removed from reality. They are, in fact, misinterpretations of what I actually see. (Being absent-minded and/or nearsighted helps here.) The commonest misinterpretation, with which most of us are familiar, occurs when we wake in the night and see some familiar object in the room transformed by shadows and moonlight. A robe hanging on the bedpost becomes a dangling body or a looming spectre. A rocking chair appears to have an occupant, misshapen and frightening. My most recent stimulus of this nature came when I was driving alone a narrow country road and saw a bundle of trash lying in a ditch. (At least I hope it was a bundle of trash.) The shape suggested a human body, and all at once I had a mental image of a skeleton, dressed in a pair of overalls, sprawled by the road. The exigencies of the plot that I developed from this image demanded a female rather than a male skeleton, and the overalls turned into a calico dress.

Once you learn to spot ideas, you see them all over the place—remarks overheard on planes or buses, unusual signs in shop windows, street names, those one- or two-line fillers newspapers sometimes insert to fill out a column. Then there are satires and take-offs. Hundreds of ideas there! Having once attended a Romance Writers Convention, I knew I had to do a book about such a group. Nothing personal—I plan eventually to satirize cat shows, sci-fi conventions, and my own professional society meetings.

One purely mechanical technique you may want to develop is to write down or clip anything that seems to have potential, and file it away. I have a file bulging with cryptic notes. A few examples: a scribbled description of a mourning gown once worn by the Empress of Austria. It is a fantastic outfit, all black without a speck of color, featuring a face mask of black lace. What am I going to do with this? I don't know yet. But I have a hunch that one day a lady dressed in this fashion will make a marvelous ghost. In my file, there is also an eerie story told me by a local antique dealer about one of her customers; a notation on nuncupative wills; notes on an article on early American gravestones; and a list of terms for groups of animals (a kindle of kittens, a shrewdness of apes) from a book published in 1614. (Goodness, what a mess; I must clean this file out!)

Another file, labeled "miscellaneous," contains newspaper clippings. I keep separate files for clippings on archaeology, the supernatural, and crime. In the miscellaneous file I find, among many others, articles with the following headlines: "Twins May Have One Mind in Two Bodies"; "Switzerland's Dying Language (Romansh)"; and my personal favorite, "The Tree That Ate Roger Williams." Sooner or later I'll get a book out of one of these—maybe all of them.

But—I hear you, the reader, complain—it's a long way from your one-liner to a finished book. True, I told you that in the beginning, remember? An idea is not a plot. A "one-liner" may not even turn out to be an idea! For me, the second stage of the process loosely termed "getting an idea" is to encourage the initial image or brief sentence to develop into something a little more substantial. It's a difficult process to describe or define; perhaps an example will demonstrate what I mean.

Legend in Green Velvet started with a visual image—a view of a steep winding street in the Old Town of Edinburgh. The "idea" that popped into my mind was a single sentence: "What a super setting for a heroine to be chased in." (Grammar never concerns me at such moments.) But I was getting tired of reading and writing books about pursued heroines. Mulling this over, I thought, "How about having the heroine do the chasing for a change?"

Then I turned to my most useful source—books. I started reading about Edinburgh and its history. Before long I came across the old story of Mary, Queen of Scots' illegitimate baby, who was carried off and adopted by one of her ladies-in-waiting. If the story were true (I doubted it, but that wasn't important), Mary was not only an ancestress of the present British royal house, she was also an ancestress of a Scottish noble family. How about one of those close physical resemblances, between a young man (hero or villain, I hadn't decided which) and a Prominent Royal Personage?

I needed more. For one thing, if I decided to make my young man the hero, I needed villains. My reading turned up another intriguing story— that of the Scottish students who swiped the Stone of Scone from Westminster Abbey. The memory of a delightful conversation with an Edinburgh taxi driver who treated me to a fiery lecture on Scottish rights reinforced the idea of using a Scottish Nationalist group in my book. But I couldn't bring myself to make the Nationalists real villains. From what I knew of them, they were an amiable lot. They would, however, provide a useful red herring, and my heroine could safely pursue one of them, since he would not be inclined to harm her.

I still needed villians—genuine, wicked, evil villains. Back to the history books and eventually another piece of the plot. The ancient regalia of Scotland—vanished, during one of the periods of warfare.

By this time my original one-line idea of a heroine chasing a villain through the streets of Edinburgh had developed, not into a plot as yet, but into the skeleton of a plot. I had a heroine, a hero who bore an uncanny resemblance to a Royal Personage, and two sets of villains who were interested in the same treasure for different reasons. The Nationalists wanted the lost royal regalia for its symbolic importance; the genuine villains planned to steal it and sell it. I had strengthened and encouraged my original idea to a point where, or from which, it could be developed into a genuine plot.

There is another technique I often employ when engaged in this second stage of idea development. It is almost the exact antithesis of the active, reading-research method; one might call it a variety of free association. First, it is necessary to find an ambiance in which your mind is free to wander as it will. For me, the ideal situation is a form of mild physical activity (I never engage in strenuous physical activity) that requires minimal mental effort. Walking is ideal. Some types of housework, such as ironing, necessitate a blank mind. (If I thought about what I was doing, I wouldn't do it.) Total relaxation, flat on my back, doesn't work, because when I am relaxed I promptly go to sleep. But as I walk or push the iron across the fabric, a goodly portion of my mind takes off on a tack of its own. With a little encouragement I can turn that detached section down the track I want it to follow. "What about that girl chasing a man up a flight of stairs in Edinburgh? Why the dickens would she do that? Why do people chase people? Did she think he was someone she knew? Did she see him drop his wallet or his handkerchief?"

These methods work for me. They may not work for you, but something else will, if you experiment. And the most encouraging thing about writing is that, as with any other talent, your skill will improve with practice.

I still become irritated when people ask me where I get my ideas, not because it is a silly question, but because it is too complex to be answered in a few words. And also, perhaps, because to a writer getting an idea is the easy part. The hard part is turning that ephemeral one-liner into thousands of actual words on hundreds of actual pages in a connected, coherent manner.

21

THE MAJOR ROLE OF MINOR CHARACTERS IN FICTION

By Hans Ostrom

AFTER READING AN EARLY DRAFT of a novel I had submitted, my editor—as I expected—commented on several areas that needed improvement. One of her responses to the novel surprised me, however. She said that she had had some difficulty with several of the minor characters. In her view, I had not depicted these characters vividly enough, and when a significant amount of time had elapsed between appearances of some secondary characters, she found that her sense of those characters had become cloudy.

To be sure, the remarks about the novel's minor characters came toward the end of the editor's written evaluation, after she had commented on larger elements of the novel. I do not want to imply that a concern for minor characters should outweigh a concern for the plot, primary characters, threads of suspense, setting, and other crucial aspects of a novel.

Ironically, however, because novelists must focus so intently on these obvious concerns, minor characters may not receive the attention they deserve, especially in early drafts. And poorly conceived minor characters can weaken a novel substantially. As a newcomer to writing novels, I realized after reading my editor's letter that concentrating on the major areas of my novels did not mean that I could afford to neglect minor characters. I also realized that, perhaps unconsciously, I had made the mistake of equating "minor" with "incidental."

Revising the manuscript in response to my editor's concerns was not difficult, but my interest in the topic of minor characters did not stop there. I thought further about the essential ways in which minor characters contribute to novels in general, and I offer my observations here in hopes that they might help other new novelists.

Perhaps the most obvious function of minor characters is in advancing the plot. In basic terms, the plot consists of events in which the main character(s) take part. Nonetheless, minor characters can often play major roles in constructing the plot.

In mystery novels, they can provide a crucial bit of information to the sleuth, or they can become unwitting obstacles to the success of either a detective or a criminal, or they can trigger a memory on the part of a detective that will allow him or her to solve a puzzle or to take the right action. In mainstream novels, the contribution of minor characters to the plot can be just as important but in an even greater variety of ways. Virtually any element of crisis or resolution can be enhanced by a minor character.

Charles Dickens's novels remain an excellent example of this potential; even though ideas about "the novel" have evolved since his era, the range of ways in which he used minor characters to contribute to intricate plots still offers a model to novelists for what it is possible to do with minor characters. Compared with many contemporary novels, Dickens's works may sometimes seem crowded or "overpopulated" with minor characters, and yet the portraits and functions of those characters are always painstakingly precise. Dickens is beyond imitation, but he may be the best example of how seriously a novelist must take lesser characters. His works reinforce the platitude about a chain being as strong only as its weakest link: A minor character, even one with a bit part, can be the most important link in a chain of events that constitutes the plot of your novel.

A second major contribution minor characters can make to a novel is to enhance the development of the main character(s). We learn much about main characters *only* from main characters—from seeing them in action or from listening to their interior voices. However, we can learn as much about them from the way they behave in encounters with secondary characters. Even when such brief encounters are not crucial to the plot (and they often are), they show us how the main character functions in "ordinary life." Furthermore, the whole concept of "round" or "three-dimensional" characters depends on the existence of "flat," "two-dimensional" characters who allow primary characters to stand in relief. As in motion pictures, such characters literally "support" the major roles in novels.

Another way of describing this function of minor characters is to say that they add texture to a novel. In fact, one of the discoveries I made in my transition from writing short fiction to writing novels is that novel writing allows me more latitude to work to enrich the texture of my fiction. Generally speaking, one can employ a larger cast of characters in a novel than one can in a short story. This situation makes for more freedom, but it also asks the writer to think more extensively about what to *do* with the freedom and, more specifically, what to do with additional minor characters in the cast.

Minor characters can also contribute to the development of suspense, either in a scene or in a whole novel. Consider one example from a classic of the suspense genre, Dashiell Hammett's *The Maltese Falcon.* In Chapter 16, when "the black bird" suddenly falls into the hands of Sam Spade, it is delivered by a mysterious, dying stranger:

> The corridor door opened. Spade shut his mouth. Effie Perine jumped down from the desk, but a man opened the connecting door before she could reach it. . . . The tall man stood in the doorway and there was nothing to show that he saw Spade. He said, "You know—" and then the liquid bubbling came up in his throat and submerged whatever else he said. He put his other hand over the hand that held the ellipsoid. Holding himself stiffly straight, not putting his hands out to break his fall, he fell forward as a tree falls.

The scene itself is suspenseful, for as readers we sense the mixture of confusion and terror that Spade and his secretary feel when the dying man appears at their door. Moreover, in relation to the entire plot, the appearance of this minor character adds enormously to the suspense. Who is he? How did he get the Maltese Falcon? Who killed him? Will Spade be accused of killing him? What should Spade do now? To a great extent, suspense is uncertainty, and Hammett uses a minor character to dump a truck load of uncertainty on Sam Spade's doorstep.

Minor characters can contribute to suspense not just in mystery and action fiction but in virtually every kind. Rust Hills, in *Writing in General and Short Story in Particular,* applies the idea of suspense to all good fiction, saying that it "can function in literature as subtly and effectively as it does in music." Minor characters are one important source of such subtlety and effectiveness. In James Joyce's classic story "Araby," for example, the minor character of the uncle is an enormous problem for the main character, the boy who wants to go to the bazaar to buy something for the girl he worships. In coming home late and generally being difficult, the uncle delays the boy's departure, adding to the suspense of the story (will the boy make it to the bazaar or not?)

and to the sense of disillusionment and disappointed desire that Joyce creates.

Still another way minor characters can be useful to fiction writers is to help evoke a sense of place and atmosphere. Whether it's Conan Doyle's London, Raymond Chandler's Los Angeles, William Faulkner's Mississippi, or Ann Beattie's New York, our sense of place depends on the people in the place. Authors can use minor characters to help convey the flavor of a region or a city quickly and convincingly. Fog and gaslights add to our sense of Holmes's London, but Mrs. Hudson, cabbies, bobbies, and a legion of other minor characters contribute as much, if not more, to our mental picture of the fictional London Conan Doyle creates.

Finally, minor characters can be interesting in and of themselves. A quick sketch of a minor character can (and should) be vivid and entertaining—should stand on its own in some way. Moreover, like all characters, minor ones grow in surprising ways, demanding more attention from the author during revisions, competing for greater roles as novels or stories take shape. In my own novel, a bartender (of all people) who I thought would be almost incidental became more crucial to the plot and to the sleuth (a sheriff) than I had ever imagined. He became more of a confidante and a representative of sorts of the ordinary people in the rural county. Such "independence" on the part of minor characters may be even more likely to occur in novels than in short stories.

These, then, are several significant roles minor characters can play in fiction. In addition, there are some rules of thumb a writer should keep in mind during the revision process:

1. Beware of stereotyping. Because minor characters *are* minor, and because authors cannot afford to spend more than a few sentences describing them, a stereotype can be tempting. A waiter or a cop or a librarian need not be a stock character. Don't call Central Casting; instead, draw on your own experience and your notebook for a not-so-typical sketch.

2. Beware of the time lapses between appearances that minor characters make. If the interval between appearances is substantial (several chapters, for instance), it is even more necessary for the first appearance to be striking. As mystery novelist Lillian O'Donnell has remarked, "Clue: If I have to go back into the early pages of a first draft

to find out a character's name, that character is not real." O'Donnell's observation applies to mainstream fiction as well, of course, and one might add that if a reader's memory of a minor character's first appearance is fuzzy, how well is that character really functioning in the novel?

3. Give minor characters memorable but not outlandish names, and make sure the names and initials of your minor characters are sufficiently different to avoid confusing the reader. Don't make your reader wonder which character was Ron Ryan and which was Bryan Ray. Most of us are unconsciously attracted to a very narrow range of names, and we need to broaden that range in our fiction.

4. Don't be afraid to eliminate a minor character entirely. The fact that minor characters can themselves be interesting cuts both ways because a minor character can upstage a major one without contributing to plot, character development, suspense, or atmosphere. He or she may be engaging without being genuinely functional.

Ask yourself whether the character ought to appear at all. (If you are moving from short fiction to a novel, you may find that the comparative freedom of the novel creates a greater temptation to clutter the stage with characters; the clutter springs not so much from the number of characters as from the purposelessness of characters.) Such characters need not disappear forever. They may turn out to be useful in other stories and novels, and may even become main characters in other works.

Ultimately, the nature of minor characters in fiction is something of a paradox: although such characters are by definition secondary and often two-dimensional, they add depth to various elements of stories and novels.

22

AGAINST NOSTALGIA

By Sumner Locke Elliott

HAVING BEEN born in Australia but having lived in the United States since 1948 and having written four-and-a-half novels with settings in Australia (the other half of one is set in California and New York), I am sometimes lauded, sometimes berated, for writing nostalgia. To both I object strenuously. *Webster's* defines nostalgia as "homesickness, a sentimental or morbid yearning for the past." In nearly forty years, I have never had a twinge of homesickness and most certainly no morbid yearning for the past, the past being generally the reason that I fled Australia. I am not prone to tears at "Waltzing Matilda" nor the smell of rain on eucalyptus leaves, and I am not bound to compare every harbor in the world to Sydney's. Possibly because I was born not unpatriotic, but un-nationalistic. I have never been easily aroused by the marching bands, the flags and confetti, or the insistence of mass enthusiasm. But I am moved more often by trivia, by hearing in my mind the raucous sound of thousands of green locusts (which is what they call cicadas there) in the quickening mornings of the marvelous Australian summers, which, unlike the summers of the east coast of America, are invigorating. I'm moved by the gift of a little mountain devil, which is a face of a small pointed elf with horns and which grows on a prickly bush in the Blue Mountains of New South Wales.

Of course there must be a trace of nostalgia in all memory. But even memory is fiction. The delineation of the past becomes the copyright of the individual and subject to his or her arrangement of the circumstances (as in Alan Jay Lerner's song, "Oh Yes, I Remember It Well"); what passes for the memory in my mind is not the same as in someone else's remembrance. Fiction, of course, frees us from the boundaries that confine us and undernourish the inherent drama in our work. It is the combination of memory and fiction that makes the work more readable in every way than the account even of some sensational event told with every facet of truth intact.

For me, at any rate, what memory does is impel the resolution of some action, and the memory is of no use without the resolution. Here, for instance, is the beginning of a short story that I have not yet written but the memory of the incident is vividly stored in my mind:

I am about seven years old. I am watching from a short distance two women in a lighted room. One is standing, the other seated in a chair. The one standing is my aunt. She is middle-aged and becoming stout; she has never been good-looking, and a heart condition has drawn little scarlet veins across her nose and cheeks. She wears her graying hair drawn back into a bun. She is dressed in a wool skirt and with a tweed cardigan covering a beige cashmere sweater or what Australians then called a "jumper." I have never liked her, and in some dim response out of starvation, she has poured gifts and protestations of love on me, which have only served to widen the gulf between us, because sometimes the responses of children are unmitigating. Her responses to my unrelenting disapproval have been expensive toy trains and riding boots of exquisite styling and leather, but she is wont not to risk exposure of herself in embraces or kisses. I watch her and the other woman deep in soft conversation. The other woman's back is turned to my aunt. Without warning, my aunt leans suddenly over the chair and kisses the top of the woman's head. I am appalled.

What could it mean? A simple demonstration of affection? Sublimated perversion? But the incident itself, the memory, is of no use unless it is projected into the scheme of a story, so that it becomes a link in the chain of emotional jousting that took place between aunt and nephew; it must be realized in the fuller context and resolved.

In my first novel, *Careful, He Might Hear You,* the same aunt is a major character, and in that book (the thought occurs to me more than occasionally that it was deliberate homicide), I contrived to have her die in a ferry accident. In real life (never as authentic to me as the fiction), she died as a result of the heart condition she had had for many years, and to my astonishment I wept inconsolably. She was in deadly fear of thunder and lightning, and when I visited her grave in 1974 on a trip back to Australia, as I alighted from the suburban train, a thunderstorm of such sudden ferocity broke that I thought, "Aha, she knows I am coming to her." But this is too pat for consideration in a book; it is the kind of trite metaphor that should be instantly rejected.

As I have said, memory is fiction. *Careful, He Might Hear You* was denounced by the only living person who could remember the event and who knew most of the participants. "Not the people *I* knew," she said. Naturally enough. I was disconcerted at first, foolishly believing she would have recognized every nuance of the time and of the characters that I had so carefully reproduced. It was through a different lens that she had looked at my world. This is part of the reason most people fail to recognize themselves as the original models of fictitious characters. How delightful it would be to know that the original Mr. and Miss Murdstone read *David Copperfield* in all innocence.

In a different sense the "I" character of the first-person novel is never really the author. Up to now I have avoided the use of the first person because I find it confining, and not being able to get into the minds of other characters is an irretrievable loss to me. This is especially so in the autobiographical novel, and in mine the principal character was myself as a child. I always felt completely disassociated from this child, never more so than when I first saw the film version of the book. It was not unlike looking at a photograph of one's self as a child.

I look at the photograph. It is in sepia. The upward-turned face with the carefully brushed clean hair is seraphic, trusting, virginal. I remember that at that age I was in love with a little girl named Beryl Garside. We were in Sunday school together. I recall the circle of baby chairs we sat in. In those days, little girls wore their best hats to Sunday school, and the hats were confections. Beryl had—to me—the most wonderful hats in the world, and many of them. Each Sunday she would be there resplendent in straw and ribbons that extended down her back. I loved to see Beryl's hats, I dreamed about them at night. Then one shocking rainy Sunday, Beryl appeared in a plain black felt hat, so unadorned and ugly that I could scarcely believe my eyes, and Beryl's pretty face mostly hidden under the wide brim seemed to have taken on an ugliness also. Without a second's thought, I leapt up, and snatching off the offending hat, slapped Beryl in the face, screaming, "I hate your hat, Beryl." Her consternation was more shock at my outrageous action than at the slap itself. Fancy dear little Putty Elliott doing such a thing, an angel like him! We are subject to the stranger in all of us.

Fifty years later, I was to write a scene in which a drunken bully

103

snatches the new hat off a frightened girl, yelling, "I hate that hat you're wearing," and throws it into a fountain. The bully's tipsy sycophants laugh loudly, and the wretched girl is forced into laughter also until the rich bully's fiancée says cuttingly to him, "Pay her. Pay her for the hat." The scene, which was in a book called *Signs of Life,* passed through my mind and onto the typewriter without the ghost of a memory of Beryl Garside until months later, when, reading the galleys, I almost tripped over the fact that I had resurrected my Sunday school disgrace.

It is easy to blame it all on the unconscious, which stores away everything that we would most like to forget. Often it is through our unconscious memory that we find the inspiration without knowing. But that fortunately is not nostalgia.

Occasionally, try as I may, I cannot fit the memory in. Or else it does not belong to the book. There is a little string of rather plaintive memories that I have considered for several books but which refused steadfastly to be included, or else were later wisely omitted. Again I see my plain aunt weeping to my good-looking male violin teacher, while I am told to wait outside in the corridor where somebody in the distance is practicing Kreisler's "Caprice Viennois."

The importance of balance can often be vital. For instance, I am usually opposed to scenes in which a major event or anything of a tragic or dramatic nature takes place during bad weather: In fiction writing, never have the storm outside when there is a storm within. At the picnic in ideal weather, the water rippling in sunlight, the drowsy hum of bees, the tablecloth laid out with the tempting food, the baby lamp chops grilling on the twig fire, wild flannel flowers and blue sky—then the child can be beckoned away behind a tree to be told of a terrible death in an accident.

Possibly this is a finnicky, old-maidish trickery. There are no rules to writing, and what is law to one writer can be anathema to another. I abhor descriptions of good-looking people, especially of beautiful women, often found in novels. Margaret Mitchell disposed of a leading character in American fiction in her opening sentence: "Scarlett O'Hara was not beautiful, but men seldom noticed it."

But the risk is that we do look back on the past with nostalgia. When I was growing up, I used to spend the long Christmas holidays with my cousins on a farm in another state. I had to travel overnight to Melbourne on the express. No more glamorous experience in memory

104

could outdo the excitement of that train. I can still smell the musty odor of the compartments and see the sleeping cars with their softly lighted corridors over the dark red carpeting with the words "NSW Railways" woven into them, and the dark green leather seats, half of which let down out of the wall and became the upper berth, reached by a small ladder with velvet-covered steps, and I can feel the rhythm and sway of the train and the thick brown blanket that smelled faintly of smoke. In a moment, in a word or two, if I am not careful, I will be on a journey of such nostalgia as to make Dickens's Little Nell seem brittle. Nostalgia must be used only as background (and not go on for too long), the sounds of the rushing train must be there only to conceal partially the sounds of weeping in the next compartment, and then . . .

But I cannot write about the past and not mention the trams. Sydney used to be a tram city (Melbourne still is), and it was the most generally used public transport to and from the city to the suburbs. The trams were big, gray and dirty cream-colored, lumbering but capable of fairly high speed, attached by long poles to the overhead electric wires. They were not dinky and pretty like the San Francisco trolleys, and they were not trolleys; they were *trams*. Shirley Hazzard has described them as "toast racks," which is accurate—the open compartments at either end, the rows of seats, doors with windows that opened in the middle, and the narrow wooden running-boards on which the conductors with their heavy bags of change clung perilously to the sides of the rocking vehicle in all weather. Wedging his shoulder firmly into the door against the swaying of the tram, the conductor gave out the tickets and made change, walking along the little footboards not more than eight inches wide. I can still hear the snap of the leather strap he pulled and the tinkle of the bell in the driver's cabin when the last people had gotten off and others got on. I can see the names of the suburbs on the roller in front: BALMORAL, THE SPIT, TARONGA PARK ZOO, CROW'S NEST.

It is six in the evening. I am in a big two-storied white house overlooking the harbor, and I can hear the Dover Road tram climbing the upward curve of the hill outside with a grinding noise. I am in bed having bread and milk off a tray. I am four, and I am filled with delight.

That is nostalgia.

23

HOW DO YOU LEARN TO WRITE?

By Ruth Rendell

POPULAR FICTION no more needs a formula than does the highest art in the mainstream novel. Indeed, I have always maintained that genre fiction, so-called, is better written as if it were mainstream fiction and that fitting it into a category is best forgotten. And one should write to please oneself. When I consider the number of readers who have written to me to ask why I bother about style and characters when all they need is the mystery, others who have written asking for more murders or fewer murders, those who have demanded only detective stories, and those who have asked for anything but detective stories, I wonder where I should be now if I had aimed to please a public rather than suited my own taste.

One myth I used to believe in has been thoroughly debunked. This is the illusion that writing cannot be taught. The truth of it is that the desire to write cannot be taught, and that desire, that longing, must be there. Perhaps it is all that must be there, for with care and awareness, and yes a certain humility, the rest may be learned. Innumerable books exist on the writing of fiction. There are more and more courses available. But I believe that the aspiring writer—come to that, the working writer—cannot do better than learn by reading other works of fiction. I read and read, more now than ever, and if my attitude to what I read has changed over the years, it is in that gradually I have brought to bear on my reading an analytical eye, a developing critical faculty, a hunger to learn more of the craft. Perhaps I have lost something thereby. Escape in fiction is less easy for me; identification with characters comes less readily; I no longer lose myself in the story. But I am first a writer. And I think these things well lost for my gain in knowledge of how to write, though I see how far I still have to go.

So what kind of fiction do I as a writer of crime novels read? Not crime fiction, not mysteries. Not any longer. I used to, and then I became afraid that I would come upon the plot I was currently writing or the twist in the tail I was so proud of. The best crime fiction anyway—always excepting the pure detective story—is simply fiction with crime in it. I read and reread the great Victorian classics that once afforded me sheer pleasure and now teach me how to evolve and develop a story and cliff-hang my protagonist at the end of a chapter. I read the best contemporary British and American masters of fiction, every novel that comes out and gets acclaimed by reviewers or wins a prize or gets itself talked about, everything we see adapted for television. My favorite novel used to be Samuel Butler's *The Way of All Flesh,* and I still love it and reread it, but its place in my top admiration stakes has for two or three years been occupied by *The Good Soldier,* by Ford Madox Ford. It has been called the finest novel in the English language, at least the best constructed. I read it once a year. Its structure, its author's skill in dealing with time, the smooth swift movements of its narrative through and in and out of the years, its curiously intimate, despairing, aghast creating of suspense—these are all marvels.

I recommend *The Good Soldier* to everyone who asks me how to write. I hope it has taught me something. It ought to have imparted some of its own subtlety, its wonderfully understated withholding from the reader—until nearly the end—of a chain of secrets, an interwoven carpet of mysteries. Victorian ghost stories also have a lot to teach us. M. R. James knew all about the power of reticence in building tension that is an essential element in my kind of fiction. And more than any modern master of horror, Perceval Landon teaches the writer all he needs to know about fear and how to create it in "Thurnley Abbey," the most frightening story I have ever read.

I am always a little dismayed by people who ask me where I get my ideas and go on to say that though they want to write, they don't know what to write about. Any aspiring writer of the sort of fiction that aims to entertain and be exciting should begin at any rate with more ideas than he or she knows what to do with. They want to tell a story, don't they? Isn't this what it's all about?

I never base my characters on real people. I mean this; I am being quite sincere. And yet, and yet . . . all we know of people is through the men and women we are close to or have met or those we have read of or seen on film. Heaven forbid that we should base our characters on those printed or celluloid personages others have created. So only reality and living people remain. I suppose that we create amalgams, taking an appearance here, a quality there, and eccentricity from elsewhere. Increasingly, I look through books of pictures, the works of old or modern masters, for my characters' faces: to Rembrandt's "Juno," Greuze's "The Wool Winder," Picasso's "Acrobats," and Titian's dark sorrowful handsome man with the gloves. And for characters' names I go not to the telephone directory but to the street names in the back of a gazetteer.

It is interesting how a character begins to form itself as one gazes at some marvelously executed portrait. Slyness must lurk behind those eyes surely, cruelty in that thin-lipped mouth, subtlety and finesse revealed by those long thin fingers. I wish I had known of this method when I first began and struggled unwisely to make a character fit the plot instead of the plot growing naturally out of the behavior of the characters. I wish I had known then the abiding satisfaction of contemplating, say, Umberto Boccioni's self-portrait and seen there a young man's inner doubts, suspiciousness, intellect, hyper-nervousness, and begun to see my way to putting his counterpart into a book.

From the first, though, I listened to people talking. My friends tell me that my books are full of the things they have said. "We had that conversation in your house with such-and-such and so-and-so." It's true. I don't use my friends for my characters, but I use what they say for my dialogue. I listen in pubs to people talking and in restaurants and at airports, in trains, in shops. And when I write down what they say, I repeat it in my head, listening with that inner ear for the right cadence, the ring of authenticity. Is this how it really sounds? Is this the rhythm? Would my man with the thin body and sad face of Picasso's harlequin, the thin lips and the delicate upturned nose, would he use quite that word in quite that way? And if not, it won't do, must be changed and listened to all over again.

A publisher friend once said to me that the next time he received a manuscript that began with the protagonist waking up, feeling depressed, and going down to make himself a cup of tea, he wouldn't read on. All too many first books do begin like this. My experience of reading the manuscripts of unpublished writers is not that they are badly written or unreal or silly or badly constructed, but they are deadly boring. They are dull. The characters have no life and are undifferentiated; every piece of information is fed to the reader in the first chapter; no care has been taken over accuracy or authenticity. If they are not exactly plagiarisms of other more exciting works, they are deeply derivative. Originality is absent. There is no evidence of the writer's own experience being put to use.

Of course, few of us have first-hand knowledge of violence, even fewer of murder. How many of us have had a child kidnapped or know of anyone to whom this has happened? We should be thankful for our lack of experience. And the writer's imagination will supply what is needed here. We all know what it is like to walk alone along a dark road at night, be alone in a house and suspect the presence of a marauder outside, hear a footfall or a door close where there should be no footfall and no closing door, suffer the suspenseful anxiety of waiting for some loved person who is late home, long for the phone to ring yet dread it, miss a train and a date, fear flying, suffer jealousy, envy, love, and hate.

These are the raw materials the writer must use. Journalists ask me if I have known many murderers, visited courts and prisons. I have known none, and it is twenty-five years since I was in a court. But I can read the great psychiatrists, the newspapers, look at faces in pictures, and I can use my imagination. If a would-be writer doesn't have an imagination, he or she should find it out young and serve the world in perhaps a worthier way by making a career in a government office or a hospital. Newspapers as sources of stories and portraits of psychopathic perpetrators of violence have their value but to my mind have been overrated by teachers of mystery writing. Sociological case histories and transcripts of trials supply better models.

I have never been much interested in writing about heroes and villians, and I think the time for a blackness and whiteness of characters, a Dickensian perfect good and utter evil, has long gone by. We have all read novels in which our attention has flagged halfway through. Sometimes this is because the characters are all so unpleasant that we lost interest in their fate. For even the worst character in a novel should inspire in the reader some fellow-feeling. It is an intriguing fact that in order to make readers care about a character, however bad, however depraved, it is only necessary to make him love someone or even something. A dog will do, even a hamster will do. I once had a character called Finn in a novel, a psychopathic hit man, almost irredeemable, one would have said. My aunt read the book and told me that for all his vices and all his crimes, she couldn't help liking Finn because he loved his mother.

Structure and the movement of my characters I used to find hardest. Moving people about I still find hard. It was Graham Greene, I think, who in giving advice on how to write about violent or dramatic action, recommended the paring down of the prose into brief sentences without adjectives or adverbs. And nothing else must be allowed to intervene, no descriptions of the room or the terrain or the people or the weather. While X is killing Y, let him do it bare, in Anglo-Saxon nouns and verbs, in short brisk sentences. This way the action will come across swift and shocking.

I've never had problems moving my characters in time. The associative process takes care of this beautifully for the writer. We all understand it; it works for us in reality. The stray word, the seldom-heard name of person or place, the sight of something or the scent—all these can evoke the past, and in fiction at any rate carry the protagonist back in time days, months, or years to when that was last heard, smelt, mentioned. There are subtler ways, but these will be learnt along the way.

Writing begets writing. Successful writing—and I mean not only worldly success but that private satisfaction that comes from doing something well—inspires the writer to do better, to attempt the scaling of greater heights, hitherto daunting obstacles. So when a technique has been mastered, instead of sitting back to rest and preen himself or herself, the writer should investigate more subtle methods. Smoother transitions in the matter of flashbacks, for instance, subtler differentiations of character by means of dialogue alone, atmospheres created without violent words or hyperbole but on a lower, more fearful key. And how to make that which is very, very hard look easy.

24

A SENSE OF PLACE

By Mary Elmblad

SETTING IS FREQUENTLY mentioned as one of the important elements of fiction, but sometimes we're inclined to overlook the fact that although setting can be sketchy in a short story, it is essential to the novel. By establishing a sense of place, the writer can invite his reader into the world of the book and can introduce him to the characters who inhabit that world and the conflicts that will develop into plot and theme.

A visitor in my house will learn much about me from my personal setting. The furniture I've chosen, the pictures on the wall, and the titles of the books on my shelves—all are clues to the sort of person I am. From the aromas wafting from the kitchen, he or she can make a fair guess at my cooking expertise—or the lack of it. In the same way, setting helps the reader get to know and understand the characters in a novel.

Here are the first few paragraphs of my novel *All Manner of Riches*:

The clearing in the scrub oak woods lay silent in the sullen noonday heat. The sun beat down on the rusty corrugated iron roof of a tenant house, a shack built of rough-sawn pine planks grayed to splintered silver by the cold wet winters and burning summers of Eastern Oklahoma.

There was not much to the place: the shack, a rough tool shed and a privy that leaned to the east. Down the hill from the house, a garden patch withered in the August sun.

A tall post oak cast a puddle of shade on the packed red earth of the dooryard, and in the shadow a little girl surrounded by a scatter of objects: a cardboard box with a torn feed sack trailing out of it, a cracked enameled pan, and the metal head gasket from a Model A Ford. She hugged a rag doll with a crooked, penciled smile and laid it in the box.

The raucous cry of a crow broke the silence, and, as if on cue, the girl began to sing in a thin, tuneless voice.

The description of Cassie Taylor's world tells the reader quite a lot about her. She is a child who lives in a sharecropper's shack in Eastern

111

Oklahoma. She plays with a part from a Model A Ford, which implies that the time is the 1930s. The mood is established: the deprivation of poverty and a dry, mean summer. But the child hugs her doll and sings, which suggests that she is loving and imaginative. I've used setting to place a happy child in a hostile environment. I have invited readers into Cassie's world, and I can hope that they will hang around long enough to find out what happens to her.

Along with beginning characterization, I have tried to plant the germ of the plot. We see an imaginative child living in abject poverty. Will she grow up there, marry a sharecropper like her father, and bear sickly children? Can she escape from the tenant farm? Creating the plot of a novel, in effect, lies in presenting the protagonist with a series of alternatives from which to choose and, at the same time, with a compelling reason to make a choice.

The theme of the book, too, has appeared in the description of the setting. Cassie Taylor is in "a barren and dry land where no water is." The importance of water and the land recurs throughout the novel.

I begin this book with a static description because it is set in place and time likely to be unfamiliar to the reader. Once the time and place are established, however, I can weave the setting into action and character development:

> When Cassie and her grandmother went blackberry picking in August . . . Granny carried two lard buckets, and Cassie . . . darted here and there like one of the white butterflies in the ditch, pausing now and then to squish her feet in a pocket of red dust or to squat down to examine a roly-poly bug.

Setting is particularly important when the action of the novel moves away from reality. The best horror writers know this and anchor their plots in the everyday world: a vampire is frightening in Transylvania, but at the checkout at K-mart, he is truly terrifying. In *All Manner of Riches,* Cassie has a visionary experience at a country church. To prepare the reader to accept this development, I intentionally describe a matter-of-fact setting. The church, "surrounded by dried-up corn-fields," is "a white frame building as simple as a child's drawing, four-square and without complications." Cassie's grandmother and the other ladies sit in the shade of the trees and fan themselves delicately "with paper fans imprinted, OCHULETA FUNERAL HOME." As the fantasy unfolds, I ease the reader's way by adding a note of the mystical. Cassie and her schoolmate peek "through a crack in the wall of the church to watch dust motes drifting down the slanting beams of sunlight" and listen to "the hushed mysterious talk of woman things, of fevers and births and deaths." I wanted to lead the reader into Cassie's experience and into acceptance of the notion that uncommon events can occur in a commonplace world.

A careful description of the setting can establish mood better than any number of adjectives. In this section of the novel, Cassie is seventeen and has moved to town. At night she takes long walks:

> People left their windows open to catch the breeze, and as Cassie walked along Maple Street and Oak and Spruce, she saw scenes like frames cut from a reel of movie film. A fat woman with her hands poised in midair over the keyboard of a piano. A man bending down to adjust an electric fan. A boy and girl at a window, two silhouettes against the light of the room, his short hair and protruding ears and her fluffy curls backlit at the edges. Children doing their homework under the light of the dining room fixture. A mother holding a plate of cookies. A father lifting his small daughter high, in a frozen moment of laughter. If they argued and screamed at each other, they did it in the kitchen or the bedroom, away from the street. Cassie saw only the good scenes, the homey scenes. In the dark, she wrapped her arms around her chest and passed by alone.

This passage does double duty by defining Cassie's mood as a lonely outsider and by describing what we like to think of as a simpler life: an American neighborhood in 1942.

How many times have we, as readers, skipped over a few paragraphs of static description? If we are going to interweave setting with character and plot and theme, we certainly do not want our readers to skip over it. The way to keep the reader's attention is by writing a description of the setting just as we write every other part of the novel. We try to make sure that our language is fresh and that what we are saying is of interest to the reader. A setting can be described in shorthand—"She lived in a cheap boarding house"—but here I use the setting to enhance the mood.

> Cassie was stopped in the doorway by the gray smell of the place, a pervading odor of stale cooking and decayed wood, as if the walls had soaked up the smell of every pot of cabbage, of every strip of slightly rancid bacon, and of the slow demise of the house itself.
> It was the smell of poverty.

A sense of place is created from a careful selection of specific details. The opening sentence of my novel places the sharecropper's cabin "in a clearing in the scrub oak woods." It would be easier to use the first word that comes to mind—"the forest," perhaps—but specific detail carries specific weight. "The scrub oak woods" is specific, as are "the aspen grove" and "the cypress swamp." When it comes to describing setting, we don't want to see the forest. We want to take a good close look at the trees.

To use specific details, however, we must have them stored in our memory banks. An ornithologist once told me, "Sit on your back steps and listen. Don't read or drink coffee, just listen. The birds are there, but you have to take the time to hear them and see them." That advice is as good for a writer as a bird watcher. Sit on the back steps and listen, and look. The details are there. Take a walk around the neighborhood and sniff occasionally, not with disdain but with curiosity. How does your town smell just before rain or when fog rolls in or when a stiff breeze blows away the smog? Do you hear a foghorn, or city traffic, or rooster crowing far away? Is the wind blowing? Is it a gentle breeze or a Force 8 gale? To help train your powers of observation, you might go for a walk with a three-year-old. He will see everything, from the tiniest bug on the sidewalk to the biggest dog on the block. Through his eyes you will see a world full of startling, wonderful things. If we add to our fund of details, they will be there when we need them. Whether the setting of our novel is an actual place or one that exists only within our creative minds, by knowing it intimately we can select the details that will establish it within the reader's mind.

Here, too, the age-old advice to writers applies: read, read, read. If a novel seems thin to you, think about it. Did the writer give you a sense of place? For a practical exercise, look back and see where a more specific description of setting might have intensified a scene. Think what you might have chosen from your fund of details.

In my novel, for example, I could have written: "Cassie awakened the next morning." Instead, I wrote:

In the early morning, a pair of phoebes perched in the cedar tree outside the bedroom window and woke Cassie with their noisy cries. She came up from sleep slowly, as if waking from a lovely, peaceful dream.

The use of detail ties Cassie's actions and feelings to the setting and at the same time foreshadows later action in which her dream will be destroyed by an intrusion as sudden and as unexpected as the cry of a bird.

Finally, test your own novel-in-progress. Does your setting enhance plot, theme and character development? Is it based on specific details? Is it fresh and interesting? If it can pass these tests, you can be sure that you have brought your reader into the world of your novel. What is more important, however, is the fact that you have fulfilled an essential duty of the novelist.

You have created a sense of place.

25

"COMMERCIAL" VS. "LITERARY"—THE
ARTIFICIAL DEBATE

By Jean M. Auel

NOT LONG ago I received a letter from an English teacher. My books
are on her Required Reading List, and she mentioned that it pleased her
that today's college students could get stirred up enough to ask questions about them. But one question came up repeatedly in one form or
another in both her lit and creative writing classes, and she wondered if
I would take a few moments to respond.

"My students, who are aware of the difference between what we
English teachers refer to as 'literary' and 'commercial' writing, would
like to know if you yourself classify your writing as commercial, and
how do you see it as differing from literary work. They think it lies
solely in amounts of imagery and symbolism. I think it is in the nature
of the storytelling. I see you as a master storyteller appealing to mass
audiences (commercial), who makes generous use of techniques (literary). But my students, who are convinced for some reason that a writer
cannot be both commercial and literary, see you solely as a commercial
writer."

This is a question that deserves an answer. It is especially telling that
those who are in the process of learning how to discern the quality of
writing, and still able to ask such questions, are doing so.

In his introduction to Masterpiece Theater's latest adaptation of
Goodbye, Mr. Chips by James Hilton, Alistair Cooke recalled that the
year before *Goodbye, Mr. Chips* appeared in print, Mr. Hilton was being
hailed as a distinguished literary newcomer with the publication of his
Lost Horizon. Then, Mr. Cooke noted, "he wrote this thundering best
seller and was instantly relegated by the critics to the lowly ranks of a
successful popular author."

When my novel, *The Clan of the Cave Bear,* was first published, it was
nominated for Best First Novel by the American Book Awards and

116

was given two other awards for "Excellence in Writing." But then it started to sell, and my next novels even more, and the knee-jerk response from certain critics was, if everyone likes them, they can't be any good.

This is nothing new. Shakespeare was a very popular writer in his day, who was disparaged because he wrote for the "masses." I doubt that even he imagined that his work would still be popular—and acclaimed—four hundred years later. Who, today, can say what books will still be around four hundred years from now, or even forty? History will decide that, not contemporary critics.

Probably long before they entered their present English teacher's class, those bright, questioning students, who are aware of the difference between what "English teachers refer to as 'literary' and 'commercial' writing," learned the accepted rules of the writing game. But there must be some nagging doubt, something that doesn't quite fit, since they want to know if I "classify my writing as commercial," and how I see it as "differing from literary work."

Why are students given such a narrow, limiting viewpoint from which to base their judgments, as though nothing else exists except "commercial" or "literary"? Not only must everything written be forced to fit within these two narrow slots, but the slots might even be mutually exclusive. A book, or a writer, might be put into one slot, but as soon as some arbitrary number of copies are sold, it is jammed into the other slot.

There is so much more to be gained by trying to understand what the author's purposes were in writing the novel and judging how well the work succeeded in accomplishing those goals. Think of the possibilities. Is the story meant to entertain? To educate? To clarify? To experiment? To express beautiful words? To search for meaning? To demonstrate the importance of some concept? To show the value of humanity, or the lack of it? Is it meant to scare you? To please you? To excite you? To sadden you or make you happy? None of these requires exclusivity. Novels can include any combination of these and other purposes, and whether or not a book is popular has nothing to do with it. Commercial vs. literary is an artificial criterion for establishing the value of a book, based on economics, not merit.

But what about imagery, symbolism, and storytelling? How do they fit into good writing, and why do some books sell better than others?

Before we get too much farther into this, there is one subject that should be dealt with immediately. To some people, any book that includes detailed sexual descriptions was written to be "commercial." Most of the mail I get is positive, but I do get a few letters from people who object to the sexual content, and those range from mild to vociferous. The comment made most often is, "Your stories are good enough without it, you didn't have to put that sex in there to sell books."

That's entirely true. I did not have to put it in there to sell books—nor did I. It was a carefully considered decision based on research, story line, and personal philosophy. As a writer, I feel that any human activity is proper for a novelist to explore, in all its ramifications, if it is essential to the story. The sexuality was used partly to define character, but more importantly to define a culture that certainly had to be different from our own. Looking at both archeological and anthropological evidence, I believe my interpretation is close to the reality of the era. I don't think they viewed this life-creating act as evil or dirty, nor were they ignorant of their own natural responses. The sexual content is not gratuitous; it is there because it was necessary to keep control of the images, to make sure that a reader did not bring a misperception to the story.

Why should anything be important to the story? Is story important? The students think that the difference between literary and commercial "lies solely in the amounts of and types of imagery and symbolism." The teacher thinks it "is in the nature of the storytelling," and sees me as a "storyteller appealing to mass audiences (commercial), who makes generous use of techniques (literary)."

Does that mean, as it seems to imply, that story or "storytelling" cannot be "literary"? If the literary category excludes stories, what are literary writers supposed to write? Just imagery and symbolism? Is that what is taught in textbooks? Is that, perhaps, why students (and many critics) are convinced that a writer cannot be both commercial and literary? That if the story is strong, particularly if it communicates in some way with many people, the work must be "solely commercial"?

What is imagery? Is it only figurative language? A clever metaphor? A pretty simile? Is the purpose of imagery to make readers stop and admire some author's wonderful words? Or is it that when they read a scene or a description, they are stimulated by the words to create an image in their minds?

118

I'm a visual writer. I see the story unfolding, I have a mental image of the setting, the characters, the action, then I search for the words to show it. I don't care about the clever metaphor that is going to impress some critic; I don't write for critics. I want the perfect word; the one to make you see or smell or taste, to feel what the characters are feeling, and to suggest more. I want to draw you into the scene, but be in control of it. I want every word to count, to move the story forward, unless I want it to slow down to change the pacing, or to make an important point about the story or the world it is set in. I use the imagery that best serves my purposes.

And what about symbolism? I went to the dictionary for this one. Webster's *New Collegiate* defines it as, "The art or practice of using symbols, especially by investing things with a symbolic meaning or by expressing the invisible or intangible by means of visible or sensuous representations." Language itself is symbolic. But does the author or the reader decide the symbolic meanings of a writer's work?

If they are successful, readers will discover it, but serious writers don't usually make conscious efforts to put "symbolism" into their work. It comes about as a result of their trying to suggest an idea or to develop a theme.

What about storytelling? One point seems to be overlooked when that word is applied to authors. "Storytelling" is no less writing than any other kind of writing. Authors don't actually *tell* stories. They are story writers. You don't see a person speaking to you; you see little black marks on a page. But if it is done well, you won't see the words. Instead, you will believe, for a while, that imaginary characters, living in a make-believe time and place, actually exist.

Some people have the impression that a book that reads effortlessly was also effortless to write. It is not true. I strive for that goal, but it takes thinking, planning, technique, and writing and rewriting and rewriting. Others think that a book that reads easily cannot be good, because good books are supposed to be hard to read. Yet, more than once I've picked up a dense and obtuse book, only to realize that most of the so-called complexity was the result of laziness. The same thing could have been said so much more simply, but the author hadn't bothered to rewrite. I like the definition for a professional that a ballet dancer once gave me: It is someone who can make the difficult look easy.

The best judge of good stories and, by far, the toughest critic is that tiny percentage of the total population that is the reading public. You can't con the collective reader into pretending a book is wonderful, and paying for it, because someone with literary prestige says it is. People understand stories, enjoy them, and probably have from the beginning of time. A particular work may have other worthwhile qualities, but if it's not a good story, readers won't tell other people about it, or buy additional copies to give to friends and relatives.

From that point of view, you can define a "commercial" book as one with a good story, but then does "literary" mean any book that does *not* have a good story? The techniques or qualities that are considered when determining the value of good writing are used, though perhaps in an altered form, when writing stories, too. Not all stories are written to be commercial.

I wanted to write good stories, partly because I enjoy story, but I had another purpose, which was equally important, that required good stories and strongly affected the way I wrote. The Earth's Children series started with an idea for a short story, I thought, of a young woman living in prehistoric times with people who were less advanced. I don't know where the idea came from. Though I quickly decided writing the story was fun, I was soon frustrated because I didn't know what I was writing about.

That led me to the library for research, and there I made a discovery. Our prehistoric ancestors were not brutish, half-ape savages, "cavemen" barely struggling for existence. The world of the Ice Age Cro-Magnon was fascinating, a stone-age technology and a hunting-gathering culture that was rich, complex, and surprisingly sophisticated. At first I was amazed, and then a little angry. Why didn't I know this? Why don't we all? Those first modern humans shared their cold ancient world with another kind of Homo sapiens, Neanderthal, whose brain was actually larger, though not quite the same. Two different kinds of advanced humans, living at the same time in the same place; what a perfect setting for fresh, new, and exciting fiction.

There was my story idea, but grown and expanded. It fired my imagination. I wanted to share this exciting new vision. It was time someone took the new, updated version of "caveman" out of the dry scientific books and made it accessible to people. I decided that someone was going to be me! It had to be accurate, but I knew the only way to do it right was through fiction.

I've been a wide and eclectic reader, and learned long ago that the real power of fiction is its ability to make you feel. Nothing else can capture you, absorb you, and literally make you live the life of the characters the way fiction can. Because of this, fiction can be a powerful teaching tool. Our education system tries to teach using primarily intellectual processes, but it is much easier to learn if your emotions are engaged. Heightened emotions aid memory; incidents remembered most vividly are invariably associated with strong feelings. Primitive peoples have known this for a long time. That's why so much knowledge and information that had to be memorized was passed on through ceremony and story.

I set as my goal to write an accurate and convincing story that showed the humanity of those ancient ancestors in such a compelling way that ingrained perceptions would be changed when people read it. I was too excited to realize what a big order that was—or too ignorant. I didn't even know how to write fiction, and I was forty when I began.

I have never taken a class in creative writing, but then I'm not sure anyone could have taught me how to write these stories that are part novel, part historical fiction, part science, part speculation. I gleaned and selected what I needed from books about writing and from fiction, including literature textbooks. To draw readers in and make them feel that world, I had to learn about character, scene, description, theme, story, pacing, texture, and more. I had to learn to cram in detail, to build it in along with the characters, and incorporate it into the story line, so that it would enhance the vision without stopping the story.

And I certainly didn't want to freight these stories with obscure techniques or obvious literary gimmicks; can you imagine using mini-malist criteria, for example? They would have bogged down completely. It would have been entirely inappropriate and would not have served my purposes. With the weight of physical detail, they have enough to carry as it is. Even the philosophies and new concepts were tucked in with the story detail so they would be assimilated unobtrusively as they were read. My novels have much to consider on several levels, but I want it to sneak up on the readers, make them think, in spite of themselves, later.

Have I fulfilled my purposes, achieved my goals? I'm not sure; I don't think any author ever really is. I tried to create an accurate, if spec-ulative, world that would capture the readers' interest. I wanted them to get caught up and carried along by the story, and not only suspend their sense of disbelief while reading, but to think about it afterwards. Are the images strong; do the words make them see, and even more, feel? Are the characters complex and memorable? Can readers find a common reference or a symbolic relationship to their own lives? Does the story stay with them after they've closed the book? Has it changed their perceptions of our stone-age ancestors?

I have had very positive responses from the academic community praising the accuracy of these novels, and since the books are popular, I think the stories must be reasonably good, so perhaps I have succeeded in some measure. But that doesn't answer the question I was asked: Do I classify my writing as "commercial," and how do I see it as differing from "literary" work?

Consider this: If I had planned to write a commercial best seller, would I have chosen Upper Paleolithic "caveman" as my subject? A spy thriller, perhaps, or a Hollywood glitzy, a type of story already proven to be enjoyed by many readers, but how many bestselling "caveman" books were there ten years ago? When I decided to write, whether it would be "commercial" or "literary" was not even a consideration. In fact, that artificial debate never entered my mind.

26

MAGICIAN, ACTOR, RUNNER ➡ WRITER

By Peter Lovesey

IT'S A PARTY and my host has steered me across the room to meet some people he says he knows I'll like. After we exchange names one of them asks, "What line of work are you in?"

"Ah." A pause for thought. Shall I admit to being a writer, or take some diversionary action, such as spilling my drink, or shouting "Fire!" or singing a couple of verses from "Some Enchanted Evening"? If not, I must face the inevitable questions; inevitable and always the same:

"Where do you get your ideas?"

I don't know the answer to this, so I generally say, "Anywhere I can."

The next is usually phrased in the form of a statement: "It must take a lot of self-discipline."

Then the questioning takes a personal turn.

"What did you say your name is?"

I give it.

There is a moment of silence, followed by,

"Should we have heard of you?"

A tough one, that. I can escape embarrassment by side-stepping ("No, it's not obligatory. What's your line of work?") or lying ("Oh, I don't often write under my own name."), because it only gets worse:

"Did you always want to be a writer?"

Actually, I didn't. I wasn't born with inky fingers. I didn't have a toy typewriter, and I didn't publish a book until I was past thirty.

The honest answer to that question is no. But what did I want to be as a child? Life before thirty must have had some relevance to my present way of life. What ambitions did I have in those so-called formative years? My earliest was to be a magician. I wanted to amaze and baffle my family and friends by sawing ladies in half. And, I'd better add, restoring them.

I was persuaded to give up conjuring for acting. I started as Joseph in a Nativity play and was sacked for overacting. I was a pure-born Method actor; I pushed the Innkeeper through the scenery when he told us there was no room. It was meant to provoke a genuine response, and it did. After the fight we were both demoted to humiliating non-speaking roles as angels. But I'd caught the acting bug, I wanted to be up there with Gielgud and Olivier.

The urge to act was eventually supplanted by an ambition to be a great long-distance runner, Great Britain's main hope for the 1956 Olympic marathon. I suppose I was one of the first joggers, running through dark suburban streets speaking a radio commentary as I went. I had to endure some strange looks. And there was more humiliation: After months of training, I finished last in the school cross-country race.

As it turned out, running made me into a writer. Facing the fact that I was constitutionally ill equipped for the marathon or even the 100 meters, I channeled my enthusiasm into supporting people who *could* run brilliantly. I made idols of the track stars I watched. I shouted for them, drew pictures of them, put them into ranking lists, and kept press clippings about them. Soon I started to catch out journalists in their facts. I don't suppose it helped them at all, but it helped my confidence. It made me believe that I could do better than they, but nobody else believed it. I wasn't an expert. I hadn't won an Olympic medal. I hadn't even coached an Olympic medalist. I was *Mr. Nobody.*

How do you become an expert overnight? Why, by picking out an area of knowledge that nobody else has bothered to investigate. I went to a newspaper museum and looked up reports of running events a century ago, fascinating to a twentieth-century reader: full of character, color, and eccentricity. I turned my discoveries into off-beat articles for track and field magazines. In a short time I was being described as "the world's foremost authority on the history of athletics." At that time, I was the *only* authority, so it was true beyond dispute.

Unfortunately, the magazine who dubbed me the world's foremost didn't pay me a cent. They published my articles for five years, and I was happy just to get into print. However, at the end of that time I looked at my best work and decided to tailor it into a book on long-distance runners. I went to a lot of trouble to get good illustrations. To his eternal credit, and may his tribe increase, a publisher picked it out of the "slush pile" of unsolicited scripts and liked it enough to publish it as *The Kings of Distance.*

The next year I was encouraged to enter a competition for a first crime novel. I used a nineteenth-century running background; what else would you expect from the world's foremost authority? *Wobble to Death* was unlike anything else in the competition and won the prize. I was launched as a mystery writer. I'm still writing mysteries, seventeen years later.

So what happened to those dreams of my childhood, to be a magician, an actor, or a marathon runner?

Magician, actor, marathon runner: As a mystery writer, I'm all of these. In my own way I'm doing the things I first dreamed of doing.

A magician? A mystery writer repeatedly performs tricks, showing the reader something that turns out to be misleading. Call it trickery, sleight-of-hand, or illusion, it comes down to unexpected effects. The best trick I ever pulled was bringing someone back to life after he'd appeared to be dead. The result was dramatic, but I can't claim any originality. Many fine writers used the device long before I did: I'm not giving too much away if, as examples, I mention Thomas Hardy in *Far From the Madding Crowd*; Evelyn Waugh in *Decline and Fall*; and, of course, Sir Arthur Conan Doyle in "The Empty House," the first story in *The Return of Sherlock Holmes*. Such a marvelous effect has to be used sparingly, or the element of surprise is lost. But there are numerous smaller illusions most of us try. There's the character who turns out to be someone else; the ambiguous suicide note; the poison that is also a cosmetic; the spy who is a double or triple agent.

Every conjurer is asked, "How is it done?" and he's supposed not to reveal his secrets. However, by the end of a book, every writer's secrets are laid bare. It's possible to look back and see exactly how it was done. The magic is in the plotting. May I suggest a useful way to learn how to be a successful writer-magician? Take a plot that has succeeded in surprising you. Study it again, analyze it, and summarize the main course of the plot on one side of a sheet of paper. Then have another look at the trick that surprised you. See how the facts were first presented to you and how the writer achieved the illusion. I promise you won't be wasting your time.

The magic, as I said, is in the plotting. Some writers will tell you that plotting is itself a mysterious process that happens without much conscious effort on their part. The book develops as they write it, and they don't know where the next day's writing will lead them.

125

My approach couldn't be more different. I believe in working out the entire plot before I start writing page one. Otherwise, I'd feel like a conjurer going out on stage without preparing his program. It's slow, agonizing, frequently unproductive work. Sometimes I worry at an idea for weeks and then reject it because I've proved to myself that it won't come out convincingly. The plot must be an excellent one, or why spend months or years of your life shaping it into a book?

I'm happy to pass on a few tips about plotting. I find it helps me at an early stage to give the characters real names, rather than A, B, or C, or "old man" or "blonde." It also helps to think up real locations, preferably places you know. Sometimes a particular setting, its streets and buildings, suggests twists that you wouldn't otherwise have thought about. And when you've reached an impasse, as I frequently do, it helps if there's someone in your life who won't mind having you explain the problem. Often the process of talking about it will clarify the difficulty. Even as I'm explaining why I'm stuck, inspiration strikes, and I see the way ahead. But choose someone *very* sympathetic, or he or she will think you quite mad.

My second ambition, you'll recall, was to act. As a writer, I'm acting all the time, with the bonus that I can invent my own dialogue as I go along. If the characters in a novel are to come alive, you need to give them convincing things to say in a realistic form. So I speak the conversations aloud as I write them, playing the parts and seeing if they have tension and drama.

The whole question of voice is crucial. After you've worked out a satisfactory—no, let's say it—brilliant plot, you need to decide what voice the writing will have. My latest mysteries have been written in the first person, with the narrator telling a tale in which he plays a leading part. In this way, the reader learns a lot about the character, whether he's forceful or unassertive, cynical or naive. It all shows through in the telling. And to get it right, I speak the lines aloud.

Even if I write in the third person, I invariably tell the story from the point of view of one or more of the characters. Once I rewrote an entire novel because I thought it would work better from someone else's point of view, and it did. I wouldn't want to give myself that task again, so now I spend time at the beginning deliberately deciding how to get it right: whose voice will tell the story.

Most actors will admit that in preparing a role they draw on their observation of people they know. The same, I am certain, is true of most writers. I wouldn't recommend telling your friends that you based this or that character on them, but I believe in doing it. Even if they bother to read my books, they don't recognize themselves in the obscure settings I put them in. Besides, I make them do things my friends probably wouldn't admit to, anyway.

Ambition number three was long-distance running, and that, too, has relevance to my life as a writer. It's about endurance and fitness and pacing yourself. The prospect at the start, faced with that first blank sheet, is daunting, but once I'm ready, I set off and take it in my stride, and after two or three weeks Chapter One is complete. I don't care to think too much at the start about the time I'm likely to take, but as I go on it sometimes helps to have a finishing date in mind. My mysteries take anything from eight months to a year to finish. I'm slow for a full-time writer working eight or ten hours a day, but I rarely rewrite, so it's all progress.

Of course, it's a very hard slog. Hemingway said it was sometimes like drilling rock and then blasting it out with charges. Peter De Vries wrote, "I love being a writer. What I can't stand is the paperwork." Ask any marathon runner why he does it when he suffers constantly from blisters and leg pains, and you're likely to be told that it's about achieving something and the joy of getting there. For me, writing is compulsive for similar reasons. However hard it appears, it's still a fun run.

And the moral of all this? If you ever meet me at a party, don't ask me if I always wanted to be a writer, because you'll have heard it all before.

May your writing be magical, dramatic, and long-lasting.

27

TOO GOOD TO BE TRUE: THE FLAWLESS CHARACTER

By Mary Tannen

MY MOTHER ONCE BOUGHT a new table that came with a card printed on buff-colored heavy stock explaining that the table had been "distressed" with artful gouges and well-placed worm holes to give it a patina of age. We (her four children) thought this was hilariously funny and said that if we had only known she wanted distressed furniture we would have been happy to oblige and that clearly we had misinterpreted her screams of anguish every time we left a soda bottle on the coffee table or ran a toy car up the leg of the Duncan Phyfe chair.

The very phrase "character flaw" makes me think of that distressed table, as if characters were naturally shiny new and perfect and needed only the addition of a flaw or two, artfully placed, to make them more realistic. To me, a personality, whether actual or fictional, is not solid but liquid, not liquid but airborne, as changeable as light. What looks like a flaw might turn out to be a virtue. Virtue might, under certain circumstances, prove to be a fault.

When my daughter was reading *Billy Budd* and having a hard time with it, she came storming into my room to protest, and seeing the book I was working on in galleys, took it into her room to read. She brought it back the next day and announced that it was "better than *Billy Budd*."

"Better than *Billy Budd*!" I could see it emblazoned across the book jacket. Actually, my novel isn't better than *Billy Budd,* but the style was a lot more congenial to my daughter. She was appalled by Melville's heavy symbolism, by the way Billy Budd was the representation of an idea, not an actual man.

Billy Budd had no flaws, physical or moral (except for his stutter). He was illiterate, of noble but unknown birth, untainted by the corrupting influence of either family or literature. He was a myth, "Apollo with his

128

portmanteau"! Melville never intended to create a realistic character. Billy Budd was Adam before the fall.

Sometimes when reading over a draft of a fiction piece I am working on, I realize that one of my major characters is suspiciously lacking in flaws. She is usually a person like me, but she is lacking in defects as well as in color and definition. When this happens in a piece of fiction I'm writing, it is a sign that I am identifying too closely with her. Just as I try to show my good and hide my bad, I am protecting this fictional person.

Recently I discovered a trick that helped me correct this. I was working with a character, Yolanda, a woman my age who ran a bookstore. Yolanda was nice. She was good. A nice good woman, and very bland. I couldn't get a grip on her or who she was. I went to my local swimming pool to do a few laps and take my mind off my troubles, when I saw a woman I'd seen many times before but don't know very well—a tall skinny woman with short elfin hair and wide-awake eyes. I decided to steal this woman's body and give it to Yolanda.

It worked miracles because now Yolanda was no longer me. She was this woman I didn't know very well. She began to exhibit all kinds of personality traits. She was allergic to almost everything and purchased her meals at the New Age Take-Out Kitchen. This explained why she was so thin. She spent lonely nights watching the families in the apartments across the street. The strange thing was that although Yolanda had many more weaknesses than she did before I discovered she wasn't me, I liked her better.

Another way to break the spell of the flawless character is to elicit the opinion of another character in the novel or story, one who dislikes, resents, or holds a grudge against the paragon of virtue. In *Second Sight,* I had a perfectly lovable older woman, Lavinia, who refused to believe that her philandering husband, Nestor, had left her for good. Instead of selling the house and investing the proceeds in order to live off the income, she managed on very little so that she could keep the house intact for Nestor's return.

Nestor (who had flaws to spare) had another version of the story. Lavinia's loyalty enraged him. He saw it as a ploy to make him feel guilty and remain tied to her. Indeed, at the end when Nestor asked Lavinia to take him back, Lavinia realized she no longer wanted to return to her old life with Nestor. She wondered if perhaps instead of being noble and true all those years, she hadn't actually been taking out a genteel and subtle revenge.

A character without flaws has nowhere to go. He can't change or grow. In Philip Roth's *The Counterlife*, the novelist Zuckerman, who used himself as a character in his books, was writing about his younger brother Henry. Because Zuckerman had given all the faults to himself-as-character, he had doomed his brother-as-character to a life of virtue. Henry had always been the good son, the good husband, father, dentist. Writing about Henry at thirty-nine, Zuckerman imagined him as the suffocating prisoner of his perfect but shallow life. The only way Henry could break the pattern was to escape altogether, leave his family and practice in New Jersey and begin anew in Israel. Zuckerman went to visit Henry in his kibbutz on the West Bank and found that his younger brother had simply exchanged one slavish system for another. He was still the good brother. He could change the scene, but he couldn't change himself because he was a character without flaws.

I realize I have been using the term "flaw" as if it could mean anything from nail-biting to one of the Seven Deadly Sins. I think of a flaw as a personality trait I wouldn't confess to, except on a dark and stormy night to a stranger passing through. And then there are the flaws we hide from ourselves, or lack the insight to see, but which help determine the course of our lives.

When I'm writing, the flaws that interest me are not the ones I assign ("Q kicks small dogs"), but those that emerge in the course of the story. Take Yolanda, who tries to be good, to be virtuous, to do no harm to others: I was amazed to discover, somewhere near the end of the first draft, that she had used someone, a man, a friend, to get over a wound suffered long ago, and in using him had hurt him. Yolanda didn't see how she could hurt this friend whom she considered much more powerful and attractive than she. The more I work on that novel, the more I see that Yolanda's major flaw is her modesty. She lets people down because she cannot conceive that she means as much to them as they do to her.

In *Second Sight*, the opposite was true: a character's flaw proved to be her saving grace. Delia, the widowed mother of a twelve-year-old son, lacked all marketable skills. She lived on welfare and whatever she could make telling fortunes over the phone. Everyone, but especially

Delia's career-minded sister Cass, faulted her for not taking her life in hand and finding a way out of the dead-end life of poverty she and her son had fallen into.

But Delia operated on another level from her more rational friends and relatives. She was watching for signs and portents, for signals that the time was right. She refused to force the unfolding of her life.

Delia did manage finally to bring about a change for herself and her son, to the amazement of the others, who began to see a glimmer of wisdom in her otherworldliness. Cass, however, could never accept that Delia's passivity had enabled her to recognize and receive love when it came her way. Cass would continue to take charge of her life, as Delia said, captaining it as if it were a ship, but never allowing for the influence of wind or tide or current.

People, fictional and real, are not perfect, like fresh-from-the-factory tables. They come with their faults built in, mingled and confused with their virtues. Whenever I find I am dealing with a character without flaws, and I am not intending a twentieth-century rewrite of *Billy Budd,* I take it as a sign that I have not done my work. I have not imagined my character fully, have not considered her through the eyes of the other characters. Finally, I have not cut the umbilical cord. I am protecting her, shielding her, and, at the same time, imprisoning her in her own virtue. It is time to let her go so she can fail and change and grow.

28

LET FICTION CHANGE YOUR LIFE

By Lynne Sharon Schwartz

THE LURE OF USING our own experiences in fiction is almost irresistible—not only for beginners but for seasoned pros as well. What could be more natural, or more inevitable? To tell what has shaped us, to cast the incidents of our lives in the form of narrative, with ourselves as heroes and heroines, is instinctive: It shows itself as soon as children acquire language. And personal experience is a vital source of fiction, one might even say the only source: what else *can* we write of but what we have seen, felt, thought, done, and as a result, imagined? As readers, we're touched most deeply by stories that possess, in Henry James's phrase, the sense of "felt life," stories the author has cared about and lived with and presented in all their intensity; the others lie stone cold on the page. Indeed, a corollary to the old saw, "write what you know," could be, "write what you care about."

But if all of the above is true, then fiction might be no more than faintly disguised autobiography, an indulgent exercise in self-expression. Fiction would be a sorry, impoverished thing indeed, deprived of the rich and incomparable offerings of the imagination and the unconscious, with their enigmatic leaps and turns. Thankfully this isn't so.

How do we make use of the tremendous stores of material our lives provide, and at the same time avoid boring our readers by being that most tedious of companions—the kind we all know and dread—who talks only of himself, by himself, and for himself?

The lamest excuse beginning fiction writers give in response to criticism is, plaintively, "But that's what really happened." Who cares, I'm tempted to ask. To put it more tactfully: If you want to write fiction that others will love to read, you have to be willing to sacrifice parts of your life. Or if that sounds rather extreme, let's call it giving up "the way it really happened" in favor of a greater truth. For a story, in some unaccountable fashion, makes its own demands, like a child outgrowing the confines of the parental home. When you're willing to let the story's life take precedence over your own and go its way, you've taken the first step to becoming a successful writer.

Once you've embarked on that journey, the urge to tell what happened is slowly transformed into the desire to give events pattern and significance, to construct a *thing,* almost like a free-standing sculpture whose shape and contours are clear to all, with the power to delight, or amuse, or provoke, or disturb. Above all, to draw in an entrance. In its final form, while the construction may have been inspired by happenings in the writer's own life and may still contain their germ, it has taken on its own life. It has, sometimes in most surprising ways, gone beyond the writer's experience.

This doesn't mean you can't allow your deepest concerns into your fiction—quite the contrary. Look at the work of Jane Austen, who has left us the most witty, thorough, and painstaking account of nineteenth-century courtship and marriage rites in the middle classes; no sociological study could be more informative, not to mention enchanting. Little is known of Austen's personal life; we cannot say for certain who were her suitors or why she did not marry; we cannot point to episodes in her novels and trace their origins. What we do know is that she scrutinized the mating game in all its aspects, with a unique blend of irony, skepticism, and mellow acceptance. In other words, Austen managed to put her individual sensibility into her work in a far more profound way than by merely drawing on actual events.

As a humbler example, since it's what I know best, I'll use my own novel, *Rough Strife,* which also happens to be about a marriage. The story follows some twenty years in the life of a couple, Caroline and Ivan, who meet in Rome then return to the United States to live in Boston, Connecticut, and finally New York City—settings I chose because I knew them and felt on "safe" territory. During the time I was writing *Rough Strife,* a spate of novels appeared in which married women, weary and disgusted with the inequities of family life, were cutting loose to find independence and adventure. Something about the ease and abruptness of their flights from home bothered me; much as I sympathized with the problem of constraint, the solution seemed oversimplified. I was determined to write about a heroine who stayed to see it through, to learn where that route could lead. At the same time I, too,

133

was determined not, fashionably, to abandon my marriage, a fact that surely influenced the book.

I suppose I planned, in some imprecise way, to have Caroline and Ivan face many of the issues my husband and I faced. But in the end the couple bypassed me to lead their own lives. Caroline, for example, surprised me by having a difficult time conceiving their first child. A mathematics professor, she has an affair with a graduate student, which leads to an abortion; later on, her second child with Ivan turns out to be hyperactive. Why, I wondered as I wrote, did I invent all that? Why did it invent itself, might be more accurate. Well, I wanted to illustrate the enormous effects that bearing and raising children have on a marriage, and those events heighten the illustration. They apply pressure and create tension. They arose from the imagination, wisely, I think, to serve the story.

At still another point the characters escaped me, quite against my will. I was writing a scene of a marital quarrel, with some rather acidic repartee. No one could have been more alarmed than I when Ivan suddenly turned violent, pushing Caroline to the floor. It was not at all what I had intended—not with these characters, anyway, civilized people, incapable of such behavior. In shock and horror, I watched a rape scene unfold. How much more shocking that it was coming from my own pen! And Caroline's reaction was equally horrifying. Instead of being indignant and repelled, she thinks she invited it in some way. She even feels sorry for Ivan in his guilt and remorse! The whole incident contradicted my beliefs as well as my experience—in real life I would have shaken them both to their senses. But this was not real life. This was the utter mystery and excitement of fiction, where characters rebel and demand their own errors and their own destiny, and we had best not stand in their way.

In the end, I had a novel about a couple whose story barely resembled my own. The only autobiographical elements left were a certain analytical turn of mind and a sense of the complex, ambiguous accommodations involved in living with another person. Whatever my original aims, I had written about the gradual process of accepting the results of one's uneducated choices. With the benefit of several years' hindsight, I can see that this notion of process, not the details of the plot, is what makes the book personal as well as, I hope, universal.

The same shifts occur in writing stories, only on a smaller scale. How well I remember lying awake one entire night with a gray spot jiggling before my eyes—something the doctors call a "floater," I later learned. It didn't let me sleep, and as the hours passed, I slipped into a miserable, unreasonable state of mind, berating myself for all the mistakes of my past, wondering what it all meant, if anything. . . . Anyone who's spent a sleepless night recently will know what I mean. The experience was so powerful and disturbing that naturally I wanted to write about it. The result was a story, "Acquainted With the Night," whose main character turned out to be a male architect ten years older than I. Why, I can't say. He too lies awake, victim of a floater, examining and agonizing over his past, which, needless to say, has nothing in common with my own. (I took the opportunity to give him a life full of moral crisis, without the straints I might have felt about detailing mine.) Again, the common and personal element, as well as the universal one, is simply the insomniac's painful and—in the light of day—distorted trip, a trip almost every reader has taken at one time or another.

The path leading to a newer story was more circuitous. Several years ago, a fire forced my husband and me out of the apartment building where we had lived for twenty years and raised our two daughters. Besides the shock and pain of losing our home, we and our fellow-tenants were outraged at the behavior of the landlord, Columbia University, in the aftermath of the fire. A lengthy court case ensued, with the tenants ranged against the power and willfulness of a large institution. Two years later I completed a book about the fire, the legal proceedings, and the social implications of institutions as landlords. Since I had written mainly fiction till then, I was prepared when friends asked why I hadn't turned my experience into a novel—what an ideal story it seemed, full of drama and conflict. My answer was, first, that the truth was topically urgent and needed to be told precisely as it happened; and second, that the story (plus the research it would entail) really didn't interest me as a novelist. I had been writing long enough to know that real estate practices, demographics, and the nature of bureaucracy were not my subjects.

Some time later, though, probably under the influence of many newspaper and magazine articles about homelessness in New York City, an imaginary family moved into my mind. Little by little their features became clear: they were newcomers from the Virgin Islands, the father was an electrician but temporarily working at a lunch counter, they were black, they were very proper and conventional, there were three young children. . . . They too had been forced out of their apartment by a fire, but unlike my family, they had had to accept the city's offer of a welfare hotel, a dismal and dangerous environment. The father, a proud man, found that intolerable, but with so little money what could he do? I became obsessed with the family until their story virtually wrote itself—"The Last Frontier," in which George and Louise Madison and their children move onto the stage set of a situation comedy, contrasting the whitewashed TV image of family life with their own reality.

None of the details about the Madisons corresponded to my own life—none, that is, except their condition of homelessness, and the resulting anger, frustration, and bewilderment. In those feelings that give the story its life, we were identical. One might say it is auto-biographical in the deepest sense.

The ability I've been discussing—giving up the facts for the broader reaches of the imagination—may sound daunting, but it comes with experience, and with the confidence and willingness to let the story take control. For almost always, at some point in the arduous process, the inner voice will whisper, "What if . . . instead of . . . ?" The secret is to listen, and to yield.

But that's not the only way. Some fiction gets written backwards, so to speak. In the case of *Balancing Acts* (my first novel, though it was published second), I was on the third draft and puzzled over why it wouldn't come right, when I finally grasped what the book was about and what its connection was to me.

I had begun it after a friend told me about her ten-year-old daughter's strong attachment to an elderly man, a volunteer teacher in her school. The man had just died, and the child was suffering the sort of grief—for the loss of a close friend—that most of us don't know till later in life. The story stayed with me—I didn't know why; one often doesn't—and I constructed a novel around it, with background and details far different from those of my own life. I couldn't help but notice, though, that the man in my novel had much in common with my father, and the thirteen-year-old heroine, with me. Not circumstantial matters in common, but affinities of temperament and attitude. Only on that third draft, when I realized that book was a particular emotional struggle on my part, connected with my aging father, could I rewrite it with coherence and conscious design. Plot, setting, and characters all remained the same,

136

but I had found the autobiographical impulse at the core and could work outwards, using its energy.

Giving the imagination free reign, or conversely, locating the fertile source of a story, is exhilarating as well as productive. But it has its negative side (doesn't everything?). The upshot of letting fiction change the events of your life is losing parts of your past. It's not an overstatement to confess that looking over my work, I occasionally note bits that sound familiar, yet I can't quite remember whether they happened or whether I made them up. Did the neighbors down the street when I was nine years old really shout those awful things out the window, or did I imagine it? Or exaggerate it? Did that man in the boat really look at me in that seductive way? Was the path behind the country houses really as dark and lush with greenery as I wrote? And were my grandmother's glasses of tea with lumps of sugar as wonderful as I've made out? The line between memory and invention blurs; I can't say for sure what happened, and I have the sinking feeling that I've erased parts of my life in order to write stories over them. I may have given up more than I expected, becoming a writer. The only relief for such doubts is to go back and write some more. Because in the end, as the Roman poet said, life is short, but art is long.

29

FICTION AND JOURNALISM: SHARED TECHNIQUES

By Russell Working

THE CALL CAME OVER the scanner in the newsroom, and everyone was stunned and stared at each other from over their computer terminals for an instant. Someone jumped up and turned up the volume to make sure we had heard it right: "An officer has been shot in front of the Eagles Lodge."

I grabbed a notebook and my camera. "Where did they say?"

"The Eagles Lodge."

"Where is that?"

"Right across the street."

Another reporter and I ran over to the parking lot where a squad car sat with its door open. The officer was sprawled across the front seat. Your first inclination is to help, but a lieutenant is already there doing everything he can. So you shoot pictures of the officer—sitting up now, having taken a gunshot—and the squad cars and ambulance screeching into the lot and the policemen with their pistols drawn, running up an alley where the gunman fled.

Then you notice a woman lying between two cars with her head in a pool of oil. A bouquet of yellow roses lies nearby on the pavement. (Later your editor will say, Did you get the woman? Did you get the flowers? We've got to have a picture with the flowers. They tell the whole story.) An ambulance worker kneels in the oil beside the woman. But the oil slick is expanding on the pavement, and too maroon in color, and you realize it is coming from the woman's head.

You lower your camera, thinking, Jesus. Jesus have mercy.

The murder happened a year and a half ago in my town; a husband killed his estranged wife and shot the officer who arrived a moment too late to help. The crime was front page news, and we played it up big for reasons that go beyond the cliché about trying to sell newspapers: It was shocking, explosive human drama. It is the kind of drama that makes good fiction.

Journalism (along with a habit of reading literature) has taught me how to write, even to write fiction. The daily task of pounding out copy has provided dozens of lessons. You learn that words are not sacred, that your copy can be cut and put back together again and even improved. And you learn two skills that can easily be transplanted into the field of fiction writing: news judgment, and the ability to observe.

The fiction writer, who has weeks to craft a story, might be tempted to dismiss the quality of newspaper writing, the columns of gray that smudge off on your fingers as you sip your morning coffee. News judgment may sound alien to someone whose concerns are primarily aesthetic, and a reporter's objectivity appears to run counter to the very nature of art, which is subjective.

Journalists, too, often fail to recognize their kinship with fiction writers. When I told one reporter that I was working on this piece, he asked, "Are you going to tell them you make up your stories for the paper?" Fiction is often bandied about as a synonym for *false* (has none of the drab officials and Congressmen who use the term that way ever read *War and Peace* or *The Sound and the Fury*?), and this usage has sullied the term in a field where accuracy is essential. Editors fire reporters who can't get their facts straight. *The Washington Post* was humiliated a few years ago when a reporter admitted that she had made up her Pulitzer Prize-winning story.

So what I am talking about is the shared techniques. The fiction writer and journalist both make use of news—the ability to recognize compelling drama, and arrange a story in a way that interests readers.

Great literature is filled with the material you find in interesting newspaper stories, from heroism to murder and betrayal. Even things that appear sensational and therefore "low" have profound fictional potential. Imagine a newspaper (or more likely, a supermarket tabloid) reporting a story under this headline: Crazed student ax-murders sisters in fourth-floor bloodbath. The topic sounds grotesque. But in the hands of Dostoevsky, *Crime and Punishment* became one of the great novels of all time.

Fiction writers must find dramatic subjects worthy of spending their time on. Newspapers contain a wealth of possibilities. Look over the headlines for a week and see what catches your eye. Read the stories that interest you, and ask why that is so. Students and young writers are often told, "Write what you know," and this advice is reasonably sound. But get to know the world around you, the interesting situations and people. Shakespeare's subjects included regicide, suicide, daughters banishing their father to the heath, a beautiful woman falling in love with a man who has the head of an ass. Drama, not technique, is the primary tool for building a story.

As I worked on my book *Resurrectionists,* I struggled with a story set in a pulp and paper mill. The story grew to an unwieldy size, and I came to realize that the main character, Clay, lacked motivation. But after I stumbled onto the wounded cop and the woman's corpse in the parking lot, something sparked in me, and I rewrote the story. Clay became a cop who had been wounded while failing to stop a murder. Unable to come to grips with his life after the shooting, he quit the police force and went to work in the mill, where he found himself unconsciously taking deadly risks amid the pounding machinery. The drama of a murder had added interest to my story.

Objectivity is another journalistic technique that can inform the work of a fiction writer. Drama may provide the impetus for a story, but it is in the quality of its writing that a story will be measured aesthetically. The ability to detach yourself from what you know, to observe rather than draw conclusions, can strengthen your fiction.

Good writing requires an intensity of vision that runs counter to most learning. While knowledge (geometry, philosophy, theology) tends to consist of abstract thought, storytelling demands detail. The image, not the idea, is supreme. Great writers have the ability to focus their powers of observation, and to describe the images that contribute symbolically or aesthetically to the whole of their work (the shadows of the leaves on the wall in Hemingway's "A Clean, Well-lighted Place"; Pierre's spectacles at the opening of *War and Peace*; Queequeg's tattoos in *Moby Dick*).

Such writing requires a kind of objectivity, an ability to detach yourself from your subject and simply observe. Writers are sometimes content to slog about in abstractions on character, rather than offering telling detail. Step back from your character and observe his actions (and please, leave the cigarettes on the table; they are dreadfully over-used—"She lit up a Marlboro and puffed nervously."). Notice how a character stands, how he gestures with one hand while tucking the other in his belt, the twitch in his left cheek. Does he keep touching his hair in front to make sure it's covering the scar on his forehead? Tell the reader.

When I was an intern at *The Daily News* in Longview, Washington, I spent a night in jail on assignment. The state of Washington had just passed a law requiring a mandatory jail sentence for drunken drivers, and I was there to write about what they faced behind bars. After I got out, my city editor asked me how I felt. Afraid? I said yes, perhaps a little. He said, "Then don't write that. Just write about what happened."

So I wrote about the man with the long braided hair and ribbons sewn to his shirt, who scooted across the floor of the holding cell and sat beside me. I glanced at him, and he smiled. I wrote about how the man across from me began describing the prisoner sitting beside me: "He's in for murder," said the bearded man with Aryan Brotherhood tatoos covering his arms. "He probably killed the guy with a chain saw."

The man beside me smiled modestly. "It was a Bowie knife." I shrugged. A Bowie knife. No problem. That's different. Here I was worrying. The man said, "People get nervous when I tell them I'm in for murder. They keep watching me. Whenever I move, they jump."

I wrote about how the prisoners began questioning my cover story: What color was the van they transported you in? Was it green or orange? Did you see the deputy who had the artificial arm? And they're shipping you to Oregon? Why are they taking you across state lines without an extradition order?

As I began describing what had happened, discussions of what I had been feeling became less and less necessary. An objective discussion of the situation set the mood better than gushing on about my sensations.

To be able to observe objectively, you must keep an open mind about your characters and about ideas you disagree with or even find repugnant. Fiction writers sometimes lose track of this. It is hard to find an interesting religious character among the works of many nineteenth- and twentieth-century writers. If you create a character simply to ridicule an idea, he becomes cardboard. A reporter is compelled almost daily to interview people and write about ideas that run counter to his own beliefs. It's a healthy practice.

Objectivity might seem like a hindrance in a fiction writer's repertoire

141

of techniques. The strength of fiction over other forms of art—most notably its cousin drama—is the intimacy of authorial voice. The reader flits in and out of characters' minds, reads their thoughts, understands situations and motivations in ways that the characters themselves do not. But intimacy can be an excuse to avoid description, and the prose becomes mushy.

A reporter's notebook is an essential part of observation, alien though it might seem to a fiction writer. Avoid the temptations to procrastinate writing your observations down. Keep a notebook with you always. When I visited Haiti in 1983 to write for a relief organization's new service, I walked through the slums and rural villages and hazy, dusty streets and Iron Market of Port-au-Prince, scribbling notes on everything I saw: a guitar player who uses wads of paper to tauten his strings, meat hanging unrefrigerated in the heat, clothes, piles of rice and beans for sale, baskets of trinkets for tourists who no longer came since the AIDS scare, toys, paintings of Christ and Pope John Paul II and the Virgin Mary. I described the colorful arabesques and painted scenes from the lives of saints that decorated the sides of vans. I made Homeric lists of the everyday life around me: cracks in the wall plaster, creaking boardwalks, beggars, posters of the now-deposed President-for-Life Jean-Claude Duvalier. Aware of the limitations of public relations writing and journalism, I saved most of my notes to use in fiction. I held back the material I knew I could not treat in a few hundred words; my story described the rural hospital and sick children, but not the piles of corpses in the morgue.

And this, too, is something that journalism teaches you: to understand, as you observe, the differences of tone and voice in different stories; that a piece on a television star spending a day fishing on the Rogue River may demand a smart-aleck voice, but the visual richness of Haiti, contrasted with its anguish, malnutrition, and poverty, requires an almost baroque complexity and an intensity of perspective that you do not want to squander in a press release. Journalism teaches you to observe suffering unflinchingly, with a quiet professional sympathy, to interview the prisoner who witnessed a rape in the common room of his cell, and then breathe the pain and outrage that you have suppressed into a story that rises, walks, and lives on its own.

This flinty perspective of the writer at times slips into cynicism. But as with your recognition of the news value in situations of great drama and even suffering, it is a characteristic that allows you to observe, to silence your pain until you sit alone at a typewriter or computer terminal and consider how to make people believe what you have seen and heard and lived, what you hope to bear witness to.

30

GETTING *OFF* THE SUBJECT

By Ellen Hunnicutt

GREAT DISCOVERIES OFTEN come at odd moments, and without warning. Several years ago when I was a beginning writer, I drove a friend to the dentist and waited in the car for her. Here was an opportunity to write, and I opened my notebook. At that time, my fiction was failing. While I'd had some of my articles published, every story I submitted came back with a rejection slip, and stories were what I longed to publish.

Since nothing else was working for me, I had tried "writing exercises," dull and dry assignments I prescribed for myself. I had written pages in very long sentences and in very short ones, pages in which no adverbs appeared, pages with only active verbs. I had written passages that imitated writers I admired. I was a little surprised at my ability to keep on inventing these exercises. Did they help? I believe they all helped; one in particular helped a great deal, in an unexpected way.

As I waited in the car that day, I looked around at perfectly ordinary houses and chose a non-descript chimney as the subject of my exercise. I would write as many descriptive sentences as I could about the chimney, and I would force myself to write at least two pages. "The chimney was red brick," I began with a sigh. "The mortar between the bricks had grayed with age." What made the exercises dull was knowing they could never be real stories. Stories were about people and their emotions, about love, fear, courage, endurance—all of the great subjects of literature. Even a beginner knew that stories were not about chimneys.

I labored on, completed my two pages, and really had to force myself to read them over. To my surprise, I found they had produced a curious result. Focused on the chimney, I had—by accident, it seemed—written several subtle and telling things about an imaginary family who lived in the house. Their love was in the wisps of warm smoke that curled from the chimney, their struggle in the aging mortar that failed in places, their courage in the solid corner that held firm against the prevailing wind. The sentences "suggested" these things, and I saw for myself that "suggestion" was more powerful than "declaration." It would be several more years before another writer, novelist and story writer Sara Vogan, told me the formal name for this technique: I had written *off the subject*. My two pages never became a finished story and were lost long ago, but in writing them, I took a giant step forward in my fiction writing.

I had a wonderful new tool. I began "suggesting" all sorts of things in stories, turning from the main discourse of the narrative to write about trees, water, old school papers, odd pieces of furniture and, yes, more chimneys. I was still learning, still being rejected, but my work assumed a subtlety and a resonance it had not had before. I stopped writing "declarations" like these:

"He was an honorable man."

"She put duty before self."

"They knew life would be better now."

Good fiction, and especially the short story, has always been marked by subtlety, and as readers become more sophisticated, they insist that stories be increasingly artful. My creative writing students, especially if they have not been reading contemporary fiction, often object when asked to write with this sort of "indirection." "Why can't you say straight out what you mean?" they demand to know.

It's because readers don't want to be "told." The greatest joy of story reading always comes at that magic moment when the reader sees into the heart of the mystery and grasps the significance of events. (Some literary theorists say all good stories are mystery stories.) Readers are much like crossword puzzle fans, and good stories are like good puzzles, full of challenge but not so difficult that they defeat the reader entirely. Reading my sentence, "He was an honorable man," is exactly like picking up a crossword puzzle with all the letters filled in. What we want from the puzzle—and from the story—is not just the answer, but the journey of discovery that brings us to the answer. We want charged language that rings through several meanings. Once we write, "He was an honorable man," the charge is spent; there is nothing left for the reader to ponder.

Then there's the old bugaboo about the abstract versus the concrete.

Abstractions like *honor, courage,* and *love* don't give the reader a picture. They sound like sermons or political speeches. Concrete details flash pictures. Real life doesn't oblige us with pat conclusions; we don't have neat little signs popping up telling us "well done," or "you have failed." We make our way, day by day, through a sea of details, and try to draw meaning from them. Fiction needs to reflect this aspect of life if it is to "feel" real. Looking at a chimney and getting a hunch about the people living in the house "feels" real. It's the sort of thing we do all the time.

In my story "When I Was Married,"[1] I wanted to show that a young woman was beginning to understand she needn't be a carbon copy of her mother. Written flat out *on* the subject, the passage might have read:

It occurred to her she didn't have to be like her mother.

Instead, the passage reads:

[She glanced furtively at her reflection in a shop window.] It occurred to her she looked a little like photographs she had seen of her father.

The second version is completely "off" the subject because the father, who disappeared years before, plays no role in the story, but it lets us "see" the character and "catch on" to what she is thinking. And the latter version gives us the bonus of a second meaning. Besides getting the new information, the reader learns how the character "feels" about what's happening. People who glance furtively at their own reflections are not very confident; the process of understanding is just beginning. Writing off the subject often produces this resonance of two or more meanings.

In "Perhaps Even the Chinese,"[2] Ezra wants to be a professional musician. Getting married would bring responsibility and probably end his career. Yet, he is powerfully drawn to the warmth and security of marriage. Expressed directly, the passage would have said exactly that:

He was surprised at how powerfully he was drawn to the idea of marriage.

---

1. Originally published in *Prairie Schooner.* Reprinted in author's collected stories, *In the Music Library* (University of Pittsburgh Press).
2. Originally published in *The Rectangle.*

146

This version gives us no picture; it is a direct statement. The reader gets no sense of what that powerful urge "feels like."

The published version reads:

[When he considered his desire to marry], he thought of swiftly flowing water hidden by trees.

The reader can see, feel, and even hear the strength and power of that swift stream. And again, there is the bonus of a second meaning. The passage suggests that the forces of nature are so powerful, they challenge reason and logic. The sentence is completely "off" the subject. There is no river in the story. The character, in fact, is sitting in a cemetery.

Off-the-subject writing can even be used in titles. My story "The Bengal Tiger"[3] has no tiger in it. Early in the story, Clayton lectures his brother Harvey about extravagance and finally, in desperation, shouts at him:

"Buy anything you like! [cars, clothes] Buy yourself a Bengal tiger!"

What Harvey buys is a fox farm. The "tiger" is the diabolical set of circumstances that develop from that project, lie in wait like a predatory beast, and then "leap out" to attack the characters at the story's climax. The title reinforces the story's theme, that evil—in this case racial prejudice—is devious, not easily overcome, and always ready to reappear and spring out at us. The tiger symbolism is more powerful, more chilling than having one of the characters declare:

"We thought we had overcome our prejudice toward blacks. We were really surprised to discover it still lurked in our hearts."

While writing off the subject can be used anywhere in fiction, it is a real lifesaver in writing endings. The end of a story must tell the reader what the story means, and still avoid all the pitfalls of overwriting or of preaching a sermon. My story "There Is a Balm in Gilead"[4] recounts a

---

3. Originally published in *The Rectangle*. Reprinted in author's collected stories, *In the Music Library* (University of Pittsburgh Press).

4. Originally published in *Mississippi Review*. Reprinted in author's collected stories, *In the Music Library* (University of Pittsburgh Press).

woman's recovery from divorce. At the end, I wanted to show that Emma had found the courage to go on with her life. Here are several "on the subject" phrases that I *didn't* use, because they just won't work for endings in the 1980s (They probably never worked very well.):

She came to realize. . . .
Now she saw clearly. . . .
She understood her mistake. . . .
She had found the courage (strength, direction, etc.). . . .

Emma is a musician. At the story's end, she is talking with a young man who sings in a church choir. He tells her:

"There are eleven people in my choir, but I'm the only bass baritone."

Emma considers for a moment and then replies:

"Never mind, one strong voice can carry the part."

The single voice, of course, symbolizes Emma's single state; the sentence expresses her confidence about her own future. The passage *suggests* both loneliness and courage, more powerfully so because those overworked words are not used.

To be sure, writing with this sort of subtlety is not as easy as writing those flat-out declarations. Once in awhile, we get lucky: The phrase or image we need tumbles out fully formed. But most of my off-the-subject passages, even very brief ones, come only after I've worked them out on seven or eight—often more—work sheets.

Are there techniques to help us write with more "suggestion," less "declaration"? I think so. I believe the problem is that we have focused on those big ideas like *honor* and *courage,* and we have to trick our minds out of those grooves. I use what I call my "motorcycle and cello trick." That is, I deliberately introduce an odd object, idea, or word into the story. If you don't like motorcycles and cellos, try firecrackers, apple cider, penicillin, a map of Tibet, or a butter churn. Write a sentence containing the odd element, then start playing back and forth between that sentence and the story, looking for a relationship, a metaphor. Let one thing lead to another. A butter churn might become a butter horn, which might turn into a French horn, then a trumpet. It could end with a character looking at a trumpet vine growing on an old stone wall.

My other trick is to pick up any book of fiction, open it at random, and begin reading words or phrases until a "bell sounds" in my mind.

What I find this way are interesting words or word combinations: *bottomless grief, murk, striding on, tweed, sunburst, fly into summer, hinge of their relationship.* From there, once again, I let one thing lead to another, look for metaphors, and scribble away at work sheets. These are just "starters." When the process is done, the borrowed elements are always gone. But they work very well to steer me around my mental blocks.

Stories, of course, really *are* about people and their emotions, about love, fear, courage, endurance—all of the great subjects of literature. I knew that was true as I sat writing sentences about a chimney, and it will always be true. There is really only a handful of "big ideas" in human experience. That is why the writer must search constantly for fresh and interesting ways to present them. Writing *off* the subject, with implication rather than declaration, is a useful tool in accomplishing this task. It is especially useful in reaching today's sophisticated reader.

31

USING IMAGINATION IN PLOTTING

By Joan Aiken

IT'S PERFECTLY possible, of course, to construct a plot *without* the use of imagination. A plot is a mechanical thing, like a coat hanger—the structure upon which the garment of fiction will be hung. You can look up a made-to-measure plot in Georges Polti's *The Thirty-Six Dramatic Situations,* and in that useful and amazing work of reference, almost any book or play that has ever been written will be found in embryo: "The Loved One Hated by Kindred of the Lover," for instance. Let's see . . . *Romeo and Juliet,* of course, *Pride and Prejudice, Beauty and the Beast.* "Recovery of a Lost One" covers *The Winter's Tale, Huckleberry Finn,* and *The Three Little Pigs.*

The point I am trying to make is that the plot itself need not be of great importance; the plot is the least of the writer's problems. When I was a child, an editor called Fothergill had the notion of passing out the same plot to a dozen different authors and persuading them to write a short story based on it. Then he published them in an anthology called *The Fothergill Omnibus.* All the stories were completely different, as each writer had handled the theme in his own way. The only drawback was that most of them were rather dull. Whatever its potential, a plot has no value unless it appeals to you personally. In which case, the simplest and most basic themes—Remorse, Mistaken Judgment, Unreasonable Jealousy—are sufficient for your coat hanger.

Where the use of imagination comes in is at the next stage: how you arrange your viewpoint, your time scheme, your characters; which feature will stand out and remain in the reader's mind. We all have our favorite books into which we dip from time to time. What do we choose? Not always an essential part of the plot. Often it is a side scene, or just a bit of description.

I'm going to discuss here a few aspects of plotting where imagination can be brought into play (naturally there are uncountable others). The

elements I have chosen are time, character, deliberately setting yourself a problem, and some odds and ends, such as story order, incident, and how to give your imagination a prod.

Time, first. You have an idea for a plot, but it drags.

How about changing its pace and momentum by interweaving a causally connected story from an earlier period?

I'll illustrate with an example.

My novel *Midnight is a Place* is a riches-to-rags story of two children in an English Stately Home setting, who suddenly find themselves destitute and not only that, but ostracized and hated by everyone about them. An adequate plot, but nothing out of the common. Feeling this, I made use of the causal strands that had brought about this situation: a wild wager between two young rakes in which one of them had cheated, and the exile and death in poverty of one of them. This story is not told flat out in one piece but is revealed to the reader in fragments, interspersed between the present-day account of how the two children struggle to keep alive in highly adverse circumstances. The account of the past, coming through in this way, has the effect of enriching the contemporary thread of plot by giving it more dimension as well as verisimilitude. In real life, after all, we receive our information from newspapers, television, and from friends in just this way—not in one consecutive saga, but in fragments we must piece together to make a coherent account.

So if a plot seems to lack the richness that imagination can provide, *start further back.* What are the causes that brought your characters to the predicament they are in at the outset of your story? You must know a great deal about them before you begin—their history, their parents, even their grandparents. Having created this material, make use of it. Don't go back to the earlier point in time and start from there, but find a means of weaving those earlier strands into your present-day fabric.

Another use of imagination can be for problem-solving. How to set this up? Construct for yourself an apparently insoluble problem and then wait to see how your imagination will deal with the challenge.

Dorothy Canfield did this masterfully in the novel *Her Son's Wife*. The plot is extremely simple. A widowed schoolteacher, left with a young son and anguished memories of her revered husband, rears the son with such rigid, obsessional authority that he turns into a weak, obedient mother's boy, who then, in one feeble spurt of resistance while

151

halfway through college, marries a selfish, illiterate slut whose only asset is vulgar prettiness. What *can* the mother do? The young pair have no money, they must live in her cherished, carefully tended house, which they reduce to a shambles. The setup is portrayed with excruciating fidelity. The mother decides that she can't endure it and accepts a better job in another town, leaving her beloved home to the feckless pair. But a few years later a chance glimpse of her adored little granddaughter, age three, left in the charge of good-time girls and street louts, obviously destined to grow up into just such another floozie as her mother, draws the grandmother home again. With an immense effort of will, she subdues her own feelings and refrains from adverse criticism or interference. But the situation is still just as bad: the son weakly unhappy, aware of his wife's defects but still infatuated by her; the daughter-in-law unfaithful, selfish, slovenly, self-pitying, hypochondriacal; and the child, bright, sweet-natured, but growing up wan and unhealthy from poor feeding, with terrible habits picked up from her mother.

What can the grandmother do? The reader honestly cannot imagine. The situation appears insoluble. The grandmother has already submerged her own nature to an almost incredible degree. Anything she does will be disruptive, almost bound to hurt the child or her son. Yet she is a strong-minded, capable woman. How can she liberate herself from this impasse?

It seems almost unfair to reveal her solution, for it is so startling, and yet, in essence, so simple, completely inevitable, built precisely upon existing foundations. The mother-in-law proceeds to exploit the wife's self-pitying disposition, and persuades her to take to her bed with an imagined ailment of the spine. There she is pampered and coddled with every possible attention, while order and routine return once more to the household, the son is able to find a better job, and the grandchild can grow up healthy and unaffected by her mother's slatternly influence. Soon the mother, fat and debilitated, could not get up even if she wished to. Thus, evil is done that good may come: The grandmother, aware that she has committed what amounts to a moral murder, condemns and despises herself, yet still feels it was the only thing to do. Her penance is on the way in any case: When son and granddaughter have left home, for another job and college respectively, and the protagonist (the grandmother) is making plans to take off to lead the independent, professional life that she has craved for so long, she finds that she is trapped. Her daughter-in-law can't do without her; she has, indeed, learned to love. "Don't leave me, Momma!" is her final cry.

Imagination can also be used to strengthen character. You have your plot—a good, workable story about an elderly man who holds a well-paid public position with practically no duties. Political events quite unrelated to him suddenly focus on him and his comfortable sinecure, and a disapproving newspaper article is written about it. Conscience-stricken, he decides to resign, and finally does so.

This, in essence, is the plot of *The Warden,* Trollope's first Barsetshire book: an exceedingly plain, straightforward plot. What turns it to magic, so that it will be read forever, and again and again by addicted readers, are the characters of the hero and his son-in-law. The hero, Mr. Harding, is a delightful old man, unworldly, musical, given to playing the cello for slightly longer than his auditors would wish, but humble, and, when he comes to think about them, absolutely certain about issues of right and wrong. We should recognize him if we met him in China. Mr. Grantly, the archdeacon, his son-in-law, is another absolutely three-dimensional character—acerbic, worldly, with hardly a grain of humor in his make-up, not at all a person with whom one would wish to live. And yet we absolutely love him. How did such characters leap into Trollope's mind, when some of his others—particularly his callow heroes—are so flat that they are no more than clothes-pegs?

An animal or an object may also be used as the imaginatively transforming agent. Peter Dickinson, a highly original writer, makes use of both. Quentin, a rat gifted with ESP, who can be used like a laser beam to kill people who believe in his power, is a notable feature of the thriller *Walking Dead,* about corruption and dictatorship in an imaginary Caribbean state. In *The Gift,* by the same author, telepathy also plays a part. The boy hero inherits this "gift" from his father's family, and so unwillingly tunes in on arrangements for a heist planned by the feckless father and some dangerous accomplices. One of these is hardly sane; it is the wild disruptiveness of his thought patterns, much more powerfully beamed out than those of normal people, that first alerts the boy to what is going to happen. But among these frantic transmissions, there is one that is beautiful and serene, the image of a stone, smoothly shaped and streaked with color, and it is the use the hero makes of this

153

image and its reappearance at the close that make the story moving and memorable.

Can a writer deliberately harness imagination? It is certainly a faculty that all writers possess (otherwise they would never have taken to the profession in the first place). So how can it be invoked? What can be done if a piece of work seems flat and uninspired and clomps along rather heavy-footed?

First, critical processes must be brought into play. We are all our own best critics; if we take the pains, we can decide which are our better works. Any writer knows that feeling of awestruck astonishment on reading an earlier work thinking, "What a perfectly marvelous invention! How in the wide world did I ever think of that?" Sometimes it really does seem as if inspiration from some other source had temporarily taken over the typewriter.

Having refreshed your memory by a glance back at one of those really inspired pieces of writing, review your present work in a critical and comparative spirit. What element that was present *then* is lacking *now*? Are the characters ready-made and uninteresting, taken out of stock rather than created expressly for this story or novel? Is the style flat, uninspired? Are the events mechanical, or the outcome too predictable, too improbable? Often the fault can be traced to one particular ingredient, one episode, one character that is not pulling its weight (like the sister Mary Bennet in *Pride and Prejudice,* a minor flaw in an otherwise nearly perfect work). Can the character be replaced by some other person, perhaps even by an animal, or taken out altogether? Can the weak incident be replaced by some other happening or narrated from a different viewpoint, or—this is often the solution—simply deleted? Leave a line-space, take a deep breath, and write "twenty years passed." Then see what happens.

A leisurely pace is often the most important factor in this kind of revision. The imagination is a balky faculty; it will not be hurried. Sometimes it is simply waiting for new material. Then you witness a scene in a bus: a repulsive little girl, unpleasantly cute, is kicking up a fiendish fuss because she has to give up her seat to an elderly lady and sit on her father's lap. "I *wanted* to sit on that seat, *very much!*" she is yelling, and the fat, placating father is beseeching her: "Don't *be* like this, sweetheart. You are hurting Daddy's feelings very much!" Or you see an elderly man and woman on a railroad platform, at odds with one another. The husband keeps making some snarling remark, then walking out of earshot toward the platform edge and angrily shouting, "What? I can't hear you?" when his wife comes back with a riposte. At once, after some such experience, you can see how the relations between a pair of characters in your story can be handled. They may not be old and young, husband and wife, father and daughter: The creatures who finally appear in your work may appear to have no connection at all to the scene in the bus, on the station. Yet the flash was there, and it came just when you needed it.

Very, very often I find that the message is transmitted in a dream, or comes in one of those brief, acute waking flashes in the middle of the night. The unconscious has known, all along what the solution was to be but has not been able to make itself heard above the clatter of your typewriter.

Why should I have dreamed about a kitchen with black corrugated walls and ten copper stoves in it, with beer-making equipment in the room next door and a strong smell of brewing, perceptible even in the dream? I write my dreams down in my notebook, and then forget about them. Sometimes, weeks later, it suddenly becomes clear what part one of them has to play. Why should I dream about K.N.'s sitting room full of water? Why of a man with a coat hanger through the shoulder of his pullover and a hat on the coat.

In writing my novel, *If I Were You,* I discovered, just before it was too late, the lack of solidity in one character. The story is about substitution: The heroine, who wants time and peaceful surroundings in which to write a novel, is persuaded to take the place of another, richer girl, whom she closely resembles and who wishes to go off to become a missionary. (Period, 1815; the other girl's parents will not permit their daughter missionary aspirations.) I knew from the start how the story was going to end: The other girl's ambitions were going to be deflected the very first time a young man proposed to her. But I thought the young man who proposed was of no importance; I had planned him as a minor character, perhaps remaining offstage altogether, or, at most, appearing only once. But, then, why did I wake up in the middle of the night, announcing to myself, "His name is Lieutenant Dunnifage"? Surely, with an emphatic name like that, he must be destined to play rather more of a part in the plot? It was not until my editor had read the story and suggested that the ending, as it then stood, was both too abrupt and too implausible, that I saw how Lieutenant Dunnifage could be worked properly into the story and turned into a highly instrumental part of the climax.

Sometimes imagination can be constructively applied to the *order* of your story. Told chronologically, it is adequate, but unremarkable; how would it be if turned back-to-front, or posed in the form of a question?

I came across a delightful example of this recently in a picture book for very small children, *The Sneeze,* by David Lloyd and Fritz Wegner. "Once upon a time," it begins, "there were a hat, a ball, a bench, a girl, a man, a dog, a newspaper, and a suitcase." Then it proceeds to ask questions. "Who wore what? Did the girl wear the newspaper? Who threw what? Did the man throw the bench? Who jumped over what? Did the man jump over the dog?" In the end, it is all sorted out with great precision and charm, so that a simple sequence of events is transformed into a shapely, rounded narrative. But what was the genesis of such a method of storytelling? Why, the imagination, of course.

Imagination is such a tremendously strong part of us that it seems a pity we harness it so little to our daily needs. Like electricity during the Middle Ages, it is there, all around us. Like medieval man, we rub a bit of amber on a coat sleeve and observe with mild wonder that it will attract particles of paper to itself. We see the lightning strike the church steeple, but we have only the most rudimentary conception of how this force can be employed to run railways or warm whole populations or transmit messages across continents. Our imagination is dying to help us, if only we would listen to its urgent cries to be heeded.

32

THE TRUTH, THE WHOLE TRUTH, MAY BE ANYTHING *BUT* THE TRUTH

By Janette Turner Hospital

OVER THE PAST FEW YEARS, in teaching writing workshops across Canada and the U.S. and in serving as a judge for several short story contests (a task that has required me to read hundreds of manuscripts), I have become convinced that one of the biggest stumbling blocks for beginning writers is this sticky matter of "the truth."

To put it another way, the pained cry, "But that's what really happened; that's the truth!" may be exactly what is giving your writing a curiously unconvincing, inauthentic, *ineffective* air.

This was something I learned early, the hard way, on my own first novel, *The Ivory Swing*. It is set in India, and I had just returned from living in that fascinating country when I began to write the book. I was a walking encyclopedia on Indian customs, politics, religious practices, attitudes toward women, and so on. Mentally (and, I'm afraid, with naïve arrogance), I appointed myself as some sort of truth-bearer, a mediator between east and west. I spent months honing my cultural vignettes, my insights; I revised endlessly to achieve the most finely nuanced portrait of South Indian life.

The first editor who read my manuscript told me bluntly: "At least a third of this, possibly half, has to be cut."

I felt demolished. I felt outraged. Doesn't anyone want to know the *truth*? I stormed. It took me almost a year of nursing that manuscript before I could admit to myself: Yes, all this cultural material is fascinating. Yes, you have lived in India in rare circumstances and have learned truths that very few Westerners could know. Yes, you have written these chapters beautifully, with delicacy and precision. Nevertheless, they do not belong in this novel. As far as the essence of this book is concerned, these chapters are so much clutter.

It was painful, cutting out those pages. But it was worth it. The radically pruned novel went on to win Canada's $50,000 Seal Award.

157

I still have about 100 unused pages of the earlier draft sitting in a box. I still think they are beautifully written, and one of these days I'll reshape them into short stories or travel pieces—but somehow I always seem to be too caught up in the project in hand to get back to them. Too absorbed, perhaps, in the pleasures of pointing my workshop students in the right direction, of urging them to unshackle themselves from the facts in order to get at the truth.

Let me illustrate with some case studies:

Example 1: A middle-aged woman in a Calgary workshop is looking at my editorial pencil markings, which suggest a substantial cut. Her story is about the death of a grandmother and about differing family reactions to that death. I suggest that several peripheral characters be dropped entirely, and that a certain action be transposed from character A to character B.

Her eyes widen with bewilderment and shock. "But this is about an actual death in my family," she says. "This is what really happened. I *can't* let character B do this, because . . . because he wasn't the one who did it."

Example 2: A student at M.I.T. has written an absorbing story about a fencing tournament. With considerable flair, he has superimposed the physical thrusts and parries of the rapier-wielders onto their academic and sexual rivalries—giving a particularly cutting edge, so to speak, to their championship bout.

Feedback from the class is largely positive, but almost everyone agrees that the preliminary bouts, and certainly the page of information on the structure of a fencing tournament, should be dropped. They interfere with the pacing of the narrative, and detract from the impact of the final contest between arch rivals.

"But if I cut all that," the student in the hot seat says plaintively, "I'm not being true to the way a fencing tournament works."

Example 3: A young woman at a summer workshop is waiting nervously for my opinion on the manuscript of her first novel, which draws on her own experience of growing up in an immigrant community. Her novel charts the conflicts between Old World and New World, especially as these affect the daughters of traditional patriarchal fathers.

I tell her that the novel is beautifully written, and very promising indeed—especially if she deletes her entire final chapter and ends at that dramatic and poignant moment when the heroine, having defied her father and run off with a man who does not belong to the immigrant community, finds herself promptly abandoned and back on her father's doorstep. She rings the doorbell; her father answers it; they stand there staring at each other.

"End it there," I suggest.

The young woman gasps. "But the next chapter is what *happened*!" she says. "Actually—I don't know whether you realized—it's autobiographical. I had my rebellion, I learned the family was right, I married the man they chose for me."

Listen, I tell her. I'm enormously curious about that young woman standing on the doorstep. I know a great deal about her; you've seen to it that I'm very involved with her. I know the strength of her drive toward individuality and freedom, and also the magnetic pull of family and tradition. I have enough information to realize that the future behavior of both father and daughter is a 50-50 toss-up. If my last view of her is that moment on the doorstep, when she and her father stand staring at each other, I'm going to go on and on wondering: did he forgive her? On what terms? Which choice did she make? Weeks later, I'll find myself still thinking about your novel and your protagonist.

But once you tell me what the choice was, and I find myself coasting pleasantly enough (a little somnolently, perhaps) through the details of a hand-sewn wedding dress, the feast prepared by the aunts, the toasts made by the uncles, et cetera, et cetera, well . . . I've pretty much lost interest in that young woman. There's no mystery left in her, nothing to keep me thinking about her.

Do you see what I mean?

For most people, the first impulse to write comes in the wake of some powerful personal experience. There is a desire to explore the meaning of that experience, to impose order upon it, to elicit the shock, or sympathy, or understanding of fellow human beings. And since *what actually happened* is of such enormous significance to us, we assume that the most potent way to convey the essence of the experience is to stick close to those literal events. That is the error.

Consider again my first example. If you are writing about a death in the family, what is it, exactly, that you wish to convey? I asked my Calgary writer this question.

As she thought about it, her hand began to tremble a little, she pressed her lips tightly together, and only after several seconds was she able to say: "I just felt so . . . so *bereft*. And I thought: Doesn't anybody care? Is this all a life is?"

I pointed out to her that those three sentences and her body language had affected me far more powerfully than her story had. She had let extraneous details interfere with the *essence* of the experience. She had wanted to convey the lurching awareness of mortality, of loss, of the fragility of our hold on those nearest to us. She had wanted to make the reader catch his breath, to feel the same dizzy moment of fear that she had felt.

All of that was lost in the thicket of "what actually happened."

If you want to make a reader understand what you felt when your mother died, you have to jolt him into a sense that *his* mother is dying. Don't *tell* the reader you felt frightened and lonely; set the stage so that the reader is lured onto it as actor, so that *he* feels frightened and lonely. And to do that, you need to pare your story down to the bare essentials, the universal elements.

Eventually, following our discussion, the Calgary woman rewrote her story in a radically different way. There was no deathbed scene, no gathering of the relatives, not even a glimpse of a dying grandmother. The readers were, instead, watching a lone woman in her kitchen on the day following the death of her mother. In her distracted body movements, in the way she forgets the kettle and lets it boil dry, in the way she accidentally cuts her finger while peeling potatoes at the sink, stares at the blood, feels sick, walks shakily outside, vomits, leans against the house and remains there staring blankly into the distance, the reader has a powerful and almost unnerving sense of loss and mortality. None of this "actually happened" but it was, ultimately, far truer to the writer's experience.

Remember: to get at the essential truth, you may have to fiddle with the facts.

33

YOU'RE THE JUDGE

By Sarah Juon

I CAN'T BE OBJECTIVE about my own work. What I need is an editor like Maxwell Perkins to tell me how to fix it.

When I heard a writer friend make this plaintive remark, I thought, Yes, isn't that every writer's fantasy: to be discovered by some patient, kind, all-knowing editor who will nurture our talent while gently pointing out our mistakes—with detailed instructions, of course, for how to correct them?

Some writers enroll in courses or workshops, hoping to find this kind of special attention. Others cultivate a trusted friend, or husband or wife, as their "ideal reader"—not realizing that this role sometimes can be more of a burden than an honor! Certainly, for the writer in quest of constructive criticism, these may be worthwhile avenues.

Sooner or later, however, you realize that no one—and probably not even Maxwell Perkins, were he available—is the "ideal reader." Every individual who reads your writing will have his or her own notion about what good writing should be, and no two will be alike. And even if you did manage to attract the interest of a wise and kind editor on the staff of some magazine or publishing house, chances are that editor would be too overworked to give you more than the most general sort of criticism ("I found the characters too flat." "This needs to be cut." Or, "The novel sort of dies around page 150.")

The longer you've been writing, the more evident it becomes that you must become your own ideal reader. This makes sense for a couple of reasons: First, no one else knows what you are trying to convey as well as you do. It's to your advantage to develop the ability to judge whether you have succeeded in conveying your idea or not.

Second, like eating carrots, the discipline of evaluating your own work is good for you. You will gain confidence as a writer if you can analyze why a manuscript works or doesn't and how to remedy its flaws. To avoid that panicky feeling that often comes when someone you respect says those three paralyzing words—"It doesn't work"—it's important to learn how to view your own writing with a cold, objective eye. This will give you a feeling of control. Then, when an editor scratches her head and says, "It doesn't really work here," you can reply, confidently, "I was afraid of that. I think I know why. What if I try such-and-such instead?"

Assuming you've spent a fair amount of time reading all kinds of literature and especially the kind you are most interested in writing, you've developed a reader's standards for evaluating work, whether you realize it or not. You know when a story or article bores you. You recognize the symptoms of puzzlement when a writer isn't communicating his ideas clearly. You also know that you feel vaguely uncomfortable when a writer keeps calling attention to himself or making asides that divert your attention.

The same criteria you apply to other people's work must be applied to your own writing. You know you are being objective when you can pick up a manuscript you've written, read it straight through as though it were written by a stranger, and answer candidly the following questions: *Does the writing hold my interest? Does it flow smoothly? Does my attention wander at any point? Are the characters believable? Interesting? Is the story line plausible? Is there a satisfying climax and resolution, or am I left hanging?*

Needless to say, this kind of objectivity is not easy. It took me several long years of writing to learn, first, that I even had an objectivity problem, and second, what I could do about it! But more on that later.

We'll assume that you've acquired some basic skills as a writer. If you write fiction, you know something about how to develop character and plot and how to establish a setting. Still, you feel you have some distance to go before you're over the hurdle of becoming a published author. You may have received some nice rejection slips ("Sorry—try again"); or, perhaps you have published but haven't made the transition to publishing regularly.

Perhaps all you lack is some skill in viewing your work as would an agent or an editor—or more important, the audience for whom you're writing. From personal experience, I've discovered four routine stumbling blocks to developing that cool, objective reader's eye, and they all have to do with attitude.

1) Overattachment to your writing

Overattachment occurs under certain conditions. Say you've just spent three months writing endless drafts of a 20-page story, laboring over each sentence backward and forward. Naturally, you are attached to this writing, after spending so much time on it. Furthermore, you will be reluctant to find anything wrong, because that might mean further agonizing changes. Chances are you won't be able to read this story objectively for quite some time—at least, not until you've totally forgotten the sweat and tears behind each sentence! The best thing to do, in this case, is to put it away and turn to something else.

Overattachment occurs when you're particularly fond of a certain story line or a scene—often for the wrong reasons. Perhaps you have fun relating to your friends an intricate plot or a comic episode. Gradually, you find yourself committed to the way you've told it—whether or not it works on the page—and are reluctant to make changes.

In general, overattachment causes you to focus on small units rather than the overall structure: on paragraphs rather than chapters, or on chapters instead of a unified book.

2) Obsession with a particular idea

No doubt you have strong feeling about certain topics or people, and, as a writer, naturally want to share them. Out of writers' obsessions come some of the most interesting literature. Faulkner wrote a series of novels about Yoknapatawpha County. Fitzgerald wrote about his wife, Zelda.

The trick is not to let your strong feelings distort your perspective. If you are obsessed with an idea and want to write about it, it's your task to find its universal component, so that your readers can relate to it as well.

You know what a turn-off it is to listen to someone narrate a long, rambling dream he had the night before. You shake your head, wondering why on earth your friend is punishing you with such boring stuff. An obsessed writer sometimes leaves the same impression in the reader's mind. The peeved reader might ask: Does this writer have a secret ax to grind? Or, um-m-m, I wonder if this has a hidden Oedipal component somewhere?

When you read over a work-in-progress, ask yourself: Would this material interest someone who doesn't know me or share my passion for this idea or person? (We can't please everyone with our writing, but we also need an audience of more than one!)

To give an example: I once wrote a story about my Aunt Laura, whose life had an impact on me. Several years later, I discovered the story in my drawer and read it over. I was shocked. The woman in the story was a giant cardboard figure with a halo around her head. There were hundreds of memories and details about her life squeezed in, but no real drama or emotion—just bathetic sentimentality. In my own passion, I had forgotten to give the reader any reason to share my admiration for Aunt Laura. A healthy dose of perspective could have saved me much time in writing a more effective story.

3) Too little self-confidence

Our current mood will color our feelings about our writing as surely as it does our reaction to a film or a new acquaintance.

Perhaps you've just received your third rejection slip this week. Or your mother read your poem and said, "Have I made you so unhappy that you can't write in plain English?" If you read over a work-in-progress at a moment when you are determined to find proof that you are a terrible writer and, furthermore, worthless as a human being, you will surely be rewarded with "evidence"!

Under the circumstances, it is best simply to put the draft away and wait until your state of mind improves. Otherwise, you might do something you later regret. I'm still irritated with myself for succumbing to a black mood and shredding the draft of a story that might have been salvaged with a little reworking.

4) Too much self-confidence

This is also a state-of-mind problem that usually occurs after some success: a story's been accepted for publication; everyone liked the scene you read in class; you've been awarded a literary prize. You approach your works-in-progress with a heady sense that you can get away with just about anything. Perhaps a section needs a little reworking—no one will notice! Or you find a character who requires some

164

fleshing out—why sweat over it! They liked that story you wrote in just two days, didn't they? Let's face it, you're *great*!

Laziness and carelessness are two products of this attitude. We are all guilty of wanting to make things a little easier for ourselves, and that applies especially to writing, because it's so difficult. But ultimately, it's self-defeating to forget that success comes from hard work and that with each new project we must once again evaluate it by the same old rugged standard: Does it work for the reader?

To achieve a neutral attitude toward your work, you first must find a way to distance yourself from it. This can be done through *time,* or *distraction.* I rely on both methods.

Whoever said "Time is a writer's best friend" wasn't exaggerating. Time performs the minor miracle of allowing you to forget all the joy, passion, and smiles of amusement you experienced while writing; all the frustration, irritation and sheer hard-work tedium that went into shaping ephemeral thoughts and images into words on a page. Once you truly forget, you will be able to read over your work as you would someone else's, and ask those important questions discussed above.

How much time should pass? Only you can be the judge of that. If you read a draft and sense that you still have some residual feelings—either negative or positive (or merely a strong *wish* to find it as good as you remember)—you will benefit by giving it more time to cool off.

There are manuscripts I still cannot look at, even though in some cases a decade has passed. I'm not always sure which emotion is involved—fondness for a pet idea, nostalgia, embarrassment? Whichever it is, I know I'll have to wait until that emotion is completely overpowered by disinterested curiosity before I can see what is truly there.

From personal experience, I offer this rule of thumb: The longer you've been working as a writer and finishing up projects, the shorter amount of time you will need to wait before evaluating a work-in-progress. And the converse: If you are a beginner, allow yourself more time between drafts.

Now for the second method: distraction. What the passing of time does naturally, you can speed up by giving yourself more than one project at a time to fret over.

Over the years I've developed what I call the slow-cooking system of

165

writing. I visualize a stove range (my desk) with four to six burners. On the front burners I have several bubbling pots of stew (folders containing short stories, articles, or book manuscripts), which I stir and taste frequently. On the back burners are more stews, not as thick, the flavors still raw and unblended. (Sometimes, one of these back-burner stews will begin to heat up and thicken on its own, and then I'll quickly shift it to the front so I can watch over it.) Gradually, if I'm lucky, all the stews will thicken and blend, and before long be ready to serve.

Your working process will, of course, be suited to your individual needs and temperament. If you are working on a long project straight through, you might think about other ways of "distracting" yourself to gain distance and perspective.

What counts in the end is that you find a method that will enable you to approach your own work with a clear, fresh eye.

34

LOVE FROM THE NECK UP

By Eva Ibbotson

I BEGAN my literary life in the fifties, as a writer of short stories for women's magazines.

To write those kinds of stories then was to accept the conventions that prevailed. If the hero and heroine kissed, they did so chastely, without physiological descriptions; they were presumed, at the end, to have come together in order to marry and, having done so, to live happily ever after. Love-from-the-neck-up-with-the-mouth-closed was the phrase I coined for their activities, mocking myself and making clear to my intellectual friends that I was well aware of the absurdity of what I was doing.

But secretly I very much enjoyed my work. I have always liked the discipline of working within limits and found total freedom hard to bear. (Consider the boredom one so often feels during "dream sequences" in musicals or films, where the rules of storytelling are suspended, and everything just goes on and on and on.)

And even more than limits, I liked love. I really loved love, from the word go. Romantic love with all its absurdities, its ludicrous determination of one man and one woman to commit themselves, each to the other, till the end of time. The forms this commitment has taken throughout history have been, for me, a never-ending source of fascination. Christian marriage, with its grandiloquent assumption that the partners can be all in all to each other till parted by death. . . . The orthodox Jewish tradition, in which a woman, shorn of virtually all legal rights, becomes—by the consent of those who love her—the kingpin, the lodestar (and frequently also the bane!) of her family. . . . The subtle, sensual delight that girls of the Orient took in serving their men. . . .

Of course, the feminists are right to be appalled by much of this, but I doubt if one can choose one's obsessions, and I—the child of parents who separated when I was three years old—was stuck with an abiding interest in this kind of love. Altogether, I think I'm with the Jesuits when they say that a child is there, *entire,* by the time it's seven years old. I'll bet that Tolstoy, trotting beside his nursemaid through the Russian forests, was already shaking his fist at God. I wouldn't be surprised if Charles Dickens was still in ringlets and knickerbockers when he began to grind his (milk) teeth at the fate of the poor. And I can see the elders of Venice hurrying by with averted faces to avoid the questions of that brat, Marco Polo, about what happened when one left the city and went East.

The fifties turned into the sixties. I wrote my stories, and the mouths of my heroines stayed closed. My own marriage was a happy one, my four children were a delight. There was nothing in England at that time to make romantic love seem obsolete. The hippies, the flower children, might not be much concerned with marriage, and when they loved, it was clear that they proceeded from the neck down and with the mouth open—but I felt in no way alienated from their world.

My stories sold. I wrote my way gradually "upwards" into anthologies and "proper" books; I published two novels for children. Then, as my own children grew up, I decided to write a full-length romantic novel. But not *only* romantic: the book was to be funny, well-researched and intelligently written, and if a man picked it up by mistake, I intended that he should go on reading.

A Countess Below Stairs took me two years to write. It's about a young Russian countess, Anna Grazinsky, who comes to work as a housemaid in an English country house after the Revolution. In it, I treated my reader to a number of my minor obsessions: for music, for ballet, for the landscape of the English countryside. . . . But, yes, the heroine does marry the earl who owns the house, and, yes, her bodice remains unripped, her mouth closed.

Here is an exchange between Anna and the earl after she hears him cry out in a nightmare (he has been wounded in the war) and has gone to his room to offer comfort:

"Do you realize if this were two hundred years ago I could keep you here? Exercise my *droit de seigneur.* What would you do then?"

"I should scream," said Anna, disengaging her wrist. She got up and went lightly to the door; then she turned and said, grinning, "I 'ope!"—and was gone.

168

This novel was published on the understanding that I write two more. Tessa, the heroine of *Magic Flutes* (set in Vienna in the twenties), has the same half-humorous awareness of her potential for passion, but she too remains chaste until the end. In my latest novel, *A Company of Swans,* Harriet, traveling to the Amazon with a ballet company at the time of the rubber boom, does go to bed with the hero, but if her mouth is open, it is rather with wonder and awe, and marriage follows. And, since to describe the act of love is to risk describing some complicated aerobic workout, I show Harriet's feelings afterwards as she tries to memorize the room in which the miracle of her "ruin" occurred:

. . . Because she had to remember this room. It was Rom's own room to which he had carried her from the Blue Suite, and she had to remember every single thing so that years later she could come back here in her mind. Even on her deathbed, she must be able to come back here and walk across the deep white carpet . . . particularly on her deathbed . . .

The years rolled by. My daughter married; I was a grandmother. And with my contract for three books fulfilled, I woke up in the mid-eighties and looked about me at the world of entertainment.

I watched plays and films in which love prided itself on bringing about intricate cruelties and pointless betrayals, ensuring for everyone a miserable end. I watched thrillers in which the "goodies" perished horribly and the "baddies," as often as not, went merrily on. I read children's books in which teen-age sex and the shoddiness of adults were the main theme. (Great authors must of course deal with serious themes—with incest and murder as much as with glory and endeavor—but I'm talking about *entertainment.*)

I tried to fit in . . . started a novel about child abuse, another about abortion . . . and abandoned them both. "I'm finished," I said to my husband and to anyone else who'd listen. "I'm out of touch."

Out of touch—that dread phrase! How often I've heard it . . . on the lips of young people who thought they were not mature enough to matter as writers, or old ones who thought life had passed them by . . . from women who lived in the provinces and believed that "real" life happened elsewhere, or men whose religious faith isolated them in a world of rationality. . . . Now it was my turn.

I became quite seriously depressed, paid attention to my physical ailments, and talked of giving up writing. I would keep chickens, run a bookshop, go to India and find a guru—anything except practice the craft I'd laboriously taught myself for thirty years.

What saved me was a girl called Shirlene.

On the train to York, on a visit to my mother, I sat opposite a homely woman of about my own age. Inevitably, we began to talk about our children. The woman had an only daughter, Shirlene, who was clearly the apple of her eye. Though a popular and friendly girl, "Our Shirlene" would never go out when they were showing old films on television. Shirlene loved these vintage movies; she liked the way there was a proper story and an end you could understand.

What sort of films, I asked, and Shirlene's mother said, "Oh, you know, Shirley Temple and Deanna Durbin and Fred Astaire. And those ones where James Stewart's putting things right. She likes things to be *nice*," said Shirlene's mother.

The train stopped at York and Shirlene was waiting on the platform. My image of her had been quite clear: one of those simple, homespun girls you still find in the north of England, wearing a tweed skirt and a cardigan. So the safety pin through her nose surprised me. Her hair surprised me too: puce on top and emerald green at the sides. Shirlene's ripped tousers were viciously studded, chains hung from her leather jacket.

And this was the girl who stayed home to watch Doris Day protect her maidenhood or watch Fred and Ginger waltz together in a cloud of tulle!

The scales dropped from my eyes. I remembered a number of things I'd heard and put out of my mind: A publisher telling me that those inordinately depressing and fashionable novels that win literary prizes are bought in quantity as Christmas presents but seldom actually read. . . . The experience of a friend who'd gone to see a much-hyped film about gang rape and found himself alone with an old bag lady who'd come to rest her feet. . . .

I remembered, too, a Jewish story of which I've always been very fond. An old rabbi is comforting a lost and bewildered member of his flock. "Remember, Moyshe," says the rabbi, "when you get up to heaven, God won't ask you if you've been Abraham or Moses; he'll ask you if you've been Moyshe Finkelstein. If you've been *you*."

I decided to be me: To have faith in the thousands of people all over

170

the world who still want to read about men and women pursuing, with humor and tenderness, a high ideal of love. To be grateful for the lifting of taboos, the broadening out of topics, to use the new techniques that films and television have brought to us as writers, but to be true to my own vision of what it is that entertains.

So I started a new book. This time my heroine's mouth will almost certainly be open, because that's the way mouths are these days, and it will be nice for her. But for all her faults and frailties, she'll be concerned with fidelity and goodness—and in the end she'll have her reward.

And those of you who have also felt discouraged—who are "out of touch"—too young, too old, too far away—won't you please join me?

After all, we owe it to Shirlene!

35

CHOOSING AND USING TENSE IN FICTION

By Ann Harleman

TIME, EINSTEIN SHOWED US more than half a century ago, is relative. Our location in time, like our location in space, can change. Whether an action is in the past or the future, whether it lasts a long time or an instant, whether it happens once or over and over—all these matters depend on the position of the observer.

We fiction writers knew this all along. For Proust, the action of dipping a biscuit in tea and eating it lasts for seven volumes; for Jerzy Kosinski, in *The Painted Bird,* the destruction of an entire village along with the rape and murder of several dozen inhabitants takes only five pages. The relativity of time in fiction goes far beyond that of "real" time. Fictional time is as elastic as taffy.

In working with fictional time, the first rule to keep in mind is, *Choose your basic time frame to suit your story's needs.* Tense, the device language provides for expressing time, offers the choice of past, present or future. In choosing the base tense for your story, you are choosing more than just time. The tense you select affects the distance from which your reader views the action, the intensity of identification between your reader and your characters—even the voice in which you tell the story. Choice of tense—like choice of plot, setting, and characters—is a decision at the heart of your story's design.

Let's look closely at the three choices. The *past tense,* because it is the most natural, has traditionally been the tense of most fiction. It is the tense most readers expect to find when they open a novel. "It was the best of times; it was the worst of times," puts the reader securely in the position of hearing a tale unfold: events that have already occurred, a story whose ending the teller knows. The past tense puts readers at a distance from the story. The distance may vary—from the remote, "Once upon a time there lived a beautiful princess," to "Yesterday I finally realized what I had to do"—but the distance is there.

172

The advantage of the past tense is its flexibility; it works with any point of view. With a first-person narrator, past tense implies some development on the character's part. A narrator who doesn't develop, learn, or change comes across as blind or unreal—the "unreliable" narrator that Poe was so fond of. But how close your reader feels to your main character is up to you. How formal or colloquial your language is, whether your voice is lyrical or ironic—the past tense leaves these decisions open. And because it's the tense most commonly used, you run less risk of diverting your readers' attention from the story itself to your technique ("Look, Ma, I'm writing!").

The *present tense* lets you achieve special effects with distance, immediacy, and pace. It can plunge your reader right into the action, virtually eliminating the distance between reader and story—and, often, the distance between reader and character. In my story "Limbo," the point-of-view character is an eight-year-old girl whose fear of dying motivates the story's action. I wanted the reader to identify with her right away (the story is only 3,000 words long) and to feel the weight of her fear—otherwise the action wouldn't be believable. The story opens this way:

> She's had the dream again. The dream that she can never remember once she wakes up, that leaves behind only its vinegar taste in her mouth. Her heart clatters heavily in her chest. The swell of her own breathing, raspy and tight, fills her ears.

Here, the readers are with the character from the first word, and her feelings have great immediacy even before the dream is described.

Bringing your reader close to action and character doesn't mean your story has to be fast-paced. If you want to create an effect of stopped time, the present tense can work as a "freeze-frame" device. In my story "Adam and Eve," told in the past tense by a young woman looking back to her fourteenth summer, I use the present tense for the moment when the narrator learns that her much-loved great-aunt, with whom she lives, has cancer—a moment that seemed to last forever at the time and that lives on, frozen, in her memory.

Or suppose you want another kind of timelessness—a sense of actions repeated over and over, forming a backdrop for the events of your story. The opening sentence of Toni Morrison's *The Bluest Eye* takes the reader right into the setting of the novel, a setting made up not of objects, but of endlessly repeated actions: "Nuns go by as quiet as lust, and drunken men and sober eyes sing in the lobby of the Greek hotel." Like her characters, readers are caught and held in an inescapable cycle.

The *present tense* works best with a first-person narrator—someone your readers feel so close to that it seems natural for them to experience each event as it occurs, without benefit of hindsight. If you use present tense with the third-person, shifting from outside your point-of-view character to inside can be awkward. "He walks up the path. He puts his hand on the gate. It swings open, and he steps into the yard." But suppose you want to convey your character's feelings. "He thinks, I don't like this" is too abrupt. "He is frightened" is telling rather than showing. All right, how about, "His hand is trembling"? Fine—but you're still *outside* the character. Your story is turning out to be imitation Hemingway.

What about the *future tense*? A stretch of future tense longer than a sentence or so tends to create an ominous voice. At its best, it is mysterious and prophetic. While the past tense conveys a solid sense of reality, describing events as if they had already happened, the future tense emphasizes the visionary, imaginative quality of events that haven't yet occurred. Mary Gordon uses the future tense for a narrator imagining the aftermath of nuclear war:

I will have to kill her to keep her from entering our shelter. If she enters it, she will kill us with her knife or the broken glass in her pocket. Kill us for the food we hide, which may, even as we take it in, be killing us. Kill us for the life of her children.

The future tense pushes your storytelling voice toward the abstract and the general. Details like the knife and the broken glass ground your vision in the concrete and the specific, so that your readers can see it.

At some points in your story, you'll probably want to depart from your base tense to show events that take place before the story begins (flashback) or after it ends (flash-forward). This brings us to the second rule in working with fictional time: *When you depart from your basic time frame, make it logical.* Events earlier than the main action of your story need a tense more "in-the-past" than your base tense; events later than the main action need a tense more "in-the-future."

Flashbacks fill your reader in on your characters' pasts. When the base

174

tense of your story is the past, flashbacks have to be in the past perfect. This can involve you in a lot of syllable sludge:

That day at the beach two summers before, George had been swimming out beyond the breakers and had seemed to be in trouble. Martha had had to swim out to rescue him, and when she had reached him, he had been being pulled by the undertow, which had . . .

And so on, and so on. One way around this is to reduce the bulkiness of the verb forms by using contractions—"when she'd reached him, he'd been being pulled by the undertow." Another way is to enter and leave your flashback using the past perfect, but switch unobtrusively to simple past in between:

That day at the beach two summers before, George had been swimming out beyond the breakers and had seemed to be in trouble. Martha had to swim out to rescue him, and when she reached him, he was being pulled by the undertow . . . That was how they'd met. Now, thinking about it, Martha sighed.

When the base tense of your story is the present, the whole flashback can simply be in the past tense. Easing in and out of flashbacks is no problem:

That day at the beach two summers before, George was swimming . . . Now, thinking about it, Martha sighs.

If your story is going to have several flashbacks, you may want to choose the present as the base tense.

Flashbacks involve a trade-off. They enrich your narrative by providing your characters with a history and your events with a context. Your story gains depth and a greater sense of reality. But a flashback interrupts your story's momentum. It turns your reader's attention toward the past rather than pushing it in the direction your story is heading.

Flash-forwards describe something that happens *after* the main action. But future time has to be logical within your story's time frame. If the base tense of your story is the past, you'll cast your flash-forward in the subjunctive:

Mary, who in years to come would win the national rope-jumping competition and later go on to become world champion, had no time for play or idle chatter with the other little girls.

You'll use the future tense for glimpses of the future only if the base tense of your story is the present:

Mary, who in the years to come will win the national rope-jumping competition and later go on to become world champion, has no time for play or idle chatter with the other little girls.

Be even more sparing with flash-forwards than you are with flash-backs. Not only do they interrupt the flow of your narrative, they also cut down on suspense—the element that keeps your readers reading. If you can, make your flash-forward *ask* a question rather than answer it. Give just enough of a glimpse of future events to arouse your readers' curiosity. For example:

Years later, when I had a son of my own, I would finally understand why my father did what he did; but at the moment when I found him, I only knew that he hadn't cared enough about me to stick around.

Logic—replicating the "real"-time sequence of events—isn't the only reason to depart from the base tense of your story. Sometimes the story itself—because of subject matter, mood, distance—demands a shift in tense. The third and last rule in working with fictional time is: *Keep your time frame flexible*. This is where the relativity of fictional time can really work for you. Give yourself the freedom to shift tense, keeping it relative to your fictional effect—subject matter, action, mood, distance.

In my story "Someone Else" (runner-up in the *Chicago Tribune's* Nelson Algren Contest), I have the first-person narrator tell her story in the past tense. As the story opens, she's looking back on a series of events that span fifteen years. I wanted the story to begin with an opening sentence that would hook the reader right away. "Mary Lee Chase fell in love with my husband when she was twelve months old." That meant the story moved toward an outcome the reader already knew, so suspense would have to come from *how* it happened rather than from *what* happened. The final scene, in which the girl, on her sixteenth birthday, comes for the narrator's husband, was flat and anti-climactic. But how to avoid that, given the opening sentence? To see how it would sound, I shifted the final scene to future tense. It became the narrator's vision of what was going to happen three years after the moment that she's speaking—the *now* of the story.

176

The whole scene resonated; it came alive. But the new ending left the story's *now* too unclear. The entire story seemed to "float" in time. To anchor it, I added a sentence or two at the beginning of each scene (except the opening one), in the present tense, describing some aspect of the setting—the edge of a lake in Minnesota in early spring—where the narrator was walking as she told her story.

Play with tense the same way you play with setting, character, plot. Don't lock yourself into a set pattern. Don't decide that every section will open with the present and close with the past, for example. Or even that every flashback must be in the past. (Some flashbacks need to shift to the timeless present of frozen memories.)

Experiment. Change a section from past to present, from present to future, and see whether you like the result. And if you find yourself unintentionally writing a section in a tense that's not the one you started with, don't automatically go back and change it. Stop and look at how it works. Maybe your instincts are sounder than you think.

Your choice of tense is a way of locating your readers in time—giving them a position from which to view the characters and the action—just as setting is a way of locating your readers in space. Why not vary your temporal setting just as you do your spatial setting, to suit the needs of your story? By doing so, you can turn the relativity of fictional time to your advantage.

36

GETTING YOUR NOVEL STARTED IN TEN DAYS

By Genni Gunn

You've always wanted to write a novel but can find neither the time nor the starting point. You have unique experiences to record, hundreds of characters struggling to come out of your pen on to paper. What you need to do is make time to write and, perhaps most important, have a clear idea of *what* you are going to write.

A book is not written in one sitting. Even assuming you have a busy schedule, you need not wait to begin until you can afford to take a year's vacation from work. If your ideas are well organized, you can begin your novel now, by setting aside one hour a day in which to write.

Think of your novel as a jigsaw puzzle. Every day, you will examine one piece and put it in its proper place. The events, characters, and actions that first appear as a jumbled mass too big to tackle can be organized to make sense. You will need discipline and persistence.

Here's how to begin:

1) Set aside one hour a day for writing, if possible, the same time every day, so that eventually writing will become a habit.

2) Set up a place to write (preferably a desk where you can leave notes, typewriter, and necessary files) and return there every day to write.

Now you're ready to explore your novel idea. Where do you start? It is important to set realistic, achievable goals for each day. Here is a sample schedule for the first ten days:

Day 1. DEFINE YOUR IDEA. A novel begins as an idea. This can take the form of a character, an isolated event, or a lifetime struggle worth recording. Begin by asking yourself, "What is my novel about?" Write a one-sentence summary. If you can't do this right away, write down all the things you think your book is about. Read these over and condense them until you have *one sentence only*. Try to be as specific as possible.

At the end of your hour, type your finished sentence and tape it over your desk so it will always be visible as you write.

Day 2: LIST YOUR CHARACTERS under two headings: *Major Characters* and *Minor Characters*. Describe their relationship to one another. New characters may emerge as you write. Add them to your list. Fill in their descriptions later.

Day 3: LIST LOCATIONS AND SETTING in your novel: cities and towns (real or imaginary), houses, fields, roads, schools, etc., in which major events will take place. Fill in the detailed descriptions later.

Day 4: DEFINE YOUR CHARACTERS' GOALS. Your main characters must want something that they are unable to get. In one sentence, define *what* each of your main characters wants—tangible or intangible. As an example, here are three characters from an unwritten novel, and their three goals. At the end of Day 4, you should have a completed page that resembles the following:

GOALS

Paul wants: 1) money to settle pressing debts.
2) a means to live; a job.
3) a way to defend himself against his sister's accusations.
Alice wants: 1) to prove Paul's a swindler. She believes that before their aunt's death, Paul took money from their aunt that rightfully belonged to Alice.
2) her share of the money.
3) to keep Paul away from her adopted daughter, Judy.
Judy wants: 1) Paul.
2) her mother (Alice) to like Paul.
3) Paul to make a new start.

Day 5: LIST OBSTACLES that will prevent the main characters from getting what they want. These should be difficult for your characters to overcome; they can be other characters or physical or emotional impediments. Here, for example, are obstacles the characters described may have to surmount:

OBSTACLES

Paul: 1) Aunt Sophia, who was to leave him an inheritance, died penniless.
2) He has no skills with which to make a living. He is in his late thirties and feels he is too old to begin a trade.
3) His sister Alice.
Alice: 1) Paul won't divulge any information regarding his relationship with their Aunt Sophia prior to her death.

179

2) Paul is secretive about his financial affairs—she can't prove he has the money.
3) Her adopted daughter, Judy, is in love with Paul.

Judy: 1) Paul is not in love with her—he considers her his little niece.
2) Her mother distrusts Paul and won't let Judy see him.
3) Paul doesn't believe in his own ability to make a fresh start.

Day 6: PLAN THE CONCLUSION. Make up an ending for your novel. Write it in paragraph or point form and tape it over your desk. Characters often take on a life of their own and do things that are not what you had originally intended. Don't be afraid to rewrite the ending if your original version doesn't ring true.

Day 7: MAKE AN OUTLINE. The outline will serve as your guide while you're writing. (Update your outline if your story plot changes along the way.) When you are stuck in a chapter, choose something from the outline that interests you and begin writing about that event. It is not necessary to write chronologically. You may prefer to write separate sections of your novel and fill in the transitions later.

List the major events that will occur in your novel, not necessarily in detail.

Day 8: MAKE CHAPTER HEADINGS. Examine the events you listed yesterday. Separate them into chapters—with each chapter covering one major event. Now, write a one- or two-sentence summary description of what happens in each chapter. Tape the revised outline over your desk.

Day 9: SET UP FILES. Today will be an organizational day. Take blank file folders (either letter or legal size) and make a label for each one, using the following headings:
1) Characters
2) Locations
3) Chapters (one for each chapter heading)
4) Mannerisms
5) Speech patterns
6) General observations

These files will give you easy access to your information as well as suggest what to write about on those days when you lack inspiration. When you begin writing your novel, fill these files with the following information:

a) *Characters:* Write detailed descriptions—physical characteristics, emotional needs, family background, etc.—*know* your characters.

b) *Locations:* Where do your characters live? Where does the action take place in your novel? Think of writing as a visual art—write pictures for the reader.

c) *Individual chapters:* For your chapters in progress, notes, and ideas.

d) *Mannerisms:* Be observant. Record the way people show their emotions by body movements. To say, "He was angry" is vague and weak, but "He stamped his foot" *shows* the anger.

e) *Speech patterns:* Listen to people speak—the sound of their voices, the way they shape sentences, etc. This will be invaluable when writing dialogue, but remember that conversation is not dialogue. Give each of your characters distinct characteristics, perhaps a favorite phrase to repeat, short clipped sentences—whatever seems appropriate.

f) *General observations:* Keep a record of any thoughts you have about your novel or about human nature. You can always use these, even if not in your current project.

Make up you own file headings for other things that are important to your novel.

Day 10: WRITE YOUR OPENING PARAGRAPH. Begin your novel at that point at which your main character is faced with his or her major problem. Try to make your opening paragraph intriguing. Here is a possible opening for the novel example given earlier:

Paul had waited twenty years for his inheritance. He had squandered his time and what little money he'd earned with odd jobs on gambling and physical pleasures. After Aunt Sophia's funeral—a dull, dreary affair in which he'd been unable to feign sorrow—the will was read. Aunt Sophia died penniless.

This opening includes:

1) The main character

2) His predicament—therefore his problem

3) The necessary background to show the reader the gravity of his problem

If you're dissatisfied with your opening paragraph, put it aside and as you get new ideas, revise it.

181

From now on, each day, when you sit at your desk, you'll have a choice of things to write about. Look through your files for something that interests you. Describe characters, locations, mannerisms, or speech patterns and fit these into your novel later. Don't worry about the order. Get your story down on paper. You can fine-tune when you begin rewriting.

Set yourself realistic goals: One page a day for a year will yield 360 pages—a book-length manuscript. Half a page each day is even more realistic. Some days you'll write several pages; other days you'll struggle just to fill one. Most important, *stick with it!* Do nothing but write in the hour you've set aside, even if you only repeat a word to fill the page.

There are no easy ways to write a novel, no secrets, no shortcuts. It takes hard work, perseverance, and the belief that you have a story to tell.

37

USING IMAGES IN FICTION

By Merrill Joan Gerber

The word "image" means "picture," and all of us have been advised just how many words a picture is worth. Yet we know it's true that a picture strikes us as "whole" and stays with us in ways that dialogue and narrative do not. Using images in fiction writing allows us to vivify and illuminate as well as highlight and frame the actions and intentions of our characters.

Evocative images in a story are graceful signposts to the reader, pointing out to him (but not telling), suggesting to him (but not insisting), what we as writers mean to convey. Like symbols, images are effective on more than one level: They move the story along in a functional way, working on a concrete, literal level, while they also serve as an indicator in a more subtle way, giving clues to deeper meaning without seeming to lecture or explain.

In the title story of my collection of stories, *Honeymoon,* I introduce the "newlyweds" Cheryl and Rand by presenting the reader with images that work in a purely literal and physical way, but also serve to suggest the nature of the characters' relationship:

On their way out of the Bun Boy coffee shop in Baker, Rand gave Cheryl a quarter to buy a Bio-Rhythm fortune card from a vending machine. She stood in the hot desert wind, her skirt lashing about her legs like a whip, strands of hair flying into her mouth, while she laughingly read him the news that the biograph rated her low on luck, low on sex, and low on leisure plans, while it rated her high on health, endurance and driving.

My intention was to use images to give the reader a sense of who these two characters are and to hint at what their relationship to one another is like. In the first line of the story, Rand, who is old enough to be Cheryl's father, gives her a quarter, just as a father might give a child money to buy some little bauble out of a vending machine. I definitely meant to convey that idea—and found I could present it quite economically with that image. Furthermore, two other words, used innocently enough to describe the effects of a hot desert wind ("lashing" and "whip"), suggest something of what is to be revealed in the nature of this new marriage—a certain corruption. After they get into the car, Cheryl asks . . .

"So can I drive the rest of the way to Vegas now? . . .It's so boring just to look out the window. There's no scenery."

"Get in the car, please," Rand said, his pants legs flapping like banners in a used-car lot, ". . . and don't put another ding in my door."

"I didn't put the first ding in," she said, getting into his red Corvette. She automatically took a sip of water from the insulated cup hanging in a holder on the dash and made a face. "Yuck—hot."

"You just had a milkshake," Rand said. "Why do you have to drink old water?"

"I don't know," she said, shrugging. "I just saw it there. Don't worry about it."

More images: the man's pants legs flapping like banners in a used-car lot, to suggest what? A used-car salesman, perhaps; maybe a certain lack of integrity. And by his accusation that his wife "put a ding in his door"—he is suggesting that she broke his toy, the red Corvette. Cheryl's taking a sip of the hot water (and her subsequent "yuck") is the kind of thing a child would do. So the reader understands certain things without being told: Both characters are immature. He is petty, impatient, easily angered; she is easily bored (which may be why she married him—to get out of some other boring situation).

Later, when she thinks about why she married Rand, in defense against her mother's opinion of him ("more than twice your age, after you because you're a gorgeous young girl, you ought to be dating his sons!"), she describes boys her own age:

What did they know? The guys her own age were nothing, invisible, scarecrows on hangers. They glugged beer and walked to some drumbeat in their heads; she was sick of faded jeans and running shoes and guys who couldn't wait to turn you on with grass or with their own throbbing bodies . . . half of the guys she knew thought they would be famous rock stars; they couldn't even carry a tune.

At least for that moment we can identify with Cheryl, seeing the young men as she sees them, "scarecrows on hangers, glugging beer . . ."

When the newlywed couple get to Las Vegas, Rand instructs her to:

"Call room service and order us each a big shrimp cocktail," Rand said, his body reflected a dozen times in the mirrored room as he hung up his clothes in the alcove.

"I don't know if I want that," Cheryl said. "Maybe I want a hamburger."

"Call! Call!" he said. "Hurry up. When I get out of the shower I want it to be here."

And when it came, big white shrimp with pink tails and pink veins arched in a goblet over a snowball of ice, heads swimming in luscious red cocktail sauce, she knew he was right. It was exactly what she wanted. She chewed in a luxury of wanting the shrimp, grateful to him. When he came out of the shower she had eaten half of his shrimp, too—and he looked at the bloody plate and laughed, and peeled off his damp towel and swatted her. "That's what I love about you," he said. "Your healthy appetites, all of them."

The images here are sensual, the words are sensual: "luscious," "red," "luxury"; and there's an undertone of sexual suggestion—the bloody plate, his peeling off his damp towel, his "swatting her," his referring to her "healthy appetites, all of them." Also, his "body reflected a dozen times in the mirrored room" suggests a certain power he has over her; to her he is bigger than life.

All of this is accomplished without ever "telling" the reader what Rand's inclinations are, or how exactly Cheryl is attracted to him—but it's all there, in the evocative images of what he does and how he appears to her.

In another story in the collection, "At the Fence," we have the situation—simply put—of Anna, a middle-aged woman who is disturbed by a barking dog who lives with a young couple in the house next door. Anna hates the dog; he is ruining her peace, ruining her life. (Or so she thinks. But here is her first view of the dog):

The young man looks behind him, and there comes the dog—a sleek black Doberman trotting right to the door, his long snout coming up against the screen, his stubby tail wagging.

Not so bad, really, thinks the reader. Can it be that this animal, described rather pleasantly, is really ruining her life? But a moment later the young man's wife . . .

swings into view, wiping her hands on her blue jeans. She is perhaps a year or two younger than her husband, about nineteen . . . yet she comes to the door as

185

if she owns not only this rented house, but also the world with Anna in it. She puts her hand on her husband's bare shoulder; only then is Anna aware of the thick black hair on his chest, the private hole of his navel looking at her eye. The girl has cornsilk blonde hair, long and thick, and she twists it, rope-like, over one shoulder as she stands there looking out. Her breasts are heavy and loose inside a blue T-shirt.

It is not the dog so much that Anna resents, as it is the mocking presence of this vital young couple who take for granted what Anna is losing: her youth, her joy in life. She sees herself as the victim of a great injustice: she is getting old too soon:

Anna thinks that it was just yesterday she was newly married, and now she's old. She doesn't believe the problems she's been thinking about these days could really be her problems. She hasn't had enough of starting out, she's just getting used to being grownup, being married.

The reader begins to understand that Anna feels trapped in her life, just as the dog is trapped in his yard. Therefore, it seems logical that each time Anna hears the dog begin to bark, she identifies with him.

. . . he begins a thin wailing, less eerie than the coyotes' wailing she hears at night from the hills, but burdened enough, an outward spiraling tornado of loneliness and misery. Then it will pause briefly before turning into an explosion of staccato barks, getting shriller and more panicky, till finally the animal is running from one end of the yard to the other, rattling the fence, clawing at the spaces between the boards, yipping and yapping in a frenzy that can go on, easily, for several hours without pause.

Anna says to her husband . . .

"No one has a right to do this, to destroy a person's peace, just because he likes the idea of having a dog. A man and his dog!—what a dumb romantic notion." At the same moment she is thinking that she would like [her daughter] to marry a man like the one next door. A man who has a dog—a man, who, with his woman and his beer and his ballgame, seems like the sort of man a woman should have, a man who protects his rights, who doesn't back down, who stands firm. She thinks of his hairy chest, and to her surprise something clutches low down in her abdomen in the place where the estrogen is running low.

So we see, by the images presented, a certain contradiction here. Anna thinks she hates the dog, perhaps hates the young man who owns him—and yet, there is some great ambivalence in her. She thinks about the dog:

186

. . . hardly a watchdog, hardly a man's best friend, just a whimpering, crazed, abandoned creature, without a mate, without a friend.

This is not really a description of the dog, it is the way Anna thinks of *herself.* Late one night, thinking that she will get even with the dog . . .

. . . Anna gets her two biggest pot covers and takes them out into the backyard. She holds them, poised like a cymbal player waiting for her cue in the pit of a great orchestra . . . Anna waits, counting the beats, as breathless as if the stars are her vast audience and this is her debut. And when it comes, first the whine, then the howl, then the full-fledged bass and treble of the mad dog's great range, she runs in her nightgown, barefoot, across the damp grass of the yard, runs to the fence and crashes the pot covers together in a series of clashes, bangs and shrieks till the night sky shakes with the lightning and thunder of her fury.

What the images here really convey is her yearning to have an audience, to have her debut, to enter the world, to be the center of attention. To count as a person! And yet whatever she does comes to a lessening, to destruction and misery:

Then . . . silence. She has terrified him. She feels her lip curl. Hah, good. She imagines the dog to be like a native in the jungle who witnesses a meteorite fall . . . Back in the house . . . Anna replaces the pot covers in the cabinet under the stove, but not before a sliver of silver metal, shredded from the edge of one of the covers by her wild banging, pierces her finger, drawing bright blood . . . The next day she buys a pair of ear plugs, little cylinders of wax and foam, and at night jams them into her ears as if she is corking up her vital fluids.

Anna's grief is immense—she rails at the gods and what does she get? More loss, her life's blood leaking from her, and more than ever, her sense of all she is missing, and losing, in life. The presence of the barking dog only underlines this emotion. By now she identifies completely with him; even as she goes out to see where at the fence she can best poison him, he trots into view and

pushes his snout against the space between the boards in the side gate. . . . The dog is licking her hand, dancing with pleasure at her company, his rear end wiggling in rippling convulsions. No one has been that happy to see her in a long time. . . .

These images convey the many things he means to her. He is her enemy, but he is also her precious friend and, like her, is lonely, desperate for friendship, and helpless to do anything about his plight.

187

He is also warm, alive, beautiful . . . sexual—all the things Anna wishes to be. Finally, after her husband, goaded by her, confronts the dog's owner, she fears that . . .

a real man has a dog and a gun. He will blast her children in the yard. Or strangle her cats . . . she imagines the young man right now stroking the polished barrel of his shotgun, and she feels herself arc out of bed and land on her toes like a ballet dancer. She hurries into the backyard. The stars are as sharp as at the beginning of creation. A tall palm at the far end of the yard is fanned out against the moon. There is a rustling in the brush on the other side of the fence as she approaches it. She whispers, "Here boy, come here," and the beautiful black dog with his princely face comes to the fence and thrusts his warm nose through the crack till it is cupped in her fingers.

Once again we have the image of her as performer as she "arcs out of bed and lands on her toes like a ballet dancer." The "beginning of creation" suggests a new life; she is going to take some action. The images that describe the dog have evolved so that the dog has changed from a crazed animal whom Anna hates to a beautiful prince whom Anna loves. And what is the function of the handsome prince in any fairy tale?

By the light of the moon she pulls and pries at a board in the fence until she wrenches it from the bottom rail. Making a tiny kissing sound with her lips she holds it aside and the dog pours through like a waterfall, shimmering and coursing down the length of her leg. She kneels and puts both arms around him, long enough to feel his hot breath on her face.

The "kissing sound" suggests the moment in the fairy tale when the animal (the beast, the donkey, the frog) is changed into the handsome human prince. Now the image of the dog—almost as her lover—takes on greater strength as she pulls him into the house with her, "leading him by his red collar."

He follows her out the front door and into the wide street where they both stand in silence panting in the cool air. His ears are up, his hind legs spread slightly apart. She bends quickly and gives him a sharp rap on his rump.
"Go!" she commands. "Go!"
He starts forward like a thoroughbred, like a whippet, a black arrow flying into the dewy night. She watches him gallop till his image begins to fade against the slurry blacktop. She doesn't breathe as she sees him pause, tense, and then leap in a single bound over the horizon. At that moment she realizes she has forgotten to climb upon his back.

188

The story ends there, with that image. In her brave moment of intimacy with the dog, she loses him. The woman is left behind.

Show—don't tell is an old truism taught by writing teachers to their students. Old truths are often the best. Using images to tell your story is an effective technique, eliminating the need for tedious exposition while opening up the mind (yours and the reader's) to poetry and picture.

38

BEYOND THE IDEA: PROJECTING THE FUTURE IN SCIENCE FICTION

By Roger Zelazny

WRITERS IN GENERAL and science fiction writers in particular dislike the question, "Where do you get your ideas?" I have always felt that a far better question would be, "What do you do with your ideas after you get them?" but I have to acknowledge that I have learned some useful things from responses to the first one.

You see, I once asked someone where he got his ideas. You'd think I'd have known better, for I was already writing professionally at the time. I had heard the question dozens of times myself, and I knew that my own answers were seldom satisfactory. But, I told myself, this was a special situation. The man was neither a novelist nor a short story writer. He was a cartoonist, and I was impressed by his ability to come up with a fresh gag for every day of the week, every week of the year.

He smiled, he told me, I believed him, and I've gotten a lot of mileage out of his answer.

He informed me that he used the Yellow Pages of the telephone directory. For me, it was one of those moments when insight actually flashes. There was light. He was not kidding. He saw the Yellow Pages as a complete compendium of the goods and services available in modern society, and meditation on a few entries invariably stirred something in his mind in the way of a comment on the society that had engendered them. My own use of this routine has varied only to the extent that science fiction writers generally use the future as a means of talking about the present. Ergo, whenever I played the Yellow Pages game, I would project fifty years into the future the first half dozen or so entries to which I turned, and then I would ask myself just how that sort of business would be run a half-century from now.

I would make some guesses about what society might be like— simple, straight-line, if-this-goes-on assumptions. Then I would try the

190

"what if?" variations; e.g., what if some of the customers (or employers) aren't human—are aliens, computer intelligences, dolphins. . . . Finally, I would try shifting the business to another world, testing it in an even stranger setting. My story, "The Doors of His Face, the Lamps of His Mouth," actually owed something to a bait-and-tackle ad.

Sure, it's only a gimmick. It is also one of the best gimmicks I have ever come across, a technique capable of generating genuine story ideas. But so what? I come, finally, to my point: Ideas are not enough. Not for a story of any length.

Science fiction has often been called a literature of ideas. I am not denying this. I am just returning to the question, "What do you do with your ideas after you get them?" The post-idea approach has grown steadily in importance for me for a couple of decades.

It was possible for Kingsley Amis to refer to much of the science fiction of forty years ago as literature in which the idea is the hero. Novelty, shock value, and spectacle were the substance of much early writing in the sf field: a description of weightlessness in outer space might occupy several pages; long discussions of the relativistic effects of high velocity interstellar travel might be in order; the paradox involved in traveling back through time and killing one's ancestor might be detailed at great length. The characters involved in these situations could be stock figures. Who cared? The situations were intrinsically interesting.

But jokes are less funny the second or third time around. Much that was substance becomes convention, to be dealt with in a phrase or two—such as, "We engaged the interstellar drive and jumped into hyperspace" or "We settled in for the generations-long cold sleep between the stars" (for those writers who don't care much for hyperspace).

Ideas from the "softer" social sciences were brought into science fiction in the fifties, and the sixties saw the focus shift to story values themselves—with greater attention to characterization and more sophisticated narrative techniques. From our present vantage point, the seventies could probably be viewed as a period of synthesis, when all of these things fused to produce a more mature literary form. At this time, the considerations involved in writing a science fiction story are the same as those for writing any other sort of story, with extra attention paid to all the things that make it science fiction.

191

To discard any of the tools or to abandon any of the concerns we have acquired since the forties would be foolish. Science fiction iş still a literature of ideas, but one generally needs more than an idea to make it work. A fresh and exceptionally clever idea *could* still carry a novel— and certainly a short story—on its own, invoking something of the imaginative power of earlier days, if that's all that one cared to do. . . . I am thinking here of top-of-the-line ideas, such as the planetary engineering of Larry Niven's *Ringworld,* the wild biochips of Greg Bear's *Blood Music,* the cyberspace of William Gibson's *Neuromancer,* and the genetic engineering for an open-space culture in John McLoughlin's *Helix and the Sword.* In each of these instances, the author has gone beyond concept and written a strong story with interesting characters.

One must always remember that today's fresh and exceptionally clever ideas are already on their way to becoming tomorrow's conventions, and the real staying power of the tale will be predicated upon story values as well as the ideas. Therefore, one must think about the special problems of settings and consider the unusual opportunities the area holds for character development when deciding what to do with one's idea.

I feel that the greatest difficulty, as well as one of the greatest challenges, in writing science fiction lies in settings. One cannot simply indicate New York, Paris, San Francisco with a few impressionistic strokes and get on with the action. Or, if one can, the problem will usually crop up someplace else. If it is a future setting, we must show what is different about it. If we are describing another planet, there is a lot of material to get across. If it is a parallel world or if the viewpoint character is a person whose vision runs on different wavelengths from the human norm, we have much to indicate. The problem obviously lies in detailing these things in a sufficiently interesting or at least acceptable fashion to hold the reader's attention through what amounts to protracted exposition. For me, the best way of doing it usually involves dividing this material into several segments and slipping it in among passages involving action or fairly lively dialogue. Also, it can in part be used to bait the narrative hook. To choose two examples—one science fiction and one fantasy—from my bookshelves:

If a man walks in dressed like a hick and acting as if he owned the place, he's a spaceman.

(*Double Star,* Robert A. Heinlein)

192

It was in that year when the fashion in cruelty demanded not only the crucifixion of peasant children, but a similar fate for their pets, that I first met Lucifer and was transported into Hell; for the Prince of Darkness wished to strike a bargain with me.

(The War Hound and the World's Pain, Michael Moorcock)*

Anything that can be made to serve a double purpose in narrative, also serves a third purpose: esthetics. If you can deal with more than one narrative necessity by means of a single statement—say, background explanation plus characterization, or plot as well as setting—you are streamlining your tale in the direction of elegance. Such economy is most valuable in a short story of any sort—but in science fiction, where the burden of additional background is always present, it is a quality worth cultivating at any length.

. . . And then there is character. If setting is the burden of science fiction (though there is always someone like Jack Vance to turn it into a rare and peculiar virtue), then character is one of the rewards. Science fiction is the only area of modern prose in which characters of the sort Northrop Frye referred to as high mimetic mode (greater than one's fellows) and mythic mode figures (greater than others and also greater than one's environment) are still employed. In addition to the realistic or ironic characters who inhabit much of modern fiction, science fiction often has justifiable need for figures normally found in mythic literature or classical tragedy—in the persons of aliens, mutants, androids, robots, sentient computers, cyborgs or individuals who are the products of genetic engineering. The range of character, I maintain, is greater in science fiction than anywhere else in fiction today.

It is possible to let your fingers do the walking and to come up with a neat little idea. However, I have always considered ideas a relatively cheap commodity. While some editors act as if the ideas are what they care most about, the cagier ones know that it is really the writing that they are buying.

If, therefore, you wish to toughen your writing for the long haul, practice clever ways of injecting background material, and consider the infinite aspects of character and the conflicts it might take to reveal something about it. The great new ideas will one day be a footnote to someone's dissertation. The character, if you have done your job well, may be someone worth remembering.

193

Unfortunately, I have never found a Yellow Pages equivalent for character. For sound characterization, observation, introspection, and reading of good examples is the best preparation I can suggest. If you follow this counsel, I believe that one day you will find that your best ideas will emerge from the consideration of character rather than external influences.

39

THE BIRTH OF A SERIES CHARACTER

By George C. Chesbro

For most writers of so-called genre fiction the quest is for a successful series character—a man or woman who, already completely brought to life in the writer's and readers' minds, leaps into action at the drop of a plot to wend his or her perilous way cleverly through the twists and turns of the story to arrive finally, triumphantly at the solution. Great series characters from mystery and spy fiction immediately spring to mind; Sherlock Holmes, James Bond, Sam Spade, Lew Archer, Miss Marple, et al. These characters may simply step on stage to capture the audience's attention, with no need for the copious program notes of characterization that must usually accompany the debut of a new hero or heroine.

Almost two decades ago, when I was just beginning to enjoy some success in selling my short stories, I sat down one day to begin my search for a series character. Visions of great (and some not-so-great) detectives waltzed through my head; unfortunately, all of these dancers had already been brought to life by other people. The difficulty was compounded by the fact that I didn't want just any old character, some guy with the obligatory two fists and two guns who might end up no more than a two-dimensional plot device, a pedestrian problem solver who was but a pale imitation of the giants who had gone before and who were my inspiration. I wanted a *character*, a detective with modern sensibilities, whom readers might come to care about almost as much as they would the resolution of the mystery itself. Sitting at my desk, surrounded by a multitude of rejection slips, I quickly became not only frustrated, but intimidated. I mean, just who did I think I was?

It was a time when "handicapped" detectives were in vogue on television: Ironside solved cases from his wheelchair and van; another was Longstreet, a blind detective. Meditating on this, I suddenly found a most mischievous notion scratching, as it were, at the back door of my

195

mind. I was a decidedly minor league manager looking to sign a player who might one day compete in the major leagues. What to do? The answer, of course, was obvious; if I couldn't hope to create a detective who could reasonably be expected to vie with the giants, then I would create a detective who was unique—a dwarf.

Believing, as I do, that it's good for the soul as well as the imagination, I always allow myself exactly one perverse notion a day (whether I need it or not). I'd had my perverse notion, and it was time to think on. What would my detective look like. What kind of gun would he carry, how big would it be, and how many bullets would it hold?

Scratch, scratch.

Would his trenchcoat be a London Fog or something bought off a pipe rack? What about women? How many pages would I have to devote in each story to descriptions of his sexual prowess?

Scratch, scratch.

The damn dwarf simply refused to go away, and his scratching was growing increasingly persistent. But what was I going to do with a dwarf private detective? Certainly not sell him, since it seemed to me well nigh impossible to make anybody (including me) believe in his existence. Who could take such a character seriously? Who, even in a time of dire need, would hire a dwarf detective? Where would his cases come from? He would *literally* be struggling to compete in a world of giants.

Scratch, scratch.

No longer able to ignore the noises in my head, I opened the door and let the Perverse Notion into the main parlor where I was trying to work. It seemed there was no way I was going to be able to exorcise this aberration, short of actually trying to write something about him.

Observing him, I saw that he was indeed a dwarf, but fairly large and powerfully built, as dwarfs go. That seemed to me a good sign. If this guy was going to be a private detective, he would have to be more than competent at his work; he would need extra dimensions, possess special talents that would at least partially compensate for his size.

Brains never hurt anyone, so he would have to be very smart. Fine. Indeed, I decided that he was not only very smart, but a veritable genius—a professor with a Ph.D. in Criminology; a psychological and spiritual outcast. His name is Dr. Robert Frederickson. Now, where could he live where people wouldn't be staring at him all the time? New York City, of course.

196

So far, so good. The exorcism was proceeding apace.

Fictional private eyes are always getting into trouble, and they have to be able to handle themselves physically. What would Dr. Robert Frederickson do when the two- and three-hundred-pound bad guys came at him? He had to be able to fight. So he'd need some kind of special physical talent.

Dwarfs. Circuses. Ah. Dr. Robert Frederickson had spent some time in the circus (in fact, that was how he had financed his education!). But he hadn't worked in any side show; he'd been a star, a headliner, a gymnast, a tumbler with a spectacular, death-defying act. Right. And he had parlayed his natural physical talents into a black belt in karate. If nothing else, he would certainly have the advantage of surprise. During his circus days he had been billed as "Mongo the Magnificent," and his friends still call him Mongo.

Mongo, naturally, tended to overcompensate, to say the least. He had a mind of a titan trapped in the body of a dwarf (I liked that), and that mind was constantly on the prowl, looking for new challenges. Not content with being a dwarf in a circus (albeit a famous one), he became a respected criminology professor; not content with being "just" a professor, he started moonlighting as a private detective.

But I was still left with the problem of where his cases were going to come from. I strongly doubted that any dwarf detective was going to get much walk-in business, so all of his cases were going to have to come from his associates, people who knew him and appreciated just how able he was, friends from his circus days, colleagues at the university where he teaches and, for good measure, from the New York Police Department, where, his *very* big brother, Garth, is a detective, a lieutenant.

I set about my task, and halfway through the novella that would become "The Drop," hamming it up, I discovered something that brought me up short: Dr. Frederickson was no joke. A major key to his character, to his drive to compete against all odds, was a quest for dignity and respect from others. He insisted on being taken seriously as a human being, and he was constantly willing to risk his life or suffer possible ridicule and humiliation in order to achieve that goal. Dr. Robert Frederickson, a.k.a. Mongo the Magnificent, was one tough cookie, psychologically and physically, and I found that I liked him very much.

And I knew then that, regardless of how he was treated by any incredulous editor, I, at least, would afford this most remarkable man the dignity and respect I felt he so richly deserved. I ended by writing "The Drop" as a straight (well, seriously skewed actually, but serious) detective story.

"The Drop" was rejected. The editor to whom I'd submitted it (he had published my short stories) wrote that sorry, Mongo was just too unbelievable. (Well, of course, he was unbelievable. What the hell did he expect of a dwarf private detective?)

That should have ended my act of exorcism of the Perverse Notion. Fat chance! On the same day "The Drop" was rejected, I sent it right out again to another editor (after all, Mongo would never have given up so easily), who eventually bought it.

The next day I sat down and started Mongo on his second adventure. Mongo was no longer the Perverse Notion; I had created a man who intrigued me enormously, a man I liked and respected, a most complex character about whom I wanted to know more, and who fired my imagination.

My Perverse Notion in that second story was to include a bit of dialogue in which Garth tells Mongo; after some particularly spectacular feat, that he's lucky he's not a fictional character, because no one would believe him. "High Wire" sold the first time out—to the first editor, and this time he never mentioned a word again about Mongo's believability. Four more Mongo novellas followed and were published. In the seventh, "Candala," it seemed I had sent Mongo out too far beyond the borders defining what a proper detective/mystery story should be, into the dank, murky realms of racial discrimination, self-hate and self-degradation. I couldn't place "Candala" anywhere, and it went into the darkness of my trunk.

But Mongo himself remained very much alive. I was still discovering all sorts of things about the Frederickson brothers, and the curious psychological and physical worlds they moved in; they needed larger quarters, which could be provided only in a novel.

Six Mongo novels later, Mongo and Garth continue to grow in my mind, and they continue to fire my imagination. In fact, that Perverse Notion proved to be an invaluable source of inspiration. Mongo has, both literally and figuratively, enriched my life, and he and Garth are the primary reasons that I was finally able to realize my own "impossible dream" of making my living as a writer.

"Candala" finally appeared in print, between hardcovers, in an anthology entitled, *An Eye for Justice*.

It is always risky business to try to extrapolate one's own feelings or experiences into the cheap currency of advice to others (especially in regard to that most painfully personal of pursuits, writing). However, the thought occurs to me that a belief in, and a respect for, even the most improbable of your characters in their delicate period of gestation is called for. That Perverse Notion you don't want to let in, because you fear you will waste time and energy feeding and nurturing it for no reward, may be the most important and helpful character, series or otherwise—you'll ever meet in your life.

40

ALWAYS A STORYTELLER

By Mary Higgins Clark

THERE'S A THEORY that our lives are set in seven-year cycles. Vaguely, I remember that the basis for that belief is that in seven years every cell in our bodies has replaced itself. In case that's mountain-folk legend, I hasten to apologize to the more learned in the scientific fields. Recently I reread an article on suspense writing that I wrote just seven years ago to see what I've learned since.

My conclusion is that the more you know, the more you don't know. I've written three books, short stories, a novella, and film treatments since then, and I'm not sure I've gained any greater insight into this wondrous, complex and tantalizing field we call writing.

However, we must start somewhere, so let's go with the basics. How do you know that you are supposed to be a writer? The first necessity is that utter yearning to communicate, that sense that "I have something to say"; reading a book and knowing, *knowing* that you can write one like it; the sense that no matter how well ordered your life is, how thoroughly you delight in your family and friends and home and job, something is missing. Something so absolutely necessary that you are constantly swallowing ashes. You want to write. You must write.

These are the people who just might make it. That yearning is usually accompanied by talent, real talent, often native, undisciplined, unfocused talent, but certainly it's there. The degree of yearning separates the *real* potential writer from the truism that everyone has one story in them. How many times are professional writers approached at seminars or parties with the suggestion, "I've got a great story to tell. You jot it down for me, and we'll split the royalties."

Face the yearning. At some point, you'll have to or else eventually go to that great beyond unfulfilled. My mother always told me that my grandmother, struggling to raise her nine children and an orphaned

200

niece, used to say, "Oh, how I'd love to write a book." On her deathbed, she was still regretting that she'd never tried.

Now you've acknowledged that you've simply got to try. Where do you begin? Most of us have a sense of what we want to write. If you don't, a terrific clue is to analyze what you like to *read*. I hadn't the faintest idea that I could write suspense, but after my first book was published, a biographical novel about George Washington that was read by the favored few, I knew that if I tried again, I'd really want to look forward to that lovely mailing from the publisher known as a royalty statement. I cast about for a story idea and looked at the bookshelf. I was astonished to realize that ninety percent of the books I'd read in the last couple of years had been mysteries. I did further soul-digging and began naming my favorite authors: Mary Roberts Rinehart, Josephine Tey, Agatha Christie, Charlotte Armstrong, and on and on. That was the clue that helped me decide to try a suspense novel. The one I launched was *Where Are the Children?* It's in its forty-second printing right now.

Footnote, just so I don't forget. Judith Guest's first novel was turned down by two publishers. She then looked at her bookshelf and realized that many of the books she read were published by Viking Press. She sent her manuscript to them. Months later she received a telegram. "Viking Press is honored to publish *Ordinary People*." The point is that the books you like to read give you a clue to what you may write best. The publisher of the books you read may turn out to be the best potential publisher for you.

Back to the beginning. Having determined whether you want to begin the writing adventure in the field of suspense or romance or science fiction; mainstream novels or books for children or adolescents; or poetry or articles, the next step is to treat yourself to several subscriptions. *The Writer* is the best at-home companion for the aspiring and/or achieving writer I can suggest.

I sold my first short story on my own. It went to forty magazines over the course of six years before it found a home. Which leads to the next question the new writer invariably asks. "How do I get an agent?" It's the chicken-and-egg query. In my case, in 1956 a young agent read the story and phoned me, saying, "I'd like to represent you." We were together thirty years until she retired two years ago. I'm still with her agency and the terrific people she put in her place. The point is, I think it's a lot easier to get an agent after you've proven yourself, even if your success is a modest one. That story brought me one hundred dollars. But remember. No story or book should ever sit in your drawer. If you get it back from one editor, send it out to the next. And don't sit in never-never land waiting for that one to sell. Start on the next project.

O.K. You have the determination; you know what you want to write; you're gathering the tools. I think it's fundamental to set aside time every day. Even one hour a day creates a habit. When my children were young, I used to get up at five and work from five until seven. I have the whole day to write now and don't get up that early, but I'm tempted to start setting the alarm again. There is something exhilarating about the world being quiet and you're somehow alone in it knowing that the phone won't ring or someone won't stop by. On the other hand, maybe you work best at night. Take that extra hour after everyone else in the family has been tucked in and use it to work on the story or poem or novel. No matter how tired you are when you start, I promise you that the sense of accomplishment of seeing even a page or two completed will make your dreams blissful.

I urge you to join some kind of writing group. Writing is one of the most isolated professions in the world. Your family can be marvelously supportive, but it's not the same. One of two things happen. They see the rejection slips and urge you not to keep banging your head against a wall. "Give it up, dear. It's just too tough to break into that field." Or they think that every word you write is gospel and expect a massive best seller any minute. Your local college or library may have writing courses available. Sign up for one of them. Don't worry about the fact that you'll inevitably miss three or four classes during the semester. You'll make the other ten or twelve. Listening to a professional, getting to know people who are in the field or aspiring to it is balm to the soul. When you begin having contact with others who share your need, you'll experience the feeling Stanley must have had when he said, "Dr. Livingston, I presume."

Be aware that there is probably an organization in your general area you should join: mystery writers, science writers, poets, among others. They're waiting for you. After that first story sold, I joined the Mystery Writers of America. I still remember my first meeting. I didn't know a soul. I was in awe of the name writers around me. Many of my best friends today I met at MWA meetings. And oh the joy of talking shop! Besides that, at these professional organizations you get to meet editors and agents who otherwise would be behind closed doors.

That's how it should be in the beginning. The determination. The quest to know what to write. The studying of the craft. The fellowship of other writers. And then in the quiet of that study or the space you cleared for yourself in the corner of the kitchen or bedroom, begin to write. Always remember that what you are is a storyteller. No matter how elegant your prose, how descriptive your passages, how insightful your eye, unless you tell a story people want to hear, you're not going to make it. A story has a beginning and a middle and an end. It tells about people we all know and identify with. It tells of their hopes and dreams and failures and triumphs. It tells of the twists of fate that bestow fortune on one person and rob another who is equally deserving. It makes us laugh and mourn and hope for the people whose lives we are sharing. It leaves us with a sense of catharsis, of emotion well spent. Isaac Bashevis Singer is a dedicated mystery reader. Several years ago at the Mystery Writers annual banquet, he received the award as Mystery Reader of the Year. This great writer offered simple yet profound advice. It was that the writer must think of himself or herself primarily as a storyteller. Every book or story should figuratively begin with the words "Once upon a time." Because it is as true now as it was in the long ago days of wandering minstrels, that when these words are uttered, the room becomes quiet, everyone draws closer to the fire, and the magic begins.

41

ONE CLUE AT A TIME

By P.D. James

FOR ME one of the keenest pleasures of rereading my favorite mysteries is their power to transport me instantly into a familiar world of people, places and objects, a world in which I feel at once comfortably at home.

With what mixture of excitement, anticipation and reassurance we enter that old brownstone in Manhattan, that gentle spinster's cottage in St. Mary Mead (never fully described by Agatha Christie but so well imagined), that bachelor flat in London's Piccadilly where Bunter deferentially pours the vintage port [for Lord Peter Wimsey], that cozy Victorian sitting room on Baker Street.

A sense of place, creating as it does that vivid illusion of reality, is a necessary tool of any successful novelist. But it is particularly important to the fabricator of the mystery: the setting of the crime and the use of commonplace objects help to heighten by contrast the intruding horror of murder. The bizarre and the terrifying are rooted in comforting reality, making murder more believable.

There is probably no room in crime fiction that we enter with a keener sense of instant recognition than the claustrophobic upstairs sitting room at 221B Baker Street. Baker Street is now one of the dullest of London's main thoroughfares, and it is difficult, walking these wide pavements, to picture those foggy Victorian evenings with the inevitable veiled lady alighting from her hansom cab outside the door of the celebrated Sherlock Holmes.

But we can see every detail of the room into which Mrs. Hudson will usher her: the sofa on which Holmes reclines during his periods of meditation; the violin case propped against the wall; the shelves of scrapbooks; the bullet marks in the wall; the two broad windows overlooking the street; the twin armchairs on each side of the fireplace; the bottle of 7-percent-cocaine solution on the mantel shelf; the desk with the locked drawer containing Holmes's confidential records; the central table with "its white cloth and glimmer of china and metal" waiting for Mrs. Hudson to clear away.

The mental scene has, of course, been reinforced countless times in films and on television, but what is remarkable is that so vivid a picture should be produced by so few actual facts. Paradoxically, I can find no passage in the books that describes the room at length and in detail. Instead, Sir Arthur Conan Doyle builds up the scene through a series of stories object by object, and the complete picture is one that the reader himself creates and furnishes in his own imagination from this accumulation of small details.

Few things reveal the essential self more surely than the rooms in which we live, the objects with which we choose to surround ourselves, the books we place on our shelves, all those small household goods that help reaffirm identity and provide comfort and a sense of security. But the description in crime fiction of domestic interiors, furnishings and possessions does more than denote character; it creates mood and atmosphere, enhances suspense and is often crucial to the plot.

In Agatha Christie, for example, we can be confident that almost any domestic article mentioned, however commonplace, will provide a clue, either true or false. A loose door number hanging on its nail; flowers that have died because no one watered them; an extra coffee spoon in a saucer; a picture postcard lying casually on the desk. In *Funerals Are Fatal,* we do well to note the bouquet of wax flowers on the malachite table. In *Murder at the Vicarage,* we can be sure that the tall stand with a plant pot standing in front of the window isn't there for nothing.

And in *The Murder of Roger Ackroyd,* we shouldn't be so intrigued by the corpse that we fail to notice how one chair has been strangely pulled out from its place by the wall.

All writers of mystery fiction use such devices, but few with such deceptive cunning. It is one of the paradoxes of the genre that it deals with that great absolute, death, yet deploys the trivia of ordinary life as the frail but powerful instruments of justice.

Because in a Christie mystery the puzzle is more important than either the characterization or the setting, she seldom describes a room in great detail. Hers is the art of the literary conjurer. How very different is the loving care and meticulous eye with which a novelist such as Margery Allingham creates for us her highly individual domestic interiors.

In *More Work for the Undertaker,* how brilliantly she describes every room of the eccentric Palinode family, so that the house itself is central to the plot, its atmosphere pervades the novel, and we feel that we know every secret and sinister corner.

But my favorite Allingham rooms are in *The Tiger in the Smoke,* with its opposing characters of the saintly Canon Avril and the psychopathic killer Jack Havoc. How simply described and how absolutely right is the Canon's sitting room. "It was the room he had brought his bride to 30 years before, and since then . . . nothing in it had ever been changed. It had become a little worn in the interim, but the good things in it, the walnut bookcase with the ivory chessmen displayed, the bureau with 13 panes in each glass door, the Queen Anne chair with the 7-foot back, the Persian rug which had been a wedding present from his younger sister, Mr. Campion's mother, had all mellowed just as he had with care and use and quiet living."

Right, too, in its very different style, is the sitting room of his dress-designer daughter, Meg, littered with its sketches of dresses and strewn with swaths of material and samples of braids and beads. "Between the demasked grey walls and the deep gold carpet there ranged every permissible tint and texture from bronze velvet to scarlet linen, pinpointed and enlivened with draining touches of Bristol blue."

This is a highly individual room in the grand manner but without pretentiousness, and I'm not in the least surprised that after a dubious sidelong glance, Chief Inspector Luke decided that he liked it very much indeed.

A room I like very much indeed is Lord Peter Wimsey's sitting room in his flat at 110A Piccadilly. We see it most clearly through the eyes of Miss Murchison in Dorothy L. Sayers's *Strong Poison.* She is shown by Bunter into a glowing, book-lined room "with fine prints on the walls, an Aubusson carpet, a grand piano, a vast chesterfield and a number of deep, cozy armchairs upholstered in brown leather.

"The curtains were drawn, a wood fire blazed on the hearth, and before it stood a table with a silver tea service whose lovely lines were a delight to the eye." No wonder Miss Murchison was impressed.

After his marriage, of course, Lord Peter honeymooned with his

Harriet at Talboys, an Elizabethan farmhouse in Hertfordshire that Lord Peter bought as their country retreat, complete with inglenooked fireplace, ancient beams, tall Elizabethan chimneys, erratic plumbing and the inevitable corpse in the cellar. Meanwhile, the dowager Duchess of Denver was busying herself collecting the chandeliers and tapestries for the Wimseys' town house in Audley Square and congratulating herself that the bride "was ready to prefer 18th-century elegance to chromium tubes." I am myself partial to 18th-century elegance, but I still feel more at home in that bachelor flat at 110A Piccadilly.

Incidently, Talboys was modernized and completely refurnished, including the installation of electricity and the provision of additional bedrooms, before the murderer of its previous owner had been executed—in England a matter then of only a couple of months. That was remarkably speedy even for the 1930's. Today I am doubtful whether even the son of a Duke would be able to command such speedy service.

I myself work in the tradition of Margery Allingham and share her fascination with architecture and domestic interiors; indeed, it is often the setting rather than a particular character or a new method of murder that sparks my creative imagination and gives rise to a novel.

In my last book, *The Skull Beneath the Skin,* the setting is a restored Victorian castle on a lonely offshore island. Here the owner, obsessed with violent death, has created his own private chamber of horrors, a study decorated with old woodcuts of execution scenes, Staffordshire figures of Victorian murderers, mourning regalia and the artifacts of murder.

Here I have used the setting to fulfill all the functions of place in detective fiction; to illustrate character, create atmosphere, provide the physical clues to the crime and to enhance that sense of unease, of the familiar and ordinary made strange and terrible, which is at the heart of detective fiction.

And it is surely the power to create this sense of place and to make it as real to the reader as is his own living room—and then to people it with characters who are suffering men and women, not stereotypes to be knocked down like dummies in the final chapter—that gives any mystery writer the claim to be regarded as a serious novelist.

42

SCIENCE FICTION TODAY

By Isaac Asimov

SCIENCE FICTION has changed enormously since I first began writing it, professionally, nearly fifty years ago.

When I submitted a story for the first time on June 21, 1938, there were three magazines in the field; only one of which, *Astounding Science Fiction,* was, in my opinion, quality. There was nothing else to speak of. An occasional amateur publisher put out a tiny printing of some poorly written science fiction novel. There were a few comic strips, notably *Buck Rogers* and *Flash Gordon,* and an occasional very primitive movie serial.

But now?

In the print media, science fiction novels are commonly found on the best-seller lists, both in hardcover and softcover. The book stores have shelves full of them. The movies and television find science fiction to be profitable blockbusters. Science fiction courses are taught in high schools and colleges. Short story anthologies exist by the hundreds. Science fiction is *big time*.

It might seem to you, then, that it must be a great deal easier to break into the science fiction field now than it was fifty years ago. After all, the target is so much larger now.

Unfortunately, I don't think that's so. Let us analyze the situation more closely. Fifty years ago, when sf consisted of three magazines and virtually nothing else, there were many other outlets for fiction. It was the heyday of the pulp-magazine craze. Every newsstand had dozens of them in every conceivable category: romance, mystery, western, jungle, war, horror, adventure. Some came out monthly, and some biweekly, and some even weekly. There were also "slick" magazines that published a great deal of fiction and paid much more than the pulps did.

Of them all, the science fiction magazines were the smallest in number, the least lucrative, the most specialized, and the least regarded segment. Almost none of the myriads of young people who had the itch to write considered science fiction as a possible outlet. The science fiction magazines drew their new prospects from among their own long-time fanatic readers, who had been reading science fiction since they had learned to read and had no interest in anything else. They didn't care for either fame or wealth, but wanted only to write that wonderful stuff they were reading and see their name in print in a science fiction magazine. There weren't many of those fanatics (usually abbreviated as "fans"), but I was one of them. I had been reading science fiction avidly from the age of nine, and I was eighteen when I made my first sale.

Under those circumstances, it was not necessary to be a great writer, you understand. There were few science fiction writers of any kind in those days, and still fewer good ones. If you were eager to write science fiction, knew grammar and spelling, and had read enough science fiction to know a new idea from an old one, that was about all that was needed.

Nowadays, all that has changed also. In the first place, the fiction market has contracted violently in the last fifty years (a result of the coming of the comic magazine, and then, even more important, television). The pulps are gone. What slicks exist publish very little fiction. In fact, the only branch of popular fiction that has expanded wildly in the last half century has been science fiction. (Mysteries and romances have done no more than hold their own over the long run.)

This means that of all the youngsters who grow up with the itch to be writers, a sizable percentage tend to flood into science fiction in large numbers. There are hundreds of excellent science fiction writers today, whereas, half a century ago, there were mere dozens of not-so-excellent ones. In addition, many of those who entered the field years ago are still there. The "big three"—Isaac Asimov, Arthur C. Clarke, and Robert A. Heinlein—whose books are sure-fire best sellers today, have been writing steadily for nearly fifty years. Clarke and Heinlein, despite their advanced years, show no signs of slowing down and I, of course, am still a youngster.

What's more, all these writers tend to write novels. That's where the money and fame are. And novels are precisely what a beginner would find difficult to do. A novel has a complex structure, with interlocking plots and subplots, with room for characterization to be developed and dialogue to show a certain depth and wit. If a beginner throws caution to the winds and determines to tackle a novel anyway, he finds it represents an enormous investment of time and effort, all of which (the chances are) will be thrown away except for what good the writing experience will do him.

The natural way in which science fiction writers broke into the field in my early days was to turn out short stories for the magazines. (There was, after all, nothing else to do since, at most, two or three novels were published each year as magazine serials.) Clarke, Heinlein, and I all got our start as writers of science fiction short stories for the magazines. We worked our way up to novels by stages.

Well, then, are there not science fiction magazines that publish short stories today, to say nothing of science fiction anthologies?

Yes, but skip the anthologies. The vast majority of them include reprints—stories that have already appeared in the magazines. That leaves only the magazines.

Unfortunately, the magazines have not expanded along with the rest of the field. There are four magazines today that specialize in science fiction. In order of age, they are *Amazing Stories* (previously *Amazing Science Fiction Stories*); *Analog Science Fiction/Science Fact* (which had once been *Astounding Science Fiction*); *The Magazine of Fantasy and Science Fiction;* and *Isaac Asimov's Science Fiction Magazine.* In addition, there are a couple of other magazines, which publish some science fiction. Most notable of these is *Omni,* which publishes two or three stories in each issue. It pays much higher rates than the others do, and consequently seeks its stories from among the established writers. (And there are a number of little magazines in the field, a good place for beginning sf writers to try, though payment rates are low.)

The magazine field, therefore, is not much larger than it was fifty years ago, and the competition is keener. The level of writing in the magazines is consequently substantially higher than it used to be, and my 18-year-old self, if transported into the present with no more talent than I possessed then, might not have been able to break in.

However, all is not lost. In the old days, when a writer established himself as a science fiction short story writer, he stayed there having nowhere else to go, and left that much less room for newcomers. Nowadays, as soon as a science fiction writer begins to make a name for himself in the magazines and has gained the necessary expertise, he shifts to writing novels. The result is that the magazines are forced to be on the continual lookout for new young writers. These new writers have to be good, to be sure—it is no longer enough that they feel warm to the touch—but the fact that they are unknown is not held against them.

But so what if the competition is keen? That makes the task the more challenging, and the triumph sweeter in the end. The rules are the same. You have to read a great deal of science fiction so that you gain some insight into what science fiction is and what makes it good. And you have to write a great deal of science fiction, because only by writing can you gradually learn the tricks of the trade. And you have to have an inhuman perseverance and develop a thick skin against disappointment and frustration. And don't think the world is picking on you. I suspect that Homer and Aeschylus had all the same experiences you had in getting started.

Perhaps something else occurs to you. It may seem to you that when I was just beginning (back in the Middle Ages) hardly anything was known about science and I could write freely about interplanetary travel and robots and all that stuff. Nowadays, however, we *have* interplanetary travel and robots, so what is there to write about? Hasn't science caught up to all the science fiction plots? Isn't science fiction dead?

Not at all! Nohow! The science fiction writer is tied to the front end of a locomotive that is speeding across the landscape. No matter how far and how fast the locomotive is going, the writer is looking ahead and sees an endless vista.

Scientific advance provides writers with fascinating new backgrounds. We used to think Mars had canals; now we know (not "think") it has extinct volcanoes. And we know Io has active volcanoes. And we know that Venus is as hot as hell—literally—and has no oceans. We can turn away from the tired old planets and make use of brand-new ones, and have the satisfaction of knowing that there's less guesswork and more knowledge now.

Again, we think of all the new concepts science has given us. We have neutron stars, and black holes, and quasars, and exploding galaxies, and big bangs. We have mesons, and hyperons, and quarks, and gluons. We have DNA and biogenetics. We have computers and microchips. We have jet planes and satellites of every kind and probes and shuttles. We have seen close-ups of Uranus and its satellites. We had *none* of that when I was starting out.

When I think of all these new scientific items there are to play around with now—and how little I had back in 1938—I am amazed that I was able to think up any stories at all in that medieval period.

Of course, we have to be careful of fashion. When I first started reading science fiction, it was all adventure and Sunday supplement science. It was written in primary colors and in jagged lightning streaks. It was ideal for a bright nine-year-old to get started on.

By the time I began to submit stories, however, it became fashionable to load them down with authentic science and to try to make the characters sound like real scientists and engineers. The 1940's and 1950's were the heyday of "hard science fiction" and that was my forte, and (to tell you the truth) I still write it even though it sounds old-fashioned today.

In the 1960's, there came a period of stylistic experimentation called "the new wave" which, it seems to me, made hard reading and wasn't very successful. However, it settled down into the literary style we have today.

So however much you may want to read the "old classics" (like Asimov) and however much you may enjoy them, you had better also read, and pay close attention to, the kind of material that is appearing in the magazines *now*. That is what you should be writing.

Of course, you may be asking yourself if you should be writing for the print media at all. Shouldn't you be breaking into movies and television, where the BIG money is?

Frankly, I don't know how that's done. I've never worked in the visual media myself except on two or three minor occasions when I was talked into it much against my will.

It is my experience that when you write for the print media, what you write is what gets published. If there is a need for revision, the editor asks *you* to revise, and the chances are even good that you will get to see a galley proof so that you can make sure that any last-minute editorial changes meet with your approval.

When you write for the visual media, however, you must apparently meet the requirements of the producer, the director, the various actors, the office boy, strangers who pass in the street, and the mother-in-law of any or all of these, each of whom changes your product at whim. If you are a real writer, money isn't going to compensate for never being free to write as you wish.

212

43

NOTEBOOKS AND NOVELS

By Thomas Fleming

WHEN I FIRST THOUGHT about writing novels, I had the romantic notion that you just sat down and let it pour out. A novel was a kind of eruption of imagination and emotion, I thought, not much different from a lyric poem. Just longer.

Then I started writing novels. I soon found out that the craft was a lot closer to planning and building a house than to gurgitating a ten-line poem. It required a lot of thought and a lot of research. It was at that point that I created my notebooks, two of them: one for my thoughts, where I talked to myself with absolute candor about my plot, my problems with my editor, my uncertainties about this or that character. My other notebook was for my research, for I am convinced that there is virtually no novel, even the most hermetically sealed, intensely personal romance, that cannot profit from an infusion of factual research. It can add solidity to descriptions, authenticity to a character.

The plot notebook, as I call it—though the term is inadequate—can be more valuable than the friend to whom many writers submit their work before sending it to an editor. That friend inevitably has some personal axes he or she may try to grind in your book. The notebook is you, facing up to the problems in your book. It is you doing a profile in courage.

This notebook can also be a marvelous memory bank. Anyone who gets into a novel starts having what I call "flash aheads." Often I have leaped out of bed in the morning with the core scene for a chapter that I will not get to for another four weeks pulsing in my mind. What to do? Abandon all method, order, and spend the day writing it? That way leads to the most demoralizing sensation you can experience—loss of control of your book.

No, confide it to your friend, the notebook, in condensed fashion. It will be there, waiting for you, when you are ready to write it out in all its putative brilliance. By the time you get to it, you may have developed some new insights that deepen it—make it superfluous.

The notebook is also a wonderful antidote to that bugaboo, writer's block. If you are completely stalled on your story, turn to the notebook and start writing about how you are stalled, why the various alternatives in the plot are driving you crazy. Nine times out of ten, you will soon be back in your book, no longer a frozen victim of your doubts.

The deeper you get into your novel, the more intricate your "notebook" should become. I usually write two- or three-line condensations of the finished chapters in the front of my plot notebook, after the halfway mark. Again, this is a marvelous way to maintain that vital feeling of control of your book. A glance through this outline can give you a grasp of the parameters of your plot; it can refresh your memory of what your main characters have already experienced.

A novelist friend, another notebook devotee, puts elaborate descriptions of his main characters in the front of his plot notebook. They are virtually personal histories of these people, with more detail than he will use in his novel. He wants to feel he knows them better than his readers. This is still another way of using your notebooks to build up your confidence.

The best time to write in your plot notebook is at the beginning of the working day: the thoughts you have had about your main characters, positive or negative, new insights into minor characters, glimpses of flash-aheads. Get it all down quickly, in a half hour, no more. The one danger of the notebook is the temptation to lavish too much time on it, to the neglect of your novel. That can turn your notebook into your worst enemy.

Thumbing through the notebook I kept for my novel, *Time and Tide* (set in the Pacific during World War II), I found all sorts of things leap out. On June 2, 1986, I wrote:

Still grappling with Lieutenant West. Now he's Joseph Lyman Shuck. His name does not reveal his Jewish past. I still find a yearning for the Captain to have a Jewish mother. But it's too unlikely. Probably too obvious.

A few days later:

Time for another sermon on the dangers of impatience. Calm down. This is not finished. Think harder and longer about certain characters and events.
The next day:

Ending. Awoke this a.m. wondering why Homewood swam away, killed himself. Couldn't he have hung onto the raft? Why this passion for immolation?

A week later:

West starts well but seems to blur out. What is his problem? Simply trying to find out who he is? What does that mean? In the end, he's simply a Navy officer. That's not enough. I don't want these characters to embrace the "narrow nobility" of the military ethic.

The next day:

Thoughts on the novel this morning: need more on the smells, the lousy food, the tiny lockers, the 120-degree heat in the engine room. Make the reader feel he's there!

That gives you a glimpse of the many faces of my friend, my plot notebook. Sometimes he's a cheerleader (every writer needs one of those occasionally). Sometimes he's a prosecuting attorney. Sometimes he's a consulting psychiatrist. Above all, if you've done right by him, he's that most invaluable of writing resources—a friend who tells you the truth.

My research notebook not only helps add authenticity to novels, but also can substantially alter the direction of a story. My novel *Spoils of War* was a very ambitious book about the impact of the American Civil War on the North. It spanned the last three decades of the 19th century and included scenes set in Europe as well as in many parts of the United States.

In my files were no fewer than four hundred pages of research notes, condensing and annotating the hundreds of books and newspapers I had consulted. When I wrote my novel *A Cry of Whiteness,* about a white policeman in a black ghetto, I spent dozens of hours interviewing friends on the New York police force about procedures and routines and slang terms. Later, I got a number of letters from readers who presumed I must be a retired cop.

Research can, as I have said, change the plot of your novel. When I was writing *Dreams of Glory,* a novel about espionage in the Revolution, I discovered there had been an abortive revolt against Spanish rule in New Orleans in 1768. I suddenly saw that if I connected my main character, Flora Kuyper, to that tragic episode—the Spanish crushed the revolutionists with ruthless cruelty—it would explain her doubts about the American Revolution. Eventually, the New Orleans experience broadened—Flora met an Englishman there who rescued her from the Spanish after her father was killed. He took her to England, which led to some vivid scenes (and more research) about high life in London

215

in the 1760's. The New Orleans revolt, which I knew nothing about when I began the book, became one of the central episodes of the novel.

In *Promises to Keep,* my novel about an aristocratic American family, my plot called for Paul Stapleton, the main character, to meet his wife Maria in Mexico in 1916, while he was serving with the American army that pursued the guerilla leader, Pancho Villa, across the border. My research into Villa's operations produced one of the most exciting scenes in the novel. Villa and his men murder Maria's father and plot to ambush the Americans at their hacienda. She finds her father's gun and fires a warning shot as they ride into the courtyard. A wild gunfight ensues in which Paul Stapleton displays both leadership and courage. The episode, *based on an actual event* (which I had recorded in my research notebook), explained their attraction to each other with an immediacy I could never have achieved with pages of romantic dialogue.

While researching my novel, *The Officers' Wives,* about the post-World War II U.S. Army, I discovered a Ph.D. thesis done at Harvard by a West Pointer, who demonstrated in overwhelming detail why the United States should never fight a war of attrition against an Asian nation where life is cheap. In the novel, this thesis is written by one of the main characters, Adam Thayer. When the Army bureaucracy ignores it (as they ignored the real thesis) and the United States goes to war in Vietnam, Adam's bitterness destroys his career and his marriage.

So, not only can research enrich your novel in these various ways—it can add a valuable dimension of confidence to your writing. Every novelist wants to believe he is penetrating reality with his book. That feeling can be a byproduct of your research notebook. It is also one of the main purposes of your plot notebook: Each contributes to the other to make your story feel authentic and your characters real.

44

SAYING IT ALL

By Catherine Aird

DEFINING EXACTLY WHAT CONSTITUTES good dialogue is a great deal easier than actually writing it. This is a fact of life that most authors discover for themselves very early in their careers. That good dialogue does not always receive the recognition it deserves is perhaps because it is one of the elements of a well-crafted novel that is usually taken for granted by the reader. Reading good dialogue is probably an almost unconscious pleasure for the reader, who is more likely to be aware of the bad than specifically to identify the good.

Nevertheless, the essential elements of dialogue in fictional writing can and should be analyzed and practiced. There are three distinct aspects of constructing it that I think novelists should bear in mind.

First and most important, the words "spoken" should be completely in the character of the fictional person uttering them. Men and women, northerners and southerners, scientists and artists, professional and lay people . . . speak quite differently from one another. So do children and adults, educated and illiterate people, the ill and the well, Europeans and Americans—the comparisons are endless.

In real life, they use different words, phrases, idioms, and figures of speech, and so they should in fiction. It therefore follows that if, as you write about them, you are not absolutely sure how your fictional characters would speak and what they would say in the circumstances you have created for them, these people may not yet be clear enough in your mind, and you should give them further thought before putting them on paper.

Secondly, you, the writer, should be aware that different types of people express what they want to say in quite distinct ways. The words—often short—of nervous, excitable, high-strung people under pressure usually come tumbling out in a hurry. Those of a mature professional man who gives guarded advice in an office setting would normally be delivered in a calm and measured manner. So, as well as using words appropriate to the character saying them, how they are delivered should also be appropriate to the situation.

The ideal test of dialogue is to see if the reader would know who in your story is speaking by reading only what is said and how it is delivered. This is, I know, a counsel of perfection, but applying this touchstone can have quite a salutary effect on us all.

An interesting and suprisingly revealing parallel to this is the attention you have to pay to the degree of familiarity with which people address each other on your pages. In everyday life, we all make instant and almost unconscious judgments of the degree of formality we should use in social conversation with others. This perception must similarly be transferred to paper and will require all your attention, because it should instantly tell your reader the relationship between the characters in your novel as they speak to one another.

The third important aspect of dialogue is the way in which it moves the plot forward. The two great masters of this art were Ivy Compton-Burnett and P. G. Wodehouse. Their plots are almost totally subsumed in dialogue, but doing this successfully takes great skill.

Nevertheless, talking for talking's sake has no place in fiction. There should be some purpose in each spoken exchange in your novel, even if, at the very least, it is only to reveal what sort of person the speaker is. (This is even more important in a short story, where there is less "elbow room.")

Carefully written dialogue can build up tension much more quickly than prose because the reader is sharing the experience with the character rather than with the narrator. This identification between reader and character makes the mounting anxiety, tingling spine, and sinking feeling in the pit of the stomach more realistic than the same idea delivered by the omniscient but necessarily impersonal author as narrator.

There is another bonus in using dialogue to convey action and emotion: Both can be shown to the reader through the words of more than one character. There is inevitably only one narrator: Any number of dimensions can be introduced through dialogue.

There are, though, traps for the unwary in writing dialogue. One of these is the use of dialect. Dialect is very difficult to handle successfully

218

and in my view should be used as sparingly as salt. Very few touches will usually suffice to convey the effect of strictly local or regional speech. Too much dialect almost automatically restricts your readership to the limited number of persons who can understand it. It is also extraordinarily difficult to convey dialect accurately solely by the use of phonetic spelling. In addition, many readers are put off by dialect in fiction, because they find it irritating; very, very few people read a novel for its dialect. I think that for the most part dialect should be heard and not written.

Another pitfall to keep in mind is that some puns or plays on words are aural rather than visual and are therefore unsuitable for the written page. Splendid confusion was caused in a book by D. E. Stevenson by the almost identical sound of "The County Surveyor" and "The Countess of Ayr," and the natural excitement in one by British novelist Danford Yates was heightened by the French word "ici" being mistaken for the initials "E.C." These authors were masters of their craft, but in general, writers should treat with great care the temptation to use verbal humor in a medium designed for the eye.

It is not possible to isolate entirely the dialogue in fiction from that in two other forms—the stage play and the radio play—but it is important both to contrast and compare all three. Words used on the stage have the added force of being delivered live by an actor whom the audience can see and hear in a setting relevant to the action. Words used in a radio play (sometimes described as "a stage play for a blind man") are emphasized by having the tonal contrast of human voices spoken by trained actors, aided by appropriate sound effects to suggest the background.

In the stage play, body language, a gesture, or a pause or inflection reinforces what is said. Words on the printed page have to create their own atmosphere in the imagination of the reader, unaided by any of these adjuncts.

This may sometimes lead the author to believe that the adverb is the most important weapon in his armory. Do be careful about this. Some things are not suitable for this purpose, as, for instance, " 'I must operate at once,' said the surgeon incisively," or " 'Give me that gun,' said the policeman disarmingly." Adverbs must be considered carefully for their appropriateness. Had the novel been well established in

Jonathan Swift's day, I think he would have extended to adverbs his proposal to keep all adjectives under lock and key and issue them to writers only on request on payment of a heavy fee!

If you remain in doubt about this, I suggest that you study the transcripts of examinations and cross-examinations in the Famous Trials series—or, indeed, in any court proceedings. There are never any adverbs recorded in these, and yet, there are few more gripping exchanges to be read. Such reading reinforces the view that there is nothing inherently wrong in using "he said" and "she said."

Good dialogue needs no adverbial embellishment, but, in my opinion, some of the alternatives to such modifiers do merit exploration. For example, short descriptions of mannerisms of the character speaking can be just as effective. So can the building up of the rhythm of an exchange of dialogue: We all know how satisfying good conversation is in real life. It should be so in your writing, without, of course, attempting to reproduce everyday talk verbatim. Actual human speech will seem very strange in print. A hidden tape recorder will reveal how inconsequential and mundane much daily conversation often is.

So let your fictional people speak for themselves in a way that is always in character for *them,* with as little intrusion from you, the author, as possible.

Make it apparent to your readers who is speaking, from *what* is said and *how* it is said.

Be sure that the dialogue you write in your fiction has a definite purpose in the story. Be sure, in fact, that it says it all.

45

TEN STEPS TO TOTAL TERROR

By William Schoell

THE FULL-LENGTH HORROR FICTION market is stronger today than
ever. Most publishers will at least consider horror novels, and there are
even a few firms whose lists consist almost entirely of works in the
genre. Naturally, the competition is fierce. It is advisable to be a fan of
the genre before attempting to write horror material. Read the work of
as many different authors as possible. Then take these "ten steps to
total terror." You may find that your manuscript has a better chance of
attracting the attention of an editor.

Step One: *Getting ideas*
   While it may be true that it isn't so much the idea that counts as what
you do with it, a truly original or striking premise is certainly a plus.
Many writers create fantastic, behind-the-scenes explanations for true
historical incidents, "solve" such puzzles as the Bermuda Triangle or
the Easter Island statues, or work up new variations on old legends,
such as the Loch Ness Monster or mythological gods. The more you
read about history and other, perhaps ancient, cultures, the more ideas
you'll get. There are still plenty of primitive deities who have not yet
"starred" in a horror novel, and many bizarre, lost cultures that have
yet to be fully explored.
   Ideas can come from many sources. A nightmare I had about a
sinister island led to my novel *Late at Night*. *Spawn of Hell* was
inspired by all the then-current talk of recombinant DNA research, and
Shivers came from a long wait for a train at a spooky subway station in
Brooklyn.

Step Two: *Choose your category*
   Or make up your own. There's more to horror than the supernatural.
You can chill your readers with mythical or modern-day monsters,

raging beasts, prehistoric creatures, or malevolent insects. The creepier the better. Although there have been "straight" horror novels featuring the most outlandish, even comical, beasties imaginable, whatever monster you come up with should be reasonably plausible and decidedly sinister.

Psychological terror—mad slashers on the loose; protagonists who are slowly being driven crazy; serial killers with macabre M.O.'s—has its own rules. The world your story operates in must be less fantastic, more rational, than one of far-fetched fifty-foot behemoths. You have much more leeway than in a straight mystery or detective story, but you still must play fair with the reader. Contemporary shockers of this type provide in-depth motives and backgrounds for their psychotic killers and tend to make them more three-dimensional than they used to be.

Medical horror, which derives its scares from current or speculative science, requires authentic-sounding details: Everything from hospital operating procedures to the more bizarre kind of medical experiments must at least *sound* convincing, or the story will collapse.

Step Three: *Putting your plot together*

First ask yourself if your idea will really work best full-length or as a short story. Long, drawn out, padded tales devoid of suspense or surprise will not do much to galvanize an editor. Try *combining* several ideas as I did in *Bride of Satan*. I knew I wanted to deal with the current controversy over graphic violence in horror films, but I was also itching to write a wild tale about a cult of sinister nuns. Another idea I had on my note pad was about a train whose passengers disappear overnight. By putting these three ideas together, I came up with an admittedly convoluted but bizarre novel that was more interesting than it would have been had I developed only one of those premises.

Instead of writing the umpteenth story about a modern-day vampire loose in Los Angeles, look through your notes and plot ideas, and try to come up with something different: a vampiric rock star who heads a cult of snake worshippers; a shape-changing vampire that assumes the form of everyone's ideal love mate, but actually resembles a larva. All of his victims become zombies who terrorize the city.

Robert R. McCammon combined the legend of the Amazons with his basic "small town with a dread secret" premise and came up with the unusual *Bethany's Sin*. In her novel *The Portent*, Marilyn Harris went a step beyond the usual nature-runs-amok story line and made our planet—nature itself—the villain instead of the usual outsized flora and fauna.

Step Four: *Streamlining*

Once you've chosen your ideas and blended them into a strong, multi-faceted plot line, it's important to work up a very smooth outline or synopsis. There is nothing more damaging than trying to make your novel make sense *after the fact,* hastily inserting bits and pieces that speciously explain the loose ends. Work out as many of the details as possible in advance. Are you getting as much out of your idea as you can, or are you missing opportunities? Don't just throw in a scene because it sounds exciting—it has to *fit.*

The outline should be the place where you try out, reject, or incorporate different scenarios. You can't have a scene in which your monster attacks your hero in broad daylight when you've already established that the beast is strictly nocturnal. If you're going to have this sequence, you'd better have a good explanation for *why* and *how* the monster has suddenly changed its habits. It will save you a lot of time scrabbling for answers and doing much rewriting later on.

Step Five: *Your characters' haunted pasts*

While there is a danger of overdoing this, it is wise to strengthen your characters by giving them backgrounds that may relate—or contrast— to the main story line. A hero who simply happens upon some weird conspiracy, demonic cult, or raging monster is less interesting than someone who has led a strange life to begin with. It can also help suspend disbelief in both your characters and your readers. It might be interesting to read about a grizzled trapper hunting down Big Foot in the mountains. But suppose the protagonist is a chic, urban newswoman who's hardly set foot out of Manhattan before? And suppose her parents were killed years ago on a camping trip—by Big Foot? This adds intensity and immediacy to your story.

Characters in horror novels are often haunted, shattered individuals who find strength by overcoming adversity, or are more susceptible to the call of the unknown because of their unstable mental states, illness, grief, or despair. The horror novel *does* present a dark view of the

223

world. Puerile, happy-go-lucky types in such settings can be jarring and unbelievable.

Step Six: *Style*

While the style of your novel may not affect whether it winds up in hardcover or paperback, as many believe, it should be suited to your story line and your ability. Stephen King and other writers have helped create a kind of "literary" horror, a blend of horror and mainstream in which plot and characters can sometimes stand on their own even without horrific overtones. These stories often encompass a more subtle kind of psychological horror that only hints at unseen evils.

"Pulp" horror is more visceral, graphic, and may have strong sexual undercurrents. This doesn't necessarily mean the characters are cardboard, but that the author is mainly out to jolt the readers at regular intervals rather than delve deeply into his or her characters' backgrounds and motivations. Some novels are a combination of literary and pulp.

Whatever style you decide to write in, there's more to consider than your command of the English language. If you have a strong, convoluted plot with twists and turns and lots of grisly action, the pulp style may work best. If the book is more thoughtful than "active," if the plot proceeds slowly and is supported mostly by characterization and atmosphere (as in T.E.D. Klein's absorbing *The Ceremonies*), the "literary" style may be required.

In any case, remember this: An unpublished writer should *get right into things*. This doesn't mean that you should have a murder in the first paragraph and twenty-five people dead by the end of chapter one, but you must write opening pages that will grip an editor. Stephen King can build slowly to his horror because readers know he'll get to it eventually, and they can look forward to it; but the same patience is not, unfortunately, accorded to the work of a neophyte. It might also help to keep early chapters short and to end each one with a hook or cliffhanger.

Step Seven: *The gore question*

While there isn't the controversy surrounding graphic violence in novels as there is in films, there's always the question of how much is too much. Hints of evil, lurking presences and mere intimations of violence can be quite effective in some types of books, but there's always a danger of losing the reader who is accustomed to more blatant gruesomeness. Horror writing should be vivid, and that means not *too* squeamish. Let your style and plot dictate how graphic your violence should be. It might be best to have a mixture of raw shocks with a more subtle sense of creeping menace. In any case, there'll always be an editor who prefers gore over subtlety, and vice versa, so you're pretty safe no matter what route you travel.

Step Eight: *Research*

After developing your synopsis, sit down and draw up a research list, including anything you're not personally familiar with. You can simplify matters, at least in your first attempt, by setting your story in the city where you live, or a variation of the town where you grew up. Your protagonist can have the same job that you or one of your friends or relatives has. Avoid setting the whole story in countries and time periods that are foreign to you.

Atmosphere is essential to a horror story, so you must be able to describe what your haunted house looks like, the flora and fauna in your monster-infested jungle, the inside of the sewer where your maniac brings his victims. Furthermore, you may have to become familiar with new terms and tools so you can add convincing details. Don't put *everything* you learn into your story; use only what you need. You're writing a book, not a lecture.

As work on your book progresses, you may find you don't have to spend nearly as much time in the library as you thought. What you'll need primarily are bits and pieces to lend veracity to your story. Don't use plot lines that you could not possibly tackle until you become a virtual *expert* in some subject.

Step Nine: *Writing it*

Make a schedule and stick to it. Write the rough draft at your own pace, and plan to have it completed in a reasonable and realistic amount of time for you. Set it aside long enough to allow you to look at what you've written objectively, from a fresh perspective. I cannot emphasize enough the importance of going through the rough draft slowly and carefully, to smooth over trouble spots, polish the writing, revise weak sections, and add more research and details where required. Make your manuscript as strong as it possibly can be.

While you're writing, minor characters and details about these characters or places will crop up. Jot these and any other nagging questions down on another piece of paper as you go along. You can tackle these problems and clear up any small details later on, or go back over the rough draft filling in and revising as necessary.

Step Ten: *Marketing*

Beginning writers can sell to this popular market without using an agent. Take note of the publishers of horror novels that you see in bookstores or libraries, and submit queries to them, and sample chapters if requested, before you send the whole book. However, until you've sold several books, it is unlikely that a publisher will go to contract on anything less than a complete manuscript.

Hardcover sales are always possible, but a beginner's best chances are in mass market paperback. Some ideas—marauding giant blobs, for instance—are simply too trivial to be published in hardcover (though there are always exceptions). Paperback publishers tend to go in for "pulp" horror but also bring out "literary" horror novels on occasion. Don't expect to get rich immediately. Advances for beginners start in the low four figures, or a publisher may even offer to buy your book outright. Always aim for a royalty contract!

The strength of the horror genre in the publishing world ebbs and flows, but it has an enduring popularity. If you have a feel for the quiet chill of the out-of-place footfall, the monstrous horror of the rampaging carnivore, perhaps you can get that big break by taking a few easy steps toward terror.

46

SOME PROBLEMS FOR THE HISTORICAL NOVELIST

By Laurie McBain

THE KEY TO A SUCCESSFUL NOVEL is to capture and hold the interest of the reader till the last page, whether you want to write contemporary, historical, fantasy-adventure, or science fiction. Each of these types of novel presents its own special problems for a writer.

Since I write historical novels, I can discuss only the problems I have faced in setting my stories in the past rather than in the present.

How do you work historical facts into a novel so that the reader absorbs the history while primarily enjoying the story?

How do you know when to work historical facts into the story?

How do you get the reader to identify with and feel for a character living in another century?

How do you overcome these obstacles while keeping the action moving forward, the characters interesting, and the plot intriguing and credible?

Prologues, epilogues, and the beginnings of chapters offer the writer the best opportunity for descriptive narrative, including passages full of historical detail to help create the right atmosphere. But, all too often, just when you think you have to insert some details, you find yourself right in the middle of a chapter, in the heart of an exciting action sequence, or a vital exchange of dialogue. You can't stop the momentum to describe some event or object, even though it may affect your plot or add necessary historical color.

What you can do is let your characters do some of the work for you. To convince the reader that these people of your imagination might actually have lived, you must have them experience real-life experiences, react to and be affected by the conditions prevalent at the time the novel takes place. By doing so, you will make your readers feel they know and can understand them.

In one of my novels, I had an English country-woman tell how to make mead, but did not list the ingredients and measurements and give step-by-step directions. In her own words, Mrs. Taylor explains how she'll go about making mead:

"I'll mix honey and ginger and a couple of handfuls of elder flowers in this pot of water and let it boil for an hour. Then, after it's been skimmed, I'll pour it into a tub and let it cool off so I can add the yeast . . . best thing around on a warm afternoon when you're bone-weary and parched with thirst . . ."

Thus, the reader knows exactly what mead is and what a person living in 18th-century England might drink on a warm afternoon.

To reveal attributes of an Elizabethan gentlewoman as well as set up a scene of confrontation between two women in my novel *Wild Bells to the Wild Sky,* I had a meddlesome, snobbish woman declare grandly:

". . . a woman must be well accomplished in all of the skills and graces of being a lady and a gentleman's wife. . . . Her reputation must be beyond question, her deportment never faulted. She would, of course, be an accomplished needle-woman, well versed in the art of lace-making, silk-spinning, and fine embroidery. For entertaining, she would indeed have to be a competent singer and musician, well skilled with lute, and virginal. But, most important, she should have a working knowledge of the household, for she would be required to handle the affairs of the family and staff at all times. . . ."

The reader now understands some of the demands made on a woman of "good family" in 16th-century England. However, the information was conveyed to the reader in the form of dialogue filled with undercurrents directed at the heroine by her rival.

In *When The Splendor Falls,* a novel set during the American Civil War, I had a scene in which the heroine, Leigh Travers, is looking through a blanket chest. Touching various items belonging to family members—a pair of gauntlet gloves and slouch hat, a packet of letters, a sketch book—she remembers the long years of the war and its devastating effect on her family. Until this point in the novel, the reader has not known what fate has befallen members of the Travers family. All of these characters were introduced earlier in the novel when the family lived an idyllic life at Travers Hill, their Virginia farm. Leigh holds a fringed officer's sash and the reader now learns of her brother's death, and also about one of the many battles of the war—a skirmish in the Shenandoah Valley, during the Romney Campaign when the brother rode with Stonewall Jackson. Leigh glances at a letter, and the reader remembers the laughter-loving sister who wrote it and the halcyon days that are no more, and also learns about life in the Confederate capital of Richmond during the war.

In another scene in *When The Splendor Falls,* I had a group of Union raiders become trapped behind Confederate lines. It is winter, and they are holed up in the stables at Travers Hill. Cold, tired, and frightened, these Yankees face almost insurmountable odds as Rebel troops close in around them. How do you bring this scene to life so the reader will feel the tension of their predicament and care what happens to them?

As these men sit huddled together in the stables, I have them going through their haversacks and finding comfort in personal belongings. One soldier looks at a treasured daguerreotype of a loved one; another thumbs through his New England *Almanac,* wondering if he'll be home in time for the spring planting; a couple of others play poker with a set of Miss Liberty playing cards, while another soldier stares down at the theater tickets for a performance he'll never attend. Then I have the reader see these men through Leigh Travers' eyes. She has discovered them in the stables. Although embittered, she tends to their wounds. Listening to them talk and joke, seeing the pain and suffering on youthful faces, she is reminded of her own brothers, and she cannot betray them.

Not only has this provided historical color and atmosphere, but this approach has now fleshed out the characters and advanced the story. The reader will respond and identify with these fictional people, who have become more than cardboard cut-outs. Their triumphs and tragedies become the readers', who will laugh with them and cry with them, and wait anxiously to find out what will happen next in their lives.

In *Tears of Gold,* my novel about Gold Rush California, I wanted the reader to appreciate fully the dangers and difficulties encountered in reaching those golden shores. I had to show the three routes the adventurers, prospectors, and settlers chose to reach California. To work that information into the story without making it sound like a history textbook, I had each of the three main characters travel by a different one of the perilous routes. The heroine and her family sailed around Cape Horn by clipper; the hero crossed the Isthmus of Panama, traveling up the Chagres River through mosquito-infested jungle, before catching a coastal steamer to San Francisco; a third character came by

229

wagon train across the plains, mountains, and deserts of the continental United States. Each route was described through the experiences of the characters. The reader shared these experiences and gained a keener insight into the lives of these people.

When is the proper time to insert historical detail? To guide you in deciding when you need historical description, ask yourself exactly *what* the reader needs to know. What is the focal point of the scene?

At the beginning of *Tears of Gold,* when my heroine, Mara O'Flynn, was traveling to California, I described the voyage around Cape Horn this way:

It had taken them two weeks to round the Horn, their sails furled as they struggled against the head winds and through the cross seas, the ocean surging into the ship as heavy swells broke over the bow . . .

Later in the story, however, when the heroine sails from San Francisco, en route to New Orleans, I did not need to describe the voyage back around Cape Horn in detail. This time I wrote, ". . . they sailed southward toward the tip of South America and the passage around Cape Horn that Mara dreaded even worse than the first time, for now she knew what she could expect. . . ." So does the reader.

At a point like this in your story, you might want to make use of a condensed description, or one more poetic than detailed. The reader already knows about close-reefed sails and the lee lurch of a ship in heavy seas. Once again, ask yourself, what is the focus of the scene? What is the importance of it? What purpose does it serve?

In *Wild Bells to the Wild Sky,* I described a sea voyage this way:

The *Madrigal*'s sails had seemed to sing, catching the wind and billowing with a thundering song. The curving sheets of canvas had been burnished by the sun from dawn till dusk, while shimmering sea had stretched as far as the eye could see.

The focal point of this scene is not the voyage, but what will happen to the characters at the end of it. The scene serves merely to bring the characters safely back to England and to give the reader a feeling of the triumphant destiny that awaited some—and the deadly reckoning that awaited others.

Wild Bells to the Wild Sky begins when the heroine, Lily Christian, is only six years old. The ship she is sailing on is sunk during a battle at

230

sea, and she is stranded, along with members of her family, on an uninhabited island in the Caribbean. The focal point of the story, however, is Lily's life a decade later, after she has been rescued and returned to England. And yet, the reader will want to know something about the heroine's life on the island. But does the reader need a day-to-day account of what took place in that ten-year period?

The reader learns about Lily's life on the island when I bring her back into the story at the age of thirteen. Sitting beneath a scrubby pine, Lily remembers:

> . . . Basil kept a careful record of the passing days. He always knew exactly how long they had been on the island. He had even set up a sun dial to tell them the time of the day. Although stranded in the wilderness, they could continue to live as civilized human beings, he declared, causing them to giggle because he was standing barefoot before them as he said it . . . Up at dawn, hunting and fishing for the day's food, lessons, then a few hours to do as one pleased, then sunset. . . .

So, through Lily's recollections, the reader learns the fate of the castaways and how they managed to survive. The reader's curiosity has been satisfied and the momentum of the story has not been slowed.

Why will readers care what happens in your novel? You have to establish a bond of understanding and sympathy between the reader and your characters. This bond of sharing is how the characters become real, and why the reader will care about those characters and what happens on the final page.

But how does a writer make them real? Your characters are reacting to a period in history. They are living it. By working the historical details into the very fabric of their lives, by having the characters aware of what is happening around them and influencing their lives, you are making them real. These characters respond to what concerns them, whether in Elizabethan England, Gold Rush California, or Civil War Virginia, in the same manner in which readers today react to what concerns them—emotionally.

The characters are also responding to each other. You have taken a period of history and filled it with people, most of them from your imagination. The hero and heroine don't exist alone; they respond and react to the other characters that you have created. That is why I try to fill my fictional worlds with an assortment of characters from every walk of life: the innocent bystander, the best friend, the serving maid,

231

the hot-headed young brother, the garrulous innkeeper, the inquisitive neighbor, and countless others. These secondary characters watch and listen and become involved in the exciting lives of the heroes and heroines. Readers, who can't always relate to the hero and the heroine, or understand what they are feeling or the emotions we as writers wish them to experience, do so through the eyes of these other characters. In this way, they can recall and relive similar incidents in their own lives.

Secondary characters also provide an excellent opportunity for integrating historical detail into the story in a credible manner. The unperturbable butler knows far more about the household affairs on an English estate than the grand duchess or fashionable lord he serves, and the reader, following in the butler's footsteps as he goes about his duties, will, too. An old soldier's reminiscences to a group of impressionable young military officers allows for a colorful and exciting firsthand account of a significant battle in which historical information is related to the reader.

The problems encountered in trying to bring another period of history to life are what I find intriguing and challenging in writing the historical novel, which, according to Webster's, is ". . . based on or suggested by people or events of the past. . . ." Those are the factors that should be influencing the characters, plot, and atmosphere of your novel. How successful you are in recreating history and in capturing the imagination of your readers—to the extent that they believe they are part of another century and share the experiences of the characters— will ultimately determine the credibility and readability of your novel.

47

THE FIRST PERSON AT THE SCENE OF THE CRIME

By William G. Tapply

When I began scribbling on my first mystery, I knew something wasn't working. I had all the scenes down: the beautiful girl discovers the corpse washed up on the beach, the salty detective arrives on the scene, the mild-mannered pathologist performs the autopsy to determine the cause and manner of death, the family lawyer investigates. But taken together, the scenes lacked coherence.

I was plagued, I finally realized, by a typical novice's problem—the wandering point of view. I hadn't decided whose story it was, and I hadn't settled on a voice with which to tell it.

When I created Brady Coyne, my Boston-based lawyer/sleuth, and allowed him to tell the story, it began to come to life. His first tale, *Death at Charity's Point,* became my first published novel. Three others have followed. Brady has served me well. He allows me to present and withhold clues at will, putting my readers into the position of participating in the story almost as if they were the sleuths. The focus is sharp and clear. Readers know only what Coyne tells them. They are encouraged to outguess him. They know whose story it is.

A magical sort of reader-narrator bonding occurs with the first-person storyteller that is generally absent with the more remote third-person narrator, provided the narrator/sleuth fulfills certain requirements.

He must wear well. Readers must like, trust, and respect him. They must care about him, root for him to succeed. He must have an appealing and unique voice, a voice that doesn't call attention to itself too blatantly, but is neither bland nor boring. At best, it will be conversational. The first-person narrator speaks to his readers as a friend, up close.

Readers should be able to identify with the narrator, who may be strong, admirable, even a hero—but never larger than life. He must be

233

fully drawn, multi-dimensional. He should have expertise, speak authoritatively. But nobody likes a know-it-all.

The narrator must have credible motivations. An occupation such as private investigator, policeman, or reporter easily places him in the center of mysteries, and for an immediately understood reason: It's his job, and he gets paid for it. At the same time, there ought to be a twist to that job. My Brady Coyne is a lawyer. Conventional enough, but he specializes in the legal affairs of the very rich. He is willing to do things for his clients that other lawyers might refuse, because he emphasizes personal service and discretion in his practice. As he says, "I spend very little of my time arguing interesting points of law in courtrooms. I work on retainer plus fees. Generous fees. Outrageous fees, really." For this, he does what his clients ask him to do, even if it isn't, strictly speaking, legal work.

It serves my purpose. It gives him stories to tell.

For all the appeal of the first-person narrator, the budding mystery writer should understand the peculiar plotting problems this approach creates.

The narrator must be present at the scene of the crime much of the time, and he must be there for believable reasons. He must observe events firsthand. Things must happen to him. The writer's task is to put his narrator on the scene without contrivance. Readers must know and accept the reasons he's there. Because the narrator is more than an observer. He is a participant in events.

Sometimes this is neither possible nor even desirable. Readers will not accept the likelihood of the sleuth always being where the action is, and for mystery to be sustained, important events must sometimes occur offstage. One way to solve this problem is to have the narrator reconstruct events as he imagines them to have happened. This is both straightforward and effective. For example, when Brady Coyne decides to tell readers about the suicide of a character years earlier, he says "I have imagined what Dud did then." To reinforce it, the next paragraph begins, "I can still see Dud in my mind's eye, striding down the hallway . . ." *The Dutch Blue Error* begins with a five-page prologue written in the third person. Then Brady's first-person voice informs the reader, "That is how I imagined it happened. Of course, I wasn't there." This technique allows the narrator to be absent from some scenes he describes. It also invites readers to read on and to challenge the narrator's version of things.

Because he can't be everywhere at once, the narrator will, of necessity, learn some things secondhand—typically, via conversation. Beware. The writer risks the twin disasters of boredom and contrivance. In an early chapter of *Death at Charity's Point,* Brady Coyne must learn a number of technical details about a dead body. He goes to the office of Dr. Clapp, the pathologist who performed the autopsy. Despite the inherent appeal of the gory details, the scene could easily founder on a routine question-and-answer format. In many ways, it's the sort of scene made for the third person, putting the reader at the shoulder of the doctor as he cuts open the corpse. In a first-person format, this immediacy is not possible. One way or the other, Coyne has to ask questions, and the doctor has to answer them.

The trick in sustaining reader interest in what amounted to a lengthy conversation between two men sitting in an office was to give Dr. Clapp an interesting and authoritative voice, to have Coyne ask the right questions (the very questions the reader would want to ask), and to interject some grisly wit and human dimensions into the scene. Readers must not view Dr. Clapp as simply a vehicle for conveying information, even if he never appears in the story again. Offbeat details can sustain readers through such scenes. For example, in this case Coyne, a heavy smoker, notices on the doctor's desk "a large glass jar. Inside it, a dark grayish mass swam in a yellowish solution. It looked like a big, dirty jellyfish. Dr. Clapp followed my gaze. 'A smoker's lung,' he said. 'I keep it as a reminder. Better than will power.' "

But too many telephone conversations, too many discussions over lunch (regardless of how appetizingly described), or too many meetings (no matter how colorful the locations) will quickly wear thin. Readers want action, and they want the storyteller in the middle of it.

The suspense of the story will be sustained as long as readers feel they know as much as—but not more than—the narrator. A mistake I made in the early versions of my first novel, in my misguided effort to "be fair" to my readers, was to leave too many obvious clues scattered across the landscape, which Coyne dutifully reported to his readers but stupidly failed to recognize as significant. Readers of these flawed drafts rightfully complained that they had the mystery solved long before

Coyne did, and had lost respect for my narrator/detective in the process—both unpardonable sins for suspense writing.

There comes a time in most mysteries when the narrator/sleuth holds in his hand the last piece to the puzzle. He thinks he's solved the mystery. It's time to confront the criminal. This is the one time in the mystery story when the narrator can legitimately manipulate his readers. He cannot spoil the climax for his readers by revealing what he knows. What does he do? In effect, he tells them, "Now I think I know. But I'm not going to tell you. Not yet. Just come along with me and watch what happens next."

In *The Dutch Blue Error,* Coyne gets that last puzzle piece over the phone. It would destroy all suspense for him to report that conversation verbatim to his readers. So instead, he says:

"As Schwartz talked I jotted notes onto a yellow legal pad. He talked for fifteen minutes or more in that precise diction of his. My mind swirled with possibilities. I underlined several words on my notepad, drew arrows from this point to that, punctuated some of Schwartz's bits of information with question marks and exclamation points."

Do readers object to being maneuvered this way by the narrator they have come to trust? Do they think it unfair that Coyne refuses to report immediately what Schwartz tells him? Not at all. Mystery readers want to guess, and then read on to see if they've guessed correctly. And they secretly hope they haven't. Readers want to be surprised. In surprise comes delight.

Because the burden of sustaining reader interest falls entirely on the shoulders of the narrator, he must grow and change, within a single book, and through a series. He continues to reveal new dimensions of himself. Subplots related to his personal life accomplish this. So does a setting richly populated with a variety of minor but interesting characters, who are foils for the narrator and who reappear in each of his adventures. Brady Coyne regularly falls in and out of love, to the bemusement of Julie, his secretary, whose challenge is to teach her boss a few things about women. Coyne has an ex-wife and two almost-grown sons whom he adores but resists getting close to. He goes fishing and plays golf with his Yale Law School chum Charlie McDevitt, who has a fondness for shaggy dog stories. He exchanges gibes, and tests his liberalism, with Xerxes Garrett, a young black lawyer.

236

It is Coyne's interactions with these permanent members of the cast, perhaps as much as the mystery he's trying to solve, that prompt readers to ask the question this writer hopes they will ask: "I wonder what's going to happen to Brady next?"

In the course of pursuing a mystery, the first-person narrator will get into scrapes. When he's at the center of the action, as he must often be, he will find himself in danger. Readers want this. Brady Coyne has been kicked in the (to put it euphemistically) groin. He's been drugged with chloroform, shot in the thigh ("There'd be an unsightly scar to mar the classic beauty of my leg"), smashed over the head with the barrel of a shotgun, and stabbed in the arm with a pickle spear.

That the narrator will escape from these brushes with death is never in doubt, of course, and it would be an error for him to tell his story as if it were otherwise. Readers know he has lived to tell it, and they will resent his efforts to create suspense where it cannot exist. The suspense for mystery readers lies in wondering how he's going to escape. This is quite enough.

If you want to write mystery fiction, start by creating your sleuth. Give him a unique voice and let him tell your story. Imagine his life fully. Populate it with minor characters, also fully imagined. Give him a job with built-in motivation to pursue mysteries. There's no better motivation than fat fees. Then give him a problem, and allow him to grapple with it.

And while you're at it, you might as well think big. Imagine a series of adventures. Editors and publishers think this way, so you should, too. Imagine a long shelf stacked with mystery books, all with your name on the spine. Because if your first one catches on, if your first-person narrator speaks beguilingly to your readers, they'll want more of him.

Just be sure to put him at the scene of the crime.

48

HOW TO KEEP THE READER TURNING THE PAGES

By L. R. Wright

A PROFESSIONAL WRITER IS—among other things—a writer who has found a way to work. But I want to emphasize at the outset that what works for some writers doesn't work for others. If what works for me doesn't help you one bit, that only means that you need to find a way of working that is not like mine.

So, with that proviso . . .

A novel that keeps its readers turning the pages probably first created that same kind of hungry curiosity in its writer, for writers write, just as readers read, in order to find out what happens next.

The trick—if there is one—is for the writer to believe so thoroughly in his characters and their situations that they are capable of surprising him.

I read a great deal, as all writers do, and I sometimes make bad choices, as all readers do. I occasionally find myself reading not very good books in which characters are threatened with the most dreadful fates, the most horrifying consequences, but I do not care, because these things are happening to people who have not convinced me of their reality. If I were to sneak around behind them, I would see that they're merely cutouts, existing in a single dimension. My attention flags, my mind wanders, I become impatient. I begin flicking through the pages quickly, and finally I throw the book aside.

But richly drawn characters absorb me into their lives. I feel, as I read about them, like a visitor who has been permitted to become invisible; I have been given the keys to all the rooms in the house and am now courteously ignored while other people's lives swirl about me, and I am free to watch and listen, to become absorbed and involved.

The first and the most important thing, then, are the people, fictional yet real, through whom you tell your tale.

For it is, in fact, a joint effort. You get them going, send them on their way, and then with great care, you follow them and tell their stories.

But there is nothing supernatural about being an author. Characters do not appear out of the ozone layer and whisper in our ears. We make them up, we fashion their lives, we engineer their fate.

Yet it is true that the characters we create can and do surprise us. I'll give you some examples.

In my first book, called *Neighbours,* there is a chapter in which the central character, a somewhat deranged, but at that point only mildly frightening person called "Betty," is being visited by a cat. She shows the animal around her house, following it through various rooms. When I wrote the chapter I had just taken them through Betty's bedroom when I found myself typing: "The cat didn't see all of her things, of course. She saw no reason to show him everything. He probably wouldn't have been interested, anyway, she thought. Not in my tools."

I stopped, amazed. I said to my typewriter, "Her 'tools'? *What* 'tools'?"

The same thing occurred in the first chapter of my fourth novel—and my first mystery—*The Suspect*. I got to the end of the chapter (in which George Wilcox murders a man named Carlyle Burke) and saw that I had written as the last sentence: "It wasn't until he had washed off the shell casing and put it on his living room windowsill with its mate, changed his clothes, and put the kettle on for tea that he suddenly remembered Carlyle's goddamn parrot."

I hadn't known, until then, that Carlyle *had* a parrot.

Writing is something like acting. In order to make a character live, the author has to *become* that character. You sit at the typewriter (or the word processor, or at the kitchen table clutching your pencil) and you pretend that you're somebody else. At least that's how I do it, in the early stages of writing a novel. It's the only way I can get to know these people as well as I have to know them.

So make your characters real by fusing them to you so solidly that when you speak *for* them, you speak *as* them, thereby leaving the door wide open for them to surprise you.

But there are some technical things at work here, too. Most how-to-write books will tell you that each chapter should end with a "hook," and that's good advice. The hook doesn't have to be a cataclysmic

239

event, however. It's just something that creates a specific curiosity about the characters and what is going to happen next. But this curiosity can be mild indeed. For example, returning for a moment to *The Suspect,* what possible difference can it make to George Wilcox, whom we already know to be a murderer, that his victim had a pet bird? When I got to that point I stopped work for the day, because I was so delighted to have been "hooked." Now I had to keep on writing in order to find out why the parrot was important. It gave me a starting place for the next day's work.

There's not much difference between writing a mystery and writing a mainstream novel. People read both—and write both—in order to find out what happens in the lives of the characters who populate the book. But a mystery does have some particular requirements. When I decided that *The Suspect* was to be a mystery, I had to stop for a while to assess my responsibilities as a writer from a slightly different point of view. There are unwritten (actually they're probably written, somewhere) rules about mysteries—established, perhaps, by readers but agreed to by writers, too. I didn't want to break the rules. But I liked George, even though he had killed someone, and I didn't want him to go to prison. I liked the policeman, too, and I didn't want him to be or appear to be stupid, which meant that he had to somehow solve the mystery without being able to arrest George. It was a dilemma that could be resolved only by the characters themselves. Things had to happen strictly in accordance with the natures of the people in the story. And there was only one way that I could find out how the dilemma would be resolved, and that was to write the book.

There comes a time in the writing of every novel, whether it's a mystery or not, when I stop and look carefully at what I've written to see if I can figure out where I'm going. It usually happens after about one hundred pages. By then the characters are firmly established; I am confident that I can put them into any situation and know how they would react. By then there is at least some semblance of plot—sometimes not much more than a semblance, though. It's at this point that I attempt to work out the logical consequences of the events about which I've written so far, and the logical reactions of my characters to these consequences. I hesitate to call this activity "plotting," since it's so sketchy and tentative, but I guess that's what it is.

And although it's never possible, even while I'm "plotting," to manufacture hooks for the ends of chapters, it is obviously possible to decide to end a chapter at the place where the flow of the story has naturally produced a hook.

For example, in my novel, *Love in the Temperate Zone,* the elderly father of one of the protagonists disappears. His son, Casey, is frantically worried, and not much less so when he begins receiving postcards from a glum and restless parent who writes that he is aimlessly traveling the continent on a succession of Greyhound buses. I knew that the father (Donald) was eventually going to show up on Casey's doorstep. But I deliberately didn't decide *when* this would happen; the idea stayed in my mind, hovering, waiting for the right moment, and finally delivered itself upon the page as the proverbial last straw, at the end of a chapter in which all sorts of bad things happen to poor Casey.

As fiction writers we walk a fine line between truth and fact: We must speak only truth, or people won't believe us; but we seldom deal in fact. We should also be walking, with our characters, the fine line that exists between authority and insurrection; between control and disorder. We have to be able to impose discipline upon ourselves and our characters, because without discipline, there is no control, and without control a manuscript is chaos. Yet we must always be ready to relinquish this control temporarily; we must always be eager to entertain disorder— temporarily.

Let your characters rebel, when they want to. Follow them, when they struggle to lead you away from wherever it is you think you want to go. Permit them to surprise you. Then stand back and have a look at what's happened to your story.

If you don't like it, strike it out and start over.

But if you're hooked . . . then your readers will be hooked.

49

PLOTTING ADVENTURE FICTION

By John Keeble

FIRST THE TRUTH—the demands of writing good adventure fiction are mainly the same as those for writing any kind of fiction. When one moves from one genre to another, though, certain elements seem to receive more emphasis. In the case of the adventure novel, the emphasis is upon a vigorously paced plot, and as a part of this, upon a test or series of tests that the protagonist must endure.

Adventure fiction is often set outdoors. Manifestations of the natural world—sandstorms, typhoons, precipitous mountain slopes, etc.—may cause some of the protagonist's hardship, but a warehouse, a city street, even an apartment, and certainly a war zone could serve equally well as the setting for an adventure tale. The important thing to remember here is that setting will become inextricably tied up with the story, that it will become an adversary, in a way, and that at some stage the writer will need to think of it as a part of plot.

There are three things—or principles, perhaps—that I've come to consider important about plot: plot is thought; it is rhythmical; and it will call the characters into action. Stated this way, the principles might seem a little abstract, but I'll take them up in order and try to explain what I mean by each.

I've listed first the notion that plot is thought because I don't think a book truly gets underway until the writer begins to think systematically about action. I will have begun to write the novel before reaching that point, working out of a rough sense of who a few of my main characters are, what the book is to be about, what problems I want to spend a long time exploring.

In the case of my novel, *Yellowfish,* a book about the transportation of illegal aliens to the United States via Canada, I began with an interest in national boundaries. Like most good subjects, this one probably found me, since I am Canadian by birth and continue to live near the border. I was aware, of course, of several things about that border: that it was the longest ungarrisoned border in the world, that it was easy to cross—surreptitiously or otherwise—and that, like many borders, there was a certain arbitrariness to it. Vancouver and Seattle, for example, have more in common with each other than either has with Montreal or New York. It seemed to me that there was an intriguing historical irony here, one that placed nationality at odds with culture, and that this had resonances that went beyond the immediate subject. That is how I always start, with some such inviting rumination, and with a sense of character.

But of course once the writing begins, one must move on to concrete detail. Before I can get very far with that, I have to formulate at least one good question. With *Yellowfish,* it came to be this: So you're going to use the border. In fiction what does one do with a border? The answer to that was easy: Bring something across it. The next question was, what? This took some hard thought because the decision would affect my book in all of its detail. I discarded various types of contraband until I finally hit upon an idea that clicked—people, illegal aliens—far more interesting than a load of drugs or military hardware, and a great deal more likely to enrich the book.

I decided that the people would come from Hong Kong, which I knew in fact to be a source of illegal immigration, and which—happily—extended my initial preoccupation with national boundaries still farther. I decided that my protagonist, who was the "escort," would pick the people up in Vancouver. From there I was able to take the first really important step toward constructing the novel: to imagine an ending, a target toward which the book would be aimed.

My protagonist would have to deliver his passengers to San Francisco. There were details attached to this, of course, certain vivid images I held in my mind as I worked, and which changed form several times. There came to be many more twists on the initial situation than I had first thought possible, especially as the adversaries—those who did not wish my characters to reach San Francisco—began to emerge. Even the ending I'd imagined turned out instead to be the penultimate scene. The point, however, is that once I had set up a target for ending the book, I could structure the book by imagining a series of events that would lead to that end. I could attend to the causality and order that is required by any plot.

243

This involved thinking, which may sound patently obvious. I feel, though, that writers, including me, sometimes neglect the need to think systematically (or strategically) about their novels. Plot construction, especially, requires the writer to pull back periodically from the page-by-page work and carefully think through what happens in the book, how one thing leads to the next. But I do not outline. My opinion is that anything as mechanical as an outline, with its headings and sub-headings, is too much needless work in the first place and ultimately anti-thetical to good writing. Good writing is fluid and best left to seek its own directions.

I do make lists, though, and some time ago I was thunderstruck to hear novelist Diane Johnson say she also kept lists, that lists were actually a form of outline. Just so. By the time I've finished a book, I'll have lists everywhere—in my notebook, on scraps of paper, in the margins of the manuscript. What I like about lists is that they also are fluid, and tentative, even easily destroyed, lost, or neglected, and that they act as triggers rather than as prescriptions. The making of lists about what should happen, where, and when in the story, about facts I need to know, about causality and about things that connect, begins in earnest once I have an ending to the story. Such lists enter freely into the play of the writer's thinking, and a well-constructed plot, carefully attuned to its ending, is finally an intricate and complete system of thought.

In an adventure story, the ending not only defines all the events that precede it, but it should also exert a very strong pull on them. This is one source of pace, or of rhythm. The very best prose writers, I think, show a strong sense of rhythm in at least two ways—in the wording, the sentence and paragraph construction, and in the overall rhythm of the story. Much of a novel's impact upon the reader is felt by virtue of the rhythms of the writing.

Writers should listen to their sentences and feel the rhythms of the narrative as it moves forward on that level of detail. An adventure story, especially, needs to have a strong pulse. If the story is good to begin with, if it has been *thought through,* and if scenes are placed in a way that heightens suspense, much of this pulse will emerge as a matter of course. At certain points in the process of revision, however, I have found it useful to think of the book in terms of its basic units, which for me are usually chapters. For another writer, these units might be scenes. Or there may be several different types of units—scenes, chapters, groups of chapters.

What the writer wants, then, is for the units to rise like waves. Early in the novel each chapter will swell strongly, but terminate before the wave begins to show white. A wave that shows white is breaking its surface tension. For the sake of suspense, it's important in an adventure tale to hold the tension as long as possible. Later on, or in a particularly crucial early section, a line of white may appear, and then, of course, as the book moves to its conclusion, the wave will come nearer and nearer to breaking apart and crashing against the sand. This process—the sense of the large rhythm that runs through an adventure tale—is actually more complicated than I have described it here, because of subplots that may come to completion at various points in the novel. These are like smaller waves, rolling in more rapidly. These establish a counterpoint to the central, overriding pulse of the book.

The writer needs to feel the movement of the story, the rising pulse of each succeeding chapter. I know that I have a chapter (or scene, or dramatic unit) close to completion when I can work through it in one sitting without getting bogged down, and by bodily experiencing its movement. This is incidentally, one of the great pleasures of writing— the physical and emotional engagement. It is also one of the things that makes writing novels difficult—the toll that an extended project can take upon the body.

Since plot is so important to adventure fiction, it follows that the characters will be expressed in large part through action. They will be best understood in terms of what they do. I might insert here that I never considered myself a writer of adventure fiction until I was told so by my publisher and the reviewers, following the publication of *Yellowfish*. I have always been most concerned with ideas and politics, with the emotional life of the characters, and with language. But maybe I also knew that such concerns when overwrought could cause the reader to close the novel—the most dreaded of all effects.

An advantage of writing so-called adventure fiction is that as soon as the basic shape of the adventure is grasped, then the writer has the framework for creating a line of action. In *Yellowfish,* the characters travel from Vancouver to San Francisco by car. My subsequent novel, *Broken Ground,* which concerns the construction of a prison in the Oregon desert, had an equally inescapable (but more complicated)

245

"process" built into it. Once the writer builds the framework, he must respond to the necessities posed by the material—the route of the journey, for example, where stops are made, how long the stops are, who dies or gets hurt, and in any case, what hardships, tests, and opportunities for suspense the journey presents.

In addition, since most adventure fiction is "realistic," particular attention needs to be paid to accuracy, especially when real places and things are used. Remember that setting is tied up with the story, and that it often joins forces with adversary characters to work against the protagonist. Research may be required. Such accuracy lends credibility to the story and connects the world of the story to the world of its readers.

Even more important, the writer must respond honestly and cleanly to the deeper aspects of character—those traits, quirks, principles, and emotional qualities for each of them that become increasingly defined as the novel develops. The characters have been drawn outward through interaction with other characters. Also—and this is most critical—they will be drawn out by the demands of the fictional world in which they discover themselves. They will be changed by this world, and yet at the same time, even as they emerge, they must remain themselves.

The plot, or line of action, that has caught up the main characters and compelled them to act fills the story with detail, with movement, drama, and, not insignificantly, with moral substance. Because of its emphasis on action and conflict, adventure fiction always has a moral dimension. As the writer is drawn more and more deeply into the novel, dealing with all these problems can be challenging. This is where the lists come in again. By this time, however, as the characters and story have increasingly asserted themselves, an interesting thing has happened to those lists: Where once they were wish-lists, so to speak, or projections, they've become lists of things the writer must deal with. This is a sign that at last the writer, like the characters, has also been forced outward.

When the adventure tale starts to work well, it and the characters, who are delineated through action, take over. What was set in motion so long ago, what demanded all that systematic thinking, now proceeds on its own power. But there's a danger here, too. It's as if one had added garlic to stew. Left in long enough, the flavor pervades everything. It's too late to make certain changes. The writer has to keep thinking, and

246

be alert, and patient, but so far as I'm concerned, reaching this stage is the reason for writing—because of the sense of discovery, the exhilaration, and sometimes the strangeness of what those first ruminations have led to.

50

HOW DO YOU TELL A GOOD SCIENCE FICTION STORY?

BY SUSAN B. WESTON

LISTENING to Isaac Bashevis Singer on a radio program recently, I heard advice useful to any writer, but especially important to those of us writing science fiction and fantasy stories. If you sit down to send a message, Singer warned, you'll probably ruin your story; but if you sit down to tell a story, you might just send a message.

The temptation to preach seems particularly hard to resist for writers extrapolating futuristic stories from present situations. "Change your ways!" many science fiction writers seem to be shouting. "Repair this"—acid rain, the greenhouse effect, midwestern drought, the exhaustion of fossil fuels . . . you know the list. It includes any massive environmental change that would wreak social havoc. But of course the message—"Don't let this happen, or else!"—is implicit in the material. The novelist's job is to tell a good *story*.

How do you tell a good science fiction story?

Remember that familiar chestnut, "write about what you know"? It seems such sensible and obvious advice. After all, literature is a feat of realization—making real with words. How can you possibly realize what you *don't* know? Is it possible to write fully realized science fiction? But you must become a "literalist of the imagination," to quote from Marianne Moore's famous poem, "Poetry." In that poem, she also suggests that a good poet must be able to create "imaginary gardens with real toads in them."

The first step in my writing begins with that imaginary garden. When I write, those toads won't come to life until they're perched on palpable rocks and shaded by chlorophyll-producing leaves. I have to create a richly detailed and plausible setting, because my characters emerge from it, interact with it, are defined by it. For me, setting leads to character leads to plot.

248

My science fiction novel, *Children of the Light,* is set in a small midwestern farming community three generations after a nuclear war. I had done one kind of research, studying government documents and various books on the consequences of a limited nuclear war; now I had to turn abstract knowledge into reality that could be felt. To transport myself to that faltering future community, I did focused "imagination exercises." Everywhere I went and everything I did was dissociated from its context here and passed through the filter of that imagined future. In front of my suburban house, for instance, I walked on a sidewalk buckled from winter freezing; grass grew up in the cracks. Suppose no one repaired this concrete ever again? What would it look like twenty winters from now?

There'd be no electricity, of course, no fuel delivery. Anyone surviving the disaster would need to gather fuel. Perhaps the wooden houses would be dismantled for firewood. I imagined my house dismantled, the basement exposed to the elements, all the useless machines rusting. And my neighbors' houses, all dismantled. As I washed dishes or tossed clean laundry into the drier or removed a convenience food from the freezer, I'd think: Oh, no running water. No washing machine. No refrigeration.

For weeks, I did these preliminary exercises, trying to set my feet firmly on that future ground by continually rehearsing what would be altered in the daily routines of my own comfortable middle-class life. Though the characters were still an indistinct communal band, I was beginning to know them because I knew the hard ridge of callouses raised along their palms, their knotted shoulder muscles. I knew what they did all day long, and how, and where.

To individualize this raggedy malnourished crew, I rather arbitrarily assigned each character some distinctive physical trait. There was a dwarf with a big booming voice. A mute with a tremor. A sallow young woman with a strident infectious laugh. And so on. Their somewhat grotesque physical traits were useful to the reader as "identifying tags" that also served to emphasize the genetic and environmental damage these people had to cope with. Each distinctive trait became my starting point for more fully developing the character. When does the dwarf's voice shrink to fit his real size? Why does the mute get so excited about pictures of windmills and generators? What makes the sallow young woman laugh?

I wrote the novel from the third-person point of view, using an omniscient narrator for descriptions and transitions, and moving into the limited third person—inside someone else's head—to gain emotional immediacy and closeness. No matter whose point of view controlled any given scene, I made sure that everyone else in the scene was either interacting or sleeping. But sometimes a character threatened to remain a lifeless comic book figure, flattening out a scene or dulling the edge of a conversation. Then I resorted to "monologue exercises," rewriting the entire scene from that person's point of view.

The first-person monologue is a basic tool in characterization. It helps you hear a character's distinctive voice, imagine what it's like inside someone else's head, and walk the proverbial mile inside someone's ill-fitting shoes. If a monologue exercise failed to bring a recalcitrant character to life, I knew I had to delete that character from the story. When it succeeded, the mystery characters emerged from the shadows so vigorously that they often surprised me with the things they said and did.

Letting the characters dictate the plot—and have priority over it—often yields some unexpected results. I used the oldest device in the writers' manual when I made my central character a stranger to the community, a time-traveler stunned by the grimness of the future he has stumbled into. The "stranger in town" device is usually coupled with an obligatory conversation in which someone *explains* all about this dreary world. Exposition presented in such a conversation is apt to be dull and awkward. I tried, instead, to imagine Jeremy's first scene in Idamore from the perspective of all the characters.

How would *you* react if someone began insistently asking about things you take entirely for granted? Suppose someone asked, "What do you call these little houses on wheels that are all over the place? Cars? Where'd they come from anyhow, all these cars?" When Jeremy poses similar questions to Helena, she thinks—not surprisingly—that he's slightly retarded. Only a dimwit could wonder what had happened to the birds, or why the trees were so small, or what time of year it was.

I might have had Helena explain to Jeremy that the birds were killed off by a radioactive dust cloud generated by a nuclear explosion in the year such and such, just after the twenty-six-minute war started by so and so over such and such an issue. More interesting—and ultimately

250

more plausible—is a dramatic exchange between the bewildered representative of our world and the future citizen possessing only distorted information. Here's part of the exchange:

> "The birds," said Jeremy. "Why did the birds go away?"
> "Dim, dim," Helena said to herself, looking at the ground and shaking her head. "You remember, Jeremy," she said in her false-patient voice. "The birds left after the time of the light."
> "What light?"
> Helena rolled her eyes. Then she rubbed her nose—less a scratch than a gesture of impatience. "You know. The light."

By staying close to the way this scene would feel to each person in it, I found a surprising vein of light humor. This comic ingredient persisted, at first making me uneasy. Who's ever heard of comedy in a post-nuclear holocaust novel? There were several scenes I almost chucked into the wastebasket for their inappropriate tone. After prying tubers from the icy water of the pond, for example, Helena basks bare-breasted in the sun. Jeremy is unaccustomed to casual conversations with half-naked women, so we get this silly sequence:

> Something soft fell on her, and she let out a shriek as she clawed it off. "Sorry I startled you," said Jeremy, once again walking away. "I brought you a dry shirt. Put it on. I need your advice."
> "I thought you put on a thinking *hat*," she said.
> "Huh?"
> "Is this a *thinking* shirt?"
> "I'm in no mood for jokes, Laney."
> They were obviously having one of their misunderstandings, so Helena fell silent, buttoning the large shirt stiff with soap and fresh air. "I have on the shirt," she said, but Jeremy continued to pace around the edge of the pond with his hands in his pockets.

What I soon discovered through the prism of comedy was the tension inherent in these scenes: eroticism, anger, tenderness, sadness, and frustration were all lurking there. Comedy became my own key to unlocking the full human dimensions of this future world.

I wrote *Children of the Light* scene by scene, groping my way closer to the characters, letting the story emerge from their conflicting experiences and concerns. Obviously I'm not one of those efficient writers who start with a plot outline and proceed to time lines and flow charts.

For writers whose creative processes resemble mine, I'd recommend Constantin Stanislavski's *An Actor Prepares*. I've found that Stanislavski's exercises can help the fiction writer who has to be an inspired actor creating not just one authentic character, but an entire society.

51

ELEMENTS OF THE POLICE PROCEDURAL NOVEL

By Rex Burns

GIVEN the development of the writer's sense of which words live and which don't — a development that for me comes as much through reading as through writing — I think the areas most pertinent to a successful police procedural are four: research, setting, plot, and character.

These divisions are, of course, artificial. As in any "recipe," the elements blend and influence each other; and in any art such as cooking or writing, the whole is greater than the sum of its parts. But though each writer must discover for himself this sense of life or wholeness, some of the basic elements contributing to it can be distinguished. Let's begin with research.

The kind of research I favor is quite basic: my main source for information is the daily newspaper. I figure that if a newspaper article about a crime interests me, it will interest other readers. Naturally, the newspaper story must undergo a metamorphosis before it comes out as fiction. For one thing, there are the questions of libel and plagiarism; and, for another, too great a reliance on the facts as reported can cause a story to become quickly dated.

More important is the question of a good yarn — an interesting newspaper article is only a germ, a bud. It provides a sequence of events and an indication of setting for the full-grown fiction. For example, the following paragraph from a UPI newswire release was the nucleus of a chapter of a novel I was working on: "The raids in Cordoba began when a small airplane, circling the city to apparently coordinate the attacks, threw a bomb that exploded without causing injuries near a provincial bank about 11 A.M." In short, a newspaper article can provide a rich source of actual whats, wheres, and whens. The whys and the whos are the novelist's responsibility.

A second good source of information for the police procedural writer is court records. Affidavits, depositions, and transcripts — in addition to

253

the writer's sitting in on court hearings — help provide not only events and incidental tidbits for a story, but also the language of narration. Increasingly, a cop, especially a senior officer such as a detective, must understand the technology of the law. Every technology has it jargon, and this can be found in legal records and in courtrooms.

Both newspaper stories and court records are as valuable for what they leave out as for what they offer. To get some of that which is left out, read the story with the questions "how?" and "why?" in mind. For instance, that favorite phrase of reporters, "police, acting on a tip from an informant . . ." gives rise to such questions as: Which policeman? Who was the informant? What incentive did he have for informing? What kind of communication — telephone, written, conversational? Who believed the informant? Who didn't? How much time passed between the tip and the raid? These and similar questions come up when the novelist begins creating the fictional world which will embody any actual events he chooses to use.

Though the writer's imagination furnishes the answers to such questions as those asked above, that imagination can be stimulated by a third kind of research which I've found to be most beneficial: interviewing. A policeman, like almost everyone else, enjoys talking about his work, and most municipalities have programs for bettering police-community relations. And a writer — despite what his neighbors may think — is a member of the community. In a larger town, check with the department's public information office. Departments in smaller towns tend to be less formal, and I think somewhat less accessible, perhaps because their manpower tends to be insufficient and the training less professional, generating a defensive attitude. The prosecutor's office and the sheriff's office are also worthwhile avenues of approach. For me, this interviewing tends to be quite casual and takes place during a duty watch; there's a lot of time for conversation during eight hours of riding in a patrol car.

Armed with some specific questions derived from reading newspapers and reports, the interviewer can start filling in those blanks found in the documents. The answers don't have to be related to the same cases read about — in fact, I like it better if they aren't. The novelist deals with probability, and patterns of common behavior offer more freedom for the invention of particulars than does the mere reporting of facts, which is where the journalist ends and the novelist begins. Unlike what takes

254

place on most television talk shows, an interviewer-novelist should be a good listener and, speaking for myself, a copious but surreptitious notetaker. It also helps to train your eye for such minutiae as manufacturer's labels, model numbers, organization charts — in short, anything that gives quick specific detail for your story's setting. Interviewing also provides the latest slang and technical jargon.

The manner of introducing those technical terms into the narrative varies. If a character honestly might not know what a particular device or procedure is called, he can simply ask someone in the story. The character and the reader become informed together. I use this device sparingly, since my characters in the Gabe Wager books are generally professional and well-trained. (Moreover, as a reader, I get damned irritated when a story's development is continually interrupted by some idiot who needs everything explained to him.) Another means of introducing technical terms is to use the phrase in normal dialogue and let the descriptive passage carry the explanation: " 'Let me have the Kell-Kit,' said Wager. Sergeant Johnston handed him the small body transmitter. . . ." Or, for variation, the equation may be reversed: " 'Let me have the body transmitter,' said Wager. Sergeant Johnston handed him the small Kell-Kit." I'm not sure if police departments have yet surpassed the federal government in the use of acronyms and arcane initials, but these are an essential part of bureaucratic jargon. It is a rule of thumb in writing first to use the full phrase, then, in the next sentence or two, the more common initials: "Wager turned to his little book of Confidential Informants. The first C. I. was. . . ." No explanatory passage is needed, and the action moves without interruption.

Research, then, is the foundation for the police procedural, and on that foundation are built in setting, plot, and character. Setting is, of course, easiest to create if it's well known to the writer. For the Gabriel Wager stories, that means Denver. Ironically, my editors more than once pointed out that a street which I invented wasn't on their map of Denver, or an odd-numbered address should be on the north rather than south side of a particular avenue. But the familiarity I mean is as much in flavor as in fact, and its manner of presentation is — for me — impressionistic. The single well-chosen detail that captures the flavor of the setting and gives focus and life to an otherwise sketchy scene is part of the economy I associate with the "grittiness" of a police procedural. A gothic, a novel that explores states of mind, or a sci-fi fantasy may call for more sweeping and panoramic descriptions to create a mood or sustain a romance. But I find harmony between a spare style and the realistic police story. Since this descriptive technique tends to emphasize action rather than setting, and since a police procedural is akin to a report — and a report is usually about "what happened" — the emphasis on concrete and concise detail feels right to me.

The concern with what happened brings us to plot. Plot is not just *what* takes place but *why* it takes place. The police procedural may or may not use the mystery as the basis of suspense. If the police do not know who the perpetrator is, then unraveling the mystery becomes the plot — i.e., the gradual revelation of motive and opportunity. But often, in life as well as in fiction, the police do know who the villain is, and the plot centers on gathering enough evidence for a viable court case. The manner of getting this evidence is quite tedious and even dull — questioning fifty or a hundred witnesses, long hours of surveillance, studying accounting records. The problem for the storyteller in the police procedural field becomes one of remaining true to reality without boring the reader. One technique that fits the police procedural is focusing attention on new methods of surveillance or on the ever-changing avenues of legal presentation. Here, research is indispensable. Another device is to give your detective more cases than one. This is by no means unrealistic, but a good story requires that the cases somehow work together toward a single conclusion. That's the old demand of art for unity, a unity seldom apparent in real life.

Another very familiar technique for maintaining interest is the foil — someone who offers byplay for the protagonist. A foil should serve a variety of purposes, all contributing toward the unity of the novel. The character used as a foil — a rookie, for instance — may be a device not only for explaining police procedure, but also for revealing the protagonist's character through his reaction to the foil's activities.

I try to make character as interesting as case. The strongest novels are those with living characters to whom the action is vital, and this holds true for any tale, even a plotless one. But whether it's a who-done-it or a how-to-prove-it, the police story is fundamentally an action story, and in it the development of character should not impede the action. Ideally, character development and action should coincide; but where they do not, I tip the balance in favor of action, possibly because I envision the Gabe Wager series as one long novel of perhaps fifteen volumes, and this view gives me plenty of room to let the character grow.

There are several other concrete devices that aid the quick presentation of character without interrupting the action. One device especially useful for creating secondary characters is the "signature" — a distinctive act, speech pattern, or habit of thought that identifies and distinguishes one character from another. This signature may be simple: one secondary figure from *The Alvarez Journal* smokes cigars, another has an old man's rumbling cough, a third speaks administrative jargon. Or, if the character is of more importance to the story, a combination of signatures may be used to flesh him out. At its worst, this device generates cliché characters — the western bad man with his black hat and sneer. At best, the signature makes the character become alive and individualized — the girth, thirst, and cowardice of Falstaff. The problem, of course, is to characterize without caricaturing — unless your aim is satire. The novelist's ability to create real characters can be improved by reading other writers who are very good at it: Shakespeare, Flaubert, Faulkner. Another means is "reading" friends and neighbors: What exactly is it that distinguishes one of your acquaintances from another? Given universal human qualities, what makes one individual different from another?

Minor and secondary characters, while absolutely necessary, do not give life to the action. Rarely can any story, police procedural or other, do without a protagonist. Again, because of the importance of action in police procedurals, the writer is faced with the need for an economical development of his main character. The technique I have chosen for my Gabe Wager series is by no means new: It's the familiar "recording consciousness" of Henry James, the restricted third-person point of view, in which every event and concept in the story is presented from the perspective of a single protagonist. I've found several advantages to this device: The action proceeds and the protagonist's character is revealed at the same time. The reader is faced with the same limitations of knowledge as the protagonist, and thus the element of suspense is heightened. Using third person rather than first person puts distance between the reader and the protagonist and offers another dimension to the story, which helps the reader through those necessary and authentic but often slow stages of a case's development.

This narrative technique also has shortcomings. The author can't give the reader any information that the protagonist does not have, thus leaving little chance for irony or depth. For this point of view to work, the author must also have a total understanding of the protagonist. While it may not be relevant to the story, it is nonetheless necessary if the character's actions are to be consistent.

First-person narration achieves many of the same results but brings an even closer identification between author and character. Think of the popular image of Mickey Spillane, for example. I prefer third person because it enforces objectivity and quite possibly because, unlike Gabe Wager, I'm not a good cop.

Focusing all the action through Wager's perspective, then, contributes to a unity of action and characterization in which action dominates but character development follows quite closely and, I hope, unobtrusively. I try to achieve this by placing a heavy emphasis on dialogue. By its very nature, dialogue is dramatic — the characters are onstage talking rather than being talked about by a narrator. Again, the signature is very important, and I play a little game of trying to see how many lines of dialogue I can put together without having to state who is speaking. The idea is that each character's voice should be distinct enough to indicate the speaker.

I place the police procedural in the category of literary realism. The contemporary, the probable, the routine, determine my choice of a realistic subject. Once I select my subject, the elements of research, setting, plot, and character are indispensable, and, in my Gabe Wager police procedurals, all of these elements must contribute to the action.

52

WRITING REALISTIC WESTERN FICTION

By Elmer Kelton

IDEALLY, the only major difference between a Western and any other good, serious novel should be the subject matter, the setting. A good story is a good story, and a bad story a loser whether the setting is Paris or London, Cape Cod or Dodge City. The same general principles of characterization, plot and movement apply.

Being set in the West automatically bestows upon a story certain advantages and certain limitations. The main advantage is a loyal if sometimes-too-small readership receptive to the Western scene. The principal limitation is that it is unlikely to be taken seriously by most of the critical establishment, making it a stepchild in the literary family.

Because of this old prejudice—call it snobbery if you wish—much fine writing has been accorded the "averted gaze," ignored in favor of "relevant" material not half so well written.

The cliché view of the classic Western is a story built around a strong, unsmiling hero who stands seven feet tall and invincible against the worst of villainy, unselfishly sets all wrongs right, and then rides away into the sunset.

Certainly, such Westerns exist. They started in the days of Ned Buntline a century ago, and they continue to appear. There is an audience for the "utility Western," typical of the Saturday-matinee "B" Western film, in which the same frontier-town set and the same outdoor scenery are interchangeable, whether the story is set in Texas or Oregon.

But I am convinced there is a larger audience for a Western novel firmly and accurately grounded in history, the story growing out of conditions inherent in and peculiar to a specific time and place, its conflicts not falling neatly into black and white.

I made my first Western short story sale, to *Ranch Romances,* in 1947. Even so, after some fifty magazine stories and twenty-six published novels, I still consider myself a learner. I continually read and watch for a good story idea, for an interesting character I can interpolate into a novel.

Most of the rules that apply to other fiction apply to the Western. A writer who approaches the Western with a down-the-nose attitude is unlikely to get far in the field. Like any other form, the Western deserves the respect of its writer—respect for the rules of good storytelling and for the realities of history around which the story revolves.

Nothing turns me off faster than to get into a story and find anachronisms and inaccuracies about the time, the place and the people. Any serious writer of historical fiction studies the history that will be the foundation of his novel. The Western deserves no less. This study does not have to be drudgery. Doing the historical research is often the most pleasurable aspect of writing fiction. A writer who does not love history has no business writing about it.

A majority of my novels have been strongly grounded in history. Before I start to write, I study the setting of the story, the historical situations that will form the framework, and the people of the time and place, their problems, their beliefs. Old newspapers, diaries, and written reminiscences are invaluable.

Intricate plots have never been my long suit, though I admire writers who can bring them off. Rather, I rely upon characters and the historical situation to set the pattern. I like the story to grow out of the history to such an extent that the plot could not be transferred to some other time and place without radical surgery.

An example is an early novel of mine, *Massacre at Goliad,* still reprinted periodically in paperback. Two brothers emigrate to Texas from Tennessee some years before the Texas revolution against Mexico. They live through the situations and events that gradually build the atmosphere for revolution. In modern terms, one is a hawk, the other a dove. They become estranged because of their political differences. However, once the fighting begins, they are brought back together by their concern for one another.

My biggest historical novel has been *The Wolf and the Buffalo,* about the lives of a black cavalryman on the Texas plains in the 1870s and a Comanche warrior against whom he is pitted, the black man fighting the red man so the white man can have the land. This novel gave me an opportunity to dramatize the daily life of both the buffalo soldier and

260

his enemy. Gideon Ledbetter, the former slave now in uniform, is on a gradual ascent, while Gray Horse, the Comanche, is witnessing the twilight of his people's way of life.

It struck me that the two characters had a great deal in common. It was a temptation to have them realize it and perhaps come together in some way, but in real life it did not happen. The fact that it should have but did not is one of the ironies of history. I *did* let one black trooper in the story see the parallel and try to act upon it, deserting the army and riding out into Indian country with the idea of proposing an alliance against the white man. What happens to him is what would have happened in real life, more likely than not. The first Indians he encounters shoot him out of the saddle. They see him as an enemy, simply a white man with a black face.

At the end of the story the two characters come together in the only way they would in real life: in combat to the death.

This brings me to what I consider the most important element in a Western, or in almost any other type of fiction: characters.

I wrote the final scene of *The Wolf and the Buffalo* with tears in my eyes. Working with those characters for two years, I had come to care about them as real people. I gloried in their triumphs and felt deeply their personal tragedies.

Well-developed characters have a way of taking charge of a story and leading the writer in directions not anticipated. Often they change details, and sometimes they cause major alterations to the intended plot line. Usually I let them go their own way, for my unconscious is quietly telling me this is the natural and spontaneous thing for them to do.

In a recent question-and-answer session, a reader said she did not understand why I should let characters take over. "They are your creation," she declared. "You can make them do what you want them to."

But to force them into my preconceived plan makes the story seem mechanical and contrived. When in doubt, I follow the character. He knows himself.

In *Stand Proud*, I started with a young Texan forced into frontier service for the Confederacy late in the Civil War, carried against his will into an ill-considered Indian fight (a real one, incidentally) that gave him a wound he would have the rest of his life. Wherever other men led him, he invariably suffered. As the years passed, he increasingly resisted

261

advice; he ignored any judgment not his own. His stubbornness caused him to make mistakes, a few with dreadful consequences. Not until almost too late in his life did he begin to acknowledge his dependence upon others.

Sound like a typical shoot-'em-up plot? I hope not.

These are not men seven feet tall and invincible. These are men five-feet-eight and nervous. They are vulnerable; they can lose, and the reader knows it.

What is more, their opponents, by and large, are not the dog-kicking villains of the old "B" Western. Often they can evoke a certain sympathy and understanding. Sometimes the reader is not sure how he wants the story to come out because he can feel empathy for both sides.

This brings up the question of conflict. The traditional image of the Western is a simple white-hat vs. black-hat yarn, a tall, strong, silent hero against a dyed-in-the-wool villain. It is an old war-horse plot, though one that a gifted writer can still make seem fresh and alive. I am not that gifted. When I have tried to use it, the old horse has shown all his ribs.

Somebody once suggested looking for plots at periods of traumatic change, when an old order is being pushed aside by something new. You can find these anywhere in history. We see them all around us today.

I like to use these periods of change as the basis for historical Westerns, for they set up a natural and understandable human conflict, often between honorable people, each side convinced that it stands for God and the right.

This type of conflict may be cataclysmic, like the clash of the Union and Confederate armies at Gettysburg. Or it may be small and intimate, like the conflict between a modern elderly couple who want to hang onto the family farm or ranch despite all of today's rural economic misery, and their grown children who want them to sell the homestead and retire to town.

At either extreme, the conflict is the same: change vs. resistance to change. It is the oldest plot in the world, and yet it is always fresh.

The conflict may be intensified when it is within the character himself as much as or more than between him and others.

There is a built-in hazard in doing a historical Western, or a historical novel of any kind: the possibility of losing the characters and the story amid all the spectacle. A few years ago we had a rash of 100th anniver-

262

sary celebrations of towns and counties in Texas. Many paid tribute to their past by staging historical pageants, parading costumed people, wagons, coaches, horses, mules, even Longhorn cattle and buffalo past the audience. The spectacle was grand, but with rare exceptions it was only that: a spectacle. The audience came away with little feeling for what it would have meant to be one of the historic personages represented. We saw them only from afar.

History provides the stage. The writer must provide the characters and make them walk and talk and breathe, feel joy and anger, exhilaration and despair. If he does not, he has simply a historical pageant, not a story.

A lot of myth surrounds the West, but the truth is there for the writer who wants to seek it out. The Western story does not deserve to be locked into any set pattern, any formula. It can be as varied as the land from which it springs.

It must be, if it is to survive in its second hundred years.

53

SEEING AROUND CURVES

By Martha Grimes

SOMETIMES I wonder if painters and potters are asked, "How far along are you?" with that portrait or vase, or "How much have you done?" with that landscape or bowl. Such well-intentioned inquiries into the progress of a novel make me feel a little cross and, in a way, slightly stupid, as if I, naïve traveler on the Orient Express, were asked to describe the Venetian canals before my feet had left the platform in Victoria.

People seem to grasp the idea that a painter does not see an orange or an ear floating in his mind's eye, and a potter does not see a neck or a handle. But perhaps because we all "write" in some sense, there is a certain familiarity about pages, and they think progress can be charted by counting them. Perhaps paintings and pots are seen spatially, as a whole, but stories and novels are seen as linear. An eye doesn't "follow" an ear in a portrait, but it's a dead cert that page two will follow page one in a book. And because of this, when I say "a hundred and fifty pages," my interrogator might answer, "Ah. Halfway through, then." No, definitely not, I tell him, no more than I'd have painted half a face if I had got down the eye and the ear.

But if one sees writing in this way—as linear—it is understandable that one might be more likely to look at it as a trip, with marked distances to go between colorful chapter stop-offs. And the mystery writer especially may lean toward this idea of inventing a sort of TripTic or map or other means of charting the territory he intends to cover, then peopling it with characters, and drenching it with atmosphere. Since it is true that in a mystery there should be no loose ends and no clues unaccounted for, it is likely that one might think all story plot problems are resolved in good time.

This assumption that the emphasis in the mystery novel is on eventful happenings or crises—like the murder itself, for it is most often

264

murder—sometimes obscures the fact that the ax doesn't hang in the air, but must be dropped by someone's hands on someone's head. It also assumes that we who write it must know about Venice before we leave Victoria Station. Yet few people know exactly what their destination will look like before they get there or even if they will reach it. So we don't know where we are until we see what it looks like, and we don't know who we are until we see what we do. No one can see around curves no matter how far he sticks his neck out the window. Plot—the territory we want to chart—depends on the characters as much in a mystery as it does in any other novel; character directs the whole journey.

Many writers apparently do very well by mapping out the trip before they start, by sorting out what we might think of as the central elements of plot in a mystery—the perpetrator, the victim, the means, and the motive—and getting them into place by means of outlines, summaries, and synopses. On the other hand, there are writers who just go ahead and climb aboard the train, uncertain even of their destination, perhaps taking their chances that some unknown factor will keep the train from derailing.

I suppose I work this way because I find it so difficult to untangle plot from character, to invent crises for strangers. Nor do I think the device of the character sketch written ahead helpful, because what Tony had for tea when he was seven doesn't interest me unless at twenty-seven he's going to lace someone else's tea with cyanide. Plot, character, setting all seem one huge tangled skein when we set out to write. And because it's difficult to untangle the elements, you might think that the Grand Design should be set down before you have characters bumping into one another on the platform. Line them up and make them behave, for heaven's sakes! There goes the Colonel, making for the café. *Thwack!*

Now let's say that the sketches, the outlines, the synopsis, or the plot summaries are all approaches that you feel will at least get you aboard the Orient Express. You take your character-sketched people along and thus you and Sybil and Grimthorpe and the Colonel manage to get into the dining car (oddly lacking in ambiance since you would hardly have included that in your plot synopsis). The four of you are having a good gossip and being quite friendly, all of you with copies of the outline/sketch/synopsis before you.

You're all in a pretty good mood, except when the Colonel becomes rather churlish because he can't get the waiter's attention. Of course he can't because there is no waiter; he was not in the TripTic.

Now, Sybil, Grimthorpe and the Colonel read over the outline/sketch/synopsis. And there the trouble begins. Fortunately, the dining car is unpeopled—since the background passengers weren't in the synopsis—and the four of you can have a high old time:

Sybil is furious because you're having her marry Grimthorpe when the Orient Express hits Venice. Sybil claims she wants to marry Anthony.

Who's Anthony, you wonder? watching her dampen her finger and plaster a spit-curl to her cheek as she gazes out at the empty (truly empty) countryside.

"Sybil," you ask patiently, "*why* must you marry Anthony?"

"Well, *I* dunno, do I?" Then she rolls her eyes and adds, "I s'pose because he's ever so 'andsome. . . ." She swings her leg and twirls a cheap sequined bag. . . .

But Sybil's supposed to be a marchioness. Why is she coming on like a shopgirl?

Grimthorpe's mouth twitches as he looks down his knobby nose at Sybil and announces he wouldn't have her on a bet.

The Colonel's face is beet-red because he can't find a waiter, yell as he might.

You now realize something's wrong and wonder how the devil you're going to get out of this mess as the Orient Express chugs along to Paris. The only thing you're sure of is that they'll all detrain in Venice—

Until the train rolls into Paris, and Sybil just gets off. Anthony lives in Paris. . . .

The reader is certainly familiar with what is practically a cliché—that after a while the "characters simply take over." This is actually one of those wonderful remissions (or reprieves) for the writer, when everything seems to be on automatic pilot, and the people in your book "come alive," and appear to know what they're going to do and how they're going to do it. You would be willing to believe that the Muse indeed visiteth at such times. The Muse or Tinkerbell or Inspiration or something. But since you know that characters do not clear the mental compartments and take over themselves, it must be some other part of your mind doing it, and all of the scenario above is probably the

266

unconscious ditching the lovely plot complications of the conscious mind. In other words, Sybil (part of you) has a reason for tuning out all of that highbrow marchioness stuff; you simply don't know what it is, any more than you can see around curves. But you will eventually know why, and eventually round the curve. That you will either go mad at worst or type away in a state of controlled hysteria (at best) is something writers like me have to put up with if they want to get to Venice.

All of this revolves pretty obviously around another question that makes me cross: "Where do you get your ideas?" *Idea* is a word that seems frighteningly all-encompassing and makes me think of Carl Sagan neatening up the cosmos. *Idea* really does sound as if the interrogator is asking you where you got your *plot*. And the whole point is—how on earth do you know what people are going to do (correction, what you're going to *have* them do) until you see what they've done so far?

Perhaps I'd opt for the word (if there must be one) of "notion." That sounds far more frivolous, something rather small and capable of being grasped. It could be *anything*. The "notion" for *The Man with a Load of Mischief* came purely from the name of a pub. That a pub would have such strange name led me on the further notion that a mystery set in England and having something to do with pub names might be interesting. My original detective was an effete, snobbish aristocrat, whose only saving grace was the wit of Oscar Wilde. Unfortunately, I had to toss that one out, since I don't have the wit of Oscar Wilde. Anyway, this character ultimately became Melrose Plant, and by that time, Scotland Yard had insinuated itself into the mystery in the person of Richard Jury. Perhaps the reason I am so fond of British pub names is that the germ of an idea can be found in so many of them. *The Anodyne Necklace* was irresistible for this reason. The notion of someone's killing for a necklace with curative powers was all I climbed aboard with.

The initial "notion" might be anything concrete—scene, sound, smell. I think if you confuse "notion" with "theme," you are definitely on the wrong platform, and you'll be sitting on your suitcases forever. *Theme* is an abstraction; it is not a cause but an effect.

The notion for my novel *The Old Fox Deceiv'd* was nothing more than a mental image of a youngish woman walking along a dark and cobbled street. In this case, it was a setting that attracted me, and memories of the quintessential English fishing village called Robin Hood's Bay that I had visited ten years before. I was writing this plotless book when in one day I saw, in three different places, a woman dressed in black and white. It was Halloween, and one of them, in a black cape, was walking across a low-rising hillside. The three became a composite that begins the story:

> She came out of the fog, her face painted half-white, half-black, walking down Grape Lane. It was early January and the sea-roke drove in from the east, turning the cobbled street into a smoky tunnel that curved down to the water. . . . The wind billowed her black cape, which settled again round her ankles in an eddying wave. She wore a white satin shirt and white satin trousers stuffed into high-heeled black boots. The click of the heels on the wet stones was the only sound except for the dry *gah-gah* of the gulls.

Here, it was setting and atmosphere that intrigued me. I liked the idea of a young woman walking along the pavement of an English fishing village, and that someone be waiting in either a door- or alleyway, and that a knife come slashing down. I had no idea (1) who the girl was, (2) why she was being murdered, (3) who was murdering her. When I wrote the opening quoted above, the only additional thing I knew was that the young woman was either going to or returning from a costume party. That made me think of the various "disguises" and the endless possibilities arising therefrom for murder and mayhem.

I have probably used about every banal convention of the British novel of detection I can think of (hoping, of course, nothing appears to be banal in the end) simply because I like them. Bodies dumped in snow, letters dipped in vitriol, corpses stuffed in trunks. I have not actually used the near-holy device of the train schedule for some reason, but I imagine it will come up at some point.

When I sit down to write a book the only thing I'm sure of is that I'm there at the moment. Talent isn't guaranteed, but discipline is at least dependable, like any other habit. Fortunately, it's more productive than smoking and drinking. Flannery O'Connor said that although she might not come up with an idea for the allotted time she was there, at least she was there in case one happened along.

I have been asked (sometimes accusingly) why in the world I, an

American, would set her books in England. Like Sybil, "I dunno." Probably I was on my way to Venice and got off, by some quirk, in Little Grousdean, where I sit around in the local pub with Sybil and Grimthorpe and the Colonel, arguing over train schedules and drinking Old Peculier.

54

WRITING THE UN-HISTORICAL NOVEL

By Gary Jennings

I AM REGARDED as an author mainly of "historical novels," though I have never in my life sat down to write any such thing. I staunchly maintain—and in these very pages I have said so before—that there really *is* no such thing as an "historical novel."

Unless a writer chooses to write about some imagined future, he or she *has* to write about the past, even if only yesterday's. Consider: It is not just a matter of tradition or convention that most novels are told in the past tense. The most up-to-date, hip and trendy "contemporary novel," about to be published tomorrow, is already a story about the past. I myself have toyed with the notion of doing a novel based on my adventures on Madison Avenue in the late 1950's—when all of us bright young admen considered ourselves the last word in up-to-date, hip and trendy—and, with some chagrin, I realize that the times, our society, our culture, all have changed so much in thirty years, that *that* would now be regarded as an "historical novel," if not a prehistoric artifact.

However, the novels that I have so far written have been set in more distant pasts—*Aztec,* 500 years ago; *The Journeyer,* 700 years; *Spangle,* 100 years—but only because, like any other novelist, I have chosen subjects, events, or characters that I knew would make a good story. It just so happened that those subjects were best represented, or those events occurred, or those characters lived in the past. I did not choose them because they were "historical."

And neither do the characters in my novels regard *themselves* as "historical," which brings me to the main point I want to make here. My fictional characters, as well as those drawn from real life—the Aztec named Mixtli and the journeyer Marco Polo and the circus troupers of *Spangle*—all think of themselves as up-to-date, hip and trendy, never once as "partakers in history." I may seem to be stressing the obvious, but I believe the point cannot be overstressed: that a writer writing about the long-ago must constantly be aware that it was not *then* the long-ago. That deliberate and constant awareness may be the most important of all the factors that go into the writing of such a novel, and sometimes it can also be the most difficult factor to manage.

The author of a Napoleonic-era novel has remarked that the hardest thing she had to do, while writing it, was to bear in mind that on the night before the battle of Waterloo, nobody knew who would win it. No author is likely to have his Babylonian hero carrying a purse of coins dated "B.C.," or to have his Westphalian hero say to the heroine, "Well, goodbye, dear, I'm off to the Thirty Years' War." But the temptation is ever present to give our long-ago characters a foreknowledge they could not have possessed.

Even when an author copes adequately with that time-frame aspect, there is another horn to the dilemma. Write about Napoleon, and you expect nearly every reader to be familiar with the history. But write about even an obscure person or era, and you have to assume that *some* readers will be familiar with it. In other words, they already know, to some degree at least, "how the story comes out." That being so, how do you simultaneously stay true to history, keep your characters properly in their time frame, *and* still make the story grip a reader who has the advantage of 20/20 historical hindsight? Well, sometimes that can be done by playing the two horns of the dilemma against one another.

And that has never been better done than by Frederick Forsyth in his *The Day of the Jackal.* Every reader of that novel knew, from page one to the end, that that story never happened at all in real history; that Charles de Gaulle never got assassinated by a sniper; that he was, in fact, still alive and feisty when the novel was published. However, *none of the novel's characters knew that,* and that was what gave such a headlong urgency to the race to intercept the jackal sniper.

Still, that would not have been enough to rivet the interest of the reader already aware that de Gaulle never got shot. So Forsyth did more. He so persuasively took us through the sniper's preparations and made his modus operandi so likely to succeed, that the reader willingly suspended the disbelief of "this never happened," and came to believe that "by damn, this scheme *could* have worked," and voraciously read on to find out "how the hell did this *not* happen?"

Forsyth managed this so superbly because (1) he made his characters believable persons with believable motives and believable responses;

(2) he had done his homework, on everything from ballistics to the most minute details of the story's time and locale; and (3) by the accretion of those realistic details he achieved a verisimilitude that no reader could fault or resist, that convinced every reader to believe "this could have happened."

Now, on the art of delineating character, I will not expound; the subject is too vast to go into here. But the other two techniques—the accretion of details and the achievement of verisimilitude—are well within the capability of even the beginning writer, if he or she is willing to put in the labor they entail.

Reality cannot be flattened down onto a two-dimensional printed page, but verisimilitude can—the *illusion* of reality. It is done by (1) knowing every last detail of your story's time and place, from architecture to climate to customs, etc., (2) knowing every last thing about your characters, from birth to story-time: their upbringing and education, their trades and the tricks thereof, their look and dress, their individual traits and crotchets . . . and then (3) immersing yourself so thoroughly in them, their surroundings, and their story that you forget they are in any sense "historical" and you live their lives and adventures right along with them.

You do not, of course, shovel into your narrative every last detail you have unearthed in your research. It is fatal to let the reader see how hard you have worked—and it is unnecessary. If you know your characters, the period and the locale inside out, believe me, your own assurance will convey that to the reader—but *only* if you know all those things inside out. When you do throw in some detail of curiosa, try to do it offhandedly, not obtrusively, and please do make sure it's a detail that your reader would not also be likely to know. (For a simplistic example: everybody knows that Roman senators wore togas and Greek bacchantes wore chitons, but who knows what they wore *under* them?)

Here again, it is equally important to know what your characters could *not* have worn or used or mentioned in dialogue, lest they step out of their time frame and destroy the story's verisimilitude. A recent novel about England's William Rufus lamentably dispelled its 12th-century mood when the author (more than once) had this or that character remark of another that he was "as flighty as a hummingbird." (No Englishman ever saw a hummingbird until he got to the New World, four hundred years or so after King William's time.)

By the way—and not at all incidentally—be sure to double-check your sources of any information from times past. A reader of my *Aztec* wrote to castigate me because I had mentioned bees and honey in that novel, and, said she, the *Encyclopedia Britannica* avers that there *were* no bees in the New World. If any edition of the *Britannica* makes any such statement, it is dead wrong. (True, the Aztecs did not have domesticated honeybees, but it is likewise true that, if the New World had had no wild bees to do the job of pollinating, it would also have been a world almost nude of vegetation.)

If you can adroitly manage the accretion of enough realistic details, and thereby achieve verisimilitude—whether you are writing a novel or trying to placate an irate spouse by inventing an excuse for some misbehavior on your part—you stand a good chance of being believed, whatever lie you're embedding in the story. And, come right down to it, fiction is nothing but expert and believable lying.

In each of my novels set in the past, I have tried to employ that method—details = verisimilitude—but in the case of *Spangle,* it led me to use a system of organization that I had never used before, and some of you might also find it useful.

First, of course, as we all must do, I did my bookwork and legwork research. The bookwork was to bone up on the history, geography, dress, customs, etc., of a hundred years ago. The legwork meant visiting and traveling with actual circuses to learn from their experts the tricks of their trades—the details of everything from lion-taming to tightrope-walking. That took me to circuses all over the world, from Nashville to Leningrad, and I have to admit that it was fun. Or most of it was. Less glamorous aspects of the circus were also necessary to my story—things like the setup and teardown of the Big Top (sometimes in terrible weather); the logistics of supply, transport, scheduling; even details like the shoveling of menagerie manure.

On occasion, I found myself instructing the experts—and this illustrates what I have said about a novelist's having to know what his characters could *not* have known. An Italian trapeze artiste told me that he supposed his act would have been done no differently a hundred years ago. I had to correct him. At that time no trapezist had ever done any such feat as a triple or quadruple somersault; the trapezist Léotard had just then introduced the simple leap from one bar to the other. Also, not Léotard or any other circus performer of that time had glitzy chrome-plated rigs, amplified music, strobe lights, etc. ("Per Bacco," muttered the artiste. "That's right, they didn't.")

Finally, home again and possessing far more information than I could ever cram into one novel, I conceived a curious system of organizing it all—the most outlandish-ever outline for a novel. It consisted of a sheet of brown wrapping paper, five feet wide and twenty feet long, scribbled and scrawled and diagrammed all over in different-colored inks. It might have been mistaken for the tracklines and timetables of every railroad in creation. The notes and diagrams began at one end of one side of the paper, with April 1865, ran all the way along that side of the paper, around the far edge and to the end of the other side—forty feet, in all—to June 1871.

To explain that, I must tell something about the story of *Spangle*. The circus that is the novel's collective "chief protagonist," finding itself impoverished and stranded in Virginia after the American Civil War, makes its way to Baltimore, sails to Europe, and there—traveling all over the continent—gradually recoups its fortunes, until it winds up in Paris just in time to be trapped in that city's siege during the Franco-Prussian War. The circus comprises a varying but always numerous cast of performers and crewmen and hangers-on, and they naturally have dealings with even greater numbers of "outsiders," including many real-life characters of the time. The circus travels through every kind of country, from the Shenandoah Valley to the Hungarian puszta and the Russian northland, and to cities as various as Baltimore, Florence, Vienna, Budapest, and St. Petersburg, before arriving in Paris.

Not only did I have to keep track of the whereabouts of each of my multitude of characters, their doings and interrelationships, the whole circus's triumphs and disasters and so on, during 1800 pages of typescript—I also had to keep track of significant dates and events, landscapes and locales in the world that the circus travels through. And in those days it was a world of infinitely shifting political situations, alliances, even national boundaries. In brief, that Bayeux-tapestry thing plotted *Spangle* from the first page to the last and enabled me to have the circus always authentically situated in real time and place.

The outline truly was woven, like a tapestry, of warp and weft and intricate design. The long sheet of wrapping paper was divided by vertical lines, according to date and locale, and in those vertical spaces I scribbled the notes from my research as to what was going on then

274

and thereabouts (just telegraphic code reminders to refer me to my more copious notebooks and file cards). Horizontally across those vertical warp lines, I wove the weft—long lines representing every one of my major characters, fictional or real, with notations along each line as to what each was doing at each time and place (for example, the developing complexity of an artiste's circus act), plus all of those characters' adventures and misadventures. Additional lines—diagonal, wiggly, criss-crossing—connected characters, to keep straight their interactions, romances, rivalries, enmities, etc. The tapestry, I am sure, would have been totally incomprehensible to anybody but its creator.

However, that peculiar outline did more than help me remember where everybody was—and when—and what he or she was doing at any specific point. It also enabled me to "live with" my characters, wherever and whenever they found themselves, and I could keep *them* from ever disrupting the time frame and mood of the story by having any pre-vision of what was to occur in the future. Also, in the occasional place where the circus itself did not provide enough action, incident, perilous situation or whatever, to keep the story lively, I could jump from the "horizontal-weft" to the "vertical-warp" notes, and bring in either true or based-on-true incidents from "outside" the circus. That was not often necessary—a circus is a perpetual adventure—but there *were* spots where real-life history was being even more dramatic than anything fictional that was going on under my Big Top.

Most of my writing colleagues and friends consider me woefully old-fashioned. I still prefer to compose (and even to do the grueling finished-typing of 1800 pages) on a manual typewriter, while they—ever so much more up-to-date, hip and trendy—have graduated to sophisticated computer word processors. Nevertheless, some of them have expressed awed admiration of the precision and flexibility with which I could work, using that "cumbersome, archaic, handwritten" roll of wrapping paper. It gave me an overview of *Spangle* that would be beyond the scope of any computer screen. As I say, I've never before resorted to any such system, and I may never do so again. (My next novel has a far less numerous cast of characters and covers a lot less territory.) But the Bayeux-tapestry layout worked splendidly for *Spangle,* and I hold no patent on it. If it appeals to you, and seems applicable to whatever novel you have in mind, feel free to imitate it. I wish you all success, and I won't even ask an acknowledgment.

55

HORROR FICTION: EXPLORING THE DARK SIDE

By William F. Nolan

OVER THE PAST DECADE, I have chosen to concentrate on writing short horror fiction. I've often been asked why. Simple. Horror fiction offers the serious writer a wonderful opportunity to explore a wide variety of characters under stress, characters faced with bizarre situations, within the commercial framework of terror-suspense.

I am challenged as a writer as I explore the dark side of the human animal. We are all capable, under pressure, of aberrant behavior, and the more strain our minds are subjected to, the more we revert to that darker self. The thing that has always frightened me most is a human mind out of control—and I often write about people who have slipped over an emotional edge.

In my "Saturday's Shadow," I move inside the head of a cop who has gone over that edge; he kills his own sister to save her from what he believes to be a deadly shadow, which is, of course, only in his mind. In "One of Those Days," my protagonist hears mice singing in the walls, watches a cat with a baby in its paws cross a busy street, and finally realizes that his psychiatrist has turned into a shaggy dog. But these are all in his mind. . . .

My story "Ceremony" deals with *group* madness. It concerns a professional hit man, a killer for hire, who is lured to a small village in Rhode Island and who himself becomes a victim—trapped by sweet-talking "normal" folk who are actually as mentally twisted as the killer himself. Yet they *seem* so nice.

Which brings us to characterization. As writer, it is my job to make certain that the readers *accept* these people, not as monsters, but as individuals who have adjusted their moral values to fit their own desperate needs. This makes them all the more frightening.

Many beginning horror writers make the mistake of thinking that if the scare elements are horrific enough, then the story will succeed. Put in enough vampires and ghouls, they say, and you don't need to worry about creating real people. In truth, horror fiction cannot be separated from mainstream fiction in this regard. Solid characterization always serves as the core, or central pillar, of any really effective story. In order to frighten a reader, you must create people your readers can recognize and identify with. Once they are willing to accept your characters, once you have won their emotional rapport with characters they believe in, they'll go along with you as storyteller. They'll follow your characters from a sunny street into the darkest alley—from sanity to nightmare. You must, therefore, graft a muscled skin of reality over your skeleton of terror.

The more realistic the external elements of your story, the more effective it becomes when you let loose the horror. Stephen King's great success in the terror genre can be attributed, mainly, not to the horrors he creates, but to the *people* he creates. In his novel, *The Shining,* he did not take his characters into the nightmarish hotel until he had fully established them as three-dimensional human beings. It took him 100 printed pages to do this. Then, and *only* then, was he ready to engulf his characters in the real terrors of the book.

In my short story "Trust Not a Man," I spend 98% of the story in building my character—a lonely young girl searching for a man she can love and trust. The reader identifies with her troubled past, her sadness, her empty life. Then she discovers she has become involved with a man who is about to assault her—and she reacts by feeding him to a large, flesh-eating thing in her greenhouse. I devote only four paragraphs, at the end of the story, to the horror. The rest is all buildup to this moment. By then the reader is ready to accept the horror *emotionally.* My skeleton has been fleshed with reality.

Beyond character, mood is an all-important factor in effective horror fiction. Atmosphere. The stage must be set for the events that follow. Very early, most often on the first page, I try to establish a sense of disquiet, of something *wrong,* an aura of dread, however subtle. Let me cite some openings from my work to demonstrate this.

Here's how I begin "The Yard":

It was near the edge of town, just beyond the abandoned freight tracks. I used to pass it on the way to school in the mirror-bright Missouri mornings and again in the long-shadowed afternoons coming home with my books held tight against my chest, not wanting to look at it.

277

The key words here are: *abandoned . . . long-shadowed . . . not wanting to look at it . . .* These words convey an atmosphere of isolation, darkness, and fear. Or let's look at the opening of "Dead Call":

Len had been dead for a month when the phone rang. Midnight. Cold in the house and me dragged up from sleep to answer the call. Helen gone for the weekend. Me, alone in the house. And the phone ringing . . .

Again, the key words: *dead . . . midnight . . . cold . . . alone.* What I'm demonstrating here is that terror has to be constructed as carefully as an office skyscraper or a fine automobile. A terror tale must be layered, with one effect built over another; it must achieve a *cumulative* effect just as, with music, a good symphony builds in intensity. Terror, then, must be carefully orchestrated.

Consider what may well be one of the most terrifying scenes ever written—the "woman in the room" scene in King's *The Shining*. It's five pages long, and each paragraph builds toward the author's horrifying climax. King starts with the boy, Danny, standing outside the room he fears. He has a pass-key but doesn't want to use it. His body trembles. He hums to himself. A stream of thoughts and images races through his mind. He opens the door, and we get a description of the room. Dark. Turns on a dim light. The bathroom door is ajar. Danny is scared because he knows *something* awful is in there. Big white tub in there, with a shower curtain drawn around it. Danny goes in, draws back the curtain. A long-dead woman is in the tub. Bloated and purple. She *sits up*. Horrified, Danny bolts from the bathroom, runs to the outer door. But it's closed. He hammers on it, telling himself that this corpse can't really hurt him, that it isn't real. And just when he almost has himself convinced, a pair of fishy dead hands close on his neck. . . .

King has *layered* this scene to gain his impact. Each sentence takes us deeper into the boy's nightmarish encounter. By the time those dead hands touch him we have been emotionally prepared to react *with* him, to be frightened and shocked.

Another key element in effective horror fiction is what I call "the echo effect." A good horror tale must leave the reader with something to think about beyond what is obvious in the story on the surface. It must resonate within the reader's psyche. I often construct a subconscious "basement" beneath the main floor of my narrative, creating a double level.

Example: In "The Halloween Man," the *surface* narrative concerns the frantic efforts of a young girl to escape from what she believes to be a ghoulish creature who appears on Halloween night to collect children's souls. She ends up, at the story's climax, hiding in her room—and when her father attempts to calm her increasing fears, she is certain that *he* is the Halloween Man. The reader is left with the question of the ghoul's ultimate reality. Did he actually inhabit the father's body or did he exist *only* in the mind of this frightened girl? Thus, my echo effect.

In another of my terror tales, "Fair Trade," the narrator, under arrest for murder, describes a bizarre journey into town with an animated dead man who attacks and kills a citizen. The narrator *could* be telling the truth or he could be making up a lurid story to cover the fact that he is indeed the real killer. The reader is left to ponder both levels of reality. The tale leaves an echo behind in the reader's mind.

There are, of course, many ways to construct a plot, but a favorite method of mine is to begin with a very ordinary situation and allow it to become more and more offbeat. Take my story "The Partnership." I begin with a folksy fellow named Tad Miller, who's chatting idly with the waitress in a roadside café. Tad tells us all about himself, and we *like* the guy. He's a good ole boy. He tells us that Sally, who runs the place, likes him. ("Most folks do. And that's nice. Person wants to know he's liked, even if he keeps mostly to home.")

Tad also tells us about his partnership with Ed. All very homey and comfortable. Stranger comes in. He and Tad get to talking. Tad ends up taking the stranger out to show him through an abandoned funhouse near the lake, in an old, closed-down amusement park. That's where we meet Ed—who just happens to be a giant half-rat-half-water creature with a razor mouth and glowing red eyes. Ed gets the stranger for dinner, and Tad gets the guy's fancy wristwatch. A partnership. My plot has taken the reader from light into darkness, from the ordinary to the extraordinary. And our guide has been good ole Tad.

Try not to give the reader what the reader may expect. The more familiar the situation, the easier it will be to take your reader wherever you wish. In my "Dark Winner," a man takes his wife back to Kansas City to visit his old neighborhood. Ordinary, right? Not quite—because the man discovers that his evil childhood self is waiting inside the house of his youth, waiting to claim him, body and soul. Adult is absorbed by child, leaving the wife alone and powerless.

What about a party? We've been to countless parties in our lives. Why not start with a man invited to one late at night? I did just that in my tale "The Party," in which we meet David Ashland, a hard-drinking man with an unhappy past, who is attending what seems to be just another cocktail party but which quickly takes on a surreal aspect. The party builds to a feverish pitch, and Ashland flees but finds he cannot leave the building. To his horror, he finds that the *same* party, with the same people, is going on in every room of every floor—a party that will never end. And, final irony, all the booze is watered! David is trapped in his own special hell.

And, as author, I took the reader there by saying, hey, let's go to a party.

Stories such as these sneak up on the reader; they are, in a sense, almost playful. But they have hidden teeth. They bite.

Let me sum up with my feelings about art versus exploitation. I've been asked what I think about the "slice and dice" school of horror, the films and stories that drench the audience in blood and gore. I have strong feelings about them. They anger and nauseate me. They fail to examine the human condition; they simply exploit it. The true art of fear is achieved through a layered use of sensual effects as the writer (or filmmaker) manipulates mood, atmosphere, and character to his subtle purposes. And, for me, that's the operative word: subtle. I have found that with horror less is often more.

As writer, I prefer to allow my audience to fill in the graphic details of horror, since nothing on paper or on film can match the horrific images we can conjure up inside our own heads. And that's the prime target: the human mind.

Your audience is out there, waiting to be frightened. So go ahead, sneak up on 'em and scare their socks off.

They'll love you for it!

56

PLOTTING THE REALISTIC DETECTIVE NOVEL

By Marcia Muller

RECENTLY I WAS having dinner with a fellow writer, and for once we were not talking shop. Instead, we were discussing a mutual friend who was having problems. After a while my friend looked thoughtful and said, "Maybe we shouldn't be talking like this. After all, remember what Sharon said about her last case: You can't understand what goes on in another person's life unless you exist inside it."

Sharon is my private detective, Sharon McCone, who to date has appeared in seven novels. And what my writer friend didn't realize at the time is that she had just paid me one of the greatest compliments of my career. Her casual quoting of Sharon told me that I had created a real character and a real situation—ones that could be remembered and applied to situations in everyday life!

In the course of our reading we've all run across characters and stories that have such reality that we remember them long after we've forgotten our best friend from high school or what happened to us in the summer of '62. In many detective novels, we encounter situations so strange that any investigator would insist they couldn't possibly happen; yet we believe in them implicitly, cheer for the hero the whole way, and heave a sigh of relief when everything is finally resolved. What makes these stories so believable? Why do we remember some novels long after we turn the last page, while we dismiss others as mere gimmickry—and often don't bother to read to the end?

The answers to these questions lie in the novels' characters. A realistic detective novel is *not* about cardboard characters sitting around a drawing room, puzzling over mechanical clues to a bloodless murder. It *is* about real people who exist in a world that is not all that dissimilar to the reader's world. What happens to these people in the course of the novel is extraordinary, and their response to the events may be unusually courageous or clever, but the realistic backdrop against which they act convinces the reader that the story actually could happen.

To make your reader believe—and become involved in—the plot of your detective novel, not just your hero but also your villain and your secondary characters must be believable. These are the people who will develop as you plan and write your book; who will interact with one another; and whose actions will suggest plot twists, red herrings, or even a better ending than the one you had first envisioned.

The development of the plot of my novel *There's Nothing To Be Afraid Of* is an example of how characters create a story. I wanted to write a book set in San Francisco's Vietnamese refugee community. I had researched the subject and knew that many of the refugees had been resettled in the Tenderloin district of the city—an area previously the sole turf of the poor and homeless, prostitutes and pimps, drug addicts and pushers. I knew that the refugees were changing the character of the neighborhood, and that the changes, while positive, had caused resentment and conflict with the long-time inhabitants. My research provided a factual basis from which I could begin to speculate: What if that resentment flared into violence—a campaign of terror directed against a group of Vietnamese living in one of the Tenderloin hotels? What if the campaign resulted in a murder? That, I decided, was the problem Sharon would be asked to investigate.

I now had a real setting for my novel and a situation that could very well occur in real life. I also had in mind several types of people who were likely to become involved in such a conflict, but I needed to create distinct characters. I made a list, named individuals, removed a few who didn't quite fit, added a few more. The final cast included a Vietnamese family, the Vangs; a street preacher, Brother Harry; a homeless man who quoted poetry, Jimmy Milligan; a flower seller, Sallie Hyde; and a porno theatre owner, Otis Knox. But at this point, these were merely names on paper. Next, I had to make them real.

To be truly believable, every fictional character must have a past, a present, and hopes for the future. Some of these details may be relevant to your plot, some may not. Some you may reveal to your reader, others you may choose to conceal until the unraveling of your mystery. But you should be aware of all of them. They are what flesh out your characters, give them a frame of reference, and allow them to act and react to the situation around them. And in turn, the acting and reacting of the characters help you to structure your plot.

In writing the detective novel, it is essential to remember that you are not merely creating a sleuth, or a victim, or a criminal; instead, you are writing about a real flesh-and-blood person who also *happens* to be a sleuth, victim, or criminal. This person does not exist in a vacuum; he has a life outside of the immediate story, consisting of a family, home, romantic entanglements, friends, political opinions, food preferences, hobbies—and much more. You may choose not to bring in all of these facts—they may not be relevant—but you should be aware of them, since they may come in handy at some point in your book. For instance, Sharon is an amateur photographer, able to read negatives, a skill that allows her to discover the motive for the murder in her fourth case, *Games To Keep the Dark Away*. I did not invent this hobby merely for the purpose of solving that case; it was something I had always known about her, but I had not mentioned it in the earlier books because it was not relevant.

Creating an existing context for your character is particularly important in the case of a series character. When I began writing about Sharon McCone (several years and many abortive attempts before she finally saw print), I created a biography for her. This contained details about her family and upbringing, her educational and work history, and such other things as political leanings, likes and dislikes in food, what she finds attractive and unattractive in men, even color preferences and the style of furniture she favors. As the series has progressed, many of these details have altered, because in fiction, as in real life, people change in response to the conditions around them. For example, Sharon originally preferred modern furniture, but after a case involving Victorian houses, she recognizes a fondness for older things. And, as each of her cases brings her into contact with violent death and evil, she becomes more worldly-wise and perhaps a shade more cynical.

The milieu in which your character exists should also include details of home life and friends. Sharon once lived in a rundown studio apartment in San Francisco's Mission district; she recently bought a house in the Glen Park area and has the usual first-time homeowner's problems. At All Souls Legal Cooperative, she is surrounded by friends and co-workers: her boss, Hank Zahn; her close friend, tax attorney Anne-Marie Altman; Ted, the efficient secretary and intrepid worker of crossword puzzles. In addition, she meets people through her cases: former lover Lt. Greg Marcus, current love Don DelBoccio, and antique dealer Charlie Cornish—to name three who reappear from novel to novel. This supporting cast lends Sharon's world an air of authenticity, and often provides fodder for subplots or the main plot. These friends' actions and reactions affect Sharon, providing further impetus for character change, which is the stuff life—and a good story—are made of.

An example of character development from *There's Nothing To Be Afraid Of* may further clarify how this process works. Hoa Dinh never appears before the reader; he is a murder victim when we first see him. But it is essential that we know a great deal about him: first, because he has been murdered, and the motive for a murder is usually personal; and second, because the reader needs to care about Hoa in order to care about the search for his killer.

From my research about the Vietnamese refugees, I knew what Hoa's past and present typically would have been. On that factual basis, I built specific details. Hoa is only sixteen at the time of his death. He has fled Vietnam with his family, narrowly escaping drowning when their boat almost sank in the South China Sea; he has been shunted between refugee camps and temporary housing; he has finally achieved some stability in his permanent home in the Tenderloin, and is attending electronics classes. Hoa's hopes for the future should have been bright, but he is murdered before he can realize them. Hoa now has a past, present, and shattered hopes for the future. He is now a tragic human being, not just an anonymous victim. Other details, concerning Hoa's feelings toward his present situation and the activities these feelings prompted, were essential to the unraveling of the plot and had to be concealed until the proper moment came to reveal them.

I developed the other characters on my list in a similar manner, giving them unusual pasts, problematical presents, and, in some cases, fears rather than hopes for the future. And eventually the circumstances of one of them suggested a motive for the harassment of the Vietnamese and the murder of Hoa Dinh. From that, I was able to project a tentative solution to the case.

The first five or six chapters of my novels are usually devoted to developing the situation and the characters and setting up complications. During this stage—even though I have the motive and solution firmly in mind—I like to keep the plot fairly flexible and open to change. The characters begin to act and interact, sometimes in unusual and surprising ways that suggest red herrings and further complications. These complications always lead to a richer plot than I've originally envisioned; often they can lead to a totally new solution.

In *There's Nothing To Be Afraid Of,* the interaction between two characters in the subplot acted as a catalyst that enabled Sharon to put several pieces of information together, leading directly to the solution of the crime. I decided that the subplot would concern All Souls Legal Cooperative, Sharon's employer: A dissident group of attorneys is trying to wrest control of the co-op from the group that founded it.

My first character was Hank Zahn. I know Hank well: He is from an upper-middle-class background; he fought in Vietnam, returned home disillusioned, and joined the protest movement. After law school, he founded All Souls. That is Hank's past. His present is troubled: Some of the attorneys want to "bring all Souls into the eighties" and do away with the concept of low-cost legal services for the underprivileged upon which the co-op was founded. Hank's hopes for the future are to continue serving his clients along those lines.

The other faction is led by Gilbert Thayer, a new partner. Gilbert's background is similarly privileged, but he is younger than Hank, has recently graduated from law school, and hopes to make a great deal of money. At present, he sees All Souls as a vehicle for furthering that ambition and is trying to turn it into a big-time law firm—and do away with the sliding fee scale.

Given Gilbert's character, it is logical that he go about his plan in a bombastic, abusive manner—which he does. On the other hand, Hank has a low-key, contemplative personality. He withdraws to think things over and then emerges with a clever plan designed to force Gilbert's hand, resolving the situation at the co-op—and in doing so, providing Sharon with the nudge she needs to solve her case.

In the above example, both men act and react in ways that are logical and consistent with their particular frames of reference. Gilbert always blusters and alienates others; Hank always thinks things through and devises clever plans. It is this logic that makes the solution to the take-over attempt at All Souls believable.

Your plot should always be based on your characters acting in ways that are logical with the past, present, and future you have devised for them. The body-finding scene (one of the most difficult to write in crime fiction) provides a good example of this. When Sharon McCone discovers a body, she does not panic, scream, or run away (as I might do), because she has discovered bodies before and is aware of what to do—check to see if the person is really dead. On the other hand, Sharon is

285

an emotional woman, so she does not conduct herself casually or coolly at a murder scene; she feels and reacts with the appropriate seriousness and sadness.

How can you ensure that your characters are acting in a logical and realistic manner? The best way is to put yourself in their shoes, keeping in mind the frame of reference you have created for them. In *There's Nothing To Be Afraid Of,* one of the minor characters also finds a body. She is not a professional investigator, nor is she experienced with this sort of violent death, so she would not check the person's pulse and call the police as Sharon would. To figure out what her logical reaction would be, I first reviewed what I knew of the young woman: She was easily frightened, had a family to whom she was close, and was not overly trusting of the police. Then I put myself into the situation: It's dark, there's a dead person on the floor, I'm scared. What would *I* do—given this young woman's background? Panic and run to get help from my family, of course. And that's exactly what my character did.

In all your characters' actions—whether as momentous as those on finding a body or as simple as deciding what to have for breakfast—place yourself in the situation, *keeping in mind the person's particular frame of reference.* This is sure to help you come up with a logical reaction that will also move your plot along to a realistic conclusion.

In assessing how plausible the plot of your detective novel is, you may want to ask yourself the following questions: Is my story based—however loosely—upon actual fact? Have I created a situation that—given those facts—could probably happen? Are my characters representative of types who would be likely to become involved in such a situation? Have I developed them fully, with an eye to the larger context in which they live? Are their actions—and thus the movement of my plot—logical and consistent with their particular frames of reference?

Once you have answered "yes" to these questions, you will feel confident about allowing your characters' interactions to create the clues, red herrings, and plot twists that will make your plot truly baffling. These, however, are merely mechanics, and only as good as the people who discover the clues, fall for the red herrings, and untangle the twists. In the detective novel, the crime is only as interesting as the person who commits it and the person who solves it.

57

WHAT IS A QUERY LETTER?

By Sondra Forsyth Enos

LET'S SAY THAT YOU HAVE never been published. You want to break into article writing, and you have an idea for a piece on helping a child deal with the untimely death of a significant person in his or her life. You're neither a psychiatrist nor a social worker, just an ordinary person interested in this topic, for whatever reason. What now?

Your first step is to select "target markets"—those that would logically print a piece like the one you want to write—by checking *The Writer* Magazine or an annual market guide to find the names of the editors to whom you should write, the length requirements for manuscripts, and the pay scales. Next, read several issues of your potential target publications—in our sample case, religious magazines, parenting magazines, major and smaller women's magazines. (Many magazines are in your library, indexed in *The Readers' Guide to Periodical Literature*.) Smaller, specialized magazines may not be found in libraries and are often difficult to find on newsstands, but on request, the editors will usually send you sample copies free or for a small fee.

Now you're ready to pitch your piece, preferably to one market at a time. Multiple queries, at least to the major magazines, are really not a good idea unless the piece is timely. Smaller magazines, on the other hand, are more receptive to multiple queries, but you should tell the editors that you have sent the query to several magazines at once. Editors don't like spending time considering your query, only to learn later that you've accepted an offer from a competing magazine in the same field. (The trick is to have plenty of queries on different topics out to different markets at any given time, so you'll always have enough work and won't be waiting for that one story to click somewhere.)

Let's say you've decided to aim for a major magazine called *Today's Parents*. (I made this magazine up.) Should *Today's Parents* reject your query, you can always try a more modest-paying magazine such as *The Episcopalian* or *Marriage and Family*.

First of all, do *not* try to skip the query letter by phoning the editor, unless you've written for the magazine before. After all, he has no idea whether you can write, not having seen anything by you on paper.

What is a query letter, anyway? It is a one- or two-page summary of your proposed article, showing that you have the style, the skill, and the necessary access to experts or authorities to write it. I believe that the most effective letter begins with a "grabber"—a titillating paragraph that might even be the lead to your article. Avoid the stiff format of an ordinary business letter, as in "I am interested in writing an article for your magazine on the topic of helping a child cope with the death of a relative or close friend." Far better to catch the editor's attention with something like:

Jennifer Wilson is an eight-year-old charmer with enormous brown eyes, blond pigtails and a fair share of freckles. Like her third-grade classmates, she is learning about American Indians and memorizing her multiplication tables. She's a budding gymnast, and she likes to make clothes for her dolls. To a casual observer, then, Jennifer is a normal little girl. But those close to her know that she is wrestling with one of the gravest traumas a young life can sustain: the recent death of her mother.

Now that you've piqued the editor's attention he will go on reading, so you've cleared the first hurdle. Your next job is to convince him that you can deliver all the elements of a first-rate article. Let me list them and then give you an example of what the body of the letter ought to look like:

1. Give statistics or expert quotes showing that the problem of children coping with the untimely death of important people in their lives is widespread enough to deserve discussion.

2. Let the editor know that you are prepared to substantiate and enliven your article with case histories—that is, anecdotal passages with quotes from people who have experienced whatever it is you are writing about. There are three ways to accomplish this:

a. *Interview people who agree to have their real names published,* and who may also agree to supply photographs or submit to photography sessions. This is the ideal, and is most easily accomplished when you are asking people to say what they would say in ordinary conversation anyway. For example, I once did

288

a piece on how the media affect today's youngsters, and I got a number of mothers and fathers (neighbors of mine, cousins of friends in the Midwest, and so on) to give taped interviews over the telephone, and to agree to have their names published with their quotes. People said such obvious things as, "I limit my children's TV viewing to one hour a day, and I monitor which shows they watch"; or "I read reviews before I take my kids to the movies, and even then, I'd yank them out of the theater if anything offensive came on the screen." In this case, I simply taped the interviews, with the interviewees' permission recorded at the beginning, and then wrote up the quotes practically verbatim. I did not use a printed release form,* although this can be an extra precaution and there would be no harm in doing so. If you interview people about a controversial topic, release forms signed by them are mandatory. I also did not allow the interviewees to see my manuscript or galleys, since the people were not quoted extensively, nor portrayed in any way that could be construed as negative.

b. *Interview people who ask that their names and other details be changed to conceal their identities* and indicate this either in the text or in a footnote. This approach is common when the topic is sensitive and personal, such as marital and sexual problems, substance abuse, domestic violence, compulsive disorders (kleptomania, nymphomania, bulimia, compulsive gambling or shopping), and mental or emotional illness. I would suggest giving each interviewee a fictitious first name ("Carol") or first name and surname initial ("Carol P.") or title and surname initial ("Mrs. P.").

Similarly, change occupations, but keep them within the same socioeconomic group, making a waitress into a repairman, a receptionist into a typist or secretary, a doctor into a lawyer. Selectively change or omit other details, such as color of hair and eyes, name of hometown or college attended, number and gender of children or siblings, provided that such changes will not affect the story. Definitely have your interviewees sign release forms.* Once again, there is no need to allow the people you interview to see your manuscript, although you may do so if you wish, with the written proviso that you are under no obligation to make changes.

c. *Use quotes you hear (or overhear) in real-life conversations.* When I was doing a piece on working mothers, I not only interviewed people who agreed to be quoted, but I also became an inveterate eavesdropper. I caught exchanges between women at the supermarket, on the commuter train, etc. I either made mental notes, or actually jotted quotes down in my notebook as I heard them (in a bus, plane or restaurant) or shortly after hearing them, and I gave them anonymous attributions, such as "said one overwrought young mother as she stood in the checkout line. . . ."

This should not be your sole method of gathering anecdotal material. Do not be tempted to sit at your desk and make up quotes that you imagine people would say regarding your topic, and don't merge a little of one person with a little of another person for a "composite" case history that more neatly serves your purposes than anything you have managed to dig up in the real world.

---

*See end of chapter for release form.

289

In the case of interviews with people who give their names, editors will ask for telephone numbers so facts can be verified. If you have given them fictitious case histories, they'll either send you back to the field or kill the piece. They will also find it hard not to remember you as inexcusably unprofessional.

3. To help the editor understand the scope of your piece, indicate what each case history will illustrate. Let's say Jennifer's mother died of cancer, so this little girl gives you the opportunity to talk about the death of a parent as well as about the problem of witnessing a long, progressive illness. Or if Kevin's revered soccer coach was killed in an automobile accident, the boy opens up a discussion of children losing important adults—"heroes," in a way—other than family members, and he also sets the stage for a look at the problem of unexpected death. Show that you have a thorough but manageable story in mind, one that can be competently told in about 3,000 words.

4. Explain that you will contact the appropriate experts for interviews: In our sample case, these experts would include pediatricians, child psychologists, hospice workers and others who work with the terminally ill, clergy, and authorities on death and dying. Do some preliminary research in the library, and give the names of respected people in the fields you plan to cover. Don't worry about eventually getting through to the top experts. If you get a go-ahead from a magazine, that will open the door for you. And I'm not just talking about major markets. If you want to write for specialized markets—*Chess Life* or *Scale Woodcraft* or *Yoga Journal*—you'll find that you'll easily get interviews with the most important people in those fields.

In the meantime, by listing the recognized authorities, you've showed that you're up on your topic. If at all possible, magazine editors want quotes from the reigning experts in whatever subject area you're writing about, so take the time to find out who those headliners are. By the way, don't choose to interview *your* child's pediatrician, *your* child's school psychologist, and *your* minister—or your hometown chess champ, woodcraftsman or yoga instructor—simply because they're easily accessible. No matter how knowledgeable these people are, unless they are widely known in their fields, they aren't the ones to approach for interviews. (The obvious exception, of course, is when you are writing for a regional or local publication, in which case you would not only want to interview the people right in your own backyard, but you might do a whole personality profile on a particularly colorful character.)

5. Mention whether you plan to add any service information. Boxes listing the names and addresses of support groups or books or government pamphlets pertaining to the topic often run alongside the appropriate article.

6. Sign off. I am personally opposed to the often recommended closer, "I can have this piece ready within six weeks." Of course you can, if you're any good. I also object to "May I have this assignment?" That sounds so pushy and canned, somehow. I'd rather read something original and sincere, such as "I'm confident that the proposed article will touch the hearts of all who read it, and more important, fill a real need for information about this sensitive topic."

Now, let's see how these points ought to be handled in a brief, rejection-resistant query:

Martin Jones
123 Some Street
Appleton, Wisconsin 54914

January 15, 1989

Leonard Smith, Articles Editor
Today's Parents
One Park Avenue
New York, New York 10016

Dear Mr. Smith:

Jennifer Wilson is an eight-year-old charmer with enormous brown eyes, blond pigtails and a fair share of freckles. Like her third-grade classmates, she is learning about American Indians and memorizing her multiplication tables. She's a budding gymnast, and she likes to make clothes for her dolls. To a casual observer, then, Jennifer is a normal little girl. But those close to her know that she is wrestling with one of the gravest traumas a young life can sustain: the recent death of her mother.

Jennifer is not alone. While the loss of a parent is a particularly stressful event, the death of any significant person in a child's life can be traumatic. According to a study done by Elaine Cummings, former co-ordinator of education and training at the St. Francis Center for Thanatology in Washington, D.C., a majority of children under the age of eighteen report having had to come to grips with the untimely loss of a relative, friend, or teacher. Countless more, of course, know the inevitable but nonetheless devastating pain of losing elderly grandparents. Yet, for most of us, death is a difficult topic to discuss with anyone, let alone a child. I propose a 3,500-word article aimed at helping people get children through the deaths of those close to them with as few psychological scars as possible.

Four families—including Jennifer's—have agreed to cooperate with interviews for the article. Jennifer's mother died after a long battle with lung cancer. The other three families are those of thirteen-year-old Kevin Stockright, whose revered soccer coach was killed instantly in an automobile accident; ten-year-old Kirsten James, whose younger sister died of leukemia; and fifteen-year-old Lauren Johnson, whose best friend died of muscular dystrophy.

I also plan to interview top experts in the field of death and dying, including Dan Schaefer and Christine Lyons, authors of *How Do We Tell the Children?* (New York: Newmarket Press, 1986); Eric E. Rofes, editor of *The Kids' Books about Death and Dying* (Boston: Little, Brown, 1985); and Elisabeth Kubler-Ross, author most recently of *Living with Death and Dying* (New York: Macmillan, 1981). I would also try to get in touch with such well-known people as the family of teacher/astronaut Christa McAuliffe.

In addition to the text, I would include a service box listing the names, addresses and telephone numbers of key support organizations across the country, as well as a box listing the best books and pamphlets on the topic.

I'm confident that the proposed article will touch the hearts of all who read it, and more important, fill a real need for information about this sensitive topic.

A stamped, self-addressed envelope is enclosed for your convenience in replying. I look forward to hearing from you.

Cordially,

Martin Jones

I can assure you that if a query like that had landed on my desk during my editing days, I would have given it far more than casual attention, even if it had come from an unknown, unagented and unpublished writer. I imagine that Leonard Smith at *Today's Parents* would, too.

SAMPLE RELEASE FORM

I, _____
(name of interviewee)

give permission to _____
(name of author or interviewer)

to use all information supplied by me, regarding my personal and professional life, for the preparation of (name of article or feature), to be published in (name of publication).

I understand that to help protect my anonymity, (name of publication) may make changes in the information so released.

Signed_____

Home Address_____

Social Security Number_____

58

TRAVEL WRITING, ANYONE?

By Bob O'Sullivan

TRAVEL WRITING is *not* fun, but getting paid for an article and being patted on the head and told what a clever person you are, now that *is* fun. And if you're going to write, the travel field has something going for it that's a real plus—traveling.

There are two basic markets for travel articles: newspapers and magazines. What follows is mostly about newspapers, which represent by far the larger market; however, the writing aspects apply to magazines, too.

Before you decide whether you want to try travel writing, it might be a good idea to consider just what it is.

1. Travel writing is the stuff in the travel sections of newspapers and magazines that keeps those big ads from smashing into each other.

2. Travel writing is what makes those travel sections attractive to the advertisers, offering them an almost pre-sold readership, people who are interested in travel.

3. Travel writing is what lets people write their travel expenses off their income taxes. However, some "travel writers" have been learning lately that the IRS expects them to make a sale once in a while.

4. Travel writing is any travel-related story an editor will accept. It could be about places, it could be humor, even a childhood reminiscence as long as it's bright enough to get an editor's attention.

I'm no expert in the field of travel—I'm just a writer who's currently specializing in travel—but I've been on enough trips and done enough writing about them to know that the concepts above are all correct.

Like every other kind of journalism, travel is a tough way to make a living. If you're writing professionally now, you probably know that; if you're not, consider yourself warned. "Writing for a living" is close to being an oxymoron, which, in case you don't know, is the combination of two words that tend to cancel each other out, like thunderous silence, English cuisine, bitter sweet, kindly editor, unbiased opinion. "Writing" and "making a living" just seem to argue with each other.

Thirty years ago I worked in the radio, television, and motion picture industries. Then, I married a lovely lady, and we had four children. Now, this is where the oxymoron comes in. The "living" I was making as a writer was slowly making it impossible for the six of us to keep on living.

I joined the Los Angeles County Sheriff's Department, and as I gradually moved up through the ranks, keeping bread on the table ceased to be a problem. After the kids were out of college, my wife and I started spending money on ourselves by doing what we'd wanted to do for years. We traveled.

As I approached the Department's mandatory retirement age, I started getting nervous. "Now what do we do?" I asked myself.

The question was answered by Dan Byrne, a boyhood friend, who had been both an editor for the *Los Angeles Times* and the boss of the Los Angeles Times Syndicate.

"You used to be a writer," he said. "Why don't you do some travel writing about some of your trips?"

"What's travel writing?" I asked. He told me and offered to edit my first few articles. I took him up on it.

"If you really want to succeed, you've got to find an area within the travel field that's not already crowded." Having been a dramatist 25 years earlier, I picked human interest and humor.

Thanks in no small part to his editorial tightening—that is, cutting out every word that didn't advance the story—my travel articles sold pretty well.

Travel is a multi-billion dollar, worldwide industry and there just might be a piece of all that money with your name on it. Either way, you'll increase the scope of your work, have more to write about, and a brand-new, world-sized market in which to sell what you write.

But, there are rules to the game, and there are a few things I've picked up that might help. Let me give you some of both.

1. First, you've got to travel, and you've pretty well got to like it.

2. Travel editors receive a lot of free-lance submissions, so you have to get the editor's attention quickly. If you haven't got it in your first five

lines, chances are you won't get it at all. If you start your piece on the Philippines with, "Imelda's shoes were burning . . ." you've probably got him for the next few lines, at least.

3. Be businesslike. Always send a brief letter with the article. Include your Social Security number. This assumes the editor's going to buy it and removes any doubt about whether you expect to be paid for it. (This is child psychology, but it's O.K. as long as the editors don't know we're using it on them.)

Though some writers' guides say the average editor will accept two mistakes per page, they really don't. They're just like the rest of the reading public: A mistake in the piece, factual or typographical, makes the reader doubt everything else in your article.

4. If you want unaccepted stories back, enclose a self-addressed, stamped envelope. But, I think the psychology that goes with the SASE is a bummer. I always send a Xerox copy, never an original manuscript, and a self-addressed postcard with, "Yes, I'll take it," "Not at this time," and "Comments" rubber stamped on it. Then, in the letter I say that I don't need the copy back but would appreciate the editor using the response card.

5. Never nag, argue with, go over the head of, or *re*submit a story to an editor without his expressed permission.

6. Try to write tight. If your piece is fifteen hundred words, go through it again to see if you can chop a couple of hundred more words out.

My editor friend, Dan, on a good day, could edit *War and Peace* down to just *War*. In those beginning days, he also gave me a few tips that might be useful to you. I remember one conversation quite well.

"Forget about adjectives," he said. "I see you use 'very' a lot. Don't. 'Very' is a very, very weak adjective."

I was pretending that what he was telling me was old stuff, but I was sneaking a few notes.

"You taking notes?"

"Just doodling."

"Don't use 'cute' or unusual words. If you've got a narrative going and a word comes up that's cute or out of the ordinary, it'll yank the reader out of the story faster than a punch in the nose."

"Will you tell me something I don't know?" I pleaded, doodling "no

296

cute words." He ignored me and went on. "As Sam Johnson said, 'If you write a word or a phrase you particularly like, strike it out.' You have enough to fight without becoming a victim of your own ego."

"Does that about cover it, Dan?"

"No, it'll take you years to cover it." Then he told me about such things as "white space," "multiple submissions," "self-syndication," "collecting tear sheets," "keeping my sense of humor," "forgiving the mailman," and "not giving up." I'll try to make it brief.

What you leave out can be (you should pardon the expression) *very, very* important. Give the editor *white space*. Double-space your copy and make lots of paragraphs, use wide margins. If you're using a word processor, leave the right side ragged, that is, don't use the Right Justification key.

The first reader, the editor, needs all the help he can get, so try to make your pages easy to read and easy on the eyes.

When I first heard about multiple submissions I thought it meant not sending more than one article to the same editor at one time. What it really means is, some newspaper editors just don't want a piece that is also being sent elsewhere.

These days, most of them realize that multiple submissions are an absolute necessity if the writer is going to make a living. Hence, syndication. Bombeck, Baker, Royko, Dear Abby appear in hundreds of papers, here and abroad, and all the editors in their individual market areas know that they have an exclusive *only* in their particular market.

For the beginning travel writer, self-syndication is the answer. A former *Los Angeles Herald Examiner* travel editor advised me to send my work out in "flights of twenty-five to fifty." Advise each editor that you are offering only "first serial rights" in his or her area. To be on the safe side, figure a market area to be a hundred-and-fifty-mile radius. Be sure you don't submit it to more than one publication in that area. Breaking this rule is a mortal sin.

(Most magazines want rights for all of North America for one year. *The Washington Post, Wall Street Journal,* and *The New York Times* want national first publication rights and won't settle for anything less.)

Tear sheets, or the section of the paper containing your article, will be mailed to you almost automatically by most papers and magazines. Keep them. Xerox them. Work to get some, even if you have to sell a few of your first pieces to weekly newspapers for absolute minimum payment. Magazine travel editors will usually ask to see a few of your tear sheets before committing themselves on a projected story.

Magazine editors also prefer queries to finished stories. Writing an editor to ask how he or she would feel about reading a piece on a certain subject saves the magazine editor a lot of time, but *it's your time.*

If you find yourself hating the mailman or mail-lady (is that an oxymoron?), don't. Though they may dump a rejection slip or two on you in the beginning, they'll be your readers someday.

DON'T GIVE UP. If you're just expanding your options by travel writing, a lot of this is old stuff; you know how the world works. But if you're just starting out, don't be discouraged. If editors don't reply, or never send back your response cards, keep sending submissions until they get to feeling guilty about seeing your stationery so often and not reading your work.

Of course, it also helps if you can write.

59

THE Q'S AND A'S OF INTERVIEWING

By Mary Crescenzo Simons

EVERY TIME YOU ASK a question, whether you are just chatting on the telephone, conversing at a party, or simply asking someone's opinion, you are conducting an interview. The key to successful interviewing is sincere interest and attentive listening, which encourage dialogue and elicit relevant responses. This attitude is an important part of your job as an interviewer, but your first task is preparation. Fortunately, interviewers have the opportunity to gather information, materials, and questions *before* they begin their interviews.

Although thorough preparation gives you a feeling of confidence, you must always expect the unexpected. Don't try to map out the exact direction of an interview; you can only *guide* the interviewee to some degree toward the answers you are looking for.

One of the first things to do is to research the interviewee and his area of expertise. If you do not know much about his field, resource material and knowledgeable individuals, friends, and associates can brief you on the vocabulary and basics. Evaluate the information and compare various perspectives.

At the library, you may find clippings and additional background data on the interviewee. Also, previously published articles or interviews by or about him or her often provide quotes you may wish to refer to, asking the interviewee to comment on an earlier statement in the context of the current situation. Such articles may also offer information about other aspects of a person's life to help you create a multifaceted profile.

For an interview with wildlife artist Daniel Smith, I had material only on his artistic background, but in a hometown publication, I discovered that he was also a body builder. This led to my asking him during the interview how he balanced these two contrasting disciplines. He pointed out that they are actually similar: both require a strong sense of individuality, ego, and a drive for perfection. Later, in writing the article, I was able to use this new insight to give me a distinctive angle.

As you acquire background information in the course of your research, you should begin to compile and organize your questions by topic or in chronological order, covering such areas as childhood, family life, work, achievements, associates, rivals, challenges, problems, leisure activities, and expectations.

Leave wide spaces on your paper between questions for on-the-spot notes. Writing down summarized versions of questions with key words underlined or highlighted will help you ask your questions in a spontaneous manner, producing a relaxed atmosphere and fuller responses. Allowing the interviewee to speak freely and informally will give you more information than you would otherwise elicit. Showing interest in and knowledge of the interviewee's field and being prepared to follow the direction the interviewee may pursue with extemporaneous questions will produce dividends for you.

If your questions are dull, predictable, and abstract, the answers will be, too. Ask questions that require more than yes-or-no answers. Investigative yet thoughtful questions will lead the interviewee to tell you what he really thinks and feels.

I like to begin an interview with a warm-up question, something general but imaginative, personal without being probing, a question that will trigger pleasant thoughts or memories and will put the interviewee in a reflective, responsive mood. In an interview I did with Tina Turner before her reemergence into the mainstream of the rock-and-roll scene, rather than asking her at the outset about her musical and personal breakup with Ike Turner, I asked her if she could remember how she felt the first time she saw Ike's band on stage, before she joined the group. Later, I asked about phases in her personal life, her current work on the road as a woman, alone and independent, and her future goals.

You can start an interview by asking how your subject got started in his career or profession. For an article called "Is There a Collector in the House?" I interviewed three art collectors and asked why and how they began collecting. What was the first object or item they collected? This led to a lively discussion (which I later drew on for my piece) on how a novice collector can begin, what to look for, and what cautions to take when making purchases.

Ask the interviewee what his or her typical day is like. Whether you

300

are focusing on someone's career, personal experiences or a specific incident or event in his life, initial questions should not be threatening or too personal.

Sometimes the best bits of information surface when your pen—and the interviewee's guard—are down. Gems are often dropped in the course of informal conversation, while you are still settling down for your talk or after you've packed up your material and are about to leave. As I left the office of the president of a local junior college after a long interview, I noticed there was no name plate on his door, although his name as founder and president appeared on bronze plaques throughout the campus. When I mentioned this, he told me that when the school first opened, his then young son scribbled "President" on his father's nondescript door in a temporary building. He went on to say that he still had that scrawled sign, and just never had a permanent one made. I used the anecdote in the opening and ending of my article about him to illustrate the unpretentiousness of the man and his close family ties.

About halfway into an interview, you can introduce more probing questions, but remember, when moving into controversial areas ask your questions with confidence and genuine concern. This is the point at which you can ask the interviewee to explain something you've learned or heard about his work or personal life, something he may not have known had been disclosed, or something he may wish to refute. Going on to less sensitive matters, you can ask what is the most rewarding and most frustrating part of the interviewee's work.

While interviewing syndicated cartoonist Dave Simpson, I noted a great deal of marine paraphernalia decorating his office. He later told me that scuba diving and model shipbuilding were his hobbies. In the corner of the room, behind his desk, stood a whaling harpoon. I decided to use this visual clue as a theme in my title, "Dave Simpson: Political Angler," and in the opening and closing statements, relating them to his stinging cartoons.

The opening paragraph began:

In the corner of his cluttered office rests an old whaling harpoon, overlooking the drawing table behind his desk. He is outspoken, witty, younger than you'd imagine, and to the point.

The article ended with his quote and a last tie-in phrase:

301

"I've mellowed through the years. I don't like to hit them over the head anymore to make a point. I'd rather prick them with a pin." Or maybe a harpoon.

Well into this interview, I said, "Someone told me you can be difficult. As an artist myself, I can understand how people sometimes react to creative people. Why do you think this comment would be made about you?"

"Because I say what I think."

Because I shared a bit about myself, he was encouraged to elaborate on this point. Through this exchange, I learned of a hilarious run-in with his boss, his determination to follow his own convictions, and the complimentary as well as hateful mail he receives from readers.

As your interview draws to a close, you want to be sure you have asked all of your questions and that the interviewee feels you have covered what is important. Questions that look toward the future or reflect on an aspect of the person's work or life are good ways to conclude the interview. Two examples are: "Who influenced you most in your life?" and "If you weren't working in this profession, what do you think you might be doing?" That kind of question allows the interviewee to reveal his personality through his fears, hopes, mistakes, and achievements. Other good closing questions: "What is the most important thing in your life?" "What do you see yourself doing 20 years from now?" "Is there anything you wish I had asked you about?"

When and where you conduct your interviews can have an effect on the results. It should always be at a time and place convenient to the interviewee. My interview with the legendary, elderly blues singer John Lee Hooker took place, at his suggestion, at his hotel, the day *after* his concert, since he was obviously tired immediately after his show. After the interview, the band joined us, and I had the opportunity to chat with them about their road experiences with Hooker and to observe the group's interaction with their leader. Later, as I reorganized my notes, I was able to incorporate the band's perspectives and relationship in my profile.

If you cannot interview someone in person, a phone interview can provide adequate information for a full and detailed profile. One advantage of a phone interview is that you can take detailed notes without distracting the interviewee. Unfortunately, it is more difficult by phone to gauge when someone is finished speaking; without face-to-face contact, you miss out on body language and facial expressions.

In-person interviews add warmth and informality to a conversation. The interviewer can look the interviewee in the eye as well as watch for nonverbal cues. In the early stages of a well-known musician's career, he wore dark sunglasses (long before the style was remarketed as fashionable) during my interview with him. This guarded signal alerted me to tread lightly, at least at first, in order to make the artist feel more comfortable. He never removed the glasses, but he did respond with increasing ease as the interview progressed.

One of the disadvantages of an in-person interview is that you must rely less on your note reading and taking, in order to keep the interview conversational and the interviewee paying attention to you rather than to your materials.

Some simple do's and don'ts of interviewing may seem minor, but these hints will help to enhance your professionalism and manner of creating comfortable surroundings for both you and the interviewee.

• Bring a tape recorder to record quotes and conversation accurately. The tape will free you to note other informative details, like mannerisms and surroundings.

• If you make an incorrect statement, be confident enough to acknowledge the error, apologize, and go on.

• Be on time with the necessary materials (pens, pencils, tape recorders, extra tapes, batteries, extension cords, notes, etc.).

• Reword a question if it is not understood, or bring it up later, in a different manner.

• Don't chew gum, smoke, mumble, keep your eyes glued to your notes, talk too much about yourself, or go over your allotted time.

• Don't ask for information from the interviewee that you can find through research.

• In trying to contact a person for an interview, don't take no for an answer. "He doesn't do interviews" usually means you have to try another, more determined approach.

As a writer obtaining information, whether for research data, a personality profile, or a question-and-answer article/interview, mastering the art of interviewing will help you discover the desired information plus additional facts, opinions, and observations that will enhance your work.

60

TRICKS OF THE NONFICTION TRADE

By Donald M. Murray

UNDER the apprentice system still practiced in most crafts, a beginner has the opportunity to work beside an experienced worker and pick up small but significant tricks of the trade. Few of us, however, observe a writer at the workbench turning a phrase, cutting a line or reordering a paragraph so that a meaning runs easy and runs clear. Here are a few of the tricks I've picked up during more than forty years of trying to make writing look easy.

Before writing

An effective piece of writing is a dialogue between the writer and the reader, with the writer answering the reader's questions just before they are asked. Each piece usually has five or six questions that must be answered if the reader is to be satisfied.

I brainstorm and polish the questions first, then put them in the order the reader will ask them. For example, if I am doing a piece on diabetes, I list such questions as:

- What is diabetes?
- How can I tell if I have it?
- What's the latest treatment?
- Do I have to give myself shots?
- Where can I get that treatment?
- How dangerous is diabetes?

Then I reconsider, refine, and reorder the questions:

1. *Lead:* What's the latest treatment for diabetes?
2. How dangerous is diabetes?
3. What is diabetes?
4. How can I tell if I have it?

5. Do I have to give myself shots? No. New treatment.
6. Where can I get it?

As I write, I may have to reorder the questions if I "hear" the reader ask the question earlier than I expected, but that doesn't happen very often. It is also helpful to write these questions down before revising a draft—especially a confusing one. Just role-play a reader and put down the questions you would ask, combining them if necessary, and then put them in order. This trick will help you understand what readers want to know and when they want to know it.

Professional writers, however, don't wait until they have a completed draft to read what they have written. They learn to pay attention to lists, collections of information, partially drafted sentences and paragraphs, abandoned pages, notes, outlines, phrases, code words that constitute the kind of writing they do on the notebook page and in their heads before the first draft.

Reading those fragments, the writer discovers a revealing or organizing specific around which an article can be built, a pattern of action or argument on which a meaning may be hung, a voice that tells the writer what he or she feels about the subject and that may be used to communicate that feeling to the reader.

Many writers write everything at the same distance from the subject. It becomes an unconscious habit. Academic writers may stand too far back from the subject, so that the reader feels detached and really doesn't become involved with the content. Magazine writers usually move in close, many times getting too close, so that readers are lost in the details of a particular person and are not able to understand the significance of the piece.

The writer should use an imaginary zoom lens before writing the first draft and decide the proper distance for this particular article, the point from which the reader will see the piece clearly, understand its context, and care about the subject. The writer may stand back and put the winning play in the context of all Army-Navy football games or move in close and tell the story of the game in terms of the winning play itself, concentrating on the fifty seconds that made the difference.

Leads and endings
The first line, the first paragraph, the first ten lines of an article establish its direction, dimensions, voice, pace. "What's so hard about

305

the first sentence is that you're stuck with it," says Joan Didion. "Everything else is going to flow out of that sentence. And by the time you've laid down the first *two* sentences, your options are all gone." It's worth taking time to get those sentences right.

The more complicated the subject the more time you may need to spend on the lead to make sure that you are giving the readers the information they need to become interested right away. You can't start too far back with background, and you can't plunge into the middle of the story so that the readers do not know what they are reading. You have to start at the right point in the right way, and the more time you spend drafting new leads, and then refining the leads you choose, the faster you will be able to write the whole piece. Most of the major problems in writing an article are solved when the right lead is found.

When I worked as writing coach at *The Boston Globe,* I found that the best writers usually knew where they would end. They had a quote, an anecdote, a scene, a specific detail with which they would close. It would sum up the piece by implication. The good writer has a sense of direction, a destination in mind. The best endings are rarely written to solve the problems of a piece that just trails off. The best endings are usually seen by the writer as waiting just ahead for the draft to take the writer and the reader there.

The right voice

Experienced writers rarely begin a first draft until they hear in their heads—or on the page—a voice that may be right. Voice is usually the key element in effective writing. It is what attracts the reader and communicates to the reader. It is that element that gives the illusion of speech. Voice carries the writer's intensity and glues together the information that the reader needs to know. It is the music in writing that makes meaning clear.

Writers keep rehearsing possible first lines, paragraphs, or endings, key scenes or statements that will reveal how what is to be said may be said best. The voice of a piece of writing is the writer's own voice, adapted in written language to the subject and audience. We speak differently at a funeral or a party, in church or in the locker room, at home or with strangers. We are experienced with using our individual voices for many purposes. We have to learn to do this same thing in

306

writing, and to hear a voice in our head that may be polished and developed on the page.

The voice is not only rehearsed but practiced. We should hear what we're writing as we write it. I dictate most of my writing and monitor my voice as I'm speaking so that the pace, the rhythm, the tone support what I'm trying to say. Keep reading aloud as you draft and edit. To train yourself to do this, it may be helpful, if you use a word processor, to turn off the screen and write, listening to what you're saying as you're saying it. Later you can read it aloud and make the changes you need to develop a voice that the reader can hear.

Put your notes away before you begin a draft. What you remember is probably what should be remembered; what you forget is probably what should be forgotten. No matter; you'll have a chance to go back to your notes after the draft is completed. What is important is to achieve a draft which allows the writing to flow.

Planning allows the writer to write fast without interruptions, putting a space or TK (to come) in the text for the quote or the statistic that has to be looked up later. There are some writers who proceed slowly, but most of us learn the advantage of producing a draft at top speed when the velocity forces unexpected connections and makes language twist and spin and dance in ways we do not expect.

When you finish your daily stint or if you are interrupted during the fast writing, stop in the middle of a sentence so you can return to the text and start writing again at a point when you know what you have to say. It's always a good idea to stop each day before the well is drained dry, when you know what you'll try to deal with the next day. This is the best way to overcome the inertia we all suffer when returning to a draft. If we know how to finish a sentence, the chances are the next sentence will rise out of that one, and we'll be writing immediately.

Planning is important, but it isn't writing. You want to be free enough in writing a draft to say more than you expect to say. Writers do not write what they already know as much as they write to know. Edward Albee echoes many writers when he says, "I write to find out what I'm thinking about." Writing is an act of thinking, and the process of writing adds two and two and comes up with seven.

An effective article usually has one dominant theme or message; everything in it should advance that meaning. Other meanings collect around the dominant one, but in the process of revision, the writer must make sure that everything in the piece relates to the main idea, cutting what does not move the reader forward.

The inexperienced writer cuts a piece of writing by compression and produces a package of tight language that can be difficult to understand and is rarely a pleasure to read. The professional writer selects those parts that most efficiently and effectively advance the meaning and then develops them fully so that the reader understands the significance of the anecdote, the full strength of the argument.

Writing in which the meaning is not clear often occurs because writers bury the most important information. One way to make an article clear is to look at the most significant paragraphs and move the sections around so that the most important information is at the end of the paragraph, the next most important at the beginning, and the least most important in the center of the paragraph.

We need important information at the beginning to attract the reader, but what the reader remembers is usually at the end of the paragraph. This pattern doesn't work for every paragraph, and shouldn't. But it is a way of clarifying a complicated and significant paragraph, and the same rule may be applied to an entire piece of writing.

I find that I am a more efficient editor of my own draft if I read it three times and have a specific goal for each reading. *First,* I read it to see if I have all the information I need. Do I have the facts, statistics, quotations, anecdotes I need to construct an accurate, persuasive article? And do I understand that information? If I don't have the information or understand it I must stop my editing and deal with these problems.

Second, I read for organization. Does the article, as I have mentioned earlier, answer the readers' questions in the order they will ask them? Does the article flow naturally from beginning to end, with each part of the article fitting what has gone before and leading to what follows?

Third, I read the article line by line, listening both to what is said and how it is said, making sure, by reading it aloud, that my voice carries the meaning to the reader. I hope that my articles will be accurate and have the illusion of speech, the rhythm, music, and ease of an ideal conversation.

Those are a few of the tricks of the nonfiction trade. Try them out to see if they work for you. Collect others from your writer friends, and become aware of those devices that you have used to make your meaning clear, so that you will be able to call on them as you continue your lifelong course in learning how to write.

61

THE CHALLENGES OF SCIENCE WRITING

By Isabel S. Abrams

Do you find worms, or stars, or liverworts fascinating? Are you intrigued by radioactivity, recombinant DNA technology, or the workings of the human brain? Then you have the makings of a science writer.

A science writer's primary task is to demystify science. You look for connections between what happens in the laboratory and the outside world. You probe the secrets of nature, investigate research, talk about technology, and relate all this information to your reader, showing the impact it has on his or her life. Since you always aim for accuracy and clarity, you tread the thin line between overdramatizing events and putting your reader to sleep.

Before you write about how research affects everyday life, you have to do research yourself. A good starting point for your research is the children's library. A book written for 6- to 9-year-olds will give you the basic concepts of atomic physics or the human body without the clutter of formulas and graphs. This clarifies the main ideas and makes you eager to obtain more detail from encyclopedias and other adult books.

In addition to general encyclopedias, a good public library will have the *Encyclopedia of Science and Technology,* nature encyclopedias, and other scientific reference books. However, because science changes so quickly and information in books is usually five years old, your research must go beyond books. To find out what is new in a particular area of science, consult your reference librarian, who may direct you to the *Readers' Guide to Periodical Literature,* or to articles published in professional journals. Other sources include *Biology Digest* and *Science News,* which abstract articles from many science journals; and *Nature, Science,* and *Scientific American,* which report research in many fields. For background on a famous scientist, look in *Who's Who* and other biographical indexes. The *Encyclopedia of Associations* is another valuable source, for it lists scientific, engineering, environmental, and medical organizations to which you can write for information.

For odd facts about technology, space, geology, the human body, animals, or plants, see *The Guinness Book of Records,* books of amazing facts, and various almanacs. A world atlas provides information about oceans, forests, mountains, climate, and other aspects of the environment.

If you have done your research well, you'll have more questions than you had when you began. (That is what keeps scientists in their laboratories and science writers at their computers!) You need to read enough to feel comfortable with the subject, then use unanswered questions as part of an interview with a scientist. Speaking directly with scientists who work in the laboratory or in the field helps your science article come alive.

How do you find a scientist who knows your subject? Ask teachers in your local high school science department; contact the public relations person at a nearby university, museum, drug company, or other related business. Look up your topic in the yellow pages of your phone directory, or find the appropriate scientific group in the *Encyclopedia of Associations.* When you've tracked down a scientist in the field you are writing about, send him or her a one-page letter mentioning the article you are working on and request an interview—or ask if you may call him at his convenience to arrange an appointment, stating how long you think the interview will take. (A face-to-face interview is best, but if time or distance is a problem, ask the scientist if he would agree to a telephone interview.)

During an interview, you will collect quotes and anecdotes, and in order to be accurate, bring a tape recorder, with extra tapes and batteries. Always ask the expert's permission to record the interview on tape (this is required by law). During the interview, if the scientist tells you something "off the record," turn the tape recorder off. You may want to take notes, as well; this avoids embarrassment if the tape recorder doesn't work and is helpful when you are dealing with unfamiliar scientific terms.

Begin the interview by verifying the scientist's name, title, address, and phone number (this will enable you to check quotes or ask more questions later, if necessary). Asking for the scientist's approval of

311

quotes before publication ensures that you've conveyed his meaning correctly. (Checking for accuracy is essential to science writing.) You may want to have him sign and date a release form saying, "I approve the quotes as written in the article _____." (If you also send a copy of the printed article, the scientist will welcome you in the future.)

Interview questions should be worded so they require an explanation rather than a "yes" or "no" answer. Instead of asking "Are you working on photosynthesis?" ask, "What aspect of photosynthesis are you investigating?" In asking your questions, go from the general to the more specific. Caution: "What's new in oceanography?" is too general; instead, ask "What kind of investigations did you do when you were 10,000 feet under the sea?" Then become more specific with "What method did you use? What were your results? Your conclusions?" Your last question, "Do you have anything to add?" often brings surprising insights.

Build trust during the interview by progressing from "safe" questions to controversial or personal ones. Preface a controversial question by saying, "Someone has said — —. Would you care to comment?" Never argue with an answer. Your job is to listen, not to debate. If you are uncomfortable with some of the answers given, get a second opinion by interviewing another authority on the subject. Then when you write the article, you can present two points of view and let the reader decide the issue.

Many people think science consists of unchangeable fact or truth. This is not so. For example, at one time the atom was described as the smallest bit of matter. Atom smashing changed all that. Science is a process as well as a body of knowledge, in which ideas about nature are continuously tested and refined by researchers. Scientists try to explain how nature operates, using the best available evidence, gathering information with their eyes and ears and other senses, and taking measurements. This data or information is summarized and interpreted in formulas, graphs, computer models, theories and laws, and retested as new technology and new information are acquired.

As you report on an experiment or technology, show how it fits in with scientific theory and how it affects the world. For example, demonstrate the principles of electricity by showing how electrons travel through the wire of a lamp. Using examples from the "real world," make scientific theories clear to your reader.

312

You must define all scientific terms so non-scientists will understand them; if readers are puzzled by a word or term, it will become a road block for them. It is easy to explain that a toxic substance is a poison, but how do you define quarks? Practice by taking an unusual scientific or technical word or term from the daily newspaper and explain it in a phrase or a sentence. For instance, you might try to define the following:

biodiversity
cancer
desertification
ecosystem
magnetic resonance imaging
nuclear fission
pancreas
photosynthesis
recombinant DNA technology
strategic defense initiative
virus

Lay readers often resist science articles because they believe that science is too hard to understand. You can overcome such "science anxiety" by explaining the reasoning behind an experiment, or the process of a technology, step by step. Picture yourself looking over the shoulder of a scientist in the laboratory, or an engineer in a power plant. Then describe what you see.

As you begin to write your science article, you may be surprised to discover that the sequence of ideas is similar to the steps of the scientific method:

1. *Ask a question or present a problem.* This is the lead that hooks your reader. It may be an anecdote, a quote, or a series of questions that presents the theme or key idea in your article.

2. *State the hypothesis.* This is the theme of your article, what you think is the answer to the question. A hypothesis is a scientific hunch or guess based on some evidence, and posed in a way that will allow it to be tested.

3. *Test the hypothesis with observations and experiments.* Take your reader into the laboratory or the field and show the events that lead to discoveries.

4. *Summarize the data,* the results of the observations and experiments. Give statistics and other evidence. Present your case. (Scientists often use formulas and graphs.)

5. *Verify results.* Cite more than one source of information, and use quotes from several scientists. Scientists perform the same experiments over and over

again to see if they obtain the same results, or they debate concepts with other scientists in conferences or in publications.

6. *State the conclusion.* This is the answer to the question, or the solution to the problem. Be sure to mention any remaining unsolved questions and related issues.

7. *Discuss the practical applications of the discovery.* How might a new technology change society? How will it affect a person's everyday life? What are the costs and benefits? How do research results alter concepts about the way nature works?

As you follow the pathways of research, you will discover some of nature's secrets. This is the joy of science—and of science writing.

62

REFLECTIONS OF A BIOGRAPHER

BY ELIZABETH LONGFORD

INSPIRATION COMES to biographers as much as to novelists but cannot be commanded by any cerebral tricks. Nevertheless one can do something to help it breathe.

In the last 20 years, I have worked out a "writing day" for myself. I write best in the morning, though not immediately after breakfast. I use that first hour to write letters or shopping lists; even the laundry list loosens me up and gets me going with a pen. Writing out-of-doors suits me best, either in the Sussex garden or on the Chelsea balcony. Outdoor sounds seem to absorb the distractive parts of my brain and leave the rest free to concentrate. It may be that I have got used over the years to writing in some degree of noise indoors: children in the same room or myself on a train journey. The only place I can't perform is at a desk on a straight-backed chair. Writing late at night seems more inspirational than it is. I seldom find the results come up to scratch when I reread them next morning. Indeed, problems that appear insoluble at midnight have a way of smoothly solving themselves at midday.

Structure and chronology are among the perennial problems. How to deal with the subject's personal and public life? They happen simultaneously, whereas in the biography there may have to be some measure of separation. Should it be separate chapters? Or separate sections within the same chapter? I have used both methods, though the former more with public male characters who tend, conveniently for the biographer, to compartmentalize their lives. Women, even public women, are more "open plan."

I reread endlessly what I have written and make continual corrections: sometimes substantial ones involving rearrangements of material, more often verbal changes. Really obstinate problems have to be solved with the help of manual labor—preferably gardening. Clearing the ground for a rosebush clears away the mental rubbish as well.

315

All these techniques to be developed for what? Biography. Not for the (superior) arts of fiction or history. I think biography chose me, as it chooses most of its operators. And chose me because I wanted to write in the ways it had to offer. Michael Holroyd, author of *Lytton Strachey*, has said that biography is the nearest art to the novel. It is about people, and it thrives on imagination, to decipher them if not to create. I prefer to work on people who were or are *there*, as a doctor or teacher does, not so much on might-have-beens. I like to see them in my mind's eye as a novelist does but also to see the actual letters they wrote, the clothes they wore. There is a special excitement in handling their possessions that seems to generate extra perceptiveness.

I like my subject to be encapsulated in a life, as history is not. All the same, my biographies must always to some extent be a "Life and Times of . . ." The balance between "Life" and "Times," however, is one of the most difficult to achieve. A reviewer said there was not enough historical background in my first biography (*Queen Victoria*); when I tried to repair that omission in my second (*Wellington*), another reviewer said there was too much. Can one win? Help has come, notwithstanding, from two guidelines, the first offered by Cecil Woodham-Smith, biographer of Florence Nightingale: "Always keep your narrative moving." That means, among other things, avoidance of too much argument with other historians, a pastime in which academics delight. My second rule is never to lose sight of my subject for more than a page or so. I aim at the maximum of background detail with the minimum of digression.

Another elusive question of balance concerns sympathy with one's subject. I could never write a biography of, say, Hitler, though I recognize the need for such works; perhaps the author's righteous indignation supplies the adrenaline usually produced by enthusiasm. Every self-respecting biographer tries to avoid hagiography like a plague of treacle.

Perhaps the thing I am really striving for is empathy. While sympathy merely means fellow feeling, empathy means "the power of projecting one's personality into, and fully understanding, the object of contemplation." I can do this only with someone I like. Incidentally, the one thing that makes biography unreadable is to lecture or rebuke one's subject.

Detection is another aspect of biography that I like: both the probing into character and the weighing up of fact versus legend. A Catch-22

316

situation is often involved at the beginning of these researches. If one reads secondary sources first—other authors' books—one may be prejudiced by them before one has had time to form one's own opinion; but if one goes straight into the original sources—letters and diaries—one may not be sufficiently well equipped to detect the hidden evidence on some controversy or problem. My own solution has been to read (or reread) *one* general account first and then dive into the primary sources.

Questions of fact or legend require exhaustive research but are sometimes solved by accident, occasionally too late, alas, for one's current book. I could not decide, for example, whether Queen Elizabeth II kept a real diary or merely a brief engagement record. After the publication of *The Queen,* I happened to mention this doubt during a lecture to a conference of American university women in London. One of them came up to me and said: "I *know.* When our group was introduced to Her Majesty, I asked: 'Ma'am, do you keep a diary? If so, how do you find the time?' The Queen replied, 'Prince Philip and Prince Charles read in bed. I write my diary. And it's a great deal more honest than anything you'll find in the media.' "

In the decade when I became a biographer—the 1960's—a double revolution in the art took place, the matrix being American universities. First, the availability of sources suddenly increased with the large-scale collecting of archives and the development of photocopying.

Second came the distinction between narrative and analytical-psychological biography. While I myself did not abandon narrative, I have learned from the disciplines of in-depth research. Forget all we ever knew about biography from *The Oxford Dictionary of Quotations,* especially Disraeli's "Read no history: nothing but biography, for that is life without theory." Today in certain quarters biography has become theory without life. As far as possible, the life *story* is ignored; even dates of birth and death may be hard to find. There is instead a wealth of interpretation of the subject's own words, which should eventually lay bare the naked self, the "inner me." Individual lives being incoherent, there must be no attempt at continuous narrative, but everything should be "discontinuous" and open-ended.

In still safeguarding narrative, I accept the need to add to my duties as biographer the roles of interpreter, mediator between other writers' views, and analyst. My chief fear is that the analytical game may become too facile, too seductive.

Biography is too important to become a playground for fantasies, however ingenious; I believe its future is safe with the reading public, who will keep it human, not too solemn.

63

BREAKING INTO PRINT AT YOUR LOCAL NEWSPAPER

BY LIZ GREENBACKER

THE BEST PLACE for a beginning article writer to get started is the local newspaper." That's good advice, but how does a writer do it? It's harder than that short sentence implies—but it's easier than you think! You have to know three things: *what* to write, *how* to write, and *how* to sell it. Let's start with what to write.

Don't try to cover the same event the paper is already covering. The fast-breaking news story is not the best place for you to start. Unless you actually find yourself at the scene of a major accident, natural disaster, train wreck, or political payoff, the newspaper will have heard about it and covered it before you can. Although many papers buy book and movie reviews and celebrity interviews from a news service—or they are staff written—many local newspapers, with small staffs and smaller budgets, are hospitable to book reviews, reviews of cultural events, etc., by free lancers. Payment is minimal, but this is an excellent way for a beginner to get started.

Take another look at your local paper. Sandwiched between that story of the Palace Theater fire, the latest election scandal, and the review of a new movie are articles that fall into the broad category of "general interest." There are man-bites-dog stories, profiles, interviews with local heroes, forthcoming yet little known community events, community anniversaries. They add the flavor, the spark, the tears and laughter to your local paper. General interest stories are a wide-open door for free lancers, because small newspapers don't have the staff to cover everything that happens in your town. You can fill the gap by supplying your paper with sidelights on local life. Explore the nooks and crannies of the town. The stories are there—in abundance! Now, to get specific.

Though you may not be able to do celebrity interviews, such features as profiles, how-tos, unusual, unique special events, even recipes are all found in the leisure/living section of most local papers. The "Accent Page" at my local paper always wants articles on family activities. I have covered an American Indian powwow, cast a dinosaur footprint in plaster of Paris, visited a castle decorated for a Victorian Christmas, taken a ride on a steam train with Santa Claus, explored the South Street Seaport Museum in New York City, toured West Point, fed the animals at Catskill Game Farm, and I've written articles about all of them for the local paper. You get the idea.

Do you want to write profiles? Start talking to friends, relatives, and service suppliers. My doctor is the town's equivalent of Fred Astaire, and my "Dancing Doctor" query brought an immediate go-ahead from the local newspaper editor. So did the idea for a piece about a World War II veteran who collected enough memorabilia, books, and clippings about submarines to start his own museum. I've interviewed children on scholarships to summer camp; a Chinese woman with a nursing degree who wants to volunteer at a hospital but must first learn English; a minister and his wife; a woman print shop owner who encounters sexual discrimination on her sales calls; a rape survivor; a Boys' Club volunteer; and mental health patients at a local Friendship Club.

What about special events? When a sixty-foot Hermaphrodite schooner anchored in the Connecticut River one summer, I wrote about it and made a sale. I also sold an article on how to run a successful quilt show, an annual event at my church. My favorite so far was the photo essay I did about our veterans' monuments. Spread throughout the city, the monuments provided a tour that was as emotionally fulfilling as a trip to Washington, D.C. I've covered recreational opportunities for women and written the history of our oldest farm.

You can write any or all of these articles for your local newspaper. Poke around! Find small, lesser-known museums; learn about the educational system; make friends with the librarian. Talk to your friends, relatives, your doctor; find people with unusual hobbies, talents, backgrounds, and associations, and start there. Do you know of some event in your town that doesn't get the coverage it deserves? The stories are there, just waiting for you to recognize them. If an idea appeals to you, it's likely to appeal to a great many others—and to an editor as well.

Advertising supplements are an often overlooked source of ideas for article writers. My paper runs supplements on cars, weddings, home improvements, a back-to-school issue, and dining guides throughout the year. Articles for these supplements give consumers information about local businesses, another golden opportunity for free lancers!

Ad supplements also include how-to articles. I've written pieces on how a couple moved and reconstructed an 18th-century house; how to hire a building contractor; what a bride forgets when planning her wedding; and how to survive first grade. Many how-to articles are purchased from news services, but your paper has to publish some stories with a local slant, and they need *you* to write them. Keep track of the publication dates of these supplements. Make a list of how-to ideas for each one. At least a month before publication, select an idea from your list, and query the special section editor.

This brings us to how to sell your ideas to a newspaper editor. Introduce yourself by sending a letter, including samples of your writing. Note the omission of the word "published" from the previous sentence. Newspaper editors want samples that prove you can write *for them*. Even if you don't have any published clips to send, you can still send writing samples. Here's how:

Find, research, and write at least two articles designed for the leisure-time section or a specific ad supplement. These should be written in the style and length of those that appear in the section you've targeted. Enclose the samples and your resumé with a short letter of introduction asking for the opportunity to query with article ideas. The editor does not want your life story. Editors are interested only in your experience, training, and background as it pertains to writing for their papers.

When you get a positive reply, your next step is to write a query letter on a specific idea. One page is sufficient. Here is the query I wrote for this piece:

Dear Editor:
I am proposing a piece titled, "Breaking into Print at Your Local Newspaper." My lead is:
The best place for a beginning writer to get started is the local paper. That's good advice, but just how do you do it?

The article will cover the following points:

1. Finding article ideas.
2. Writing query letters.
3. Writing the article.

The article would be approximately 1800 words and can be completed in one week. I am willing to write the piece on speculation. I have enclosed a self-addressed, stamped envelope for your reply.

A query letter should be short and direct. I use the above style for all my queries to newspapers and magazines. I like to include the lead to my proposed article, because it shows that I've already done some work on the piece and that my beginning will catch the reader's attention. When you get a go-ahead, don't think that the quality of your writing can be less than the best just because the market is small. Forget flowery phrases and first person. Newspapers demand objectivity. But you don't have to stick to the strict, rigid format of the front page, either. Forget including the *who, what, where, when* and *why* in the first paragraph. You're writing general interest, not news.

Learn to write briefly. Lengths vary from 200 words for the advertising supplements to 1,000 words for the leisure section. The average length is 800 words, which is less than three double-spaced typed pages. You can't include everything—stick to the most interesting highlights.

Be thorough. Readers may plan vacations, visit museums, and add on to their houses following your advice. Make sure every fact is correct and every quote is accurate. Use the best in research and interviewing techniques.

When you're writing for your local paper, your lead and tone can be as varied as they would be if you were writing for a hundred different publications. Just keep in mind your editor's tastes. Editors appreciate the different voices and styles free lancers use, so don't become predictable—another reason free lancers are in demand at local papers.

Find the bizarre, the interesting, the out-of-the-ordinary, the unique all around you. Every town has its share of interesting and unusual people, places, and things that will make it easy for you to break into print at your local paper.

64

WRITE TO SELL
A 3-Point Checklist That Works

By Samm Sinclair Baker

WHY do some writers make sales and collect sizable checks again and again . . . while others, perhaps you, are beaten back repeatedly by discouraging rejections? Is there some "magic" by which rejected writers can be transformed into published professionals? Is there immediate help for you if your work isn't selling?

Yes . . . the reasons for rejections are often surprisingly clear and simple—once you know how to identify and correct them for your own benefit. You'll gain some valuable eye-openers by applying these three basic checkpoints. They can open new pathways to selling what you write.

The primary reasons for failure to sell were affirmed vividly for me when I was the judge of a contest for beginning writers. Employing these practical insights has worked for me and for other selling writers. They're bound to work for you, if you'll follow through with them intelligently—*never giving up.*

Take advantage of these three checkpoints in analyzing any manuscript before you submit it for publication, and you'll uncover crucial, costly flaws. Making necessary corrections and revisions before you submit your article can mean the difference between sale and turndown.

First, study these recommendations; then apply them to the piece you've just finished—and to others that didn't sell. Concentrate on reading your article objectively, line by line, as though you were the editor. Now, as editor rather than writer, *you* must decide whether or not to buy the piece for publication. Be ruthlessly honest as you ask yourself, "Is the manuscript faulty, judged by any or all of the checkpoints?"

If yes, revise, rewrite—or start all over again. It often pays to discard the entire piece if it doesn't measure up. Finally, you'll be thrilled by the improvements you can readily make, once you realize exactly what is wrong. That's *self-help in action,* since you'll have a simple method to use profitably in planning and completing everything you write to sell from now on.

CHECKPOINT # 1

Will This Subject Interest Enough Readers?

The great editor of *Good Housekeeping,* John Mack Carter, enlightened me about editorial needs. He said that there are three subjects of outstanding interest to most women and many men today. Readers, he emphasized, are constantly seeking new, usable information about: *Diet . . . Sex . . . Money.*

If you write in the categories of these prime subjects—offering fresh, easily grasped approaches—you'll certainly have a better chance to sell than if your piece is about something as far-out as "The Prevalence of Fire Ants in Abyssinia." Obviously that's a wild exaggeration to make an essential point: *Write what interests most others, not just what pleases you.*

Of course, you don't have to confine yourself to those three basic themes. Yet, even within that seeming limitation, the possibilities for writing that sells are practically unlimited. For example, consider the many variations, such as:

DIET: "DROP POUNDS NOW WITH 12 DELICIOUS NEW RECIPES."

SEX: "ENCHANTING NEW HAIRSTYLES BOOST SEX APPEAL."

MONEY: "ADD INCOME WITH EASY NEW WORK-AT-HOME IDEAS."

It comes down to the old saw: Feed your pets what *they* want to eat, not what *you* like. Similarly, choose a subject that is of high interest to other people, realizing that editors are people, too. Analyze carefully in advance the interests of the specific reading audience you're trying to reach. Otherwise, you'll waste time and effort and invite discouragement and frustration. Smart subject selection is fundamental if you *write to sell.* Clearly, selling interests you. . . . or you wouldn't be reading this.

A common mistake of beginners is the I-I-I approach—writing about

324

your personal experiences. That's relatively easy, but get it out of your head that anything that happens to you is of interest to others, unless it will appeal to a wide audience. Editors groan when a manuscript begins, "I remember Aunt Clara very well. I loved her deeply, and I'll always treasure sweet memories of her. . . ."

How many magazines readers care about your Aunt Clara or your Uncle Ted? How many of the same readers would be interested in an article that begins: "The weekend reducing spa business is booming, but what can a brief stay at a spa do for you realistically? Can it help you lose weight, keep on taking off pounds and inches, and stay slim from then on? For the answers, I interviewed five men and five women who had been to various weekend spas a month earlier. Here's what they reported. . . ."

Aren't your chances of selling the spa piece infinitely better? Checkpoint #1 is clear: Before you write on any theme, think of where you're going to aim for publication. Then consider the subject through the editor's eyes. Realize that, as editor, you must interest the largest possible number of your readers, so you'll buy only articles most likely to do that. To sell the articles you write, *you must fulfill the editor's needs.* For a men's magazine, for example, you would interview mainly men.

CHECKPOINT #2

Are Your Opening Lines "Reader-Grabbers"?

An editor of a mass circulation magazine (a neighbor) brought home for the weekend a huge briefcase loaded with articles submitted for publication. He said, "Before I take you sailing, help me weed out which of these pieces have possibilities for an issue coming up soon." I protested, "It will take me forever to get through these."

"You'll be finished in less than a hour," he assured me. "You can usually tell by reading just the first paragraph whether to discard it or go further. If the opening sentences don't hook you, reject it—the writing rarely gets any better."

Here are a couple of examples to show how much the opening sentences matter in the articles you write. Again, read them as though you're the editor examining the two following submissions on the same general subject. Based on the opening paragraphs alone, which manuscript would you have read with greatest attention?

(A) "Everyone in the neighborhood spoke well of Maryann Browne. She could usually be seen sitting in the old rocker on her front porch, swaying slightly as she knitted patiently hour after hour. We were all deeply shocked when we heard that her family doctor, whom we all knew, let it be known through the grapevine that she had cancer."

(B) "I'm a cancer patient, in the midst of that uneasy purgatory known as remission. After a year that would make the cast of *Dynasty* shake its collective head in disbelief, I am trying to get well. I *will* get well. That is, if people let me. The cancer may not kill me. But I'm not at all sure about the public."

The article that was bought, and appeared in a leading magazine, was "B." As a casual reader, I turned the pages rather idly, but the opening brief paragraph grabbed me. The writer telling flat out that she is afflicted with the dread disease led me on with the promise of hope in "remission." I was hooked further by the unexpected challenge in the surprising dramatic twist that "the public" might keep her from getting well. The public? That's *me!* Now *I* was involved. How could I stop reading?

It's obvious why I—or you—as editor, would, if offered a choice, probably reject "even without reading any further than that first paragraph. Why should I care or be particularly interested in someone I don't know—Maryann Browne—just because people "spoke well" of her? There's nothing very thrilling about a woman sitting in an old rocker on her front porch, knitting patiently hour after hour. Sure, I (and you) feel sympathy for anyone with cancer—but that's not enough to *compel* me to read more. Result: rejection. I'll bet that the discouraged writer never realized why her piece didn't sell—as you understand the reason now.

What's your next step? As an aspiring, determined writer, you'll gather all of your rejections for reexamination as soon as you can. You'll reread the opening paragraphs carefully, objectively, with fresh, clear-sighted analysis—as if through the editor's eyes. Do your opening lines reach out and grip readers, pulling them into the rest of the article? If not, rewrite until you have created a solid reader-grabber, even if it means rewriting a dozen times. You'll have a far better chance of having your writing read and bought.

Here's one more self-teaching example to help you avoid rejection slips in the future, or turn your past rejects into sales: A fine professional writer wanted to sell an article on beauty care to one of the best-paying, top-circulation women's magazines. But she knew there was tremendous competition in the beauty article field, not just from other free-lance writers, men and women, but from the magazine's staff writers.

She put her creativity to work and sought out one of the most popular photography models, who agreed to coauthorship. There was just one problem, as she knew too well: Most women might feel that they couldn't learn from a model who started with "perfect features." So the writer tackled the dilemma head-on with this opening paragraph:

You don't have to be born with perfect features to have a model's face. [Really? Tell me more. . . .] Many of the world's highly paid models are not necessarily natural beauties, but they do have the ability to put their best face forward. That means skin care and carefully applied make-up. I'd like to share with you some of the very special beauty secrets I've learned during my career as a model.

That's the hook—the grabber—the promise from a top model to share her beauty secrets with you. Possibly you're asking yourself, "Why didn't I think of a creative idea like that, and write an opening that would make the sale to an editor?" From now on, I hope you will.

I've reworked the opening paragraphs of my books up to twenty and more times, until I felt as sure as I could be that I'd fashioned an irresistible promise, the hook that would seize and hold the reader. One of the best examples I know is the start of the best-selling diet book of all time, *The Complete Scarsdale Medical Diet* (which I coauthored with Dr. Herman Tarnower). The opening proved a salesmaker.

The doctor is speaking:

"I, personally, explain *The Complete Scarsdale Medical Diet*'s phenomenal popularity in two words: 'It works.' A slim trim lady said to me recently, 'Your diet is beautifully simple, and the results are simply beautiful.' I just say, 'It works.'"

A reader-grabber like that can work for you. Check your opening lines repeatedly to make sure they convey convincing promise of worth-while reading ahead.

CHECKPOINT #3

Have You Done Enough "Self-Editing"?

"A superb cook knows when to take a dish out of the oven so it's neither underdone nor overcooked," an editor commented. "But most of the manuscripts I reject are either underwritten—not enough thought and work put into them—or overwritten—too many words to say too little, not enough careful cutting."

When I've been involved on the editing end, I've found that many 20-page manuscripts would have been more acceptable if cut to 15 or even 10 pages. Yet, when I've suggested this to earnest individuals, the reaction usually has been, "You want me to cut out what I've worked so hard to put in? The writing is good, isn't it?"

Yes, the writing may be good—but, as the cliché affirms, it can be "too much of a good thing." Any word that isn't effective and essential should be eliminated. Stop and think what "edit" means. According to dictionaries, "to edit" means "to make written materials suitable for publication." Next time you're about to send out a manuscript you've written, ask yourself . . .

• *Have I worked this over specifically, so it's "suitable for publication," saying exactly what the reader needs and wants to know?*
• *Have I been too lazy to go back and cut again and again?*
• *Am I too much in love with my own words to edit sufficiently?*

A big part of successful professionalism grows from enough self-editing. It pays to review and rework every page repeatedly, asking each time, "Is this word necessary?" This chapter was more than three times as long before I cut-cut-cut, to make it most understandable and useful for you. Yes, it hurts to cross out words, paragraphs, pages you've sweated over, but it's essential to successful editing.

After over thirty years of writing and selling, I still check every piece according to all three of the preceding checkpoints. That discipline keeps working for me. There are other factors that can make or break a sale. Some, such as timing and a magazine's overstock, are often out of your control. Regardless of such unforeseeable obstacles, these three basic checkpoints can and will work remarkably for you—when you *write to sell.*

65

HOW TO WRITE GOOD ARTICLE LEADS

BY MARSHALL COOK

IF YOUR article lead doesn't catch the reader's attention immediately, your article doesn't stand a chance in the marketplace. That makes the first words of an article the most important ones you write. And it puts a lot of pressure on you to write them well.

First, your lead should issue a clear invitation to the reader by promising useful or interesting information and an enjoyable reading experience. Never try to trick your readers by promising more than your article will deliver. And there's no use trying to coerce them, either. You can't force your readers to participate in your visions. You can only show them how interesting and exciting those visions are.

Next, your lead should establish the focus of the article by introducing the subject and conveying the main idea or slant.

Finally, your lead should establish the tone of your article. If you plan to take a light, humorous approach, for example, your lead should provoke a chuckle.

Here are seven approaches that can help you create compelling leads.

The startling statement

"Your English teacher lied to you." That's how I started an article on advertising copy writing for an in-house publication. My point was not that English teachers are liars, but that good ad copy often breaks the sacred grammar rules we dutifully learned. "Ad copy often breaks grammar rules" didn't strike me as an especially effective lead, however, so I chose a statement that I hoped would generate more interest.

A study skills article I wrote for *Directions,* a regional college campus magazine, began, "The good grades don't necessarily go to the smartest students." They go, I pointed out, to those who have learned how to study most effectively.

The startling statement should convey the focus or slant quickly while evoking a positive attention and arousing curiosity.

The quote lead

It's often best to let the subjects speak for themselves. Quotation marks around a lead signal readers that the show is about to begin.

My profile of architect Kenton Peters for *Wisconsin Trails* magazine began with Peters' assertion, "We have the fundamental right not to be confronted by ugliness." I thought it a fine quote to lead with, because, though the words are easy to understand, the context isn't clear at once. It should pique the readers' curiosity without befuddling them.

Provide the context, along with attribution for the quote, as quickly as possible. If you leave your readers hanging too long, they may feel manipulated or become confused.

Sometimes the quote can be commonplace and close to home. For my humor piece, "Fraction Action," for *The Milwaukee Journal Green Sheet* (check your local newspapers as potential markets), I quoted my son:

"Hey, Dad. I need help with my homework."
Words to strike terror into any parent's heart.

Your best quotes come from your own sources, because they supply material that has never been in print. Occasionally, however, you may want the richness of allusion that a familiar quote can provide. I've used Mark Twain's, "If you can catch an adjective, kill it," and the immortal advertising slogan, "Plop, plop, fizz, fizz. Oh, what a relief it is," to bring the readers closer to my subjects.

The anecdotal lead

Perhaps the most effective but often the hardest to develop, the anecdotal lead shows rather than tells. The anecdote is a small, human story used to illuminate the point of the whole article.

I began my profile of a thriving acrylics company for *Business Age* magazine with the story of how Jim Lynn started the company with a $200 power saw and a few scraps of wood and plastic in the basement of his home. It provided a simple, human introduction to the complexities of the business and illustrated my theme, that a $2.2 million-a-year business could begin without planning and, indeed, almost by accident.

330

As with quotes, the best anecdotes come from your own sources. Probe for anecdotes in your interviews. When your subject gives you a generalization such as "You meet the most interesting people in my line of work," your response should be, "Describe some of those interesting people."

It's almost always best to keep yourself out of the article, but it may occasionally be effective to begin with a personal anecdote in order to make contact with your readers. I began my article "Holiday Hassles/ Holiday Happiness" for *Catholic Digest* by describing my 24-hour wait at the Milwaukee airport while my parents, snowbound in Denver, tried to get through for a Thanksgiving visit.

It's all right to make up an anecdote, as long as you make it clear to the reader that you're doing so. For my piece "Personal Publishing," I walked the reader through the experience of submitting a manuscript and having it rejected, to illustrate that the hardest work for the writer sometimes begins when the actual writing is done.

The cliché with a twist

Ordinarily, clichés have no place in your work, and especially not in the lead, where freshness is a must. But a good, hard twist can squeeze new life from a seemingly wrung-out phrase.

I began my article on physical fitness for *Directions* with an old saw with a couple of new teeth: "Caution: College may be hazardous to your health."

I've never forgotten the newspaper article on dieting that began, "Despite all the diets, pills and potions, heft springs eternal" or the baseball story that led with, "Things were so quiet in the Brewers clubhouse last night, you could hear a batting average drop."

Direct address

Often the best approach is the most direct one, a lead that puts the reader directly into the action.

I wanted to begin my description of a Mercury-Marine outboard motor plant for *The Yacht* magazine with the surprising fact that "Many yachts have their beginnings in an aluminum recycling plant in Fond du Lac, Wisconsin." I think I made the lead much stronger by rewriting it in direct address: "Your yacht may have begun as a mound of aluminum cans in Fond du Lac, Wisconsin."

One widely used variation on direct address is the question lead, but be careful here. Writers have overworked this technique, using it as an "if-all-else-fails" catch-all. Especially worn out is the "What do Sylvester Stallone, George Bush and Mother Theresa have in common?" format. Avoid it.

Avoid, too, the rhetorical question, one that clearly manipulates the reader into giving a predetermined response. "Do you want your children to have a good education?" (No, I want my kids to be illiterate bums!)

If the question provokes reader curiosity and introduces a genuine search for answers, it may be an excellent lead.

The narrative lead

For a long time, I thought there were two kinds of writing, "creative" (as in short stories and poetry) and "journalistic" (as in stuff you wrote for money). I've learned better. There are two kinds of writing, all right, writing that works and writing that doesn't. Effective writing uses any appropriate means to tell its story. If description and narration, primary tools of the fiction writer, work best in opening your nonfiction piece, you have both the right and the responsibility to use them.

I began an article on the old Boston Blackie television series for *Airwaves,* a public television programming guide, by describing the opening sequence of each episode, with the mysterious detective's silhouette looming ever-larger at the end of a darkened alley. I did so to try to evoke the rough charm of a 1950s low-budget production.

My profile of National Book Award winner Herbert Kubly for *Wisconsin Trails* began with a panoramic sweep, almost like the opening of a movie, panning from the tiny town of New Glarus, where Kubly grew up, out along a country road to the fourth-generation Kubly family farm. I wanted to show the author's tie to the land and the effect that tie has had on his writing. What better way than to describe that land?

Description for its own sake merely delays the true start of the article and makes the readers impatient—if it doesn't chase them away completely. Effective description must be thematic, revealing the focus of the article.

The comparison lead

Metaphor, simile, and analogy are effective tools for making sense out of nonsense and rendering the abstract concrete. Don't save them for later. Use them in the lead.

I've described a Wisconsin street as a carnival, compared a writer's query letter to a job interview, likened the process of scanning a magazine article to standing back to take in an entire mural before moving closer to study details, all to try to shine a light on the darkness of a new subject.

The effective comparison startles readers with new insights, makes them nod in agreement and murmur, "Ah-ha!" As with all good writing, it helps us to see familiar realities in new ways.

These seven lead categories often overlap. A metaphor may arrive wearing quotation marks. Direct address may also twist a cliché. Strict categorization isn't important. Finding the best lead for your article is.

Begin the search early. As you gather material, ask yourself, "What is unique about my subject?" Constantly and consciously look for quotes, anecdotes, and bits of thematic description that might illustrate this uniqueness in a memorable lead.

Trying to write the lead before you're ready can leave you staring into space, too worried about getting off to a good start to get off to any start at all. Work with the material you're comfortable with until lead possibilities begin to emerge.

When you're ready to tackle the lead, write not one but several. Let your imagination play with the idea. See how many possibilities you can generate. Don't be too quick to settle on one. The more choices you give yourself, the more likely you are to discover the best approach.

Finally, never impose a lead on your material. Let the lead emerge from the material.

It's worth the time and effort it takes to craft a compelling lead. It can make the difference between an article that never sees print and one that entertains and informs your readers.

66

BIG AS ALL OUTDOORS

BY CHARLES NICHOLSON

ARE YOU LOOKING FOR a market that publishes new and little-known writers every month and pays well? One with a constant demand for straight expository articles, personal essays, fiction, humor, and even poetry and cartoons? One where editors truly want you to succeed and often go out of their way to encourage a talented novice? If you are, the outdoor sports market might be for you.

Ask yourself these two questions first, and answer them honestly. One: Can you write clearly and concisely in one or more of the forms mentioned above? You don't have to be a Hemingway, but his sparse, action-packed prose is some of the best outdoor writing ever published. Two: Do you truly love the outdoors? You don't have to be a Daniel Boone, but you should have more than a passing interest in outdoor sports—fishing, camping, skiing, hiking, outdoor photography, boating, golf, tennis, or any one of the dozens of outdoor recreational activities. If you can answer yes to both these questions, however tentatively, then the outdoor sports market may be for you. Let's see how you go about breaking into it.

There is an irritating myth about outdoor writing that I want to debunk right now. An old friend with whom I've fished and camped since we were kids asked to read a piece I was working on for a national sports magazine. It was about fishing and had a humorous reference to Captain Ahab and Moby Dick.

"Nice story," he commented, "but do you think the kind of people who read that magazine will know who Moby Dick was?"

I could hardly believe that he would say that. It would be disastrous for a writer trying to break into the outdoors market to have such a misconception. Readers of sports magazines are educated, literate, affluent enough to indulge in one or more expensive hobbies—and they read! Big words and literary references won't confuse them (but may turn them off). Make your article easy to read; concentrate on big thoughts, not big words.

Before you sit down to write, you should take time to read Ernest Hemingway's *The Old Man and the Sea* and *Green Hills of Africa.* Then read "The Bear" and "Delta Autumn," from William Faulkner's *Go Down, Moses.* Get a good translation of Ivan Turgenev's *Sketches from a Hunter's Album,* and read all of it, paying special attention to the stories called "Kasyan from the Beautiful Lands" and "Forest and Steppe." Study the very different ways each of these master craftsmen evokes the beauty of nature. Then discover the common bonds that unite such diverse characters as Santiago and Kandisky and Sam Fathers and Kasyan. When you understand these things, you will have found the essence of all good outdoor writing.

Next, study the magazines. You can find a complete listing of those currently being published at any major library. Look in *IMS Directory of Publications* under the section headed "Outdoors" for a list of publications with addresses, editors' names, frequency of publication, and circulation. If the sheer volume of periodicals overwhelms you, or you want more detailed information about editorial requirements, look in the market section of this book under "Sports, Outdoors, Recreation" and "Fiction." Other outdoor writing opportunities can be found even in literary journals! One of my best outdoor stories was first published in a small journal, although I prefer to sell to magazines that pay more.

When you've found a few magazines that interest you, buy the current issues, if available on the newsstands, or write for sample issues, which you can usually get for a dollar or two, and sometimes free. Go to the library and read all the current and back issues of magazines you may not find for sale. Keep in mind that each outdoor magazine has its own distinctive personality. To get to know those you want to write for, read the editorials in such magazines as *Field & Stream, Sports Afield, Southern Outdoors,* and *Outdoor Life,* among others. Read the ads and the letters to the editors, too, to find out what's on readers' minds. I've come up with more than one good story idea from those sources.

Read the magazines from cover to cover. Compare the table of contents to the masthead so you will know which articles are staff written and which are free-lance. Generally, the larger magazines publish more staff-produced material than smaller ones, but I know of no outdoor sports magazine that does not use some free-lance material. Technical articles are most often done by staff writers, while the more general pieces (the most fun to write) are more open to free lancers. Also, be aware that most of these magazines have very strict taboos. Almost all of them will send you free writers' guidelines if you send an SASE.

Now you're ready to write. Choose a form—essay, fiction, etc.— you've already had some success with. If you're unpublished, choose the form you most enjoy reading. Pick a subject you know, and try to come up with a unique angle. At this point, it is probably best to write a clear, short query letter to the editor of your target magazine. Send a rough outline of your idea, your qualifications to do the piece, and clips of your published work. If you want an answer, don't forget the SASE.

An unpublished writer has little chance of getting the go-ahead on a query unless he has an extremely unusual idea and impressive credentials, but don't let that deter you.

I've sold unsolicited manuscripts to *Sports Afield* and *Southern Outdoors* in less time than it took me to sell one I had queried *Field & Stream* about. I find that my chances of making a sale are better now if I query, but if I have a piece I feel is right for a particular magazine, I don't hesitate to submit the completed manuscript without querying first. The key is to know the market, and the only way to do that is to read the magazines.

A well-written query or finished piece about a unique subject, or a common subject handled uniquely, is difficult for an editor to reject. You don't have to go fly fishing on the Nile; just think about what you like to do and how to tell about it in a way that will intrigue a jaded editor.

The how-to article is the mainstay of outdoors magazines, but many also devote space to fiction and humorous or thoughtful essays. Again the key is uniqueness and originality. Don't suggest a story about a weekend camping trip unless you were attacked by a bear or mountain lion while you were there. Go to a remote area and do something unusual—not necessarily exotic, just different. Shed new light on an old subject, and, if you can do it well, take pictures. Articles with quality photographs are always welcome, and magazines usually pay more for them than for straight text pieces.

Now that you have the idea, go ahead and write the article or story.

336

But remember two things: Make it timely, and keep it short. The outdoors field is seasonal, and most material is purchased six months to a year before publication. The outdoors magazines rarely publish anything over 2,500 words, and if it's a humorous piece, better keep it below 1,500 words or risk automatic rejection. The editors won't try to cut it and won't ask you to do it: It just doesn't work and will be rejected.

I cured my wordiness, and a few other problems, in an unusual way. I had received rejections for every conceivable reason but bad writing, when an editor at one of the top outdoor magazines suggested I find a local newspaper editor to write for. So I wrote our local weekly newspaper, included clips of my published work, and described an eclectic, outdoors-oriented column I wanted to write for them.

As a result, I now write that column, "Up the Creek," on a regular basis, and the experience has been invaluable. I am limited to 500 words, which is a darn short space to say anything worthwhile. You learn to choose your subject matter carefully and edit your work wisely. My writing has become tighter and is rejected much less frequently. It's the only writing course I've ever had, and they pay me for taking it.

The outdoor sports market isn't an easy one to write for, but outdoor sports magazines pay well—from 10¢ to $1 per word and up. They have a high turnover of writers, so they are always looking for new talent.

I was lucky enough to sell a story when I was sixteen, but after that, I didn't write anything for several years. Then I wrote a deer-hunting story, put it aside, and almost forgot about it. Over a year later, I took it out and rewrote it. From a market listing, I learned that *Sports Afield* sometimes buys fiction related to outdoor sports. I thought about the story for a while, rewrote the ending again, and finally typed a short cover letter and submitted my unsolicited manuscript to that magazine. And waited.

A month later, the business manager of *Sports Afield* called me. It seems I had not put my Social Security number on the manuscript, and they had to have it before they could issue my check! When I asked how much I would be paid, the figure quoted was so high I thought there had been a mistake. I couldn't believe my work could be worth that much, but they thought it was. Yours could be, too, in the outdoor sports market.

67

HAVING FUN WRITING HUMOR

By Gene Perret

IRONICALLY, writing and selling humorous magazine pieces follows the classic "good news-bad news" joke form. The good news is that editors want good, funny pieces. "We need good humor," or "We're constantly searching for people who can write humor," editors say. The bad news is that humor is one of the most difficult things to sell to those same editors.

That contradiction may seem as if it were created by a humorist, but it is logical. It's because magazine editors are so selective in buying humor that they're constantly in need of it. If humor were easy to write and sell, they'd have plenty.

Why are the editors so selective? First of all, comedy is an elusive art form. It is to writing what jazz is to music. It's innovative, often rebellious and more often than not, will break tradition rather than follow it. The standard rules might not apply to a humorous piece. Therefore, it can confuse and frighten editors.

With a conventional article, the editor can analyze the form and structure and can grade each piece, calculating whether it will hold the reader's interest. With humor, those hard-and-fast rules become only guidelines. The editor can only guess how effective the article will be.

The basis of judgment changes, too. It's no longer whether the article is well written and well constructed. It's whether the article is entertaining or not. Most editors are less sure of themselves on that ground. Consequently, they're more hesitant about buying.

Secondly, comedy is very subjective. A joke or story is funny only to the person hearing it. That person forms a picture in the mind. If that picture is amusing, the reader laughs; if it isn't, he doesn't. One article can be funny to reader A and not funny to reader B. Since editors are first of all readers, you can see the confusion.

I asked one managing editor how she bought humor for her magazine.

338

She said, "We pass it around to the various editors. If they all laugh, we buy it." If they ALL laugh! That's formidable veto power for a humorist to face.

None of this should discourage the aspiring comedy writer, though. Rather, it should be encouraging for several reasons:

1) Since humor writing is admittedly difficult to sell, it automatically cuts down the competition. If it were easy, everybody would be doing it. Lighter pieces may be a way of reaching editors who have their favorite writers for the more conventional articles.

2) There is a demand for humor. Those magazines that use it often admit that it usually finishes very high in their reader surveys. People enjoy a chuckle. They like comedy in the movies, on TV, and in their reading. And good humor is not easy to find. The demand is high, and the supply is low—that's a situation that every free lancer dreams of.

3) There is probably less rewriting demanded on light pieces than any other type of writing. Why? Because, again, it's an area that is foreign to most editors. They can strengthen a traditional piece with suggestions for rewrites or restructuring, but can they make something funnier? They're writers or journalists and usually not humorists. They leave that fine tuning to the wits. Also, there is less rewriting requested because the piece was basically amusing. If it weren't, it would have been rejected sooner.

4) Comedy is a rewarding type of writing. It's cathartic for the writer as well as the reader. It helps you get many little peeves out of your system and onto the paper. Humor also forces you, by definition, to search out the fun in any topic. Any time I suggest a humor project to a fellow comedy writer, regardless of whether it's a touch project or not, whether it has an unmeetable deadline or not, I always say, "Have fun with it."

Earlier I noted that humor writing was like jazz. It has rules, as jazz does. Music has mathematical rules of scales and rhythms, but sometimes the creativity comes from violating or bending those precepts.

It's difficult to define rules for writing humor. There are almost as many different forms of the art as there are humorists. Erma Bombeck is different from Art Buchwald is different from Stephen Leacock is different from H. Allen Smith. To limit one's style of writing is to restrict the innovation that creates the fun.

One way to create a humorous style is to read and study those humorists you enjoy. Then try to duplicate their style. Within a short time you'll be adding a flair of your own because humor demands that . . . it needs spontaneity. Soon you'll see that their style combined with your variations has created a new and different style.

A humor writer needn't be afraid of experimentation. Comedy has to be unpredictable. If it weren't, it wouldn't be as funny. People don't laugh as hard at a story they've heard before. The surprise element is part of the humor. It's fun writing that says to you, "Try anything."

While there may be few if any rules about the writing of lighter pieces, there are some universal truths about comedy that may keep your humorous writing more salable.

1) The best humor is based on truth. I used to write funny lines for Phyllis Diller. It's hard to imagine anyone more outlandish or bizarre than Phyllis. Yet she would say to me often, "Honey, if the jokes aren't true, don't send them to me." She knew what she was talking about.

Any humor you attempt should be based on a truthful premise. Like Phyllis Diller, you may then distort that truth. You can bend it, twist it, exaggerate it, carry it to extremes—even unbelievable extremes. The basic truth on which it was based remains.

To illustrate, suppose we do a comedy piece on where all the socks go that we lose in the wash. That's basically a truthful premise. Every household has had one unmatched sock show up after the family wash is done. For some reason the other one never does return. From that basic truthful premise you might hypothesize in your article that it goes down through the earth to Australia. You might conjecture that creatures from outer space feed on single socks. You might even suppose that they run off to join some sort of "sock circus." These are all wild, preposterous fantasies, but based on a totally believable, relatively truthful premise.

That's much more effective comedically than any humor based on a false, manufactured premise. For instance, suppose you were to do a hilarious treatise based on the fact that all people who own black dogs as pets are grouches. You may have some funny, plausible stories about people who own black dogs, but the basic premise is flawed. You created the premise to support your funny stories. Whereas in the first instance, you created the outrageous tales based on a believable premise.

340

Your humor will generally be stronger if it's based on truth.

2) Recognizable humor is usually more fun for a reading audience. Earlier I said that humor is graphic. A joke or story generates a picture in each reader's or listener's mind. If the picture is amusing, they laugh. If they can see themselves in that picture, they laugh harder.

In my lectures I tell the audience that humor is already around them. For example, I say, "If you see a man open the car door for his wife, you know right away either the car is new or the wife is." That line gets a quick response because so many listeners recognize themselves in that scene. The wives see their husbands, and the husbands see themselves. It has a high recognizability factor.

I once read a statement attributed to some vaudeville comic. I don't remember his name, nor do I know if he was a successful comic. I hope he was, because he knew what he was talking about. He said, "A good joke is saying what everybody else is thinking, only you say it better."

The best humor writers look at commonplace, everyday events from a fresh, oblique angle. The topic may be commonplace; the humorist's view of it is original.

3) Remember your readers. Again, the humorist can only suggest. The humorist paints the picture in the reader's mind. The reader then passes judgment on whether that scene is funny or not. You'll score higher if you know what your readers want to see. You do that by knowing who your readers are. Editors admonish us time and time again to "read the magazine." It applies as much in writing humorous pieces as it does in any other writing.

Since humor writing is different from conventional article writing, it also has some slightly different rules for marketing.

"Query first" is almost an absolute in dealing with magazine editors. It's not in selling humor. Editors have told me that they don't want to see a query letter or a proposal for lighter pieces. Why? Because they tell the editor practically nothing about how funny the piece will be. One writer may do a piece about the socks missing from the family wash and make it a masterpiece. Another may use the same premise and never generate a snicker. The value of a humorous piece is the humor. Editors can't tell how funny it is until it's written. So, humor writing will have to be submitted on speculation. Do the piece and then send it to the editors. It's wise to select subjects that have wide appeal—premises that would be of interest to many magazines. As an example, a piece on some aspect of cooking could be sent to all of the family and women's magazines. Then one rejection isn't catastrophic. It just means typing up a new submission envelope.

Try writing humor. The editors claim they want it and need it. We all know the world certainly could use a few more chuckles.

68

RESEARCH TIPS TO HELP YOU WRITE

By Alden Todd

IT HARDLY NEEDS stating that research is essential to good writing, because our words must convey authenticity, accuracy, and precision if we want readers to give us their confidence. This is true both in fiction and in non-fiction. Carelessness in research can lead to all kinds of embarrassments—misplaced dates, incorrect names, impossible meetings, and so on. We must, therefore, lay a solid groundwork of carefully researched facts for your writing, and sometimes this process requires considerably more time than the writing itself. The following tips can be helpful in improving and speeding the research that underpins good writing.

1. *Thinking through a research plan.* In doing research for writing, the beginner often makes the mistake of rushing to the first possible source of information that comes to mind, instead of considering several possibilities and then choosing the best order to follow. This order can be written down as a research plan and revised as work progresses.

In researching history, biography, and events of the recent past, particularly when looking for material in written form, a writer can get good results by playing detective and asking these questions:

Who would know? Who could care? Who would care enough to have it in print? The answers can often lead directly to the printed matter or to the people you'll need to interview.

Thinking through your plan of research may save you an hour or day, or even longer. Too much time is often spent in hunting for the written materials that might be spent more productively in actually doing the research. An important element in research skills lies in getting one's hands on the right material fast. Therefore, the writer whose work is based on solid research and who wants to be most productive should learn everything possible about the available reference books and periodicals, the local libraries, and what specialists to ask for the necessary information.

2. *Finding the right library.* It is natural to turn to the town or city public library as the first source of resource material. Because it must serve the entire community, the public library generally holds a much larger collection of reference books and other materials than the ordinary card holder realizes. So it is always a first good step to find out what standard reference works your public library has. In many places, counties have organized interlibrary loan systems; the local staff can tell you which cooperating public library can supply the books you need.

Bear in mind that the biggest library in your community is not always the best for your purposes. If your subject is art, you care only about the depth of its art reference collection. In fact, the small, specialized library often has a far better collection for your specific purpose than the large public library does. It is usually less crowded and staff members are more likely to know the collection thoroughly. The same is true of a departmental library of a large university system.

To find out about special libraries near you, ask the reference librarians whether they have a local or regional directory of the Special Libraries Association (SLA). Such directories are compiled for many metropolitan regions of the country for interlibrary loans and job placement. Librarians usually keep their SLA Directory behind the desk and show it only on request. The local directory of special libraries in law firms, medical centers, social work agencies, businesses, clubs, and many other places can be of great help to the writer. If the local SLA Directory is not available, ask for the national library directory and look in it for all the libraries in your area.

Writers often ask whether a person not connected with a company, professional school, or organization that maintains its own library can gain admission to it. In every case, I have found that if one asks permission to use such a library for a special purpose, such as writing an article, the librarians have been friendly and cooperative. Do not be timid: Special libraries can give you more help per hour spent in research than the large general library.

In localities where there is a college library, it is worth exploring the possibility of using that collection—either through a friend with a

344

college connection or perhaps under a program that permits local residents to use the library for a fee. And within many universities, one often finds subsidiary libraries on special subjects (e.g. medicine, law, business, astronomy) in different parts of the campus, each with its own admission policies.

3. *Finding reference books.* The best way to find if there are standard reference books on your subject is to consult an experienced professional librarian acquainted with your field, if possible in a special library devoted to that field. Do not waste time browsing through reference book shelves in the hope of finding what you want. It's much more efficient to find people who know their collections, then state precisely what you want to find out, and ask for reference books that will help you.

Of course, you can start out by looking in the library catalogue under various subject headings to see which books the library carries on your subject. You may find a dozen books that are useful, or you may draw a blank. It's a matter of how broad or narrow your subject is, and how detailed the subject categorizing is.

The standard directory of reference book titles is the *Guide to Reference Books,* issued by the American Library Association and revised regularly. This is a comprehensive, 1,000-page, two-column work containing brief descriptions of books on all kinds of subjects. An experienced librarian can help you find the headings and pages relevant to your topic. It is worth the time of any serious researcher/writer to become generally familiar with the contents and organization of this valuable sourcebook.

A particularly useful and inexpensive guide to reference books that writers would do well to acquire for themselves is the paperbound *Reference Books: a Brief Guide,* by Bell and Swidan, published by the Enoch Pratt Free Library (400 Cathedral Street, Baltimore, MD 21201). This is the best low-price guide to reference works that I know, and it has been kept up to date by dedicated editors who are professional librarians.

One fast method of making at least a preliminary choice of books to consult on much-explored subjects is to look at the brief bibliographies that are appended to articles in major encyclopedias, such as *Encyclopedia Britannica.* You might not otherwise know where to begin among the many books that have been written on such subjects as George Washington or heart disease. Also, the sources suggested in the encyclopedia articles have passed the scrutiny of specialists and are authoritative.

Another useful reference work for your research is *Subject Guide to Books in Print,* an annual that lists more than 600,000 book titles currently in print and available from U.S. publishers. They are indexed with cross references under 63,500 subject headings. Here you can find all U.S. books in print on a particular subject. A companion guide is *Paperbound Books in Print,* which lists current books by title, author, and subject. Subject headings are not as numerous as in the subject guide to hardcover books, so within the more than 100 listed subject-areas, you must search for suitable titles.

Finally, the *Guide to American Directories* will tell you whether there is a directory in your field that would help you in your research.

4. *Finding periodical articles.* Most libraries subscribe to the *Readers' Guide to Periodical Literature,* which indexes by author and subject the articles published in about 200 periodicals. But for a comprehensive index of subjects published in other periodicals, academic publications, and learned society journals, the *Readers' Guide* is not sufficient, because it mainly indexes articles in general circulation magazines and covers relatively few others. To find such specialized articles, the researcher/writer should consult one or more other indexes that cover specialized magazines and journals. Examples are *Applied Science & Technology Index, Art Index, Business Periodicals Index, Education Index, Index to Legal Periodicals,* and the like. Ask a professional reference librarian what specialized periodical indexes are available, and you will discover how much depth they add to your research.

Note: You may have to visit a special library to locate some of these indexes as well as the back issues of periodicals to which they refer.

5. *Finding specialists and people who know.* There is, of course, more to research than turning to what others have written. Much that the writer wants to find out has not been put on paper, so he must frequently locate experts who can be interviewed, whether in a face-to-face meeting, by telephone, or by letter. It all depends on how accessible the expert is. As a writer you should, however, always remain a bit

skeptical, remembering that what you learn from someone else may only be that person's version or opinion of a past event and should be subject to the same critical scrutiny as that with which you approach a book or article.

One very handy way to find experts and specialists in all parts of the country is to use the *Encyclopedia of Associations,* which can be found in good reference—and sometimes business—libraries. The 1987 edition contains information on more than 23,000 national and international organizations operating in the U.S., including hobby clubs, professional societies, trade associations, labor unions—in fact, every sort of association in which members have a common purpose. Each entry in this multi-volume encyclopedia includes an association's address, purpose, activities, executive officers, and the titles and frequencies of publications. By writing or calling the association headquarters, you can locate a chapter or individual members in your city or region, and call on them for information in their special field.

Another way to find people with a special knowledge in a different part of the country is to consult *Editor & Publisher International Yearbook,* an annual directory of the daily and weekly newspapers of North America. For daily newspapers, it lists the editors and specialized reporters in various departments—music, sports, gardening, theater, and others. There is also the newspaper library, which contains clippings and memos about important happenings in the locality. I have called on newspaper editors and reporters several times in the course of my research and have always found them cordial and helpful.

6. *Using public relations sources.* Public relations professionals can be of great help to the researcher and writer. Their offices go under various names—public relations, PR, publicity, public information (the term used in government), press relations, and, in embassies, press attaché. Whatever the title, these are people whose job it is to supply information to the press and public on behalf of an organization, institution, or individual.

In recent years, the PR function has become so important in the U.S. that the person best equipped to supply information about an institution is often the PR director—not the president or chief executive officer. But no one seeking information from a PR source should park his critical faculties at the door. Researchers should be as careful in accepting what PR professionals tell them as they would about statements read in a journal article or a book. Similarly, one must be cautious and critical dealing with the public information officer of a university, government agency, manufacturing company, or airline. It is the researcher's job to separate the factual and valid from what may be exaggerated or even untrue.

Writers may sometimes become so fascinated and engrossed in their research that they lose their sense of time and purpose. The writer must recognize that the final purpose is writing, and that research is a subsidiary though necessary means to reaching the final goal.

69

ARTICLE OUTLINES BRING SALES

By William E. Miles

"Put it before them briefly so they will read it, clearly so they will appreciate it, picturesquely so they will remember it and, above all, accurately so they will be guided by its light."

Give Joseph Pulitzer a prize for this nearly century-old advice to reporters! Although the publisher of the New York *World* was referring to newspaper stories, his remarks are just as applicable today to magazine article outlines. Brevity, clarity, color, accuracy—that's the gift-wrapping of the package you are inviting an editor to open when you submit an outline of a subject you hope will spark his interest in your article.

An outline should be kept as short as possible, preferably one page single-spaced. Sometimes, of course, the subject demands more detailed explanation—but try not to let it exceed two pages. Within this framework, fill it with enough colorful facts and figures to catch the editor's eye and indicate the authenticity of the material.

Typed on a separate page or pages, the outline should be accompanied by a brief covering letter and sufficient return postage. A sample covering letter might read like this: "Would you be interested in taking a speculative look at a 2,000-word article on the order of the attached outline? My articles have been published in . . ." (naming some of the magazines you have sold to or listing whatever other qualifications you may have). Then, paper-clipped to the covering letter, the outline itself. For example:

Pranks for the Memory

Practical jokes are probably so-called because they are practically never a joke to the victim—who often winds up on something funny as a crutch. Even Mark Twain, an inveterate practical joker much of his life, confessed in his later years that he "held the practical joker in limitless contempt."

349

The late Bennett Cerf, another humorist who held practical jokers "in low esteem," once waxed particularly indignant over the dirty trick perpetrated on a Chicago bridegroom. After passing out at a bachelor party, he awakened to find his right arm in a cast. His fun-loving friends told him he had broken it in a brandy-inspired brawl—forcing him to spend his entire honeymoon with a perfectly good arm in a painfully tight cast.

Such practical jokers, according to Cerf, are "under no circumstances to be confused with humorists." But American history, dating back to pre-Revolutionary War days, is filled with hundreds of other examples of more harmless exercises in hilarity that don't deserve the harshness of his critical verdict.

One of the earliest of these was conceived by General Israel Putnam, a hero of the French and Indian War, after being challenged to a duel by a British army officer. Putnam selected as his choice of weapons two powder kegs into which he bored holes and inserted slow fuses. When the fuses burned down to an inch of the kegs, the British officer beat a hasty retreat—from barrels filled with onions!

But some practical jokes turn out to be really practical—as in the case of a "green" engineer at the General Electric plant who was assigned by old-timers as a prank the "impossible" job of frosting light bulbs on the inside. Marvin Pipkin not only found a way but, at the same time, devised a method of strengthening the bulbs so they would last much longer—cutting the cost to consumers in half!

An article of mine, based on this outline, appeared in *Elks Magazine*.

If this makes the outline approach to article sales sound easy, it isn't. An outline is only the bare bones of an article and no skeleton key guaranteed to unlock all editorial doors. For every idea that clicks, you may receive a dozen or more rejections. And sometimes the article itself is rejected after the outline has received a speculative O.K. For one reason or another, the article may just not live up to its billing.

But whether it does or not, outlines are not only attention-getters, but time-savers. A complete article can take a month or so to research and write and another month or so languishing in editorial offices awaiting a decison. An outline, on the other hand, requires only cursory research—enough to establish an intriguing lead and some supporting information. Only after the "go-ahead" (if you get it) do you need to start researching the subject in depth.

Editors also answer queries far more rapidly than they return articles—so even a rejection has its bright side. If the query is turned down, you've saved yourself unnecessary work in more ways than one. When outlines are returned, as they usually are, there's no retyping involved (except for another covering letter), if you decide to try elsewhere.

Another important aspect of an outline is that an editor, who likes the general idea, may have some suggestions of his own as to how he'd like it handled. An article I sold to *The Lion* is a good example of this. My original idea was to take a swipe at juries because of the way they were influenced by clever lawyers (and sometimes their own ignorance) into returning strange, far-out verdicts. I had no solutions to the problems in mind when I submitted the following outline to the editor:

THE TROUBLE WITH JURIES

FBI statistics show that 90 out of every 100 murderers are arrested, 50 receive some sort of punishment, and two are sentenced to death. This means that almost half of all accused killers are acquitted after their mandatory trials by jury in cases of first degree murder—presumably the guilty as well as the innocent.

This assumption was borne out by an investigation of the jury system in Pennsylvania which disclosed some juries had reached their verdicts by drawing straws or flipping coins. Other jurors were found to have rushed through their deliberations in order to get to a dance or a lodge meeting on time.

Although Thomas Jefferson described juries as "the best of all safeguards for the person, the property and the reputation of every individual," many legal experts regard them as outmoded relics in this modern age. Trial by jury stems from trial by oath in which the accused, swearing to his innocence, was supported by twelve "oath-helpers," or compurgators, who attested to their belief in his statements. This "jury of peers" was intimately acquainted with the defendant and the circumstances of the alleged crime. But in our day, as Dr. Joseph Catton points out, an attempt is made to select persons who know *nothing* about the offense. "There are those who believe," he adds wryly, "that today's jurors know nothing about anything."

Other criminologists contend that a modern jury is generally made up of persons unfamiliar with the law who often miss the significance of technical rulings by the judge. Even in cases where court rulings are simple and understandable, the jury sometimes ignores them. There is one actual case on record in which members of the jury, disregarding the evidence and the judge's charge, all knelt in prayer—and came up with a verdict!

The editor replied: "I'd be happy to consider your article 'The Trouble with Juries' with one important condition. I'd like to see the piece conclude with some constructive recommendations from authorities on how the jury system could be improved and/or replaced by better systems."

Further research incorporated his suggestions into the article whose whole thrust was changed, including the lead, when it appeared in *The Lion* under the new title, "Of Juries and Judgments."

The lead (aside from the idea) is probably the most important part of an outline, because it's the first thing to attract an editor's eye. One good means of accomplishing this is to tie it to a particular city or state even though the actual subject matter may range far afield. Here's an outline with just such a lead that resulted in a sale to the *Chicago Tribune Sunday* Magazine:

Chicago's long history of accomplishments includes the honor of being the first city to introduce what some engineering experts have called one of the ten most complex and ingenious inventions of the past hundred years. Back in 1893 it put the "zip" in the zipper when a sample of the original slide fastener was placed on display at Chicago's Columbian Exposition for use by the Fair's hootchie-kootchie dancer, Little Egypt, as a rapid skirt-release.

But it was the zipper, not the stripper, that caught the eye of a visitor to the Fair—Colonel Louis Walker of Meadville, Pa.—and he hired the inventor, Whitcomb L. Judson, to improve his original patent on a "locker or unlocker for automatically engaging or disengaging an entire series of clasps by a single continuous movement."

After years of experimentation, the device was finally perfected in 1913 and, four years later, a Brooklyn tailor made the fastener famous by attaching it to money belts which he sold to sailors at the Brooklyn Navy Yard. The Navy itself was soon using the fastener on flying suits. And during the depression, a dress company tried out the novelty as a sales booster—taking the industry by storm. Soon the zipper's long story of "ups and downs" was over. Its slide to success had begun!

Leads come in all shapes and sizes and there are dozens of other ways of writing that all-important first paragraph whose purpose is to sell a particular editor on a particular idea. For instance, the "striking statement" lead:

Lightning, the silent partner of thunder, has frightened more people—and killed fewer—than any other common danger. In fact, your chances of being killed by a lightning bolt are one in a million.

The editor liked this outline lead well enough to keep it intact when my article "Striking Down Lightning Myths" was published in *Wheels Afield*.

Another editorial eye-opener is the "news peg" approach—tying the article to a current happening or upcoming event—or the "anniversary angle" like this outline lead for my article "Meters By The Mile" that appeared in *The Rotarian* more years ago than I care to remember:

Ten years ago last October 1,500 parking meters went on trial in New York City. They were immediately found guilty by protesting motorists who charged that they interfered with their constitutional privileges of life, liberty and the pursuit of free parking space . . .

But why go on? The point is that, varied as they were, all of these leads had one thing in common—an ability to grab the editor's attention and keep him reading. From these examples, you can see that I like to write a

352

lead (and sometimes an ending) that will be used more or less "as is" in the finished article if the outline receives an editorial O.K.

This gives the editor a good idea of what to expect—not only of the subject but of the style in which it will be written. For an outline must persuade the editor that you not only have a good idea, but possess the ability to handle it well.

70

THE POET WITHIN YOU

BY DAVID KIRBY

I FIGURE POETRY is a way of beating the odds. The world is never going to give you everything you want, so why not look elsewhere? In a wonderful book called *The Crisis of Creativity* (now regrettably out of print) by George Seidel, it is stated that the artist will always have one thing no one else can have: a life within a life.

And that's only the start. If you have talent and luck and you work like a son of a gun, you might even end up, as the poet John Berryman says, adding to "the store of available reality."

But at least you can have a life within a life, no matter who you are. Not all of us can be great poets. If that were so, the Nobel Prize would be in every box of breakfast cereal—you'd get up, write your poem for the day, and collect your prize. But every literate person has it in him- or herself to be a good poet. Indeed, I have wonderful news for you— each of us is a poet already, or at least we used to be. It's just that most of us have gone into early retirement.

Seriously, when interviewers ask the marvelously gifted William Stafford when he started to write poetry, Stafford often replies, "When did you stop?" All children put words together imaginatively; just talk to one and you'll see what I mean. But then they grow up and enter the world of bills and backaches. They start chasing that dollar, and suddenly their time is limited. Poetry is usually the first thing to go. People get so busy with their lives that they forget to have a life within a life. But you have a life anyway, right? So forget about it for a minute—it'll still be there when you come back—and let's talk about the poet within you.

The first thing you need to do is forget that all poets are supposed to be erratic or unstable. Flaubert was quite clear on this point. He said, "Be regular and orderly in your life, like a bourgeois, so that you may be violent and original in your work." In other words, there's no point

354

in sapping your resources by pursuing some phony "artistic" lifestyle. First, the outer person has to be calm and self-disciplined; only then can the inner one be truly spontaneous.

And that means getting organized. Here are a few rules I use to make my life as orderly and bourgeois as possible, so that the poet within me can be as wild as he wants to be.

1) *Start small.* Most beginning writers tackle the big themes: love, death, the meaning of life. But don't we already know everything there is to know about these subjects? Love is wonderful, death is terrible, life is mysterious. So start small and work your way up. Take a phrase you overheard, a snippet of memory, a dream fragment, and make a poem of that. Once the details are in place, the big theme (whatever it is) will follow, but the details have to come first.

2) *Write about what you remember.* It is a commonplace that you should write about what you know, but usually the present is too close for us to see it clearly. We have to move away from the events in our lives before we can see them in such a way that we can write about them engagingly. Don't waste time on the guy you saw talking to his dog this morning; take a few notes, if you like, but if he's memorable, he'll pop into your mind later, when you really need him. Instead, why not write a poem about the girl in your third-grade class who could throw a baseball better than any of the boys and all the problems that caused? By putting these memories down on paper and shaping them, you're enriching not only your own life but also the lives of others.

3) *Be a sponge.* Shakespeare was. His plays are based on historical accounts and on lesser plays by earlier playwrights. So what are you, better than Shakespeare? I once wrote a poem called "The Last Song on the Jukebox" that was published in a magazine and then in a collection of my poetry and now in an anthology that is widely used on college campuses; people seem to like it pretty well. Looking back at the poem, I can hear in it echoes of two country songs that I used to be able to sing in their entireties but have since forgotten. Somebody says something in my poem that is a variation on something a character says in a novel called *Ray,* by the talented Barry Hannah. And the overall tone of "The Last Song on the Jukebox" owes much to a poet I heard reading his own work one night. His voice was perfect—it had just the right twang to it—so I used it for the speaker in my poem. Now that I

think about it, I realize that I didn't like the guy's poetry that much. That didn't stop me from adapting his twang to my purpose.

4) *Play dumb*. Just about anything can be turned into a poem if you play dumb about it, because when you're smart, everything makes sense to you and you go about your business, whereas when you're dumb, you have to slow down, stop, figure things out. Recently, in Chicago, I saw a man being arrested. The police had cuffed him and were hauling him away while an elderly woman shook with rage and screamed after them as they all climbed into the paddywagon. "Liar!" she shouted, "liar!" You mean you can get arrested just for lying, I said to myself? Is that only in Chicago, or does the law apply everywhere? Now if I were a smart person, I might have figured out what really happened: Probably the guy grabbed her purse, and she called the cops, and he said he didn't do it, and she said he *did* do it, and so on. But by being dumb, I got a flying start on a poem. I haven't finished the poem yet, but as you can see, I have already given myself a lot to work with, thanks to my astonishingly low IQ.

5) *Reverse your field*. When you catch yourself on the verge of saying something obvious, don't just stop; instead, say the opposite of what you were going to say in the first place. Listen to the poet within you. If you want to eat a chocolate bar, that's not poetry; everybody likes chocolate. But suppose the chocolate bar wanted to eat you? Now that's a poem. Here's another example: I'm thinking of ending my liar-in-Chicago poem with something about husbands and wives and how they have to be truthful to each other, and I can see myself heading toward a stanza in which the speaker wonders what his wife really means when she says (and this would be the last line of the poem), "I love you." The problem is that that's too pat for a last line, too cloying, too sentimental, an easy out. Instead, since people who are really crazy about each other sometimes kid around in a mock-hostile way, why not have the speaker wonder whether the wife is telling the truth or not when she laughs and hits him on the arm and says, "I hate you, you big lug!" Such an unexpected statement would come as a surprise to the reader, although first it will have come as a surprise to me, who was heading in the opposite direction before I realized that I needed to reverse my field.

6) *Work on several poems at once.* For one thing, you won't end up giving too much attention to a poem that doesn't need it—like children, some poems do better if you don't breathe down their necks all the time. For another, if you're working on just one poem and it isn't going anywhere, you're likely to feel terribly frustrated, whereas if one poem is dying on the vine and three others are doing pretty well, you'll feel as though you are ahead of the game (because you will be). Also, sometimes our poems are smarter than we are, and a word or a line or a stanza that isn't right for one poem will often migrate to another and find a home for itself there. Poems are happiest in the company of other poems, so don't try to create them in a vacuum. You probably wouldn't try to write four novels at once, but there's no reason why you shouldn't take advantage of poetry's brevity and get several poems going simultaneously.

7) *Give yourself time.* This is actually related to the preceding rule, since you wouldn't tend to rush a poem if you were working on several of them at once. I have a friend whose daughter is learning how to cook. But she's a little impatient, so when she has a recipe that says you should bake the cake at 350 degrees for thirty minutes, she doesn't see why you can't cook it at 700 degrees for fifteen minutes. If you take this approach to poetry, your poems are going to end up like my friend's daughter's cakes, charred on the outside and raw in the middle. If you saw a stunningly handsome stranger walking down the street, would you run up to him and shout, "Marry me"? Of course not—he might say yes! Poems are the same way, and if you try to make them yours too soon, you won't be happy with the results, I promise you. Be coy, be flirtatious; draw the poem out a little and see what it's really about. There's no hurry, because you've got all those other poems you're working on, remember?

8) *Find a perfect reader.* A perfect reader is like a perfect tennis partner, someone who is a little better than you are (so you feel challenged), but not that much better (so you don't get demoralized). And like an ideal tennis partner, a good reader is going to be hard to find. You don't play tennis with your mother, so don't expect her to critique your writing.

Anyway, what kind of mother would tell her own child that his poetry is terrible? That's what friends are for. So no parents. And no roommates, either: people are always saying to me, "You're going to love this poem; my roommate says it's the best thing I've ever written." What else would a roommate say? You can hardly go on living with someone after you've told him to throw his notebook away and take up basketweaving. Just as you would play tennis with a couple of dozen people before you pick the one you want to play with every Saturday, so too should you pass your poems around until you find the one person who can show you their strengths and weaknesses without inflating or deflating your ego too much. If you're lucky, you'll then do what I did when I found my perfect reader—you'll marry her (or him).

If you have a knack for language and you follow these rules and you get a break from time to time and you look both ways whenever you cross the street, after a while you will find you have created for yourself a life within a life. You will have awakened—reawakened, actually—the poet within you. And even if this isn't your year to win the Nobel Prize, I have to say that I never met anybody who didn't break out into a big happy smile when I introduced myself as a poet. I don't know what it is; maybe people associate me with Homer or Milton. At any rate, everyone seems happy to know there is a poet in the neighborhood.

Well, not everybody. Once I was negotiating with a man to buy his house, and I was getting the better of him. So the man lost his temper and said I didn't know what I was doing, I *couldn't* know, because I was a poet and I ought to go back to my poems and leave business affairs to men like him, practical, level-headed men. For a couple of days, I felt pretty rotten, although the whole thing turned out spledidly for me, since I later found another house I liked even better than his. Meanwhile, the practical level-headed fellow had lost a great buyer; like Flaubert, I believe in paying my bills on time.

And I got my revenge: I wrote a poem about him.

71

MAKING A NAME IN POETRY

By X. J. Kennedy

As POETS KNOW only too well, trying to sell poetry to paying magazines and book publishers is a rough task, often impossible. Even giving away poems may be difficult: Some little magazines that pay in free copies can be choosey. And as John Ciardi once observed, it is hard for poets to prostitute their talents. There just aren't that many buyers around.

It would be hypocritical for me to claim that for a poet to see print shouldn't matter. Of course it matters. If you write poems, having them accepted helps convince you that you are right to believe in yourself. Disappointments notwithstanding, just being published once in a while encourages a poet to stick to what William Butler Yeats glumly called "this sedentary trade."

That poems are hard to peddle isn't terribly depressing—to poets who live for the pleasure of making poems. "Well, so Editor X has bounced my sublime ode," they'll tell themselves. "The benighted creep." But to writers who aren't yet widely published and who fiercely crave to be, writers who live not necessarily to write good poems but to see their names in print, this difficulty leads to chagrin.

Writing poetry is radically different from writing articles, stories, or fillers. Most moneymaking writers—that is, writers who aren't poets— scout for a likely market. Then, they often shrewdly adapt their product to suit that market's needs. Their lives make sense: They can supply a demand. Poets, however, if they are serious about writing good poems, have to think differently.

Poetry is probably the one field of writing in which it is a mistake to try to psych out editors. In fact, specific marketing advice can some-times harm the novice poet by enticing him to pursue fashions. The poet's best hope is to sound like *nobody* else: The finest, most enduring poetry constructs a new marketplace of it own.

Excellent poems are like better mousetraps: Build one, said Emer-

359

son, and the world will beat a path to your door. It always amazes me how quickly a good, original book of poetry becomes known: W. D. Snodgrass's *Heart's Needle,* for instance, a book acclaimed soon after publication and laden with a Pulitzer, despite the fact that its author had published relatively little before.

Evidently, it is much simpler to chase after fashions than to transform yourself into a fine poet, the likes of whom the world hasn't seen before. It is easy to advise anyone whose poetic ambition goes no further than to achieve publication. To such a person, I'd suggest the following strategies:

1. Center your poem on your experience, your family, your everyday concerns—however drab. If you write a poem about your cousin's case of AIDS, you will surely find an editor who will accept it, no matter how bad it may be, for he fears that if he doesn't, you will think him a coarse, unfeeling swine who won't sympathize with your cousin. I'm serious!

2. Write in the first person, in the present tense. Not long ago, Peter Davison, poetry editor for *The Atlantic,* remarked that most of the poems he currently receives are like that. Some other, less discriminating editors mistakenly believe that the present tense lends everything a kind of immediacy.

3. Brainstorm, force your unconscious to yoke together disparate things. In the midst of a dull poem on your grandfather's old antimacassar, throw in a mention of something completely far-out and unexpected, such as a fur-lined frying pan.

4. Include a dash of violent realism, preferably straight out of current news. If you can relate your workaday world to, say, war-torn Nicaragua, you've got it made.

5. Give your poem a snappy title to catch an editor's eye. With a little more brainstorming, you can readily invent titles of poems for which many editors, the dolts, will be pushovers: "Contracting Chicken-pox in a First Kiss," "A Lesbian Mother Tells Her Daughter the Facts of Life." Titles like that either promise something interesting, or else reek of Significance with a capital S.

6. Don't, whatever you do, write in traditional forms. To do so will only slow your rate of production. Even worse, you might reveal your

lack of skill. Traditional forms, such as sonnets and blank verse, which held sway over English-speaking poetry for five centuries (up until about 1960), can still nourish wonderful poems—as witness recent work by Seamus Heaney, Derek Walcott, Gjertrud Schnackenberg, and Timothy Steele. But remember, I'm not talking about quality. If you write in traditional forms, you had better be good. In rhymed metrical stanzas, mediocre poetry tends to look shoddy in an obvious way, while bad poetry looks really horrible. On the other hand, bad poems in open forms (or "free verse") tend to seem passable. And—I hate to say this, but it's true—mediocre poems in open forms look like most poems appearing nowadays in respectable places.

7. Study an annual that lists poetry markets such as the *International Directory of Little Magazines and Small Presses* (found in the reference section of many libraries). Then zero in on the less competitive markets, like *Superintendent's Profile & Pocket Equipment Directory,* a monthly for highway superintendents and directors of departments of public works. Although it uses only poems about snow-plowing and road repairing, the magazine prints two out of every three poems it receives.

If indeed all you care about is becoming a widely published poet, those hints may be as good as any. What I hope, of course, is that you will ignore all those suggestions.

For a poet who cares about the art of poetry, merely to be published isn't enough. The first time you see your name in print, it may seem to scintillate on the page like a Fourth of July sparkler. Karl Shapiro once recalled the joy of seeing rows of his own book on a shelf, "saying my golden name from end to end." But after you see it a few times, your own name may not prove especially interesting. At the moment, the problem for a poet in this country isn't to get published. A couple of thousand markets now publish poetry, some of whose editors have no taste. And anyone who can't get published can, for $200, start his own little magazine and generously heap his own work with acceptances. Unfortunately, the problem, in this time of dwindling attention spans, is to find attentive readers.

Poets whose work is widely published may still be widely ignored. The poetry star system that produced household names like Robert Frost, Dylan Thomas, and E.E. Cummings passed away twenty years ago, so there is no longer much point in a poet's trying for celebrity. The celebrity that a poet may attain isn't the tenth part of one percent of the celebrity that a rock songwriter can attain from a single video. If you are going into the poetry writing business, you might as well forget about fame and fortune and seek other rewards.

Some writers think that bringing out that first collection of poems will be an experience far superior to beholding the beatific vision. This view is distorted. Publishing a book can be a lot of fun, but it may not transform your life. Having published a volume of poetry, you, unlike Michael Jackson or Madonna, can walk the streets and not be overwhelmed by autograph-seekers. Moreover, you can publish a book of poems and continue to suffer from any ailment or lacks that afflicted you.

Poetic fame, like sea water, isn't worth thirsting for. Poets, if they are any good, compete for space in books not only with their peers but with the giants of the ages. They race not only with John Ashbery and Tess Gallagher, to name two deservedly admired contemporaries, but with John Milton and Emily Dickinson. Let them not imitate the plumage of any currently acclaimed poet. Let them discover their own natures, however disappointing the discovery, and stay faithful to whoever they may be.

At the risk of appearing to hold myself up as a sterling example, I shall recall that as a whitehat in the Navy back in the early fifties, just beginning to fool around writing poems, I made plenty of mistakes. (One mistake was trying to write like Dylan Thomas, an attempt that rendered my work thick, fruitcake-like, and impenetrable.) One mistake I didn't make was to crave premature publication. I resigned myself to just writing, piling up poems, not showing them to anybody. Pigheadedly, I believed that one day an editor would print my work, or some of it. At least that attitude kept up my morale: I didn't have to cope with the rejection slips I would certainly have received. And when I finally started licking stamps and getting poems rejected, I was a little (but not a whole lot) more competent.

For a poet, there can be no greater luxury than to work as a complete unknown. When you are an undiscovered gem, there isn't the least bit of pressure on you to publish, to become better and better and stun your critics, to win prizes, and all that debilitating responsibility. All you need care about is writing good poems. Too many college sophomores

362

and also a few grandparents who have never read any poetry other than Hallmark greeting card verse assume that if their first stumbling efforts don't get published, they have failed miserably. But that Sylvia Plath won a noteworthy prize when she was a college student, that Amy Clampitt published her first book in middle age and won immediate accolades, doesn't mean that they should feel any grim duty to succeed. America is full of excellent poets who have had their poems published for years, despite the fact that they receive little notice. Luckily for our poetry, they persist.

Nowadays, lust for hasty fame takes root early. The other day I was talking with a bunch of fourth-graders in a public library in Quincy, Massachusetts, and a lad of ten asked me again and again—insistently rephrasing the question—how you get poems published. I wanted to tell him, Kid, forget it. I'll bet your stuff at the moment, while it may show flickers of something good, is not much good yet; you will be smart to shelve your ambition for another ten or fifteen years. But, too craven to hit him with the hard truth, I pointed out how rare it is to publish poems in nationwide places when you are ten. Myra Cohn Livingston in her wonderful book *The Child as Poet* tells some horror stories about fledgling poets whose parents goaded them into print at an early age.

All right, call me a sourpuss. I'm trying to dash a little cold water on the notion, so dear to many unpublished writers, that publication is the be-all and end-all of existence. This attitude makes such people push-overs for racketeers: for contests that charge forty-dollar entrance fees, accept everything, then try to sell the contestants a bound volume containing their supposedly winning work for $38.95, or $62.95 for the gold-edged edition. It makes them suckers for vanity publishers who, appealing to their pride and frustration, urge them to subsidize an edition of their own poems, which will sell to nobody, or to practically nobody, unless they themselves sell the copies, and which no reviewer in a national magazine would touch with a thirty-foot flagpole.

Letting oneself be the victim of such con games is all right if seeing your name in print is your one aim. And with any luck, sheer, tireless stamp-licking will result in *some* kind of publication. But sometimes, if viewed as fortresses to be stormed and overpowered, poetry magazines tend to resist. I can recall when, as poetry editor for the *Paris Review,* I kept getting a tide of manuscripts from a poet who had published little but whose name must have been known to every poetry editor. His manuscripts came in *daily* showing the wrinkles of many previous rejections. Always folded and refolded sixteen times, sometimes looking as if they'd been given a fresh press with a steam iron, always in envelopes saying Biltmore and Statler and Hilton (pilfered, it seemed, from writing desks in hotel lobbies). If only the contributor had devoted as much time to learning to write as he spent stuffing envelopes!

Why is it that hundreds of thousands of people want to be poets? I don't know, but I have a hunch. In this anonymous society in which we feel like zip codes or social security numbers, writing a poem and publishing it is one way to stand up on your hind legs and sass the universe. A printed poem proclaims, "I exist." There is something powerfully appealing in the thought that you can seize paper and pencil in an odd moment and scrawl a few lines that might make you immortal in anthologies. Immortality is all very well, but it is more interesting to think about the problems of writing good poetry. You don't need to publish a thousand poems in order to become immortal; you need publish only one poem, if it is good enough.

Literary history is full of cases of great poets who garnered no fame or praise or significant publication in their lifetimes. Gerard Manley Hopkins, whose strange masterpiece "The Wreck of the Deutschland" was rejected by a small Jesuit magazine, showed his poems to only a tiny handful of correspondents. Emily Dickinson, after local newspaper editors rewrote the few items she submitted to them, evidently said the hell with them and stitched her poems into little packets that she stashed away in her attic, as is well known. Hopkins and Dickinson, to be sure, were superb poets whose work refused to die. But my point is that they placed quality first and bravely turned their backs upon celebrity.

Sometimes, when I look at the current spate of forgettable poems, I think it would be a great idea if literary magazines were to declare a moratorium on by-lines for a few years. Just suppose every poem were printed anonymously. By and by, of course, the real original poets would be recognized by the character of their work, as surely as "The Pearl" poet of the Middle Ages. But the great mass of poems, undistinguished and forgettable, would slip into oblivion. And there would be fewer of them, since people who now publish poems in order to boost their egos would have no reason to.

I think it is a good idea for young poets to start having their poems published in the very smallest magazines, those read by few people. If in later years they should decide that their maiden works were poor, they can comfort themselves with the knowledge that practically nobody will have read them. Most poets I have known have come to regard their first works as pretty embarrassing. John Ciardi, who won a prize in a student writing contest at the University of Michigan, once told me he longed to burgle his found manuscript from the library and burn it.

Those poets willing to try the most onerous route of all—growing in depth and in skill—might cultivate an aloof coolness toward publication. No formula, no market tip, no advice from me or anybody else will help you write a great poem. But you can take action. You can try reading. Most poets do too little of that. Talk to any editor of a poetry magazine, and you will learn that the would-be contributors usually outnumber paying subscribers by at least five to one. Many poets want to heap their outpourings upon the world, expecting the world to take them gladly. Too impatient to read other poets, they never find out how poetry is written, and they keep repeating things that have already been done well, and so do not need redoing.

If you haven't been published and deserve to be, you might make a personal anthology of poems you admire—the dozen or twenty poems you'd swear by. This task will concentrate your attention, make you aware of your own standards, and reveal your nature to you. I made such a anthology once and learned to my surprise that the poems I most cherish in all of literature are religious ones. You might also try writing a lot—and throwing most of it away. Delmore Schwartz said that a poet is wise to write as much, and to publish as little, as possible.

Keats put it beautifully in a letter to a friend: "I should write for the mere yearning and fondness I have for the beautiful, even if my night's labors should be burnt every morning and no eye shine upon them." That is, I think, a noble attitude. Rejections—or critical attacks—could not thwart a Keats; they simply had no great power over him. For a poet, the only sure reward is the joy of making a poem. Any reward besides—fame, prizes, publication—is like money found in the street. If you see a silver dollar gleaming on the sidewalk, you pick it up. But you need not roam the streets desperately looking for that gleam.

72

FORM AND EXPERIMENTATION
IN POETRY

By Liz Rosenberg

THE WAR between poetic form and poetic license has been raging for a long time and continues to this day. In 1668 the poet John Milton threw down one gauntlet, in his blank verse poem *Paradise Lost:* "This neglect of Rhyme so little is to be taken for a defect, though it may seem so perhaps to vulgar Readers, that it rather is to be esteem'd an example set, the first in English, of ancient liberty recover'd to Heroic Poem from the troublesome and modern bondage of Rhyming."

Three hundred years later Robert Frost dropped the other glove in his now-famous scorn of unrhymed verse: "I'd as soon play tennis with the net down."

Rhyme has been the chief net over which the opposing sides slug it out, maybe because it is the most instantly noticeable musical aspect of English poetry and poetic form, though by no means the only formal element available to the poet. Anglo-Saxon poetry, which was highly regimented, depended upon a certain number of stressed beats per line, and alliteration. Chinese poetry uses pitch. Other formal elements have held precedence at various times—the controlled musicality of Sapphic verse, syllabics, cinquains, haikus, William Carlos Williams's "variable foot," and so on. Between structure and freedom the pendulum swings widely and regularly, one way, then another. We tend to think of our own time as the absolute reign of free verse: unrhymed, unmetered, personal, brief, as jumpy as a gesture by James Dean—yet there are already signs of a swing leading the other way, in poems one feels an urge to call "verse"—the formal, rhymed, structured and ornamented work of poets like Amy Clampitt, Philip Booth, Gertrude Schnackenberg, and others.

As we draw closer to the end of the twentieth century, I suspect that the tendency both to poetic structure and poetic freedom will grow more exaggerated. Ends of centuries produce extremes, as witness

Alfred, Lord Tennyson on the one hand and Walt Whitman on the other, at the end of the nineteenth century. That these two poets had a great interest in and admiration for one another's work should come as no surprise. It's at both ends of the spectrum—extreme formal control, extreme poetic freedom—that the poet is pushing at boundaries, struggling to discover the necessities of the craft. It is exactly this pitched battle, *in extremis,* that produces great art, this pushing against limits, exploration of what is possible. The poet must write only according to internal necessity. The danger lies with those caught in the middle, like Dante's souls forever caught in the ante-chambers of hell, following first one flag and then another. This is the only mistake one can make in regard to poetic form: to allow the form to choose you. And it is as easy, as we have all lately discovered, to be the stooge of free verse as of formal verse. The worst one can do is to write in a particular form out of habit, intimidation, or laziness. There is an equal slackness in the doggerel rhyme of greeting cards or the nebulous free-form of Rod McKuen and his imitators. What one feels lacking in both is the tension of discovery, of necessity. And these are achieved only by a continual questioning of the status quo, by relentless experimentation and invention.

By "experimentation" I don't necessarily mean those finger exercises that are the stock in trade of many creative writing workshops. I'm not sure it's a good idea to get in the habit of just fooling around with poetry this way. It encourages a small kind of achievement; it puts a great emphasis on competence and cleverness, whereas great poetry is more like an explosion, built up under great pressure over a long period. One might practice with some of the tools of poetry—to sharpen musical and linguistic skills—but the poem, the thing itself, is not much good diluted.

Poets who practice with exercises must have a deep, nearly inexhaustible well of vital material. In this case, it will be impossible for anything the poet writes not to turn to poetry. But there is a frigidity in most poetic exercise, a sense of withholding that is deadly to real art. Poets shouldn't write villanelles or sonnets the way we are told we "should" write bread-and-butter letters or thank-you notes to Aunt Claire. This again is an encouragement to fall into the trap of thinking about form as somehow prescribed and habitual, as something one "really ought to do," rather than something one must do, having exhausted all other possibilities. It is only when this internal combustion forces one into new forms that something strange and lovely takes place.

"New" forms proceed from an intuition of potentialities, of something lurking around the corner, a sense that what *is* is not enough. "Mine deeper, that's the ticket!" wrote Melville, and his remains the one true battle cry of all art. Experimentation is as natural to poetry as breathing is to life. If one were content with the old forms, with things-as-they-are, and with things-as-they-have-been-said, one could not write poetry at all.

Invention is the almost incidental by-product of this constant chafing against what is, an emergence into discovery. Invention need not be new to the world; it need only be genuinely new and fresh to the writer, who discovers his or her form alone, in solitude, after many failures and much self-doubt. It is absurd to imagine that Robert Frost did not grope his way toward the lyrical, rhyming, colloquially American language that evolved as his own. All of the so-called traditional or classical poets were wildly inventive and outrageous in their day. Milton, with his thundering blank verse, is only one example. Dante dropped from the "acceptable" elevated language of great poetry—Latin—to the mundane Italian spoken by street vendors, fishwives, soldiers, and farmers, and he did it against the advice and imprecations of his friends. Shakespeare careens from blank verse to formal sonnets to prose, all within a single play, and anyone who believes that his verse was written in strict iambic pentameter has a tin ear: "Howl, howl, howl, howl!" or "Bare ruined choirs, where late the sweet birds sang."

Invention is playful, but it is not merely play. My one objection to Frost's famous remark on free verse is that poetry seems to me an infinitely more important and complex "game" than tennis. Invention is the one true genius child of necessity, and it comes with the kind of passion and power that we may imagine first breathed life into the planets and spun them, the impulse that is always behind birth and creation. It is not strange, but familiar and fundamental to the very fact of our existence. Perhaps this is why great "new" poetry feels at the same time shocking and yet inevitable. There is nothing alien or rarefied about poetry, in whatever form. It is indeed at its best when it is closest to the mundane mysteries, when it is fresh with its own discoveries, with invention, and therefore brings us close to the common, creative wellspring of all being.

73

BUILDING CONFIDENCE IN YOURSELF AS A POET

BY JAMES APPLEWHITE

THE WRITING OF A POEM from first draft to publishable version tends to fall into several phases. Getting a first draft down on paper is, or ought to be, a pleasurable process. Poetry incorporates an element of play. Word-sounds that echo against each other (in internal and end-line rhyme, consonance, assonance, and alliteration) are a kind of technical signature of this play, which extends through image, metaphor and whole narrative contour. That is, the poet's mind in the process of composing allows itself the child-freedom of lip-and-tongue eroticism, of language indulged *as if* in nonsense syllables. The idea of a poem is itself a playful invention, a bending or troping away from the literal into the figurative. "God a mighty," I still hear the field hand saying, "this here morning is cold as blue blazes." I *saw* the cold—materialized, active—in those "blazes," in those flames.

I like to alter Coleridge's image of the poet as a charioteer driving onward with loosely held reins. Instead of a horse as representative of that bodily, kinetic, spontaneous source of sound, association, and undisclosed motive, I propose the more contemporary machine of the bingo parlor. It is a kind of glass-sided till, within which numbered ping pong balls are steadily blown upward, like bubbles in the muses' fountain. You, the conscious half of the writer, are standing above, receiving into your hands these syllables of an evolving riddle breathed from beneath. It is like a popcorn machine, sounds a bit like one, and maybe the smell of popcorn blows through the tent. You don't accept every proposal for a word in your poem, or every rhythmic impluse, that so "pops up." You select, take some but push some back, asking for better imagination, a fresher number. Language, after all, is generic, a possession in common, and every sound and sense has been used to death. Some of "what comes" is inevitably cliché.

This is my image for stage one of the writing, and a point for appreciating a delicate balance. Coleridge had his driver—my caller of numbers—hold the reins loosely. The horse must, to some extent, have its head. A kind of momentum, expressed most obviously in the rhythm and sound, needs to develop, If the caller waits for too long to pick out one of the balls, they may pile up in frustration and cause a blockage. What wants and needs to be said has to get itself in motion. Altering the image, the words that begin to come are like the knotted scarves pulled by the magician from his hat. One is linked to another, and pulling them into motion the first time is necessary for the whole strip to unfurl.

For this stage of composition, then, I advise a willing suspension of disbelief in the validity of what you are saying. I don't mean that you should be wholly uncritical, but I do mean that you should allow yourself the freedom and self-approval to write without inhibition. You can't hit a golf or tennis ball or skate or dive if you are so self-conscious that your movements are deliberate and forced. You learn how to do it by practice, then *do* it, in a movement that is whole, feels spontaneous, and causes a certain delight.

The times to put the harder pressure on yourself are *before* this first writing, and after. What is available to you as you write is in part dependent upon your preparation. Wide reading, study, and analysis of poetry, reading aloud, developing access to your deeper sources of subject matter, all help enrich the mix of what is bubbling up from "below." Discriminating insight into language—sound as well as sense—should have become habitual in you *before* this moment. Put pressure on yourself to read and to understand, to know yourself, to begin the extraction of insights that lead to the richer interior. But don't freeze up when you should be intuitive. Admit to yourself that you love this verbalization of the irrational, this bingo game in which you fill in for yourself the missing columns of self-knowledge.

Getting down the first draft is phase one. You may, for a lyric-length poem, write it in one sitting, or begin it in one session, in the morning, and then continue for a bit more that evening before going to bed. *Phase one* goes on for as long as conception is still glowing inside your head. At this point, the text is illuminated by what you intended.

Here is the first draft of my poem, "Clear Winter." The reader will note that the published version (see page 373) is a few lines shorter, and that changes have been made in word order, word choice, and above all, in the rhythmic momentum or "flow." The finished poem runs on more swiftly, as I had from the beginning intended. But in the first attempt, I was unable quite to capture in writing the seamless movement I had felt. Still all the elements of the final poem are present in this first draft. This is a remarkably complete first version, for me. Even so, the poem had to go through a series of versions, before I was able to bring back those spontaneous phrases and movements from the manuscript and give them a more finely tuned setting.

Clear Winter
(First draft, January 8, 1985)

Confusion of seasons is over.
Today was clear winter.
Light that on trunks was warm
Looked bare and bleak
On chill limbs against chill air.
I saw everywhere corpses of trees
Piled mercilessly by past
High water, crotch-chunk
Of one upon trunk of another.
I worry about my brother.
Angular cedars with crowns
Thinned of needles in death
Seem some desert tribe
Overtaken by an angel of death.
Finally I climbed clear
Of the river valley where memory
Surrounded with its proxy history
Tree-corpses. I saw air clear
In its isolation and pure
As a star. We are unable
to endure this light
The cold whets like a knife.
I stand above this used,
Abused river land and
Hypothesize the being
We cannot undertand, who
Begins springs with fire of a star,
Who is the clarity of air
And the far zero dark.
I sniff for the scent of some fire,
For coffee or leaf smoke or
cigarette scent. All are purely
Absent. I turn toward home,
Alone as a pane of ice
This keen sun shines through.
I will kiss my warm wife,

And under the first star,
Gather cedar for a fire.

Phase two begins when the first glow has faded, or has begun to. *Then* there is the shock of recognition, as you encounter the text you have produced. It is not necessarily disappointing. You may be happily surprised by the electricity in some phrases. You may also note lapses, stretches of dead language, redundancy. Now, with the text in hand, you apply maximum pressure. The poem won't be inhibited. It already exists. *Always* keep the first draft. You aren't a painter who loses the early version in revision. Be as self-critical as you can be. Call everything into question. Go from self-love to self-hate. But avoid extremes. A *balanced* appreciation, an objective appraisal of weaknesses and failings in your own writing is needed. It is essential for you to recognize excellence as well as to admit fault.

You want to see the poem clearly, as it is, and for many poets (including myself), this requires part of phase two to be a revision that questions everything, that entertains the possibility that the whole poem may be a failure. I tend to over-revise at this point, possibly to over-rationalize, and perhaps to make the poetic statement artificially complete, too explicit. Since I seem to need to do this, I allow it to happen, knowing that it is part of phase two: critically confronting the poem.

Phase three emphasizes the fact that the "real poem" knows more than "I" do, that ideally it combines the phase-one spontaneity and the phase-two appraisal. Thinking too much about it, trying all possible combinations of key words in troublesome phrases, is only another effort on your part to see the essence of the poem clearly. Thus, phase three involves a kind of "forgetting" of this highly conscious, trial-and-error revision. I let the text rest, like dough between kneadings. This may be for weeks or months. Then something will reawaken interest. I will recall the true poem, the real poem, from the confusion of various versions. Sometimes I literally recall the poem by writing it out afresh as I remember it at this point, perhaps with help from earlier drafts, especially the first. Often I find that the revision has helped pare away the nonessential, and to prepare a place for what in the first draft was really final. I cherish the sense that for each real poem there is some absolute, inevitable form toward which I have been fumbling through successive drafts. This is in part an illusion, for even "final" texts get revised. You should never turn down what you consider better insight. The real poem seems to gather up into itself the many competing glimpses scattered through various versions. I think of prose as linear, a link through time, but a poem is more a circle, which, when completed, does not end. It looks forward and backward, resisting the erosion of more revisions.

I am myself a runner, and *River Writing: An Eno Journal* was largely composed while I was running along the Eno River in all seasons, all weathers. It started accidentally, but once begun, my premise came to be that the poem would be founded on whatever I saw or thought during the run. The river is over the ridge behind my house, so I could go out and return without interruption. (By the way, *shield* yourself from interruption during the time you set aside to write. If writing is as important to you as you think it is, treat it as such. Give it that central importance in your life.)

The finished version of "Clear Winter" is four lines shorter than the first draft, and words have been cut or substituted in a number of lines that remain. These changes help allow the rhythm of lines to fuse one into the other, so that the whole seems a single movement. For example, "chill limbs against chill air" becomes "chill limbs high in chill air." The first draft let the word *death* appear twice at the ends of lines, and the word *star* appears twice. It also allows the word *corpses* to come in too soon. It was as if my first impulse had known generally what it wanted, but had had to move toward that goal by trial and error. But notice that except for a change in tense, the ending stands as first imagined and drafted.

Here is the published version of "Clear Winter":

Clear Winter
(Published in *River Writing: An Eno Journal*,
Princeton University Press, 1988)

Confusion of seasons is over.
Today was clear winter.
Light that on trunks seemed warm
Looked bleak and bare
On chill limbs high in chill air.
I saw bodies of trees
Piled mercilessly by past
High water, crotch-chunk

373

Of one upon trunk of another.
Angular cedars, their crowns
Thinned of needles by drought,
Seemed a desert tribe
Overtaken by an angel of death.
Finally I climbed clear
Of the valley which memory
Stocked with its proxy
Corpses. I saw air
In its isolation now pure.
We are unable to endure
This light the cold whets to steel.
I stood above river land
And hypothesized the being
We cannot understand, who
Begins things with flame of a star,
Who is the zero far dark.
I sniffed for scent of some smoke,
For coffee, leaf-smolder or
Cigarette odor. All unendurably
Absent. I turned toward home,
Alone as a pane of ice
The keen sun shines through.
I kissed my warm wife
And under the first star
Gathered cedar for a fire.

Here is the lesson I learned from the poems in *River Writing*. It is good sometimes to let the cadences and larger structures of your poetry and its emotional momentum build. Learn to write with ease, with relaxation. You can't really run faster or farther over the long haul simply by bearing down harder. You have to raise the level of your effort, then relax, and trust that preparation. Then perfect the draft later. With joy. As Fred Astaire said to a new partner, "Don't be nervous, but don't make a mistake." Learning not to be nervous, not to make yourself nervous, because of your relaxation and confidence in revision, will help you prevent making a mistake. And remember that the only real mistake in poetry is not ever to get the poem written.

But the key element for most poets who are learning the process is knowing when and how to apply the pressure. Writing poetry is like training for athletic competition. Performance in the event—the writing of the poem—is largely a product of conditioning, associated with analysis of form and technique. But you don't perform that analysis in the act of writing. You somewhat analyze the problem before you, but

374

finally you have to get in there and perform. You don't sit there anxiously wondering whether the last word was really the right one. You don't sit there worrying whether the poem will finally be any good. Time will tell.

74

EVERYONE WANTS TO BE PUBLISHED, BUT...

By John Ciardi

At a recent writers' conference I sat in on a last-day session billed as "Getting Published." Getting published was, clearly, everyone's enthusiasm. The hope of getting published will certainly do as one reason for writing. It need not be the only, nor even the best, reason for writing. Yet that hope is always there.

Emily Dickinson found reasons for writing that were at least remote from publication. Yet even she had it in mind. She seems to have known that what she wrote was ahead of its time, but she also seemed to know that its time would come. If Thomas H. Johnson's biography of her is a sound guide, and I believe it is, she spent her last ten years writing her "letters to the future." The letters, to be sure, were addressed to specific friends; yet they were equally addressed *through* her friends to her future readers. As Hindemith spent ten years composing his quartets and then ten more creating the terms by which they were to be assessed critically, so Emily spent ten years writing her poems (1776 of them, if I recall the right number), and then ten more years stating the terms for their reception.

Even she, then, had an audience (which is to say, publication) in mind. Nor do I imply that the desire to publish is an ignoble motive. Every writer wants to see himself in print. No writer, to my knowledge, has ever been offended when his published offerings were well received. The desire to publish becomes ignoble only when it moves a writer to hack and hurry the work in order to get it into print.

Poetry, of course, is relatively free of commercial motive. Every generation has its Edgar Guest. Ours, I suppose, is Rod McKuen. These are writers whose remouthing of sentiments catches some tawdry emotional impulse in commercial quantities. Yet such writers—or so I have long suspected—must come to believe seriously in the inanities they write. I doubt that they have sold out to the dollar sign: more tragically, they have sold out to themselves.

376

Such writers aside, it is hard to imagine that anyone would think to bribe a poet to write a bad poem. It would follow then (all temptation to cheat being out of the equation) that the only reason for writing a poem is to write it as well as one possibly can. Having so written it, one would naturally like to see it published.

I was, accordingly, in sympathy with the conference members—but I was also torn. For I had just spent days reading a stack of the manuscripts these people had submitted, and I had found nothing that seemed worthy of publication. I sat by, thinking that session on getting published was an exercise in swimming in a mirage. I even suspected a few of those present of drowning in their mirages.

Then one of the hard-case pros on the conference staff delivered a statistic. "You want to get published?" he said. "Fine. Look at the magazines. What are they publishing? The answer is, roughly, 98 percent nonfiction and not quite half of one percent poetry. Yet of the manuscripts submitted at this conference, seventy-six are poetry and only two are nonfiction." He paused. "Now you tell me," he said, "where are you going to get published?"

The hard case, as it happened, was a successful nonfiction writer for the large-circulation magazines; he had dismissed from consideration the literary quarterlies that do publish poetry, sometimes without payment, but sometimes with an "honorarium." To the quarterlies, I would certainly add our two excellent poetry tabloids, *The American Poetry Review* and *Poetry Now*.

For poetry does get published, though not on terms that would be attractive to the big-circulation pros. Poets *qua* poets do not run into serious income tax problems. So be it. If a little is all one asks, then a little is enough. I have never known of anyone who turned to poetry in the expectation of becoming rich by it. Were I to impersonate the hard-case pro at that conference, I could argue that a writer writes as an alcoholic drinks—which is to say, compulsively, and for its own sake. An alcoholic expects no special recognition for being helpless in his compulsion: Why should a poet expect money and recognition for his compulsion?

The fact is that the good poets do generally find their rewards and recognitions. Ego being what it is (and the poet's ego more so), any given poet may think his true merit has been slighted. For myself, whatever I have managed to make of my writing (and it has been a love affair, not a sales campaign), I have always felt that my own

377

satisfaction (or at least the flickering hope of it) was a total payment. Whatever else came has always struck me as a marvelous bonus. And there have been bonuses—grants, prizes, even a small, slow rain of checks. How could I fail to rejoice in that overflow of good? I wish it to every writer, and wish him my sense of joy in it.

But there is more to it. The hard case's manuscript count stayed with me. Can seventy-six poets and two nonfiction writers be called a writers' conference? He hadn't mentioned fiction, and I never learned how many fiction manuscripts had been turned in. But why, I asked myself, would seventy-six turn to poetry and only two to nonfiction? All writing is writing; all of it is part of one motion. I have enjoyed trying different sorts of writing. This present piece, for example, is nonfiction. It is part of the same exploration that poems take me on.

I asked myself the question, but I know I already had the answer —at least part of it—from the poems I had read and criticized. The poems had been bad, and I had fumbled, as one must, at trying to say why I thought they were bad. I wished on that last day that the conference were just starting and that I had ahead of me another chance to identify the badness of the poems. But perish that thought: I was emotionally exhausted.

Yet on that last day the reason so few of the conference members had turned to nonfiction seemed clear to me. Even to attempt nonfiction a writer must take the trouble of acquiring some body of information. The poems I had read lacked anything that could be called a body of information. The writers seemed to have assumed that their own excited ignorance was a sufficient qualification for the writing of poetry.

I wanted to go back and say to my conferees, "Your poems care nothing about the fact!" Isn't that another way of saying they were conceived in ignorance? Not one of the poets I read had even tried to connect fact A to fact B in a way to make an emotional experience of the connection. The writing lacked *thingness* and a lover's knowledge of thing.

Consider these lines by Stanley Kunitz (the italics are mine):

> Winter that *coils* in the thickets now,
> Will *glide* from the fields, the *swinging* rain
> Be *knotted* with flowers. On every bough
> A bird will *meditate* again.

The diction, the rhyming, the rhythmic flow and sustainment are effortless, but how knowledgeably things fall into place! Winter *coils* in the thickets because that snow that lies in shade is the last to melt, thinning down to scrolls of white by the last thaw. Winter will then *glide* from the fields—and what better (continuous, smooth) motion for the run-off of the last melt? The *swinging* rain (what word could better evoke our sense of April showers?) will then be *knotted* (as if) with flowers while birds (as if) *meditate* on every bough. The rain, of course, will not literally be knotted with flowers, nor will birds, literally, meditate. Yet what seems to be a scientific inaccuracy is of the central power of metaphor. Metaphor may, in fact, be conceived as an exactly felt error.

Metaphor is supposed to state the unknown in terms of the known. It is supposed to say X equals Y. Yet when we say "John is a lion," we do not think of John with a mane, with four clawed paws, nor with a pompon tipped tail. We extract from "lion" the emotional equivalent we need and let the rest go. The real metaphoric formula is X does-and-does-not-equal Y. Kunitz understands this formula. His knowledge of it is part of his qualification as a master poet.

There is more. More than can be parsed here. But note how the italicized words *hearken* to one another, each later term being summoned (by some knowledge and precision in the poet) by what went before. The italicized words form what I will dare to call a chord sequence by a composer who has mastered musical theory.

The passage, that is to say, is empowered by a body of knowledge of which I could find no trace in the poets I had been reading at the conference. My poets had been on some sort of trip. Their one message was "I feel! I feel!" Starting with that self-assertive impulse (and *thing* be damned), they then let every free association into the poem. They were too ignorant even to attempt a principle of selection.

I do not imply that I know what any given poem's principle of selection ought to be. To find the principle that serves best and to apply it in a way to enchant the reader is the art and knowledge of the poet. Everything in a good poem must be *chosen* into it. Even the accidents. How else could it be when one stroke of the pen will slash a thing out forever? All that has not been slashed out, it follows, is chosen in.

Ignorance, as nearly as I could say it (too late), was what had really stifled the poems I had read. The writers had not cared enough to learn their own art and use their eyes.

They will, I suppose, get published. Some of them somewhere. But have they earned the right to publication? I ask the question not to answer it. It is every writer's question to ask for himself.

POETIC DEVICES

By William Packard

THERE is a good story about Walter Johnson, who had one of the most natural fast balls in the history of baseball. No one knows how "The Big Train" developed such speed on the mound, but there it was. From his first year of pitching in the majors, 1907, for Washington, Walter Johnson hurtled the ball like a flash of lightning across the plate. And as often as not, the opposing batter would be left watching empty air, as the catcher gloved the ball.

Well, the story goes that after a few seasons, almost all the opposing batters knew exactly what to expect from Walter Johnson—his famous fast ball. And even though the pitch was just as difficult to hit as ever, still, it can be a very dangerous thing for any pitcher to become that predictable. And besides, there were also some fears on the Washington bench that if he kept on hurtling only that famous fast ball over the plate, in a few more seasons Walter Johnson might burn his arm out entirely.

So, Walter Johnson set out to learn how to throw a curve ball. Now, one can just imagine the difficulty of doing this: here is a great pitcher in his mid-career in the major leagues, and he is trying to learn an entirely new pitch. One can imagine all the painful self-consciousness of the beginner, as Johnson tried to train his arm into some totally new reflexes—a new way of fingering the ball, a new arc of the elbow as he went into the wind-up, a new release of the wrist, and a completely new follow-through for the body.

But after awhile, the story goes, the curve ball became as natural for Walter Johnson as the famous fast-ball pitch, and as a consequence, Johnson became even more difficult to hit.

When Walter Johnson retired in 1927, he held the record for total strike-outs in a lifetime career (3409), and he held the record for total pitching of shut-out games in a lifetime career (110)—records which have never been equaled in baseball. And Walter Johnson is second only to the mighty Cy Young for total games won in a lifetime career.

Any artist can identify with this story about Walter Johnson. The determination to persist in one's art or craft is a characteristic of a great artist and a great athlete. But one also realizes that this practice of one's craft is almost always painstakingly difficult, and usually entails periods of extreme self-consciousness, as one trains oneself into a pattern of totally new reflexes. It is what Robert Frost called "the pleasure of taking pains."

The odd thing is that this practice and mastery of a craft is sometimes seen as an infringement on one's own natural gifts. Poets will sometimes comment that they do not want to be bothered with all that stuff about metrics and assonance and craft, because it doesn't come "naturally." Of course it doesn't come naturally, if one hasn't worked to make it natural. But once one's craft becomes second nature, it is not an infringement on one's natural gifts—if anything, it is an enlargement of them, and an enhancement and a reinforcement of one's own intuitive talents.

In almost all the other arts, an artist has to learn the techniques of his craft as a matter of course.

The painter takes delight in exploring the possibilities of his palette, and perhaps he may even move through periods which are dominated by different color tones, such as viridian or Prussian blue or ochre. He will also be concerned, as a matter of course, with various textural considerations such as brushing and pigmentation and the surface virtue of his work.

The composer who wants to write orchestra music has to begin by learning how to score in the musical notation system—and he will play with the meaning of whole notes, half notes, quarter notes, eighth notes, and the significance of such tempo designations as *lento, andante, adagio,* and *prestissimo.* He will also want to explore the different possibilities of the instruments of the orchestra, to discover the totality of tone he wants to achieve in his own work.

Even so—I have heard student poets complain that they don't want to be held back by a lot of technical considerations in the craft of poetry.

That raises a very interesting question: Why do poets seem to resist learning the practice and mastery of their own craft? Why do they protest that technique *per se* is an infringement on their own intuitive gifts, and a destructive self-consciousness that inhibits their natural and magical genius?

I think a part of the answer to these questions may lie in our own modern Romantic era of poetry, where poets as diverse as Walt Whitman and Dylan Thomas and Allen Ginsberg seem to achieve their best effects with little or no technical effort. Like Athena, the poem seems to spring full blown out of the forehead of Zeus, and that is a large part of its charm for us. Whitman pretends he is just "talking" to us, in the "Song of Myself." So does Dylan Thomas in "Fern Hill" and "Poem in October." So does Allen Ginsberg in "Howl" and "Kaddish."

But of course when we think about it, we realize it is no such thing. And we realize also, in admiration, that any poet who is so skillful in concealing his art from us may be achieving one of the highest technical feats of all.

What are the technical skills of poetry, that all poets have worked at who wanted to achieve the practice and mastery of their craft?

We could begin by saying that poetry itself is language which is used in a specific way to convey a specific effect. And the specific ways that language can be used are expressed through all of the various poetic devices. In "The ABC of Reading," Ezra Pound summarized these devices and divided them into three categories—phonopoeia (sight), melopoeia (sound), and logopoeia (voice).

SIGHT

The image is the heart and soul of poetry. In our own psychic lives, we dream in images, although there may be words superimposed onto these images. In our social communication, we indicate complete understanding of something when we say, "I get the picture"—indicating that imagistic understanding is the most basic and primal of all communications. In some languages, like Chinese and Japanese, words began as pictures, or ideograms, which embodied the image representation of what the word was indicating.

It is not accidental that our earliest record of human civilization is in the form of pure pictures—images of bison in the paleolithic caves at Altamira in Northern Spain, from the Magdalenian culture, some 16,000 years B.C. And there are other records of stone statues as pure

383

images of horses and deer and mammoths, in Czechoslovakia, from as far back as 30,000 years B.C.

Aristotle wrote in the "Poetics" that metaphor—the conjunction of one image with another image—is the soul of poetry, and is the surest sign of genius. He also said it was the one thing that could not be taught, since the genius for metaphor was unaccountable, being the ability to see similarities in dissimilar things.

Following are the principal poetic devices which use image, or the picture aspect of poetry:

image—a simple picture, a mental representation. "That which presents an intellectual and emotional complex in an instant of time." (Pound)

metaphor—a direct comparison. "A mighty fortress is our God." An equation, or an equivalence: A = B. "It is the east and Juliet is the sun."

simile—an indirect comparison, using "like" or "as." "Why, man, he doth bestride the narrow world/Like a Colossus..." "My love's like a red, red rose."

figure—an image and an idea. "Ship of state." "A sea of troubles." "This bud of love."

conceit—an extended figure, as in some metaphysical poetry of John Donne, or in the following lines of Shakespeare's Juliet:

> Sweet, good-night!
> This bud of love, by summer's ripening breath,
> May prove a beauteous flower when next we meet...

SOUND

Rhythm has its source and origin in our own bloodstream pulse. At a normal pace, the heart beats at a casual iambic beat. But when it is excited, it may trip and skip rhythm through extended anapests or hard dactyls or firm trochees. It may even pound with a relentless spondee beat.

In dance, rhythm is accented by a drumbeat, in parades, by the cadence of marching feet, and in the night air, by churchbell tolling.

These simple rhythms may be taken as figures of the other rhythms of the universe—the tidal ebb and flow, the rising and setting of the sun, the female menstrual cycles, the four seasons of the year.

Rhythm is notated as metrics, but may also be seen in such poetic devices as rhyme and assonance and alliteration. Following are the poetic devices for sound:

384

assonance—rhyme of vowel sounds. "O that this too too solid flesh would melt..."

alliteration—repetition of consonants. "We might have met them dareful, beard to beard, And beat them backward home."

rhyme—the sense of resonance that comes when a word echoes the sound of another word—in end rhyme, internal rhyme, perfect rhyme, slant or imperfect rhyme, masculine rhyme, or feminine rhyme.

metrics—the simplest notation system for scansion of rhythm. The most commonly used metrics in English are:

iamb $(\smile\,')$
trochee $('\,\smile)$
anapest $(\smile\smile\,')$
dactyl $('\,\smile\smile)$
spondee $('\,')$

VOICE

Voice is the sum total of cognitive content of the words in a poem. Voice can also be seen as the signature of the poet on his poem—his own unmistakable way of saying something. "Only Yeats could have said it that way," one feels, in reading a line like:

That is no country for old men...

Similarly, Frost was able to endow his poems with a "voice" in lines like:

Something there is that doesn't love a wall...

Following are the poetic devices for voice:

denotation—literal, dictionary meaning of a word.

connotation—indirect or associative meaning of a word. "Mother" means one thing denotatively, but may have a host of other connotative associations.

personification—humanizing an object.

diction—word choice, the peculiar combination of words used in any given poem.

syntax—the peculiar arrangement of words in their sentence structures.

rhetoric—"Any adornment or inflation of speech which is not done for a particular effect but for a general impressiveness..." (Eliot)

persona—a mask, an assumed voice, a speaker pretending to be someone other than who he really is.

385

So far these are only words on a page, like diagrams in a baseball book showing you how to throw a curve ball. The only way there can be any real learning of any of these devices is to do endless exercises in notebooks, trying to master the craft of assonance, of diction shifts, of persona effects, of successful conceits, of metrical variations.

Any practice of these craft devices may lead one into a period of extreme self-consciousness, as one explores totally new reflexes of language. But one can trust that with enough practice they can become "second nature," and an enhancement and reinforcement of one's own intuitive talents as a poet.

76

WRITING POETRY FOR CHILDREN

By Myra Cohn Livingston

I NEVER intended to write poetry for children. It was a complete accident, and even today I marvel that it happened at all. I was eighteen, in college, and writing what I considered far more important—poetry about love! My instructor at Sarah Lawrence College, Katherine Liddell, had given us an assignment; we were to use alliteration and onomatopoeia. I turned in some verses. "These," she said to me in her converted closet-conference room, reeking with the odor of Sano cigarettes, "would be wonderful for children. Send them to *Story Parade*" (a magazine for boys and girls published by Simon & Schuster). I grudgingly followed her instructions—the accompanying letter, the self-addressed stamped envelope. Several weeks later the envelope came back. I threw it onto a pile of papers and three weeks later became so angry with Miss Liddell's folly, that I ripped it open to confront her with her error. I caught my breath. The editor had carefully clipped three of the poems, and there was a letter accepting these for publication.

It took me eleven years for my first book, *Whispers and Other Poems,* written when I was a freshman, to be accepted for publication by the same editor, Margaret K. McElderry, who had seen the manuscript when I was in college and encouraged me to continue writing. I know now that during the war years few new books were published, and certainly poetry for children was far down on the list of desired manuscripts. In those days, I read *The Writer* religiously, hoping to find someone who would want my work, and collected a sheaf of rejection slips.

But I did not write and never have consciously written *for* children. I cannot understand why the world appeared to me from the start as through the eyes of a child—of my own childhood—or why, even today, most of the poetry I write comes out that way. The only clue I have is that, even as an anthologist, I am drawn to (or write) those poems that speak to the subjects, emotions, and thoughts of children in a diction they understand.

My own poems have often been called "deceptively simple"; the first review of *Whispers* scathingly accused me of writing about "simple, everyday things," as though this were some sort of evil. Perhaps this is because many adults forget that to the child, these very things are what pique his curiosity, engage his attention. As the poet-in-residence for our school district, in my visits to schools and libraries throughout this country, and in teaching courses for teachers at U.C.L.A. Extension, I note that today's child is very different, in many respects, from the child I was, or that my children are, but that many things remain eternal. Children may know more facts, be more worldly wise, but the curiosity, wonder and fresh way of looking, the joys and pains and doubts, seem just as they always were.

I would like to suggest that anyone who wishes to write poetry that children might enjoy face up to a few basics about this vocation. The climate today is far more receptive to poetry than it was a number of years ago when the English—Walter de la Mare, Robert Louis Stevenson, and A. A. Milne—dominated the field. America has given us Elizabeth Madox Roberts, David McCord and Harry Behn, to mention but a few—and there are many exciting middle-aged and young poets publishing today whose work is excellent. We no longer have to take second place to the English, but we do have to recognize that poetry is still somewhat of a stepchild in juvenile literature. Children, themselves, are more apt to read a story in a picture book than to read poetry, for most adults and teachers feel uncomfortable about presenting it. Even Mother Goose is not as well known as once she was. And poetry demands an involvement of the emotions, whether it be laughter or wonder or a more serious way of viewing the world.

The crisis we seem to face now is the mistaken notion that *anyone* can write a poem. The Poets-in-the-Schools program, in many areas, has too often, in my opinion, fostered undisciplined writing, that which John Ciardi has called "a spillage of raw emotion." Any word or series of words written down are called "poems." This, as I see it, is a great disservice to the children who are falsely praised, but it also applies to older aspiring poets. Many of the high school and college students have had no real discipline. Metrical feet, scansion, forms are

388

unknown. Of course, we do not want didactic, sing-song verse, the moralizing of a Henley's "Invictus" or the elusive fairies of Rose Fyleman. What we do need is true poetry that takes into account the interests and yearnings of the young and leads them toward a process of humanization.

In offering suggestions to the person who wishes to write such poetry, I would ask that he ask himself if anything of the child remains in him—a way of looking, tasting, smelling, touching, thinking; if he is in touch with the contemporary child and his way of viewing the world, if he is truly comfortable with children. I would also suggest that he make the commitment to learn the basics of writing in disciplined forms and meters. One cannot, for example, attempt a limerick without knowing how to use the iambus and anapest correctly, nor even free verse without knowing why it *is* free verse.

Another, and perhaps more elusive point, is that the writer understand and believe that poetry for children is not second-best; there is a tendency on the part of many to feel that a so-called children's poet is one who has failed in writing adult poetry, or that it is "easy" to do. The poet who writes for children exclusively is a sort of second-class citizen.

Although I have spent almost twenty years sharing with young people poetry ranging from Mother Goose to T.S. Eliot, it is difficult to give any definite answer as to what sort of poetry children like best. We know through experience that levity is always high on the list, and humor is important, for it counters the view of poems as soul-building messages in high-flown diction. But many a child prefers the more serious. The more a young person is exposed to poetry, the more refined is his taste in this, as in all arts. I would hope that any writer aspiring to publish poetry would not write for what he thinks is the juvenile market, but rather concentrate on his own strengths. The word-play of David McCord is something that comes naturally to his art; curiosity and a love for nature are intrinsic to Harry Behn's work; and Elizabeth Madox Roberts wrote about experiences of her own as a child.

My own poetry has gone through a series of changes. Trained in the traditional rhyme/meter school, I have at times broken away to free verse, knowing that the force of what I wished to say had to dictate the form. Yet I do not feel I could have made this break without a sure knowledge of the disciplines, taught to me by Robert Fitzgerald and Horace Gregory. I know that there are many who would take issue with me, who feel that anything one wishes to put down, if arranged in a certain order, is a poem.

This change may best be shown by contrasting my first published poem, "Whispers," to later work:

Whispers
   tickle through your ear
   telling things you like to hear.

Whispers
   are as soft as skin
   letting little words curl in.

Whispers
   come so they can blow
   secrets others never know.

Most of my verse in *Whispers, Wide Awake, Old Mrs. Twindlytart* and *The Moon and a Star* was written in traditional forms. But in *A Crazy Flight* (published in 1969), what I wanted to say suddenly refused to be confined by rhyme. The need to use repetition and a freer form of expression asserted itself in a poem that also picked up some current speech patterns of the children I was then teaching:

THE SUN IS STUCK

The sun is stuck.
I mean, it won't move.
I mean, it's hot, man, and we need a red-hot
   poker to pry it loose,
Give it a good shove and roll it across the sky
And make it go down
So we can be cool,
Man.

Yet, *The Malibu,* my poem inspired by the moon landing and America's concerns with litter, combined both the rhyming couplet and some elements of free verse:

Hey moonface,
man-in-the-moonface,

do you like the way
we left your place?

can you stand the view
of footprints on you?

is it fun to stare
at the flags up there?

did you notice ours
with the stripes and stars?

does it warm you to know
we love you so?

moonface,
man-in-the-moonface,

thanks a heap for the rocks.

In *The Way Things Are,* the meter follows a child's pattern with a different rhyme pattern, in "Growing: For Louis."

It's tough being short.

Of course your father tells you not to worry,
But everyone else is giant, and you're just the
way you were.
And this stupid guy says, "Hey shorty, where'd
you get the long pants?"
Or some smart beanpole asks how it feels to
be so close to the ants?
And the school nurse says to tell her again how
tall you are when you've already told her.
Oh, my mother says there's really no hurry
And I'll grow soon enough.

But it's tough being short.

(I wonder if Napoleon got the same old stuff?)

But the rhymed couplet creeps up again and again in *4-Way Stop* (published in 1976):

Ocean at Night

Mother Wave sings soft to sleep
the fish and seaweed of the deep

black ocean, and with quiet hands
pats to peace her tired sands,

her kelp and driftwood; fills her shoals
with gleaming tides, and gently pulls

across her bed the pale moonlight.
And this is night. And this is night.

Throughout these later books are outcroppings of free verse with which I am still experimenting, but there is an inherent pull that constantly draws me back to the containment of fixed forms. I have finally begun to tackle the haiku and cinquain, most demanding in their use of words:

Even in summer
bees have to work in their orange
and black striped sweaters.

Like any other poet, I feel that the most important factor in my poetry writing is not that I set out to write in any given form, but that I must find the right form for the subject matter. For this is when —and only when—the poem "comes right" for me.

What is right for me is not so for everybody. There are no surefire methods, although I do believe that one must know the basics and rules before breaking them. Even children need these rules, for without them, they flounder and grow dissatisfied with what they are doing. What we all have in common is that we are still learning, and, I hope, growing and changing.

77

GUIDELINES FOR
THE BEGINNING PLAYWRIGHT

By Louis E. Catron

YEARS OF teaching playwriting probably have been more educational for me than for my students. Several hundred young playwrights have taken one or more of my classes since I first started teaching at the College of William and Mary in 1966, and they have taught me that writing a play can be simplified—maybe not made "easy," but certainly "easier"—if certain boundaries are imposed.

We began experimenting with guidelines because so many playwrights were expending too much creative energy chasing nonproductive fireflies. We found that these limitations help playwrights over difficult hurdles. More, they are highly important for the overall learning process.

To be sure, for some writers the very idea of imposed limits appears to be a contradiction in significant terms. How, they ask, can I do creative writing if you fence me in?

Their objections have merit. Limitations often inhibit the creative mind, and many creative people expend a great deal of effort seeking clever ways of circumventing the rules. Certainly I've had students react to the guidelines with the fervor of a bull to a red flag and we've had to arm wrestle about the rules.

Nonetheless, imposition of limitations is a way of life in all creative arts. Theatre is no exception. As a play director, for example, I have found that one key portion of my job is establishing parameters of character for actors, holding these walls tightly in place during rehearsals, and encouraging the performers to create depth within those limitations.

We're talking about the contrast between the casual and sloppy meandering of a Mississippi River versus a tightly confined Colorado. The former changes directions so often that it confuses even experienced riverboat captains, but the latter is held so tightly in direction that it cuts the Grand Canyon. Discipline is essential for the creation of beauty.

393

The beginning playwright is encouraged to accept the following guidelines to write his or her first play. Later plays can be more free. Indeed, deliberately breaking selected guidelines later will help you better understand the nature of dramatic writing. For now, however, let these guidelines help you in your initial steps toward learning the art and craft of playwriting.

1. *Start with a one-act play.* A full-length play isn't merely three times longer and therefore only three times more difficult. And that a one-act is simpler doesn't mean it is insignificant. The one-act play can be exciting and vibrantly alive, as has been shown by plays such as *No Exit* (Sartre), *Zoo Story* (Albee), *The Maids* (Genet), *the Dumb Waiter* (Pinter) and *The Madness of Lady Bright* (Wilson).

Starting with the one-act lets the writer begin with a canvas that is easily seen at a glance, instead of a mural that covers such a huge space perception doesn't grasp it all.

The one-act typically has only a few characters, is an examination of a single dramatic incident, and runs about half an hour in length. It usually stays within one time frame and one place. Because there are fewer complexities, you'll be able to focus more upon the actual writing, and you'll have less concern about a number of stage problems which come with full-length plays.

2. *Write about something you care about.* Writing manuals usually tell the beginner to write "about what you know best." I think that can lead a beginner to think in terms of daily, mundane events. Better, I believe, is for the beginner to *care;* if the playwright is involved with the subject, that interest will pull an audience along.

3. *Conflict is essential to drama.* Quibble me no quibbles about plays which may not have conflict. For *your* first play, there should be conflict. Drama is the art of the showdown. Force must be opposed by force, person (or group) by person (or group), desire by desire.

If there's no conflict, the dramatic qualities are lost. The result may still hold the stage, but the odds against it are increased. More important, even if the one-act has no conflict and yet holds the stage, the playwright hasn't learned that all-significant lesson about showing conflict. You'll want to know that when you write more.

394

4. *Let there be emotion.* People *care,* in your first play, I hope; people feel strongly, whether it is love or hate, happiness or despair. If you are able to get them emotional, your characters more than likely are going to be active and going somewhere. The audience will care more about emotional people than those dull-eyed, unfeeling dramatic deadbeats.

5. *Stay within the "realistic" mode.* Realism deals with contemporary people, the sort who might live next door, in their contemporary activities, and with selective use of ordinary speech. It avoids the aside and the soliloquy. It is quite comfortable inside the traditional box set. Realism is selective, and sometimes critical, in its presentation of objective facts.

Realism is the familiar mode you've seen most often: it dominates television, and only a handful of movies break away from realism. No doubt you've also seen it on stage more than any other mode. Because you know it best, your first play will be easier to write if you stay in realism. Expressionism, absurdism, symbolism, epic: avoid these for your first experience with playwriting.

(Examples of realism would be full-length plays like *Ghosts* or *A Doll's House,* both by Ibsen, or one-acts like *Ile* and other sea plays by O'Neill. More recent plays tend to be eclectic—primarily but not totally realistic, like the full-length *Death of a Salesman,* by Arthur Miller, or the one-act *Gnadiges Fraulein* by Tennessee Williams.)

6. *Limit the number of characters.* Too many characters and you may lose some: they'll be on stage but saying and doing nothing, so you'll send them off to make dinner or fix the car while you focus on the remaining characters you like better. Consider eliminating those who are dead.

Strenuously avoid "utilitarian" characters—those people who make minor announcements (in older drawing-room plays they say little more than, "Dinner is served"), or deliver packages or messages (Western Union's delivery boy, remember, is as much a relic as the butler). Such characters tend to be flat and no fun for playwright, performer or audience.

Some utilitarians are confidants, on stage to serve as ears so the protagonist will be able to speak inner thoughts without resorting to the soliloquy. The confidant in this sort of case turns out to be about as vital as a wooden listening post.

Confidants, by the way, are easily recognized: their faces are covered with a huge question mark. They seem to be asking questions eternally, without any apparent interest in question or answer. The playwright uses the confidant to get to the answer. If such a person is necessary, let the character be more than a pair of ears.

Just how many characters should be in the play?

Three is a good number for the first play. The triangle is always helpful; three characters allow development of good action and conflict and variety. More, and there's the risk of excess baggage; less, and the characters may quickly become thin and tired.

7. *Keep them all on stage as long as you can.* All too often I've seen plays developing potentially exciting situations, only to be deflated by the exit of a prime character. The audience will feel let down—promised excitement evaporated through the swinging door.

A flurry of activity with entrances and exits is deceptive. There may be a feeling of action but in truth there's only movement of people at the door. The more such business, often the less the drama: in class we begin to comment jokingly about wanting a percentage of the turnstile concession.

The beginning writer needs to learn to keep all characters alive and actively contributing to the play's action. So, then, you need to try to keep them all on stage as long as you possibly can. If you have a character who keeps running out, perhaps he ought to be eliminated.

You needn't invent a supernatural force to keep them in the same room, by the way, although I've seen my student writers come up with fascinating hostage or kidnap situations and locked doors in order to justify keeping everyone present. All of that is clever, but all you need is action that involves all the characters.

8. *No breaks: no scene shifts, no time lapses.* Just as some playwrights have people leaving when stage action is growing, so also are there authors who cut from the forthcoming explosion with a pause to shift scenery or to indicate a passage of time. There is a break in the action and that always is disappointing. Such lapses are all too often barriers to the play's communication with the audience.

If you have in mind a play that takes place first in an apartment, then in a grocery store, then in a subway, you have let the motion pictures overly influence your theatrical concept. It just won't wash, not in a one-act stage play; with so many sets and breaks producers will shy away from your script. (Yes, yes, you can cite this or that exception, but we're talking about a beginner's first play, not a script by someone with an established reputation.)

Reduce the locales to the *one* place where the essential action occurs, and forget the travelogue. So also with the jumps in time: find the *single* prime moment for these events to take place.

Later you can jump freely in time and space, as Miller does so magnificently in *After the Fall*. Your first play, however, needs your concentrated attention on action, not on inventive devices for jumping around through time and space.

9. *Aim for a thirty-minute play.* One-act plays are delightfully free of the restrictions placed upon full lengths, and can run from only a few minutes to well over an hour. The freedom is heady stuff for a beginning writer.

Aim for around half an hour. Less than that and you probably only sketched the characters and action; much longer, and you might exhaust your initial energies (and your audience!). Your goal, of course, is to be sure you achieve adequate amplification; too many beginners start with a play only eight or ten minutes long, and it seems full of holes. Your *concept* should be one that demands around half an hour to be shown.

10. *Start the plot as soon as you can.* Let the exposition, foreshadowing, mood and character follow the beginning of the plot (the point of attack). Get into the action quickly, and let the other elements follow.

11. *Remember the advantage of the protagonist-antagonist structure.* Our era of the anti-hero apparently has removed the protagonist from the stage. Too bad. The protagonist is a very handy character indeed, and the protagonist-antagonist structure automatically brings conflict which, you recall, is essential for drama.

The protagonist is the "good guy," the one with whom we sympathize and/or empathize, the central character of the play. A better definition: *The one whose conscious will is driving to get a goal.* The antagonist stands firmly in the way. Both should be equal forces at the beginning of the play: if one is obviously stronger, the conflict is over quickly and so should the play be.

(If you do not fully understand the personality of a true protagonist, look at Cyrano in Hooker's translation of Edmond Rostand's *Cyrano de Bergerac*. Cyrano is so strongly a conscious will moving actively that it takes several antagonists to balance him.)

12. *Keep speeches short.* Long speeches often grow boring. Sometimes they are didactic; the playwright delivering The Play's Message. Always they drag the tempo. But the worst sin of a long speech is that it means the playwright is thinking just of that one character and all the others are lying about dead.

Short speeches—quick exchanges between characters—on the other hand keep all of them alive and make the play appear to be more crisp and more vital. The play will increase in pace and you'll automatically feel a need to increase the complications.

How long is "short"? Let the dialogue carry but one idea per speech. Or, to give you another answer, let your ear "listen" to the other characters while one is talking, and see who wants to interrupt. A third answer: try to keep the speeches under, say, some twenty words.

One grants the effectiveness of the "Jerry and the Dog" speech in Albee's *Zoo Story*. It makes a nice exception to this guideline. But there are very few such examples, and there are many more examples of plays where the dialogue is rich and effective because the playwright disciplined the talky characters.

13. *Complications are the plot's heartbeat.* John wants Mary. Mary says fine. Her family likes the idea. Her dog likes John. His parrot likes Mary and the dog. So John and Mary get married. They have their 2.8 kids, two cars, a dishwasher, and they remember anniversaries. Happiness.

Interesting? Not very. Dramatic? Hardly.

John wants Mary. Mary is reluctant, wondering if John simply is in love with love. John is angry at the charge. Mary apologizes. John shows full romanticism. Mary worries again. Mary's grandmother advises Mary to take John to see what love really is by visiting Mary's older sis who everyone knows is happy in marriage. Mary and John visit. Sis and her husband Mike are having a violent fight; mental cruelty; damning ac-

398

cusations. Sis gets John to help her and he unwillingly does; Mike pulls John to his side; Mary yells at John for causing trouble.

That's the first ten minutes.

I think you'll grant it has more potential than the first sketch. *Complications* keep it vital, moving, alive. *A play depends upon conflict for its dramatic effect, and complications are the active subdivision of the basic conflict.*

So, then: the traditional baker's dozen—thirteen guidelines which will help you with your first play. They will help you avoid pitfalls which have lamed so many playwrights, and they will give you a basic learning experience which will help you with future plays.

78

CONFLICT: THE HEARTBEAT
OF A PLAY

By D. R. Andersen

EVERY PLAYWRIGHT is a Dr. Frankenstein trying to breathe life into a page for the stage. In a good play, the heartbeat must be thundering. And the heartbeat of a play is conflict.

Simply put, conflict exists when a character wants something and can't get it. Conflict may sometimes be internal—as when a character struggles to choose between or among opposing desires. For example, Alma in Tennessee Williams's *Summer and Smoke* longs to yield to her sexual yearnings but is prevented by the repressed and conventional side of her nature.

Conflict in drama may also be external—as when a character struggles against another *character* (Oscar and Felix in Neil Simon's *The Odd Couple*); against *society* (Nora in Ibsen's *A Doll's House*); against *nature* (the mountain climbers in Patrick Meyers' *K2*); or against *fate* (Sophocles' *Oedipus*).

In most plays, the conflict is a combination of internal and external struggles. In fact, internal conflict is often externalized for dramatic impact. In Philip Barry's *Holiday,* for instance, the hero's inner dilemma is outwardly expressed in his attraction to two sisters—one who represents the safe but boring world of convention, and the other who is a symbol of the uncertain but exciting life of adventure.

Granted that a conflict may be internal or external; that a character may be in conflict with another character, society, nature or fate; and that most plays are a combination of internal and external conflict, many plays that have these basic elements of conflict do not have a thundering heartbeat. Why? These plays lack one, some, or all of the five magic ingredients of rousing, attention-grabbing-and-holding conflict.

The five magic ingredients

I. *Never let your audience forget what your protagonist wants.*

You can achieve this in a number of ways. Often the protagonist or another character states and periodically restates in dialogue what is at stake. Or in some plays, he explains what he wants directly to the audience in the form of a monologue. As you read or watch plays you admire, take note of the obvious and ingenious techniques playwrights use to tell the reader or audience what the characters' goals are.

Sometimes the method used to keep your audience alerted to your protagonist's goal/concern/need is a direct reflection of the protagonist's personality. In the following three short passages from my play *Graduation Day*,[1] a mother and father with very traditional values have a conversation while waiting to meet their rebellious daughter, who has told them she has a big surprise. Notice how the protagonist—Mrs. Whittaker—nervously and comically manipulates the conversation, reminding her husband and the audience of her concern for her daughter Jane:

MRS. WHITTAKER
(Knocking on the door)
Jane. Jane. It's Mom and Dad.
(Pause)
No answer. What should we do, Tom?
MR. WHITTAKER
Let's go in.
MRS. WHITTAKER
Suppose we find Jane in a compromising situation?
MR. WHITTAKER
Nobody at Smith College has ever been found in a compromising situation.

*   *   *

MRS. WHITTAKER
Tom, you know, this was my freshman room.
MR. WHITTAKER
Of course, I know.
MRS. WHITTAKER
And Jane's. It was Jane's freshman room too, Tom. Remember?

*   *   *

MR. WHITTAKER
Mary, you get in the craziest moods at these reunions. I may never bring you back again.

---

1. First produced by Playwrights Horizons in New York, starring Polly Holliday.

MRS. WHITTAKER
Do you know why you fell in love with me, Tom?
MR. WHITTAKER
I fell in love with you the minute I saw you eat pancakes.
MRS. WHITTAKER
That's a sound basis for a relationship. Tom, where do you suppose Jane is?
And more frightening, what do you suppose she wants to tell us? She said just
enough on the phone to suggest that she's going to be bringing a boy here for us
to meet.
MR. WHITTAKER
A man, Mary, a man.
MRS. WHITTAKER
Oh, God. I never even considered that possibility. Suppose Jane brings a
fiancé—our age—like Pia Zadora did.
MR. WHITTAKER
Don't you want Jane to live her own life?
MRS. WHITTAKER
No. Especially not her own life. Practically anyone else's. But not her own.
MR. WHITTAKER
What *do* you want for Jane?
MRS. WHITTAKER
I don't see why Jane can't fall in love with a plain Harvard Business School
student, let's say. Someone who'll be steady and dependable.

And so it goes. The protagonist discusses a number of topics, but she
inevitably leads the conversation back to her overriding concern. Mrs.
Whittaker's desire to see her daughter do the right thing and marry
wisely is always uppermost in the mind and conversation of the
character.

In this one act, a comic effect is achieved by having Mrs. Whittaker
insistently remind the audience what she wants. Once you have clearly
established what a character wants, you can then write powerful and
often hilarious scenes in which the audience, already knowing the
character's point of view, is able to anticipate his reaction.

II. *Show your protagonist struggling to achieve what he wants.*

This principle is, of course, the basic writing advice to *show,* not tell,
and it was a major concern for me when I was writing *The House Where
I Was Born.*[2]

The plot: A young man, Leo, has returned from the Vietnam War, a
psychosomatic mute because of the atrocities he witnessed. He comes
back to a crumbling old house in a decaying suburb, a home populated

---

2. First produced by Playwrights Horizons in New York.

402

by a callous stepfather; a mother who survives on aphorisms and by bending reality to diminish her despair; a half-crazy aunt; and a grandfather who refuses to buckle under to the pressures from his family to sell the home.

I set out to dramatize Leo's painful battle to free himself of memories of the war and to begin a new life. However, each time I worked on the scene in the play when Leo first comes home, his dialogue seemed to trivialize his emotions.

Then it occurred to me that Leo should not speak at all during the first act; that his inability to speak would *show* an audience his suffering and pain far better than his words could.

At the end of the third act, when Leo regains some hope, some strength to go on, every speech I wrote for him also rang false. The problem, I eventually realized, was that as playwright, I was *telling* the audience that a change had taken place, instead of *showing* the change as it took place.

In the final draft, I solved this dramatic problem by having Leo, who had loved music all his life, sit down at the piano and begin playing and singing Christmas carols while his surprised and relieved family joined in.

First silence, then singing, served my play better than mere telling.

III. *Create honest, understandable, and striking obstacles against which your protagonist must struggle.*

Many plays fail because their characters' problems seem too easily solved. I wrestled with this issue when I was writing *Oh Promise Me!*[3] a play that takes place in a private boarding house for the elderly. The play's original title was *Mr. Farner Wants a Double Bed*. The plot involved the attempt of an elderly man and woman—an unmarried couple—to share a double bed in a rooming house run by a repressed and oppressive owner. I wanted to explore contemporary attitudes toward the elderly, particularly as they concerned sexuality.

The more I played with the idea, the more I repeatedly heard an inner voice saying, "Chances are the couple could find some place to live where nobody cared if they were married or not." This voice—like the

---

3. Winner of the Jane Chambers Memorial Playwriting Award.

audience watching a play without an honest, understandable, convincing obstacle for the protagonist—kept saying, "So what?"

The writer's response: "Suppose, instead of a man and a woman, the couple is two men." Here was a real obstacle: Two elderly, gay men, growing feeble, want to sleep together in a double bed under the roof of an unsympathetic and unyielding landlord.

Suddenly, the play was off and running.

IV. *In the final scene or scenes, make sure your protagonist achieves what he wants; comes to understand that there is something else he wants; or accepts (defiantly, humbly, etc.) that he cannot have what he wants.*

If we spend time in the theater watching a character battle for something, we want to know the outcome—whatever it may be.

In my psychological thriller *Trick or Treat,*[4] Kate, a writer in her forties, has been badly burned in a love affair and is unable to decide whether to accept or reject a new relationship. She is involved at present with Toby, a younger man, but—as the following dialogue reveals—she insists on keeping him at a cool distance.

KATE
That does it, Toby. We're getting out of this place.
TOBY
Okay. Tomorrow we'll check into the local Howard Johnson's.
KATE
I want to go home—to New York—to my own apartment.
TOBY
Okay. Okay. If you insist. Besides, Howard Johnson's is not to be entered into lightly.
KATE
Huh?
TOBY
It's an old college rule. You'd never shell out for a room at Howard Johnson's—unless you were *very* serious about the girl.
KATE
I'll remember that. The day I agree to check into a Howard Johnson's—you'll know I've made a serious commitment to our relationship.

In the course of the play, Kate faces a number of trials—including a threat to her life—as she tries to expose the fraudulent leader of a

---

4. First produced by the Main Street Theater, New York, New York.

religious cult. Through these trials—with Toby by her side—Kate comes to realize that she's ready to forget the past and give herself over to a new relationship. This critical decision is humorously expressed in the last seconds of the play:

KATE

Do you love me, Toby?

TOBY

Yes, I do. I found that out tonight . . . when I thought I might be losing you forever. Do you love me?

KATE

Yes. And I can prove it.

TOBY

How?

KATE

Take me to Howard Johnson's—please! Take me to Howard Johnson's!

The curtain falls and the audience knows that the heroine has made an unequivocal decision.

V. *Make sure that the audience ultimately sympathizes with the protagonist's yearning to achieve his goal, however outlandish his behavior.*

This may be the most important of the five magic ingredients of conflict. It may also be the most elusive. To oversimplify, in a good play, the protagonist must be very likable and/or have a goal that is universal.

In the plays I've had produced, one character seems to win the sympathy of the audience hands down. In my romantic comedy *Funny Valentines*,[5] Andy Robbins, a writer of children's books, is that character. Andy is sloppy, disorganized, and easily distracted, and—this is his likable trait—he's painfully aware of his shortcomings and admits them openly. Here's Andy speaking for himself:

ANDY

Judging by my appearance, you might take me to be a complete physical and emotional wreck. Well, I can't deny it. And it's gotten worse—much worse—since Ellen left. You know that's true.

---

5. Published by Samuel French; winner of the Cummings/Taylor Playwriting Award; produced in Canada under the title *Drôles de Valentins*.

Andy is willing to admit his failings to old friends and strangers alike. Here he's talking to an attractive young woman he's just met.

ANDY

You don't have to be consoling just because I haven't finished a book lately. I won't burst into tears or create a scene. No. I lied. I might burst into tears—I'm warning you.

ZAN

I didn't mean to imply . . . (*She laughs.*)

ANDY

Why are you laughing?

ZAN

You stapled your shirt.

ANDY

What's so odd about that? Millions of derelicts do it every day.

ZAN

And your glasses are wired together with a pipe cleaner.

ANDY

I didn't think twine would be as attractive.

In addition to liking Andy, audiences seem to sympathize with his goal of wanting to grow up and get back together with his collaborator and ex-wife, Ellen.

Whether you're wondering where to find an idea for a one-act play or beginning to refine the rough draft of a new full-length work or starting rehearsals of one of your plays, take your cue from the five magic ingredients of conflict. Whatever your experience as a playwright and whatever your current project, understanding the nature of dramatic conflict and how to achieve it will prove invaluable at every point in the writing and staging process.

* * *

Five exercises for creating dramatic conflict

Try these exercises to develop your skill in handling conflict.

1. Choose five plays you like. Summarize each in one sentence, stating what the protagonist wants. For example, Hamlet wants to avenge his father's murder.

2. Write one page of dialogue in which character A asks character B to do something that character B doesn't want to do. Have character A

406

make a request in three different ways, each showing a different emotion—guilt, enthusiasm, humility, anger.

3. Write a speech in which a character talks to another character and conveys what he wants without explicitly stating his goal.

4. Choose a famous play you enjoy. Rewrite the last page or two so that the outcome of the conflict for the protagonist is entirely different from the original.

5. Flip through today's newspaper until you find a story about a person—famous or unknown—who interests you. Then summarize the story in one sentence, stating what the person wants. For example: X wants to save an endangered species of bird. Next list the obstacles the person is facing in trying to get what he wants:

   • A developer wants to build a shopping mall where the remaining members of the endangered species live.

   • Pollution from a nearby factory is threatening the birds' food supply.

Finally, write several short scenes in which X (the protagonist) confronts the people (the antagonists) who represent the cause of each obstacle. (In this example, the antagonist would be the developer or the owner of the factory.) Decide which of the scenes you've written is the most dramatically satisfying. Identify the reasons you think it is the best scene.

79

TEN GOLDEN RULES FOR PLAYWRIGHTS

By Marsha Norman

Budding playwrights often write to ask me advice on getting started—and succeeding—in writing plays. The following are a few basics that I hope aspiring playwrights will find helpful.—M.N.

1. Read at least four hours every day, and don't let anybody ask you what you're doing just sitting there reading.

2. Don't write about your present life. You don't have a clue what it's about yet. Write about your past. Write about something that terrified you, something you *still* think is unfair, something that you have not been able to forget in all the time that's passed since it happened.

3. Don't write in order to tell the audience how smart you are. The audience is not the least bit interested in the playwright. The audience only wants to know about the characters. If the audience begins to suspect that the thing onstage was actually written by some other person, they're going to quit listening. So keep yourself out of it!

4. If you have characters you cannot write fairly, cut them out. Grudges have no place in the theatre. Nobody cares about your grudges but you, and you are not enough to fill a house.

5. There must be one central character. One. Everybody write that down. Just one. And he or she must want something. And by the end of the play, he or she must either get it or not. Period. No exceptions.

6. You must tell the audience right away what is at stake in the evening, i.e. how they know when they can go home. They are, in a sense, the jury. You present the evidence, and then they say whether it seems true to them. If it does, it will run, because they will tell all their friends to come see this true thing, God bless them. If it does not seem true to them, try to find out why and don't do it any more.

7. If, while you are writing, thoughts of critics, audience members or family members occur to you, stop writing and go read until you have successfully forgotten them.

8. Don't talk about your play while you are writing it. Good plays are always the product of a single vision, a single point of view. Your friends will be helpful later, after the play's direction is established. A play is one thing you can get too much help with. If you must break this rule, try not to say what you have learned by talking. Or just let other people talk and you listen. Don't talk the play away.

9. Keep pads of paper near all your chairs. You will be in your chairs a good bit (see Rule 1), and you will have thoughts for your play. Write them down. But don't get up from reading to do it. Go right back to the reading once the thoughts are on the paper.

10. Never go to your typewriter until you know what the first sentence is that day. It is definitely unhealthy to sit in front of a silent typewriter for any length of time. If, after you have typed the first sentence, you can't think of a second one, go read. There is only one good reason to write a play, and that is that there is no other way to take care of it, whatever it is. There are too many made-up plays being written these days. So if it doesn't spill out faster than you can write it, don't write it at all. Or write about something that does spill out. Spilling out is what the theatre is about. Writing is for novels.

80

HOW TO SELL YOUR TELEVISION SCRIPT

By Richard A. Blum

MARKETING a television script requires strategy, determination, and a realistic understanding of the industry. The marketplace is extremely competitive, and even the best projects written by established professionals might end up on the shelf. Still, an *excellent* original script—submitted to the right person at the right time—might suddenly break through all barriers. The key word is *excellent*. It makes no sense to submit a script unless you feel that it is in the most polished form (even then it will be subject to rewrites), and that it represents the highest calibre of your creative potential. One might think producers are inclined to see the masterpiece lurking behind a rough draft script. More likely, they'll focus on the weaknesses, compare it to top submissions, and generalize about the writer's talents. So, if you feel uncertain about the professional quality of a work, hold off submitting it. Your next work might show you off to better advantage.

Since unsolicited scripts tend to be lost or "misplaced" by production companies, it's a good idea to have a sufficient number of copies. The *minimum* number you will need is three—one for your files, one for submission, and one for inevitable rewrites. More realistically, you'll probably want additional copies for two or three producers, an agent or two, and your own reserve file for unanticipated submissions. Incidentally, fancy covers and title designs are totally unnecessary. Three inexpensive brads can be punched through the left hand margins of the manuscript. Scripts are usually printed or photocopied to avoid the smudged look of carbons.

The Writers Guild

The Writers Guild of America protects writers' rights, and establishes minimum acceptable arrangements for fees, royalties, credits, and so on. You are eligible to join the Guild as soon as you sell your first project to a signatory company (one who has signed an agreement with the Guild). A copy of your contract is automatically filed and you will then be invited to join the membership. Before you sell the new project, you *have* to be a member of the Guild; otherwise, no signatory company can hire you.

The one-time membership fee for Writers Guild of America, West (Los Angeles) is $1,500, plus 1% of yearly earnings as a writer (or $25 quarterly, if you earn less than $1,000 as a writer). The membership fee for Writers Guild of America, East (New York) is $1,000. Dues are $62 per year, plus 1½% of annual earnings as a writer.

Any writer can register a story, treatment, series format, or script with the Writers Guild of America. The service was set up to help writers establish the completion dates of their work. It doesn't confer statutory rights, but it does supply evidence of authorship which is effective for ten years (and is renewable after that). If you want to register a project, send one copy with the appropriate fee ($15 for nonmembers; $5 for members) to: Writers Guild of America West, Registration Service, 8955 Beverly Blvd., Los Angeles, CA 90048, or Writers Guild of America East, Inc., 555 West 57th Street, New York, NY 10019.

You can also register dramatic or literary material with the U.S. Copyright Office—but most television writers rely on the Writers Guild. The Copyright Office is mainly used for book manuscripts, plays, music or lyrics, which the Writers Guild will not register. For appropriate copyright forms (covering dramatic compositions), write to: Register of Copyrights, Library of Congress, Washington, D.C. 20540.

The release form or waiver

If you have an agent, there is no need to bother with release forms. But if you're going to submit a project without an agent, you'll have to send to the producer or the production company for a release form—or waiver—in advance. (Addresses of selected production companies are listed at the end of this chapter.) Most production companies will return your manuscript without it. The waiver states that you won't sue the production company and that the company has no obligations to you. That may seem unduly harsh, but consider the fact that millions of dollars are spent on fighting plagiarism suits, and that hundreds of ideas are being developed simultaneously and coincidentally by writers, studios, and networks.

The waiver is a form of self-protection for the producer who wants to avoid unwarranted legal action. But it also establishes a clear line of communication between the writer and producer. So rest assured, if legal action is warranted, it can be taken.

The cover letter

When you prepare to send out your project, draft a cover letter that is addressed to a *person* at the studio, network, or production company. If you don't know who is in charge of program development, look it up in the trade papers, or telephone the studio receptionist. If she says, "Mr. So-and-So handles new projects," ask her to *spell* "Mr. So-and-So." That courtesy minimizes the chance of embarrassment, and maximizes the chance that the project will wind up at the right office.

The letter you write should sound professional. There's no need to offer apologies for being an unsold writer, or to suggest that the next draft will be ten times better than this one. If a cover letter starts off with apologies, what incentive is there to read the project?

Here's the tone a cover letter might have:

Dear_____

I've just completed a mini-series called FORTUNES, based on the book by Frank Tavares. I've negotiated all TV and film rights to the property, which is a dramatic adventure series about a family caught in the California Gold Rush. I think you'll find the project suitable for the mini-series genre. It's highly visual in production values and offers unusual opportunities for casting.

I look forward to your reaction. Thank you for your cooperation.

Sincerely,

The letter doesn't say I'm an unsold writer in the midwest or that Frank Tavares is my friend and let me have the rights for a handshake. Nor does it take the opposite route, aggressively asserting that it is the best project the studio will ever read. There's no need for such pretentions. The cover letter sets the stage in a simple and dignified manner. The project will have to speak for itself.

Submitting a script

Independent producers represent the widest span of marketing potential for the free-lance writer. If one producer turns down an idea, there are many others who might still find it fresh and interesting. However, the smaller independent producer is not likely to have the financial resources to compete with the development monies available at the network or studio.

Production companies do have that bargaining power. The distinction between smaller independents and larger production companies is their relative financial stability and current competitive strength on the airwaves. Production companies form and dissolve according to the seasonal marketing trends and network purchases. The more successful production companies have become mini-studios in their own right, with a great number of programs on the air and in development. Some of the more recognizable entities are M. T. M. Enterprises (Mary Tyler Moore), Embassy TV (Norman Lear), and Lorimar Productions (Lee Rich).

The major motion picture studios are in keen competition with production companies. Only six major film studios have aggressive and viable television divisions: Columbia Pictures—TV; Paramount Pictures—TV; Metro-Goldwyn-Mayer (M.G.M.)—TV; 20th Century-Fox—TV; Universal—TV; and Warner Brothers—TV. (Addresses at the end of this chapter.) They represent highly fertile ground for program development; strong deals can be negotiated by agents for the right project.

At the top of the submission ladder is the network oligarchy: ABC, CBS, NBC. Once a project is submitted at this level, there's no turning back. If a project is "passed" (*i.e.,* turned down), it's too late to straddle down the ladder to independent producers. *Their* goal is to bring it back up to the networks (who in turn must sell to the sponsors).

The closer the project comes to the network, the more limited the number of buyers. As the submission moves up the ladder, it faces stiffer competition and fewer alternatives. So you see that the marketplace is highly competitive, although not totally impenetrable. Your submission strategy will depend on knowing the marketplace trends and organizing a campaign to reach the most appropriate people and places.

There's no better way to stay on top of marketing and personnel changes than reading the trade papers—*Daily Variety* (1400 N. Cahuenga Blvd., Hollywood, CA 90028) and the *Hollywood Reporter* (6715 Sunset Blvd., Hollywood CA 90028). The trades reflect the daily pulse of the entertainment industry on the West Coast. Moreover, each paper offers a weekly compilation of production activities ("TV Production Chart," "Films in Production," etc.), which lists companies, addresses, phone numbers, and producers for shows in work. A careful scrutiny of those lists will provide helpful clues to the interests and current activities of independent producers, production companies, and studios.

A similar resource is the "Television Market List," published regularly in the *Writers Guild of America Newsletter* (8955 Beverly Blvd., Los Angeles, CA 90048). It lists all current shows in production or pre-production, and identifies the story consultant or submission contact for each show. The WGA's market list states whether or not a show is "open" for submissions, and whom to contact for assignments. A careful reading of these and other publications, such as *Ross Reports Television* (40–29 27th St., Long Island City, NY 11101), a monthly magazine that lists new television programs and their producers, can help bring you closer to making knowledgeable and practical decisions about marketing your own projects and scripts.

In the network marketplace, you have a choice of submitting a script to a great number of places at the same time or sending it selectively to a few individuals. The specific strategy depends on the needs of the marketplace at the time. You should determine which producers and production companies are particularly interested in the type of project you have developed.

Options, contacts, and pay scales

If a producer is interested in a project he or she will propose a *deal,* *i.e.,* the basic terms for a contract. If you have no agent, now is the time to get one. *Any* agent will gladly close the deal for the standard 10% commission. An attorney would be equally effective, or if you have an appropriate background, you might want to close the deal yourself. The need for counsel depends on the complexity of the proposed deal, and the counter-proposals you wish to present.

On the basis of your discussions, a *Deal Memo* is drawn up which outlines the basic points of agreement—who owns what, for how long, for how much, with what credits, royalties, rights, and so on. The deal memo is binding, although certain points may be modified if both parties initial it. The *Contract* is based on the terms of the deal memo and is the formal legal document. If you're dealing with a producer who is a signatory to the Writers Guild (most established producers are), the contract will adhere to the terms of the Minimum Basic Agreement (M.B.A.) negotiated by the Writers Guild of America.

A producer can either option your work, purchase it outright, or assign you to write new material. If the property is *optioned,* the producer pays for the right to shop it around (which means the project can be submitted by the producer to a third party, e.g., the network). During the option period, you can't submit the project to anyone else. Typically, option money is relatively small; perhaps $1,500 or $2,500 for a six-month period. But the writer will be paid an additional sum of money if the producer elicits interest and moves the project forward. If the producer fails to exercise the option (*i.e.,* if the option expires), the rights revert back to the writer.

A *Step Deal* is the most common form of agreement between producers and free-lance writers. It sets forth fees and commitments for story and teleplay in several phases. The first step is at the *story* stage. When the writer turns in a treatment, the producer pays for it—at least 30% of the total agreed upon compensation—but the producer does not have to assign that writer to do the script. If the writer *is* retained, the producer exercises the *first draft* option. When that draft of the script is turned in, the writer receives a minimum of 40% of the total agreed upon compensation. Now the producer has the final option—putting the writer to work on the *final draft.* Once that script is received, the writer is entitled to the balance of payment. The *Step Deal* is a form of protection for the producer who can respond to the quality of content, the inviolability of delivery dates, and the acceptability of the project to the networks. It also guarantees the writer that his or her work will be paid for, whether there is a cut-off or a go-ahead on the project.

How to get an agent

A good agent is one with a respectable track record, a prestigious list of clients, and a reputation for fairness in the industry. There is no magical list of good agents, although the Writers Guild does publish a lists of agents who are franchised by the Guild. (Send $1.00 to Writers Guild West, *Attn: Agency List,* 8955 Beverly Blvd., Los Angeles, CA 90048.) Names and addresses of literary and dramatic agents appear in *Literary Market Place* (Bowker), available in most libraries. A list of

415

agents can also be obtained by sending a stamped, self-addressed envelope to Society of Authors' Representatives, 39½ Washington Square South, New York, NY 10012.

If you have no agent representing you, it's difficult to get projects considered by major producers. One of the best ways is to submit your work to an agent who already represents a friend, a professor, a long-lost uncle in the industry. If you are recommended by someone known to the agency, it makes you less of an unknown commodity. If you have no contact, make a list of possible agents for your project, and prioritize them in your submission status file. You might send the project to one top agency for consideration, or to a select number of agencies at the same time.

A brief cover letter might introduce you as a free lancer looking for representation on a specific project. If you don't get a response within six to eight weeks, you can follow up with a phone call or letter, and submit the project to the next agent on your list. Don't be discouraged if you get no response at first; just keep the project active in the field. If the script or presentation is good enough, you might eventually wind up with some positive and encouraging response from the agency.

If an agent is interested in your work, he or she will ask to represent it in the marketplace. If the work sells, the agent is entitled to 10% commission for closing the deal. If the work elicits interest but no sale, you have at least widened your contacts considerably for the next project.

The larger agencies offer an umbrella of power and prestige, but that elusive status is seriously undermined by the sheer size of the agency itself. Many clients inevitably feel lost in an overcrowded stable, and newcomers can hardly break into that race. In contrast, a smaller literary agency provides more personalized service, and is more open to the work of new talent. If you're going to seek representation, the smaller agency is the likely place to go. But don't be fooled by the label "small." Many of these agencies are exceptionally strong and have deliberately limited their client roster to the cream of the crop. In fact, many smaller agents have defected from executive positions at the major agencies. So you'll have to convince them you're the greatest writer since Shakespeare came on the scene—and that your works are even more salable.

How do you prove that you have the talent to be a star talent? It's all

416

in the writing. If your projects look professional, creative, and stylistically effective, you're on the right track. Indeed, you can call yourself a writer. If the artistic content is also marketable and you back it up with determination and know-how, you might just become a *selling* writer.

And that is the "bottom line" for success in the television industry.

Networks, Studios and Production Companies

(Note: New submissions should be addressed to the Head of Program Development.)

NETWORKS

ABC-TV
4151 Prospect Ave.
Los Angeles, CA 90027
or, 1330 Ave. of the Americas
New York, NY 10019

CBS-TV
7800 Beverly Blvd.
Los Angeles, CA 90036
or, 51 West 52nd St.
New York, NY 10019

NBC-TV
3000 W. Alameda
Burbank, CA 91523
or, 30 Rockefeller Plaza
New York, NY 10020

MAJOR STUDIOS

Columbia Pictures-TV
3000 Colgems Sq.
Burbank, CA 91505

MGM-TV
10202 W. Washington Blvd.
Culver City, CA 90230

Paramount Pictures-TV
5555 Melrose Ave.
Los Angeles, CA 90038

20th Century Fox-TV
10201 W. Pico Blvd.
Los Angeles, CA 90064

Universal Studios-TV
100 Universal City Plaza
Universal City, CA 91608

Warner Bros.-TV
4000 Warner Blvd.
Burbank, CA 91505

SELECTED INDEPENDENT
PRODUCTION COMPANIES

Embassy Television Corp.
100 Universal City Pl.
Universal City, CA 91608

Lorimar Productions
3970 Overland Ave.
Culver City, CA 90230

M.T.M. Enterprises
4024 Radford Ave.
Studio City, CA 91604

Aaron Spelling Productions
1041 N. Formosa
Los Angeles, CA 90046

81

ROLES IN COLLISION:
A PLAY BEGINS

By Jeffrey Sweet

MY SON CAME BACK from his visit to a department store Santa Claus with a handout from an elf—one of those infernal little plastic doodads containing three tiny BB's. On the floor of the container is a picture pocked by three shallow indentations. The object is to tip the container to and fro so as to propel the three BB's into the three indentations and thus complete the picture (in this case—a juggler with three balls overhead).

I had better things to do. So of course I picked up the game. More than half an hour evaporated as I jiggled and jostled and cussed. Finally, after countless near-misses, I had two of the three BB's snugly placed. Only one to go. I held my breath and tapped gingerly. And, with lazy grace, the third BB rolled across the face of the picture and settled into the third indentation with a plop.

There was something very familiar about that plop. It is with a similar sound that I find that the premises of my plays usually come together. After analogous jiggling, jostling, and tapping in my imagination, some small element drops into place, and I suddenly know how I'm going to be spending the next several months. Mind you, this is not primarily a matter of luck (though luck is never entirely absent in writing). Just as there is skill (however trivial) involved in the BB game, there is skill involved in taking images, hunches, and impulses that have lodged in one's mind and manipulating them into an arrangement that is sufficient grounds for typing "Act One" onto a piece of paper.

Different dramatists arrive at their starting points in different ways. Many rely on instinct and intuition, but I've always held to the belief that when performing surgery you're more likely to have a successful outcome if the lights are on in the operating room so you can see your

418

tools. I'd like to share a tool that I've found of particular use in building plays.

I had long ago been fascinated by the blacklisting of entertainers that occurred during the McCarthy era and wanted to find a way to deal with the subject dramatically. A friend of mine named Kate Draper had told me that her father Paul had been among those blacklisted in the fifties, so I asked her if we could arrange to get together so that I could fire a few questions at her. She was agreeable, and soon after, in a local coffee shop, she told me how her father, a famous dancer, had seen his career all but destroyed when someone accused him of being a Communist. After she had shared details of her family's ordeal and answered all of my prepared questions, the conversation shifted to chat about what was going on in our lives at the moment. She had good news. She had just been cast in a Broadway musical. Idly, I asked how she thought her father would react if it turned out that the director of the musical had been one of those who had cooperated with the House Committee on Un-American Activities, one of the forces responsible for the blacklist.

"The director didn't," said Kate.

"I know," I said. "I'm asking 'if.' "

She paused for a second, then replied, "He probably wouldn't say much of anything. He tends not to talk too much about those days."

My reaction was, "That's not dramatic."

This led me to wonder what would make it dramatic. The answer, of course, was if the father had quite a strong reaction indeed. Plop. There was the premise of my play. A year or so later, my play *The Value of Names* opened at the Actors Theatre of Louisville and has since been staged by a number of other companies and been published.

Thinking about the matter later, I realized that what I did when I asked Kate that question was construct the dilemma that would result if two important roles in her life—those of actress and daughter—were to come into conflict. This dilemma—the conflict between two or more of a central character's roles—is the dynamic element in most of the plays I write as well as those I admire.

Everybody plays several roles. Among the ones I count in my personal repertoire: my son's father, my wife's husband, my father's son, my mother's son, my agent's client, my students' teacher, and so on. Frequently, these roles come into conflict. For instance, as any dedicated writer who is married knows, there inevitably come times when your spouse asks, "Are you married to me or your work?" How one responds to this question may determine whether one retains the role of husband and wife or takes on the challenge of the new role of a divorced person.

Characters in plays, too, must choose between roles. Their choices and the resulting fates are the stuff of drama.

Let's dive into the deep and look at *Hamlet*. Shakespeare loads him with several conflicting roles. Hamlet is simultaneously the ghost's appointed avenger, Gertrude's son, Claudius's nephew, Ophelia's boyfriend, Rosencrantz and Guildenstern's schoolmate, and so on. The impossibility of being all of these things at the same time and the choice he has to make between these roles are what make the action of the play possible. One of the many things Hamlet and the audience discover is that his role as avenger ultimately supersedes all of the other roles. Because he embraces this role and the attendant responsibility, Gertrude is poisoned, Claudius is stabbed, Ophelia drowns, Rosencrantz and Guildenstern are executed, and Hamlet himself dies.

In Sophocles' *Antigone,* the title character must choose between two mutually exclusive roles. Creon, the king of Thebes, has refused to allow the slain rebel Polyneices the dignity of funeral rites and has decreed that anybody contravening his order is to be executed. Antigone's dilemma is that she is both a citizen of Thebes (and thereby bound to obey Theban law) and Polyneices' sister (and thereby bound by family obligation to give her brother a proper funeral). The play centers on her determination that her role as sister takes precedence over her role as citizen. In burying her brother she condemns herself to death.

Much has been written about why one experiences a catharsis watching tragedy. How is it that witnessing the destruction of heroes produces in the audience not a profound depression but a kind of elation? My theory is that this feeling is a result of our knowledge that Hamlet, Antigone, Iphigenia, Romeo and Juliet, Macbeth, and Medea (to name but a few) meet and embrace their true natures. "To thine ownself be true" is an injunction few in real life have the courage to fulfill, and there is something liberating about seeing characters who, in full knowledge of the frequently cataclysmic consequences, choose to be their truest selves.

But this business of characters choosing their true selves is not limited to classical tragedy. Neil Simon's *The Odd Couple* is a comedy in which characters, again, have to determine their real roles. Felix and Oscar must battle their way to the understanding that their relationship is more truly that of good friends than bad roommates. The title character in Molière's *Tartuffe* meets his deserved comeuppance when he gives free rein to his usually-hidden lecherous nature. At the end of Ibsen's *A Doll House,* Nora walks out on her marriage having resolved to put aside the degrading part of Torvald's "doll-wife" in favor of the role of a mature and self-respecting adult.

I have found this construct useful not only for the analysis of others' plays, but for the synthesis of my own. Before I begin to write a script, I ask myself a number of questions about my central character's options. A play depicts the actions taken by the central character or characters. It is not enough, however, to know what my protagonist does. I have to know what my protagonist chooses *not* to do. After all, the choice of one road necessarily implies the rejection of at least one other. If a character's choice is to have any tension or resonance, the case for the road not taken must be very strong. In the case of *The Value of Names,* Norma, the daughter, knows that if she chooses to stay in the cast of the play being directed by her father's enemy, she puts her relationship with her father at risk. If she resigns from the play, she jeopardizes her career. It is the difficulty of the choice that attracted me to the story.

Because Norma ultimately decides to stay with the play, Benny, her father, then is faced with a choice: either to accept and forgive what he sees as a betrayal or to hold fast to his bitterness and, in essence, blacklist his daughter from his affections. During the writing of the play I found that this choice became the central question of the piece.

To summarize the process, what started as my speculation about which choice Paul Draper would make in a hypothetical situation led me to wonder which choice my character Norma would make if confronted over this issue by her father Benny, which, in turn, led me to wonder which choice Benny would make in reaction to Norma's choice.

I am not suggesting that one should blithely appropriate the private lives of friends. (As I hope I've established, my play, though derived from a speculation about how Kate and her father would handle a certain situation, is in no meaningful way a reflection of Kate's rela-

421

tionship with her father.) But everybody lives with contradictions in his or her life. Most of us are fairly nimble about keeping these contradictions from coming to too much of a head. But drama is found in the exploration of these contradictions, in asking what would happen if push were indeed to come to shove.

Get into the habit of this kind of speculation, and you may also find the third BB dropping into place in your imagination.

82

THE S-N-A-P-P-E-R TEST FOR PLAYWRIGHTS

By Lavonne Mueller

WHENEVER I finish a play, I check to see that I have applied to it every point from what I call the "S-N-A-P-P-E-R Formula." Here is my "Snapper" checklist.

Secret

Everyone loves to hear a secret. Have the main characters in your play tell something about themselves that is revealing and intimate.

In my play *The Only Woman General*, Olive Wiggins tells us that when she was in combat, she couldn't tell the winning from the losing; all battles seemed the same.

The secret Anne reveals (but only to her diary) in *The Diary of Anne Frank* is the physical change in her body that turns her into a woman. Willy Loman, in Arthur Miller's *Death of a Salesman*, tells Ben about his life insurance policy and also what his funeral will be like:

They'll come from Maine, Massachusetts, Vermont, New Hampshire! All the old timers with strange license plates.

In Tennessee Williams' *The Glass Menagerie*, Laura tells the Gentleman Caller her secret humiliation when she was going to school with a brace on her leg:

My seat was in the back row. I had to go clumping all the way up the aisle with everyone watching.

How would *Death of a Salesman* change, for example, if Willy's secret was that he wanted to be an artist? How would *The Glass Menagerie* change if the secret Laura confides to the Gentleman Caller was that she had successfully hid from the world the brace on her leg?

423

Names

Give your characters interesting names. Names can define a character. They can also function ironically and humorously. A cowboy in my play *Little Victories* is called Double Ugly because he's been in a fight that cut his face in two places. In *The Only Woman General,* the woman general is ironically named Olive—olive for peace.

Big Daddy in Tennessee Williams's *Cat on a Hot Tin Roof* is the head of a wealthy household, and not only does he command obedience and servitude, but the humorous overtones of his name add an ironic dimension. Big Daddy's sons are Gooper and Brick—the first is simpering, the second headstrong.

How would *Cat on a Hot Tin Roof* change if Tennessee Williams had named Big Daddy Herbert or Leslie or reversed the names of his sons?

If you wrote a one-act play about a dermatologist, would you want to call him Sam Lumpkin?

Action

Every play must have action. Drama is like a boxing match. Two characters go at each other until one is shoved up against the wall. Or knocked out. The image of a boxing match is actually used by author Shirley Lauro in her excellent play, *Open Admissions.* Ms. Lauro states: "The audience's experience from the start should be as if they had suddenly tuned in on the critical round of a boxing match."

In *Little Victories,* Joan wishes to be a successful general. She has to convince her adjutants that she is competent. She is constantly being pressured by them. In desperation, she uses many tricks of common sense that she learned as a farm girl. Her main goal is always a source of action: Joan pulls soldiers out of mudholes with the same skill she used on her cows. Because she can't read, she uses the lines in the palm of her hand as a map. She struggles to win over her troops. Action.

Make sure your main character wants something, and make sure somebody is keeping him/her from getting it. In *Cat on a Hot Tin Roof,* Big Daddy wants a son from Brick. Brick is obstinate. They struggle. Action!

Props

Props can be very effective. They are visual messages to the audience, and they are an extension of the character's personality. Try to think of props that are genuinely important to the development of your play. You don't want to use a prop that is gratuitous.

In my play *Breaking the Prairie Wolf Code,* Helen, a pioneer woman, takes a tea set with her on the westward journey. At every wagon stop, she has tea to remind herself of a former gentility. As the trip progresses, parts of the tea set are broken and lost. I use this prop to show graphically the hardships of the journey.

Hamlet speaks to the skull of Yorick. The Moor in *Othello* uses a handkerchief as proof of his suspicions of Desdemona's infidelity. In *The Diary of Anne Frank,* Anne tapes pictures of movie stars on the wall of her small hiding space. In Eugene O'Neill's *Long Day's Journey into Night,* Mary's faded wedding dress is her one tangible connection to the past.

It's hard to imagine these plays without their classic props. What if Hamlet delivered his monologue to a rock instead of Yorick's skull? What if Anne Frank had pictures of food instead of movie stars on her wall?

Plot

Plot is as important to a dramatist as it is to a novelist. The attention of the audience is held by a clear, strong story line. Shakespeare is a master of storytelling. We want to know, for example, what will happen to Romeo and Juliet. What will happen to Lear after he's turned over his power to his children?

The plot is closely related to what we call "the dramatic question." This question is something an audience wants answered. In *Hamlet,* the dramatic question is: Will Hamlet avenge his father? The answer to that dramatic question keeps each person interested enough to come back after the intermissions.

The plot/dramatic question does not have to be complex. In *Little Victories,* the question is simply: How will Joan win the battle? In the musical *A Chorus Line,* the plot/dramatic question is simply: Who will get chosen for the chorus line?

If you think of a question to ask on stage, it becomes easier to structure a plot around it. In *Breaking the Prairie Wolf Code,* my question is simply: Will the wagon train get to California? After I came up with the question, I began to imagine all the things that could prevent this journey and make it more difficult. I invented obstacles and characters to "hang" on the story line of my dramatic question.

Ending

Give your characters a well-planned exit. They've come to the end of their tale, and it's very effective if they can leave the stage with some relevant words or actions.

Again, in *Little Victories,* the drama ends when Joan tells Susan that she must reach into the future and find somebody who can help her. Joan takes Susan's hand and points it to the audience, saying: "Take the dark."

In *Cat on a Hot Tin Roof,* Maggie says to Brick at the end of the play: "Oh, you weak, beautiful people who give up so easily. You need somebody to hand your life back to you like something gold."

Anne's father in *The Diary of Anne Frank* reads a last line from her diary entry: "In spite of everything I still believe that people are really good at heart."

How would *Cat on a Hot Tin Roof* change if the ending line were Brick's—perhaps saying that he didn't know if he had the strength to go on?

How would *The Diary of Anne Frank* change if her last diary entry were that people are basically corrupt?

Relatives

Let the characters tell us something about their relatives or background. It helps us to understand how they came to be the people they are.

Esther Bibbs, an ex-slave on the wagon train in *Breaking the Prairie Wolf Code,* tells us:

I used to make this pea soup for the Fenchler family. They were my marsters in Georgia. My folks was took to the South from Africa and sold into the Fenchler family, ya know. Course the North whupped the South and they made the Constitution signed. That's why I'm free—here in the west.

In *Death of a Salesman,* Willy tells us that his father lived for many years in Alaska and was an adventurous man. Willy adds: "We've got quite a little streak of self-reliance in our family."

Mary, in *Long Day's Journey into Night,* tells us that she was in a convent school for girls when she was young:

At the Convent I had so many friends. Girls whose families lived in lovely homes.

How would *Death of a Salesman* change if Willy's father had been a college professor? How would *Long Day's Journey into Night* change if Mary had gone to a public school?

Now you know the formula. It works for me, and it can work for you. Don't mail out your script until you give it the S-N-A-P-P-E-R test. And after you do so and send it off, begin immediately to think of your next play. Don't wait for the mail. Let your mind work on new ideas. The following test may help get your imagination rolling again. It is not meant to be an indicator of your creativity, but only a vector to point the way to your creative potential.

How's Your I. Q. (Imagination Quotient)?

(Give yourself 5 points for each YES answer. Give yourself 2 points for each SOMETIMES answer.)

1. When I see a person for the first time, I always observe the color of his eyes and hair.
YES   SOMETIMES   NO

2. I like to think about a person's name and how it is appropriate or not appropriate for that person.
YES   SOMETIMES   NO

3. I would definitely laugh (to myself) if I became acquainted with a Japanese man named John Smith.
YES   SOMETIMES   NO

4. When I look at a cloud in the sky, I often see more than just a cloud.
YES   SOMETIMES   NO

5. When I'm observing the behavior of animals, I am often reminded of certain human characteristics.
YES   SOMETIMES   NO

427

6. If I came across an empty food tray in a cafeteria, I would find it fun to *guess* by the leftovers what kind of person belonged to that tray.
YES SOMETIMES NO

7. If a person sits across from me on a bus or train or airplane for any length of time, I like to guess the occupation of that person by his appearance.
YES SOMETIMES NO

8. I find it fun to sit in an outdoor restaurant or park bench for long periods of time just to peoplewatch.
YES SOMETIMES NO

9. When I go into a person's house, I like to observe how that person added his own personality to the house by means of furniture, art objects, and color scheme.
YES SOMETIMES NO

10. If I see a person reading a particular book, I imagine what kind of person he is by the book he is reading.
YES SOMETIMES NO

11. If I observe a person carrying a large, wrapped box, I often imagine quite a few things that could be inside that box.
YES SOMETIMES NO

12. When someone I don't know is on the phone, I try to imagine what that person is like from the tone of his voice.
YES SOMETIMES NO

13. When I am at a large function such as a ball game, concert, or picnic, I often like to strike up a conversation with someone next to me because I find it interesting to know what they are thinking or what they might say to me.
YES SOMETIMES NO

14. If I see a movie I really like, I like to imagine what happens to the main character after the movie ends.
YES SOMETIMES NO

15. I always see variety in a rainy day. Rainy days are not all alike.
YES SOMETIMES NO

428

16. If I am outside and hear a jet going over, I like to imagine what the inside of the jet looks like and the people on it and what they might be doing at that instant.
YES   SOMETIMES   NO

17. I like to look at other people's picture albums and piece together their lives from the various photos.
YES   SOMETIMES   NO

18. I like to try strange and exotic foods just for the experience.
YES   SOMETIMES   NO

19. Whenever I go through a department store or grocery store, I have a strong desire to "touch" things so that I can feel as well as see objects.
YES   SOMETIMES   NO

20. An interesting smell such as that of perfume or food or flowers can suddenly bring back a memory to me.
YES   SOMETIMES   NO

WHAT IS YOUR IMAGINATION SCORE?

100–80 = Excellent
79–60 = Very Good
59–40 = Average
Below 40 = You need to be more observant about ways to improve your imagination.

83

THINK PICTURE BOOK

By Eve Bunting

THE BAD NEWS IS THAT NO, picture books are not easy to write. The good news is that there are some useful guidelines in picture book writing, and although they will never guarantee a sale, they will at least put you on course if writing a beautiful picture book is your heart's desire. So let's think picutre book.

Most obviously, *think pictures.* Perceive your story as a moving slide show, vivid, arresting, and dramatic. Give the illustrator something to work with. If you are both author and illustrator you will be doing yourself the same favor. Incidentally, it is not necessary for you to provide the pictures. The publisher will take care of that for you.

Remember, static scenes without variety do not make a good slide presentation.

I once had a friend show me a picture book manuscript she'd written.

"It's so cute," she said. "But I've sent it out and sent it out, and no one wants to buy it. Why?"

In the book, a cat stands before a mirror, trying on hats—a cowboy hat, a fireman's helmet, a baseball cap, etc. One character, one scene, one action, repeated over and over.

"He could be a very cute cat," I said. "But nothing happens."

My friend looked puzzled and a little irritated by my lack of perception.

"Something does happen," she said. "He changes hats."

I amended my words. "Not enough happens."

That cat in the mirror would make a dull slide show and a dull picture book.

An art director in a major publishing house once told me: "The words in a picture book should be a gift to the illustrator."

I had always believed that the illustrator's paintings were gifts to the writers, adding dimensions often undreamed of. And that is true. But it has to work the other way around, too. What the art director meant was that if the scenes in the text are varied, imaginative, plentiful, the illustrator doesn't have to struggle and the book is what it should be, a happy collaboration. To achieve this, keep in mind that the scenes should roll forward in an ever-moving diversity of character and action. This does not always happen naturally for me. I have to work at it. You can, too.

When you've finished your manuscript, divide it by drawing lines across the text to mark what you see as the natural ending of a page. Or set up a dummy by taking eight sheets of blank paper and folding them horizontally to make a 32-page book (32 pages is the usual picture book length, less three or four for front matter: title page, copyright, and dedication). Write your text on each dummy page. Do you have enough pictures? Do you have too many words? Look for balance. Visualize your little reader, or listener, impatient to get on with it, to turn the page to find out what happens next.

If I see an ungainly chunk of text in my own work, I deliberately set out to "break" it up with picture possibilities.

For instance, in *The Mother's Day Mice,* there is a scene in which the three little mice are watching Honeysuckle Cottage, waiting and hoping that the cat on the porch will go away. It is important here that I give the impression of time passing, since Little Mouse needs to hear many repeats of the song being played on the piano inside the cottage. When I read what I'd written, I realized I had a static scene. So I added:

(Middle Mouse) set his strawberry on the ground and a beetle came on the run. Middle picked it up again and shooed the beetle away.
Little Mouse began creeping toward the cottage on his belly.
Biggest yanked him back by his tail.

These few lines add action and a little humor. They use all three mouse characters and a new peripheral character, the beetle, is placed on the scene. But better, better, better, they add two picture possibilities. And Jan Brett, the illustrator, used both charmingly.

Adding scenes is not that difficult. But it is harder because of the second unbreakable law of the picture book—*think short*. Think 1,000 words, or less. Think concise. Say what you need to say in the most economical way possible that makes sense and that sounds poetic, because a poetic telling is the essence of the picture book.

A few weeks ago I visited a school where examples of "pretty sentences from picture books" were pinned on the wall of the library.

"We talk about them," the librarian told me. "We ask: 'Why did the author say it this way instead of another way?' We listen to the sounds of the words and the cadence of the sentence and look for images."

So "pretty" sentences are a must, if we want to make it on the wall. Not overblown, though. Not gushy or sentimentally sweet.

Isn't it more breathtaking to read, "The air hissed to the beat of wings" *(The Man Who Could Call Down Owls)* than, "There was the sound of wings in the air"? Try to use the actual "sound" word. The air *hissed;* the bus *wheezed;* the leaves *flurried* in the wind.

Long passages of undiluted description are out in the picture book. But I believe short descriptions add immeasurably to the texture of the story and enhance the word awareness of even the youngest reader. A line or two can set the scene:

Milk bottles stood on front steps, waiting to be let in. The sky was the color of his mother's pearl brooch. The one she wore on Sundays. *(St. Patrick's Day in the Morning)*

Crows cawed in the white air. The arms of the trees scratched at the sky. *(The Valentine Bears)*

Our table seemed monstrously big. Chairs, hump-backed, clawed and crouched around it. *(Ghost's Hour, Spook's Hour)*

Enough description, but not too much.

A picture book, then, must be short, not abrupt. It must be pure, not sterile. There is room for a story and for a few beautiful word pictures, too.

There is also room to say something valuable. A picture book that does not has no value of itself. Heavy or deeply moralistic, no. Worthwhile, yes. The treasure is well hidden, but it's there for the child to feel and understand. In *Ghost's Hour, Spook's Hour,* I am saying: "No need to be afraid of the dark. The scary things can be explained away. See? No need to be afraid." Those actual words never appear in the text. They are self-evident as Jake and his trusty dog, Biff, search the dark house for Mom and Dad while in the hallway the big clock strikes midnight—ghost's hour, spook's hour.

On a trip to mainland China a few years ago, I spent some time browsing in a bookstore and brought back with me a picture book entitled *A Boy and His Kitten* (for children from 4 to 8). The story is about Maomao who will not go to bed. He and his kitten play through the night hours, disturbing his good little sister.

"How troublesome are those children who do not go to bed," the text says.

In the morning, little sister, who presumably got some sleep, is up at dawn doing her morning exercises. Alas for Maomao and his kitten who are now sleeping the day away:

> For them, it is too late
> To breathe the fresh morning air,
> Or hear their teacher's interesting stories.
> Oh, what a great pity it is
> for Maomao and his kitten!
>
> Our little friends,
> Be not like these two.
> Early to bed,
> And early to rise,
> Keeps you fit and wise.

One has to hope that the story lost a little something in the translation!

You must try not to do this in the picture books you write. In fact, I venture to say, do this and you'll never have a picture book. So *think subtle*. The worthwhile thing you have to say will come across just as clearly and much more palatably.

The picture book writer, perhaps more than writers in any other genre, must *think original*. The field is overflowing with books about cats and dogs, horses and ponies, dinosaurs, rabbits, ducks, mice; boys who are having terrible, awful days, girls who can be anything they want to be; moms, dads, pesky little sisters—all subjects that interest little kids. But writers need to find the *new* angle. As in Carol and Donald Carrick's book: *What Happened to Patrick's Dinosaurs?* The dinosaurs, Patrick says, liked helping people to build houses and lay roads. But after a while the people were willing to sit back and let the dinosaurs do it. They didn't help themselves. So the dinosaurs, for the sake of the people and still helping them, took off in space ships. And *that's* what happened! A nice, original touch and a theme that is there without being belabored.

When I wrote *Scary, Scary Halloween,* I knew of the numerous picture books about this popular holiday. What was there to say that hadn't already been said? So I did trick or treating from a cat's point of view, a mama cat, hiding under the house with her baby kittens, waiting fearfully for the monsters, who are the children in costume, to leave. When they do—

It's quiet now, the monsters gone
The streets are ours until the dawn.
We're out, we prowlers of the night
Who snap and snarl and claw and bite.
We stalk the shadows, dark, unseen . . .
Goodbye 'til next year, Halloween.

A different angle? I think so, and the editor agreed.

When you think picture book, think lasting and forever, because that is what the best picture books are. How many children have been frightened and reassured by *Where the Wild Things Are* (Maurice Sendak)? How many have learned to read for pleasure through the good graces of Dr. Seuss and *The Cat in the Hat* or *Green Eggs and Ham*? How many have gone to sleep to the lullaby lull of *Goodnight Moon*? How many will? A picture book is not temporary, it is not ephemeral. It is as lasting as truth itself and should, said Arnold Lobel, "Rise out of the lives and passions of its creators." It should be unique and ageless and seemingly effortless in its smooth, easy flow.

For all the effort involved, the pruning and shaping and sculpting of words, you will be rewarded with joy as you hold in your hand this small polished jewel that is *your* picture book.

84

WRITING NONFICTION BOOKS FOR YOUNG READERS

By James Cross Giblin

WHERE do you get the ideas for your nonfiction books?" is often the first thing I'm asked when I speak to writers. My usual reply is, "From anywhere and everywhere."

I've found a good place to start in the search for ideas is with your own interests and enthusiasms. It also helps if you can make use of personal experience. For example, the idea for my *The Skyscraper Book* (Crowell) really had its beginnings when I was a child, and loved to be taken up to the observation deck of the Terminal Tower, the tallest building in my home city of Cleveland.

Years later, after I moved to New York, I rented an apartment that was just a few blocks away from the Flatiron Building, one of the city's earliest and most striking skyscrapers. No matter how many times I passed the building, I always saw something new when I looked up at the carved decorations on its surface.

Although I had edited many books for children, I'd never thought of writing for a young audience until I was invited to contribute a 500-word essay to *The New York Kid's Book.* I chose the Flatiron Building as my topic because I wanted to find out more about it myself.

That piece led to an expanded magazine article (for *Cricket*) called "Buildings That Scrape the Sky," and then to *The Skyscraper Book.* In the latter I was finally able to tell the story behind Cleveland's Terminal Tower, the skyscraper that had fascinated me forty years earlier.

Besides looking first to your own interests and knowledge, you should also be open to ideas that may come your way by luck or chance. The idea of *Chimney Sweeps* (Crowell) literally came to me out of the blue when I was flying to Oklahoma City on business.

The plane stopped in Chicago and a tall, rangy young man carrying what I thought was a musical instrument case took the seat next to me. We started to talk, and I discovered that the man—whose name was Christopher Curtis—was a chimney sweep, and his case contained samples of the brushes he manufactured at his own small factory in Vermont. He was on his way to Oklahoma City to conduct a seminar for local sweeps on how to clean chimneys more efficiently.

Chris went on to tell me a little about the history of chimney sweeping and its revival as a profession in the last decade, because of the energy crisis. In turn, I told him I was a writer of children's books, and that he'd fired my interest in chimney sweeps as a possible subject.

We exchanged business cards, and a month or so later I wrote to tell him that I'd followed up on the idea and had started researching the book on chimney sweeps. I asked him if he'd be willing to read the manuscript for accuracy. He agreed to do so and volunteered to supply photographs of present-day sweeps that could be used (and were) as illustrations in the book.

According to an old English superstition, it's lucky to meet a chimney sweep. Well, meeting Christopher Curtis was certainly lucky for me!

Evaluating an idea

Once you have an idea for a book, the next step is to decide whether or not it's worth pursuing. The first thing I do is check R. R. Bowker's annual *Subject Guide to Children's Books in Print*, available in the reference department of most libraries, to see what else has been written on the subject. With *Chimney Sweeps*, there was nothing at all. In the case of *The Skyscraper Book*, I discovered that there were several books about *how* skyscrapers are constructed, but none with a focus on *why* and *by whom* they're constructed, which was the angle of the book I wanted to write. There may be many books on a given subject, but if you find a fresh or different slant, there'll probably be room in the market for yours, too.

Another thing to weigh when evaluating an idea is the matter of levels: A subject worth treating in a book usually has more than one. For instance, when I began researching *Chimney Sweeps*, I soon realized that besides the obvious human and social history, the subject also touched on economic and technological history. Weaving those different levels together made the book more interesting to write—and I believe it makes it more interesting for readers also.

436

A third important factor to consider is what age group to write the book for. That decision has to be based on two things: the nature of the subject and a knowledge of the market for children's books. I aimed *Chimney Sweeps* at an older audience, because I felt that the subject required more of a sense of history than younger readers would have. At the same time, I kept the text as simple and compact as possible, because I knew that there's a much greater demand today for children's nonfiction geared to the upper elementary grades than there is for Young Adult nonfiction.

After you've checked out your idea and decided what slant to take with it, and what age group to write for, it's time to begin the research. An entire article could be devoted to research methods alone. The one thing I feel it's safe to say after writing seven books is that each project requires its own approach, and you have to discover it as you go along.

When I was researching *The Scarecrow Book* (Crown, 1980), I came up against one stone wall after another. It seemed no one had ever bothered to write anything about scarecrows. Research became a matter of following up on the skimpiest of clues. For example, a brief mention in a magazine article that the Japanese had a scarecrow god led me to the Orientalia Division of the Library of Congress, where a staff member kindly translated a passage from a Japanese encyclopedia describing the god and its relation to Japanese scarecrows.

The Skyscraper Book presented the opposite problem. There was so much background material available on skyscrapers that I could easily have spent ten years researching the subject and never come to the end. Choices had to be made early on. I settled on the eight or ten New York skyscrapers I wanted to discuss and sought detailed information only on those. I did the same thing with skyscrapers in Chicago and other cities around the country.

Chimney Sweeps opened up the exciting area of primary source material. On a visit to the Economics Division of the New York Public Library, I discovered the yellowing transcripts of early 19th-century British investigations into the deplorable living and working conditions of child sweeps.

Fireworks, Picnics, and Flags: The Story of The Fourth of July Symbols (Clarion) introduced me to the pleasures of on-site research. I had spent two days at beautiful Independence National Historical Park in Philadelphia. I toured Independence Hall, visited the rented rooms nearby where Thomas Jefferson drafted the Declaration of Independence, and watched a group of third-grade youngsters touch the Liberty Bell in its pavilion. I won't soon forget the looks of awe on their faces.

Whenever I go out on a research expedition, I always take along a supply of 4 × 6-inch cards. At the top of each one, I write the subject for handy reference when I file the cards alphabetically in a metal box. I also write the title, author, publisher, and date of the book I'm reading so that I'll have all that information on hand when I compile the bibliography for my book. Then I go on to jot down the facts I think I might be able to use.

I try to check each fact against at least two other sources before including it in the text. Such double-checking can turn up myths that have long passed as truths. For instance, while researching *Fireworks, Picnics, and Flags,* I read two books that said an old bell-ringer sat in the tower of Independence Hall almost all day on July 4, 1776. He was waiting for word that independence had been declared so that he could ring the Liberty Bell.

At last, in late afternoon, a small boy ran up the steps of the tower and shouted, "Ring, Grandfather! Ring for Liberty!" The old man did so at once, letting all of Philadelphia know that America was no longer a British colony. It makes a fine story—but according to the third source I checked, it simply isn't true.

By no means will all of the facts I find appear in the finished book. Only a small part of any author's research shows up in the final manuscript. But I think a reader can feel the presence of the rest beneath the surface, lending substance and authority to the writing.

Picture research

With most of my books, I've gathered the illustrations as well as written the text, and this has led me into the fascinating area of picture research. On *The Scarecrow Book,* for example, I discovered the resources of the Prints and Photographs Division of the Library of Congress, where I located several stunning photographs of Southern scarecrows taken during the 1930s. Later, in a back issue of *Time* magazine, I came across a story about Senji Kataoka, a public relations officer with the Ministry of Agriculture in Tokyo, whose hobby was taking pictures of scarecrows. Over the years, the article said, Mr.

Kataoka had photographed more than 2000 examples in the countryside around Tokyo.

I decided to follow up on this lead, remote as it might prove to be. From the Japanese consulate in New York I obtained the address of the Ministry of Agriculture in Tokyo, and wrote Mr. Kataoka there. Six weeks later his answer arrived in neatly printed English, along with eight beautiful color snapshots of scarecrows. I wrote back saying I needed black-and-white photos for the book and Mr. Kataoka immediately mailed me a dozen, four of which were used in the chapter on Japanese scarecrows. Another appeared on the jacket. When I asked Mr. Kataoka how much he wanted for his photos, he said just a copy of the book.

Experiences such as these have taught me several important things about doing picture research. The first is: Never start with commercial photographic agencies. They charge high reproduction fees which are likely to put you in the red if your contract states that you are responsible for paying such costs.

Instead, try non-profit sources like U.S. government agencies, which provide photographs for just the cost of the prints; art and natural history museums, which charge modest fees; and national tourist offices, which will usually give you photographs free of charge, asking only that you credit them as the source.

Other good sources of free photos are the manufacturers of various products. Their public relations departments will be happy to send you high quality photographs of everything from tractors to inflatable vinyl scarecrows in return for an acknowledgment in your book.

Selling

Writers often ask me if they should complete all the research for a nonfiction book before trying to sell the idea to a publisher. That's usually not necessary. However, if you're a beginner you should do enough research to make sure there's sufficient material for a book. Then you'll need to write a full outline and draft one or two sample chapters. After that, you can send query letters to publishers and ask if they'd like to look at your material.

If a publisher is interested, you should be prepared to rewrite your sample chapters several times before being offered a contract. That happened to me with my first book, *The Scarecrow Book,* and looking back now I'm glad it did. For it helped me and my collaborator, Dale Ferguson, to sharpen the focus of that book.

Of course it's different after you become an established author. Then both you and your editors know what you can do, and generally a two- or three-page proposal describing your new book idea will be enough for the publisher to make a decision.

Once you have your contract for the book in hand, you can proceed with the writing of the manuscript. Some authors use electric type-writers, others have turned to word processors. I write longhand in a spiral notebook and mark in the margins the date each passage was drafted. That encourages me as I inch through the notebook, working mainly on Saturdays and Sundays and during vacations from my full-time editorial job.

Achieving a consistent personal voice in a nonfiction book takes me at least three drafts. In the first, I get down the basic material of the paragraph or section. In the second, I make certain the organization is logical and interesting, and I then begin to smooth out those spots where the style of the original research source may be too clearly in evidence. In the third draft, I polish the section until the tone and voice are entirely mine.

After I deliver to the editor the completed manuscript and the il-lustrations I've gathered, I may heave a sigh of relief. But chances are my work won't be over. The editor may feel that extensive revisions are necessary; sections of the manuscript may have to be reorganized, others rewritten. Perhaps the editor will want me to compile a bibliogra-phy, or a glossary of unfamiliar words used in the text.

At last everything is in place, and a year or so later—during which time the manuscript has been copyedited, designed, and set in type— the finished book arrives in the mail. That's an exciting moment, fol-lowed by a few anxious weeks as you wait for the first reviews to appear. The verdict of the critics isn't the final one, though. There's yet another stage in the life of any children's book: the reaction of young readers.

Perhaps a boy will come up to me after a library talk and tell me that he was inspired to find out more about the skyscrapers in his city after reading *The Skyscraper Book.* Or a girl will write to say that the chapter on a day in the life of a climbing boy in *Chimney Sweeps* made her cry. It's only then that I know I'm on the way toward achieving my goal—to write lively, accurate, and entertaining books for young people.

85

PEOPLE I HAVE KNOWN

By Katherine Paterson

How do you build your characters?" It's a familiar question to those of us who write fiction and, I suspect, one of the most uncomfortable. When someone asks me about "building characters," I'm tempted to remind him that characters are people, not models you put together with an erector set. You don't "build" people, you get to know them.

All human beings are born on a certain day in a particular place and from two parents. These are all givens. When I am beginning a book, the central character is little more than an uneasy feeling in the pit of my stomach. I spend a long time trying to understand who this person is— where he or she was born, when, and from whom.

When I was trying to start *Jacob Have I Loved,* I knew the protagonist was a girl of about fourteen, who was eaten up with jealousy for a brother or sister. That was all I had to go on in the beginning. When I discovered, quite by accident, that she lived on a tiny island in the middle of the Chesapeake Bay, I was well on my way to getting to know her.

(Incidentally, anyone who has written fiction knows that such revelatory accidents are a way of life for writers. This one involved a Christmas gift book about the Chesapeake Bay which I happened to read because I was desperate for reading material on the 29th of December. Time after time, writers stumble blindly upon the very secrets that will serve to unlock the story they are currently struggling with.)

Anyhow, as I discovered, life on a Chesapeake Bay island is different from life anywhere else in America. On Tangier and Smith (the islands upon which I modeled my imaginary island of Rass), there are families that have lived on the same narrow bits of land since well before the Revolutionary War. The men of the island earn their living crabbing in the warmer months and oystering in the colder. For island people, all of

441

life is organized about the water that surrounds them and even today cuts them off from the rest of our country. The speech of the people is unlike that of those in nearby Maryland or Virginia. Scholars think it may resemble the Elizabethan speech of colonial America. The islands were converted to Methodism in the 18th century and remain strongly religious communities. I could go on, but you can see how being born and spending her formative years on such an island would affect the growth of Louise Bradshaw. She could be molded by her adaptation to her environment or by her rebellion against it. Either way, the place is of vital significance to the person she is and will become.

When a character is born is another revealing point. You can see this in life. My husband and I were born at the height of the depression. Our older boy was born soon after Kennedy was assassinated. Our younger daughter was born the year both Martin Luther King and Robert Kennedy were killed. When I am trying to get to know a character, I always ask what was happening in the world when this person was born and what effect these events might have had on his life.

Usually, I determine the date of birth of all of my central characters, not just the protagonist. This was crucial to the story in my novel *Come Sing, Jimmy Jo*. James was born in 1973, and his mother was born in 1959. "But that means . . !" Yes, it means that Keri Su was fourteen when James was born. If I know that, I can begin to understand some of the problems that have always existed between them—why almost from birth James has looked to his grandma for mothering rather than his mother.

This leads directly to the question of parentage. When I first began writing *Jimmy Jo,* I assumed that Keri Su was James's mother, and Jerry Lee was his father. The fact that Jerry Lee was ten years older than his wife explained to some extent why he was the more responsible parent of the two. After all, he was already a grownup when the boy was born.

But the better I got to know this family, the more I realized that there was something there that they weren't telling. Gradually, I got a picture of Keri Su, a thirteen-year-old girl from the West Virginia hills. The mountain boyfriend who has made her pregnant has run away and joined the navy to escape the wrath of the girl's hard-drinking father. Now all of the father's anger is directed toward his daughter. She runs away with nowhere to run and happens into a tiny mountain town where the Johnson Family Singers are performing at one of the local churches.

The girl loves music, and she hangs around until the Johnsons, especially Grandma and Jerry Lee, realize the extent of her desperation and take her under their wings. She is a good-looking, spunky kid with a powerful singing voice, and Jerry Lee, with a mixture of admiration and pity and affection, marries her. James, the child that is born so soon afterwards, is a Johnson heart and soul, made so by the love of Jerry Lee and Grandma, who share with him the special love they have one another.

What happens, then, to the rest of the family members? There brother Earl, who was a young adolescent when Keri Su joined the family. He has always resented Jerry Lee, who is older, wiser, nicer, and, as Earl sees it, much their mother's favorite. Now his brother has married a girl Earl's own age, a girl, who under different circumstances, he might have liked to take out himself. Earl is jealous of the position Keri Su immediately achieves in the family and at the same time is attracted to her despite himself.

And what about Grandpa? He seems to take his wife for granted, but perhaps he, too, feels a wistful twinge when he sees how she dotes on Jerry Lee and on the fatherless child that their son has totally accepted as his own. Doesn't blood count for something? Grandpa wonders. Like most mountain men, he puts a lot of stock in good blood. He likes the boy and all, but it's not as if James were really his grandson.

So far nothing I've said is actually in the book. It is all in the background to the story—the life these people lived before they entered the pages of this particular book. But I have to know all of these things about the characters or run the risk that my characters will be as separate and inanimate as Barbie and Ken. If you let *living* people into a story, they will move each other. If you put in *constructed* characters, you'll have to do the moving yourself. The reader won't be fooled. He'll be able to tell which is which.

When it comes to deciding what about these people will actually be revealed on the printed page, I am guided, of course, by the story I want to tell, but also, quite particularly, by point of view. *Jacob Have I Loved* is written in the first person. The only point of view the reader is given is that of Louise, who is so jealous of her sister that she is blind to the affection that her parents, Call, the Captain, and even her sister have for her. Now I am not Louise. I can see what she cannot, and it breaks my heart to realize how much her mother loves her and to know how little Louise can understand or trust that love.

A wise reader will be aware of the narrowness of Louise's vision, but since I write principally for children and young people, I know that many of my readers will assume that Louise's badly skewed view is the correct view. I suppose I could have written the book differently to give Louise's mother and even sister Caroline a sporting chance, but then the power of Louise's jealousy would have been diminished. It would have been a different, and, I believe, weaker story.

Again, in *Come Sing, Jimmy Jo,* the story is told wholly from James's viewpoint. He's never been told about his origins, but that doesn't mean he doesn't feel the uneasiness of the other family members when the past is referred to.

Often children will ask me about the parents in my books. "Why are they so mean?" is a question I've gotten more than a few times about Jesse Aarons's parents in the book, *Bridge to Terabithia.* I use the occasion to try to help young readers understand point of view. All the parents in my stories are seen from their children's point of view, and it has been my experience that children are very seldom fair in their judgments of their parents. I hope I've sent all my questioners home to take another, more objective look not only at my book, but at their own parents, most of whom, I dare say, are like the parents in *Bridge to Terabithia,* doing the best they can under trying circumstances.

Characters are like people in another way. Some of them are very easy to get to know, others more difficult. Maime Trotter, the foster mother in *The Great Gilly Hopkins,* simply arrived one day full grown. She was so powerfully herself that the other characters in the book came to life responding to her immense loving energy. Gilly, who had spent her time before the book began cynically manipulating the people about her, had to learn how to reckon with a force greater than her own anger.

The actual appearance of one of the most important characters in *The Great Gilly Hopkins* takes up less than two pages of the text. She is Gilly's mother—the unwed flower child who gave Gilly up to foster care years before the book opens. Yet what she actually is and what Gilly dreams she is (two different things, as you might suspect) combine to help shape the troubled and troubling child, whom we first meet in the

444

back seat of the social worker's car on the way to yet another foster home.

There is, finally, something mysterious about the life of one's characters. In my secret heart, I almost believe that one of these days I'll meet Jesse Aarons walking toward me on a downtown street. I'll recognize him at once, although he will have grown to manhood, and I'll ask him what he's been doing in the years since he built that bridge across Lark Creek.

On the second thought, I probably won't ask. I'll smile and he'll nod, but I won't pry. Years ago he let me eavesdrop on his soul, but that time is past. He is entitled to his privacy now. Still, I can't help wondering.

86

WRITING FOR YOUNG ADULTS

By Norma Fox Mazer

WRITING for young adults today is particularly satisfying. These young people are going through the most intensely felt time of their lives. They are a devoted audience and, once caught by one of your books, they will read all of them and wait impatiently for the next one to appear. To write for this audience, it's not necessary to know their slang or the latest fad. It is important to understand their fears, dreams and hopes, but it is vital to know your *own* point of view: what you, the writer, think, feel, fear, understand and believe. You cannot write a deeply felt, satisfying book without a point of view on your material.

The storyteller brings order to events that in life might be random, purposeless, even meaningless. It's this sense of orderliness and meaning that makes the novel so satisfying. But to create that order, the writer should be aware of certain rhythms and patterns. To begin with, a story needs those simple classic elements: a beginning, a middle, and an ending. Most books have a beginning and an ending of sorts, but a great many fall down in the middle. If the writer flounders, the reader gets the sense of the writer's despair: I've come this far—what do I do now?

There are two things I think will help the new writer. One is to work with a unity of opposites as the foundation for your story—two characters locked together but intent on opposite goals. In my novel *Taking Terri Mueller,* Phil and Terri are father and daughter; that is their essential unity. They are further united by the deep love between them, and this, in turn, is reinforced by their life style, which isolates them from other people. This is the background of the struggle that ensues between them. Terri is determined to know the truth about her past. Phil is equally determined that she should not. There they are, united, unable and unwilling to get away from each other, and wanting completely different things.

446

When you first come up with an idea for a novel, test it by asking yourself a few questions: What is the basic unity? (It does not have to be two people. The unity of a character and an animal, or a character and nature, such as a landslide or a hurricane, is just as valid.) What is the opposition? Can I put the idea of the story into a paragraph that will suggest the unity of opposites? *Taking Terri Mueller* began with a single sentence. "A girl has been kidnapped by her own father."

When a writer works with a powerful unity of opposites, there are scenes that almost demand to be written. Long before I knew how I would develop the story to the point at which a confrontation about Phil's lying takes place between Terri and Phil, I knew that scene had to be written. All I had to do was work my way through the story toward that point. This key scene comes about midway through the novel, when the reader has been fully engaged with Terri's struggles and her father's painful desire to keep her ignorant of the truth.

The second thing I find helpful in writing a novel is to think in threes. Three is a magic number. Human beings respond to threes. A story must rise and fall three times to satisfy the reader. When I'm planning, I often divide the book into three sections. Then each section can also be divided twice into three parts. And in most chapters, there is a threefold rise and fall. Let me give one illustration from the key chapter in *Taking Terri Mueller:*

Terri and her father Phil have a close, affectionate and trusting relationship. Her only other relative is her Aunt Vivian. Now it's time for Aunt Vivian's once-a-year visit, a wonderful event to which Terri looks forward all year.

She wants to make the most of the visit, yet it's marred almost from the beginning. Three things happen. First, Vivian dislikes Nancy, Phil's new girlfriend, creating a strained atmosphere. Secondly, Terri sees a wallet snapshot of her aunt, who is said to have no other family, with two young boys. And finally, Terri overhears a conversation between her father and her aunt that strongly suggests there are secrets between them.

There are other ways to use the rhythm of three. For instance, a working rule of thumb for fixing a character in the reader's mind is to repeat something about that character three times. Although it needn't be a physical characteristic, the obvious and old example is the mole on the nose. Use a bit of subtlety in repeating the detail—certainly don't

447

say it the same way each time—but within the first five or six chapters, working in the "mole" helps the reader visualize the character, especially if the detail can be used to shed light on the character's personality or state of mind.

In a description of Terri, I work on her appearance, but also on her state of mind.

> She was a tall girl with long hair that she sometimes wore in a single braid down her back. . . . She was quiet and watchful and didn't talk a lot, although she liked to talk, especially to her father, with whom she felt she could talk about anything.

The end of that description reveals something much more important than that Terri has long hair: her trust in her father. That he betrayed this trust is one of the central themes of the book. In the next chapter, Nancy thinks Terri is older than she is. Terri says, "You only thought so . . . because I'm tall." Thus, through dialogue, I repeat one of the points of Terri's description. And through narration we also learn that Terri is almost always the tallest girl in her class. But what's important here is not Terri's height, but her emotional maturity. And this is reinforced when Nancy says that it isn't Terri's being tall—but her poise—that made her think Terri was older.

In creating characters, remember that key word—create. You are not making a real human being, but an illusion of a human being. It would be impossible, confusing, and boring to put down on paper all the elements that go into any one actual person. Your job as a writer is to make your readers believe. Therefore, on the one hand your character needs a certain consistency, and on the other hand those very contradictions that are part of being human.

It's good to give your readers a sense of how your characters look, but what's basic are words and actions. What the characters say. What the characters do. I, the author, tell you, the reader, that Terri is a warmhearted girl, but if what you see her do is trip up a little old lady, then you know I'm lying to you. When I'm struggling with a character, I remind myself of the basic dictum: show, don't tell. I wanted to show Terri's longing for a family. Rather than say it, I showed Terri looking at a friend's family snapshots. Terri's interest and eagerness bring home to the reader her underlying sense of isolation and loneliness.

I've been speaking here of the young adult novel, and yet most of the things I'm saying should apply to any novel. Still, the young adult novel stands in a class by itself. Briefly, I'd like to mention what, in general, distinguishes the young adult novel from any other novel.

The first and most obvious point is the age of the protagonist. Nearly always, the main character is going to be a person the same age or slightly older than the people in your audience. In the young adult novel, there tends to be a very close identification between the reader and the protagonist. A reader wrote me recently, "I hope you know your book describes my life." Literally, it couldn't have, since story, setting, and characters were all products of my imagination. Yet this reader believed in the reality of the world I created. To achieve this sense of verisimilitude, when you write you cannot stand above or to one side of the character, you cannot comment as an older, "wiser" adult, but you must see and report the world through your protagonist's eyes. This limitation, more than anything else, makes the difference between a novel written for this audience and one written for an adult audience.

Although it's important to recognize who your audience is, it's simply death to allow a patronizing attitude to creep into your writing. Your readers deserve your best. The one time I focus on the fact that I'm writing for teenagers is in the early stages when I'm searching for the right idea. Clearly, some book ideas are better than others.

I consider this early stage of writing the novel, which is really an almost non-writing stage, the most important. Concept is all. A silly or unimportant concept can mean months of wasted work.

Questions: Is the idea about young people? Is there an opportunity for the characters to work out their own problems and destinies? Is there a chance for consideration of some serious subjects? Is there also a place for the playful scene or character? I like to achieve a balance. Even in *Taking Terri Mueller,* which is about the terribly serious problem of childnapping, there are a few funny scenes with her father, a scattering of amusing dialogues with her girlfriend.

There are rewards in writing for young adults. There is hardly a subject or an idea that can't be tackled. I have written short stories, serious realistic novels, a time fantasy and, in *Taking Terri Mueller,* a mystery.

Perhaps the first real lesson I learned about writing was that not only did I have something to say, but, whether I recognized it or not, it was

449

there, inside me, waiting to be said. I'm convinced this is true for everyone. Each of us has a unique point of view on the world; the struggle is to get in touch with that uniqueness and bring it into our writing.

My method is to write a first draft in which I spill out everything. The inner censor is banished. I do not allow myself to ponder over the "right" word, to search for the felicitous phrase or struggle for the beautifully constructed sentence. For me, a first draft means putting the truth of a story before all else. It means digging down for all those unique, but what-if-no-one-else-agrees-with-me thoughts, bringing them into the light and onto paper.

Then there is your audience. Is there another group of readers who are quite so enthusiastic, who are ready to laugh and cry over your book, who will cheer you on and write to you in droves? What can compare with the thrill of receiving a letter like the one that came in my mail from a girl in Pennsylvania: "Once I began to read about Terri, I could not get my eyes away from the book."

Each time I approach the writing of a new young adult novel I wonder, "Can I do it again? Will I do this story justice? Will I write a book readers will enjoy? What does this story mean? And aren't there enough books in the world already?"

No, not as long as there are readers and writers. Not as long as there are people like me, like you, like all of us who, like the writer Katha Pollitt, believe that we "go to fiction for the revelation of character, the rich presentation of lived life and the daily clutter of things."

87

DOUBLE VISION: A SPECIAL TOOL FOR YOUNG ADULT WRITERS

By Cheryl Zach

WRITING A YOUNG ADULT NOVEL with an authentic teen voice requires the author to see the world with double vision—both as the child he was and the adult he is now. We have all lived through adolescence, endured its pains, joys, and frustrations. Delving into your own teenage memories will enable you to relive those strong, sometimes overwhelming emotions and recreate them in your fiction, producing the immediacy and validity that the genre demands.

Do you remember your first date? (Could you ever forget it?) The first time someone asked you out? The first time that special person kissed you? The sweating palms, the rumbling stomach, the anguished attempts at achieving a poise that often failed you at the most crucial moments—these feelings are universal and timeless. Attributing such emotions to your characters will give them depth and reality, propel them off the page and into full dimension.

Adolescence involves a series of stages, changing year by year. Think back to the summer you were thirteen—what were your most pressing concerns? Girls with developing figures who snubbed you unmercifully? The low velocity in your fast ball that might keep you off the team?

Now jump to your sixteenth birthday! How have you changed? Have you achieved a reputation for being "cool" that makes you the envy of all the other guys, but might be lost if you reveal your attraction for the girl who smiles at you in chemistry class—a girl that not everyone admires? Or, from the feminine perspective, have you had your first date, your first kiss, and then—horrors—lost your first love to an older, more sophisticated girl? How will you ever recover, and who wants to? Has an essay you've written or a unique science project you've prepared drawn praise from your favorite teacher, causing you to dream for the first time of attending college—even though you know your parents can't afford to send you? Remember—and put it all into the characters you create.

Then, returning to your adult perspective, examine these characters. Reliving your own emotions will give your characters validity and elicit the essential reader sympathy. As the writer, you must add the exterior polish. Emotions do not change, nor do many of the "first" experiences—first date, first kiss, first car, etc. But the outer trappings—clothes, fads, slang—do.

To make your teen characters ring true to your young adult readers, now you must substitute observation for nostalgia. Watch today's teenagers in their natural settings—schools, restaurants, movies, malls, beaches, among others. Notice that they wear Reeboks or Nikes, not saddle shoes; acid-washed denim, not poodle skirts. Note the music coming from a teenager's Walkman, the activities that attract them as participants or observers. And if you don't enjoy spending time with teens, beware: writing YA novels may not be for you. Immersing yourself in the lives of your teenage characters as you write your novel will be difficult unless you have a genuine liking for this age group.

After creating strong, believable characters, you must grapple with the related question of conflict and plot. What is your character's problem, and how will he or she solve it? Looking at this from your perspective as a teenager will help you avoid a common pitfall among would-be YA authors: an adult-centered plot rather than one that is teen-centered. Again, think back to your own teen years. What was your biggest problem and how did you handle it? Did your older sister steal your boyfriends? What did you do about it? Were you and your best friend in love with the same person? How did you work it out? Allowing your character to cope with his or her problem in a manner consistent with the character's age shapes your plot outline.

Reverting to your adult viewpoint allows you to check your plot for possible flaws. Most of all, remember that the conflict must be solvable by your teen protagonist. Having an adult, friendly or not, step in to deal with your young hero's problem is a fatal mistake. When my shy, teenaged protagonist in *The Frog Princess* is elected class president because of a cruel joke, no adult can be allowed to solve her dilemma for her. Kelly has to solve her problem by herself, gaining self-confidence as well as the respect of her classmates in the process.

Having looked at your conflict through your young protagonist's eyes

452

should also protect you from another common pitfall—the condescension that creeps in when the writer's "adult" side has not been effectively exorcised. The problems you faced at thirteen or fifteen or seventeen were real and vital and soul-shaking: they mattered. The fact that getting a date for the big dance or outshining your older brother seems a minor worry now does not lessen its original importance. Remembering this should deter you from talking down to your teen readers, or, even worse, preaching to them. Problem-solving and moments of revelation can come only through your teen protagonist, and cannot be superimposed by an intrusive author. At the end of *The Frog Princess,* Kelly receives a compliment from Tony, the good-looking classmate she has secretly admired, despite the dirty trick he played on her earlier. But by now she has realized that "Tony would smile only for party-pretty girls in new dresses," and decides this guy is not worth any heartache.

Having believable characters, a strong but age-appropriate conflict and logical plotting, what next? Dialogue is just as crucial in teen fiction as in adult novels, with an added twist—challenge of "current" teen slang. Your child's eye will remind you of basic interests—friends, school, family problems—but dialogue is one element of your novel that may benefit most from your adult/detached writer's perspective.

Sit on a park bench, on a bus, at the beach or amusement park, and listen to teenagers talk. Write down what you hear. Will this give you good dialogue? Only if you cut the inconsequential chatting that forms a large part of real conversation. Good dialogue is not the same as real speech; it only sounds that way. Listen to how teenagers really speak—using lots of monosyllables and elliptical phrases, as in the following:

> "Butt out," Pete told me, his voice thick with anger. "What's it to you?"
> "She's my sister," I said.
> "So?"
> "So she's coming home, right now."

What about current slang—often a double-edged sword? Watch out for outdated expressions. An anachronistic slang word will alert readers—and editors—that the author isn't paying attention. Teen catchwords change quickly. The expression you hear today may be "out" by the time your book gets into print. So use even the most up-to-date slang judiciously, to add flavor but not overpower the other essentials.

What about setting? Unless your book takes place during a holiday period, school will probably be part of your background. In some ways, schools are unchanging, but in others, they may have altered greatly since your own school days. Take a look at the schools in your neighborhood. What are the kids studying, what are they doing for extracurricular activities? Read student newspapers; they will inform you about student opinions, issues that concern them, their opinions, and interests.

Remember the first rule, however: Look at the school scene through the eyes of a teenager, not those of a curious adult. To a fourteen-year-old, the essential part of the school day will most likely take place before, between and after classes.

And when you return to your adult viewpoint, consider other, more novel settings. Editors sometimes complain about overused lunchroom scenes. This doesn't necessitate moving your story to exotic locales. My YA novel, *Too Many Cooks,* in which the action centers around a small catering business, won critical praise for its "vivid and unusual setting."

Last, point of view. Most YA novels are written either from first person—the "I" viewpoint—or third person limited—looking inside one or two main characters. Both have advantages and pitfalls. First person can lend an impression of immediacy and help the writer focus strongly on the protagonist. It can also be limiting, presenting only what your main character witnesses. Also, some Young Adult editors have grown tired of first-person viewpoint and are less likely to be impressed with a novel using it.

Using third person lets you present more than one viewpoint, widening the scope of your novel. But switching viewpoints must be done skillfully and not too often, or your book will sound choppy and confuse your reader. Accidental switches in points of view are one of the most obvious signs of a beginning writer and throw up a red flag to editors. While viewing the situation through your eyes as an adolescent will enable you to make the point of view authentic, you must go over your manuscript carefully from your perspective as an adult.

When you have brought your YA novel to a satisfying and believable conclusion and have rewritten, polished, and proofread it, how do you market it? With the same care that you would use for an adult novel, studying the marketplace and individual publishers' requirements.

The YA market changes just as the adult market does. Currently, series using continuing characters are "hot." While this may make it harder to sell your individual title, a strong novel may be adapted to a series concept. Why not sell four or six book ideas instead of one? And series do offer opportunities for beginning writers to break into the field, gaining valuable experience.

YA romance novels, which once occupied much of the bookstore shelf space, have lost ground to books in which romance is only one of many concerns facing teenage protagonists. Recent popular series titles reveal this diversity: *Sweet Valley High, Sisters, Sorority Girls, Roommates* all cover the full spectrum of teen life. Problem novels, dealing with darker conflicts of drugs, suicide, abortion, etc., are not presently being sought; humor, on the other hand, is very popular with readers and editors. YA hardcover sales have dropped, but the market for original YA paperbacks continues to grow.

The most essential requirement doesn't vary: a good manuscript with strong, believable characters and an authentic teen voice. Your double vision will aid you in crafting a satisfying and special YA novel.

88

REMEMBERING HOW IT WAS

BY LOIS LOWRY

I REMEMBER hitting my daughter once. Swatting her right across the seat of her jeans with a wire coat hanger, when she was nine years old.

It was back in the days when little girls still wore dresses to school, and mothers still ironed them. I had ironed a whole week's worth of those cotton, starched, puffed-sleeved horrors, placed them on hangers, and asked her to take them to her room.

And she did. When I entered her room later, I found her sprawled on her bed with a book, and all seven freshly-ironed dresses in a heap on the floor where she had deposited them.

Naturally I swatted her on the behind with the nearest available weapon.

But my point is not confession or absolution. My point is this: recently I mentioned the incident to my daughter—who is now twenty-five and has a child of her own—and asked her if she remembered it.

"*Remember* it?" she replied. "How could I *not* remember the time my own mother beat me unmercifully around the head and shoulders with a blunt instrument?"

Memory, we should bear in mind, is a subjective thing.

It always amazes me when I hear people say, as many do, that they don't remember their own childhood. What time is my doctor's appointment? What was the name of the librarian I met at that last convention? Those things I forget. But childhood? I have only to press the mental key that calls up each year: 1941 (nursery school: I snitched a blue crayon and wrote my name on my cot during naptime; Pearl Harbor, and my father in uniform, letting me try on his major's cap; my green wicker rocking chair; a book about penguins); 1945 (the fourth-grade bully named Gene; the stain on the blanket under my cat after she gave birth to kittens in the attic); 1948 (the green jumper and white blouse I wore, my first day in seventh grade; the three maids giggling together in the kitchen of our Tokyo home; "Kerria Japonica": the room I shared with my sister during a spring vacation in the Fujiya Hotel, where each room was named for a flower).

Each detail appears, and with it come back the emotions. Humiliation, at four, caught stealing a crayon. Anger at Allen, the boy across the street, who borrowed and lost my penguin book. Fear of the boy Gene, who terrorized the fourth grade. Sudden and frightening awareness, watching my cat lick her firstborn litter, that birth involves blood.

For me it is all there, and I can call it back. If that were not so, I could not write for children.

Some years ago, when working on an article about medical hypnosis, I interviewed a doctor who suggested that it would be helpful if he were to hypnotize me. I agreed, and sat there, relaxed, while he talked in a steady voice; I watched, feeling no pain, as he inserted a needle into the back of my hand.

Then he suggested that I would be regressing in age: now fifteen; now ten; now five.

"Now that you are five," his droning voice said, "where do you find yourself? What are you experiencing?"

"In my grandparents' backyard," I said without hesitation. "Barefoot, standing under the big pine tree; I can feel the dry needles under my feet. I can smell my grandmother's roses. I can hear a mourning dove."

"You're a good subject," he said, later. "Wasn't that amazing, how all those sensations came back from the time you were five?"

"But I do that all the time, without hypnosis," I told him. "If I'm writing about a five-year-old, I *remember* being five. And I can feel those pine needles, smell the roses, hear the mourning dove."

"Well," he said huffily, "somehow, then, you've mastered the art of self-hypnosis."

But I don't think it's self-hypnosis at all. For me it is simply memory, a phenomenon with which I seem to be richly endowed. And what a blessing it is for one who chooses to write for kids! Each day, sitting here at work, I call upon it constantly.

Anastasia Krupnik is a character who has now appeared in six of my books and is currently making her way through the manuscript pages of a seventh. She is fictional. She is not me. I never had her freckles, her astigmatism, her family, or what my mother would have referred to as her "smart alec mouth." But I have used my own memories again and again as I have created her and moved her through the incidents that appear on those pages.

Anastasia is ten in the first book, whose title bears her name. Writing it—specifically, writing a scene in her school classroom—I thought back, remembering my own anger at a supposed classroom injustice: for me, it was the day that the drawing of the class mural began. It was to be a mural across one entire wall, depicting a wagon train heading west.

I had looked forward to the mural so. At ten I prided myself on my drawing ability, and I had planned, in my mind, the creation of the stalwart pioneer figures: the gaunt sunbonneted mothers holding babies; the carefree children running beside the covered wagons, loyal dogs at their heels. I would draw a girl my own age, I would even make her look a little like me, skinny and blonde—turning with a look of irritated surprise as a brother pulled at her pigtails.

But my teacher took me aside in the midst of the classroom excitement as the paper was being unrolled and tacked across the wall, the art materials brought from the supply closet.

"You know," she said with a kind smile, "you draw better than anyone else in the class."

Of course I knew. But humility was appropriate, and I hung my head shyly. Inside myself, I glowed.

"And because of that," she went on, "I'm assigning you to the very hardest part of the mural."

A tiny gremlin of suspicion began to gnaw inside me where the glow had been, and I looked up at her.

"I want you to do all eight oxen for us," she explained. "All the children can draw people pretty well. But I know that no one but you will be able to draw oxen."

Oxen? Had I heard her correctly? Yes. Oxen.

And so I obediently, diligently, conscientiously, drew oxen for a week, while the other kids did the people. I researched oxen, practiced oxen, and completed oxen; and even today, forty years later, I'd bet you

458

anything that they were the best-rendered, most anatomically-accurate oxen any ten-year-old ever presented in crayon on a twenty-foot-long strip of white paper.

But oh, how I remember my resentment of the moment. Writing of Anastasia, I recreated not the moment itself, but the emotions of it. I had Anastasia's teacher, Mrs. Westvessel, assign the writing of a poem to her fourth-grade students. I tried to recapture the joy of the assignment:

. . . when Mrs. Westvessel announced one day in the fall that the class would begin writing poetry, Anastasia was the happiest she had ever been in school.

Somewhere, off in a place beyond her own thoughts, Anastasia could hear Mrs. Westvessel's voice. She was reading some poems to the class; she was talking about poetry and how it was made. But Anastasia wasn't really listening. She was listening instead to the words that were appearing in her own head, floating there and arranging themselves into groups, into lines, into poems.

. . . and the bitter disappointment of its outcome:

An F. Anastasia had never had an F in her entire life. She kept looking at the floor. Someone had stepped on a red crayon once; the color was smeared into the floor forever.

"Iworkedveryhardonthatpoem," whispered Anastasia to the floor.

"Speak up, Anastasia."

Anastasia lifted her head and looked Mrs. Westvessel in the eye. "I worked very hard on that poem," she said in a loud, clear voice.

In a later book, Anastasia is twelve. I punched my mental button to the memory section marked "12" and saw myself standing in front of a mirror, yanking a comb through tangled hair which seemed to have taken on, at puberty, characteristics of seaweed marinated in Wesson Oil. And I wrote:

. . . . Vaguely she remembered the fairy tale of Rapunzel, who had been locked in a tower, and who had hung her long hair from the window so that her lover could climb up. That was kind of neat.

But that Anastasia ran her fingers through her own hair, which had begun to be pretty long—halfway down her back—but she realized that it needed washing again. Yuck. If a lover tried to climb her greasy hair, he would slide back down.

Another book, and now she was thirteen. Almost unbidden (because surely I have repressed it; my mother is such a gracious and charming

459

lady now, at eighty) came this memory: me, thirteen, glaring at her as she appeared from her bedroom, dressed to attend a mother/daughter school event with me. I could hear my own voice: "You're not going to wear *that,* are you?" and see her look of surprise and hurt, as she stared down at her best dress. And I wrote:

"Well, I used to like you a whole lot. I thought you were really a neat mother. You used to be fun. But lately—"
"Yes? Go on. Tell me about lately."
"Well, your clothes, for example. They're embarrassing. You always wear jeans. I don't even like to walk beside you on the street because you don't look like a regular mother."

Now about the bludgeoning of my daughter. The details of memory, as I pointed out, are subjective. They are subjective because they depend upon the emotions. If my daughter remembers that I beat her mercilessly with a heavy wooden weapon, it is because she remembers not the weapon (and it *was* a wire hanger) but the overwhelming and terrifying astonishment of being physically attacked by a usually pleasant, soft-spoken mother.

And perhaps my fourth-grade teacher would be able to document that it was only six oxen, not eight; and that she let me draw a couple of people as well.

But in writing, it is not the veracity of the details that matters. As fiction writers, we lie about those anyway. The truth of the feelings is the only essential thing.

If you do not, or cannot remember those feelings, don't fake them; they're too strong, too powerful to be faked even by the best of tricksters at typewriters. And young readers are masters of phoniness-detection.

If your youth doesn't come back for you, call upon yesterday instead. Remember your rage and frustration standing at the Hertz desk in Boise after being told that they have no record of your reservation made three weeks before, and no car either? And then the clerk saying, "Have a nice day"? Use it, that memory. Apply that same pressure-cooker anger to your fictional adolescent who has just been cut from the basketball squad, or grounded for a month by his parents.

I use yesterday's—and this morning's—emotions myself, adding them to the stockpile of those that come from the past. Recently, for a short story called "Splendor," I created two sisters, thirteen- and fourteen-years-old. Writing the scene where the younger has just acquired a very special new dress, I called back the old jealousies that I remembered from my own adolescent relationship with my own older sister, and wrote:

Back upstairs, she hung the dress carefully in her closet, and looked with pleasure at the burst of color it provided there in contrast to the clothes of her ordinary life. Beside it hung an outgrown brown jumper of Angela's, and next to that Angela's old plaid skirt. It was a closet full of leftovers, Becky thought, a *life* full of leftovers—until the dress changed everything.

But for a separate scene, I used other, more recent memories as well. I remembered a very few years back, when my husband, children, and I went every Thanksgiving to the home of a brother and sister-in-law. The sister-in-law was Wonder Woman. She could do anything, and did. Every Thanksgiving there were new accomplishments to admire: a hand-hooked rug, a newly papered room, a promotion in her professional field, a new and faster finish time in the Boston Marathon. Finally, one Thanksgiving, instead of the usual turkey, she had roasted a goose. Helping her clean up after dinner, I removed a pan swimming with goose grease from the oven.

"What would you like me to do with this?" I asked her, holding it carefully so that it wouldn't drip on the vinyl floor which she had, of course, installed herself.

"Why don't you take some of it home with you?" she suggested.

I stood there for quite a while, staring at several quarts of thick yellow grease, before I finally said, "What for? What would I do with it?"

She was hanging up a dish towel. It was probably handwoven. And she replied cheerfully, "Make soap."

I sulked all the way home, two hours by car. Every now and then I muttered, "Make soap."

I didn't. Didn't make soap, that is. And I didn't save the goose grease, either. But I saved the memory. And I used it when the younger sister, Becky, thrilled with her new, expensive dress, feels that same frustrating, antagonistic rivalry.

"Mine only cost ten dollars," Angela said smugly.
"Well, you *made* yours. Not all of us can sew," muttered Becky. Or sing, she

461

thought, or cook, or play the piano, or get all A's in school. Angrily she listed her sister's accomplishments in her mind. "Not all of us are perfect."

I suppose that psychologically, using painful memories fictionally is a way of getting over them. Personally, I think it's a good way of getting even. And pragmatically, it's a nifty way of getting published.

89

ON WRITING FICTION FOR CHILDREN

By Mary Louisa Molesworth

THERE IS, WE ARE TOLD, no royal road to learning. Is there a royal road to any good thing? Are not hard work, more or less drudgery, perseverance, self-control, and self-restraint the unavoidable traveling companions, the only trustworthy couriers through the journey to the country of success? I think so.

None of the paths is "royal," in the sense of being smooth and flower-bestrewn. To literary success, there are many and varying roads. Were it not so indeed, the thing itself would be infinitely less worthy of achievement. For if literary work is to be in any sense admirable, it must be individual and characteristic; its essence must be of the author's personality.

I have the very strongest belief in every writer taking his or her own path, trusting to his or her own intuitions. Yet these intuitions, if I may be forgiven an apparent paradox, must be those of a cultivated taste, a thoughtful intellect, an imagination all the more luxuriant from having been well pruned. Therefore, I would urge upon young authors, before beginning to write, to see well to their own mental possessions. You cannot "give" out of nothing, and if you would give the best, with the best must you be furnished. Read the best books, study the best models, till in a sense they become your own. "Originality" will never be crushed by real study.

Many young writers, too modest to aspire very high, think they can "write for children." And often this is a mistake. Writing for children calls for a peculiar gift. It is not so much a question of taking up one's stand on the lower rungs of the literary ladder, as of standing on another ladder altogether—one which has its own steps, its higher and lower positions of excellence.

It is very difficult to define this gift. It is to some extent the power of seeing as children see, feeling as they feel, realizing the intensity of their hopes and fears, their unutterably pathetic sorrows, their sometimes even *more* pathetic joys, and yet—*not* becoming one of them: remaining yourself, in full possession of your matured judgment, your wider and deeper views. Never for one instant forgetting the marvelous impressionableness of the little hearts and minds; never losing sight of what is in the best sense *good* for them. Yet all this so skillfully, so unobtrusively, that the presence of the teacher is never suspected. Not perhaps till your readers are parents themselves—possibly writers!—need they, nor should they, suspect how in every line, far more than their passing entertainment or amusement was considered, how scrupulous was the loving care with which you banished from the playground you were preparing for their enjoyment, all things unsightly, or terrifying, or in any sense hurtful—all false or exaggerated sentiment in any form.

And yet you must be true to nature. Save in an occasional flight to fairyland, children's stories should be *real*—true, that is to say, to what may be or are actual experiences in this always chequered, often sorrowful, world of ours. It would be very false love for children to represent life to them as a garden of roses without thorns, a song with no jarring notes. But underlying the sad things, and the wrong things, and the perplexing things which must be touched upon in the little dramas, however simple, there must be belief in the brighter side—in goodness, happiness, and beauty—as the real background, after all. And any one who does not feel down in the bottom of their hearts that this "optimism" is well-founded, had better leave writing for children alone.

It is not always those who are nearest childhood who are the best fitted to deal with it. There is a phase of melancholy and hopelessness which youth often has to pass through, and though much mingled with false sentimentality, it is a real enough thing while it lasts. It is those who have outgrown this, who while not closing their eyes to the dark and sad side of things, yet have faith in the sunlight behind and beyond, who, to my mind, are the best storytellers for the little ones, whose own experience of life is all to come.

As to questions of "style" in writing for children, general rules hold good, with the addition of a few special ones. Your language should of course be the very best you can use. Good English, terse and clear, with perhaps a little more repetition, a little more *making sure you are understood* than is allowable in ordinary fiction. Keep to the rule of never using a long word where a short one will express your meaning as well; but do not be too slavishly afraid of using a long word—a word even which, *but for the context,* your young readers would fail to understand. In such a case, you can often skillfully lead up to the meaning, and children must learn new words. It does them no harm now and to have to exercise their minds as to what the long or strange word can mean.

It is a simple but valuable test of your writing to read it aloud when finished, even if you have no audience but yourself! In writing for children the criticism—which you may be sure will not be too flattering—of a group of intelligent boys and girls is *in*valuable.

And now as to the subject matter itself. What is the best way of composing a story for children? To me it seems, as a rule, that in writing stories for either old or young, the great thing is to make the acquaintance of your characters and get to know them as well and intimately as you possibly can. I generally begin by finding names for all my personages. I marshal them before me and call the roll, to which each answers in turn, and then I feel I have my "troupe" complete, and I proceed to take them more in detail. I live with them as much as I can, often for weeks, before I have done more than write down their names. I listen to what they talk about to each other and in their own homes, not with the intention of writing it down, but by way of getting to know them well. I seldom care to look very far ahead, though at the same time a certain grasp of the whole situation is, and has been, there from the first. It never seems to me that my characters come into existence, like phantoms, merely for the time I want them. Rather do I feel that I am selecting certain incidents out of real lives. And this, especially in writing for children, seems to me to give substantiality and actuality to the actors in the drama. I always feel as if *somewhere* the children I have learnt to love are living, growing into men and women like my own real sons and daughters. I always feel as if there were ever so much more to hear about them and to tell about them.

But this general rule of first getting to know your characters is not without exceptions. There are instances in which the most trivial incident or impression suggests a whole story—a glance at a picture, the words of a song, a picturesque name, the wind in an old chimney—anything or nothing will sometimes "start" the whole, and then the characters you need have to be sought for and thought about, and in some sense chosen for their parts. These often entirely unexpected suggestions of a story are very valuable, and should decidedly, when they occur, be "made a note of."

Remembrances of one's own childhood, not merely of surroundings and events, but of one's own inner childish life, one's ways of looking at things, one's queer perplexities and little suspected intensities of feeling, it is well to recall and dwell much upon because these memories revive and quicken the sympathy. Such reminiscences put us "in touch" again with child-world.

If you have any serious intention of making stories for children a part of your life-work, beware of "*waiting* for inspiration," as it is called. You must go at it steadily, nay, even plod at it, if you want to do good and consistent work, always remembering that your audience will be of *the most critical,* though all the better worth satisfying on that account. And rarely, if ever, does work carefully and lovingly done meet with a sweeter reward than comes to the writer of children's books when fresh young voices exclaim how interested they have been in perhaps the very story which had often filled its author with discouragement.

This chapter originally appeared as an article in *Atalanta* Magazine (England) 1893.

90

CREATING SUSPENSE IN THE YOUNG ADULT MYSTERY

By Joan Lowery Nixon

CREATING SUSPENSE in the young adult mystery novel is not just a matter of keeping the reader guessing: Suspense calls for all the nail-biting emotional responses of anxiety, excitement, and fear, as readers live through the viewpoint of the main character.

Young adult readers are impatient. They'll often read the first few lines of a book, and if it doesn't intrigue them, they'll put the book down and reach for another; so suspense must begin in the first few paragraphs, as in my book *The Kidnapping of Christina Lattimore:*

> I don't like the way he's looking at me.
> It's a kind of creepy look as though the two of us shared some kind of secret, and it's making me uncomfortable.

The story might begin with an immediate, fully written scene of terror, as in *The Dark and Deadly Pool:*

> Moonlight drizzled down the wide glass wall that touched the surface of the hotel swimming pool, dividing it into two parts. The wind-flicked waters of the outer pool glittered with reflected pin-lights from the moon and stars, but the silent water in the indoor section had been sucked into the blackness of the room.
> I blinked, trying to adjust my eyes to the darkness, trying to see the edge of the pool that curved near my feet. I pressed my back against the wall and forced myself to breathe evenly. I whispered aloud, "Mary Elizabeth Rafferty, there is nothing to be afraid of here! Nothing!" But even the sound of my own wobbly words terrified me.

It's not enough just to capture the attention and interest of young adult readers; the author has to keep them in suspense throughout the entire story, and there are a number of ways in which this can be done.

467

1. *Challenge readers with a situation that is completely new and different.* Many of us fondly remember stories from our childhood that involved buried treasure, trunks in attics, and secret passages. But those stories are familiar to today's adolescent mystery fans, too, and unless you can come up with an original, unusual twist, you'd better develop a plot based on your own ideas. Ask yourself an intriguing question and challenge yourself to find the answer.

What if a thirteen-year-old girl, who has been shot during a robbery, wakes from a semi-comatose state four years later to find that she is the only eyewitness to the unsolved crime? (*The Other Side of Dark*)

What if a girl with a serious illness has given up hope and decides not to fight for her life? Suppose her life were in danger from an unexpected direction—wouldn't she instinctively, automatically fight to live? (*The Specter*)

2. *Take a sudden, unexpected turn, making good use of the element of surprise.* In *The Seance,* another of my mysteries, the girls' nervousness during the seance builds to terror, resulting in a scene of panic, in which the candles—the only light in the house—are extinguished. During those few minutes of darkness, before a lamp is plugged in and turned on, one of the girls—Sara—disappears. It's a "locked room mystery" until readers are led to suspect that one of the other girls present must have been involved in Sara's disappearance. When it's revealed that the main character, Lauren, is the one who is responsible, it comes as a total surprise. From this point, the story shifts, and Lauren becomes a potential murder victim.

3. *Throw suspicion on someone whom the main character has trusted.* In *The Ghost of Now,* Angie's brother has been struck by a hit-and-run driver. She tries to unravel the events of that night and comes to suspect that her brother's accident had really been attempted murder. As Angie uncovers information that may lead to the identity of the killer, she confides in Del, a boy she's begun to care for. Then one night Del says something that arouses Angie's suspicions, and she begins to be afraid that Del might be the one who tried to kill her brother.

4. *Let readers know something that the main character hasn't found out yet.* In the novel of detection, a crime has been committed, and the

identity of the criminal must be discovered by both the main character and the readers. In the novel of suspense, someone is out to do away with the main character—who may or may not know the identity of this person—but readers know what is planned and watch the main character head into danger, ignorant of what awaits.

I combined these two forms in *The Stalker*. Every odd-numbered chapter is written in the form of *detection,* from the viewpoint of Jennifer, whose best friend's mother has been murdered. Circumstantial evidence points to the friend, but Jennifer enlists the help of a retired police detective to help her prove Bobbie's innocence. Every even-numbered chapter is written in the form of *suspense,* in the mind of the murderer. The murderer's identity is unknown to both Jennifer and to readers, but readers are aware that he presents an ever-growing danger to Jennifer.

5. *Let the main character become aware of some information but keep it from the reader for a while.* While you must play fair with readers by eventually giving them every clue, there is no reason you can't heighten suspense by showing your reader that your main character knows something but is not yet ready to divulge it. In Chapter One of *The Stalker,* Jennifer, still in shock with news of the murder, questions her grandmother.

"Where is Bobbie? Did they say?"
"Good question. Police don't know where she is. Looks like she up and run away. Nobody on God's earth knows where that girl's gone off to."
Jennifer clutched the (freshly ironed) shirts to her chest, ducking into the smell of starch and scorch so that Grannie couldn't see her face. "I'll start supper," she mumbled, and hurried from the room.
Where was Bobbie? Suddenly, surely, Jennifer knew.

The chapter ends as the police question Jennifer, who is so angry that she keeps her knowledge from them, too.

There was a pause. The detective with the pad and pen leaned toward her just a fraction. The other one did, too. It was coming—the question Jennifer had expected, had been afraid of.
"Jennifer," he said, "do you know where Bobbie Trax is now?"
Jennifer looked at him without blinking, as steadily as she could manage. She gripped the arms of her chair so tightly that her fingers ached as she answered, "No, I don't."

It is not until Chapter Three, when Jennifer is on her way to join Bobbie, that readers are made aware of what Jennifer has known all along.

6. *Tantalize readers by hinting at other kinds of secrets that are up to them to uncover.* In *A Deadly Game of Magic,* Lisa and three companions seek refuge from a storm in a nearby house. From the beginning, Lisa, who is intuitive, feels uncomfortable in this house, sensing that though they thought they were alone, there is some other presence in the house with them; her fear zeros in on a room at the end of the bedroom wing—the only room in which the door stands open. Throughout the story an unseen person again and again attempts to lure them toward that room, but each time they manage to avoid entering it. While readers begin to suspect what might be in that room, the final clue isn't given until the last paragraph in the book, and readers must figure out the answer themselves.

7. *Let readers see your main character make a mistake, or choose a totally wrong course of action, as a result of a personality flaw.* In *The Stalker,* Jennifer has been characterized as loyal and loving, but impulsive and stubborn, too. Readers are well aware that she should stay away from the scene of the crime, but her impatient single-mindedness causes her to make the wrong choice. Without telling her detective-partner, Jennifer goes alone to the scene, placing herself in immediate danger.

8. *Description of the setting can help to create and maintain suspense.* Highly visual writing through active picturesque verbs is the essential tool here. In *The Ghosts of Now,* an empty house holds such an important place in the story that it deserves the detailed description which begins:

The Andrews place squats alone at the end of an empty, quiet street. Maybe it's because of the overlarge lot that surrounds it; maybe it's because the house looks like an unkempt, yellowed old man who badly needs a barber, but I feel that the other houses on the block have cringed away from this place, tucking in their tidy porches and neat walkways and dropping filmy curtains over blank eyes. . . .
Someone once lived in this house and loved it, and for a few moments I feel sad that it should be so neglected, left alone to die.
But the house is not dead.

obvious that while the children were on the island, they would have
_emselves. If they waited a whole month to be rescued, what would
_here would they sleep? How would they stay warm?

_ks later, I was asked to lead a workshop on writing fiction for
_ever having led a workshop or taught anything at all, I went
_ary and found several manuals on the subject. I read them
_aking notes. Before long I was horrified. It was the first I had
_ of "P.O.V." (point of view), and I suspected there wasn't one
_ks. "Conflict" had been emphatically stressed by all the
_nd seemed to involve psychological problems unfamiliar to
_cters. And if it was true that children couldn't handle the
_y of flashbacks, I was in real trouble.

_ghly intimidated myself, I set out to intimidate the writers in
_hop. It wasn't hard. When I mentioned point of view, they
_ed. When I moved on to conflict, they turned green. One
_ student asked me to explain the conflict in *Goodnight Moon*.
_he dark?" I suggested glibly.

_ fond of my students, however, and had second thoughts. I
_red the day in a high school biology class when I told the
_esperately, "I can't find the esophagus, but I'm still sure it's a
_s I discouraging future authors by throwing unfamiliar terms
_ At the next session, I qualified the strict rules that I had
_during the first workshops. If children liked their stories, they
_g something right; it was that simple. I told them that P.O.V.
_ a matter of fashion, and that while some writers felt comfort-
_ first-person-singular narratives, others (including Newbery
_inners) stuck to the "old-fashioned," universal or omniscient
_view. I told them that if children couldn't handle flashbacks, it
_author's fault. (Who said flashbacks have to be complex?) I told
_t conflict, as far as I was concerned, was whatever made the
_rn the page.

_g as the author doesn't bore, confuse, or lose the reader, a story
_ut remember that unless a book is required reading for school,
_as only one motive to continue reading: the desire to find out
_ppens next. He didn't choose the book because it was a best
_ because he was embarrassed at a dinner party to admit that he
_r read it.

There are small rustlings, creakings, and sounds barely loud enough to be heard as the house moves and breathes with the midday heat. I feel that it's watching me, waiting to see what I'll do. Or could someone be watching, listening, just as I listen?

9. *Sub-mysteries can aid suspense.* A sudden shadow on the porch, which is accounted for in the next chapter; a character whose actions are so peculiar that they frighten your main character; an aunt who is frantic to keep something hidden—such sub-mysteries tie in with the central mystery to be solved and heighten suspense. Sometimes they can do double duty by serving as red herrings. In *The Kidnapping of Christina Lattimore,* Christina, upstairs in bed and doing her homework, thinks she is alone in the house, until:

Maybe there was the click of a doorknob downstairs. If there was, I didn't notice it. I hold my breath and listen as I become aware that softly, very softly, through the thick plush carpeting on the stairway, footsteps are padding, patting, like little slaps with a power puff. And they are coming up the stairs!

Christina, preparing to defend herself, discovers it's only her father's secretary, Rosella, and relaxes. But as they talk, Rosella's inconsistent, nervous behavior arouses Christina's suspicions.

10. *A peculiar character can add suspense whenever he or she appears.* In *The Seance,* the daily life of Ila Hughes, grandmother of one of Lauren's friends, is built around superstitions, some of them creepy, such as the cat she has buried inside the walls of her house to keep the devil away. And her hobby?

My glance fell on something that made me automatically step back. On the mantel, on a level with my eyes, was a row of little gray skulls!
There was a chuckle close to my ear, and Mrs. Hughes touched my shoulders, moving me forward again. "Those are my little birds," she said, laughing. "Aren't they precious? Little bird skulls. I began finding them in the Thicket years ago."

11. *Old tricks can still be used.* We're all familiar with the *time is running out* technique, but it can still be effective. And so can the technique of *making the readers—but not the main characters—aware that someone is sneaking toward the house or slowly turning the knob on the bedroom door.* Pull out all the stops. Readers of young adult mysteries love it.

12. *Each chapter ending should be so intriguing that readers can't close the book.* These last sentences can whet curiosity or be downright terrifying, but their job is to lead readers from one chapter into the next, nonstop:

From *The Other Side of Dark:*

If I shot Jarrod, wouldn't it be self-defense? And wouldn't it end the trials and the questions and the badgering and the harassment and the nightmares and the worries and the years and years of fear?
Carefully I aim the gun.

From *A Deadly Game of Magic:*

I would have liked to comfort her. I would have loved it if someone had tried to comfort me. All I could do was lean against the door, hoping it would hold me. My legs were wobbly. My mind seemed to tremble as much as my body, but one thought came through clearly. "Whatever Sam saw," I said, "is still in this house. And like it or not, we're trapped in here with it."

To keep readers from becoming exhausted, you must have the suspense in your mystery build and peak, drop and build again. The valleys are a good place for humor, for development of the relationships between the main character and her family and friends, for her moments of introspection and attempts to handle the non-mystery problems that are part of her life.

But it's those peaks of suspense that will cause your readers to write, "I just couldn't put your book down. When is your next mystery coming out?"

9

HOW TO MAK

BY ANNE LI

WHEN I WAS a child, I expected a
vacation: endless. Unfortunately, ev
vacation, came to a sudden stop. This
author had opened a door into a new
people who had obviously existed
would go on existing after I had closed
events, and had no business wandering
My ambition at the time was to becom
the stories abandoned by C. S. Lewis,

I had forgotten this ambition by the
lectures on "Great Books" rather tha
writing, I tried to write in the style of
grim, meandering fiction for the next t
period, a friend came to me claiming
given him a headache. "I don't believe
you hadn't written it yourself," he grum
thing you like to read?"

What did I like to read? Children's b
puritan in me naggingly asked what enj
down to write *Osprey Island*. Instinct
structure similar to that of the books I h
one adventure and usually one day per
time. It also meant a book where the
character is reacting to every other cha
the middle of page two in *Osprey Island,*
the three children and one parent was
remaining three parents, a doctor, and a d
carefully included:

But it wa
to fend for
they eat? V

Five bo
children.
to the lib
carefully,
ever hear
in my bc
manuals
my chara
complexi

Thorou
my work
were baf
rebelliou
"Fear of

I grew
remembe
teacher
frog." W
at them
imposed
were do
was ofte
able wit
Award
point of
was the
them th
reader t

As lo
works.
a child
what ha
seller, c
had nev

I took another look at *Osprey Island*. I ached to rewrite it, loosening the style and tightening the structure. Still, children had liked it. Why? Probably because I had taken my friend's advice and written the sort of thing that I liked to read: an adventure heavily dosed with magic, but with real characters with whom I could identify, so that the story seemed to be happening to me.

"Real" is the key word. The farther I venture into make-believe, the more important reality becomes for me as a writer: make-believe must be believable. The children in *Osprey Island* travel by magic on Sunday afternoons, but on weekdays they lead ordinary lives. Once the magic has delivered them to the island they are still ordinary children with ordinary needs, so they have to plan carefully before leaving home. This planning provides the practical details that inspire belief:

> When the children said the magic words that Sunday, it seemed more natural to find themselves in a patch of ferns. In fact, they weren't really thinking about the magic at all; they were thinking about the things they had brought with them. Charles had his knapsack, Amy had her sketchbook and Lizzie was carrying her mother's kettle and a home-made cherry pie.

Real children get hungry, catch colds, and quarrel. Bearing this in mind, I let August Brown make himself a sandwich before going off to spend the day with the time travelers of Pineapple Place. Zannah, in *The Hunky-Dory Dairy,* is sent back to her own time from the nineteenth-century farm after sneezing into the applesauce. Dawn and her brother Marcus are so busy bickering over a spilled milkshake at the beginning of *The Shadow on the Dial* that Mr. Bros and his magical Removers Van nearly escape their attention.

Children occasionally want to know why there is magic in so many of my stories. I tell them that once I started, it became a habit I couldn't break.

Paradoxically, I started using magic in *Osprey Island* because the situation in which I put my characters was not believable. What parents, I asked myself, would allow young children to camp by themselves on a faraway island? I couldn't include the parents as chaperones because the moment trouble arose, they would insist on taking charge. How about a shipwreck? The parents could go down with the boat while the children were washed ashore with the dog. But what children would enjoy an adventure knowing that their parents had just drowned?

I didn't want any brooding orphans on Osprey Island. Should I make the children older?

Thrashing about for a believable solution, I thought of magic. My original plan was to use it as a taxi: Magic would take the children to the island in Chapter One and bring them back at the end of the book. But it seemed a pity to let the taxi wait there with its motor running. The instantaneous slip from one place or time to another by means of a magic painting, or window, or sundial, offered tempting possibilities. Why not let the children use it to explore? My habit was formed and developed fast. The children in *Osprey Island* travel back and forth repeatedly, returning home for a sandwich, a change of clothes, or simply to baffle the grownups in the story.

Meals, clean laundry, and other reminders of everyday life are essential in order to fasten my fantasies to reality, but before entering into fantasy at all I like to give the reader a long introduction to my characters and their surroundings. If Bailey, of *Bailey's Window*, had marched straight upstairs on his first day at the farm, painted a snow scene on his bedroom wall, and stepped out of August into March, a reader might hold back doubtfully—might even close the book. I wanted to convince my readers of the total believability of the farm, the children who lived there, and the long, hot summer. I wanted them to meet the parents and the dogs. I wanted them to smoulder with indignation at Bailey's tricks. When Bailey jumped through the painted window into knee-deep snow I wanted readers to jump, too—not for a whimsical change of scene, but to keep an eye on Bailey and make sure he gets what's coming to him.

Unfortunately, it took me thirty-two pages to accomplish this, and the resulting discussions with my editor were endless. Why, I was asked, if I promise magic on the book flap does it take me five chapters to deliver? "Who's promising?" was my answer. "Let the magic come as a surprise."

When I read *Bailey's Window* now, I am surprised that my readers are willing to bear with me (and the obnoxious Bailey) until Chapter Five. The story seems to meander. Again, I wish I could tighten a bit here, loosen a bit there. But it worked.

With each new book I try to bring in the magic a little closer to the beginning. This is a matter of setting, rather than of structure. Planning for the window to be painted or the sundial to be turned in Chapter One is not enough. It's more important to create a setting so real that when magic crops up, the reader will be too off guard to step back.

Most important of all, the reality of the setting must be sustained. Make-believe is not to be taken lightly. Once you have your reader's trust, it is a betrayal to imply that the magic is a joke, a fairy tale, or a dream. As a child I could not forgive Alice's sister (or, indirectly, Lewis Carroll) for the words:

"It was a curious dream, dear, certainly: but now run in to your tea; it's getting late." So she sat on, with closed eyes, and half believed herself in Wonderland.

Why not whole belief? Why shouldn't Alice have her tea and Wonderland too?

92

A SENSE OF AUDIENCE

By Jill Paton Walsh

I FEEL DISTINCTLY uneasy about giving practical, down-to-earth advice about writing for children. There are many things in the world, like riding a bicycle, which one may be well able to do, about which one cannot offer a coherent explanation; in one sense one does not know how to do it, even while bowling along the road! Writing for children may be very like riding a bike.

Certainly in the case of the bike, if you become too self-conscious about it you fall off at once; and a similar Catch-22 really does apply to writing for children; if you think that because your audience is young, something special needs doing, or not doing, then you probably can't do it at all. I would like to pursue the heavy metaphor about bike riding a little further, because much of the advice about writing for children that one reads is like exhortations to remember your balance when riding. It is so often telling people to think deliberately about their audience, the vocabulary, the market, whereas, I believe, the sense of audience really is like a sense of balance: If you need to think about it, you haven't got it, and you can't get it by wrinkling your brows and thinking about it harder, because to do it properly you need to be thinking about something else, rather as the cyclist, unaware of how to ride, thinks about which way to take into town.

Let me elaborate on this a little further, though enough about the bike, I promise. I once read an article advising people to *"write for children as though they were your equals."* Does that startle you as much as it did me? Children *are* my equals. Many of them, in time, will turn out to be my superiors—in brain power, in sensitivity, in warmth of heart. By and large, I believe, one generation is pretty much like another, and belonging to an older one gives no ground for claiming superior status.

But, perhaps you won't feel easy with this statement. Perhaps you think that claiming to think of children as equals is a sign of lack of sophistication, or a form of swank, in the way that Damon Runyon was swanking when he said he had never met a boring person. If that is how you are reacting as you read these words, then my down-to-earth advice is that you should ask yourself whom you *do* think of as your equals, and write for them; they are your natural audience. For them you will be able to write without, metaphorically speaking, putting on a funny hat, adopting a curious vocal tone, or limiting your vocabulary.

I have often wondered in the course of what is now a twenty-year career as a children's writer, why some people instinctively take children seriously, and others—including some published writers for children—simply fool about, and I have arrived at a contentious theory, which is that it depends what sort of childhood you had. If you have half forgotten your own; if it was happy and uneventful, and nothing painful or dangerous happened, or if it tested you much until you reached your teens, then, when you write, your characters will be teen-agers or older. I was a child in the war; I think of childhood as the most important formative time of life. I don't think about children when I write; I just assume without thinking that some of the readers will be children and that things had best be told as simply as possible, because everyone, including me, prefers it that way.

You must by now be wondering what I do think about when working, and the answer is, the subject. Day and night, at the typewriter, off the typewriter, waiting at the bus stop, lying in the bath, while washing up, dusting, eating, I recommend thinking consciously about the *book*. Or, more accurately perhaps, having book-shaped thoughts about the subject. Not just any subject, either; not something concocted from worldly-wise assessments of publishers' stated needs, or deductions about what sells based on reading what has sold. Not something that someone thinks there ought to be a book about. But something that moves your mind to enthusiasm. That gives you that glow of real interest. I realize that this sounds wildly impractical—the other kind of advice sounds so *sensible;* and of course I am thinking, in what I say, · only about fiction—nonfiction may be different, or may not, I don't know enough about writing it to say—but however airy-fairy it sounds, it has always worked for me. I write about things that move me deeply, I never try to write commercially salable work, I try to write the best book I possibly can about this wonderful subject; and I honestly think that the best book you can write is your best prospect of publication and commercial success. It is also your best prospect of noncommercial success—of that letter from a child who has never managed to finish a book until he reads yours, or who has read what you say about the war and found a sudden sympathy for a dreadful grandpa, or who just wants you to look at the picture he has drawn for you, of a scene in your book.

When I ask myself if my method is successful, I think of the flaws and shortcomings in my books—none of us can write as well as we wish we could—and then I remember the hundreds of loving letters I have received from children all over the world, and I feel like the most lucky and successful person I can possibly imagine.

Of course, it's all very well for me to tell you to burn with enthusiasm for your subject. Most people do that readily for their first book. But most first books don't get published. Keeping oneself supplied indefinitely with burning enthusiasms to make books out of is a problem for published and unpublished writers alike. And here comes my most practical piece of advice, my only really useful suggestion—do as I do, keep a notebook.

A notebook is not a diary, and doesn't have to be written in every day, or contain a note of anything dull. And everyone's notebook would contain a different balance of items. A notebook is a record of the activity of that part of your mind that produces ideas. Writing is a split personality activity: a "producer," which creates a huge output of thought and story and description, and a "controller," which carves and squashes and selects, and constructs a book from the raw material thrown up by the "producer." In my experience, the "controller" is easy to advise and improve and teach, and is sitting in your conscious mind, where you can talk to it. The notebook is an attempt to talk to the producer down in the unconscious depths, where it all comes from.

So what's in the notebook? Mine contains a good deal of description. I like places and often get ideas for books just from some interesting place. But I might come back from a week at the seaside with nothing in the notebook except a few sentences about the exact color of a breaking wave, and a list of the types of seaweed on a lee shore. I often try to write very exact descriptions of unusual weather, sky formations, effects of the light, and so on. The notebook entries are fragmentary and short, but in the year of the drought, for example, I made a lot of such notes. Three years ago I wrote a novel set in the summer of the Plague, when it didn't rain for three and a half months, and I reaped the benefit.

The next most frequent entry is fragments of overheard conversation, especially in any regional or highly demotic voice. I eavesdrop ruthlessly, wherever I am. Catching the tune of real voices—the English don't speak standard English—is terribly difficult. Months and months before I began work on *Gaffer Samson's Luck,* I had noted two children talking about a mouse their cat had caught: "What did you do with that?" "She put that in the bin, haven't she . . . ." The local children in my book never say "it." But if you don't eavesdrop, how will you know?

I also clip newspapers for stories that catch my attention, as in the item about a forest fire started deliberately to provide a rare bird with the hot pine cones it needed to nest; the fire went out of control and destroyed a small North American town. Hundreds of such fascinating possible starting points are printed free in the papers—local papers especially—every week. I clip or note the ones I like.

Finally I list reactions to the books I am reading, and sometimes make notes of states of mind—especially of frames of mind about the book I am writing; there is some comfort in looking back and seeing how gloomy I was about the last one, which is now in print and doing nicely, when I am feeling suicidal about the current one.

The point about a writer's notebook is writing it, of course—not reading it. I never read mine. I don't even, very often, consult it. If you went back and copied one of those exact descriptions, or conversations, directly into a book the words would be sure to stick out like a sore thumb. The tone of voice would be all wrong. But I find I can remember things I noted down, as I remembered the dusty surface of rivers and ponds in the year of the drought, all the way through till I needed that little detail. Perhaps your memory is marvelous anyway. But writing in a notebook regularly has an astonishing effect on your attention; things you would have no reason to notice, aspects of the world for which you have no present use, and which would normally float past you on the tide of weeks and days, will collect in your notebook. You will be like a child gathering handfuls of unremarkable special pebbles from a beach, and it will gradually enhance your powers of attention, and the vividness and realism with which you can write.

For really, writers have no special expertise. The only claim we have on the reader's time is that we have learned more, thought more, looked more carefully at some aspect of the human context, the human predicament, than most people have time for. There is a teaching method for very young children called "Look and Say." Look comes before Say. Otherwise what shall we have to tell each other stories *about*?

93

WRITING FOR YOUNG PEOPLE

AN EMOTIONAL DÉJÀ VU

By Charlotte Zolotow

THE MORE I TRY to analyze children's books or children's minds, or the fusion of feelings and events that goes into writing for them, the more I realize what a mystery children's thoughts are, and what a mystery the whole process of writing for them is. Part of it is the imagery and events and feelings that are completely individual; part of it the dreamlike, almost Jungian, merging of thoughts, feelings, fantasies, and desires that are universal.

A friend of mine on the brink of divorce told me of a recurring dream: She opened a door in her house and discovered a room she never knew was there. Her dream haunted me, and I would remember it at odd times. It had such evocative power that years later I used it in my book *Someday,* where a little girl is dreaming of lovely things she would like to have come true.

Last week, Andrea, a small girl who lives on my street, rang my bell and asked if she could go through my house again. "I haven't been upstairs in a long time," Andrea said. And she climbed upstairs humming under her breath and disappeared. When her mother came to collect her, I said, "She's upstairs. She wanted to go through my house." Andrea's mother began to laugh. "Ever since she read *Someday,* she's been searching for a new room in our house. I guess she thinks since you wrote the book, she'll find it here."

What a fusion! Of my friend's dream, with her unconscious telling her of unknown new things ahead; of my own inability to forget the dream, of having it turn up years later as I was writing a book about a little girl's wish fulfillment, and then its effect on the little girl next door, who wasn't even born when my friend dreamed her dream. There's a continuity, a flow of something unexplainable, a lovely, slow, rich mystery that lies at the core of life.

It is this mystery that flows through much writing for young children, although on the surface the stories may seem to be about very ordinary things.

Some writers for children deal with the most exaggerated kinds of events. Most of my books are about ordinary, daily events: relationships between children and adults, brothers and sisters, mothers and daughters, mothers and sons, fathers and sons, and fathers and daughters—and the infinite variety of personal encounters out of which emotions arise.

Emotions, *feelings* don't change. A child's emotions are similar to those an adult experiences—anger, jealousy, loneliness, loss, hate, and love—but adults have found ways to buffer themselves against the intensity of a child's emotions, emotions that can be aroused by the most ordinary situations. Adults have learned to camouflage—through religion or withdrawal or resignation or humor or cynicism; to protect themselves from the full impact of their feelings. They have memory to help them. As children, they have felt everything before, but children have no way of understanding that sad, wise, eternal truth: "This, too, shall pass." To adults the phrase can bring comfort; but to children, it would destroy the meaning, the moment of the experience itself. And for both good and bad experiences, the more fully we feel them, the more fully we live. In a way, children live more fully, more completely than we do. They are the true existentialists of the world.

So how and why does one write for the very young? For me it is an emotional *déja vu*. My adult anger or grief or joy is intensified by its familiarity. I have felt this way before. I remember not only childhood events themselves but the feelings those long-ago events evoked. They are the same feelings I experience again as an adult. And now when I experience a sense of loss or change or love or hate, I can remember the events of childhood that gave me grief or pleasure long ago, and see the kinds of events that give grief or pleasure to the children around me, who recognize and understand these happenings. The emotion they arouse is intensified by the fact that as an adult I am reexperiencing it.

A grown person's unrequited love evokes the same misery as a child's when his big brother or sister goes off without him. The loss of a job to another person can awaken the same feeling of anger a small child gets when a dog he wanted is given to someone else. We adults are no different from the children we were—only more experienced and defensive and better able to disguise our feelings from others (if not from ourselves).

Children experience keenly feelings that arise from events that to the adult seem unimportant. But to know and remember this is to respect a child's feelings in a way that will lead to greater understanding.

When a friend of mind read *The Name of the Rose,* by Umberto Eco, she told me I *must* read it. With her increasing enthusiasm and urging, my irritation grew. Later, I realized that the second she said, "You must read it," resistance built up in me: I knew I was *not* going to read it, even though I value my friend's judgment and taste. As I examined my ornery reaction, I realized that my childish resistance to what others urge upon me is much the same resistance that some children have to certain books. In a way, it's an intrusion on our privacy. For reading is a very private affair, and that's why TV will never replace it! I have so much I want to read and reread that I want to select what fills my own emotional needs, needs that are often different from or unknown to even my closest friends.

It was not that way when I was an adolescent, or in my middle years, when I had a wide, all-encompassing, greedy desire to read everything. But when I think back, I do remember as a child wanting to read certain books over and over again, and others not at all. I think that's because very young children—like adults—want to read books that help them sort out their own most acute needs, their own questions about life.

I remember a small girl at the dinner table listening for as long as she could to adults discussing politics, and then, suddenly breaking in by saying, "Now let's talk about me." Selfish? No. Self-centered? Yes. It is intelligent to be self-centered. Being "centered" is good; it describes a healthy psychological or physical state, and this self-interest and self-knowledge help you understand the interests and needs of others. That is what little children are doing; that is why they choose certain books over others. For each book is a world into which they are trying to fit their own perception and feelings. And that is why it is good that there are so many different kinds of books being written for children today: If they don't like one, they will like another. *They* must be allowed to find the ones that answer some need of their own.

In the hundreds of letters I've received over the years from children and parents, there are two comments that please me the most. One is from the child who writes, "How do you know about me?" And the other is from the parent who complains that when he finishes reading the book out loud to the child, the child turns to the front of the book and asks to hear it again.

The reason the child thinks the book is about him or wants to hear it over and over again is that he is facing or feeling or trying to clarify something he recognizes about himself in the book. For young children this is often the most ordinary, daily event. They want to understand *why* their parents or peers do a certain thing, why they respond to it in a way that perplexes them and the people around them. They want to know that their experience exists in other people, that they are not alone. It is themselves they search for.

My first published book, *The Park Book,* illustrated by H. A. Rey, originally published in 1944, was reissued in 1986. I am especially pleased to have my early books reissued, because the emotions in these books are valid for children today. The children of the thirties, forties, fifties, sixties, and seventies felt as children do now when they are lonely or frightened, or angry or happy. Although events change from period to period, in both the world and personal history, emotional reactions are the same.

I've been talking so far almost entirely about the picture book. I've skipped over that adolescent, middle-years period when we want to plunge into all things great and small, specific and abstract; into experiences we've had, might have, will never have, but want to have vicariously through the books we read. Adolescence is that strange time of life when we have matured physically, but our experience and understanding and independence lag behind. Despite increased sexual education and open discussion and television dramas to which young people are constantly exposed today, they still suffer from not knowing how to talk to each other, or how to deal with the violence and dissipation and contradicting moral behavior of their peers and adults. They are capable of understanding more than most books before the fifties gave them credit for. Not only capable, hungry, too. They need books that deal with protagonists their own age, facing their own struggles and conflicts and joys and desires.

But how does an editor find such books? There is a certain would-be author who will ask us what kind of book we are looking for. I can write anything, they say, just tell us what themes, what trends, you want. An editor can't assign authors to write books. No genuine piece of writing ever happens without the author's total emotional belief and involvement in what he or she is writing about. It must germinate inside his own unconscious and consciousness and emotions if it is to be a truly fine book.

Some authors write out of great happiness, and theirs are warm, exciting, loving books; other books come out of some bad and troubled experiences in the author's own development. Any writer honest enough to recall and put on paper the full story of his or her turbulent adolescence—or any segment of it—will have a book intense and rich and true for any reader, young or old. Fine books like *The Catcher in the Rye* or *I Never Promised You a Rose Garden* or *My Sweet Charlie,* all published originally for adults decades ago, are read and cherished by young people everywhere. Excellent writers such as Patricia Windsor, Louise Lawrence, Mollie Hunter, Paul Zindel, M. E. Kerr, and Adrienne Jones have written magnificent books that are read by both young people and adults with equal absorption and satisfaction.

When these books are written, coming as they do from the emotional experiences of the individual writer, they often deal with issues and ideas or evoke feelings and doubts and dilemmas that have not been dealt with before in young people's fiction. Often because it is so new in content and breaks new ground, a book has a hard time making its way. And often, too, those first startling revelations of a unique reaction to experiences previously untried in books for the young are books of passion and belief, not books that pander to the public.

An editor has to be open to new ideas, new ways of writing, new styles, new approaches, new thoughts, new directions, in content and form. But, of course, we are often fallible. Sometimes it's tempting to advise an author to cut a scene, which, however effectively written, we feel might arouse the anxiety or anger of some part of the reading public. Words or scenes may shock, but the editor's criteria must be how necessary to the reality of the story these words and scenes are. When such things are thrown into a story simply for shock value, that is bad writing, and no good writer resorts to it.

When Maurice Sendak's *Where the Wild Things Are* first came out, there was an outcry from angry adults, but the monsters that horrified some adults, the children took to their hearts immediately. They recognized their honesty as an expression of a small child's rage.

Other writers deal with similar themes in different fashion. Mine is

487

down-to-earth, everyday, ordinary events. *The Hating Book* is an example. The episodes or desires that evoke the reader's emotions are accessible to young children: a broken pencil, a friend not sitting next to you on the school bus. But the emotion of anger toward someone you really liked is there, not because I knew of two little girls who quarreled, not because I knew about their quarrel with their best friend, but because at the age of fifty when I wrote that book, I had just had a quarrel with a friend across the street. My anger and hurt and hate poured out; when I sat down at the typewriter, full of adult rage, that was familiar from previous times going back to my childhood when I had experienced it. As I said at the beginning, we are not all that different, adults and children. Emotionally, we experience the same feelings. That is what makes us, whatever nationality, whatever age, adult and child alike, more human than otherwise. That is why so many children identify with the book I sat down to write, angry at my friend across the street, and began it with, "I hate, hate, hated my friend." How do you know about me, the children write and ask. I don't. I only know about myself.

94

STORYTELLING: THE OLDEST AND NEWEST ART

By Jane Yolen

SOME time ago I received one of those wonderful letters from a young reader, the kind that are always signed mysteriously "Your fiend." This one had an opening that was an eye-opener. It read:

Dear Miss Yolen:
  I was going to write to Enid Blyton or Mark Twain, but I hear they are dead so I am writing to you...

Of course I answered immediately—just in case. After all, I did not want that poor child to think that all the storytellers were dead. Because that was what the three of us—Enid Blyton, Mark Twain, and Miss Yolen—had in common. Not style. Not sense. Not subject. Not "message or moral." The link was clear in the child's mind just as it was in mine. Blyton, Twain, and Yolen. We were all storytellers.

Nowadays most of the storytellers *are* dead. Instead, we are overloaded with moralists and preachers disguised as tale tellers. Our medium has become a message.

So I want to talk to you today about the art of and the heart of storytelling; about tales that begin, go somewhere, and then end in a satisfying manner. Those are the tales that contain their own inner truth that no amount of moralizing can copy. The Chinese, the *New York Times* reported in 1968, were recruiting "an army of proletarian storytellers" who were ordered to fan out into the countryside and "disseminate the thoughts of Chairman Mao." They told the kind of stories that end: "As a result, the evil wind of planting-more-watermelons-for-profit was checked." These tales waste no time in getting their message across. But they are sorry excuses for stories. As Isaac Bashevis Singer has said: "In art, truth that is boring is not true."

Storytelling may be the oldest art. The mother to her child, the hunter to his peers, the survivor to his rescuers, the priestess to her

489

followers, the seer to his petitioners. They did not just report, *they told a tale.* And the better the tale was told, the more it was believed. And the more it was believed, the truer it became. It spoke to the listener because it spoke not just to the ears but to the heart as well.

These same stories speak to us still. And without the story, would the tale's wisdom survive?

The invention of print changed the storyteller's art, gave it visual form. Since we humans are slow learners, it took a while to learn that the eye and ear are different listeners. It took a while to learn the limits and the limitlessness of two kinds of tellers—the author and the illustrator—in tandem. And it has taken us five centuries, dating from Gutenberg, to throw away the tale at last.

Children, the last audience for the storytellers who once entertained all ages, are finding it hard to read the new stories. Their literature today is full of realism without reality, diatribes without delight, information without incantation, and warning without wisdom or wit. And so the children—and the adults they grow into—are no longer reading at all. The disturbing figure I heard only last month is that 48% of the American people read no book at all in the past five years.

And so I dare. I dare to tell tales in the manner of the old story-tellers. I do not simply retell the old tales. I make up my own. I converse with mermaids and monsters and men who can fly, and I teach children to do the same. It is the only kind of teaching I allow in my tales.

What of these stories? There is a form. First, a story has a beginning, an opening, an incipit. Sometimes I will use the old magical words "Once upon a time." Sometimes I vary it to please my own ear:

Once many years ago in a country far to the East....

There was once a plain but goodhearted girl....

In ancient Greece, where the spirits of beautiful women were said to dwell in trees....

Once on the far side of yesterday....

In the time before time, the Rainbow Rider lives....

Once upon a maritime, when the world was filled with wishes the way the sea is filled with fishes....

490

But always a story begins at the beginning. That is surely a simple thing to remember. Yet my husband begins reading any book he picks up in the middle and, if he likes it, he will continue on. He says it does not matter where he begins, with modern books—and he is right. If stories and books no longer start at the beginning, why should the reader? And if, as Joyce Cary says, "... reading is a creative art subject to the same rules, the same limitations, as the imaginative process...," then a story that begins in the middle and meanders around and ends still in the middle encourages that kind of reading.

Now I am not saying that a story has to move sequentially in time to have a beginning. One does not have to start with the birth of the hero or heroine to start the story at the beginning. Still, there must be a reason, a discernible reason, for starting a tale somewhere and not just the teller's whim. The person who invented the words "poetic license" should have his revoked.

What of the story's middle? First it should not be filled with middle-age spread. But also, it should not be so tight as to disappear. Do you remember the nursery rhyme:

> I'll tell you a story
> About Jack O'Nory,
> And now my tale's begun.
> I'll tell you another
> Of Jack and his brother,
> And now my tale is done.

Where is the middle of that story? It should be the place in the tale that elicits one question from the reader—*what then*? The middle is the place that leads the reader inevitably on to the end.

Is that not a simple task? I run a number of writers' groups and conferences, and all persuasions of writers have passed through. There are the naive novices who think that children's books must be easier to write because they are shorter and the audience less discriminating. There are the passable writers, almost-pros who have had a story or two published in religious magazines and are ready to tackle a talking animal tale or—worse—a talking prune story where inanimate objects converse on a variety of uninteresting subjects. And there are the truly professional writers whose combined publications make a reasonable backlist for any publishing company. And they all have trouble with the middles of stories.

The problem is one of caring. Too few writers today care enough about storytelling. If they should happen in the throes of "inspiration" to come upon a beginning and an ending, then they simply link the two together, a tenuous lifeline holding two climbers onto a mountain.

Of course the middle *is* the mountain. It is the most important part of the book, the tale, the story. It is where everything important occurs. Perhaps that is why so few people do it well.

What of the end? Ecclesiastes says: "Better is the end of a thing than the beginning thereof." An overstatement perhaps. But if the end is not *just* right, and is not filled with both inevitability and surprise, then it is a bad ending.

Adults are quite willing to forgive bad endings. I saw only recently a review of an adult book that said, in essence, the ending is silly, unconvincing, and weak, but the book is definitely worth reading. Children will not forgive a weak ending. They demand a rounding off, and they are very vocal in this demand. I remember reading a story of mine in manuscript to my daughter, then age seven. It was a tale about three animals—a sow, a mare, and a cow—who, tired of men and their fences, decided to live together. When I finished reading, with great feeling and taking the dialogue in special voices, I looked up at my audience of one. She looked back with her big brown eyes.

"Is that all?" she asked.

"Well, that's all in this story," I said, quickly adding "Would you like another?"

She tried again. "Is that all that happens?"

"Well, they just...I mean they...yes, that's all."

She drew in a deep breath. "That *can't* be all," she said.

"Why?" I asked, defeated.

"Because if that's all, it's not a story."

And she was right. I have not yet worked out a good ending for that story, though I am still trying. G.K. Chesterton noted this about fairy tale endings, which are sometimes bloodier than an *adult* can handle. He wrote: "Children know themselves innocent and demand justice. We fear ourselves guilty and ask for mercy."

But lots of stories can still have a beginning, a middle, and an end and not be right. If they are missing that "inner truth," they are nothing. A tale, even a small children's tale filled with delight, is still

492

saying something. The best stories are, in Isak Dinesen's words, "a statement of our existence." Without meaning, without metaphor, without reaching out to touch the human emotion, a story is a pitiable thing; a few rags upon a stick masquerading as life.

I believe this last with all my heart. For storytelling is not only our oldest art, it is our oldest form of religion as well; our oldest way of casting out demons and summoning angels. Storytelling is our oldest form of remembering; remembering the promises we have made to one another and to our various gods, and the promises given in return; of recording our human-felt emotions and desires and taboos.

The story is, quite simply, an essential part of our humanness.

95

WHAT EVERY WRITER NEEDS TO KNOW ABOUT LITERARY AGENTS

By Ellen Levine

Q. *At what stage in their careers should writers look for an agent— or will a good agent find them?*

A. Most agents prefer to begin a working relationship with a writer when there is a book-length work to market, rather than articles or short stories. Some agents prefer writers who already have publication credits, perhaps magazine publication of shorter work. However, a writer who has never published before, but who is offering a book which deals with a unique or popular topic may also have an excellent chance of securing an agent. Quite a number of agents are actively looking for new writers, and they comb the little magazines for talented writers of fiction. They also read general interest and specialty magazines for articles on interesting subjects, since they might contain the seeds for books. Some agents visit writers conferences and workshops with the express purpose of discovering talented authors who might be interested in representation.

Q. *How does a writer go about looking for a legitimate agent?*

A. Writers can obtain lists of agent members from two professional organizations—The Society of Authors' Representatives (SAR) or The Independent Literary Agents Association (ILAA)— by writing to these organizations at (for SAR) 39½ Washington Square South, New York, New York 10012 and (for ILAA) 21 W. 26th St., New York, NY 10010. Writers can also obtain a more complete list of agents by checking the "Agents" section of *Literary Market Place* (LMP), available from R. R. Bowker, 205 E. 42nd St., New York, NY 10017, or as a reference work at the local library. Finally, the Authors Guild at 234 W. 44th St., New York, NY 10036 will supply a list of agents.

Q. *How important is it for an agent to be a member of SAR or ILAA?*

A. It is not essential for a good agent to belong to either organization, but membership is very helpful and adds credibility and professionalism to the agency. These organizations schedule meetings to discuss issues and problems common to the industry and their members work together to solve them. Expertise is often shared; panels and seminars are regularly scheduled, often including key publishing personnel. There are also certain codes of professional ethics, which members of each group subscribe to. This, of course, is to the writer's advantage.

Q. *Do literary agents specialize in particular types of material— novels, plays, nonfiction books, short stories, television scripts? Are there some categories that agents could not profitably handle that could better be marketed by the authors?*

A. Most of the agents' listings in LMP specify which kind of material the agency handles. A few agencies do have certain areas of specialization such as screenplays, or children's books, as well as more general fiction and nonfiction.

Q. *Should a writer query an agent (or several agents) before sending him or her his manuscript(s)?*

A. It is acceptable for a writer to query more than one agent before sending material, but it should be made clear to the agent that the writer is contacting several agents at one time. It is even more important for the writer to clarify whether he plans to make multiple submissions of a manuscript. Most agents prefer to consider material on an exclusive basis for a reasonable period of time, approximately four to eight weeks.

Q. *What do agents look for before accepting a writer as a client?*

A. An agent usually takes on a new client based on his or her enthusiasm for that writer's work and a belief that it will ultimately be marketable.

Q. *Once an agent has agreed to take a writer on as a client, what further involvement can the agent expect and legitimately ask of the writer?*

A. It may take longer to place the work of a new author, and the client should be patient in the process. If the writer has made contact with a specific editor or knows that there is interest in the work from a specific publisher, he or she should inform the agent. The writer should feel free to continue contacts with book editors with whom he or she has worked, and to discuss ideas with magazine editors.

Q. *Do most agents today ask for proposals, outlines, synopses, etc., of a book-length work before taking on the job of reading and trying to market the whole book? Do agents ever prepare this type of material, or is that solely the author's function?*
A. This varies among agents. A popular procedure for consideration of material from a prospective client is the request of an outline or proposal and the first 50 or 100 pages. If the book is complete, some agents might request the completed manuscript. It is common practice to submit a nonfiction work on the basis of one or more chapters and a synopsis or outline. The extent of the sample material needed is often based on the writer's previous credentials. It is generally the author's job to prepare the outline and the agent's to prepare the submission letter or the "pitch."

Q. *When, if ever, are multiple queries or submissions allowable, acceptable, desirable? By agent or by author?*
A. If an author is working without an agent, multiple submissions to publishers are acceptable only if the author informs the publisher that the book is being submitted on that basis. However, this can sometimes backfire since those publishers who will read unsolicited manuscripts may not care to waste the staff's reading time on a manuscript that is on simultaneous submission to five other publishers. Multiple queries with one-at-a-time submissions upon receipt of a favorable reply are probably more effective for a relatively new author. However, if a writer has a nonfiction project that is obviously very desirable or timely (an inside story, a current political issue), it is of course expedient to proceed with a multiple submission. This should be done carefully, informing all the participants of the deadline, ground rules, and so on. Agents must judge each project individually and decide on the appropriate procedure. If more than one publisher has expressed an interest in a specific writer or project, a multiple submission is not

only appropriate, it is fair and in the author's best interest if there are competitive offers. If a book is very commercial, an auction may well be the result of a multiple submission. If other factors, such as a guaranteed print order or publicity plans are important, a multiple submission without the necessity of taking the highest bid may bring the best results. If an agent routinely makes multiple submissions of all properties, credibility may be lost. If this practice is reserved for the projects which warrant it, the procedure is more effective. It is usually not appropriate to send out multiple copies of a promising first novel. It may be for the inside story of last week's Congressional investigation.

Q. *What business arrangements should a writer make with an agent? Are contracts common to cover the relationship between author and agent? How binding should this be and for what period of time?*

A. Author-agent business arrangements vary among agencies. Some agents will discuss commission, expenses, and methods of operation with their authors, and this informal verbal agreement is acceptable to both parties. Others will write letters confirming these arrangements. Several agencies require contracts defining every detail of the business arrangements, and others require formal, but less extensive contracts. Written agreements often contain a notification of termination clause by either party with a period varying from 30 days to a full year. A few of the agency agreements require that the agency continue to control the subsidiary rights to a book even after the author and agent have parted. Most agents include what is known as an "agency clause" in each book contract the author signs, which provides for the agency to receive payments for the author due on that book for the complete life of the contract, whether or not the author or agent has severed the general agency agreement. In a few cases this clause will contain the provision mentioned above (compulsory representation of the author's retained subsidiary rights). It is important for a writer to discuss these and all aspects of the agency's representation at the beginning of the relationship. In addition to understanding clearly commission rates and expenses he or she will be required to pay, a writer might want to discuss such matters as expectations for consultation on marketing, choice of publishers, the number of submissions to be made, frequency of contact with agent, and so on. *Poets and Writers, Inc.* at 201 West

54th Street, New York, NY 10019 has published a helpful handbook entitled *Literary Agents: A Writer's Guide* ($5.95), which addresses these issues. Commissions vary among agents. The range is often between 10% and 20%. Some agencies may vary the commission for different rights, charging 10% or 15% for domestic sales and 15% or 20% for foreign sales. Certain agencies have different rates for different authors, depending upon the length of time the author has been with the agency, the size of the publishing advance, or the amount of editorial and preparatory work the agent must do before marketing the book. Some agents work more extensively in an editorial capacity than others and may make detailed suggestions and ask for revisions before marketing a work.

Q. *Can a writer express a preference to the agent concerning the particular publishing house or kind of house he would prefer for his book?*

A. Writers should share with their agents any preferences or ideas they may have about their work, including which publishers would be most appealing, and in which format they envision their books. However, writers should not be dismayed if their agents feel in some cases that a particular preference may be unrealistic or inappropriate.

Q. *How much of the business side of publishing does the writer need to deal with, once he is in the hands of a competent agent?*

A. An agent acts as a writer's business representative for his publishing affairs. Most agents do not act as a writer's overall financial manager, and if an author begins to earn a substantial income, he or she may be well-advised to consult with a C.P.A. and/or tax attorney. The prudent writer, while entrusting his business affairs to his or her agent, will want to stay informed about these matters.

Q. *How much "reporting" can a writer legitimately expect from the agent who has agreed to handle his work?*

A. This would depend on the agent's individual style and the writer's need and preference. Many agents keep clients informed about the progress of submissions by sending copies of rejection letters; others do not, and will give the writer a summary periodically. A writer

498

should be kept informed of all important events and conversations with editors and co-agents about his or her work; for instance, a favorable *Publishers Weekly* review that has come in, a substantial delay in publication, a paperback auction date that has been set. On the other hand, writers should not expect daily contact with an agent as an established routine.

Q. *What involvement, if any, should a writer have in the contract that the agent makes with a publisher? Does he have the right, responsibility to question the terms, change them, insist on higher royalty rates, advertising, etc., or is this left entirely to the agent, along with the sale of substantial rights?*

A. It is the agent's responsibility to consult with the author before accepting any of the basic terms of an offer such as the advance, royalties, subsidiary rights, and territories granted. If the author has any particular reasonable requests which he or she would like to include in the contract, such as approval or consultation on the jacket design, it is the author's responsibility to let the agent know before the start of negotiations. The choice of an agent should imply the author's trust and confidence in the agent's expertise in negotiating the contract and securing the best possible financial and legal terms for the author. Authors should read contracts carefully and ask questions about any provisions, if necessary. However, it is not reasonable for an author to ask for changes in every clause or expect provisions that are extremely difficult to obtain, particularly for authors who have not had best sellers. For instance, advertising guarantees in contracts are not common for new authors. If the author has chosen a skillful agent, he or she should have confidence in the agent's explanation of what is or is not feasible in a contract with a particular publisher.

Q. *If an agent feels that he cannot place a manuscript and the author feels that it is marketable, or, at least, worthy of publication, can the author try to sell it on his own?*

A. If this happens on occasion and the agent has no objection, the author should feel free to try after discussing what he or she plans to do. The agent will want to be informed so that no prior obligation, such as an option requirement, is breached. If the author's agent repeatedly feels that the author's manuscripts cannot be placed, perhaps it is time for the author and agent to re-examine their relationship and discuss a change.

Q. *What services, other than the marketing of the manuscripts, negotiating the terms of their publishing contracts and related business arrangements may authors reasonably expect from their agents?*

A. In addition to marketing manuscripts, agents often help authors in formulating book ideas, passing along book ideas from editors when appropriate, and making introductions to appropriate editors if the author is between projects and free of contract obligations. Agents also follow up on various details of the publication process, such as production schedules, publicity, promotion, suggestions of other writers who might offer a quote for the jacket. The agent should also disseminate reviews, quotes, and information on subsidiary rights sales such as reprint and book club sales. Agents also examine royalty statements and, when necessary, obtain corrected statements.

Authors should not expect an agent to act as a secretary, travel agent, or bank. On the other hand, it is inevitable that a more personal bond may often form in the author/agent relationship, and in certain cases, agents do become involved to varying extents in friendships with their clients. In fact, hand-holding, "mothering" and counseling are not unfamiliar to many agents in dealing with certain authors. This is really a function of the agent's personality and often a conscious decision about how personally involved with his or her clients that particular agent wishes to be. A client should not expect that agent to solve his or her personal problems routinely.

Q. *How would you sum up the major role the agent plays in selling an author's work?*

A. If a manuscript is marketable, a good agent can short-circuit the random process of submissions by knowledge of the market, publishers, and the tastes and personalities of specific editors. However, an agent cannot place unsalable work. An agent can also be effective in the choice of marketing strategy for a particular work—should the book be sold as a trade paperback? Is a "hard-soft" deal best for the project? Would the author best be served by an auction, or would select individual submissions with editorial meetings be best?

500

96

EDITOR TO WRITER

By Joan Kahn

I'll START OFF with some don'ts—don't pay any attention (or much attention) to anything I'm about to say if you're a genius. If you're a genius *you'll* know where you're going and what you're going to do. Though I don't think I've known very many geniuses and maybe—oh, well—

And don't pay any attention (or much attention) to anything I'm about to say if you feel that writing a book is a snap and that all you need is some spare time and a word processor.

Otherwise—and I'll stick to novels, mystery or non-mystery—I think the first thing you should do is try to write a book to please yourself. If you're bored with what you've embarked on, stop as soon as you realize that, and go off and do something else for a while. Often, when you come back and look at what you've been working on, you'll think, "Hey, that isn't too bad, all it needs is etc., etc." Or sometimes you'll tear it up, throw it away, and start out in another direction.

Oh, another very important thing: If you're just embarking on your novel, I hope you've been reading other people's novels, lots of them, and that you feel what you're working on isn't something everyone else has already done—that your book will have *your* observations and your point of view; that you're not going to be just an echo.

After you've decided you do like what you're working on, keep at it. The opening of a novel *is* very important—but the end of the book is *much* more important—and a good ending is much harder to come by. Much. When you have completed your book, reread it. Because you're not writing the book just for yourself, you're hoping that other people will want to read it, preferably a lot of other people. As you reread it, *try* to look at it dispassionately and see if you think you've accomplished what you set out to do, or if you've made things not clear enough for

501

your potential readers. Everything might have seemed clear and compelling while you were at work, but no one else can get into your head.

I find that a number of authors, alas, are so careless, or so stupidly smug, that they don't (apparently, considering the state of their manuscripts) bother to go back over what they're sending out into the world. And, considering how tough it is (in most cases) to get published, you should do everything *you* can to help your book before you send it on its way.

I'd better say at this point that though I can and do consider incomplete nonfiction manuscripts, because I feel that with evidence of the author's writing ability, his idea for the book, and an outline, it's safe to move ahead, I don't think an editor can help a novel *while it's coming into being*. A good novelist, the best novelists I've known—and I know some very good ones—knows that the book, however carefully he plans, will choose its own path, will change about, its people will change, in many instances, as he writes. After the book has been completed and the editor can see the whole picture, only then, I feel, can the editor be helpful in suggesting modifications, if any are needed.

Once you have given birth to your novel, a novel that pleases you, the next step is finding a publisher and the publisher's editor for your book. As is perhaps already evident, *I* don't want to see anything but the completed manuscript of a novel. Many other editors disagree with me. One of the things I do feel strongly about is that publishers should read unagented manuscripts with the same care that they read agented ones—if the manuscripts are good, of course. I'll look at *any* manuscript submitted to me. A really bad piece of work can be dismissed very quickly (and sometimes such bad pieces come in via agents!). The beginning author, especially an author who doesn't have writing friends or a good local librarian to advise him, may have trouble figuring out where he'd like to send his manuscript.

I wish (and someday I hope it will be common publishing practice) that on the copyright page of every book published, where there now is information about the Library of Congress number, etc., there will be— it can be in small type—the editor's name. So that if an author far away from available knowledge of the publishing world picks up a book he admires—a book of poetry (if he wants to write poetry), a book on the Roman emperors (if that's a subject he wants to write about), a sensitive

502

novel about a girl's sixteenth birthday (if that's what he's thinking about), or a blood-and-thunder shoot-'em-up (if that's where he's heading)—he can say to himself, "I think *that* editor would respond to my work, why don't I try him?"

An inexperienced author may need a lawyer's advice on his contract, and an author can certainly be helped by a good agent who not only can advise him financially, but can help him also by sending his manuscript on, if the first publishing house he sends it to doesn't respond. And a good agent can be a friend, and even a soothing nanny if things get rough. But sometimes a beginning author may find it hard to get a good agent. Still, no one ever said it was easy in the world of the arts, and of all the arts, the art of writing is probably the least difficult one. Hang in there. And, once you *have* published a book, I recommend joining the Authors Guild (234 W. 44th, NYC 10036) and (if it's a mystery) the Mystery Writers of America (236 W. 27th, NYC 10001).

I have just said that the writing world isn't the toughest, but after you've found your publisher and your editor, there are the book buyers (or the book borrowers from libraries) to think about. *Very* important people—actually the people you have to think about *right* after you've thought about how you feel about the book. If they want to read your book, that's all anyone can ask.

After hearing about all these things to contend with you may wonder why bother. Because you want to. And, if what you want to write is a mystery—a word of encouragement. Mystery readers read more than any other kind of fiction reader—they are (I think) more intelligent—and if you plan on writing a mystery, though you have to do a lot of homework so that the police work, the medical aspects, etc., are sound, you don't have to worry, "What *is* my theme?" It's just a matter of life and death—not unimportant elements. Plus giving your readers a chance to use their deductive skills, which I think they enjoy. But remember—the ending, as I said earlier, of any novel is *especially* important in a mystery. You can't cheat at all on your way to the solution. And, your people, as in any novel, have to be real. *You* have to know them thoroughly—or you won't have a book worth writing.

Work hard—and good luck. Luck is *very* much a part of the picture.

97

BECOMING YOUR OWN EDITOR

By Moira Anderson Allen

WRITERS SPECULATE a lot about what editors really do. Some firmly believe that we are the final barricade between writers' excellent manuscripts and publication. Others seem to believe that the job of an editor is to clean up after writers and tell them what to do next.

To a certain extent, the latter is true. When a manuscript comes along that is so magnificent that no amount of typos can detract from its impact, we clean it up, gladly. Usually, though, we must weigh whether or not this "clean-up" time will be justified by the final product. Often the answer is no.

You can avoid this, however. If you follow these four easy steps, your editor will be able to judge your work using criteria that really count. Better yet, you'll never again have to speculate about what an editor does, because you'll be doing it yourself!

Step 1: **Get to the point.** The first thing an editor wants to learn from your manuscript is its purpose. What is the story you are going to tell, and why? Why is it important? Don't shroud your purpose in three or four cleverly written but pointless opening paragraphs.

If you're writing a story about Old Sam, a three-legged border collie who was the most unforgettable dog you've ever met, don't start your article with this kind of opener:

> When I got out of college with a few courses of animal science under my belt, I had little idea how bleak the job outlook would be. I wandered from clinic to clinic, but no work was to be had. Then my old buddy Joe, who owned a sheep ranch out on the South Fork Road, offered me a job as a stablehand. . . .

This sort of opener may ramble on just like buddy Joe's ranch before the author finally gets to the point: "And that's where I met Old Sam."

All this information may be important, but it isn't the point of your piece: Old Sam is. If, on the other hand, your first sentence is "Old Sam was the most unforgettable dog I've ever met," your editor might not think you have the world's best knack for opening lines, but he will know what you plan to talk about up front, and be more inclined to read on. Find another way to work in all that background information, if it's really necessary.

Part of getting to the point is explaining to the editor, and the reader, why he should spend time reading what you have to say. Why are you writing this particular article? Why are you writing it now? The answer may lie in your credentials, your personal experience, or simply in your ability to express important ideas to the editor's readers.

Let's say you want to write an article about a new virus in cats. Why should the reader hear about this from you? The answer could be that you're a veterinarian who has handled several cases of the virus and can enlighten cat owners about it; or you might be a cat owner who chanced to learn about this new disease, and you want to share the information you've gathered about it. Or, as a writer with a "nose" for a good story, you might choose to interview both veterinarians and cat owners about the disease and its effects, providing an article with both human appeal and expert information.

The approach you choose will depend on your market and your audience, but you should make two things clear: why this topic is important, and why the editor should accept you as the best person to write about it. Then let your story tell itself.

Step 2: **Get organized.** One of my associates told me of a trick she had learned to help her organize her thoughts while writing: "Think in subheads." Just about every magazine or newspaper story of any length is broken up into smaller chunks, each set off with a subhead. These subheads make the page look better artistically and lead the reader through an organized series of ideas.

If you look at your article carefully, you'll probably find that it breaks down into three or four major component ideas. Thinking of subheads for these ideas gives you a chance to organize your thoughts into the appropriate categories, almost like creating an outline for the article after it has been written. You may find during this process that you need to flesh out one of your ideas in greater detail, cut back on another, or add yet a third. Your subheads don't have to be cute or catchy, and you may decide not to include them in the final draft; their primary purpose is to help you organize your material.

Step 3: **Get rid of the clutter.** When you break your article into subheads, you may find that you have some ideas that don't belong under any of the categories you've roughed out. This could mean one of two things: You need another subhead, or you don't need that information in the article. It might be the basis for another piece, but serves only as clutter in this particular manuscript.

It can be painful to look at a stack of notes and realize that, even though it took you hours to get the information, it just doesn't belong in your article. But part of your job is deciding precisely what is important about the material you've amassed, and presenting that—and only that—to your readers. If you leave it to an editor to pluck the gems from the clutter, he may simply pluck a rejection slip from the drawer instead.

So read through your work again. Once you've organized it, it's easier to spot ideas that are only tangential to the main subject, or identify background material that is interesting but doesn't contribute that much to the basic piece. Try pulling some of the material out of the main text and presenting it in sidebars. Suppose you are writing about cancer treatments at a particular clinic, for example, and you've found some interesting information about another clinic or some other methods that seem promising. If that information doesn't belong in the main body of your piece, write it up as a complementary sidebar. If the editor likes your sidebar and has room for it, you may even get paid extra for it. But if he doesn't, you won't have jeopardized the success of your main article by cluttering it with extra information.

Step 4: **Keep it "clean."** Whenever I receive an all-but-illegible manuscript, filled with typos, my first reaction is that the writer doesn't care enough about me or my audience to clean up his work, to present the best article he can. I'm prejudiced against that writer from the start, and he'll have to work twice as hard to prove that the content of his work outweighs his presentation.

Unfair? Maybe. But if a writer doesn't check for typos and grammatical errors—the easy stuff—I'm bound to wonder if he was any more careful where it counts. When a manuscript is littered with mis-

506

spellings, what assurance do I have that the writer has checked his facts, verified every phone number and double-checked figures and spellings of names?

Editors also get irritated by the idiosyncrasies of computers. If your computer leaves peculiar codes on the page when you try to underline or capitalize, changes your quotation marks to brackets, or leaves huge spaces between your words because it's trying to justify your right-hand margins, do something about it. Be extra careful of inadvertent changes that result from corrections: Your text may rearrange itself in ways you never anticipated. And please, please don't leave your manuscript just the way it was printed on continuous-feed paper. No editor enjoys having to tear your pages apart before being able to read them.

Finally, editors like to know that *you* know they exist, and that you know what's going on with their publications. When I receive a manuscript addressed to my predecessor's predecessor at an address that we haven't used in two years, I can't help but wonder how recently that author has examined a copy of the magazine.

The penultimate sin, of course, is to leave out your self-addressed, stamped envelope. Make sure that you put enough postage on the SASE; I have seen writers put a 25-cent stamp on a large manila envelope that would require extra postage just to be delivered empty. The ultimate sin? Letting your manuscript arrive with postage due.

So take another look at that manuscript you're about to put in the mail. Did you read it through with an editor's eyes—the eyes of someone who has never seen it before and doesn't know yet what you're trying to say? Is your ribbon clean and dark? Is there enough postage on both envelopes? If you've answered "yes," congratulations! You've just removed another major barrier between you and success.

98

A LITERARY AGENT'S PERSPECTIVE

By Anita Diamant

IN THIS AGE of proliferating conglomerates, the publishing industry has followed suit: The former cottage industry has indeed become big business. The business department, the sales and marketing departments are apt to influence the acceptance of a manuscript by the publishing house. And so literary agents, following the trends, often become interested primarily in projects bearing the promise of a six-figure advance. Where does this leave the great majority of writers and would-be writers? Is it impossible for them to secure representation?

It is true that conservatively 75% of all manuscripts are sold through agents today, but it is also a fact that there remain many bona fide agents who are more interested in representing a writer than only in securing huge advances. I can think of no greater pleasure than to place a first novel that indubitably will bring a relatively small advance. And it is important and rewarding for an agent to be an integral part of building a successful career for a new writer. Does this mean that every agent will take on any project that is sent in to him or her? Of course, we have to be discriminating, and obviously we will all take on manuscripts and ideas that appeal to us and would seem to bear the promise of a sale. I would like to start by assuring writers that it is possible even for a neophyte to obtain representation by a professional agent; but a good deal depends upon the way in which the work is presented and of course on the feasibility of selling the material.

The author-agent relationship is a very personal one. There must be complete trust and respect between the writer and the agent. This is true financially as well as editorially. The agent receives all monies due the writer, deducts a percentage, and then sends the balance to the writer. This should be done as soon as the publisher's check has cleared, but I must admit that I have heard numerous stories about an undue length of time that elapses before the writer is paid by the agent.

All of this can be avoided if a writer secures a reference before deciding to have a particular agent represent him or her.

I also feel that an agent must have enough background in the publishing world to be able to offer some editorial assistance to a writer. I do not mean that it is an agent's job to edit or rewrite, but an agent should know whether a proposal is sufficiently effective; whether plot, style, and characterization are successful; whether a theme is handled with clarity. If there are problems, the agent should be willing and able to indicate where the problems lie and perhaps offer suggestions that would help correct them. Your agent should also be your friend. This does not mean that an agent should take the place of your psychiatrist, your attorney, or your financial adviser, although we generally listen carefully to problems in all these areas.

The value of agents obviously is their knowledge of the markets, of the changing editorial staffs, and, of course, the close contact with all of the people who are in the field at any one time. And this is certainly a changing scene: This past year has seen enormous changes in ownership of the large publishing companies and in the hiring and firing of editorial personnel. It is very often important to think not solely of the suitable publishing house for a project, but also of the editor who will be most empathic and whose interests are somewhat analogous to the material presented.

The question inevitably rises, "Is it necessary for a writer to have an agent?" Of course, there are always manuscripts submitted directly to publishers, which sell, but the fact remains that many houses simply will not read unsolicited manuscripts, and in the case of a book project, I would certainly advise a writer to get an agent, if it is at all possible. All successful agents work on a commission basis—from 10% to 15% on domestic sales, 15% to 20% on foreign sales—and this is how the agent makes a livelihood.

An agent will also know how best to handle a property. If it is a book project, the question arises whether it should be a hardcover book, a paperback, or perhaps it would be best to sell to a hard/soft firm. Since in the case of most book contracts, the writer must give up 50% of the monies secured on a softcover deal by a hardcover publisher, it is often advisable to sell both hard- and softcover rights to a publisher who offers this arrangement, in which case there will not be a 50% split on the softcover sale.

509

There is always the question of multiple submissions or auctions. Not every work should be auctioned; if we feel there is a particularly appropriate publisher or editor for a certain idea, we would rather give first crack at the work to that editor. We're told by many top editors today that they are really annoyed by auctions of books that are not top properties, and it seems totally unfair and a waste of time for them to read a manuscript that is also being read by a great many other editors simultaneously. Hence, the agent's decision on how the work should be presented becomes of the utmost importance.

An agent also often assumes the role of an arbiter—between the publisher and the writer and also, more importantly, between two writers on a project. We were asked recently to handle a manuscript that had been contracted for by a major publishing house, but later rejected because of the arguments between the writers. We resold the material for a larger advance and made a very good deal with the former publisher to pay back only a portion of the money advanced. However, we spent endless hours again trying to get the parties to agree to accepting responsibility for the share each had in the manuscript. At this moment, everything is signed and we hope the new publisher will receive a satisfactory revision and the work can get underway.

Now, how does a writer go about finding an agent? First, through recommendation from other writers, perhaps from a publisher. However, three good sources are the lists offered by The Society of Authors' Representatives (39½ Washington Square South, New York, NY 10012); The Independent Literary Agents Association (55 Fifth Avenue, New York, NY 10003); and *Literary Market Place,* published by R. R. Bowker Co., available in the reference department of most good public libraries. Also, there are always agents who speak at writers' conferences and even to writers' groups.

Once you decide on having an agent, you must write a good, selling query letter, indicating just what the idea may be, outlining the idea, as well as including something about your own background and authority for writing the book; your general vita; any previous publications you have had, and why you feel there is a market for this idea. DO NOT send manuscripts, and by all means make certain that you are approaching the agent who handles the kind of material you are writing. *Literary Market Place* indicates in the agents' section the type of manuscripts the agent will accept.

When we read a query letter that is intelligently written, we will ask to see either a proposal and sample chapters, or we may even ask to see the entire manuscript. We have been fortunate in finding even best-selling writers this way, the most notable of whom was V. C. Andrews, whose novels have sold over 30 million copies in this country alone. Consequently, even though realistically an agent will prefer to handle a writer who already has a track record, it is unrealistic for us not to take a chance at reading something that evokes our interest.

Each time I speak at a writers' conference, I am bombarded with requests for my address, and I realize that this will bring in numerous proposals and a good deal of mail. But I have found several very good writers through these conferences, and I would advise writers who are not living near the major markets to attend writers' conferences, for this gives them an opportunity to meet and talk to agents and editors and in this way make a professional contact.

Often writers ask me whether it is necessary to sign a contract with an agent. Many agents do require contracts, but I personally do not feel this is necessary, for like a marriage, the relationship between writer and agent is good only if they can work amicably together. If not, then a divorce is inevitable. Also, all book contracts have an agency clause stipulating that the agent has the right to negotiate for the author, and all monies due will be sent directly to the agent.

However, if problems develop between you and your agent, first discuss the situation with him or her. If this does not resolve the problem, send a registered letter detailing your complaints and stating that you are hereby ending your agreement. Even though there may not be a termination clause in your agreement with your agent, most agents will release a client if there is a bona fide reason for disagreement.

We find that writers today are shopping for agents as they might publishers. This is certainly legitimate, but we do resent having to take the time to read manuscripts if we have not been given them ex-clusively. And frankly, many agents have told me that they simply will not read anything if they know it has been given to many other agents. It is far better to select an agent, give that person a specified time to respond to the project and to your letter, and if you are not satisfied at that point, go on to seek another agent. After all, personalities do not always mesh, and you may be happier with one agent representing you than another.

It's important for the writer to be able to keep in touch with his agent, who, upon the writer's request, must make available a record of where a manuscript has been sent and what the rejections have been. Many writers ask whether it is advisable to seek an attorney as well as an agent, or perhaps in lieu of an agent. If an attorney has been dealing with literary properties, he can of course be very helpful, but the average attorney does not know the practices of the trade, and we find (as do publishers) that the average lawyer simply does not know what is negotiable in a contract and what must remain intact. Since agents spend so many hours attempting to sort out these problems, they are more knowledgeable about them. Recently, a deal was almost killed because of the inappropriate interference of an attorney who did not understand that his client must assume responsibility for what he presents in his manuscript.

The publishing business has become exceedingly complex, and it is because of the nature of the changes that I feel it is so important for a writer to find representation with a well-established agent. A good agent knows what rights must be protected for a writer in a contract and which houses offer better contracts than others. It is an interesting fact that in selling a manuscript, we find it easier to obtain a higher advance for a writer when the idea is so exciting that many publishers want it, than for a writer who has published many books but whose sales record is not very good. The first question editors ask when we submit an idea by a published writer is how many copies his or her last book sold. The fact is that editors are looking almost exclusively for book ideas that will sell in big numbers.

Since agents receive publishers' lists of their forthcoming books, we are also in a position to advise our writers whether they are zeroing in on an idea that has been presented before, and perhaps we can save the writer time in trying to work out that particular idea. The agent must be constantly in touch with the market, and this is where a writer receives the greatest benefit from that representation.

In spite of the fact that publishers prefer best sellers and blockbusters to anything of a literary nature, the market is still open for well-written, fresh works, and any legitimate agent will welcome the submission of a work that has a *good sales potential* or reveals a writer with a future.

Certainly, any writer who has the urge, the ability, and the time to pursue such a career should not be discouraged at this time. It was George Sand who once said, "The trade of authorship is a violent and indestructible obsession."

512

99

INSIDE THE EDITOR'S OFFICE

BY PATRICIA TOMPKINS

THE EDITOR'S OFFICE. If you've never been inside one, perhaps you've imagined what it is like: a plush, spacious room, with framed photographs on paneled walls; behind a vast teak desk and leather chair, a panoramic view of the city. Outside the door to this center of serene efficiency sits a secretarial sentinel. The elusive editor is out having lunch with a writer.

For the novice free-lance writer, the editor's office may seem like an inner sanctum, a place where only writers with the right password are admitted. But you'll be closer to reality—and closer to getting inside the office—if you imagine the following: a typewriter and possibly a word processor on a little table; mismatched chairs crowded around a gray metal desk, with calendars, memos, and page layouts taped on plaster walls; through the venetian blinds, a view of a parking lot. On the littered desk, alongside an overflowing in-box, are a salad in a plastic container and a mug of cold coffee. The phone rings while the editor is down the hall, trying to fix the photocopying machine. The editor's office, in short, is usually about as glamorous as that of a free-lance writer. (I'm writing this at my "desk"—a folding card table.)

Having set the scene, let's look at what the editor does in that office. First, understand that an editor is a working professional, often overworked and underpaid, in a wonderful, competitive business. That could describe a free-lance writer, too. Well, an editor is not so very different from you. But sometimes the mutual interests of writers and editors get lost in the shuffle of manuscripts. Aspiring contributors often forget that editors can be writers' greatest allies. The following guidelines, drawn from my experience as a copy editor for a monthly city magazine, apply to most publications and will enable you to improve your chances of selling articles. These three basics will help you reach your most important reader—the editor:

(1) Show your familiarity with the magazine to which you send your proposal or query.

(2) Communicate your enthusiasm for your subject in your query letter.

(3) Understand what an editor does and expects from free-lance writers.

The clues to what the editor is looking for appear in every issue. Study several recent issues of the magazine and obtain a copy of its writers guidelines. If your public library has back issues, you may also want to look at several copies from the past year and five years ago. Note any changes in format, content, and staff.

A thorough reading includes advertisements, which give a sense of the magazine's audience. And look at the staff list. The magazine I work for lists numerous contributing editors and identifies the subjects they cover. If there is already a regular columnist on wine, you may have a tough time selling your article on wine to the editor. But regular contributors are not necessarily permanent, and the magazine may buy free-lance material as well.

Once you've done your research and are confident your proposal suits the magazine, introduce yourself in your query letter. Remember: first impressions count, and you are competing with many others; to get the editor's attention, your letter must stand out. This doesn't mean typing in red ink on purple paper; it means writing an engaging, informative letter. Perhaps you're aiming at a local publication and are tempted to skip a letter and simply telephone the editor. Your idea is so good, you think, the editor will naturally say yes. And you'll save a month waiting for a reply by getting an instant assignment. No, you won't. The editor is not sitting around waiting for unsolicited proposals by telephone from unfamiliar callers. If you're a writer, write a letter; put your idea on paper so the editor can assess it at a convenient time.

Two weeks may pass before the editor has time to look at your letter. Why? Partly because most editors can't spend their days reading; they're busy putting out a magazine. Consider an average day in the editor's office: Arrives at nine o'clock; a glance through the mail reveals that two manuscripts due today didn't arrive. Assistant calls in sick. Editor writes final headlines and captions for three articles; associate art director asks for two lines to be cut from an article to fit layout. Desk lamp burns out; no spare bulbs around. Appointment at ten with writer to discuss work needed on feature story. Meets with editorial staff at eleven to discuss possibilities for the next issue, three months away. Eats lunch at desk while returning phone calls. Writer delivers assignment and spends fifteen minutes pitching another article idea. Editor looks at an assigned article that arrived in the day's mail. Calls printer to find out why galleys are late; writer calls wanting to update her piece. Fact-checker brings in manuscript full of errors; copy editor asks how to handle a writer who refuses her suggested changes. Interview at four with potential summer intern. Discusses illustrations for cover story with art director. Selects five letters to the editor for inclusion in next issue. Leaves at six to spend half an hour at a press preview party.

Generally, the day doesn't allow time to read unsolicited manuscripts or queries. The editor I work for coordinates editorial production with two senior editors and manages a staff of two full-time assistants supplemented by six part-time helpers (free-lance copy editors and proofreaders, plus interns) in a noisy, crowded room next to her office. Rarely does she have ten minutes alone and uninterrupted at her desk—not exactly ideal reading conditions.

One assistant weeds out the inappropriate queries each week and passes along more hopeful prospects to the editor, who then reviews them, along with recent fiction submissions. When does she read? At home in the evening and on the weekends when, much as she loves her job, she wouldn't mind doing something else. Under these circumstances, she appreciates a clear, concise query, one with enthusiasm for and knowledge of the subject and the magazine.

Keep in mind that your query is one of dozens in limbo (make that hundreds or thousands for popular national publications). Although no one likes form rejection letters, they are time-savers. Unfortunately, they don't convey how close you may have come to acceptance. The difference between a positive and a negative response to a query is often a matter of timing and luck—good and bad. Once I proposed an idea for a new column in a monthly magazine; it seemed a natural, given the publication's audience. No, thanks. I still thought my idea was sound, so twelve months later, I tried again; this time the answer was yes. Why? The proposal was the same; so was the editor, but—unknown to me—he was planning a change in format, and my suggestion now solved a problem.

No can mean the editor already has a related story in the works. I've seen two pieces on the same subject arrive simultaneously; both took a similar approach to their subject. (The one chosen was by a writer long established with the magazine.) *No* can also mean the editor has a backlog of good material ready; she knows your article would sit on hold for many months—frustrating for the writer when payment is on publication, impractical for the editor when payment is on acceptance.

Suppose the editor says *yes*—on speculation—and gives you guidelines on the desired focus, length, and deadline. These guidelines are made to avoid wasting your time and the editor's. Follow them. The magazine's production schedule won't collapse if your piece is late, but the delay will be passed along to the copy editor, art department, printer, and proofreader. (The tendency to ignore basic directions is one reason editors ask new writers to submit work on speculation, rather than on assignment.) Turn your work in on time; it will save you the trouble of thinking up novel excuses for being late.

A problem even more common than missing deadlines is submitting a manuscript that is longer than requested. A maximum of 2,000 words doesn't mean that you should write 2,500 or 3,000. But isn't that the editor's job—to edit stories to the right length? No, it isn't. The right length is the requested or assigned length. The editor has other pieces competing for space and attention. Although the magazine may vary in length from issue to issue, the amount of advertising sold, not the length of articles, usually determines an issue's size. Holding to the assigned length can be an aid to keep your piece focused.

If you've done your job, the editor can concentrate on hers: critically examining the article and seeing if its parts work well together. Are the transitions adequate? Is the subject covered adequately, or is vital material missing? Does the piece start fast and finish slow? Will it inform or entertain readers? In asking such questions, the editor exercises her skills creatively, making murky prose lucid.

Once your article is accepted, the fact-checker, copy editor, and proofreader will be looking at your work closely. (With a small staff, one person may handle all three tasks.) The fact-checker verifies the statistics, the spelling of names, and the accuracy of quotes. These details are checked with primary sources when possible, usually not with the writer. Just a few misspelled names will cast doubt on your reliability;

516

substantial discrepancies and errors may put your piece in jeopardy. Check your manuscript for accuracy before submitting it.

The proofreader and copy editor will be alert to other types of errors. No one will reject a manuscript if it has a dangling participle and uses "which" where "that" is correct, but the fewer mistakes, the more professional you will look. The copy editor will ask for clarification of cryptic and confusing passages. If you're a local writer, include your home and work phone numbers, along with your name and address, on the first page of your manuscript so an editor can get in touch with you easily.

It's natural to assume your writing is perfectly clear when you know the topic. The copy editor helps ensure that everything will be clear to readers, too. I've found most writers appreciate careful editorial attention to their work, but some regard copy editors as meddlers and hacks, critics who can't write. Avoid this superiority complex and cooperate. All writers' work receives the same scrutiny. You might be surprised and encouraged if you saw the deletions and revisions on most manuscripts by the time they're ready for the typesetter. Only rarely does what appears in the magazine exactly match what the editor received in manuscript form. An acceptable manuscript doesn't have to meet impossible criteria of perfection before an editor will accept it, but the less time the editorial staff has to spend cutting and polishing your manuscript, the better they'll like it.

When you have the published version of your work in hand, compare it with your original copy. Over a period of several weeks or months between writing and publication, you may be better able to see alterations as improvements. Think of editing as a writing lesson. If you're pleased with the results, send a note of thanks to the editor.

At its best, the editor-writer relationship is a partnership of peers. If you use common sense and courtesy and treat the editor as an ally, you'll be two steps ahead of the crowd.

100

ERASING THE BLUE-PENCIL BLUES

By David Petersen

IF YOU'VE ever felt that too many of the magazine articles you've strived so diligently to create have wound up getting edited too harshly, then I don't need to tell you about the Blue-Pencil Blues. You know the ailment well, even if you've not heard the term before. While I'd never say that you should consider this potentially debilitating malady a blessing, I *will* suggest that your writing can benefit from it.

During more than a decade of straddling the publishing fence as both a free lancer and a magazine editor, I've identified five nonfiction problem areas that I feel comprise the most common reasons editors bring out their blue pencils. The good news is that by learning to recognize and weed out these troublemakers, you can significantly reduce the need for editing and—a delightful spin-off—increase sales.

Here, then, are what I perceive to be the five primary reasons editors edit—along with a few tips to help you eliminate them from your writing.

1. *Editors edit for grammar, punctuation, spelling, and all the other nuts and bolts that hold a manuscript together, but that too many free lancers too often fail to tighten.*

Many aspiring wordsmiths feel so blessed with talent that they think they needn't bother with the more mundane details of the writer's craft—things such as submitting clearly typed manuscripts free of punctuation errors, pronouns that disagree in number, misspellings, and the like. Some of these writers do show budding talent, but anyone who believes that just a good yarn is enough to win consistently at the free-lancing game is setting himself up for a fall.

The reality is that few magazine editors have the time or inclination to take on serious cosmetic surgery, no matter how beautiful the hidden message may be. Sloppily prepared pieces, peppered with mechanical glitches that could easily have been caught and corrected by the writer, are rarely going to sell—and the few that do are bound to be heavily edited.

The self-evident remedy, therefore, is to make sure that your copy is road-ready; that nary a screw that you can detect is left jangling loose for an editor to spot and tighten. If *you* don't take care of the mechanical essentials and your editors have to, consider their tinkering a blessing rather than a curse.

2. *Editors edit for style.*

No two publications speak with exactly the same voice. A serious free lancer knows this and—while making no attempt to parrot every stylistic inflection of a magazine—will avoid submitting seriously off-key articles. You wouldn't, for example, use a stiff, academic style in an article bound for a magazine whose voice is as informal and conversational as *The Mother Earth News,* but many free lancers have—only to be rejected or heavily edited for their trouble.

A submission written in a voice that's gratingly off-key tells an editor that the writer a) hasn't bothered to familiarize himself with the publication (a cardinal and surprisingly common free lancer's sin); or b) is unable to recognize a magazine's style when he sees it. An off-key article is far less likely to sell and, if it does, is certain to be returned to bring it into editorial harmony. So, familiarize yourself with your target publication's voice, and pitch your style accordingly.

3. *Editors edit for length.*

When I queried one of my favorite magazines about an article idea not long ago, the editors gave me a green light to submit the piece on speculation, but stipulated that I hold the length to around 1,500 words. Had I sent them the 2,500 tome I generated on the first draft (rather than the 1,500 words I eventually trimmed it to), I could hardly have taken umbrage had they cut the piece to the requested length—or even rejected it. The moral: When an editor is helpful enough to indicate a preferred length for an article, don't exceed it.

But many times you don't have a specified length to shoot for. What then? Here's a procedure that has worked well for me as a free lancer—and *with* me as an editor.

Begin by studying a few recent issues of the target magazine to determine the average word count of several articles similar in style and scope to the one you plan to submit. Next, send an SASE for writer's guidelines (which will probably suggest minimum and maximum lengths for different kinds of articles). Finally, a query. And in that query, suggest a length for your article based on what you've learned by studying the guidelines and the magazine itself. This procedure will significantly improve your chances of getting a go-ahead from the editor. If the editor is interested in your proposal but wants more or fewer words than you've suggested, he can say so in his response.

4. *Editors edit for accuracy and completeness.*

Consider this scenario: You've written and submitted an article in which you quote a fellow named Stewart. The piece sells, is published, and all is well . . . until the day the publication's editor sends you a copy of a letter received from Mr. Stewartt (two t's). No matter that the extra "t" is a somewhat unusual spelling; Mr. Stewartt is upset that you got his name wrong—and the editors are also upset because they feel compelled to print Stewartt's letter along with an apology. How eager do you think they'll be to purchase more of your work?

The most common inaccuracies are dates, figures, quotations, professional titles, and the names of persons and places. The free-lancing war is won or lost through many small battles. Verify, verify, verify!

Hand-in-hand with accuracy goes completeness. Never assume that readers will have sufficient foreknowledge of your topic to fill in informational blanks for themselves. When in doubt, err on the side of providing too much detail rather than too little.

5. *Editors edit for clarity.*

Clarity is the cornerstone of effective communication—and effective communication is the foundation of good writing. To achieve clarity, polish each of your manuscripts until you think it shines, then ask a reliable friend who's willing to play the part of candid literary critic to read it and point out any hazy spots. If your critic is confused by a passage, fails to chuckle at a joke you thought was an absolute knee-slapper, or otherwise misses a point you've tried to make, it's a fair bet that other readers—including editors—will have the same trouble. (If you don't have someone to read your work for you, the next best critic is *time*. The longer you can afford to let a piece rest after you've "completed" it, the more objective you'll be when you return to it for further editing.)

Sure, a good editor can shine up your slightly hazy prose for you—that's part of what he's trained and paid to do. But a serious writer won't expect him to, won't want him to, won't give him the need to. To increase sales and minimize editing, polish your product until even the filmiest patches of fog disappear. Then polish some more.

And there you have it—the five kinds of problems that most frequently prompt editors to reject or heavily edit manuscripts . . . along with a few suggestions for eliminating them from your writing.

Of course, all this talk of how to minimize having your work altered assumes that you'll be dealing with competent editors. A fair assumption, I believe. Slovenly and unqualified editors are as scarce as fur on a fish and as ephemeral as Hailey's comet. In general, you can trust career blue-pencilers to be skilled professionals dedicated to making their publications the best they can be by making their free-lance contributors perform at their best. Both are essential.

When an editor improves my words without making them sound more like his than mine, I'm unabashedly grateful. But as much as I appreciate the help, I nonetheless set my sights on leaving no loose nuts and bolts to tighten, no fat to trim away, no murky prose to clarify, no inaccuracies to correct or blanks to fill in, and no off-key voice to bring my article into line with the magazine's style. I don't always succeed, but I always try. That's my duty as a writer.

And when I'm sitting on the other side of the editorial desk, I try to make every article I work with as good as it can be without destroying the writer's voice or betraying the style of my magazine. That's my duty as an editor.

I've never known a sadistic editor, and the unqualified are few and far between. In the majority of cases, therefore, the most effective way to avoid the feeling that your work is being edited too severely by others is to bear down a little harder with your own blue pencil.

PART IV

Where to Sell

This year's edition of The Writer's Handbook includes a completely revised and updated list of free-lance markets, and writers at all levels of experience should be encouraged by the number and wide variety of opportunities available to them. Editors, publishers, and producers rely on free lancers for a wide range of material, from articles and fiction to play scripts, op-ed pieces, how-to and children's books, and they are very receptive to the work of newcomers.

The field of specialized publications, including travel, city and regional magazines, and those covering such areas as health, science, consumer issues, sports, hobbies and crafts, remains one of the best markets for beginning free lancers. Editors of these magazines are in constant need of authoritative articles (for which the payment is usually quite high), and writers with experience in and enthusiasm for a particular field, whether it's gardening, woodworking, bicycling, stamp collecting, bridge, car repair, will find their knowledge particularly helpful, as there is usually at least one publication devoted to every one of these areas. Such interests and activities can generate more than one article, if a different angle is used for each magazine, and the writer keeps the audience and editorial content firmly in mind.

The market for technical, computer, health, and personal finance writing is also very strong, with articles on these topics appearing in almost every publication on the newsstands today. For these subjects, editors are looking for writers who can translate technical material into lively, readable prose, often the most important factor in determining a sale.

While some of the more established markets may seem difficult to break into, especially for the beginner, there are thousands of lesser-known publications where editors will consider submissions from first-time free lancers. City and regional publications offer some of the best opportunities, since these editors generally like to work with local writers, and often use a wide variety of material, from features to fillers. Many newspapers accept op-ed pieces, and are most receptive to pieces on topics not covered by syndicated columnists (politics, economics, and foreign affairs); pieces with a regional slant are particularly welcome here.

It is important for writers to keep in mind the number of opportunities that exist for nonfiction, because the paying markets for fiction are somewhat limited. Many general-interest and women's magazines do publish short stories; however, beginners will find these markets extremely competitive, with their work being judged against that of experienced professionals. We highly recommend that new writers look into the small, literary, and college publications, which always welcome the work of talented beginners. Payment is usually only in copies, but publication in literary journals can lead to recognition by editors of larger circulation magazines, who often look to the smaller publications for new talent. A growing number of regional, specialized, and Sunday magazines use short stories and are particularly interested in local writers.

The market for poetry in general-interest magazines continues to be tight, and the advice for poets, as for fiction writers, is to try to get established and build up a list of publishing credits by submitting material to literary journals. Poets should look also to local newspapers, which often use verse, especially if it is related to holidays or other special occasions.

Community, regional, and civic theaters and college dramatic groups offer new playwrights the best opportunities for staged production in this competitive market. Indeed, many of today's well-known playwrights received their first recognition in regional theaters, and aspiring writers who can get their work produced by one of these have taken a dramatic step toward breaking into this field. In addition to producing plays and giving dramatic readings, many theaters also sponsor competitions or new play festivals.

Though a representative number of television shows are included in this section of the Handbook, writers should be aware of the fact that this market is inaccessible without an agent, and most writers break into it only after a careful study of the medium and a long apprenticeship.

While the book publishing field remains competitive, beginners should be especially encouraged by the many first novels published over the past few years, with more editors than ever before seeking out new works of fiction. An increasing number of publishers are broadening their nonfiction lines, as well, and editors at many hardcover and paperback houses are on the lookout for new authors, especially those with a knowledge of or training in a particular field. Writers oi juvenile and young adult books will be pleased to hear that in response to a growing audience of young readers and increased sales, many publishers are greatly expanding their lists of children's books.

Small presses across the country continue to flourish—in fact, they are currently publishing more books by name authors, and more books on important subjects, than at any time in recent years—offering writers an attractive alternative for their manuscripts.

All information in these lists concerning the needs and requirements of magazines, book publishing companies, and theaters comes directly from the editors, publishers, and directors, but editors move and addresses change, as do requirements. No published listing can give as clear a picture of editorial needs and tastes as a careful study of several issues of a magazine, and writers should never submit material without first thoroughly researching the prospective market. If a magazine is not available in the local library, write directly to the editor for a sample copy (often sent free or at a small cost). Contact the publicity department of a book publisher for an up-to-date catalogue or a theater for a current schedule. Many companies also offer a formal set of writers guidelines, available for an SASE upon request.

ARTICLE MARKETS

The magazines in the following list are in the market for free-lance articles of many types. Unless otherwise stated in these listings, a writer should submit a query first, including a brief description of the proposed article and any relevant qualifications or credits. A few editors want to see samples of published work, if available. Manuscripts must be typed double-space on good white bond paper (8 ½ x 11), with name, address, and telephone number at the top left- or right-hand corner of the paper. Do not use erasable or onion skin paper, since it is difficult to work with, and always keep a copy of the manuscript, in case it is lost in the mail. Submit photos or slides only if the editor has specifically requested them. A self-addressed envelope with sufficient postage to cover the return of the manuscript or the answer to a query should accompany all submissions. Response time may vary from two to eight weeks, depending on the size of the magazine and the volume of mail it receives. If an editor doesn't respond within what seems to be a reasonable amount of time, it's perfectly acceptable to send a polite inquiry. Many publications have writers guidelines, outlining their editorial requirements and submission procedures; these can be obtained by sending a self-addressed, stamped envelope (SASE) to the editor. Also, be sure to ask for a sample copy: Editors indicate the most consistent mistake free lancers make is failing to study several issues of the magazine to which they are submitting material.

GENERAL-INTEREST PUBLICATIONS

ALCOHOLISM & ADDICTION MAGAZINE—P.O. Box 31329, Seattle, WA 98103. Neil Scott, Ed. Articles on all aspects of alcoholism: treatment, legislation, education, prevention, and recovery. Send SASE for guidelines.

ALLIED PUBLICATIONS—1776 Lake Worth Rd., Lake Worth, FL 33460. Articles, to 1,000 words: business, management, fashion, careers, travel (foreign and domestic), beauty, hairstyling, general interest, home, family, art and artists. Photos, cartoons, humor. Write for terms of payment. Guidelines. Publishes *Trip & Tour, Management Digest, Modern Secretary, Woman Beautiful, Home, Exhibit.*

THE AMERICAN LEGION MAGAZINE—Box 1055, Indianapolis, IN 46206. Michael D. LaBonne, Ed. Articles, 750 to 1,800 words, on current world affairs, public policy, and subjects of contemporary interest. Pays $100 to $1,000, on acceptance. Query.

AMERICAN VISIONS, THE MAGAZINE OF AFRO AMERICAN CULTURE—The Visions Foundation, Smithsonian Institution Frederick Douglass House, Capitol Hill, Washington, DC 20560. Madelyn Bonsignore, Ed. Articles, 1,500 to 4,000 words, and columns, 750 to 2,000 words, on people and events that contribute significantly to black culture and heritage. Pays from $100 to $1,000, on publication. Query first.

AMERICAS—OAS, General Secretariat Bldg., 1889 F. St. N.W., Washington, DC 20006. Catherine Healy, Man. Ed. Features, to 2,500 words, on life in Latin America and the Caribbean. Wide focus: anthropology, the arts, travel, science, and development, etc. No political material. Query. Pays from $200, on publication.

AMTRAK EXPRESS—140 E. Main St., Suite 11, Huntington, NY 11743.

Christopher Podgus, Ed. General-interest articles on business, health, books, sports, personal finance, life style, entertainment, travel (within Amtrack territory), science for Amtrack travelers. Submit seasonal material three to six months in advance. Pays on publication, $300 to $700 for 1,500- to 2,000-word manuscript; $250 to $600 for department pieces of 1,500 to 2,500 words. Query with published clips.

THE ATLANTIC—8 Arlington St., Boston, MA 02116. William Whitworth, Ed. In-depth articles on public issues, politics, social sciences, education, business, literature, and the arts, with emphasis on information rather than opinion. Ideal length: 3,000 to 6,000 words, though short pieces (1,000 to 2,000 words) are also welcome. Pays $1,000 to $7,000, on acceptance.

BETTER HOMES AND GARDENS—1716 Locust St., Des Moines, IA 50336. David Jordan, Ed. Articles, to 2,000 words, on home and family entertainment, building, decorating, food, money management, health, travel, pets, and cars. Pays top rates, on acceptance. Query.

CAPPER'S—616 Jefferson St., Topeka, KS 66607. Nancy Peavler, Ed. Articles, 300 to 500 words: human-interest, personal experience, for women's section, historical. Pays varying rates, on publication.

CHATELAINE—MacLean Hunter Bldg., 777 Bay St., Toronto, Ont., Canada M5W 1A7. Elizabeth Parr, St. Ed. Articles, 1,500 to 3,500 words, for Canadian women, on current issues, personalities, medicine, psychology, etc., covering all aspects of Canadian life. "Upfront" columns, 600 words, on relationships, health, nutrition, fitness, parenting. Pays from $350 for columns, from $1,200 for features, on acceptance.

THE CHRISTIAN SCIENCE MONITOR—One Norway St., Boston, MA 02115. David Holstrom, Feature Ed. Articles, 800 words, on arts, travel, education, food, sports, science, and lifestyle; interviews, literaty essays for "Home Forum" page; guest columns for "Opinion Page." Pay varies, on acceptance. Original material only.

CLASS—27 Union Sq. W., New York, NY 10003. Rene John-Sandy, Ed. Articles, to 2,500 words, of interest to the Third World population living in the U.S., and inhabitants of the Caribbean Islands. Pays 5¢ to 20¢ a word, after acceptance. Guidelines.

CONNOISSEUR—Hearst Corp., 1790 Broadway, 18th fl., New York, NY 10019. Ellen Rosenbush, Man. Ed. Articles for readers "interested in learning about excellence in all areas of art." Topics include fine, decorative, and performing arts, architecture and design, food, fashion, and travel; include pertinent service data. Length varies; query required.

COSMOPOLITAN—224 W. 57th St., New York, NY 10019. Helen Gurley Brown, Ed. Guy Flatley, Man. Ed. Artilces, to 4,500 words, and features, to 2,500 words, on issues affecting young career women. Pays $1,500 to $2,500, for full-length articles, less for features, on acceptance. Query.

COUNTRY—5400 S. 60th, Greendale, WI 53129. Dan Johnson, Assoc. Ed. Articles, 500 to 1,000 words, for a rural audience. Fillers, 50 to 200 words. Taboos: tobacco, liquor,and sex. Pays $125 to $200, on acceptance. Query.

COUNTRY JOURNAL—P.O. Box 8200, Harrisburg, PA 17105. Francis Finn, Ed. Paula Noonan, Man. Ed. Articles, 1,500 to 3,000 words, for country an small town residents; practical, informative pieces, essays, and reports on contemporary rural life. Pays $400 and up, on acceptance. Query.

DAWN—628 N. Eutaw, Baltimore, MD 21201. Linda Harris, Ed. Illustrated feature articles, 750 to 1,000 words, on subjects of interest to black families. Pays $100, on publication. Query.

DIVERSION MAGAZINE—60 E. 42nd St., Suite 2424, New York, NY 10169. Stephen N. Birnbaum, Ed. Dir. Articles, 1,200 to 2,500 words, on travel, sports, hobbies, entertainment, food, etc., of interest to physicians at leisure. Photos. Pays from $400, on acceptance. Query.

EBONY—820 S. Michigan, Chicago, IL 60603. Herbert Nipson, Exec. Ed. Articles, with photos, on blacks: achievements, civil rights, etc. Pays from $150, on publication. Query.

THE ELKS MAGAZINE—425 W. Diversey Parkway, Chicago, IL 60614. Fred D. Oakes, Exec. Ed. Articles, 3,000 words, on business, sports, and topics of current interest, for non-urban audience with above average income. Informative or humorous pieces, to 2,500 words. Pays $150 to $500 for articles, on acceptance. Query.

EQUINOX—7 Quuen Victoria Rd., Camden East, Ont., Canada K0K 1J0. Jody Morgan, Asst. Ed. Articles, 3,000 to 6,000 words, on popular geography, wildlife, astronomy, science, the arts, travel, and adventure. Department pieces, 300 to 500 words, for "Nexus" (science and medicine), and "Habitat" (man-made and natural environment). Pays $1,250 to $2,000, for features, $100 to $300 for short piecess, on acceptance.

ESQUIRE—1790 Broadway, New York, NY 10019. David Hirshey, Articles Ed. Articles, 1,500 to 4,000 words, for intelligent adult audience. Pay varies, on acceptance. Query with published clips; complete manuscripts from unpublished writers.

ESSENCE—1500 Broadway, New York, NY 10036. Susan L. Taylor, Ed.-in-Chief. Provocative articles, 1,500 to 3,000 words, about black women in America today: self-help, how-to pieces, business and finance, health, celebrity profiles and political issues. Short items, 500 to 750 words, on work and health. Pays varying rates, on acceptance.

FAMILY CIRCLE—110 Fifth Ave., New York, NY 10010. Susan Ungaro, Articles Ed. Ellen Stoianoff, Sr. Ed., Leah Breir, Health Ed. Articles, to 2,500 words, on "women who have made a difference," marriage, family and child-rearing issues; consumer affairs, travel, humor, health and fitness, personal opinion essays. Query required. Pays top rates, on acceptance.

FORD TIMES—One Illinois Center, 111 E. Wacker Dr., Suite 1700, Chicago, IL 60601. John Fink, Ed Articles for a family audience, particularly geared to ages 18 to 35: topical pieces (trends, life styles); profiles; first-person accounts of unusual vacation trips or real-life adventures; unusual sporting events or out door activities,; food and cooking; humor. Bright lively photos desireed. "Road Show": travel and dining anecdotes; pays $50, on publication. Payment for articles, 1,200 to 1,700 words, is $550 to $800; $400 for 800 to 1,200 words; and $250 for short pieces (500 to 800 words), on acceptance. Query with SASE required for all but humor an anecdotes.

FRIENDLY EXCHANGE—Locust at 17th, Des Moines, IA 50336. Adele Malott, Ed. Articles, 1,000 to 1,800 words, of interest to the active Western family, on travel and leisure. Photos. Pays $400 to $800, extra for photos. Query preferred. Guidelines.

GENTLEMEN'S QUARTERLY—350 Madison Ave., New York, NY 10017. Eliot Kaplan, Man. Ed. Articles, 1,500 to 4,000 words, for a male audience, on politics, personalities, life styles, trends, grooming, sports, travel, business. Columns, 1,000 to 2,500 words: "Private Lives" (essays by men on life); "All about Adam" (nonfiction by women about men); "Games" (sports); "Health"; and "Humor"; also columns on fitness, nutrition, investments, music, wine and food. Pays $750 to $3,000, on acceptance. Query with clips.

GLAMOUR—350 Madison Ave., New York, NY 10017. Ruth Whitney, Ed.-in-Chief; Judith Coyne, Art. Ed. Articles on careers, health, psychology, interpersonal relationships, etc.; editorial approach is "how-to" for women, 18 to 35. Fashion and beauty material staff-written. Pays from $1,000 for 1,500- to 2,000-word articles, from $1,500 for longer pieces, on acceptance.

GLOBE—5401 N.W. Broken Sound Blvd., Boca Raton, FL 33431. Donald McLachlan, Assoc. Ed. Factual articles, 500 to 1,000 words, with photos: exposés, celebrity interviews, consumer and human-interest pieces. Pays $50 to $1,500.

GOOD HOUSEKEEPING—959 Eighth Ave., New York, NY 10019. Joan Thursh, Articles Ed. Personal-experience articles, 2,500 words, on an inspirational, unique, or trend-setting event; personal medical pieces dealing with an unusual illness, treatment, and result; personal problems and how they were solved. Short essays, 750 to 1,000 words, on family life or relationships. Pays top rates, on acceptance. Queries preferred. Guidelines.

GOOD READING MAGAZINE—Litchfield, IL 62056. Peggy Kuethe, Assoc Ed. Articles, 500 to 1,000 words, with b&w photos, on current subjects of general interest; travel, business, personal experiences, relationships. Pays $10 to $100.

GRIT—208 W. Third St., Williamsport, PA 17701. Alvin Elmer, Assoc. Ed. Articles, to 800 words, with photos, on interesting people, communities, jobs, recreation, families, and coping. Pays 15¢ a word, extra for photos, on acceptance.

HARPER'S BAZAAR—1700 Broadway, New York, NY 10019. Anthony Mazzola, Ed.-in-Chief. Articles, 1,500 to 2,000 words, for active, sophisticated women. Topics include the arts, world affairs, food, wine, travel, families, education, personal finance, careers, health, and sexuality. No unsolicited manuscripts; query first with SASE. Payment varies, on acceptance.

HARPER'S MAGAZINE—666 Broadway, New York, NY 10012. Address Managing Editor. Articles, 2,000 to 5,000 words.

INQUIRER MAGAZINE— *Philadelphia Inquirer,* P.O. Box 8263, 400 N. Broad St., Philadelphia, PA 19101. Fred Mann, Ed. Local-interest features, 500 to 7,000 words. Profiles of national figures in politics, entertainment, etc. Pays varying rates, on publication. Query.

INSIDE MAGAZINE—226 S. 16th St., Philadelphia, PA 19102. Jane Biberman, Ed. Articles, 1,000 to 3,000 words, on Jewish issues and the arts. Queries required; send clips if available. Pays $75 to $600, within four weeks of acceptance.

KIWANIS—3636 Woodview Trace, Indianapolis, IN 46268. Chuck Jonak, Exec. Ed. Articles, 2,500 to 3,000 words, on home, family, international issues, the social and emotional needs of youth, career and community concerns of business and professional men. No travel pieces, interviews, profiles. Pays $400 to $1,000, on acceptance. Query.

LADIES' HOME JOURNAL—100 Park Ave., New York, NY 10017. Jan Goodwin, Exec. Ed. Linda Peterson, Articles Ed. Jane Farrell, Sr. Ed. Articles on contemporary subjects of interest to women. Personal-experience and regional pieces. Query required. Not responsible for unsolicited manuscripts.

MCCALL'S—230 Park Ave., New York, NY 10169. A. Elizabeth Sloan, Ed. Andrea Thempson, Articles Ed. Interesting, unusual and topical narratives, reports on health, home management, social trends relating to women of all ages, 1,000 to 3,000 words. Humor. Human interest stories. Pieces for "Vip-Zip" and regional sections: consumer, travel, crafts. Pays top rates, on acceptance.

MADEMOISELLE—350 Madison Ave., New York, NY 10017. Michelle Stacey, Man. Ed. Articles, 1,500 to 2,000 words, on subjects of interest to single, working women in ther 20s. Pays from $1,750, on acceptance. Query.

MARRIAGE & FAMILY (FORMERLY *MARRIAGE & FAMILY LIVING*)—Abbey Press Publishing Div., St. Meinrad, IN 47577. Kass Dotterweich, Man. Ed. Articles, 1,500 to 1,700 words, on husband-wife and parent-child relationships; faith dimension essential. Pays 7¢ a word, on acceptance. Query.

MD MAGAZINE—3 E. 54th St., New York, NY 10022. Sharon AvRutnick, Ed. Articles, 750 to 2,500 words, for doctors, on the arts, history, other aspects of culture; fresh angle required. Pays from $200 to $700, on acceptance. Query by mail only.

METROPOLITAN HOME—750 Third Ave., New York, NY 10017. Service and informational articles for residents of houses, co-ops, lofts, and condominiums, on real estate, equity, wine and spirits, collecting, trends, travel, etc. Interior design and home furnishing articles with emphasis on lifestyle. Pay varies. Query.

MODERN MATURITY—3200 East Carson St., Lakewood, CA 90712. Ian Ledgerwood, Ed. Articles on careers, workplace, human interest, living, finance, relationships, and consumerism, for persons over 50 years, to 2,000 words. Photos. Pays $500 to $2,500, extra for photos, on acceptance. Query first.

MOTHER EARTH NEWS—105 Stoney Mt. Rd., Hendersonville, NC 28793. Articles, with photos, for rural and urban readers: home improvements, how-tos, indoor and outdoor gardening, family pastimes, etc. Also, self-help, health, food-related, ecology, energy and consumerism pieces. Pays varying rates, on acceptance. Guidelines.

MOTHER JONES—1663 Mission St., San Francisco, CA 94103. Doug Foster, Ed. Investigative articles, political essays, cultural analyses. Pays $750 to $2,000, after acceptance. Query in writing only.

MS.—One Times Square, New York, NY 10036. Address Manuscript Ed. Articles relating to women's roles and changing lifestyles; general interest, how-to, self-help, profiles. Pays market rates. Query with SASE required.

NATIONAL ENQUIRER—Lantana, FL 33464. Articles, of any length, for mass audience: topical news, the occult, how-to, scientific discoveries, human drama, adventure, personalities. Photos. Pays from $325. Query; no unsolicited manuscripts accepted.

NATIONAL EXAMINER—5401 N.W. Broken Sound Blvd., Boca Raton, FL 33431. Cliff Linedecker, Sr. Assoc. Ed. Celebrity interviews and human-interest pieces, 500 to 1,000 words. Must be well documented. Pays varying rates, on acceptance. Query required.

NATIONAL GEOGRAPHIC MAGAZINE—17th and M Sts. N.W., Washington, DC 20036. Wilbur E. Garrett, Ed. First-person, general-interest, heavily-illustrated articles on science, natural history, exploration, and geographical regions. Query required.

NEW WOMAN—215 Lexington Ave., New York, NY 10016. Pat Miller, Ed.

"Read the magazine in order to become familiar with our needs before querying." Articles on new lifestyles. Features on financial and legal advice, building a business, marriage, relationships, surviving divorce, innovative diets. Pays varying rates, on acceptance. Query with SASE.

THE NEW YORK TIMES MAGAZINE—229 W. 43rd St., New York, NY 10036. Address Articles Ed. Timely articles approximately 4,000 words, on news items, forthcoming events, trends, culture, entertainment, etc. Pays $350 to $500 for short pieces, $1,000 to $2,500 for major articles, on acceptance. Query with clips.

THE NEW YORKER—25 W. 43rd St., New York, NY 10036. Address the Editors. Factual and biographical articles, for "Profiles," "Reporter at Large," "Annals of Crime," "Onward and Upward with the Arts," etc. Pays good rates, on acceptance. Query.

NEWSWEEK—444 Madison Ave., New York, NY 10022. Phyllis Malamud, My Turn Ed. Original opinion essays, 1,000 to 1,100 words, for "My Turn" column: must contain verifiable facts. Submit manuscript with SASE. Pays $1,000, on publication.

OMNI—1965 Broadway, New York, NY 10023–5965. Patrice Adcroft, Ed. Articles, 2,500 to 3,000 words, on scientific aspects of the future: space, machine intelligence, ESP, origin of life, future arts, lifestyles, etc. Pays $750 to $3,500, less for short features, on acceptance. Query.

PARADE—750 Third Ave., New York, NY 10017. Fran Carpentier, Articles Ed. National Sunday newspaper supplement. Factual and authoritative articles, 1,000 to 1,500 words, on subjects of national interest: health, education, consumer and environmental issues, science, the family, sports, etc. Profiles of well-known personalities and service pieces. No fiction, poetry, games or puzzles. Photos with captions. Pays from $1,000. Query.

PENTHOUSE—1965 Broadway, New York, NY 10023–5965. Peter Bloch, Exec. Ed. Robert Sabat, Man. Ed. General-interest or controversial articles, to 5,000 words. Pays from 20¢ a word, on acceptance.

PEOPLE IN ACTION—Box 10010, Ogden, UT 84409. Caroll McKanna Halley, Pub. Features, 1,200 words, on nationally noted individuals in the fine arts, literature, entertainment, communications, business, sports, education, etc.: must exemplify positive values. Manuscripts should be accompanied by high-quality color transparencies. Query. Pays 15¢ a word, on acceptance.

PEOPLE WEEKLY—Time-Life Bldg., Rockefeller Ctr., New York, NY 10020. Hal Wingo, Asst. Man. Ed. Considers article proposals only, 3 to 4 paragraphs, on timely, entertaining, and topical personalities. Pays good rates, on acceptance. Most material staff written.

PLAYBOY—919 N. Michigan Ave., Chicago, IL 60611. John Rezek, Articles Ed. Sophisticated articles, 4,000 to 6,000 words, on interest to urban men. Humor: satire. Pays to $3,000, on acceptance. Query.

PLAYGIRL—801 Second Ave., New York, NY 10017. Nancie S. Martin, Ed.-in-Chief. Articles, 2,000 to 2,500 words, for women age 18 to 34. Celebrity interviews, 1,500 to 2,000 words. Pays negotiable rates. Query with clips to nonfiction editor.

PRIME TIME—2802 International Ln., Suite 120, Madison, WI 53704. Joan Donovan, Exec. Ed. Articles, 500 to 1,800 words, for dynamic, creative mid-lifers. Departments, 850 to 1,000 words. Pays $125 to $750, on publication. Query. Guidelines with SASE.

PSYCHOLOGY TODAY—1150 17th St. N.W., Suite 408, Washington, DC 20036. Wray Herbert, Ed. Lively, useful articles, 2,500 to 3,000 words, and short news items about timely subjects, based on the research findings of social scientists and the clinical insights of practicing psychotherapists; jargon free. Department pieces, 1,200 to 1,500 words, on health, work, relationships, the brain, etc. Pays good rates, on acceptance.

READER'S DIGEST—Pleasantville, NY 10570. Kenneth O. Gilmore, Ed.-in-Chief. Unsolicited manuscripts will not be read or returned. General-interest articles already in print and well-developed story proposals will be considered. Send reprint or query to any editor on the masthead.

REDBOOK—224 W. 57th St., New York, NY 10019. Annette Capone, Ed.-in-Chief. Karen Larson, Sr. Ed. Articles, 1,000 to 3,500 words, on subjects related to relationships, sex, current issues, marriage, the family, and parenting. Pays from $750, on acceptance. Query.

ROLLING STONE—745 Fifth Ave., New York, NY 10151. Magazine of modern American culture, politics, and art. No fiction. Query; "rarely accepts free-lance material."

THE ROTARIAN—1560 Sherman Ave., Evanston, IL 60201. Willmon L. White, Ed. Articles, 1,200 to 2,000 words, on international social and economic issues, business and management, human relationships, travel, sports, environment, science and technology; humor. Pays good rates, on acceptance. Query.

SATELLITE ORBIT—8330 Boone Blvd., Vienna, VA 22180. Mike Doan, Ed. Television-related articles, 750 to 2,500 words; personality profiles; and articles of interest to the satellite and cable TV viewer. Query with clips. Pay varies, on acceptance.

THE SATURDAY EVENING POST—1100 Waterway Blvd., Indianapolis, IN 46202. Ted Kreiter, Exec. Ed. Family-oriented articles, 1,500 to 3,000 words: humor, preventive medicine, destination-oriented travel pieces (not personal experience), celebrity profile, the arts, and sciences. Pieces on sports and home repair (with photos). Photo essays. Pays varying rates, on publication. Queries preferred.

SAVVY WOMAN (FORMERLY *SAVVY*)—3 Park Ave., New York, NY 10016. Analyn Swan, Ed. Profiles of successful women in all fields, and articles that relate to women, 3,000 words. Payment varies. Query.

SELF—3 Park Ave., New York, NY 10017. Anthea Disney, Ed. Articles for women of all ages, with strong how-to slant, on self-development. Pays from $700, on acceptance. Query.

STAR—660 White Plains Rd., Tarrytown, NY 10591. Topical articles, 50 to 800 words, on human-interest subjects, show business, lifestyles, the sciences, etc., for family audience. Pays varying rates.

SUCCESS—342 Madison Ave., New York, NY 10175. Scott Degarmo, Ed.-in-Chief. Profiles of successful executives, entrepreneurs; management science, psychology, behavior, and motivation articles, 500 to 3,500 words. Query.

SUNDAY JOURNAL MAGAZINE— *Providence Sunday Journal,* 75 Fountain St., Providence, RI 02902. Doug Cumming, Ed. Features and essays, 300 to 1,000 words, with emphasis on prose style; articles on some aspect of life in New England, especially Rhode Island and S.E. Massachusetts. Pays $75 to $750, on acceptance. Query preferred; send published clips.

TOWN & COUNTRY—1700 Broadway, New York, NY 10019. Address

Features Dept. Considers one page proposals for articles. Rarely buys unsolicited manuscripts.

TRAVEL & LEISURE—1120 Ave. of the Americas, New York, NY 10036. Pamela Fiori, Ed.-in-Chief. Articles, 800 to 3,000 words, on destinations and leisure-time activities. Regional pieces for regional editions. Pays $600 to $3,000, on acceptance. Query.

TROPIC— *The Miami Herald,* One Herald Plaza, Miami, FL 33132. Tom Shroder, Assoc. Ed. Essays and articles on current trends and issues, light or heavy, 1,000 to 4,000 words, for sophisticated audience. Pays $200 to $1,000, on publication. Query with SASE; 4 to 6 weeks for reponse.

TV GUIDE—Radnor, PA 19088. Andrew Mills, Asst. Man. Ed. Short, light, brightly-written pieces about humorous or offbeat angles of television. Pays on acceptance. Query.

US MAGAZINE—One Dag Hammarskjold Plaza, New York, NY 10017. Steven Redicliffe, Man. Ed. Cyndi Stivers, Sr. Ed. Articles, 750 to 3,500 words, on celebrities and entertainment-related topics. Pays from $500, on publication. Query with published clips required.

VANITY FAIR—350 Madison Ave., New York, NY 10017. Wayne Lawson, Ed. Articles. Pays on acceptance. Query.

VILLAGE VOICE—842 Broadway, New York, NY 10003. David Herndon, Man. Ed. Articles, 500 to 2,000 words, on current or controversial topics. Pays $75 to $450, on acceptance. Query or send manuscript with SASE.

VISTA—999 Ponce, Suite 600, Coral Gables, FL 33134. Renato Perez, Man. Ed. Articles, 2,000 words, for English-speaking Hispanic Americans, on job advancement, bilingualism, immigration, the media, fashion, education, medicine, sports, and food. Profiles, 100 words, of Hispanic Americans in unusual jobs; photos welcome. Pays 20¢ a word, on acceptance. Query required.

VOGUE—350 Madison Ave., New York, NY 10017. Amy Gross, Features Ed. Articles, to 1,500 words, on women, entertainment and the arts, travel, medicine and health. General features. Query.

VOLKSWAGEN'S WORLD—Volkswagen of America, Troy, MI 48099. Marlene Goldsmith, Ed. Articles, 600 to 1,000 words, for Volkswagen owners: profiles of well-known personalities; inspirational or human-interest pieces; travel; humor. Photos. Pays $150 per printed page, on acceptance. Query. Guidelines.

WASHINGTON POST MAGAZINE— *The Washington Post,* 1150 15th St. N.W., Washington, DC 20071. Stephen L. Petranek, Man. Ed. Personal-experience essays, profiles and general-interest pieces, to 5,000 words, on business, arts and culture, politics, science, sports, education, children, relstionships, behavior, etc. Pays from $1,000, after acceptance.

WEEKLY WORLD NEWS—600 S. East Coast Ave., Lantana, FL 33462. Joe West, Ed. Human-interest news pieces, about 500 to 1,000 words: human adventure, unusual situations. Pays $125 to $500, on publication.

WOMAN'S DAY—1515 Broadway, New York, NY 10036. Rebecca Greer, Articles Ed. Articles, 500 to 3,500 words, on subjects of interest to women: marriage, education, family health, child rearing, money management, interpersonal relationships, changing lifestyles, etc. Dramatic first-person narratives about women who have experienced medical miracles or other triumphs, or have overcome common problems, such as alcoholism. "Reflections": short, provocative personal essays, 1,000 to 1,500 words, humorous or serious, dealing with concerns of interest and relevance to women. Pays $2,000 for essays, top rates for articles, on acceptance.

WOMAN'S WORLD—177 N. Dean St., Englewood, NJ 07631. Gerry Hunt, Sr. Ed. Articles, 600 to 1,800 words, on interest to middle-income women between the ages of 18 and 60, on love, romance, careers, medicine, health, psychology, family life, travel, dramatic stories of adventure or crisis. Pays $300 to $750, on acceptance. Query.

WORKING WOMAN—342 Madison Ave., New York, NY 10173. Anne Mollegen Smith, Ed. Articles, 1,000 to 2,500 words, on business and personal aspects of working women's lives. Pays from $400, on acceptance.

YANKEE—Dublin, NH 03444. Judson D. Hale, Ed. Articles, to 3,000 words, with New England angle. Photos. Pays $150 to $1,000 (average $750), on acceptance.

CURRENT EVENTS, POLITICS

AFRICA REPORT—833 U.N. Pl., New York, NY 10017. Margaret A. Novicki, Ed. Well-researched articles by specialists, 1,000 to 4,000 words, with photos, on current African affairs. Pays $150 to $250, on publication.

THE AMERICAN LEGION MAGAZINE—Box 1055, Indianapolis, IN 46206. Michael D. LaBonne, Ed. Articles, 750 to 1,800 words, on current world affairs, public policy, and subjects of contemporary interest. Pays $100 to $1,000, on acceptance. Query.

AMERICAN POLITICS—810 18th St. N.W., Washington, DC 20006. Grant Oliphant, Ed. Narrative/feature articles, 1,200 to 2,500 words, on how politics affect individuals, and on "how individual or local dilemmas cast light on national problems." No op-ed or journal-style analysis. Pay varies, 30 days after publication. Query.

THE AMERICAN SCHOLAR—1811 Q St. N.W., Washington, DC 20009. Joseph Epstein, Ed. Non-technical articles and essays, 3,500 to 4,000 words, on current affairs, the American cultural scene, politics, arts, religion and science. Pays $450, on acceptance.

THE AMICUS JOURNAL—Natural Resources Defense Council, 122 E. 42nd St., Rm. 4500, New York, NY 10168. Peter Borrelli, Ed. Investigative articles, book reviews, and poetry related to national and international environmental policy. Pays varying rates, on acceptance. Queries required.

THE ATLANTIC—8 Arlington St., Boston, MA 02116. William Whitworth, Ed. In-depth articles on public issues, politics, social sciences, education, business, literature, and the arts, with emphasis on information rather than opinion. Ideal length: 3,000 to 6,000 words, though short pieces (1,000 to 2,000 words) are also welcome. Pays $1,000 to $7,000, on acceptance.

COMMENTARY—165 E. 56th St., New York, NY 10022. Norman Podhoretz, Ed. Articles, 5,000 to 7,000 words, on contemporary issues, Jewish affairs, social sciences, community life, religious thought, cultural activities. Pays about 20¢ a word, on publication.

COMMONWEAL—15 Dutch St., New York, NY 10038. Margaret O'Brien Steinfels, Ed. Catholic. Articles, to 3,000 words, on political, social, religious and literary subjects. Pays 3¢ a word, on acceptance.

THE CRISIS—4017 24th St., #8, San Francisco, CA 94114. Fred Beauford,

Ed. Articles, to 1,500 words, on the arts, civil rights, and problems and achievements of blacks and other minorities. Pays $75 to $500, on acceptance.

ENVIRONMENT—4000 Albemarle St. N.W., Washington, DC 20016. Jane Scully, Man. Ed. Articles, 2,500 to 6,500 words, on environmental, scientific and technological policy and decision-making issues. Pays $75 to $300, on publication. Query.

FOREIGN POLICY JOURNAL—11 Dupont Circle N.W., Washington, DC 20036. Charles William Maynes, Ed. Articles, 3,000 to 5,000 words, on international affairs. Honorarium, on publication. Query.

FOREIGN SERVICE JOURNAL—2101 E. St. N. W., Washington, D.C. 20037. Stephen R. Dujack, Ed. Articles on American diplomacy, foreign affairs and subjects of interest to Americans representing U.S. abroad. Pays 2¢ to 10¢ a word, on publication. Query.

THE FREEMAN—Foundation for Economic Education, Irvington-on-Hudson, NY 10533. Brian Summers, Sr. Ed. Articles, to 3,500 words, on economic political, and moral implications of private property, voluntary exchange, and individual choice. Pays 10¢ a word, on publication.

INQUIRER MAGAZINE— *Philadelphia Inquirer,* P.O. Box 8263, 400 N. Broad St., Philadelphia, PA 19101. Fred Mann, Ed. Local-interest features, 500 to 7,000 words. Profiles of national figures in politics, entertainment, etc. Pays varying rates, on publication. Query.

IRISH AMERICA—432 Park Ave. S., Suite 1000, New York, NY 10016. Sean O'Murchu, Sr. Ed. Articles, 1,000 words, of interest to Irish-American audience; preferred topics include history and politics. Pays 7¢ a word, after publication. Query.

MIDSTREAM—515 Park Ave., New York, NY 10022. Murray Zuckoff, Ed. Jewish-interest articles and book reviews. Pays 5¢ a word, after publication.

MOMENT—3000 Connecticut Ave., Suite 300, Washington, DC 20008. Charlotte Anker, Man. Ed. Sophisticated articles and some fiction, 2,500 to 5,000 words, on Jewish topics. Pays $150 to $400, on publication.

MOTHER JONES—1663 Mission St., San Francisco, CA 94103. Doug Foster, Ed. Investigative articles, political essays, cultural analyses. Pays $750 to $2,000, after acceptance. Query in writing only.

THE NATION—72 Fifth Ave., New York, NY 10011. Victor Navasky, Ed. Articles, 1,500 to 2,500 words, on politics and culture from a liberal/left perspective. Pays $75 per published page, to $300, on publication. Query.

THE NEW YORK TIMES MAGAZINE—229 W. 43rd St., New York, NY 10036. Address Articles Ed. Timely articles, approximately 4,000 words, on news items, trends, culture, etc. Pays $350 to $500 for short pieces, $1,000 to $2,500 for major articles, on acceptance. Query with clips.

THE NEW YORKER—25 W. 43rd St., New York, NY 10036. Address the Editors. Factual and biographics articles, for "Profiles," "Reporter at Large," "Annals of Crime," "Onward and Upward with the Arts," etc. Pays good rates, on acceptance. Query.

NEWSWEEK—444 Madison Ave., New York, NY 10022. Phyllis Malamud, My Turn Ed. Original opinion essays, 1,000 to 1,100 words, for "My Turn" column; must contain verifiable facts. Submit manuscript with SASE. Pays $1,000, on publication.

535

NUCLEAR TIMES—1601 Connecticut Ave. N.W., Suite 300, Washington, DC 20009. Elliott Negin, Ed. News and feature articles, 500 to 4,000 words, on the nuclear disarmament movement, the arms race, nuclear weapons, U.S.-Soviet relations, and the militarization of American culture. Pays 15¢ a word, on publication.

POLITICAL WOMAN—4521 Campus Dr., #388, Irvine, CA 92715. Sally Corngold, Ed. Well-documented, nonpartisan articles, 1,000 to 3,000 words, for "thinking women." Pays $25 to $1,000, on publication.

PRESENT TENSE—165 E. 56th St., New York, NY 10022. Murray Polner, Ed. Serious reportage and political journalism, 2,000 to 3,000 words, on contemporary developments concerning Jews worldwide. Pays $100 to $250, on publication. Query.

THE PROGRESSIVE—409 E. Main St., Madison, WI 53703. Erwin Knoll, Ed. Articles, 1,000 to 3,500 words, on political, social problems. Light features. Pays $75 to $300, on publication.

PUBLIC CITIZEN MAGAZINE—2000 P St. N.W., Suite 605, Washington, DC 20036. Catherine Baker, Ed. Investigative reports and articles of timely political interest, for members of Public Citizen: consumer rights, health and safety, environmental protection, safe energy, tax reform and government and corporate accountability. Photos, illustrations. Pays to $500.

REGARDIE'S—1010 Wisconsin Ave. N.W., Suite 600, Washington, DC 20007. Brian Kelly, Ed. Profiles and investigations of the "high and mighty" in the DC area: "We require aggressive reporting and imaginative, entertaining writing." Pays 50¢ a word, on publication. Queries required.

ROLL CALL: THE NEWSPAPER OF CAPITOL HILL—317 Massachusetts Ave. N.E., Washington, DC 20002. James K. Glassman, Ed.-in-Chief. Factual, breezy articles with political or Congressional angle: Congressional historical and human-interest subjects, political lore, etc. Political satire and humor. Pays on publication.

THE ROTARIAN—1560 Sherman Ave., Evanston, IL 60201. Willmon L. White, Ed. Articles, 1,200 to 2,000 words, on international social and economic issues, business and management, environment, science and technology. "No direct political or religious slants." Pays good rates, on acceptance. Query.

SATURDAY NIGHT—36 Toronto St., Suite 1160, Toronto, Ont., Canada M5C 2C5. John Fraser, Ed. Canada's oldest magazine of politics, social issues, culture, and business. Features, 1,000 to 3,000 words, and columns, 800 to 1,000 words; fiction, to 3,000 words; one-page puzzles for "Cryptic Crossword." Must have Canadian tie-in. Payment varies, on acceptance.

TROPIC— *The Miami Herald,* One Herald Plaza, Miami, FL 33132. Tom Shroder, Assoc. Ed. Essays and articles on current trends and issues, light or heavy, 1,000 to 4,000 words, for sophisticated audience. Pays $200 to $1,000, on publication. Query with SASE; 4 to 6 weeks for response.

VFW MAGAZINE—Broadway at 34th, Kansas City, MO 64111. James K. Anderson, Ed. Magazine for Veterans of Foreign Wars and their families. Articles, 1,000 words, on current issues and history, with veteran angle. Photos. Pays from $200, extra for photos, on acceptance.

VILLAGE VOICE—842 Broadway, New York, NY 10003. David Herndon, Man. Ed. Articles, 500 to 2,000 words, on current or controversial topics. Pays $75 to $450, on acceptance. Query or send manuscript with SASE.

536

THE WASHINGTON MONTHLY—1711 Connecticut Ave. N.W., Washington, DC 20009. Charles Peters, Ed. Investigative articles, 1,500 to 5,000 words, on politics, government and the political culture. Pays 10¢ a word, on publication. Query.

WASHINGTON POST MAGAZINE— *The Washington Post,* 1150 15 St. N.W., Washington, DC 20071. Stephen L. Petranek, Man. Ed. Personal-experience essays, profiles and general-interest pieces, to 5,000 words, on business, arts and culture, politics, science, sports, education, children, relationships, behavior, etc. Pays from $1,000, after acceptance.

REGIONAL AND CITY PUBLICATIONS

ADIRONDACK LIFE—P.O. Box 97, Jay, NY 12941. Christopher Shaw, Ed. Features, to 3,000 words, on outdoor and environmental activities and issues, arts, wilderness, profiles and history; focus is on the Adirondack region and North Country of New York State. Pays to 25¢ a word, on acceptance. Query.

ALASKA—808 E St., Suite 200, Anchorage, AK 99501. Ron Dalby, Ed. Articles, 1,500 words, on life in Alaska and Northwestern Canada. Pays varying rates, on acceptance. Guidelines.

ALOHA, THE MAGAZINE OF HAWAII—P.O. Box 3260, Honolulu, HI 96801. Cheryl Chee Tsutsumi, Ed. Articles, 1,500 to 4,000 words, on the life, customs, and people of Hawaii and the Pacific. Poetry. Fiction. Pays 10¢ a word, on publication. Query first.

AMERICAN WEST—7000 E. Tanque Verde Rd., Tucson, AZ 85715. Mae Reid-Bills, Man. Ed. Articles, 2,500 to 3,000 words, and department pieces, 900 to 1,000 words, that celebrate the West, past and present; emphasis on travel. Pays $200 to $800, on acceptance. Query required.

ARIZONA HIGHWAYS—2039 W. Lewis Ave., Phoenix, AZ 85009. Merrill Windsor, Ed. Articles, 2,000 words, on travel in Arizona; pieces on adventure, humor, life styles, nostalgia, history, archaeology. Pays 35¢ to 40¢ a word, on acceptance. Query first.

ARKANSAS TIMES—Box 34010, Little Rock, AR 72203. Mel White, Ed. Articles, to 6,000 words, on Arkansas history, people, travel, politics. All articles must have strong AR orientation. Pays to $500, on acceptance.

ATLANTA—1360 Peachtree St., Suite 1800, Atlanta, GA 30309. Lee Walburn, Ed. Articles, 1,500 to 5,000 words, on Atlanta subjects or personalities. Pays $600 to $1,200, on publication. Query.

THE ATLANTIC ADVOCATE—P.O. Box 3370, Gleaner Bldg., Prospect St., Fredericton, N.B., Canada E3B 5A2. Harold P. Wood, Ed. Well-researched articles on Atlantic Canada and general-interest subjects; fiction, to 1,500 words. Pays to 8¢ a word, on publication.

ATLANTIC CITY MAGAZINE—1637 Atlantic Ave., Atlantic City, NJ 08401. Ronnie Polaneczky, Ed. Lively articles, 500 to 5,000 words, on Atlantic City and Southern New Jersey: casinos, business, personalities, environment, local color, crime, for locals and tourists. Pays $100 to $600, on publication. Query.

AUSTIN MAGAZINE—P.O. Box 4368, Austin, TX 78765. Laura Tuma, Man. Ed. Profiles, civic affairs and general-interest articles, 750 to 3,000 words, with local business focus. Query preferred. Pays $75 to $400, on publication.

BAKERSFIELD LIFESTYLE—123 Truxtun Ave., Bakersfield, CA 93301.

Steve Walsh, Ed. Articles and fiction with local slant, 1,500 to 2,000 words. Pays $15, on publication.

BALTIMORE MAGAZINE—26 S. Calvert St., Baltimore, MD 21202. Eric Douglas, Exec. Ed. Articles, 500 to 3,000 words, on people, places, and things in the Baltimore metropolitan area. Consumer advice, investigative pieces, profiles, humor, and personal experience pieces. Payment varies, on publication. Query required.

BIRMINGHAM—2027 First Ave. N., Birmingham, AL 35203. Joe O'Donnell, Ed. Personality profiles and nostalgia pieces (to 8 pages) with Birmingham tie-in. Pays $50 to $175, on publication.

BOCA RATON—JES Publishing, Amtec Center, Suite 100, 6413 Congress Ave., Boca Raton, FL 33487. Barbara Westlake-Kenny, Ed. Articles, 800 to 3,000 words, on Florida topics, personalities, and travel. Pays $175 to $500, on publication. Query with clips required.

BOSTON GLOBE MAGAZINE— *The Boston Globe,* Boston, MA 02107. Ande Zellman, Ed. General-interest articles, interviews, and profiles, 2,500 to 5,000 words. Query required.

BOSTON MAGAZINE—300 Massachusetts Ave., Boston, MA 02115. David Rosenbaum, Ed. Informative, entertaining features, 1,000 to 4,000 words, on Boston area personalities, institutions and phenomena. Pays $250 to $1,200, on publication. Query Betsy Buffington, Man. Ed., or Janice Brand, Service Features Ed.

BOSTONIA—10 Lenox St., Brookline, MA 02146. Laura Freid, Ed. Articles (1,800 words) on politics, the arts, travel, food, and wine; life style essays (1,200 words) with regional tie-in. Pays $150 to $800, on publication. Queries required.

BOUNDARY WATERS JOURNAL—Route 1, Box 1740, Ely, MN 55731. Stuart Osthoff, Ed. Articles, 2,000 to 3,000 words, on recreation and natural resources in Minnesota's Boundary Waters region, including canoe routes, life styles of residents, hiking, and events. Pays $200 to $400, on publication.

BUFFALO SPREE MAGAZINE—Box 38, Buffalo, NY 14226. Johanna Shotell, Ed. Articles, to 1,800 words. Pays $75 to $100, $25 for poetry, on publication.

BUSINESS IN BROWARD—1040 Bayview Dr., Suite 210, Ft. Lauderdale, FL 33304. T. Constance Coyne, Ed. Small business regional quarterly; 2,500-word articles for eastern Florida county. Pay varies, on acceptance.

CALIFORNIA—11601 Wilshire Blvd., Los Angeles, CA 90025. Rebecca Levy, Man. Ed. Features with a California focus, on politics, business, environmental issues, ethnic diversity, travel, style, fashions, restaurants, the arts, and sports. Service pieces, profiles, and well-researched investigative articles. Pays $500 to $2,500 for features, $250 to $500 for shorter articles, on acceptance. Query first.

CALIFORNIA BUSINESS—4221 Wilshire Blvd., Suite 400, Los Angeles, CA 90010. Joan Yee, Ed. Articles, 500 to 5,000 words, on Los Angeles-based businesses. Payment varies, on acceptance. Query.

CALIFORNIA FOOTBALL MAGAZINE—1801 S. Catalina Ave., Suite 301, Redondo Beach, CA 90277. Dorothy Sirus, Exec. Ed. Articles, 250 to 2,000 words, related to California high school, junior college, and college football programs and standout Californians playing in other states. Pays $25 to $300, on acceptance. Query with writing samples.

CAPE COD LIFE—P.O. Box 222, Osterville, MA 02655. Brian F. Shortsleeve, Pub. Articles on current events, business, art, and gardening, 2,000 words. Pays 10¢ a word, 30 days after publication. Queries preferred.

CAPITAL REGION MAGAZINE—4 Central Ave., Albany, NY 12204. David Levine, Man. Ed. News, features, and profiles with Albany, New York, angle (1,000 to 5,000 words); fillers, shorts, and humor (250 to 500 words). Pays 10¢ a word, on acceptance. Query required.

CAPITOL, THE COLUMBUS DISPATCH SUNDAY MAGAZINE— *The Columbus Dispatch,* Columbus, OH 43216. T.R. Fitchko, Ed. General-interest pieces, essays, humorous articles, to 3,000 words. Pays varying rates, on publication.

CARIBBEAN TRAVEL AND LIFE—606 N. Washington St., Alexandria, VA 22314. Veronica Gould Stoddart, Ed. Articles, 500 to 3,000 words, on all aspects of travel, recreation, leisure, and culture in the Caribbean, Bahamas, and Bermuda. Pays $75 to $550, on publication. Query with published clips.

CHESAPEAKE BAY MAGAZINE—1819 Bay Ridge Ave., Annapolis, MD 21403. Betty D. Rigoli, Ed. Articles, 8 to 10 typed pages, related to the Chesapeake Bay area. Profiles. Photos. Pays $75 to $125, on publication. Query first.

CHICAGO—414 N. Orleans, Chicago, IL 60610. Joanne Trestrail, Man. Ed. Articles, 1,000 to 5,000 words, related to Chicago. Pays varying rates, on acceptance. Query.

CHICAGO HISTORY—Clark St. at North Ave., Chicago, IL 60614. Russell Lewis, Ed. Articles, to 4,500 words, on urban political, social and cultural history. Pays to $250, on publication. Query.

CINCINNATI MAGAZINE—409 Broadway, Cincinnati, OH 45202. Laura Pulfer, Ed./Pub. Articles, 1,000 to 3,000 words, on Cincinnati people and issues. Pays $75 to $100 for 1,000 words, on acceptance. Query with writing sample.

CITY MAGAZINE (FORMERLY *INDIANAPOLIS MAGAZINE*)—5563 W. 73rd St., Indianapolis, IN 46268. Nancy Comiskey, Ed. Articles on health, business, sports, people, etc., with regional tie-in. Lengths vary, to 12 pages. Pays $40 to $300, on publication. Query required.

CITY SPORTS—P.O. Box 3693, San Francisco, CA 94119. Jane McConnell, Ed. Northern California. Greg Ptacek, Ed. Southern California: 1120 Princeton Dr., Marina Del Rey, CA 90291. Will Balliet, Ed. New York: 140 W. 22nd St., New York, NY 10011. Peg Moline, Ed. Boston: 48 Grove St., Boston, MA 02144. Articles, 500 to 2,000 words, on participant sports and the active lifestyle. Pays $100 to $650, on acceptance. Query appropriate editor first.

CLINTON STREET QUARTERLY—Box 3588, Portland, OR 97208. David Milholland, Ed. Articles (to 15 pages) and creative fiction (2 to 20 pages) on Pacific Northwest themes: "eclectic blend of politics, culture, humor and art." Compelling first-person accounts welcome. Pays $50 to $200, on publication.

COLORADO BUSINESS—5951 S. Middlefield Rd., Littleton, CO 80123. Ann Feeney, Ed. Articles, to 1,500 words, on banking, real estate, transportation, manufacturing, etc., in Colorado. Pays 10¢ a word, on publication. Query.

COLORADO HOMES & LIFESTYLES—2250 31st St., Suite 154, Denver, CO 80216. Ania Savage, Man. Ed. Articles on topics related to Colorado: travel, fashion, design and decorating, gardening, luxury real estate, art, celebrity lifestyles, people, food and entertaining. Pays to 20¢ a word, on acceptance.

CONNECTICUT—P.O. Box 6480, Bridgeport, CT 06606. Sara J. Cuneo, Ed. Articles, 1,500 to 2,500 words, on Connecticut topics, issues, people and life styles. Pays $500 to $800, on publication.

CONNECTICUT TRAVELER—2276 Whitney Ave., Hamden, CT 06518.

Elke P. Martin, Man. Dir. Articles, 500 to 1,200 words, on travel and tourist attractions in New England. B&W photos. Pays $50 to $250, on acceptance. Query.

COOSA VALLEY VIEW—13 Public Sq., Cartersville, GA 30120. John Willis, Man. Ed. Articles, 500 to 750 words, on business and economic developments in North Georgia; profiles, 500 to 750 words. Pays 5¢ to 10¢ a word, on publication.

THE COVENTRY JOURNAL—P.O. Box 124, Andover, CT 06232. Bill Cisowski, Ed. Articles, to 2,000 words, about the Eastern Connecticut region: historical, how-to gardening, travel, and events. Pays $50 to $250, on acceptance.

CRAIN'S DETROIT BUSINESS—1400 Woodbridge, Detroit, MI 48207. Peter Brown, Ed. Business articles, 500 to 1,000 words, about Detroit, for Detroit business readers. Pays $75 to $150, on acceptance. Query required.

CREATING EXCELLENCE—New World Publishing, P.O. Box 2084, S. Burlington, VT 05403. David Robinson, Ed. Self-help and inspirational articles, profiles, and essays related to Northern Vermont. Pays $75 to $250, on publication.

D—3988 N. Central Expressway, Suite 1200, Dallas, TX 75204. Ruth Fitzgibbons, Ed. In-depth investigative pieces on current trends and problems, personality profiles, and general-interest articles on the arts, travel, and business, for upper-class residents of Dallas. Pays $350 to $500 for departments, $800 to $1,200 for features. Written queries only.

DALLAS LIFE MAGAZINE— *The Dallas Morning News,* Communications Center, Dallas, TX 75265. Melissa Houtte, Ed. Well-researched articles and profiles, 1,000 to 3,000 words, on contemporary issues, personalities, or subjects of strictly Dallas-related interest. Pays from 25¢ a word, on acceptance. Query required.

DALLAS MAGAZINE—1201 Elm., Suite 2000, Dallas, TX 75270. Jeff Hampton, Ed. Features, 2,500 words, on business and businesses in Dallas. Department pieces, 1,500 words. Pays $100 to $600, on acceptance. Query required.

DELAWARE TODAY—P.O. Box 4440, Wilmington, DE 19807. Lise Monty, Ed. Service articles, profiles, news, etc., on topics of local interest. Pays $75 to $125 for department pieces, $125 to $300 for features, on publication. Queries with clips required.

DETROIT MAGAZINE— *Detroit Free Press,* 321 W. Lafayette Blvd., Detroit, MI 48231. Articles, to 4,000 words, with a Detroit-area or Michigan focus, on issues, lifestyles. Personality profiles; essays; humor. Pays $100 to $600. Query required.

DETROIT MONTHLY—1400 Woodbridge, Detroit, MI 48207. Jack Lessenberry, Ed. Articles on Detroit-area people, issues, life styles and business. Payment varies. Query required.

DOMAIN—P.O. Box 1569, Austin, TX 78767. Catherine Chadwick, Ed. Quarterly life-style supplement to *Texas Monthly.* Articles on Texas architecture, art, design, and cuisine (to four pages). Payment varies, on acceptance. Query.

DOSSIER—See *Washington Dossier.*

DOWN EAST—Camden, ME 04843. Davis Thomas, Ed. Articles, 1,500 to 2,500 words, on all aspects of life in Maine. Photos. Pays to 15¢ a word, extra for photos, on acceptance. Query.

ERIE & CHAUTAUQUA MAGAZINE—Charles H. Stong Bldg., 1250 Tower La., Erie, PA 16505. Kim Kalvelage, Man. Ed. Feature articles, to 2,500 words, on issues of interest to upscale readers in the Erie, Warren, and Crawford counties (PA), and Chautauqua (NY) county. Pieces with regional relevance. Pays after publication. Query preferred, with writing samples. Buys all rights. Guidelines available.

FLORIDA GULF COAST HOME BUYER'S GUIDE (FORMERLY *FLORIDA GULF COAST LIVING)*—1311 N. Westshore Blvd., Suite 109, Tampa, FL 33607. Milana Petty, Ed. Articles, 750 to 1,200 words, for the active home buyer on the Gulf Coast: home-related articles, moving tips, financing, etc. Pays 7¢ to 10¢ a word, on acceptance. Query preferred.

FLORIDA HOME & GARDEN (FORMERLY *SOUTH FLORIDA HOME & GARDEN)*—600 Brickell Ave., Suite 207, Miami, FL 33131. Kathryn Howard, Ed. Features, 800 to 1,000 words, and department pieces, 500 to 900 words, about Florida interior design, architecture, landscape architecture, gardening, cuisine, fashion, trendy new products, medical/health and beauty, and home entertaining. Pays $200 to $400, photos extra.

FLORIDA KEYS MAGAZINE—505 Duval St., Upper Suite, Key West, FL 33040. David Ethridge, Ed. Articles, 1,000 to 4,000 words, on the Florida Keys: history, environment, natural history, profiles, etc. Fillers, humor. Photos. Pays varying rates, on publication. Query preferred.

FLORIDA TREND—Box 611, St. Petersburg, FL 33731. Matt Walsh, Ed. Articles, to 2,000 words, on Florida business and businesspersons. Photos. Query.

GEORGIA JOURNAL—Grimes Publications, P.O. Box 27, Athens, GA 30603–0027. Articles, 1,200 words, on people, events, travel, etc. in and around GA. Poetry, to 20 lines. Pays $20 to $35, on acceptance.

GO: THE AUTHENTIC GUIDE TO NEW ORLEANS—541 Julia St., New Orleans, LA 70130. Katherine Dinker, Ed. Articles, 1,200 words, of interest to New Orleans visitors. Pays $150, on publication. Query required.

GOLD COAST LIFE MAGAZINE—700 E. Atlantic Blvd., Suite 201, Pompano Beach, FL 33060. Fern Matthews, Ed. Articles, from 1,000 words, on life styles of southeastern Florida. Pays $50 to $250, on publication.

GOLDEN YEARS—233 E. New Haven Ave., Melbourne, FL 32902–0537. Carol Brenner Hittner, Ed. Controlled-circulation monthly for Florida residents over the age of 50. Pieces on unique hobbies, beauty and fashion, sports, and travel, 500 words. Pays 10¢ a word, on publication.

GREAT LAKES SAILOR—572 W. Market St., Suite 6, P.O. Box 951, Akron, OH 44309. Drew Shippy, Ed. Department pieces: "Destinations" (2,500 to 3,000 words, on cruises); "Trailor Sailor" (trips for day sailors, to 1,500 words); and "First Person" (profiles, 2,500 to 3,000 words). How-to pieces on sailing and navigational techniques, human-interest stories. Photos. Pays to 10¢ a word, on publication. Queries required. Guidelines.

GULFSHORE LIFE—2975 S. Horseshoe Dr., Naples, FL 33942. G. Stephen Weichelt, Ed. Articles, 950 to 3,500 words, on personalities, travel, sports, business, investment, nature, in southwestern Florida. Pays $50 to $300. Query.

HAWAII—Box 6050, Mission Viejo, CA 92690. Dennis Shattuck, Ed. Articles related to Hawaii. Pays 7¢ a word, on publication. Query.

HIGH COUNTRY NEWS—Box 1090, Paonia, CO 81428. Betsy Marston, Ed. Articles on environmental land management, energy and natural resource issues; profiles of western innovators; pieces on western politics. Poetry. B & W photos. Pays $2 to $4 per column inch, on publication, for 750-word roundups and 2,000-word features. Query first.

HONOLULU—36 Merchant St., Honolulu, HI 96813. Brian Nicol, Ed. Features highlighting life in the Hawaiian islands: politics, sports, history, people, events are all subjects of interest. Pays $400, on acceptance. Columns and department pieces are mostly staff-written. Queries required.

ILLINOIS ENTERTAINER—2200 E. Devon, Suite 192, Des Plaines, IL 60018. Bill Dalton, Ed. Articles, 500 to 1,500 words, on local and national entertainment and leisure time activities in the greater Chicago area. Personality profiles; interviews; reviews. Photos. Pays varying rates on publication. Query preferred.

ILLINOIS TIMES—Box 3524, Springfield, IL 62708. Fletcher Farrar, Jr., Ed. Articles, 1,000 to 2,500 words, on people, places, and activities of Illinois, outside the Chicago metropolitan area. Pays 4¢ a word, on publication. Query required.

IMAGE— *San Francisco Examiner,* 110 Fifth St., San Francisco, CA 94103. Articles, 1,200 to 4,000 words, on life styles, issues, business, history, events, and people in Northern California. Query first. Pays varying rates.

INDIANA HORIZONS—5563 W. 73rd St., Indianapolis, IN 46268. Jane Graham, Man. Ed. Quarterly. Articles, 750 to 2,000 words, of interest to active Indiana residents, 50 years and older. Profiles, 250 words, for "Indiana Achievers." Pays $100 to $350, $30 for profiles, on publication.

INDIANAPOLIS MAGAZINE—See *City Magazine.*

INDIANAPOLIS MONTHLY—8425 Keystone Crossing, Indianapolis, IN 46240. Deborah Paul, Ed.-in-Chief. Sam Stall, Assoc. Ed. Articles, 1,000 words, on health, sports, politics, business, interior design, travel, and Indiana personalities. All material must have a regional focus. Pays varying rates, on publication.

INDUSTRY MAGAZINE—441 Stuart St., Boston, MA 02116. Angelo Alabiso, Ed. Articles, 1,200 to 1,500 words, related to industry in Massachusetts. Pays negotiable rates, on acceptance. Queries required.

INLAND, THE MAGAZINE OF THE MIDDLE WEST—Inland Steel Co., 18 South Home Ave., Park Ridge, IL 60068. Sheldon A. Mix, Man. Ed. Articles, varying lengths, of interest to Midwestern readers. Pays on acceptance.

INQUIRER MAGAZINE— *Philadelphia Inquirer,* 400 N. Broad St., Philadelphia, PA 19101. Fred Mann, Ed. Articles, 1,500 to 2,000 words, and 3,000 to 7,000 words, on politics, science, arts and culture, business, life styles, and entertainment, sports, health, beauty, psychology, education, religion, home and garden, and humor. Short pieces, 200 to 800 words, for "Our Town" department. Pays varying rates. Query.

INSIDE CHICAGO—2501 W. Peterson Ave., Chicago, IL 60659. Barbara Young, Man. Ed. Features, to 3,000 words, on Chicago-related trends, profiles of Chicagoans, entrepreneuring, architecture (to 1,500 words). Short reports, 200 to 700 words. Department pieces, 1,000 to 1,500 words. Pays varying rates, on acceptance. Query.

THE IOWAN MAGAZINE—108 Third St., Suite 350, Des Moines, IA 50309. Charles W. Roberts, Ed. Articles, 1,000 to 3,000 words, on business, arts, people and history of Iowa. Photos a plus. Pays $200 to $600, on publication. Query required.

ISLAND LIFE—P.O. Box X, Sanibel Island, FL 33957. Joan Hooper, Ed.

Articles, 500 to 1,200 words, with photos, on unique or historical places, wildlife, architecture, fashions, home decor, cuisine, on barrier islands off Florida's S.W. Gulf Coast. Pays 3¢ a word, on publication. SASE necesary.

JACKSONVILLE MAGAZINE—P.O. Box 329, Jacksonville, FL 32201. Carolyn Carroll, Ed. Articles of interest to the Northeast Florida community: strong regional slant a must. Pays $100 to $300, on acceptance. Query required.

JACKSONVILLE TODAY—White Publishing Co., 1325 San Marco Blvd., Suite 900, Jacksonville, FL 32207. Rejeanne Davis Ashley, Man. Ed. Articles, 1,500 to 2,000 words, and features, 2,000 to 3,000 words, relating to Jacksonville and North Florida personalities, life styles, business, politics, arts, and health topics. Pays $150 to $400, on publication. Query required.

KANSAS!—Kansas Dept. of Commerce, 400 W. Eighth Ave., 5th fl., Topeka, KS 66603–3957. Andrea Glenn, Ed. Quarterly. Articles of 5 to 7 typed pages on the people, places, history, and events of Kansas. Color slides. Pays to $150, on acceptance. Query.

L/A TODAY—250 Center St., Suite 500, Auburn, ME 04210. Howard Kany, Ed. Articles, 500 to 2,000 words, on Maine-related topics, for readers in Lewiston/Auburn area: personalities, profiles, places, and activities (contemporary or historical). Short poetry and fillers. Pays 10¢ a word, on publication.

L.A. WEST MAGAZINE—Santa Monica Bay Printing & Publishing, 919 Santa Monica Blvd., #245, Santa Monica, CA 90401. Jan Loomis, Ed. Essays, travel, and life style articles, 800 to 1,000 words, for upscale, well-educated audience. Pays $75 to $500, on acceptance. Queries required.

LAKE SUPERIOR MAGAZINE—325 Lake Ave. S., #100, Duluth, MN 55802. Paul Hayden, Ed. Articles with unusual twists on regional subjects; historical pieces that highlight the people, places and events that have affected the Lake Superior region. Pictorial essays; humor and occasional poetry. Pays to $400, after publication. Query first.

LONG ISLAND MONTHLY—CMP Publications, 600 Community Dr., Manhasset, NY 11030. John Atwood, Ed. "We seek to cover all aspects of Long Island, from politics and food to fashion and personalities." Payment varies, on acceptance. Query with clips.

THE LOOK—P.O. Box 272, Cranford, NJ 07016–0272. John R. Hawks, Pub. Articles, 1,500 to 3,000 words, on fashion, student life, employment, relationships, and profiles of interest to New Jersey readers aged 16 to 26. Pays $30 to $200, on publication.

LOS ANGELES MAGAZINE—1888 Century Park E., Los Angeles, CA 90067. Lew Harris, Exec. Ed. Articles, to 3,000 words, of interest to sophisticated, affluent southern Californians, preferably with local focus on a lifestyle topic. Pays from 10¢ a word, on acceptance. Query.

LOS ANGELES READER—12224 Victory Blvd., N. Hollywood, CA 91606. Lana H. Johnson, Ed. Articles, 750 to 2,500 words, on subjects relating to the Los Angeles/Southern California area; special emphasis on entertainment, feature journalism, and the arts. Pays $25 to $200, on publication. Query preferred.

LOS ANGELES TIMES MAGAZINE—Times Mirror Sq., Los Angeles, CA 90053. Michael Parrish, Ed. General-interest news features, photo spreads, profiles, and interviews focusing on people and events of interest in Southern California, to 3,500 words. Pays to $2,000, on acceptance. Query required.

LOUISVILLE—One Riverfront Plaza, Louisville, KY 40202. Betty Lou Amster, Ed. Articles, 1,000 to 2,000 words, on community issues, personalities, and entertainment in the Louisville area. Photos. Pays from $50, on acceptance. Query; articles on assignment only. Limited free-lance market.

MAGAZINE OF THE MIDLANDS— *Omaha World-Herald,* World Herald Sq., Omaha, NE 68102. David Hendee, Ed. General-interest articles, 800 to 2,000 words, and profiles tied to the Midwest. Photos. Pays $40 to $150, on publication. Query.

MAGNETIC NORTH—Thorn Books, Inc., Franconia, NH 03580. Jim McIntosh, Ed. Well-researched, offbeat articles, 500 to 1,500 words, for residents and visitors to New Hampshire's White Mountains. Pays $50 to $150, on publication. Query with SASE.

MAINE LIFE—250 Center St., Suite 500, Auburn, ME 04210. Howard Kany, Ed. Articles, to 3,000 words, about traveling, places to see, and things to do in Maine. Of particular interest are unusual or little-known spots. Features on contemporary social, political, economic, and environmental topics. Pays 10¢ a word, on publication.

MAINLINE STYLE MAGAZINE—P.O. Box 350, Wayne, PA 19087. Articles, 100 to 1,400 words, on leisure, business, history, travel, dining, food, sports, education, real estate, lifestyles, health, etc., with regional tie-in. Pays 15¢ a word, 30 days after publication.

MARYLAND—c/o Dept. of Economic and Community Development, 45 Calvert St., Annapolis, MD 21401. Bonnie Joe Ayers, Ed. Articles, 800 to 2,200 words, on Maryland subjects. Pays varies, on acceptance. Query preferred. Guidelines available.

MAUIAN MAGAZINE—P.O. Box 10669, Lahaina, Maui, HI 96761. Joe Harabin, Ed. Informative, thought-provoking, upbeat articles, 500 to 5,000 words, about any aspect of life and times on Maui—past, present, or future. Pays $50 to $500, on publication.

MEMPHIS—MM Corp., Box 256, Memphis, TN 38101. Larry Conley, Ed. Articles, 1,500 to 4,000 words, on a wide variety of topics related to Memphis and the Mid-South region: politics, education, sports, business, etc. Profiles; investigative pieces. Pays $75 to $1,000, on publication. Query. Guidelines available.

MIAMI/SOUTH FLORIDA MAGAZINE—See *South Florida Magazine.*

MICHIGAN BUSINESS—Cranbrook Center, Suite 302, 30161 Southfield Rd., Southfield, MI 48076. Ron Garbinski, Ed. Business news features on Michigan businesses. Query. Pay varies, on publication.

MICHIGAN LIVING—17000 Executive Plaza Dr., Dearborn, MI 48126. Len Barnes, Ed. Travel articles, 500 to 1,500 words, on tourist attractions and recreational opportunities in the U.S. and Canada, with emphasis on Michigan: places to go, things to do, costs, etc. Color photos. Pays $100 to $350, extra for photos, on acceptance.

MICHIGAN: THE MAGAZINE OF THE DETROIT NEWS—615 W. Lafayette Blvd., Detroit, MI 48231. Cynthia Boal-Janssens, Ed. Articles, from 750 words, on business, politics, arts and culture, science, people, sports and education, etc., with a Michigan slant. Cover articles, to 3,000 words. Some fiction. Pays $200 to $500, on publication.

MICHIGAN WOMAN—30400 Telegraph Rd., Suite 374, Birmingham, MI

48010. Monica Smiley, Ed. Articles, 750 words, highlighting the achievements and contributions of Michigan women in helping others enjoy more fulfilling careers and personal lives. Pays 10¢ a word, on publication. Query first.

MID-ATLANTIC COUNTRY—P.O. Box 246, Alexandria, VA 22313. Anne Elizabeth Dowell, Exec. Ed. Articles, 2,000 words, related to life in the Mid-Atlantic region: travel, home, food, gardening, antiques, history, architecture, and entertaining. Photos. Pays from $250, on publication. Query.

MID-WEST OUTDOORS—111 Shore Dr., Hinsdale, IL 60521. Gene Laulunen, Ed. Articles, 1,500 words, with photos, on where, when, and how to fish, within 500 miles of Chicago. Pays $25, on publication.

MILWAUKEE—312 E. Buffalo, Milwaukee, WI 53202. Judith Woodburn, Ed. Profiles, investigative articles, and historical pieces, 3,000 to 4,000 words; local tie-in a must. Some regional fiction. Pays $400 to $600, on publication. Query required.

MPLS. ST. PAUL—12 S. 6th St., Ste. 1030, Minneapolis, MN 55402. Claude Peck, Man. Ed. In-depth articles, features, profiles, and service pieces, 400 to 3,000 words, with Mpls.-St. Paul focus. Pays to $600.

MONTANA MAGAZINE—P.O. Box 5630, Helena, MT 59604. Carolyn Cunningham, Ed. Where-to-go items, regional profiles, photo essays. Montana-oriented only. B&W prints, color slides. Pays $75 to $350, on publication.

MYRTLE BEACH MAGAZINE—P.O. Box 1474, N. Myrtle Beach, SC 29598. Toby Beckham, Ed. Features, 1,500 to 2,500 words; articles, 500 to 1,500 words. Must have local angle and be geared for residents, not tourists, in the area. Pays from $75 for features, from $35 for topical features, on publication.

NEVADA—Capitol Complex, Carson City, NV 89710. Kirk Whisler, Ed. Articles, 500 to 700 or 1,500 to 1,800 words, on topics related to Nevada: history, profiles, travel, and places—with photos. Pay varies, on publication.

THE NEVADAN— *The Las Vegas Review-Journal,* Box 70, Las Vegas, NV 89125–0070. A.D. Hopkins, Ed. Feature articles, 2,000 to 2,500 words, on social trends and people in Nevada. Pieces, 1,000 to 2,000 words, on history in Nevada, Southwest Utah, Northeast Arizona, and Death Valley area of California, accompanied by B&W photos. Pays $100, extra for photos, on publication. Queries required.

NEW ALASKAN—Rt. 1, Box 677, Ketchikan, AK 99901. R.W. Pickrell, Ed. Articles, 1,000 to 5,000 words, and fiction related to S.E. Alaska. Pays 1 ½¢ a word, on publication.

NEW ENGLAND GETAWAYS—21 Pocahontas Dr., Peabody, MA 01960. Features, 1,500 to 2,500 words, "designed to lure travelers to specific regions of New England. We are looking for specific, informational articles that will motivate the reader to explore New England and will supply the tools (addresses, phone numbers, hours of business) to make the trip easy." Pays $150 to $300, on publication.

NEW HAMPSHIRE PROFILES—90 Fleet St., Portsmouth, NH 03801. David J. Gibson, Ed. Articles, 500 to 2,500 words, on New Hampshire people, events, arts, and life styles. Pays $100 to $350, on publication. Query.

NEW HAVEN BUSINESS DIGEST—375 Orange St., New Haven, CT 06510. Kim Hanson, Ed. Feature articles, 1,500 to 2,000 words, on New Haven area businesses. Pays $2.75 per published inch, $10 per photo, on publication. Query required.

NEW JERSEY MONTHLY—7 Dumont Pl., Morristown, NJ 07960. Larry

Marscheck, Ed. Patrick Sarver, Man. Ed. Articles, profiles, and service pieces, 2,000 to 3,000 words; department pieces on health, business, education, travel, sports, local politics, and arts, 1,200 to 1,800 words, with New Jersey tie-in. Short pieces of regional interest. Some fiction. Pays $35 to $100 for shorts, $450 to $1,500 for features, on acceptance. Query first. Guidelines.

NEW JERSEY REPORTER—The Center for Analysis of Public Issues, 16 Vandeventer Ave., Princeton, NJ 08542. Rick Sinding, Ed. In-depth articles, 2,000 to 6,000 words, on New Jersey politics and public affairs. Pays $100 to $250, on publication. Query required.

NEW MEXICO MAGAZINE—Joseph M. Montoya Bldg., 1100 St. Francis Dr., Santa Fe, NM 87503. Address Ed. Articles, 250 to 2,000 words, on New Mexico subjects. Pays about 17¢ a word, on acceptance.

NEW ORLEANS MAGAZINE—111 Veterans Blvd., New Orleans, LA 70124. Sherry Spear, Ed. Articles, 3 to 15 triple-spaced pages, on New Orleans area people and issues. Photos. Pays $50 to $500, extra for photos, on publication. Query.

NEW YORK—755 Second Ave., New York, NY 10017. Edward Kosner, Ed. Laurie Jones, Man. Ed. Feature articles on New York City subjects. Payment negotiated and on acceptance. Query required.

NEW YORK ALIVE—152 Washington Ave., Albany, NY 12210. Mary Grates Stoll, Ed. Articles aimed at developing knowledge of and appreciation for New York State. Features, 3,000 words maximum, on lifestyle, sports, travel and leisure, history and the arts. Department pieces for regular columns, including "Great Escapes" (travel ideas) and "Expressly New York" (unusual places, products or events in New York). Pays $200 to $350 for features, $50 to $150 for departments. Query preferred.

NORTH DAKOTA HORIZONS—P.O. Box 2467, Fargo, ND 58108. Sheldon Green, Ed. Quarterly. Articles, about 3,000 words, on the people, places and events that affect life in North Dakota. Photos. Poetry. Pays $75 to $300, on publication.

NORTH TEXAS GOLFER—P.O. Box 162079, Irving, TX 75016. Bob Gray, Ed. Articles, 800 to 1,500 words, involving local golfers or related directly to North Texas. Pays from $50 to $250, on publication. Query.

NORTHCOAST VIEW—Blarney Publishing, Box 1374, Eureka, CA 95502. Scott K. Ryan, Damon Maguire, Eds. Fiction, 2 to 20 pages; local news articles, 4 to 10 pages; poetry. Pays $5 per typed page, on publication.

NORTHEAST MAGAZINE— *The Hartford Courant,* 285 Broad St., Hartford, CT 06115. Lary Bloom, Ed. Articles and short essays that reflect the concerns of Connecticut residents, 750 to 3,000 words. Pays $250 to $1,000, on acceptance.

NORTHERN LIGHTS—Box 8084, Missoula, MT 59807–9962. Address Editor. Thoughtful articles, 500 to 1,500 words, about the West. Occasional fiction and poetry. "We're open to virtually any subject as long as it deals with our region (the Rocky Mountains) in some way." Pays to 10¢ a word, on publication.

NORTHWEST—1320 S.W. Broadway, Portland, OR 97201. Jack R. Hart, Ed. Sunday magazine of *The Sunday Oregonian.* Articles, to 3,000 words, on Pacific Northwest issues and personalities: regional travel, science and business, outdoor recreation, and lifestyle trends. Personal essays. Local angle essential. Pays $75 to $1,000. Query first.

NORTHWEST LIVING—130 Second Ave. S., Edmonds, WA 98020. Terry

W. Sheely, Ed. Lively, informative articles, 400 to 1,000 words, on the natural resources of the Northwest: homes, gardens, people, travel, history, etc. Color photos essential. Shorts, 100 to 400 words. Pays $50 to $400, on acceptance. Query required.

OH! IDAHO—Peak Media, Box 925, Hailey, ID 83333. Colleen Daly, Ed. "Articulate, image-oriented" features, 2,000 to 2,500 words, on Idaho's history, residents, and recreation. Department pieces, 1,200 to 1,500 words, on food and travel in Idaho. Humor, 1,500 words. Pays 10¢ a word, on publication. Query.

OHIO MAGAZINE—40 S. Third St., Columbus, OH 43215. Ellen Stein Burbach, Man. Ed. Profiles of people, cities and towns of Ohio; pieces on historic sites, tourist attractions, little-known spots. Lengths and payment vary. Query.

OKLAHOMA TODAY—Box 53384, Oklahoma City, OK 73152. Sue Carter, Ed. Travel articles; profiles, history and arts articles. All material must have regional tie-in. Queries for 1,000- to 2,000-word articles preferred. Pays $100 to $300, on acceptance. SASE for guidelines.

ORANGE COAST—245-D Fisher, Suite 8, Costa Mesa, CA 92626. Janet Eastman, Ed. Articles of interest to educated, affluent Southern Californians. Pieces, 1,000 to 1,500 words, for regular departments: "Profile," "Coasting" (op-ed), "Media," "Business" (hard news about the regional business community), and "Nightlife." Feature articles run 1,500 to 2,500 words. Query. Pays $150 for features, $100 for columns, on acceptance. Guidelines.

ORLANDO MAGAZINE—P.O. Box 2207, Orlando, FL 32802. Nancy Long, Features Ed. Articles and profiles, 1,000 to 1,500 words, related to Central Florida. Photos a plus. Pays $50 to $150, on acceptance. Query required.

PALM SPRINGS LIFE—Desert Publications, 303 N. Indian Ave., Palm Springs, CA 92262. Becky Kurtz, Ed. Articles, 800 to 1,200 words, of interest to "wealthy, upscale people who live and/or play in the desert": food, travel, homes, personalities, arts, and culture. Pays $150 to $200 for features, $30 for short profiles, on publication. Query required.

PENNSYLVANIA MAGAZINE—Box 576, Camp Hill, PA 17011. Albert E. Holliday, Ed. General-interest features with a Pennsylvania tie-in accompanied by illustrations. Pays from 10¢ a word, usually on acceptance. Query preferred.

PHILADELPHIA—1500 Walnut St., Philadelphia, PA 19102. Bill Tonelli, Exec. Ed. Articles, 1,000 to 5,000 words, for sophisticated audience, relating to Philadelphia area. No fiction. Pays on publication. Query.

PHOENIX METRO MAGAZINE—4707 N. 12th St., Phoenix, AZ 85014. Robert J. Early, Ed. Articles, 1,000 to 3,000 words, on topics on interest to Phoenix-area residents. Pays $75 to $300, on publication. Queries preferred.

PITTSBURGH—4802 Fifth Ave., Pittsburgh, PA 15213. Bruce VanWyngarden, Ed. Articles, 850 to 3,000 words, with western Pennsylvania slant, 2- to 4-month lead time. Pays on publication.

THE PITTSBURGH PRESS SUNDAY MAGAZINE— *The Pittsburgh Press,* 34 Blvd. of the Allies, Pittsburgh, PA 15230. Ed Wintermantel, Ed. Well-written, well-organized, in-depth articles of local or regional interest, 1,000 to 3,000 words, on issues, trends or personalities. No fiction, hobbies, how-tos or "timely events" pieces. Pays $100 to $400, extra for photos, on publication. Query.

PORTLAND MONTHLY—578 Congress St., Portland, ME 04101. Colin Sargent, Sr. Ed. Articles on local people, fashion, culture, trends, commercial and residential real estate. Fiction, to 2,500 words. Pays on publication. Query preferred.

PRIME TIMES—Senior World, Inc., 121 Mercer St., Seattle, WA 98109. Anthony E. Thein, Pub./Ed. Articles to address active, affluent residents of King County, WA, ages 55 to 70. Pays $50 to $75, on publication.

REGARDIE'S—1010 Wisconsin Ave. N.W., Suite 600, Washington, DC 20007. Brian Kelly, Ed. Profiles and investigations of the "high and mighty" in the DC area: "We require aggressive reporting and imaginative, entertaining writing." Pays 50¢ a word, on publication. Queries required.

ROCKFORD MAGAZINE—211 W. State St., Box 197, Rockford, IL 61101. John Harris, Ed. Feature articles, 3,000 words, and fillers, 400 to 1,000 words, on local events, arts and entertainment, nostalgia and personalities as well as pieces on how national trends or news affect the Midwest. Pays 10¢ a word, on publication. Query first.

RURAL LIVING—P.O. Box 15248, Richmond, VA 23227–0648. Richard G. Johnstone, Jr., Ed. Features, 1,000 to 1,500 words, on people, places, historic sites in Virginia and Maryland's Eastern Shore. Queries are preferred. Pays $100 to $150 for articles, on publication.

RURALITE—P.O. Box 558, Forest Grove, OR 97116. Address Ed. or Feature Ed. Articles, 800 words, of interest to a primarily rural and small-town audience in Oregon, Washington, Idaho, Nevada, Northern California, and Alaska. Upbeat articles; biographies, local history and celebrations, self-help, etc. Humorous articles and animal pieces. No fiction or poetry. No sentimental nostalgia. Pays $30 to $120, on acceptance. Queries preferred.

SACRAMENTO MAGAZINE—P.O. Box 2424, Sacramento, CA 95811. Ann McCully, Man. Ed. Features, 2,500 words, on a broad range of topics related to the region. Department pieces, 1,200 to 1,500 words, and short pieces, 500 words, for "City Lights" column. Pays $300, on acceptance. Query first.

SAN DIEGO MAGAZINE—4206 W. Point Loma Blvd., P.O. Box 85409, San Diego, CA 92138. Martin Hill, Sr. Ed. Articles, 1,500 to 3,000 words, on local personalities, politics, life styles, business, history, etc., relating to San Diego area. Photos. Pays $250 to $600, on publication. Query with clips.

SAN DIEGO READER—P.O. Box 80803, San Diego, CA 92138. Jim Holman, Ed. Articles, 2,500 to 10,000 words, on the San Diego region. Pays $500 to $2,000, on publication.

SAN FRANCISCO BUSINESS TIMES—325 Fifth St., San Francisco, CA 94107. Tim Clark, Assoc. Ed. Business-oriented articles, about 20 column inches. Limited free-lance market. Pays $75 to $100, on publication. Query.

SAN FRANCISCO FOCUS—680 Eighth St., San Francisco, CA 94103. Mark Powelson, Ed. Service features, profiles of local newsmakers, and investigative pieces of local issues, 2,500 to 3,000 words. Short stories, 1,500 to 5,000 words. Pays $250 to $750, on acceptance. Query required.

SAN FRANCISCO: THE MAGAZINE—45 Belden Pl., San Francisco, CA 91404. Umberto Tosi, Ed. "Our readership is upscale. We want articles on the people, places, power, and issues of the San Francisco Bay area." Pays varying rates, half on acceptance, half on publication. Query required.

7 DAYS—36 Cooper Sq., New York, NY 10003. Adam Moss, Ed. Short articles and fiction reflecting the New York City scene. Weekly. Payment varies, on acceptance. Query preferred.

SOUTH CAROLINA WILDLIFE—P.O. Box 167, Columbia, SC 29202. Address Man. Ed. Articles, 1,000 to 3,000 words, with regional outdoors focus: conservation, natural history and wildlife, recreation. Profiles, natural history. Pays form 10¢ a word. Query.

SOUTH FLORIDA HOME & GARDEN—See *Florida Home & Garden.*

SOUTH FLORIDA HOMEBUYER'S GUIDE—2151 W. Hillsboro Blvd., Suite 300, Deerfield Beach, FL 33442. Deanna Krams, Ed. Articles on developments in the housing industry, home improvements, security, decorating, energy efficiency, etc.; advice on finding, buying, and maintaining a home or condominium in South Florida. Pays 10¢ a word, on acceptance. Query.

SOUTH FLORIDA MAGAZINE (FORMERLY *MIAMI/SOUTH FLORIDA MAGAZINE*)—600 Brickell Ave., Suite 207, Miami, FL 33131. Joseph McQuay, Man. Ed. Features, 2,000 to 3,500 words, and department pieces, 900 to 1,300 words, on a variety of subjects related to South Florida. Short, bright items, 200 to 400 words, for the "Undercurrents" section. Pays $75 to $900, 15 days before publication.

SOUTHERN MAGAZINE—P.O. Box 3418, 201 E. Markham, Suite 200, Little Rock, AR 72203. Linton Weeks, Ed. Articles, 1,000 to 6,000 words, that explore all facets of the contemporary South: news, profiles, essays, first-person adventure pieces, etc. Departments include travel ("Weekends"), food and drink ("Southern Lights"), success stories, and short news items from around the South. Some short fiction of and about the South. Pays from $50 for department pieces, to $2,000 for features, on acceptance.

SOUTHERN OUTDOORS—N. 1, Bell Rd., Montgomery, AL 36141. Larry Teague, Ed. How-to articles, 200 to 600 words or 1,500 to 2,000 words, on hunting and fishing, for fishermen and hunters in the 16 southern states. Pays 15¢ a word, on acceptance. Query.

SOUTHERN STYLE—Whittle Communications, 505 Market St., Knoxville, TN 37902. Elise Nakhnikian, Ed. Articles, 750 to 1,500 words, on fashion, beauty, celebrities, food, and related topics of interest to Southern women. Pays $350 to $1,500. Query required.

SOUTHWEST ART—Franklin Tower, 5444 Westheimer, Suite 1440, Houston, TX 77056. Susan McGarry, Ed. Articles, 1,800 to 2,200 words, on the artists, museums, galleries, history and art trends west of the Mississippi. Particularly interested in representational or figurative arts. Pays from $300, on acceptance. Query.

THE STATE: DOWN HOME IN NORTH CAROLINA—P.O. Box 2169, Raleigh, NC 27602. Jim Duff, Ed. Articles, 600 to 2,000 words, on people, history, and places in North Carolina. Fillers. Photos. Pays on acceptance.

SUNDAY— *Chicago Tribune,* 435 N. Michigan Ave., Rm. 570, Chicago, IL 60611. Ruby Scott, Man. Ed. Profiles and articles, to 6,000 words, on public and social issues on the personal, local, national, or international level. Query.

SUNDAY MAGAZINE— *Providence Sunday Journal,* 75 Fountain St., Providence, RI 02902. Berkley Hudson, Ed. Profiles, personal-experience pieces, fiction, New England features, 1,000 to 3,000 words. Pays $75 to $750, on publication. Query.

SUNSET MAGAZINE—80 Willow Rd., Menlo Park, CA 94025. William Marken, Ed. Western regional. Queries not encouraged.

SUNSHINE: THE MAGAZINE OF SOUTH FLORIDA— *The News/Sun-*

Sentinel, 101 N. New River Dr., Ft. Lauderdale, FL 33301–2293. John Parkyn, Ed. Articles, 1,000 to 4,000 words, on topics of interest to South Floridians. Pays $250 to $1,000, on acceptance. Query first. Guidelines.

SUSQUEHANNA MONTHLY MAGAZINE—Box 75A, RD1, Marietta, PA 17547. Richard S. Bromer, Ed. Well-documented articles, 1,000 to 4,000 words, on regional (PA, DE, MD, DC) history. Pays to $75, on publication. Query required. No fiction or poetry.

TALLAHASSEE MAGAZINE—P.O. Box 12848, Tallahassee, FL 32317. William Needham, Ed. Articles, 800 to 1,100 words, with a positive outlook on the life, people, and history of the North Florida area. Pays 10¢ a word, on publication. Query.

TEXAS HIGHWAYS MAGAZINE—State Dept. of Highways and Public Transportation, 11th and Brazos, Austin, TX 78701–2483. Frank Lively, Ed. Texas history, scenic and travel features, 200 to 1,800 words. Pays $150 to $800, on acceptance, extra for photos. Guidelines.

TEXAS MONTHLY—P.O. Box 1569, Austin, TX 78767. Gregory Curtis, Ed. Features (2,500 to 5,000 words) and departments (under 2,500 words) on art, architecture, food, education, business, politics, etc. "We like solidly researched pieces that uncover issues of public concern, reveal offbeat and previously unreported topics, or use a novel approach to familiar topics." Pays varying rates, on acceptance. Queries required.

TIMELINE—1985 Velma Ave., Columbus, OH 43211–2497. Christopher S. Duckworth, Ed. Articles, 1,000 to 6,000 words, on history of Ohio—politics, economics, social, and natural history—for lay readers in the Midwest. Pays $100 to $900, on acceptance. Queries preferred.

TOLEDO MAGAZINE— *The Blade,* Toldeo, OH 43660. Sue Stankey, Ed. Articles, to 5,000 words, on Toledo area personalities, events, etc. Pays $50 to $500, on publication. Query.

TORONTO LIFE—59 Front St. E., Toronto, Ont., Canada M5E 1B3. Marq De Villiers, Ed. Articles, 1,500 to 4,500 words, on Toronto. Pays $1,000 to $2,500, on acceptance. Query.

TROPIC— *The Miami Herald,* One Herald Plaza, Miami, FL 33132. Tom Shroder, Ed. General-interest articles, 750 to 3,000 words, for South Florida readers. Pays $200 to $1,000, on acceptance. Send SASE.

TUCSON LIFESTYLE—Old Pueblo Press, 7000 E. Tanque Verde, Tucson, AZ 85715. Sue Giles, Ed. Features on local businesses, celebrities, and life styles. Payment varies, on acceptance. Query preferred.

TWIN CITIES READER—600 First Ave. N., Minneapolis, MN 55403. D.J. Tice, Ed.-in-Chief. Articles, 2 to 4 printed pages, on cultural phenomena, city politics, and general-interest subjects, for local readers aged 25 to 44. Pays to $3 per inch, on publication.

VALLEY MAGAZINE—16800 Devonshire, Suite 275, Granada Hills, CA 91344. Anne Framroze, Ed. Articles, 1,000 to 3,000 words, on celebrities, issues, education, health, business, dining and entertaining, etc., in the San Fernando Valley. Pays $100 to $500, within 8 weeks of acceptance.

VENTURA COUNTY & COAST REPORTER—1583 Spinnaker Dr., Suite 213, Ventura, CA 93001. Nancy Cloutier, Ed. Articles, 3 to 5 pages, on any locally slanted topic. Pays $10, on publication.

VERMONT LIFE—61 Elm St., Montpelier, VT 05602. Tom Slayton, Ed.-in-Chief. Articles, 500 to 3,000 words, about Vermont subjects only. Pays 20¢ a word, extra for photos. Query required.

VIRGINIA BUSINESS—600 E. Broad St., Richmond, VA 23219. James Bacon, Ed. Articles, 1,000 to 2,500 words, related to the business scene in Virginia. Pays varying rates, on acceptance. Query required.

THE VIRGINIAN—P.O. Box 2828, Staunton, VA 24401. Hunter S. Pierce, IV, Man. Ed. Articles, 1,000 words, relating to VA, WV, MD, NC, and DC.

WASHINGTON—901 Lenora, Seattle, WA 98121. David Fuller, Man. Ed. Articles, varying lengths, on the people and places of Washington State. Payment varies. Query required.

WASHINGTON DOSSIER (FORMERLY *DOSSIER*)—3301 New Mexico Ave. N.W., Suite 310, Washington, DC 20016. Laura Goldstein, Assoc. Ed. Feature articles (4,000 words), profiles and department pieces (1,500 words), including "quick profiles, restaurant news, and extraordinary itineraries (200 to 500 words)." Pays good rates, on acceptance. Query required.

WASHINGTON POST MAGAZINE— *The Washington Post,* 1150 15th St. N.W., Washington, DC 20071. Stephen L. Petranek, Man. Ed. Personal-experience essays, profiles and general-interest pieces, to 6,000 words, on business, arts and culture, politics, science, sports, education, children, relationships, behavior, etc. Pays from $300, on acceptance.

THE WASHINGTONIAN—1828 L St. N.W., Suite 200, Washington, DC 20036. John Limpert, Ed. Helpful, informative articles, 1,000 to 4,000 words, on Washington-related topics. Pays 30¢ a word. Query.

WE ALASKANS MAGAZINE— *Anchorage Daily News,* Box 149001, Anchorage, AK 99514. Kathleen McCoy, Ed. Articles, 2,000 words, and features, 3,000 to 4,000 words, on Alaska topics only. Profiles, fiction, and humor. Pays $75 for articles, $300 for features, on publication.

THE WEEKLY, SEATTLE'S NEWS MAGAZINE—1931 Second Ave., Seattle, WA 90181. David Brewster, Ed. Articles, 700 to 4,000 words, with a Northwest perspective. Pays $75 to $800, on publication. Query. Guidelines.

WEST MICHIGAN MAGAZINE—7 Ionia St. S.W., Grand Rapids, MI 49503. Articles, to 2,000 words, on the people, places, issues, and events of the region. Pays varying rates, on publication.

WESTERN SPORTSMAN—P.O. Box 737, Regina, Sask., Canada S4P 3A8. Rick Bates, Ed. Informative articles, to 2,500 words, on outdoor experiences in Alberta and Saskatchewan. How-tos, humor, cartoons. Photos. Pays $40 to $325, on publication.

WESTWAYS—Box 2890, Terminal Annex, Los Angeles, CA 90051. Mary Ann Fisher, Ed. Articles, 1,000 to 1,500 words, and photo essays, on western U.S., Canada, and Mexico: history, contemporary living, travel, personalities, etc. Photos. Pays from 20¢ a word, extra for photos, 30 days before publication. Query.

WISCONSIN— *The Milwaukee Journal* Magazine, Newspapers, Inc., Box 661, Milwaukee, WI 53201. Alan Borsuk, Ed. Articles, 500 to 2,000 words, on business, politics, arts, science, personal finance, psychology, entertainment, health, etc. Personal-experience essays and investigative articles. Pays $75 to $500, on publication. Query.

WISCONSIN TRAILS—P.O. Box 5650, Madison, WI 53705. Geri Nixon,

Man. Ed. Articles, 1,500 to 3,000 words, on regional topics: outdoors, life style, events, adventure, travel; profiles of artists and craftspeople, and regional personalities. Fiction, with regional slant. Fillers. Pays $100 to $300, on acceptance and on publication. Query.

WISCONSIN WEST MAGAZINE—P.O. Box 381, Eau Claire, WI 54702–0381. Jane Hieb, Features Ed. Articles on contemporary issues for residents of western Wisconsin; profiles of towns, neighborhoods, families in the region; and historical pieces. Short humor. Payment varies, on acceptance.

WORCESTER MONTHLY—P.O. Box 300, Worcester, MA 01614. Michael Warshaw, Ed. Articles, to 3,000 words, on the arts, entertainment, fashion, events, and issues specific to Central Massachusetts. Pays $200, on publication. Query required.

YANKEE—Yankee Publishing Co., Dublin, NH 03444. Judson D. Hale, Ed. Articles and fiction, about 2,500 words, on New England and its residents. Pays about $600 for features, $1,000 for fiction, on acceptance.

YANKEE HOMES—Main St., Dublin, NH 03444. Jim Collins, Ed. Articles, 200 to 1,500 words, on New England real estate, housing, and living. Pays $50 to $500, on acceptance. Queries required.

YANKEE MAGAZINE'S TRAVEL GUIDE TO NEW ENGLAND AND ITS NEIGHBORS—Main St., Dublin, NH 03444. Elizabeth Doyle, Ed. Articles, 500 to 2,000 words, on ususual activities, attractions, places to visit in New England, New York State, and Atlantic Canada. Photos. Pays $50 to $300, on acceptance. Query with outline and writing samples.

TRAVEL ARTICLES

AAA WORLD—8111 Gatehouse Rd., Falls Church, VA 22047. Douglas Damerst, Ed.-in-Chief. Articles, 600 to 1,500 words, on consumer automotive and travel concerns. Pays $200 to $800, on acceptance. Query with writing samples only.

ACCENT—Box 10010, Ogden, UT 84409. Marjorie H. Rice, Ed. Articles, 1,200 to 1,500 words, on travel, ways to travel, and travel tips. Pays 15¢ a word, $35 for photos, on acceptance. Query first.

ADVENTURE ROAD—The Condé Nast Publications, 360 Madison Ave., New York, NY 10017. Marilyn Holstein, Ed. Official publication of the Amoco Motor Club. Articles, 1,500 words, on destinations in North America, Mexico, and the Caribbean. Photos. Pays $300 to $800, on acceptance. Query required.

AIRFARE INTERLINE MAGAZINE—25 W. 39th St., New York, NY 10018. Ratu Kamlani, Ed. Travel articles,1,000 to 2,500 words, with photos, on shopping, sightseeing, dining, and night life for airline employees. Prices, discount information, and addresses must be included. Pays $75, after publication.

ARIZONA HIGHWAYS—2039 W. Lewis Ave., Phoenix, AZ 85009. Richard G. Stahl, Man. Ed. Informal, well-researched travel articles, 2,000 to 2,500 words, focusing on a specific city or region in Arizona and environs and including anecdotes, historical references, nature, contemporary art and events, anthropology and archaeology. Pays 35¢ to 40¢ a word, on acceptance. Query with published clips. Guidelines.

BRITISH HERITAGE—P.O. Box 8200, Harrisburg, PA 17105. Gail Huganir, Ed. Travel articles on places to visit in the British Isles, 1,000 to 2,000 words. Include detailed historical information with a "For the Visitor" sidebar. Pays $100 to $200, on acceptance.

552

CALIFORNIA HIGHWAY PATROLMAN—2030 V St., Sacramento, CA 95818. Carol Perri, Ed. Travel articles, to 2,000 words, focusing on places in California and the West Coast. Pays 2 ½ ¢ a word, extra for black and white photos, on publication.

THE CAMPER TIMES—Royal Productions, Inc., Box 6294, Richmond, VA 23230. Melinda Gammon, Ed. Articles and fiction, 500 to 2,000 words, related to camping in the MD, VA, NC, and TN area. Pays $25 to $50, on publication. Queries preferred.

CARIBBEAN TRAVEL AND LIFE—606 N. Washington St., Alexandria, VA 22314. Veronica Gould Stoddart, Ed. Lively, informative articles, 500 to 2,500 words, on all aspects of travel, leisure, recreation, and culture in the Caribbean, Bahamas, and Bermuda, for up-scale, sophisticated readers. Photos. Pays $75 to $550, on publication. Query.

CHARTERING MAGAZINE—See *Yacht Vacations Magazine.*

COLORADO HOMES & LIFESTYLES—2550 31st St., Suite 154, Denver, CO 80216. Ania Savage, Man. Ed. Travel articles on cities, regions, establishments in Colorado; roundup and travel pieces with unusual angles, 1,200 to 3,000 words. Pays 10¢ to 15¢ a word, on acceptance. Query.

CONNECTICUT TRAVELER—2276 Whitney Ave., Hamden, CT 06518. Elke P. Martin, Man. Dir. Articles, 500 to 1,200 words, on travel and tourist attractions in New England. Pays $50 to $225, on acceptance. Query first with SASE.

DISCOVERY—Allstate Motor Club, 3701 W. Lake Ave., Glenview, IL 60025. Claire McCrea, Ed. Articles, 1,000 to 2,500 words, on travel topics that explore continental North America and its people. Photos on assignment only. Pays $500 to $850, on acceptance. Query and published samples required.

EARLY AMERICAN LIFE—Box 8200, Harrisburg, PA 17105. Frances Carnahan, Ed. Travel features about historic sites and country inns, 1,000 to 3,000 words. Pays $50 to $400, on acceptance. Query.

ENDLESS VACATION—Box 80260, Indianapolis, IN 46280. Helen A. Wernle, Ed. Travel features, to 2,000 words; international scope. Pays on acceptance. Query preferred. Guidelines.

FAMILY CIRCLE—110 Fifth Ave., New York, NY 10011. Susan Ungaro, Articles Ed. Travel articles, to 2,000 words. Destination pieces should appeal to a national audience and focus on affordable activities; prefer area roundups, theme-oriented travel pieces or first person family vacation stories. Pay rates vary, on acceptance. Query first.

FORD TIMES—One Illinois Center, 111 E. Wacker Dr., Suite 1700, Chicago, IL 60601. John Fink, Ed. Articles, 500 to 1,500 words, on current trends, life styles, profiles, places of interest, travel, outdoor activities, food, and humor, appealing to drivers aged 18 to 35. pays from $550 for 1,200 to 1,500 words, on acceptance. Query with SASE required.

GO: THE AUTHENTIC GUIDE TO NEW ORLEANS—541 Julia St., New Orleans, LA 70130. Katherine Dinker, Ed. Articles, to 1,200 words, of interest to New Orleans visitors. Pays to $150, on publication. Query required.

GREAT EXPEDITIONS—Box 8000–411, Sumas, WA 98295–8000. Craig Henderson, Ed. Articles, 700 to 2,500 words, on independent, adventurous, budget-conscious travel and unusual destinations. Pays $15 to $30, on publication. Guidelines.

GULFSHORE LIFE—Collier Park of Commerce, 2975 S. Horseshoe Dr., Naples, FL 33942. G. Stephen Weichelt, Ed. Destination-oriented travel articles, 1,800 to 2,400 words. Pay negotiable, on publication. Queries required.

INTERNATIONAL LIVING—824 E. Baltimore St., Baltimore, MD 21202. Bruce Totaro, Ed. Newsletter. Short pieces and features, 200 to 2,000 words, with useful information on investing, shopping, travel, employment, real estate and life styles overseas. Pays $50 to $200, after publication.

ISLANDS—3886 State St., Santa Barbara, CA 93105. Articles on island-related topics written from a historical, exploratory, or cultural point of view, 3,000 words, 2,500 words, or 1,000 words. Pays 25¢ a word, half on acceptance, half on publication. Query preferred. Guidelines.

MEXICO MAGAZINE—P.O. Box 700, Carbondale, CO 81623. Harlan Feder, Man. Ed. Articles, 2,000 to 2,400 words, that "help travelers understand, respect, and cope with cultural differences while visiting Mexico." Department pieces, 600 words, for "Pesos and Sense," "Budget Mexico," and "Essentially Spanish." Pays $50 to $250, on publication.

MICHIGAN LIVING—Automobile Club of Michigan,17000 Executive Plaza Dr., Dearborn, MI 48126. Len Barnes, Ed. Informative travel articles, 500 to 1,500 words, on U.S. Canadian tourist attractions and recreational opportunities; special interest in Michigan.

THE MIDWEST MOTORIST—12901 N. Forty Dr., St. Louis, MO 63141. Jean Kennedy, Man. Ed. Articles,1,000 to 1,500 words, with photos, on travel, transportation and consumerism. Pays $50 to $200, on acceptance or publication.

NATIONAL GEOGRAPHIC—17th and M Sts. N.W., Washington, DC 20036. Wilbur E. Garrett, Ed. First-person articles on geography, exploration, natural history, archaeology, and science. Half staff written; half written by recognized authorities and published authors. Does not review manuscripts.

NATIONAL GEOGRAPHIC TRAVELER—National Geographic Society, 17th and M Sts. N.W., Washington, DC 20036. Joan Tapper, Ed. Articles 1,500 to 4,000 words, that highlight specific places. Query with 1- to 2- page proposal, resume, and published clippings required. Pays $1 a word, on acceptance.

NATIONAL MOTORIST—Bayside Plaza, 188 The Embarcadero, San Francisco, CA 94105. Jane Offers, Ed. Illustrated articles, 500 to 1,100 words, for California motorists, on motoring in the West, car care, roads, personalities, places, etc. Photos. Pays from 10¢ a word, extra for photos, on acceptance. SASE required.

NEW ENGLAND GETAWAYS—21 Pocahontas Dr., Peabody, MA 01960. Features, 1,500 to 2,500 words, designed to lure travelers to New England; include specific information such as addresses, phone numbers, hours of business, etc. Pays $150 to $300, on publication.

NEW WOMAN—215 Lexington Ave., New York, NY 10016. Armchair travel pieces; personal experience and "what I learned from this experience" pieces, 2,000 to 3,000 words. Pays $500 to $2,000, on acceptance. Query required.

NEW YORK DAILY NEWS—220 E. 42nd St., New York, NY 10017. Harry Ryan, Travel Ed. First-person impressions, anecdotes, 600 to 1,200 words, on all manner of travel. Price information must be included. Black and white photos preferred. Pays $100 to $200, on publication, extra for photos.

THE NEW YORK TIMES—229 W. 43rd St., New York, NY 10036. Nora

554

Kerr, Travel Ed. Considers queries only; include writer's background, description of proposed article. No unsolicited manuscripts or photos. Pays on acceptance.

NORTHWEST— *The Sunday Oregonian,* 1320 S.W. Broadway, Portland, OR 97201. Travel articles, 1,000 to 1,500 words, third-person perspective. All material must pertain to the Northwest (OR, WA, ID, and MT). Include details about where to go, what to see, plans to make, with specific information about reservations, ticket purchases, etc. Pays $150 to $250, on acceptance. Query. Guidelines.

NORTHWEST LIVING—130 Second Ave., South Edmonds, WA 98020–3588. Terry W. Sheely, Ed. Articles, 400 to 1,500 words, on regional travel and natural resources. Color slides or B&W prints. Query with SASE required.

OFF DUTY MAGAZINE—3303 Harbor Blvd., Suite C-2, Costa Mesa, CA 92626. Bruce Thorstad, U.S. Ed. Travel articles, 1,800 to 2,000 words, for active-duty military Americans (aged 20 to 40) and their families, on U.S. regions or cities. Must have wide scope; no out-of-the-way places. Military angle essential. Photos. Pays from 13¢ a word, extra for photos, on acceptance. Query required. Send for guidelines. European and Pacific editions. Foreign travel articles for military Americans and their families stationed abroad. Send SASE for guidelines. Limited market.

THE ORIGINAL NEW ENGLAND GUIDE—Historical Times, Inc., 2245 Kohn Rd., Box 8200, Harrisburg, PA 17105. Howard Crise, Ed. Annual. Articles, to 1,000 words, of interest to visitors in New England; special events, sightseeing, travel destinations, and activities. Short pieces, 500 words, focusing on a particular attraction or theme. Pays 15¢ a word, on acceptance. Query with clips preferred.

SACRAMENTO MAGAZINE—P.O. Box 2424, Sacramento, CA 95812–2424. Nancy Martini, Ed. Destination-oriented articles in the Sacramento area (or within a 6-hour drive),1,000 to1,500 words. Pay varies, on acceptance. Query first, to Jan Haag.

SOUTHERN TRAVEL—5520 Park Ave., Trumbull, CT 06611–0395. Shepherd Campbell, Ed. Articles on travel in southern U.S., from 1,000 to 2,500 words. Pays from $150, on acceptance. Query.

TEXAS HIGHWAYS MAGAZINE—State Dept. of Highways and Public Transportation 11th and Brazos, Austin, TX 78701–2483. Frank Lively, Ed. Travel, historical, cultural, scenic features on Texas, 1,000 to1,800 words. Pays $400 to $800, on acceptance, extra for photos.

TOURS & RESORTS—World Publishing Co., 990 Grove St., Evanston, IL 60201–4370. Ray Gudas, Man. Ed. Features on international vacation destinations and resorts, 1,500 words; also essays, nostalgia, humor, tour company profiles, travel tips and service articles, 800 to 1,500 words. Pays up to $350, on acceptance. Top-quality color slides a must. Query.

TRANSITIONS ABROAD—18 Hulst Rd., Box 344, Amherst, MA 01004. Dr. Clayton A. Hubbs, Ed. Articles for travelers overseas; work, study, travel, budget tips. Include practical, first-hand information. Emphasis on establishing meaningful contact with other cultures: home stays and exchanges, volunteer work, etc. B&W photos a plus. Pays $2 per column inch, after publication.

TRAVEL AGE WEST—100 Grant Ave., San Francisco, CA 94108. Donald Langley, Man. Ed. Articles, 800 to 1,000 words, with photos, on any aspect of travel useful to travel agents, including names, addresses, prices, etc.; news or trend angle preferred. Pays $2 per column inch, after publication.

TRAVEL & LEISURE—1120 Ave. of the Americas, New York, NY 10036.

Pamela Fiori, Ed-in Chief. Articles, 800 to 3,000 words, on destinations and leisure-time activities. Regional pieces for regional editions. Pays $600 to $2,500, on acceptance. Query; articles on assignment.

TRAVEL HOLIDAY—Travel Bldg., Floral Park, NY 11001. Scott Shane, Ed. Informative, lively features, 1,400 to 1,600 words, on foreign and domestic travel to well-known or little-known places; featurettes, 1,000 to 1,200 words, on special-interest subjects: museums, shopping, smaller cities or islands, special aspects of destination. Pays up to $325 for featurettes, $600 for features, on acceptance. Query with published clips.

TRAVEL SMART—Dobbs Ferry, NY 10522. Short pieces, 250 to 1,000 words, about interesting, unusual and/or economical places; give specific details on hotels, restaurants, transportation, and costs. Pays on publication.

TRAVEL SMART FOR BUSINESS—Dobbs Ferry , NY 10522. H.J. Teison, Ed. Articles, 200 to 1,000 words, for company executives and business travel managers, on lowering travel costs and increasing travel convenience. Pays on publication.

VISTA/USA—Box 161, Convent Station, NJ 07961. Kathleen M. Caccavale, Ed. Travel articles, 1,500 to 2,500 words, on U.S., Canada, Mexico and the Caribbean; also, general interest, hobby/collecting, culture, and Americana. "Flavor of the area, not service oriented." Shorts, 500 to 1,000 words, on mini-trips, close-focus, American vignettes. Pays from $500 for features, from $150 for shorts, on acceptance. Query with writing sample and outline. Limited market.

VOLKSWAGEN'S WORLD—Volkswagen of America, Inc., P.O. Box 3951, 888 W. Big Beaver, Troy, MI 48007–3951. Marlene Goldsmith, Ed. Travel articles on unique places or with a unique angle, to 750 words. Pays $150 per printed page, on acceptance. Query.

WESTWAYS—P.O. Box 2890, Terminal Annex, Los Angeles, CA 90051. Mary Ann Fisher, Exec. Ed. Travel articles on where to go, what to see, and how to get there, 1,500 words. Domestic travel articles are limited to Western U.S., Canada and Hawaii; foreign travel articles are also of interest. Quality color photos should be available. Pays 20¢ a word, 30 days before publication.

WOMAN TRAVELER MAGAZINE—P.O. Box 6117, New York, NY 10150. Jeanine Moss, Ed./Pub. Detailed travel advice about America's major business cities from a woman's point of view: hotels with skirt hangers, hair dryers, fitness facilities, light cuisine; restaurants comfortable for a woman eating alone, good for entertaining; some vacation travel. Costs and specific details a must. Pays from $200, on publication. Query first.

YACHT VACATIONS MAGAZINE (FORMERLY *CHARTERING MAGAZINE*)—P.O. Box 755, Jensen Beach, FL 34957. Antonia Thomas, Ed. Articles and photography on chartered yacht vacations, 1,000 to 1,800 words. Pays varying rates, on publication. Query first.

YANKEE MAGAZINE'S TRAVEL GUIDE TO NEW ENGLAND—Main St., Dublin, NH 03444. Elizabeth Doyle, Ed. Articles 500 to 2,000 words, on unusual activities, restaurants, places to visit in New England, New York, and Atlantic Canada. Photos. Pays $50 to $300, on acceptance. Query with outline and writing samples.

INFLIGHT MAGAZINES

ABOARD—North-South Net, Inc., 777 41st St., P.O. Box 40–2763, Miami Beach, FL 33104. Christina Arencibia, Ed. Inflight magazine of nine Latin Ameri-

can international airlines. Articles, with photos, on Chile, Panama, Paraguay, Dominican Republic, Ecuador, Guatemala, El Salvador, Bolivia, Venezuela, and Honduras. Pieces on science, sports, home, fashion and gastronomy, 1,200 to 1,500 words. Pays $150, on acceptance and on publication. Query required.

AMERICAN WAY—P.O. Box 619616, MD 2G23, DWF Airport, TX 75261–9616. Barnard Collier, Ed. American Airlines' inflight magazine. Features of interest to the business traveler, emphasizing travel, adventure, business and the arts/culture. Pays from $450, on acceptance. Query.

AMERICANA WEST AIRLINES MAGAZINE—Skyward Marketing, Inc., 7500 N. Dreamy Draw Dr., Suite 236, Phoenix, AZ 85020. Michael Derr, Ed. Articles celebrating creativity, 750 to 2,000 words; regional angle helpful. Pays from $250 to $750, on publication. Query required. Guidelines.

ECHELON—Halsey Publishing Co., 12955 Biscayne Blvd., N. Miami, FL 33181. Debra Silver, Ed. Inflight magazine for Butler Aviation International. Pays one month prior to publication. Query with SASE required.

MIDWAY—Skies Publishing Co., Plaza West, 9600 S.W. Oak St., Suite 310, Portland, OR 97223. Terri Wallo, Ed. Articles, 1,000 to 1,300 words; and columns, 500 to 700 words, of interest to business travelers. Pays $200 to $400 for features, $50 to $100 for columns, on publication. Query letters preferred. Same requirements for Braniff *Destination*, United *Express, Horizon,* and *San Juan.*

NORTHWEST PORTFOLIO—East/West Network, 34 E. 51st St., New York, NY 10022. William McCoy, Ed. Features, 1,500 to 2,000 words, on travel, business, sports, entertainment, media, and profiles. Pays from $300, on acceptance.

SKY—12955 Biscayne Blvd., North Miami, FL 33181. Lidia de Leon, Ed. Delta Air Lines' inflight magazine. Articles on business, lifestyle, high tech, sports, the arts, etc. Color slides. Pays varying rates, on acceptance. Query.

USAIR—338 N. Elm St., Greensboro, NC 27401. Maggie Oman, Ed. Articles, 1,500 to 3,000 words, on travel, business, sports, entertainment, food, health, and other general-interest topics. No downbeat or extremely controversial subjects. Pays $350 to $800, on acceptance. Query first.

VIS A VIS—East/West Network, 34 E. 51st St., New York, NY 10022. Erla Zwingle, Sr. Ed. First-person articles, 600 to 700 words, on profiles, golf resorts, and luxury vacations. Pays varying rates, on acceptance. No photos. Queries required. Guidelines.

WOMEN'S PUBLICATIONS

BBW: BIG BEAUTIFUL WOMAN—9171 Wilshire Blvd., Suite 300, Beverly Hills, CA 90210. Carole Shaw, Ed.-in-Chief. Articles, 2,500 words, of interest to large-size women, including interviews with successful large-size women and self-pieces on how to cope with difficult situations. Tips on restaurants, airlines, stores, etc., that treat large women with respect. Payment varies, on publication. Query.

BEAUTY DIGEST—126 Fifth Ave., New York, NY 10011. Linda Moran

Evans, Ed. Reprints and original pieces, 1,800 to 2,500 words, on beauty, health, exercise, self-help, for women. Pays varying rates, on publication.

BLACK ELEGANCE—475 Park Ave. South, New York, NY 10016. Sharyn J. Skeeter, Ed. Articles, 1,000 to 2,000 words, on fashion, beauty, relationships, home design, careers, personal finance, and personalities for black women age 25 to 45. Short interviews. Pays $150 to $225, on publication. Query. Guidelines.

BRIDAL GUIDE—441 Lexington Ave., New York, NY 10017. Lois Spritzer, Exec. Ed. Features, 500 to 2,000 words, on wedding planning, remarriage, honeymoons, ethnic traditions, and unusual and celebrity weddings. Photos. Pays $100 to $400, on publication. Guidelines.

BRIDE'S—350 Madison Ave., New York, NY 10017. Andrea Feld, Copy and Features Ed. Articles, 1,000 to 3,000 words, for engaged couples or newlyweds, on communication, sex, housing, finances, careers, remarriage, step-parenting, health, birth control, pregnancy, babies, religion, in-laws, relationships, and wedding planning. Pays $300 to $800, on acceptance.

CAPPER'S—616 Jefferson St., Topeka, KS 66607. Nancy Peavler, Ed. Human interest, personal experience, historical articles, 300 to 700 words. Poetry, to 15 lines, on nature, home, family. Novel-length fiction for serialization. Letters on women's interests, recipes, hints, for "Heart of the Home." Jokes. Children's writing and art section. Pays varying rates, on publication.

CHATELAINE—Maclean Hunter Bldg. 777 Bay St., Toronto, Ont., Canada M5W 1A7. Elizabeth Parr, Sr. Ed. Articles, 2,500 words, on controversial subjects and personalities of interest to Canadian women. Pays from $1,200 for 1,500 to 3,000 words; from $350 for 600-word "Up-front" columns (relationships, health, parents/kids), on acceptance. Send query with outline, or manuscript with international reply coupon.

COMPLETE WOMAN—1165 N. Clark, Chicago, IL 60610. Susan Handy, Assoc. Ed. Articles, 1,500 to 2,000 words, with how-to sidebars, giving practical advice to women on careers, health, personal relationships, etc. Inspirational profiles of successful women. Pays varying rates, on publication. Send manuscript or query with SASE.

COSMOPOLITAN—224 W. 57th St., New York, NY 10019. Helen Gurley Brown, Ed. Betty Nichols Kelly, Fiction and Books Ed. Articles, to 5,000 words, and features, 2,000 to 3,000 words, on issues affecting young career women. Fiction on male-female relationships: short shorts, 1,500 to 3,000 words; short stories, 3,000 to 4,500 words; mystery and other novels; condensed books, 25,000 words. Pays from $1,500 for full-length articles, $750 to $1,500 for short stories, $500 to $750 for short shorts, on acceptance.

COUNTRY WOMAN—P.O. Box 643, Milwaukee, WI 53201. Kathy Pohl, Man. Ed. Personal-experience, humor, service-oriented articles, and how-to features, to 1,000 words, of interest to country women. Pays $40 to $150, on acceptance.

ELLE—551 Fifth Ave., New York, NY 10176. Joan Harting, Sr. Ed. Articles, varying lengths, for fashion-conscious women, ages 20 to 50. Subjects include beauty, health, careers, fitness, travel, and life styles. Pays top rates, on publication. Query required.

ESSENCE—1500 Broadway, New York, NY 10036. Susan L. Taylor, Ed.-in-Chief. Provocative articles, 800 to 2,500 words, about black women in American today: self-help, how-to pieces, business and finance, health, celebrity profiles and political issues. Short items, 500 to 750 words, on work, parenting, and health. Features and fiction, 800 to 2,500 words. Pays varying rates, on acceptance. Query for articles.

EXECUTIVE FEMALE—127 W. 24th St., New York, NY 10011. Mary Elizabeth Terzella, Ed. Features, 6 to 12 pages, on managing people, time, and careers, for women in business. Articles, 6 to 8 pages, for "More Money," "Horizons," "Profiles," and "Entrepreneur's Corner." Pays varying rates, on publication. Limited market.

FAMILY CIRCLE—110 Fifth Ave., New York, NY 10010. Susan Ungaro, Articles Ed. Ellen Stoianoff, Sr. Ed. Leah Brier, Health Ed. Articles, to 2,500 words, on "women who have made a difference," marriage, family and child-rearing issues; consumer affairs, travel, humor, health and fitness, personal opinion essays. Query required. Fiction: limited market. Seeks quality short stories that reflect real-life situations. Pays top rates, on acceptance.

FLARE—777 Bay St., Toronto, Ontario, Canada M5W 1A7. Patricia McGee, Assoc. Ed. Service articles, 1,500 to 2,000 words, on health, careers, relationships, and contemporary problems; articles on home decor, food, and entertaining for Canadian women aged 18 to 34. Profiles, 200 to 800 words, of up-and-coming Canadians. Pays on acceptance. Query.

GLAMOUR—350 Madison Ave., New York, NY 10017. Ruth Whitney, Ed.-in-Chief. Barbara Coffey, Man. Ed. Rona Cherry, Exec. Ed. How-to articles, from 1,500 words, on careers, health, psychology, interpersonal relationships, etc., for women aged 18 to 35. Fashion and beauty pieces staff-written. Submit queries to Judeth Welderholt Coyne, Articles Ed. Pays from $500.

GOOD HOUSEKEEPING—959 Eighth Ave., New York, NY 10019. Joan Thursh, Articles Ed. Naome Lewis, Fiction Ed. In-depth articles and features on controversial problems, topical social issues; dramatic personal narratives with unusual experiences of average families; new or unusual medical information, personal medical stories. No submissions on food, beauty, needlework and crafts. Short stories, 2,000 to 5,000 words, with strong identification for women, by published writers and "beginners with demonstrable talent." Pays top rates, on acceptance.

HARPER'S BAZAAR—1700 Broadway, New York, NY 10019. Anthony Mazzola, Ed.-in-Chief. Articles, 1,500 to 2,000 words, for active, sophisticated women. Topics include the arts, world affairs, food, wine, travel, families, education, personal finance, careers, health, and sexuality. No unsolicited manuscripts; query first with SASE. Payment varies, on acceptance.

IDEALS—Nelson Place at Elm Hill Pike P.O. Box 140300, Nashville, TN 37214–0300. Peggy Schaefer, Ed. Articles, 600 to 800 words; poetry, 12 to 50 lines, no free verse. Light, reminiscent pieces of interest to women over 50. Pays $10 for poems. Guidelines.

LADIES' HOME JOURNAL—100 Park Ave., New York, NY 10017. Myrna Blyth, Pub. Dir./Ed.-in-Chief. Articles of interest to women. Send queries with outlines to Jan Goodwin, Exec. Ed. (reportage/human interest/celebrities); Linda Peterson, Articles Ed. (health/medical); Lois Johnson (beauty/fashion); Marilyn Glass (decorating); Jan Hazard (food). Fiction and poetry accepted through literary agents only.

LEAR'S—505 Park Ave., 19th fl., New York, NY 10022. Audreen Ballard, Exec. Ed. "Literate, lively, and compelling" articles, 800 to 1,200 words, for women over 40, on health, finance, personalities, and leisure. Query with clips and SASE. Pays $1 a word, on acceptance.

MCCALL'S—230 Park Ave., New York, NY 10169. Andrea Thompson, Ed. Articles, 1,000 to 3,000 words, on current issues, human interest, family relationships. Pays top rates, on acceptance.

MADEMOISELLE—350 Madison Ave., New York, NY 10017. Michelle Stacey, Exec. Ed., Articles; Eileen Schnurr, Fiction Ed. Fiction and articles. Pays $800 to $1,000 for short articles, $1,750 for full-length features; $1,000 for short-short stories; from $1,500 for short stories, on acceptance.

MICHIGAN WOMAN—8888 Thorne Rd., Horton, MI 49246. Monica Smiley, Ed. Articles, to 2,000 words, that highlight the achievements of Michigan women. Fillers, to 700 words. Pays 10¢ a word, on publication. Query required.

MODERN BRIDE—475 Park Ave. South, New York, NY 10016. Mary Ann Cavlin, Man. Ed. Articles, from 1,500 words, for bride and groom, on wedding planning, financial planning, juggling career and home, etc. Pays on acceptance.

MS. MAGAZINE—One Times Sq., New York, NY 10036. Address Manuscript Editor with SASE. Articles relating to women's roles and changing lifestyles; profiles, self-help, and general interest. Poetry and fiction neither accepted, acknowledged, nor returned. Pays competitive rates.

NA'AMAT WOMAN—200 Madison Ave., 18th fl., New York, NY 10016. Judith Sokoloff, Ed. Articles on Jewish culture, women's issues, social and political topics, and Israel, 1,500 to 2,500 words. Short stories with a Jewish theme. Pays 8¢ a word, on publication. Query or send manuscript.

NEW BODY—888 Seventh Ave., New York, NY 10106. Constance Cardozo, Ed. Lively, readable service-oriented articles, 800 to 1,500 words, by writers with background in health field: exercise, nutrition, psychology, and diet pieces for women aged 18 to 40. Pays $100 to $300, on publication. Query.

NEW WOMAN—215 Lexington Ave., New York, NY 10016. Pat Miller, Ed./Pub. Self-help/inspirational articles, on psychology, relationships, money, careers. Travel features, with personal discovery angle. Lifestyle, health, and fitness features. Some fiction and poetry. Profiles of celebrities, business women. Innovative quizzes. Pays to $1 a word, on acceptance. Query with SASE.

NEW YORK WOMAN—2 Park Ave., New York, NY 10016. Betsy Carter, Ed. Articles, 500 to 3,000 words, for women age 25 to 45, living in the metropolitan New York area. Pays $1 a word, on publication. Queries required.

PLAYGIRL—801 Second Ave., New York, NY 10017. Nancie S. Martin, Ed.-in-Chief. In-depth articles for contemporary women. Fiction, 2,500 words. Humor, celebrity interviews. Pays varying rates. Query first with clips. Guidelines.

POLITICAL WOMAN—4521 Campus Dr., #388, Irvine, CA 92715. Sally Corngold, Ed. Well-documented, non-partisan articles, 1,000 to 3,000 words, for "thinking women." Pays $25 to $1,000, on publication.

QUARANTE—P.O. Box 2875, Arlington, VA 22202. The Magazine of Style and Substance. Michele Linden, Articles Ed. Features and fiction (to 3,000 words), poetry (3 to 18 lines), and short profiles for "Women of Substance" column. Topics include fashion, politics, health, cuisine, and finance geared to women over 30. Pays to $150, on publication.

REDBOOK—224 W. 57th St., New York, NY 10019. Deborah Purcell, Fiction Ed. Gini Kopecky, Articles Ed. Fiction and articles for women ages 25 to 40. Pays from $1,000 for short stories to 25 typed pages; to $850 for short shorts, to 9 typed pages; $750 for personal-experience pieces, 1,000 to 2,000 words, on solving problems in marriage, family life, or community, for "Young Mother's Story." Query for articles only. SASE required.

SAVVY WOMAN (FORMERLY *SAVVY*)—3 Park Ave., New York, NY 10016. Annalyn Swan, Ed.-in-Chief. Sophisticated articles on careers, for successful women; topical features and profiles of interesting women, 2,000 to 2,500 words. Payment varies.

SELF—350 Madison Ave., New York, NY 10017. Anthea Disney, Ed. Articles for women of all ages, with strong how-to slant, on self-development. Pays from $700, on acceptance. Query.

SOUTHERN STYLE—Whittle Communications, 505 Market St., Knoxville, TN 37902. Elise Nakhnikian, Ed. Articles, 750 to 1,500 words, on fashion, beauty, celebrities, food, and related topics. Pays $350 to $1,500. Query required.

VIRTUE—P. O. Box 850, Sisters, OR 97759. Becky Durost-Fish, Ed. Articles, 1,000 to 1,500 words, on the family, marriage, self-esteem, working mothers, opinions, food, decorating. Fiction. Pays 10¢ a word, on publication. Query required.

VOGUE—350 Madison Ave., New York, NY 10017. Address Features Ed. Articles, to 1,500 words, on women, entertainment and the arts, travel, medicine and health. General features. No unsolicited manuscripts. Query first. Pays good rates, on acceptance.

WEIGHT WATCHERS MAGAZINE—360 Lexington Ave., New York, NY 10017. Nelly Edmondson, Articles Ed. Articles on nutrition and health. Pays from $250, on acceptance. Query with clips required. Guidelines.

WOMAN—1115 Broadway, New York, NY 10010. Sherry Amatenstein, Ed. Personal-experience and how-to pieces, 1,000 to 2,000 words, for women who want to better their relationships, careers or lifestyles. Profiles of women business owners for "Be Your Own Boss." Short interviews with successful women for "Woman in the News." Short medical and legal news items for "Let's Put Our Heads Together." Pays $50 to $400, on acceptance. Query.

WOMAN'S DAY—1515 Broadway, New York, NY 10036. Rebecca Greer, Articles Ed. Eileen Herbert Jordan, Fiction Ed. Human-interest or helpful articles, to 3,500 words, on marriage, child-rearing, health, careers, relationships, money management. Dramatic narratives of medical miracles, rescues, etc. Quality short stories. Pays top rates, on acceptance. Query for articles.

WOMAN'S WORLD—177 N. Dean St., Englewood, NJ 07631. Gerry Hunt, Sr. Ed. Articles, 600 to 1,800 words, of interest to middle-income women between the ages of 18 and 60, on love, romance, careers, medicine, health, psychology, family life, travel, dramatic stories of adventure or crisis. Pays $300 to $750, on acceptance. Query.

WOMEN IN BUSINESS—American Business Women's Assn., 900 Ward Pkwy, Box 8728, Kansas City, MO 64114. Margaret E. Horan, Ed. Features, 1,000 to 1,500 words, for working women between 35 and 55 years. No profiles. Pays on acceptance. Written query required.

WOMEN'S SPORTS & FITNESS—P.O. Box 2456, Winter Park, FL 32789. Lewis Rothlein, Ed. How-tos, profiles, and sports reports, 500 to 3,000 words, for active women. Fitness, nutrition, and health pieces also considered. Pays on publication. Query first.

WOMEN'S CIRCLE—P.O. Box 299, Lynnfield, MA 01940. Marjorie Pearl, Ed. Success stories on home-based female entrepreneurs. How-to articles on contemporary craft and needlework projects. Unique money-saving ideas and recipes. Pays varying rates, on acceptance.

THE WORKBASKET—4251 Pennsylvania, Kansas City, MO 64111. Roma Jean Rice, Ed. Instructions and models for original knit, crochet, and tat items. How-tos on crafts and gardening, 400 to 1,200 words, with photos. Pays 7¢ a word for articles, extra for photos, on acceptance; negotiable rates for instructional items.

WORKING WOMAN—342 Madison Ave., New York, NY 10173. Julia Kagan, Exec. Ed. Articles, 1,000 to 2,500 words, on business and personal aspects of working women's lives. Pays from $400, on acceptance.

WORKING WOMAN WEEKENDS—342 Madison Ave., New York, NY 10173. Louise Washer, Assoc. Ed. Articles, 250 to 750 words, on weekend activities: entertaining, travel, cooking for fun, treats and retreats, recreational shopping. Pays on acceptance.

HOME AND LIFESTYLE PUBLICATIONS

AMERICA ENTERTAINS—Working Woman/McCall's Group, 230 Park Ave., New York, NY 10169. Articles on informal entertaining or home design (750 or 1,500 words), geared to women aged 30–45. Quarterly. Pays from $1 a word, on acceptance.

THE AMERICAN ROSE MAGAZINE—P.O. Box 30,000, Shreveport, LA 71130. Harold S. Goldstein, Ed. Articles on home rose gardens: varieties, products, etc. Pays in copies.

AMERICANA—29 W. 38th St., New York, NY 10018. Sandra Wilmot, Ed. Articles, 1,000 to 2,500 words, with historical slant: restoration, crafts, food, antiques, travel, etc. Pays $350 to $600, on acceptance. Query.

BETTER HOMES AND GARDENS—1716 Locust St. , Des Moines, IA 50336. David Jordan, Ed. Articles, to 2,000 words, on home and family entertainment, money management, health, travel, pets, and cars. Pays top rates, on acceptance. Query.

BON APPETIT—5900 Wilshire Blvd., Los Angeles, CA 90036. Barbara Fairchild, Exec. Ed. Articles on fine cooking (menu format or single focus), cooking classes, and gastronomically-focused travel. Query, with samples of published work. Pays varying rates, on acceptance.

CHOCOLATIER—Haymarket, Ltd. 45 W. 34th St., New York, NY 10001. Barbara Albright, Ed. Articles related to chocolate and desserts; cooking and baking techniques. Pays varying rates, on acceptance. Query required. Guidelines.

THE CHRISTIAN SCIENCE MONITOR—One Norway St., Boston, MA 02115. David Holmstrom, Features Ed. Denis Glover, Home and Family Ed. Articles on lifestyle trends, women's rights, family, parenting, consumerism, fashion, and food. Pays varying rates, on acceptance.

CONNOISSEUR—Hearst Corp., 1790 Broadway, 18th fl., New York, NY 10019. Ellen Rosenbush, Man. Ed. Articles for readers "interested in learning about excellence in all areas of art." Topics include fine, decorative, and performing arts; architecture and design, food, fashion, and travel; include pertinent service data. Length varies; query required. Pays about $1 a word, on acceptance.

CONSUMERS DIGEST—5705 N. Lincoln Ave., Chicago, IL 60659. John Manos, Ed. Articles, 500 to 3,000 words, on subjects of interest to consumers:

products and services, automobiles, health, fitness, consumer legal affairs, and personal money management. Photos. Pays from 30¢ a word, extra for photos, on publication. Buys all rights. Query with resumé and published clips.

THE COOK'S MAGAZINE—2710 North Ave., Bridgeport, CT 06604. Marc Wortman, Exec. Ed. Articles on trends in home and restaurant food and cooking. Query with brief outline, published clips, and sample recipe (for writing and recipe style). Pays $200 to $500, on acceptance. SASE required.

COUNTRY—5400 S. 60th St., Greendale, WI 53129. Address Dan Johnson. Pieces on interesting rural and country people who have unusual hobbies or businesses, 500 to 1,500 words; liberal use of direct quotes. Good, candid, color photos required. Pays on acceptance. Queries preferred.

FARM & RANCH LIVING—5400 S. 60th St., Greendale, WI 53129. Bob Ottum, Ed. Articles, 2,000 words, on rural people and situations; nostalgia pieces, profiles of interesting farms and farmers, ranches and ranchers. Poetry. Pays $15 to $400, on acceptance and on publication.

FLORIDA HOME & GARDEN (FORMERLY *SOUTH FLORIDA HOME & GARDEN*)—600 Brickell Ave., Suite 207, Miami, FL 33131. Kathryn Howard, Ed. Features, 800 to 1,000 words, and department pieces, 500 to 900 words, about Florida interior design, architecture, landscape architecture, gardening, cuisine, fashion, trendy new products, medical/health & beauty, and home entertaining. Pays $200 to $400, extra for photos.

FLOWER AND GARDEN MAGAZINE—4251 Pennsylvania, Kansas City, MO 64111. Rachel Snyder, Ed.-in-Chief. How-to articles, to 1,200 words, with photos, on indoor and outdoor home gardening. Pays 8¢ a word, on acceptance. Query preferred.

FOOD & WINE—1120 Ave. of the Americas, New York, NY 10036. Ila Stanger, Ed.-in-Chief. Warren Picower, Man. Ed. Current culinary or beverage ideas for dining and entertaining at home and out. Submit detailed proposal.

FOUR SEASONS—55 Doncaster Ave., Suite 106, Thornhill, Ont., Canada L3T 1L7. Leslie May, Ed. Coord. Four Seasons hotel chain magazine. Lifestyle articles, 700 to 2,500 words. Canadian and U.S. editions. Payment varies, on publication. Query required.

FRIENDLY EXCHANGE—Locust at 17th, Des Moines, IA 50336. Adele Malott, Ed. Domestic travel and leisure features, 1,000 to 2,500 words, for young, active families who live in the western half of the U.S. Pieces written with real people in mind, making use of anecdotes and quotes. No first person or routine destination pieces. No poetry, fiction, cartoons. Pays $400 to $800, extra for photos. Query preferred.

GARDEN—The Garden Society, Botanical Garden, Bronx, NY 10458. Ann Botshon, Ed. Articles, 1,000 to 2,500 words, on botany, horticulture, ecology, agriculture. Photos. Pays to $300, on publication. Query.

GARDEN DESIGN—1733 Connecticut Ave. N.W., Washington, DC 20009. Karen D. Fishler, Man. Ed. Articles, 500 to 1,000 words, on classic and contemporary examples of residential landscape design, garden art, and garden history. Pays $350, on publication. Query.

HARROWSMITH/USA—The Creamery, Ferry Rd., Charlotte, VT 05445. Tom Rawls, Ed. Investigative pieces, 4,000 to 5,000 words, on ecology, energy, health, gardening, do-it-yourself projects, and the food chain. Short pieces for "Screed" (opinions); and "Gazette" (news briefs). Pays $500 to $1,500 for features, from $50 to $600 for department pieces, on acceptance. Query required. Send SASE for guidelines.

THE HERB QUARTERLY—P. O. Box 275, Newfane, VT 05345. Jeanne Turner, Assoc. Ed. Articles, 2,000 to 10,000 words, on herbs: practical uses, cultivation, gourmet cooking, landscaping, herb tradition, unique garden designs, profiles of herb garden experts, practical how-to's for the herb businessperson. Include garden design when possible. Pays on publication. Guidelines.

HG: HOUSE & GARDEN—350 Madison Ave., New York, NY 10017. Nancy Novogrod, Ed.-in-Chief. Priscilla Flood, Man. Ed. Articles on decorating, style, design, architecture, and the arts. No unsolicited material.

HOME MAGAZINE—P.O. Box 92000, Los Angeles, CA 90009. Channing Dawson, Ed. Articles of interest to homeowners: architecture, remodeling, decorating, how-to's, project ideas, landscaping, taxes, insurance, conservation and solar energy. Pays varying rates, on acceptance. Query, with 50- to 200-word summary.

HOMEOWNER—3 Park Ave., New York, NY 10016. Joe Carter, Ed. Articles, 500 to 1,500 words, with photos, on home improvement, remodeling, landscaping and do-it-yourself projects. Pays $400 to $1,000 for feature stories, on acceptance. Query.

HOMEOWNERS—8520 Sweetwater, Suite F57, Houston, TX 77037. Theresa Seegers, Man. Ed. Articles, 200 to 500 words, on buying and selling real estate, mortgages, investments, home improvement, interior design, consumer and business trends: "material should emphasize the importance of consulting a real estate professional on any real estate matter." Pays 10¢ to 20¢ a word, on acceptance. Query.

HORTICULTURE—Statler Bldg. 20 Park Plaza, Suite 1220, Boston, MA 02116. John Barstow, Man. Ed. Authoritative, well-written articles, 1,000 to 2,500 words, on all aspects of gardening. Pays competitive rates. Query first.

HOUSE BEAUTIFUL—1700 Broadway, New York, NY 10019. Carol Cooper Garey, Features Dir. Service articles related to the home. Pieces on design, travel and gardening mostly staff-written. Send for guidelines. Query with detailed outline. SASE required.

HOUSTON HOME & GARDEN—5615 Kirby, Suite 600 P.O. Box 25386, Houston, TX 77265. Diane Stafford, Exec. Ed. Articles on interior design, regional gardening, cooking, art, architecture, health, fitness, and travel. Limited free-lance market. Query.

INDEPENDENT LIVING—44 Broadway, Greenlawn, NY 11740. Anne Kelly, Ed. Articles, 1,000 to 2,000 words, addressing lifestyles of the "physically challenged and disabled." Possible topics: travel, sports, cooking, hobbies, family life and sexuality. Pays 10¢ a word, on publication. Query.

LIFE IN THE TIMES—The Times Journal Co., Springfield, VA 22159. Barry Robinson, Ed. Travel articles, 900 words; features on food, 500 to 1,000 words; and short, personal-experience pieces, 750 words, of interest to military people and their families around the world. Pays from $25 to $150 for short piecs, to $350 for general-interest features up to 2,000 words, on acceptance.

LOG HOME GUIDE FOR BUILDERS & BUYERS—Hwys. 32 & 32I, Cosby, TN 37722. Articles, 500 to 1,500 words, on building new, or restoring old, log homes, especially with solar or alternative heating systems, as well as pieces on decorating or profiles of interesting builders of old homes. Pays 20¢ a word, extra for photos, on publication. Limited market. Query first.

METROPOLITAN HOME—750 Third Ave., New York, NY 10017. Barbara Graustark, Articles Ed. Service and informational articles for metropolitan dwellers in apartment, houses, co-ops, lofts and condos. Pays varying rates. Query.

MILITARY LIFESTYLE MAGAZINE—1732 Wisconsin Ave. N.W., Washington, DC 20007. Hope Daniels, Ed. Articles, 1,000 to 2,000 words, for military families in the U.S. and overseas; pieces on child raising, marriage, health, fitness, food, and issues concerning young military families; fiction. Pays $200 to $600, on publication. Query first.

THE MOTHER EARTH NEWS—105 Stoney Mt. Rd., Hendersonville, NC 28791. Bruce Woods, Ed. Articles on country living: home improvement and construction, how-to's, indoor and outdoor gardening, crafts and projects, etc. Also self-help, health, food-related, ecology, energy, and consumerism pieces; profiles. Pays from $100 per published page, on acceptance. Address Submissions Ed.

NATIONAL GARDENING MAGAZINE—180 Flynn Ave., Burlington, VT 05401. Kit Anderson, Ed. Articles, 300 to 3,000 words: seed-to-table profiles of major crops; firsthand reports from experienced gardeners in this country's many growing regions; easy-to-follow gardening techniques; garden food receipes; coverage of fruits, vegetables, and ornamentals. Pays $75 to $450, extra for photos, on acceptance. Query preferred.

NEW AGE—342 Western Ave., Brighton, MA 02135. Florence Graves, Ed./ Assoc. Pub. Features, 2,000 to 4,000 words; columns, 750 to 1,500 words; short news items, 50 words; and first-person narratives, 750 to 1,500 words, for readers who take an active interest in holistic health, personal and spiritual growth, social responsibility, and contemporary social issues. Pays varying rates. Query or send completed manuscript.

NEW HOME—P.O. Box 2008, Laconia, NH 03247. Steven Maviglio, Man. Ed. Articles, 250 to 2,500 words, "that give upscale new homeowners whatever they need to make their home more comfortable, practical, and personal." Department pieces on lawn care, roofing, and interviews with professionals in their homes. Pays $200 to $1,000, on acceptance. Query required.

THE NEW HOMEOWNER—Castlewood Corp. 222 Keswick Ave., 2nd fl., Glenside, PA 19038. Articles on resources, home care, interior design, and decorating, of varying lengths, for the affluent new homeowner. Pays varying rates, on acceptance.

1001 HOME IDEAS—3 Park Ave., New York, NY 10016. Ellen Frankel, Ed. General-interest articles, 500 to 2,000 words, on home decorating, furnishings, antiques and collectibles, food, household tips, crafts, remodeling, gardening. How-to and problem-solving decorating pieces. Pays varying rates, on acceptance. Query.

ORGANIC GARDENING—33 E. Minor St., Emmaus, PA 18098. Christine A. Rossell, Man. Ed. Articles by gardeners, well-researched, detailed: growing specific organic vegetables and fruits, annual and perennial flowers, shrubs, and trees. Profiles of experienced gardeners who use organic techniques. Pays 35¢ to 50¢ a word. Query preferred.

PALM SPRINGS LIFE—Desert Publications, 303 N. Indian Ave., Palm Springs, CA 92262. Becky Kurtz, Ed. Articles (800 to 1,200 words) of interest to "wealthly, upscale people who live and/or play in the desert." Pays $150 to $200 for features, $30 for short profiles, on publication. Query required.

PEOPLE IN ACTION—P.O. Box 10010, Odgen, UT 84409. Address Editor. Cover stories, 1,200 words, on living, renowned individuals in fine arts, entertainment, communications, business, sports, education, health, science and technology. "People featured must exemplify positive values, overcome obstacles, help others, advance culture, and create solutions." Send high-quality, color transparencies illustrating manuscript. Query first with SASE.

RELATIONSHIPS TODAY—432 Park Ave. S., Suite 504, New York, NY 10016. Lyle Benjamin, Ed.-in-Chief. Articles, to 2,500 words, that help to improve communication and provide entertainment for "people who want to get the most from their relationships." Pays to $500, on publication.

SELECT HOMES—3835 W. 30th Ave., Vancouver, B.C., Canada V6S 1W9. Pam Withers, Ed. How-to articles, profiles of building or renovations and "what's available" pieces, 750 to 1,200 words. Pays from $150, on acceptance. Query regional editors: Pam Withers, Western Ed. (address above), or Carol Besler, Homes Editor, 1450 Don Mills Rd., Don Mills, Ont., Canada M3B 2X7. Include International Reply Coupons.

WORKBENCH—4251 Pennsylvania, Kansas City, MO 64111. Robert N. Hoffman, Ed. Illustrated how-to articles on home improvement and woodworking, with detailed instructions. Pays from $150 per printed page, on acceptance. Send SASE for writers' guidelines.

YOUR HOME/INDOORS & OUT (FORMERLY *YOUR HOME MAGA-ZINE*)—P.O. Box 10010, Ogden, UT 84409. Articles, 1,200 words, with fresh ideas in all areas of home decor: the latest in home construction (exteriors, interiors, building materials, design); the outdoors at home (landscaping, pools, patios, gardening); home management; buying and selling. "We are especially interested in articles on choosing a realtor or home builder." No do-it-yourself pieces. Manuscripts, 1,200 words, with quality color transparencies. Query first with SASE to editor.

SPORTS, OUTDOORS, RECREATION

AAA WORLD—AAA Headquarters, 8111 Gatehouse Rd., Falls Church, VA 22047. Douglas Damerst, Ed. Automobile and travel concerns, including automotive travel, maintenance and upkeep, 750 to 1,500 words. Pays $300 to $600, on acceptance. Query with clips preferred.

THE AMATEUR BOXER—P.O. Box 249, Cobalt, CT 06414. Bob Taylor, Ed. Articles on amateur boxing. Fillers. Photos. Pays $10 to $35, extra for photos, on publication. Query preferred.

THE AMERICAN FIELD—222 W. Adams St., Chicago, IL 60606. William F. Brown, Ed. Yarns about hunting trips, bird-shooting; articles to 1,500 words, on dogs and field trials, emphasizing conservation of game resources. Pays varying rates, on acceptance.

AMERICAN GOLF MAGAZINE—4500 S. Lakeshore Dr., Suite 336, Tempe, AZ 85282. Michael A. Cox, Ed. Articles, 800 to 2,000 words, aimed at public golfers; "we never write about courses that the general golfer cannot play." Travel pieces (1,500 to 2,500 words), course reviews, profiles (600 to 800 words), and shorts (150 words). Pays $50 to $300, on publication. Query preferred. Guidelines.

AMERICAN HANDGUNNER—591 Camino de la Reina, Suite 200, San Diego, CA 92108. Cameron Hopkins, Ed. Semi-technical articles on shooting sports, gun repair and alteration, handgun matches and tournaments, for lay readers. Pays $100 to $500, on publication. Query.

AMERICAN HUNTER—470 Spring Park Place, Suite 1000, Herndon, VA 22070. Tom Fulgham, Ed. Articles, 1,400 to 2,500 words, on hunting. Photos. Pays on acceptance. Guidelines.

AMERICAN MOTORCYCLIST—American Motorcyclist Assn., Box 6114, Westerville, OH 43081-6114. Greg Harrison, Ed. Articles and fiction, to 3,000 words, on motorcycling: news converage, personalities, tours. Photos. Pays varying rates, on publication. Query with SASE.

THE AMERICAN RIFLEMAN—470 Spring Park Place, Suite 1000, Herndon, VA 22070. Bill Parkerson, Ed. Factual articles on use and enjoyment of sporting firearms. Pays on acceptance.

AMERICAN SQUAREDANCE MAGAZINE—216 Williams St., P.O. Box 488, Huron, OH 44839. Cathie Burdick, Ed. Articles and fiction, 1,000 to 1,500 words, related to square dancing. Poetry. Fillers to 100 words. Pays $2 per column inch.

ARCHERY WORLD—319 Barry Ave. S., Suite 101, Wayzata, MN 55391. Tim Dehm, Ed. Articles, 1,000 to 2,500 words, on all aspects of bowhunting, with photos. Pays from $200, extra for photos, on publication.

THE ATLANTIC SALMON JOURNAL—1435 St. Alexandre, Suite 1030, Montreal, Quebec, Canada H3A 2G4. Terry Davis, Ed. Material related to Atlantic salmon: conservation, ecology, travel, politics, biology, how-tos, anecdotes, cuisine. Articles, 1,500 to 3,000 words. Pays $100 to $350, on publication.

ATV SPORTS—Box 2260, Costa Mesa, CA 92628. Bruce Simurda, Ed. Articles, 1,000 to 1,500 words, relating to three- and four-wheel, all-terrain vehicles. Pays $60 per printed page, on publication. Query.

BACKPACKER MAGAZINE—1515 Broadway, New York, NY 10036. John A. Delves, Ed. Articles, 250 to 3,000 words, on backpacking, technique, kayaking/canoeing, mountaineering, alpine/nordic skiing, health, natural science. Photos. Pays varying rates. Query.

THE BACKSTRETCH—19363 James Couzens Hwy., Detroit, MI 48235. Ruth LeGrove, Man. Ed. Ann Moss, Ed. United Thoroughbred Trainers of America. Feature articles, with photos, on subjects involved with thoroughbred horse racing. Pays after publication.

BASEBALL FORECAST, BASEBALL ILLUSTRATED, BASEBALL PREVIEW, BASKETBALL ANNUAL AND BASKETBALL FORECAST—See *Hockey Illustrated.*

BASSIN'—15115 S. 76th E. Ave., Bixby, OK 74008. Tony Dolle, Ed. Articles, 1,500 to 1,800 words, on how-to and where-to bass fish, for the average fisherman. Pays $200 to $500, on acceptance.

BASSMASTER MAGAZINE—B.A.S.S. Publications, P.O. Box 17900, Montgomery, AL 36141. Dave Precht, Ed. Articles, 1,500 to 2,000 words, with photos, on freshwater black bass and striped bass. "Short Casts" pieces, 400 to 800 words, on news, views, and items of interest. Pays $200 to $400, on acceptance. Query.

BAY & DELTA YACHTSMAN—2019 Clement Ave., Alameda, CA 94501. Bill Parks, Ed. Cruising stories and features. Must have Northern California tie-in. Photos and illustrations. Pays varying rates.

BC OUTDOORS—1132 Hamilton St., #202, Vancouver, B.C., Canada V6B 2S2. George Will, Ed. Articles, to 2,000 words, on fishing, hunting, conservation and all forms of non-competitive outdoor recreation in British Columbia and Yukon. Photos. Pays from 15¢ to 25¢ a word, on acceptance.

BICYCLE GUIDE—711 Boylston St., Boston, MA 02116. Theodore Costantino, Ed. "Our magazine covers all aspects of cycling from an enthusiast's perspective: racing, touring, sport riding, product reviews, and technical information. We depend on free lancers for touring articles and race coverage." Queries are preferred. Pays varying rates, on publication.

BICYCLING—33 E. Minor St., Emmaus, PA 18098. James C. McCullagh, Ed. Articles, 500 to 2,500 words, on recreational riding, fitness training, nutrition, bike maintenance, equipment, racing and touring, for serious cyclists. Photos, illustrations. Pays $25 to $800, on acceptance. Guidelines.

BIKEREPORT—Bikecentennial, P.O. Box 8308, Missoula, MT 59807. Daniel D'Ambrosio, Ed. Accounts of bicycle tours in the U.S. and overseas, interviews, personal-experience pieces, humor and news shorts, 1,200 to 2,500 words. Pays $25 to $65 per published page.

BIRD WATCHER'S DIGEST—P.O Box 110, Marietta, OH 45750. Mary B. Bowers, Ed. Articles, 600 to 2,500 words, for bird watchers: first-person accounts; how-tos; pieces on endangered species; profiles. Cartoons. Pays to $50, on publication.

BLACK BELT—P.O. Box 7728, 1813 Victory Pl., Burbank, CA 91510–7728. Articles related to self-defense: how-tos on fitness and technique; historical, travel, philosophical subjects. Pays $100 to $200, on publication. Query required. Guidelines.

BOAT PENNSYLVANIA—Pennsylvania Fish Commission, P.O. Box 1673, Harrisburg, PA 17105–1673. Articles, 200 to 2,500 words, with photos, on boating in Pennsylvania: motorboating, sailing, waterskiing, canoeing, kayaking, and rafting. No pieces on fishing. Pays $50 to $300, on acceptance. Query. Guidelines.

BOATING—One Park Ave., New York, NY 10016. Doug Schryver, Ed. Illustrated articles, 1,000 to 2,000 words, on power boating. Pays good rates, on acceptance. Query.

BOUNDARY WATERS JOURNAL—Route 1, Box 1740, Ely, MN 55731. Stuart Osthoff, Ed. Articles, 2,000 to 3,000 words, on recreation and natural resources in Minnesota's Boundary Waters region, including canoe routes, lifestyles of residents, hiking, and events. Pays $200 to $400, on publication.

BOW & ARROW HUNTING—Box HH, 34249 Camino Capistrano, Capistrano Beach, CA 92624. Roger Combs, Ed. Dir. Articles, 1,200 to 2,500 words, with photos, on bowhunting; profiles and technical pieces. Pays $50 to $300, on acceptance. Same address and mechanical requirements for Gun World.

BOWHUNTER MAGAZINE—2245 Kohn Rd., Box 8200, Harrisburg, PA 17105–8200. M.R. James, Ed. Informative, entertaining features, 500 to 5,000 words, on bow and arrow hunting. Fillers. Photos. Pays $25 to $300, on acceptance. Study magazine first.

BOWLERS JOURNAL—101 E. Erie St., Chicago, IL 60611. Mort Luby, Ed. Trade and consumer articles, 1,200 to 2,200 words, with photos, on bowling. Pays $75 to $200, on acceptance.

BOWLING—5301 S. 76th St., Greendale, WI 53129. Dan Matel, Ed. Articles, to 1,500 words, on amateur league and tournament bowling. Profiles. Pays varying rates, on publication.

CALIFORNIA ANGLER—1921 E. Carnegie St., Suite N, Santa Ana, CA 92705. Jim Gilmore, Ed. How-to and where-to articles, 2,000 words, for freshwater and saltwater anglers in California: travel, new products, fishing techniques, profiles. Photos. Pays $75 to $350, on acceptance. Query first.

CALIFORNIA HORSE REVIEW—P.O. Box 2437, Fair Oaks, CA 95628. Articles, 750 to 2,500 words, on horse training, for professional horsemen; profiles of prominent West Coast horses and riders. Pays $35 to $125, on publication.

CANOE—P.O. Box 3146, Kirkland, WA 98083. David F. Harrison, Ed.-in-Chief. Features, 2,000 to 4,000 words; department pieces, 500 to 2,000 words, on competition, political and environmental affairs, equipment, health, how-tos, etc. Pays $5 per column inch, on publication. Query preferred.

CAR AND DRIVER—2002 Hogback Rd., Ann Arbor, MI 48105. William Jeanes, Ed. Articles, to 2,500 words, for enthusiasts, on car manufacturers, new developments in cars, etc. Pays to $2,000, on acceptance. Query with clips.

CAR CRAFT—8490 Sunset Blvd., Los Angeles, CA 90069. Cameron Benty, Ed. Articles and photofeatures on unusual street machines, drag cars, racing events; technical pieces; action photos. Pays from $150 per page, on publication.

CASCADES EAST—716 N.E. Fourth St., P.O. Box 5784, Bend, OR 97708. Geoff Hill, Ed./Pub. Articles, 1,000 to 2,000 words, on outdoor activities, (fishing, hunting, golfing, backpacking, rafting, skiing, snowmobiling, etc.), history, special events and scenic tours in Cascades region. Photos. Pays 3¢ to 10¢ a word, extra for photos, on publication.

CHESAPEAKE BAY MAGAZINE—1819 Bay Ridge Ave., Annapolis, MD 21403. Betty Rigoli, Ed. Technical and how-to articles, to 1,500 words, on boating, fishing, conservation, in Chesapeake Bay. Photos. Pays $85 to $125, on publication.

CITY SPORTS MAGAZINE—P.O Box 3693, San Francisco, CA 94119. Jane McConnell, Ed. Articles, 200 to 2,000 words, on the active life style, including service pieces, trend pieces, profiles, and business. Pays $50 to $650, on publication. Query appropriate editor.

CORVETTE FEVER—Box 44620, Ft. Washington, MD 20744. Pat Stivers, Ed. Articles, 500 to 2,500 words, on Corvette repairs, swap meets, and personalities. Corvette-related fiction, about 700 lines, and fillers. Photos. Pays 10¢ a word, on publication.

CROSS COUNTRY SKIER—33 E. Minor St., Emmaus, PA 18049. Virginia Hostetter, Man. Ed. Articles, to 3,000 words, on all aspects of cross-country skiing. Departments, 1,000 to 1,500 words, on ski maintenance, skiing techniques, health and fitness. Published October through February. Pays $300 to $700 for features, $100 to $350 for departments, on publication. Query.

CRUISING WORLD—524 Thames St., Newport, RI 02840. George Day, Ed. Articles on sailing, 1,000 to 2,500 words: technical and personal narratives. No fiction, poetry, or logbook transcripts. 35mm slides. Pays $100 to $600, on acceptance. Query preferred.

CYCLE MAGAZINE—5706 Corsa Ave., Westlake Village, CA 91362. Phil Schilling, Ed. Articles, 6 to 20 manuscript pages, on motorcycle races, history, touring technical pieces; profiles. Photos. Pays on publication. Query.

CYCLE NEWS—2201Cherry Ave., Box 498, Long Beach, CA 90801. Jack Mangus, Ed. Technical articles on motorcycling; profiles and interviews with motorcycle newsmakers. Pays $2 per column inch, on publication.

CYCLE WORLD—853 W. 17th St., Costa Mesa, CA 92627. Paul Dean, Ed. Technical and feature articles, 1,500 to 2,500 words, for motorcycle enthusiasts. Photos. Pays $100 to $200 per page, on publication. Query.

CYCLING U.S.A.—U.S. Cycling Federation, 1750 E. Boulder St., Colorado Springs, CO 80909. Diane Fritschner, Ed. Articles, 500 to 1,500 words, on bicycle racing. Pays 10¢ a word, on publication. Query first.

CYCLIST—20816 Higgins Ct., Torrance, CA 90501. John Francis, Ed. Articles on all aspects on bicycling: touring, travel and equipment. Query required.

THE DIVER—P.O. Box 249, Cobalt, CT 06414. Bob Taylor, Ed. Articles on divers, coaches, officials, springboard and platform techniques, training tips, etc. Pays $15 to $40, extra for photos ($5 to $25 for cartoons), on publication.

EASTERN HORSE WORLD—See *Horse World USA.*

FIELD & STREAM—1515 Broadway, New York, NY 10036. Duncan Barnes, Ed. Articles, 1,500 to 2,500 words, with photos, on hunting, fishing. Fillers, 250 to 1000 words. Cartoons. Pays from $800 for feature articles with photos, $250 to $450 for fillers, $100 for cartoons, on acceptance. Query for articles.

FINS AND FEATHERS—318 W. Franklin Ave., Minneapolis, MN 55404. James F. Billig, Ed. Articles, 2,000 to 2,500 words, on a wide variety of recreational activities, including hunting, fishing, camping, and environmental issues. Pays $100 to $500, on publication. Query.

FISHING WORLD—51 Atlantic Ave., Floral Park, NY 11001. Keith Gardner, Ed. Features, to 2,500 words, with color transparencies, on fishing sites, technique, equipment. Pays $300 for major features, $100 for shorter articles. Query preferred.

THE FLORIDA HORSE—P.O. Box 2106, Ocala, FL 32678. F.J. Audette, Pub. Articles, 1,500 words, on Florida thoroughbred breeding and racing. Pays $100 to $150, on publication.

FLY FISHERMAN—Box 8200, Harrisburg, PA 17105. John Randolph, Ed. Articles, to 3,000 words, on how to and where to fly fish. Fillers, to 100 words. Pays from $50 to $500, on acceptance. Query.

THE FLYFISHER—1387 Cambridge, Idaho Falls, ID 83401. Dennis G. Bitton, Ed. Articles, 500 to 3,000 words, on techniques, lore, history, and flyfishing personalities; how-pieces. Serious or humorous short stories related to flyfishing. Pays from $50 to $200, after publication. Queries are preferred. Guidelines.

FLYFISHING NEWS, VIEWS AND REVIEWS—1387 Cambridge, Idaho Falls, ID 83401. Dennis G. Bitton, Ed. Articles 500–3,500 words on flyfishing, fictions, humor, nonfiction reports, or where-tos/how- tos. Guest opinion articles, "Cheap Shots," and letters to the editor. Pays $50 to $150 for articles, $25 to $50 for prints or drawings. Queries preferred.

FLYING MAGAZINE—1515 Broadway, New York, NY 10036. William Garvey, Ed.-in-Chief. Articles, 1,500 words, on personal flying experiences. Pays varying rates, on acceptance.

FOOTBALL DIGEST—Century Publishing Co., 990 Grove St., Evanston, IL 60201. Michael K. Herbert, Ed.-in-Chief. Profiles of pro stars, "think" pieces, 1,500 words, aimed at the pro football fan. Pays on publication.

FOOTBALL FORECAST—See *Hockey Illustrated.*

FUR-FISH-GAME—2878 E. Main St., Columbus, OH 43209. Mitch Cox, Ed.

Illustrated articles, 800 to 2,500 words, preferably with how-to angle, on hunting, fishing, trapping, dogs, camping or other outdoor topics. Some humorous or where-to articles. Pays $40 to $150, on acceptance.

GAME AND FISH PUBLICATIONS—P.O. Box 741, Marietta, GA 30061. Publishes outdoors magazines for 37 states. Articles, 1,500 to 2,500 words, on hunting and fishing. How-tos, where-tos, and adventure pieces. Profiles of successful hunters and fishermen. No hiking, canoeing, camping, or backpacking pieces. Pays $150 to $175 for state-specific articles, $200 to $300 for multi-state articles, before publication.

GOAL—650 Fifth Ave., 33rd Fl., New York, NY 10019. Michael A. Berger, Ed. Official magazine of the National Hockey League. Player profiles and trend stories, 1,000 to 1,800 words, for hockey fans with knowledge of the game and players, by writers with understanding of the sport. Pays $150 to $300, before publication. Query.

GOLF DIGEST—5520 Park Ave., Trumbull, CT 06611. Jerry Tarde, Ed. Instructional articles, tournament reports, and features on players, to 2,500 words. Fiction, 1,000 to 3,000 words. Poetry, fillers, humor, photos. Pays varying rates, on acceptance. Query preferred.

GOLF FOR WOMEN—426 S. Lamar Blvd., Oxford, MS 38655. Glen D. Zediker, Ed.-in-Chief. Golf-related articles of interest to women; fillers and humor. Instructional pieces staff written. Pays from 25¢ a word, on publication. Query first.

GOLF ILLUSTRATED—3 Park Ave., New York, NY 10016. Al Barkow, Ed. David Earl, Man. Ed. Golf-related features, 1,000 to 2,000 words: instruction, profiles, photo essays, travel, technique, nostalgia, opinion. Pays $750 to $1,500, on acceptance. Query preferred.

GOLF JOURNAL—Golf House, Far Hills, NJ 07931. Robert Sommers, Ed. U.S. Golf Assn. Articles on golf personalities, history, travel. Humor. Photos. Pays varying rates, on publication.

GOLF MAGAZINE—380 Madison Ave., New York, NY 10017. James Frank, Exec. Ed. Articles, 1,500 words with photos, on golf. Shorts, to 500 words. Pays $500 to $1,000 for articles, $75 to $150 for shorts, on publication.

GREAT LAKES SAILOR—572 W. Market St., Suite 6, P.O. Box 951, Akron, OH 44309. Drew Shippy, Ed. How-to pieces on sailing and navigational techniques; human-interest stories; and department pieces. "Destinations" (2,500 to 3,000 words, on cruises), "Trailor Sailor" (trips for day sailors, 1,500 words), and "First Person" (profiles, 2,500 to 3,000 words). Photos. Pays to 20¢ a word, on publication. Queries required. Guidelines.

THE GREYHOUND REVIEW—National Greyhound Association, Box 543, Abilene, KS 67410. Tim Horan, Man. Ed. Articles, 1,000 to 10,000 words, pertaining to the greyhound racing industry: how-to, historical nostalgia, interviews. Pays $85 to $150, on publication.

GULF COAST GOLFER—See *North Texas Golfer.*

GUN DIGEST AND HANDLOADER'S DIGEST—4092 Commercial Ave., Northbrook, IL 60062. Ken Warner, Ed. Well-researched articles, to 5,000 words, on guns and shooting, equipment, etc. Photos. Pays from 10¢ a word, on acceptance. Query.

GUN DOG—P.O. Box 35098, Des Moines, IA 50315. Bob Wilbanks, Man. Ed.

Features, 1,000 to 2,500 words, with photos, on bird hunting: how-tos, where-tos, dog training, canine medicine, breeding strategy. Fiction. Humor. Pays $50 to $150 for fillers and short articles, $150 to $350 for features, on acceptance.

GUN WORLD—See *Bow & Arrow Hunting.*

GUNS & AMMO—8490 Sunset Blvd., Los Angeles, CA 90069. E. G. Bell, Jr., Ed. Technical and general articles, 1,500 to 3,000 words, on guns, ammunition, and target shooting. Photos, fillers. Pays from $150, on acceptance.

HANG GLIDING—U.S. Hang Gliding Assn., P.O. Box 500, Pearblossom, CA 93553. Gilbert Dodgen, Ed. Articles and fiction, 2 to 3 pages, on hang gliding. Pays to $50, on publication. Query.

HOCKEY ILLUSTRATED—Lexington Library, Inc., 355 Lexington Ave., New York, NY 10017. Stephen Ciacciarelli, Ed. Articles, 2,500 words, on hockey players, teams. Pays $125, on publication. Query. Same address and requirements for *Baseball Illustrated, Wrestling World, Pro Basketball Illustrated, Pro Football Illustrated, Basketball Annual* (college), *Baseball Preview, Baseball Forecast, Pro Football Preview, Football Forecast,* and *Basketball Forecast.*

HORSE & RIDER—941 Calle Negocio, San Clemente, CA 92672. Ray Rich, Ed. Articles, 500 to 3,000 words, with photos, on Western riding and general horse care: training, feeding, grooming, etc. Pays varying rates, on publication. Buys all rights. Guidelines.

HORSE WORLD USA (FORMERLY *EASTERN HORSE WORLD*)—P.O. Box 249, Huntington Station, NY 11746. Diana DeRosa, Ed. Horse-related articles of varying lengths of interest to horse enthusiasts. Pays on publication. Query.

HORSEMAN—25025 I 45N, Suite 390, Spring, TX 77380. David T. Gaines, Ed./Pub. Instructional articles, to 2,500 words, with photos, for Western trainers and riders. Pays from $50.

HORSEMEN'S YANKEE PEDLAR—785 Southbridge St., Auburn, MA 01501. Nancy L. Khoury, Pub. News and feature-length articles, about horses and horsemen in the Northeast. Photos. Pays $2 per published inch, on publication. Query.

HORSEPLAY—P.O. Box 130, Gaithersburg, MD 20877. Cordelia Doucet, Ed. Articles, 1,000 to 3,000 words, on eventing, show jumping, horse shows, dressage, driving and fox hunting, for horse enthusiasts. Pays 10¢ a word, all rights, after publication.

HOT BIKE—2145 W. La Palma, Anaheim, CA 92801. Buck Lovell, Ed. Articles, 250 to 2,500 words, with photos, on motorcycles (contemporary and antique). Event coverage on high performance street and track and sport touring motorcycles, with emphasis on Harley Davidsons. Pays $50 to $100 per printed page, on publication.

HOT BOAT—Sport Publications, 500 Harrington St., Suite I, Corona, CA 91720. Kevin Spaise, Exec. Ed. Family-oriented articles on motorized water sport events and personalities: general-interest, how-to, and technical features, 600 to 1,000 words. Pays $85 to $300, on publication. Query.

HOT ROD—8490 Sunset Blvd., Los Angeles, CA 90069. Jeff Smith, Ed. How-to pieces and articles, 500 to 5,000 words, on auto mechanics, hot rods, track and drag racing. Photo-features on custom or performance-modified cars. Pays to $250 per page, on publication.

HUNTING—8490 Sunset Blvd., Los Angeles, CA 90069. Craig Boddington,

Ed. How-to articles on practical aspects of hunting. At least 15 photos required with articles. Pays $250 to $400 for articles with B&W photos, extra for color photos, on publication.

INSIDE CYCLING—4885 Riverbend Rd., Boulder, CO 80301. Susan Eastman, Man. Ed. Articles, to 1,500 words, on competitive cycling; personality profiles and interviews with cyclists, coaches, and organizers. "We focus on the elite of the sport." No how-to or touring articles. Pays 10¢ a word, on publication.

INSIDE TEXAS RUNNING (FORMERLY *INSIDE RUNNING & FITNESS*)—9514 Bristlebrook Dr., Houston, TX 77083. Joanne Schmidt, Ed. Articles and fillers on running, cycling, and triathlons in Texas. Pays $35 to $100, $10 for photos, on acceptance.

KEEPIN' TRACK OF VETTES—P.O. Box 48, Spring Valley, NY 10977. Shelli Finkel, Ed. Articles of any length, with photos, relating to Corvettes. Pays $25 to $200, on publication.

KITPLANES—P.O. Box 6050, Mission Viejo, CA 92690. Dave Martin, Ed. Articles, geared to the growing market of aircraft built from kits and plans by home craftsmen, on all aspects of design, construction and performance, 1,000 to 4,000 words. Pays $100 to $300, on publication.

LAKELAND BOATING—1600 Orrington Ave., Suite 500, Evanston, IL 60035. Douglas Seibold, Ed. Articles for boat owners on the Great Lakes and other area waterways, on long distance cruising, short trips, maintenance, equipment, history, regional personalities and events, and environment. Photos. Pays on acceptance. Query first. Guidelines.

MEN'S FITNESS—21100 Erwin St., Woodland Hills, CA 91367. David Rivas, Ed-in Chief, Chris Weygandt, Man. Ed. Features, 1,500 to 2,500 words, and department pieces, 1,000 to 1,500 words: "authoritative and practical articles dealing with fitness, health, and men's lifestyles. Pays $200 to $400, on acceptance.

MEN'S HEALTH—Rodale Press, 33 E. Minor Dr., Emmaus, PA 18098. Michael Lafavore, Exec. Ed. Articles, 1,000 to 2,500 words, on fitness, diet, health, relationships, sports, and travel, for men ages 25 to 55. Pays 50¢ a word, on acceptance. Query first.

MICHIGAN OUT-OF-DOORS—P.O. Box 30235, Lansing, MI 48909. Kenneth S. Lowe, Ed. Features, 1,500 to 2,500 words, on hunting, fishing, camping and conservation in Michigan. Pays $75 to $150, on acceptance.

MID-WEST OUTDOORS—111 Shore Dr., Hinsdale, IL 60521. Gene Laulunen, Ed. Articles, 1,500 words, with photos, on where, when, and how to fish in the Midwest. Fillers, 500 words. Pays $15 to $35, on publication.

MOTOR TREND—8490 Sunset Blvd., Los Angeles, CA 90069. Mike Anson, Ed. Articles, 250 to 2,000 words, on autos, racing, events, and profiles. Photos. Pay varies, on acceptance. Query.

MOTORCYCLIST—8490 Sunset Blvd., Los Angeles, CA 90069. Art Friedman, Ed. Articles, 1,000 to 3,000 words. Action photos. Pays varying rates, on publication.

MOTORHOME MAGAZINE—29901 Agoura Rd., Agoura, CA 91301. Bob Livingston, Ed. Articles, to 2,000 words, with color slides, on motorhomes; travel and how-to pieces. Pays to $500, on acceptance.

MUSCULAR DEVELOPMENT—Strength and Health Publishing, P.O. Box 1707, York, PA 17405. Jan Dellinger, Ed. Articles, 5 to 10 typed pages, on competitive bodybuilding and power lifting for serious weight training athletes. Pays $50 to $200, extra for photos, on publication. Query.

MUSHING—P.O. Box 144, Ester, AK 99725. Todd Hoener, Ed. How-tos, profiles, and feautres (1,500 to 2,000 words) and department pieces (500 to 1,000 words) for competitive and recreational mushers and skijorers. Humor and photos. Pays $25 to $250, after acceptance. Queries preferred. Guidelines.

NATIONAL PARKS MAGAZINE—1015 31st St. N.W., Washington, DC 20007. Michele Strutin, Ed. Articles, 1,000 to 2,000 words, on natural history, wildlife, outdoors activities, travel and conservation as they relate to national parks: illustrated features on the natural, historic and cultural resources of the National Park System. Pieces about legislation and other issues and events related to the parks. Pays $100 to $400, on acceptance. Query. Send for guidelines.

NATIONAL RACQUETBALL—400 Douglas Ave., Suite B, Dunedin, FL 34698. Helen Quinn, Pub./Man. Ed. Articles, 800 to 1,200 words, on health and conditioning. How-tos. Profiles. Fiction. Material must be related to racquetball, health/fitness, diet, etc. Pays $25 to $150, on publication. Photos.

NAUTICAL QUARTERLY—Pratt St., Essex, CT 06426. Joseph Gribbins, Ed. In-depth articles, 3,000 to 7,000 words, about boats and boating, U.S. and foreign. Pays $500 to $1,000, on acceptance.

NORTH TEXAS GOLFER—9182 Old Katy Rd., Suite 212, Houston, TX 77055. Bob Gray, Ed. Articles, 800 to 1,500 words, of interest to golfers in North Texas. Pays $50 to $250, on publication. Queries required. Same requirements for Golf Coast Golfer.

NORTHEAST OUTDOORS—P.O. Box 2180, Waterbury, CT 06722-2180. Camillo Falcon, Ed. Articles, 500 to 1,800 words, preferably with B&W photos, on camping in Northeast U.S.: recommended private campgrounds, camp cookery, recreational vehicle hints. Stress how-to, where-to. Cartoons. Pays $30 to $80, on publication. Guidelines.

NORTHEAST RIDING—225 Palisado Ave., Windsor, CT 06095. Paul Essenfeld, Pub. Motorcycle-related articles, 500 to 1,000 words, for motorcyclists in the Northeast. Pays negotiable rates, on publication.

OFFSHORE—220 Reservoir St., Needham Heights, MA 02194. Rick Booth, Man. Ed. Articles, 1,000 to 3,000 words, on boats, people, and places along the New England, New York, and New Jersey coasts. Photos. Pays from 5¢ to 10¢ a word, on acceptance.

ON TRACK—17165 Newhope St., "M', Fountain Valley, CA 92708. Andrew Crask and Craig Fisher, Eds. Features and race reports, 500 to 2,500 words. Pays $4 per column inch, on publication.

OPEN WHEEL—See *Stock Car Racing.*

OUTDOOR AMERICA—1401 Wilson Blvd., Level B, Arlington, VA 22209. Quarterly publication of the Izaak Walton League of America. Articles, 1,500 to 2,000 words, on natural resource conservation issues and outdoor recreation; especially fishing, hunting, and camping. Pays from 20¢ a word for features, on publication. Query Articles Ed. with published clips.

OUTDOOR LIFE—380 Madison Ave., New York, NY 10017. Clare Conley, Ed. Articles on hunting, fishing and related subjects. Pays top rates, on acceptance.

OUTSIDE—1165 N. Clark, Chicago, IL 60610. High-quality articles, with

574

photos, on sports, nature, wilderness travel, adventure, etc. Pays varying rates. Query.

PENNSYLVANIA ANGLER—Pennsylvania Fish Commission, P.O. Box 1673, Harrisburg, PA 17105–1673. Address Ed. Articles, 250 to 2,500 words, with photos, on freshwater fishing in Pennsylvania. Pays $50 to $300, on acceptance. Must send SASE with all material. Query. Guidelines.

PENNSYLVANIA GAME NEWS—Game Commission, Harrisburg, PA 17110–9797. Bob Bell, Ed. Articles, to 2,500 words, with photos, on outdoor subjects, except fishing and boating. Photos. Pays from 5¢ a word, extra for photos, on acceptance.

PERFORMANCE HORSEMAN—Gum Tree Corner, Unionville, PA 19375. Miranda Lorraine, Articles, Ed. Factual how-to pieces for the serious western rider, on training, improving riding skills, all aspects of care and management, etc. Pays from $300, on acceptance.

PETERSEN'S FISHING—8490 Sunset Blvd., Los Angeles, CA 90069. Robert Robb, Ed. "We're interested primarily in how-to articles (2,000 to 2,500 words), though pieces on where to fish, unusual techniques and equipment, and profiles of successful fisherman will also be considered. Photos must accompany all manuscripts, and we prefer to be queried first." Pays $300 to $400, on acceptance.

PGA MAGAZINE—100 Ave. of the Champions, Palm Beach Gardens, FL 33418. Articles, 1,500 to 2,500 words, on golf-related subjects. Pays $300 to $500, on acceptance. Query.

PLEASURE BOATING—1995 N.E. 150th St., North Miami, FL 33181. Gord Lomer, Man. Ed. Articles, 1,000 to 2,500 words, on fishing cuising, recreational boating, travel, offshore racing, covering the coastline from Texas to New York and the islands. Special sections on Florida Keys, Bahamas, Jamaica and Cayman Islands. Pays varying rates, on publication. Query first. Study sample copies. Guidelines.

POPULAR LURES—15115 S. 76th E. Ave., Bixby, OK 74008. Tony Dolle, Ed. Articles, 1,500 to 1,800 words, on lure and techniques for catching all freshwater and saltwater fish. Pays $200 to $400, on acceptance.

POWERBOAT—15917 Strathern St., Van Nuys, CA 91406. Randy Scott, Ed. Articles, to 1,500 words, with photos, for powerboat owners, on outstanding achievements, water-skiing, competitions; technical articles on hull developments; how-to pieces. Pays $300 to $500, on acceptance. Query.

PRACTICAL HORSEMAN—Gum Tree Corner, Unionville, PA 19375. Miranda D. Lorraine, Articles Ed. How-to articles on English riding, training, and horse care. Pays on publication. Query.

PRIVATE PILOT—P.O. Box 6050, Mission Viejo, CA 92690. Mary R. Silitch, Ed. Technically based aviation articles for pilots and aircraft owners, 1,000 to 4,000 words, for aviation enthusiasts. Photos. Pays $75 to $250, on publication. Query.

PRO BASKETBALL ILLUSTRATED—See *Hockey Illustrated.*

PRO FOOTBALL ILLUSTRATED AND PRO FOOTBALL PREVIEW— See *Hockey Illustrated.*

PURE BRED DOGS/AMERICAN KENNEL GAZETTE—51 Madison Ave., New York, NY 10010. Marion Lane, Exec. Ed.; Judy Hartop, Sen. Ed.

Articles, 1,000 to 2,500 words, relating to pure-bred dogs. Pays from $100 to $300, on publication. Queries preferred.

RESTORATION—Box 50046, Tucson, AZ 85703. W.R. Haessner Articles, 1,200 to 1,800 words, on restoration of autos, trucks, planes, trains, etc. Photos. Pays from $50 per page, on publication. Queries required.

RIDER—29901 Agoura Rd., Agoura, CA 91301. Tash Matsuoka, Ed. Articles, with slides, to 3,000 words, with emphasis on travel, touring, commuting, and camping motorcyclists. Pays $100 to $500, on publication. Query.

RIVER RUNNER—P.O. Box 697, Fallbrook, CA 92028. Ken Hulick, Ed. Illustrated articles, 1,500 to 3,000 words, on canoeing, rafting, kayaking, and topics related to U.S. rivers. Pieces for departments on current legislation, short subjects, opinion, "River Towns," and "History." Pays from 5¢ a word, on publication. Query. Guidelines.

ROAD RIDER MAGAZINE—P.O. Box 6050, Mission Viejo, CA 92690. Bob Carpenter, Ed. Articles, to 1,500 words, with photos or B&W illustrations, on motorcycle touring. Pays from $150, on publication. Query.

RUNNER'S WORLD—Rodale Press, 33 E. Minor St., Emmaus, PA 18098. Bob Wischnia, Sr. Ed. Articles for "Human Race" (submit to Bob Wischia) "Finish Line" (to Cristina Negron) and "Health Watch" (to Kate Delhagen) columns. Payment varies, on acceptance. Query.

SAIL—Charlestown Navy Yard, 100 First Ave., Charlestown, MA 02129. Patience Wales, Ed. Articles, 1,500 to 3,500 words, features, 1,000 to 1,500 words, with photos, on sailboats, equipment, racing, and cruising. How-tos on navigation, sail trim, etc. Pays $75 to $1,000 on publication. Guidelines sent on request.

SAILING—125 E. Main St., Port Washington, WI 53074. William F. Schanen, III, Ed. Features, 700 to 1,500 words, with photos, on cruising and racing; first-person accounts; profiles of boats and regattas. Query for technical or how-to pieces. Pays varying rates, 30 days after publication. Guidelines.

SAILING WORLD—111 East Ave., Norwalk, CT 06851. John Burnham, Ed. Articles, 8 to 10 typed pages, on sailboat racing and cruising, regatta reports, equipment, techniques. Photos. Pays $150 per published page, on publication. Query.

SALT WATER SPORTSMAN—280 Summer St., Boston, MA 02210. Barry Gibson, Ed. Articles, 1,200 to 1,500 words, on how anglers can improve their skills, and on new places to fish off the coast of U.S. and Canada, Central America, the Caribbean and Bermuda. Photos a plus. Pays $350 to $700, on acceptance. Query.

SCORE, CANADA'S GOLF MAGAZINE—287 MacPherson Ave., Toronto, Ont., Canada M4V 1A7. John Gordon, Man. Ed. Articles, 800 to 2,000 words, on travel, golf equipment, golf history, personality profiles or prominent professionals. Pays $125 to $600 for features, on assignment and publication. Query with published clips.

SEA KAYAKER—1670 Duranleau St., Vancouver, B.C., Canada V6H 3S4. John Dowd, Ed. Articles, 400 to 4,500 words, on ocean kayaking. Fiction. Pays 5¢ to 10¢ a word, on publication. Query with clips and international reply coupons.

SEA, THE MAGAZINE OF WESTERN BOATING—P. O. Box 1579, Newport Beach, CA 92663. Linda Yuskaitis, Assoc. Ed. Features, 800 to 3,500 words, and news articles, 200 to 500 words, of interest to West Coast boating enthusiasts: profiles of boating personalities, cruise destinations, analyses of marine environmental issues, technical pieces on navigation and seamanship, news from Western waterfronts, sailing regattas, etc. Pays varing rates, on publication.

SHOTGUN SPORTS—P.O. Box 6810, Auburn, CA 95604. Frank Kodl, Ed. Official publication of The United States Sporting Clays Assoc. Articles with photos, on trap and skeet shooting, hunting with shotguns, reloading, gun tests, and instructional shooting. Pays $25 to $200, on publication.

SIERRA—730 Polk St., San Francisco, CA 94109. Jonathan F. King, Ed. Articles, 250 to 2,500 words, on environmental and conservation topics, politics, hiking, backpacking, skiing, rafting, cycling. Book reviews and children's departments. Photos. Pays from $75 to $1,000, extra for photos, on acceptance. Query.

SKI MAGAZINE—380 Madison Ave., New York, NY 10017. Dick Needham, Ed. Articles, 1,300 to 2,000 words, for experienced skiers: profiles, humor, "it happened to me" stories, and destination articles. Short, 100 to 300 word, news items for "Ski Life" column. Equipment and racing articles are staff written. Query first (with clips) for articles. Pays from $200, on acceptance.

SKI RACING—Box 1125, Rt. 100, Waitsfield, VT 05673. Tim Etchells, Man. Ed. Annual. Articles on alpine and nordic skiing and winter vacations at resorts in New England. Color photos (slides preferred). Rates vary.

SKIING—1515 Broadway, New York, NY 10016. Bill Grout, Ed. Personal adventures on skis, from 2,500 words (no first time on skis stories); profiles and interviews, 50 to 300 words. Pays $150 to $300 per printed page, on acceptance.

SKIN DIVER MAGAZINE—8490 Sunset Blvd., Los Angeles, CA 90069. Bill Gleason, Ed. Illustrated articles, 500 to 2,000 words, on scuba diving activities, equipment and dive sites. Pays $50 per published page, on publication.

SKYDIVING MAGAZINE—P. O. Box 1520, Deland, FL 32721. Michael Truffer, Ed. Timely news articles, 300 to 800 words, relating to sport and military parachuting. Fillers. Photos. Pays $25 to $200, extra for photos, on publication.

SNOWMOBILE—319 Barry Ave. S., Suite. 101, Wayzata, MN 55391. Dick Hendricks, Ed. Articles, 700 to 2,000 words, with B&W color photos, related to snowmobiling: races and rallies, trail rides, personalities, travel. How-tos, humor; cartoons. Pays to $450, on publication. Query.

SNOWMOBILE WEST—520 Park Ave., Idaho Falls, ID 83402. Steve Janes, Ed. Articles, 1,200 words, on snowmobiling in the western states. Pays to $100, on publication.

SOCCER AMERICA MAGAZINE—P. O. Box 23704, Oakland, CA 94623. Lynn Berling-Manuel, Ed. Articles, to 500 words, on soccer: news, profiles, coaching tips. Pays $25 to $50, for features, within 60 days on publication.

SOUTH CAROLINA WILDLIFE—P. O. Box 167, Columbia , SC 29202. John E. Davis, Ed. Articles, 1,000 to 3,000 words, with regional outdoor focus: conservation, natural history, wildlife, and recreation. Profiles, how-tos. Pays on acceptance.

SPORT MAGAZINE—8490 Sunset Blvd., Los Angeles, CA 90069. Kelly Garrett, Sr. Ed. Query with clips. No guidelines.

THE SPORTING NEWS—P. O. Box 56, 1212 N. Lindbergh Blvd., St. Louis, MO 63132. Tom Barnidge, Ed.-in-Chief. Articles, 1,000 to 1,500 words, on baseball, football, basketball, hockey, and other sports. Pays $150 to $500, on publicaiton.

SPORTS AFIELD—250 W. 55th St., New York, NY 10019. Tom Paugh, Ed.

Articles, 2,000 words, with quality photos, on hunting, fishing, natural history, conservation, personal experiences, new hunting/fishing spots. How-to pieces; humor, fiction. Pays top rates, on acceptance.

SPORTS AFIELD SPECIALS—250 W. 55th St., New York, NY 10019. Well-written, informative fishing and hunting articles, 2,000 to 2,500 words, with photos, with primary focus on how-to techniques: includes lively anecdotes, and good sidebars, charts. Pays to $450 for features, on acceptance.

SPORTS ILLUSTRATED—1271 Avenue of the Americas, New York, NY 10020. Rob Fleder, Articles Ed. No unsolicited material.

SPUR MAGAZINE—P. O. Box 85, Middleburg, VA 22117. Address Editorial Dept. Articles, 300 to 5,000 words, on Thoroughbred racing, breeding, polo and steeplechasing. Profiles of people and farms. Historical and nostalgia pieces. Pays $50 to $250, on publication. Query.

STOCK CAR RACING—P. O. Box 715, Ipswich, MA 01938. Dick Berggren, Feature Ed. Articles, to 6,000 words, on stock car drivers, races, and vehicles. Photos. Pays to $350, on publicAtion.

SURFER MAGAZINE—P. O. Box 1028, Dana Point, CA 92629. Steve Pezman, Pub. Paul Holmes, Ed. Articles, 500 to 5,000 words, on surfing, surfers, etc. Photos. Pays 10¢ to 15¢ a word, $10 to $600 for photos, on publication.

SURFING—P. O. Box 3010, San Clemente, CA 92672. David Gilovich, Ed. Bill Sharp, Assoc. Ed. First-person travel articles, 1,500 to 2,000 words, on surfing locations; knowledge of sport essential. Pays varying rates, on acceptance.

SWIMSUIT INTERNATIONAL—Swimsuit Publishers, 801 Second Ave., New York, NY 10017. Robert Scalza, Sr. Ed. Articles, 1,000 words, on swimwear-related topics. Pays $350, on acceptance. Query.

TENNIS—5520 Park Ave., P. O. Box 0395, Trumbull, CT 06611–0395. Alex McNab, Ed. Instructional articles, features, profiles of tennis stars, 500 to 2,000 words. Photos. Pays From $100 to $750, on publicaiton. Query.

TENNIS U.S.A.—3 Park Ave., New York, NY 10016. Liza N. Burby, Man. Ed. Articles, 750 to 1,000 words, on local, sectional, and national tennis personalities and news events. Pays $50 to $100, on publication. Query; uses very little free-lance material.

TENNIS WEEK—124 E. 40th St., Suite 1101, New York, NY 10016. Eugene L. Scott, Pub. Robin Serody, Ed. In-depth, researched articles, from 1,000 words, on current issues and personalities in the game. Pays $125, on publication.

TRAILER BOATS—20700 Belshaw Ave., P. O. Box 5427, Carson, CA 90249–5427. Chuck Coyne, Ed. Technical and how-to articles, 500 to 2,000 words, on boat, trailer or tow vehicle maintenance and operation; skiing, fishing and cruising. Fillers, humor. Pays 10¢ to 15¢ a word, on publication.

TRAILER LIFE—29901 Agoura Rd., Agoura, CA 91301. Bill Estes, Ed. Articles, to 2,500 words, with photos, on trailering, truck campers, motorhomes, hobbies, and RV lifestyles. How-to pieces. Pays to $500, on acceptance. Send for guidelines.

TURF AND SPORT DIGEST—26 W. Pennsylvania Ave., Towson, MD 21204. Allen L. Mitzel, Jr., Ed. Articles, 1,500 to 4,000 words, on national turf personalities, racing nostalgia, and handicapping. Pays $75 to $200, on publication. Query.

VELO-NEWS—Box 1257, Brattleboro, VT 05301. Marilee Attley, Ed. Articles, 500 to 2,000 words, on bicycle racing. Photos. Pays $2.65 per column inch, extra for photos, on publication. Query.

VOLKSWAGEN'S WORLD—Volkswagen of America, Troy, MI 28007. Marlene Goldsmith, Ed. Articles, 750 to 1,000 words, accompanied by color slides. Pays $150 per printed page, on acceptance. Query required. Guidelines.

THE WALKING MAGAZINE—711 Boylston St., Boston, MA 02116. Bradford Ketchum, Ed. Articles, 1,500 to 2,000 words, on fitness, health, equipment, nutrition, travel and adventure, famous walkers, and other walking-related topics. Shorter pieces, 500 to 1,500 words, and essays for "Ramblings" page. Photos welcome. Pays $500 to $1,000 for features, $100 to $350 for department pieces. Guidelines.

WASHINGTON FISHING HOLES—P.O. Box 32, Sedro Wolley, WA 98284. Detailed articles, with specific maps, 800 to 1,500 words, on fishing in Washington. Local Washington fishing how-tos. Photos. Pays on publication. Query. Send SASE for guidelines.

THE WATER SKIER—P.O. Box 191, Winter Haven, FL 33882. Duke Cullimore, Ed. Offbeat articles on waterskiing. Pays varying rates, on acceptance.

THE WESTERN BOATMAN—20700 Belshaw Ave., P.O. Box 5427, Carson, CA 90249–5427. Ralph Poole, Ed. Articles, to 1,500 words, for boating enthusiasts from Alaska to Mexico, on subjects from waterskiing and salmon fishing to race boats and schooners. Photos required. Pays $5 per column inch, $20 to $300 (cover) for color photos, on publication. Queries preferred.

THE WESTERN HORSEMAN—P.O. Box 7980, Colorado Springs, CO 80933. Randy Witte, Ed. Articles, around 1,500 words, with photos, on care and training of horses. Pays from $150, on acceptance.

WESTERN OUTDOORS—3197-E Airport Loop, Costa Mesa, CA 92626. Timely, factual articles on fishing and hunting, 1,500 to 1,800 words, of interest to western sportsmen. Pays $400 to $500, on acceptance. Query. Guidelines.

WESTERN SPORTSMAN—P.O. Box 737, Regina, Sask., Canada S4P 3A8. Rick Bates, Ed. Articles, to 2,500 words, on outdoor experiences in Alberta and Saskatchewan; how-to pieces. Photos. Pays $75 to $325, on publication.

WILDBIRD—Box 6050, Mission Viejo, CA 92690. Tim Gallagher, Man. Ed. Features, 1,500 to 2,000 words, and columns, 700 to 1,000 words, for field birders and garden birders. "No pieces on taming wild birds." Pays $25 for reader columns, from $100 for articles, extra for photos. Guidelines.

WIND SURF—P.O. Box 561, Dana Point, CA 92629. Drew Kampion, Ed. Articles on all aspects of windsurfing. Pays 10¢ to 20¢ a word, on publication.

WINDRIDER—P.O. Box 2456, Winter Park, FL 32790. Debbie Snow, Ed. Features, instructional pieces, and tips, by experienced boardsailors. Fast action photos. Pays $50 to $75 for tips, $250 to $300 for features, extra for photos. Send guidelines first.

WOMAN BOWLER—5301 S. 76th St., Greendale, WI 53129. Karen Sytsma, Ed. Profiles, interviews, and news articles, to 1,000 words, for women bowlers. Pays varying rates, on acceptance. Query with outline.

WOMEN'S SPORTS AND FITNESS—P.O. Box 2456, Winter Park, FL 32789. Lewis Rothlein, Ed. How-tos, profiles, and sports reports, 500 to 3,000 words, for active women. Fitness, nutrition, and health pieces also considered. Pays on publication.

WORLD TENNIS—Family Media, Inc., 3 Park Ave., New York, NY 10016. Peter Coan, Man. Ed. The Magazine of the U.S. Tennis Assoc. Articles, 750 to 1,500 words, on tournaments, technique, celebrities, equipment, and related subjects. Payment varies, on acceptance. Query.

WRESTLING WORLD—See *Hockey Illustrated.*

YACHTING—P.O. Box 1200, 5 River Rd., Cos Cob, CT 06807. Roy Attaway, Ed. Articles, 2,000 words, on recreational power and sail boating. How-to and personal-experience pieces. Photos. Pays $350 to $1,000, on acceptance. Queries preferred.

AUTOMOTIVE MAGAZINES

AAA WORLD—AAA Headquarters 8111 Gatehouse Rd., Falls Church, VA 22047. Douglas Damerst, Ed. Automobile and travel concerns, including automotive travel, maintenance and upkeep, 750 to 1,500 words. Pays $300 to $600, on acceptance. Query with clips preferred.

AMERICAN MOTORCYCLIST—American Motorcyclist Assn., Box 6114, Westerville, OH 43081–6114. Greg Harrison, Ed. Articles and fiction, to 3,000 words, on motorcycling: news coverage, personalities, tours. Photos. Pays varying rates, on publication. Query.

ATV SPORTS—Box 2260, Costa Mesa, CA 92628. Bruce Simurda, Ed. Articles 1,000 to 1,500 words, relating to three- and four-wheel, all-terrain vehicles. Pays $60 per printed page, on publication. Query.

CAR AND DRIVER—2002 Hogback Rd., Ann Arbor, MI 48105. Don Sherman, Ed. Articles, to 2,500 words, for enthusiasts, on car manufacturers, new developments in cars, etc. Pays to $1,500, on acceptance.

CAR AUDIO AND ELECTRONICS—4827 Sepulveda Blvd., Suite 220, Sherman Oaks, CA 91403. William Burton, Ed. "We want articles that cover complicated topics simply." Features and reports (1,000 to 2,000 words) on electronic products for the car: how to buy them; how they work; how to use them. Pays $300 to $1,000, on acceptance. Send manuscript or query.

CAR CRAFT—8490 Sunset Blvd., Los Angeles, CA 90069. Cameron Benty, Ed. Articles and photofeatures on unusual street machines, drag cars, racing events; technical pieces; action photos. Pays from $150 per page, on publication.

CORVETTE FEVER—Box 44620, Ft. Washington, MD 20744. Pat Stivers, Ed. Articles, 500 to 2,500 words, on Corvette repairs, swap meets, and personalities. Corvette-related fiction, about 700 lines, and fillers. Photos. Pays 10¢ a word, on publication.

CYCLE MAGAZINE—5706 Corsa Ave., Westlake Village, CA 91362. Phil Schilling, Ed. Articles, 6 to 20 manuscript pages, on motorcycle races, history, touring technical pieces; profiles. Photos. Pays on publication. Query.

CYCLE NEWS—2201 Cherry Ave., Box 498, Long Beach, CA 90801. Jack Mangus, Ed. Technical articles on motorcycling; profiles and interviews with motorcycle newsmakers. Pays $2 per column inch, on publication.

CYCLE WORLD—853 W. 17th St., Costa Mesa, CA 92627. Paul Dean, Ed. Technical and feature articles, 1,500 to 2,500 words, for motorcycle enthusiasts. Photos. Pays $100 to $200 per page, on publication. Query.

HOT BIKE—2145 W. La Palma, Anaheim, CA 92801. Tod Knuth, Ed.

Articles, 250 to 2,500 words, with photos, on motorcycles. Event coverage on high performance street and track and sport touring motorcycles, with emphasis on Harley Davidsons. Pays $50 to $100 per printed page, on publication.

HOT ROD—8490 Sunset Blvd., Los Angeles, CA 90069. Jeff Smith, Ed. How-to pieces and articles, 500 to 5,000 words, on auto mechanics, hot rods, track and drag racing. Photo-features on custom or performance-modified cars. Pays $250 per page, on publication.

KEEPIN' TRACK OF VETTES—P.O. Box 48, Spring Valley, NY 10977. Shelli Finkel, Ed. Articles of any length, with photos, relating to Corvettes. Pays $25 to $200, on publication.

MOTOR TREND—8490 Sunset Blvd., Los Angeles, CA 90069. Mike Anson, Ed. Articles, 250 to 2,000 words, on autos, racing, events, and profiles. Photos. Pay varies, on acceptance. Query.

MOTORCYCLIST—8490 Sunset Blvd., Los Angeles, CA 90069. Art Friedman, Ed. Articles, 1,000 to 3,000 words. Action photos. Pays varying rates, on publication. Query.

NORTHEAST RIDING—225 Palisado Ave., Windsor, CT 06095. Paul Essenfeld, Pub. Motorcycle-related articles, 500 to 1,000 words, for motorcyclists in the Northeast. Pays negotiable rates, on publication.

OPEN WHEEL—See *Stock Car Racing*.

RESTORATION—Box 50046, Tucson, AZ 85703. W.R. Haessner, Ed. Articles, 1,200 to 1,800 words, on restoring autos, trucks, planes, trains, etc. Pays $10 per page, on publication. Query.

RIDER—29901 Agoura Rd., Agoura, CA 91301. Tash Matsuoka, Ed. Articles, with slides, to 3,000 words, with emphasis on travel, touring, commuting, and camping motorcyclists. Pays $100 to $500, on publication. Query.

ROAD RIDER MAGAZINE—P.O. Box 6050, Mission Viejo, CA 92690. Bob Carpenter, Ed. Articles, to 1,500 words, with photos or B&W illustrations, on motorcycle touring. Pays from $150, on publication.

STOCK CAR RACING—P.O. Box 715, Ipswich, MA 01938. Dick Berggren, Ed. Features, technical automotive pieces, up to ten typed pages, for oval track racing enthusiasts. Fillers. Pays $75 to $350, on publication. Same requirements for *Open Wheel*.

VOLKSWAGEN'S WORLD—Volkswagen of America, Troy, MI 28007. Marlene Goldsmith, Ed. Articles, 750 to 1,000 words, accompanied by color slides. Pays $150 per printed page, on acceptance. Query required. Guidelines.

FITNESS MAGAZINES

AMERICAN FITNESS—15250 Ventura Blvd., Ste. 310, Sherman Oaks, CA 91403. Peg Angsten, Ed. Brenda Sutton, Man. Ed. Articles, 500 to 1,500 words, on exercise, health, sports, nutrition, etc. Illustrations, photos, cartoons.

AMERICAN HEALTH: FITNESS OF BODY AND MIND—80 Fifth Ave., New York, NY 10011. Joel Gruin, Ed. Lively, authoritative articles, 1,000 to 3,000 words, on scientific and life style aspects of health and fitness; 100-to 750-word news reports. Query with clips. Pays $150 to $2,000.

HEALTH—3 Park Ave., New York, NY 10016. Articles, 800 to 2,500 words, on fitness. Pays $150 to $1,200, on acceptance. Query.

INSIDE TEXAS RUNNING (FORMERLY *INSIDE RUNNING & FIT-NESS*)—9514 Bristlebrook Dr., Houston, TX 77083. Joanne Schmidt, Ed. Articles and fillers on running, cycling, and triathlons in Texas. Pays $35 to $100, $10 for photos, on acceptance.

MEN'S FITNESS—21100 Erwin St., Woodland Hills, CA 91367. David Rivas, Ed-in-Chief Features, 1,500 to 2,500 words, and department pieces, 1,000 to 1,500 words: "authoritative and practical articles dealing with fitness, health, and men's lifestyles." Pays $200 to $400, on acceptance.

MEN'S HEALTH—Rodale Press, 33 E. Minor Dr., Emmaus, PA 18098. Michael Lafavore, Exec. Ed. Articles, 1,000 to 2,500 words, on fitness, diet, health, relationships, sports, and travel, for men ages 25 to 55. Pays 50¢ a word, on acceptance. Query first.

MUSCULAR DEVELOPMENT—Strength and Health Publishing, P.O. Box 1707, York, PA 17405. Jan Dellinger, Ed. Articles, 5 to 10 typed pages, on competitive bodybuilding and power lifting for serious weight training athletes. Pays $50 to $200, extra for photos, on publication. Query.

NEW BODY—888 Seventh Ave., New York, NY 10106. Constance Cardozo, Ed. Lively, readable service-oriented articles, 800 to 1,500 words, by writers with background in health field: exercise, nutrition, psychology, and diet pieces for women aged 18 to 40. Pays $100 to $300, on publication. Query.

THE PHYSICIAN AND SPORTSMEDICINE—4530 W. 77th St., Minneapolis, MN 55435. Cindy Christian Rogers, Features Ed. News and feature articles, 500 to 3,000 words, on fitness, sport, and exercise. Medical angle necessary. Pays $150 to $900, on acceptance. Guidelines.

SHAPE—21100 Erwin St., Woodland Hills, CA 91367. Jennifer Koch, Asst. Ed. Articles, 1,200 to 1,500 words, with new and interesting ideas on physical and mental side of getting and staying in shape; reports, 300 to 400 words, on journal research. Expert bylines only. Payment varies, on publication. Guidelines.

VEGETARIAN TIMES—P.O. Box 570, Oak Park, IL 60603. Paul Obis, Pub. Articles, 750 to 2,500 words, on health, nutrition, exercise and fitness, meatless meals, etc. Personal-experience and historical pieces, profiles. Pays $25 to $300, on publication.

VIM & VIGOR—8805 N. 23rd Ave., Suite 11, Phoenix, AZ 85021. Leo Calderella, Ed. Positive articles, with accurate medical facts, on health and fitness, 1,200 words. Pays $250 to $350, on publication.

THE WALKING MAGAZINE—711 Boylston St., Boston, MA 02116. Bradford Ketchum, Ed. Articles, 1,500 to 2,000 words, on fitness, health, equipment, nutrition, travel and adventure, famous walkers, and other walking-related topics. Shorter pieces, 500 to 1,500 words, and essays for "Ramblings" page. Photos welcome. Pays $500 to $1,000 for features, $100 to $350 for department pieces. Guidelines.

WEIGHT WATCHERS MAGAZINE—360 Lexington Ave., New York, NY 10017. Nelly Edmondson, Articles Ed. Articles on nutrition and health. Pays from $250, on acceptance. Query with clips required. Guidelines.

WOMEN'S SPORTS AND FITNESS—P.O. Box 2456, Winter Park, FL 32789. Lewis Rothlein, Ed. How-tos, profiles, and sports reports, 500 to 3,000 words, for active women. Fitness, nutrition, and health pieces also considered. Pays on publication.

YOGA JOURNAL—2054 University Ave., Berkeley, CA 94704. Stephan Bodian, Ed. Articles, 1,200 to 3,000 words, on holistic health, spirituality, yoga, and transpersonal psychology; "new age" profiles; interviews. Pays $75 to $200, on publication.

CONSUMER/PERSONAL FINANCE

BETTER HOMES AND GARDENS—1716 Locust St., Des Moines, IA 50336. Articles, 750 to 1,000 words, on "any and all topics that would be of interest to family-oriented, middle-income people." Address Margaret V. Daly, Money Management, Automotive and Features Ed., *Better Homes and Gardens,* 750 Third Ave., New York, NY 10017.

BLACK ENTERPRISE—130 Fifth Ave., New York, NY 10011. Earl G. Graves, Ed. Articles on money, management, careers, political issues, entrepreneurship, high technology, and lifestyles for black professionals. Profiles. Pays on acceptance. Query.

CHANGING TIMES—1729 H St. N.W., Washington, DC 20006. Articles on personal finance (i.e., buying a stereo, mutual funds). Length and payment vary. Query required. Pays on acceptance.

CONSUMERS DIGEST—5705 N. Lincoln Ave., Chicago, IL 60659. John Manos, Ed. Articles, 500 to 3,000 words, on subjects of interest to consumers: products and services, automobiles, travel, health, fitness, consumer legal affairs, and personal money management. Photos. Pays from 30¢ a word, extra for photos, on acceptance. Query with resumé and clips.

FAMILY CIRCLE—110 Fifth Ave., New York, NY 10011. Susan Ungaro, Articles Ed. Nancy Josephson, Sr. Ed. Enterprising, creative, and practical articles (1,000 to 2,000 words) on investing, real estate, and financial planning. Query first with clips. Pays $1 a word, on acceptance.

GOLDEN YEARS—233 E. New Haven Ave., Melbourne, FL 32902–0537. Carol Brenner Hittner, Ed. "We consider articles (to 500 words) on preretirement and retirement planning, real estate, and other topics of particular interest to affluent people over 50." Pays on publication.

THE KIWANIS MAGAZINE—3636 Woodview Trace, Indianapolis, IN 46468. Chuck Jonak, Exec. Ed. Articles (2,500 to 3,000 words) on financial planning for younger families in a variety of areas; pieces on financial planning for retirees and small business owners. Pays $400 to $2,000, on acceptance. Query required.

MODERN MATURITY—3200 E. Carson St., Lakewood, CA 90712. Ian Ledgerwood, Ed. Articles, 1,000 to 2,000 words, on a wide range of financial topics of interest to people over 50. Pays to $2,500. Queries required.

MONEY MAKER—5705 N. Lincoln Ave., Chicago, IL 60659. Dennis Fertig, Ed. Informative, jargon-free articles, to 4,000 words, for beginning-to-sophisticated investors, on investment opportunities, personal finance, and low-priced investments. Pays 25¢ a word, on acceptance. Query for assignment.

THE MONEYPAPER—930 Mamaroneck Ave., Mamaroneck, NY 10543. Vita Nelson, Ed. Financial news and money-saving ideas. Brief, well-researched articles on personal finance, money management: saving, earning, investing, taxes, insurance, and related subjects. Pays $75 for articles, on publication. Query with resumé and writing sample.

SELF—350 Madison Ave., New York, NY 10017. Marion Asnes, Assoc. Ed.

Articles, 1,500 to 2,000 words, on money matters for career women in their 20s and 30s. Pays from $1,000, on acceptance. Query first.

SYLVIA PORTER'S PERSONAL FINANCE MAGAZINE—380 Lexington Ave., New York, NY 10017. Greg Daugherty, Exec. Ed. Well-researched articles on investing, taxes, financial planning, real estate, entrepreneurship, etc. Pays on acceptance. Query.

WOMAN'S DAY—1515 Broadway, New York, NY 10036. Rebecca Greer, Articles Ed. Articles, to 3,000 words, on financial matters of interest to a broad range of women. Pays top rates, on acceptance. Query first.

WOMAN'S ENTERPRISE—28210 Dorothy Dr., Agoura Hills, CA 91301. Caryne Brown, Ed. Articles, 1,500 to 2,000 words, on women who own small businesses; features on business management. "The more specific income, expenditure, and profit figures are, the better." No personal profiles. Pays 20¢ a word, on acceptance. Query preferred.

YOUR MONEY—56 The Esplanade, 2nd fl., Toronto, Ont., Canada M5E 1A7. Linda Kramer, Man. Ed. Features, 2,500 words, on personal finance for Canadians. Pays 70¢ a word, on acceptance. Query with outline required.

PROFESSIONAL/TRADE PUBLICATIONS

ACCESS CONTROL/FENCE INDUSTRY—6255 Barfield Rd., Atlanta, GA 30328. Bill Coker, Ed./Assoc. Pub. Articles on access control and fencing industry; interviews with dealer-erectors; on-the-job pieces. Photos. Pays 10¢ a word, extra for photos, on publication. Query.

ACCESSORIES MAGAZINE—50 Day St., Norwalk, CT 06854. Reenie Brown, Ed. Dir. Articles, with photos, for women's fashion accessories buyers and manufacturers. Profiles of retailers, designers, manufacturers; articles on merchandising and marketing. Pays $75 to $100 for short articles, from $100 to $300 for features, on publication. Query.

ACROSS THE BOARD—845 Third Ave., New York, NY 10022. Sarasue French, Asst. Ed. Articles, to 5,000 words, on a variety of topics of interest to business executives; straight business angle not required. Pays $100 to $750, on publication.

ALTERNATIVE ENERGY RETAILER—P.O. Box 2180, Waterbury, CT 06722. Ed Easley, Ed. Feature articles, 2,000 words, for retailers of alternative and energy products: wood, coal and fireplace products and services. Interviews with successful retailers, stressing the how-to. B&W photos. Pays $200, extra for photos, on publication. Query first.

AMERICAN BANKER—One State Street Plaza, New York, NY 10004. William Zimmerman, Ed., Patricia Stunza, Features Ed. Articles, 1,000 to 3,000 words, on banking and financial services, human resources, management techniques. Pays varying rates, on publication. Query preferred.

AMERICAN BAR ASSOCIATION JOURNAL—750 N. Lake Shore Dr., Chicago, IL 60611. Robert Yates, Man. Ed. Practical articles, to 3,000 words, that will help lawyers in small firms better their practices. Pays from $750 for features, on acceptance.

AMERICAN COIN-OP—500 N. Dearborn St., Chicago, IL 60610. Ben Russell, Ed. Articles, to 2,500 words, with photos, on successful coin-operated laundries: management, promotion, decor, maintenance, etc. Pays from 6¢ a word, $6 per B&W photo, two weeks prior to publication. Query. Send SASE for guidelines.

AMERICAN DEMOGRAPHICS—P.O. Box 68, Ithaca, NY 14851. Caroline Arthur, Man. Ed. Articles, 3,000 to 5,000 words, on demographic trends and business demographics for strategists in industry, government, and education. Pays $300, on publication. Query.

AMERICAN FARRIERS JOURNAL—63 Great Rd., Maynard, MA 01754. Susan G. Philbrick, Ed. Articles, 800 to 5,000 words, on general farriery issues, hoof care, tool selection, equine lameness, and horse handling. Pays 30¢ per published line, $10 per published illustration or photo, on publication. Query.

AMERICAN MEDICAL NEWS—535 N. Dearborn St., Chicago, IL 60610. Flora Johnson Skelly, Asst. Exec. Ed. Weekly newspaper of the American Medical Association. Features, 1,000 to 3,000 words, and news pieces, 200 to 1,000 words, of interest to physicians across the U.S.; socio-economic angle is preferred. No "clinical breakthrough" pieces. Pays $50 to $1,000, on acceptance. Queries are required.

AMERICAN PAINTING CONTRACTOR—2911 Washington Ave., St. Louis, MO 63103. Paul B. Stoecklein, Ed. Technical articles, to 2,500 words, with photos, on challenging and industrial maintenance painting, for contractors and architects.

THE AMERICAN SALESMAN—424 N. Third St., Burlington, IA 52601–5224. Barbara Boeding, Ed. Articles, 900 to 1,200 words, on techniques for increasing sales. Pays 3¢ a word, on publication. Guidelines.

AMERICAN SALON—7500 Old Oak Blvd., Cleveland, OH 44130. Jody Byrne, Ed. National Cosmetology Assn. Articles of varying lengths for salon professionals. Payment varies, on publication. Query.

ARCHITECTURE—1735 New York Ave. N.W., Washington, DC 20006. Donald Canty, Ed.-in-Chief. Articles, to 3,000 words, on architecture, urban design. Book reviews. Pays $100 to $500, extra for photos. Query.

AREA DEVELOPMENT MAGAZINE—525 Northern Blvd., Great Neck, NY 11021. Tom Bergeron, Ed. Articles for top executives of manufacturing companies, on industrial and office facility planning. Pays $40 per manuscript page. Query.

ART BUSINESS NEWS—60 Ridgeway Plaza, P.O. Box 3837, Stamford, CT 06905. Jo Yanow-Schwartz, Ed. Articles, 1,000 words, for art dealers and framers, on trends and events of national importance to the art industry, and relevant business subjects. Pays $75 plus, on publication. Query preferred.

ART MATERIAL TRADE NEWS—6255 barfield Rd., Atlanta, GA 30328. Charles C. Craig, Ed. Articles, from 800 words, for dealers, wholesalers, and manufacturers of artist mateials; must be specific to trade. Pays to 15¢ a word, on publication. Query.

ASSOCIATION & SOCIETY MANAGER—1640 Fifth St., Santa Monica, CA 90401. Helene Kass, Ed. Articles geared to people who run nonprofit membership societies and associations: features (1,500 to 2,200 words) should emphasize methods of organization management, procedures for increasing membership, conducting meetings, and related topics. Pays 10¢ a word, on acceptance. Queries are preferred.

AUTOMATION IN HOUSING & MANUFACTURED HOME DEALER—P.O. Box 120, Carpinteria, CA 93013. Don Carlson, Ed. Articles, 500 to 750 words, on various types of home manufacturers and dealers. Query required. Pays $300, on acceptance, for articles with slides.

AUTOMOTIVE EXECUTIVE—8400 Westpark Dr., McLean, VA 22102. Joe Phillips, Man. Ed. National Automobile Dealers Assn. Articles, 750 to 2,500 words, on management of automobile and heavy-duty truck dealerships and general business and automotive issues. Photos. Pays on publication. Query.

BARRISTER—American Bar Assn., 750 N. Lake Shore Dr., Chicago, IL 60611. Anthony Monahan, Ed. Articles, to 3,500 words, on legal and social affairs, for young lawyers. Pays to $700, on acceptance.

BARRON'S—200 Liberty St., New York, NY 10281. Alan Abelson, Ed. National-interest articles, 1,200 to 2,500 words, on business and finance. Query.

BETTER BUSINESS—235 East 42nd St., New York, NY 10017. John F. Robinson, Pub. Articles, 10 to 12 double-spaced pages, for the small business/ minority business markets. Query.

BOATING INDUSTRY—850 Third Ave., New York, NY 10022. Olga Badillo-Sciortino, Ed. Articles, 1,000 to 1,500 words, on marine management, merchandising and selling, for boat dealers. Photos. Pays varying rates, on publication. Query.

BUILDER—Hanley-Wood, Inc. 655 15th St., N.W., Suite 475, Washington, DC 20005. Mitchell B. Rouda, Ed. Articles, to 1,500 words, on trends and news in home building: design, marketing, new products, etc. Pays negotiable rates, on acceptance. Query.

BUSINESS AGE MAGAZINE—P.O. Box 11597, Milwaukee, WI 53211. Margaret Brickner, Ed. Articles, 1,000 to 2,000 words, on how to operate a small business effectively. Departments: accounting, finance, personnal management, taxes, marketing, technology, and planning. Queries are required. Guidelines available.

BUSINESS AND COMMERCIAL AVIATION—Hangar C-1, Westchester Co. Airport, White Plains, NY 10604. John W. Olcott, Ed. Articles, for pilots, 2,500 words, with photos, on use of private aircraft for business transportation. Pays $100 to $500, on acceptance. Query.

BUSINESS ATLANTA—6255 Barfield Rd., Atlanta, GA 30328. Barrie S. Rissman, Ed. Articles, 1,000 to 4,500 words, with Atlanta or "deep South" business angle, strong marketing slant that will be useful to top Atlanta executives and business people. Pays $300 to $800, on publication. Query with clippings.

BUSINESS MARKETING—220 E. 42nd St., New York, NY 10017. Bob Donath, Ed. Articles on selling, advertising, and promoting products and services to business buyers. Pays competitive rates, on acceptance. Queries are required.

BUSINESS MONTH—488 Madison Ave, New York, NY 10022. John Van Doorn, Ed.-in-Chief. Articles, to 5,000 words: profiles of CEOs, large corporations; articles on trends in management, the economy, finance. Pays to $1 a word, on acceptance.

BUSINESS SOFTWARE MAGAZINE—M&T Publishing, 501 Galveston Dr., Redwood City, CA 94063. Nancy Beckus, Man. Ed. Software applications for business-oriented audience; tips and techniques using popular software; reviews of new products; case studies of corporate users. Pays to $500, before publication. Query.

BUSINESS SOFTWARE REVIEW—9100 Keystone Crossing, Indianapolis,

IN 46240. Dennis Hamilton, Ed.-in-Chief. Articles, 300 to 3,000 words, on the computer business, centering on management software: productivity, profitability, return-on-investment. Pays $50 to $500, on publication. Query.

THE BUSINESS TIMES—8 Glastonbury Ave., Rocky Hill, CT 06067. Mark D. Isaacs, Ed. Articles on Connecticut-based businesses and corporations. Pays $2 per column inch, on publication. Query.

BUSINESS TODAY—P.O. Box 10010, 1720 Washington Blvd., Ogden, UT 84409. Karen E. Hill, Ed. Articles, 1,200 words; profiles of businessmen and women. Pays 15¢ a word, $35 for color photos, on acceptance. Query.

BUSINESS VIEW—P.O. Box 9859, Naples, FL 33941. Eleanor K. Somer, Pub. Innovative articles and columns, 750 to 1,500 words, on business, economics, finance; profiles of business leaders; new trends in technology and advances in management techniques. Real estate and banking trends. Southwest Florida regional angle a must. Pays $75 to $200, on publication. Query.

CALIFORNIA BUSINESS—4221 Wilshire Blvd., Suite 400, Los Angeles, CA 90010. S. C. Gwynne, Ed. Articles, 1,200 to 3,000 words, on business and econometric issues in California. Pays varying rates, on acceptance. Query.

CALIFORNIA LAWYER—555 Franklin St., San Francisco, CA 94102. Thomas K. Brom, Man. Ed. Articles, 2,500 to 3,000 words, for attorneys in California, on legal subjects (or the legal aspects of a given political or social issue); how-tos on improving techniques in law practice. Pays $250 to $750, on acceptance. Query.

CAMPGROUND MANAGEMENT—11 N. Skokie Hwy., #205, Lake Bluff, IL 60044. Mike Byrnes, Ed. Detailed articles, 500 to 2,000 words, on managing recreational vehicle campgrounds. Photos. Pays $50 to $200, after publication.

CASHFLOW—6255 Barfield Rd., Atlanta, GA 30328. Richard Gamble, Ed. Articles, 1,250 to 2,500 words, for treasury managers in public and private institutions: cash management; investments; domestic and international financing; credit and collection management; developments in law, economics, and tax. Pays $125 per published page, on publication. Query.

CERAMIC SCOPE—3632 Ashworth N., Seattle, WA 98103. Michael Scott, Ed. Articles, 800 to 1,500 words, on retail or wholesale business operations of hobby ceramic studios. Photos. Pays 10¢ a word, extra for photos, on publication. Query.

CHEESE MARKET NEWS—Gorman Publishing Co., 8750 W. Bryn Mawr, Chicago, IL 60631. Jerry Dryer, Ed. Articles, to 2,500 words, on innovative dairies, dairy processing operations, marketing successes, new products, for milk handlers, and makers of dairy products. Fillers, 25 to 150 words. Pays $25 to $300, $5 to $25 for fillers, on publication.

CHIEF EXECUTIVE—205 Lexington Ave., New York, NY 10016. J. P. Donlon, Ed. Articles, 2,500 to 3,000 words, on management, financial or business strategy, administration, investments, amenities, and unusual hobbies; travel pieces, 1,200 to 1,500 words. Pays varying rates, after acceptance. Query required.

CHINA, GLASS & TABLEWARE—P.O. Box 2147, Clifton, NJ 07015. Amy Stavis, Ed. Case histories and interviews, 1,500 to 2,500 words, with photos, on merchandising of china and glassware. Pays $50 per page, on publication. Query.

CHRISTIAN RETAILING—190 N. Westmonte Dr., Altamonte Springs, FL 32714. Howard Earl, Ed. Articles, 850 to 1,200 words, on new products, industry news, or topics related to running a profitable Christian retail store. Pays $50 to $150, on publication.

CLEANING MANAGEMENT—15550-D Rockfield, Irvine, CA 92718. R. Daniel Harris, Jr., Pub. Articles, 1,000 to 1,500 words, on managing efficient cleaning and maintenance operations. Photos. Pays 10¢ a word, extra for photos, on publication.

COLLEGE STORE EXECUTIVE—P.O. Box 1500, Westbury, NY 11590. Catherine Orobona, Ed. Articles, 1,000 words, for college store industry only; news; profiles. No general business or how-to articles. Photos. Pays $2 a column inch, extra for photos, on acceptance. Query.

COMMERCIAL CARRIER JOURNAL—Chilton Way, Radnor, PA 19089. Jerry Standley, Ed. Factual articles on private fleets and for-hire trucking operations. Pays from $50, on acceptance. Queries required.

COMPUTER & COMMUNICATIONS DECISIONS MAGAZINE—10 Mulholland Dr., Hasbrouck Hgts., NJ 07604. Robin Nelson, Ed. Articles, 800 to 4,000 words, on corporate applications of computer systems. Pays $500 to $1,500, on acceptance. Queries are required.

COMPUTER CONSULTANT—208 N. Townsend St., Syracuse, NY 13202. Articles, to 2,500 words, on innovative sales techniques, and tips for increasing profitability for computer consultants. Pays varying rates, on publication. Query required.

COMPUTER GRAPHICS WORLD—P.O. Box 1112, 119 Russell St., Littleton, MA 01460. Stephen Porter, Man. Ed. Articles, 1,000 to 5,000 words, on computer graphics technology, applications, and products. Photos. Pays $150 to $200 per printed page, on publication. Query.

COMPUTER PRODUCT SELLING—Lebhar-Friedman, 425 Park Ave., New York, NY 10022. Betty J. Taylor, Exec. Ed. How-to and professional development articles geared to computer salespeople; new product applications and reviews, industry news. Pays 30¢ a word, on publication. Queries are required.

CONCRETE INTERNATIONAL: DESIGN AND CONSTRUCTION— Box 19150, 22400 W. Seven Mile Rd., Detroit, MI 48219. Robert E. Wilde, Ed. Articles, 6 to 12 double-spaced pages, on concrete construction and design, with drawings and photos. Pays $100 per printed page, on publication. Query.

CONTACTS—17 Myrtle Ave., Troy, NY 12180. George J. Yamin, Ed. Articles, 300 to 1,500 words, on management of dental laboratories, lab techniques, and equipment. Pays from 7¢ a word, on acceptance.

CONTRACTORS MARKET CENTER—Box 2029, Tuscaloosa , AL 35403. Robert Ruth, Ed. Features, 500 to 1,500 words, for contractors who use heavy equipment; success stories. Pays $10 to $50, on acceptance.

CONVENIENCE STORE NEWS—254 W. 31st St., New York, NY 10001. Denise Melinsky, Ed. Features and news items, 500 to 750 words, for convenience store owners, operators, and suppliers. Photos, with captions. Pays $3 per column inch, extra for photos, on publication. Query.

COOKING FOR PROFIT—P.O. Box 267, Fond du Lac, WI 54936-0267. Colleen Phalen, Ed. Practical how-to articles, 1,000 words, on commercial food preparation, energy management; case studies, etc. Pays $75 to $250, on publication.

CORPORATE HEALTH—2506 Gross Point Rd., Evanston, IL 60201. Lisbeth Maxwell, Ed. Articles, 2,800 to 4,200 words, and columns, 1,400 to 2,800 words, on employee benefits, cost containment, fitness, health, and safety, of interest to CEOs and benefits managers. Payment varies, on publication. Query preferred.

CRAIN'S CHICAGO BUSINESS—740 Rush St., Chicago, IL 60611. Dan Miller, Ed. Business articles about the Midwest exclusively. Pays $10.25 per column inch, on acceptance.

CREATING EXCELLENCE—New World Publishing, P.O Box 2084, S. Burlington, VT 05403. David Robinson, Ed. Self-help and inspirational articles; profiles and essays related to personal development. "We want to accent the positive." Pays $75 to $250, on acceptance. Queries preferred.

CREDIT AND COLLECTION MANAGEMENT BULLETIN—Bureau of Business Practice, 24 Rope Ferry Rd., Waterford, CT 06386. Russell Case, Ed. Interviews, 500 to 1,250 wods, for commercial and consumer credit managers, on innovations, successes, and problem solving. Query.

D & B REPORTS—299 Park Ave., New York, NY 10171. Patricia W. Hamilton, Ed. Articles, 1,500 to 2,500 words, for top management of smaller businesses: government regulations, export opportunities, employee relations; how-tos on cash management, sales, productivity; profiles, etc. Pays on acceptance.

DAIRY HERD MANAGEMENT—P.O. Box 2400, Minnetonka, MN 55343. Edward Clark, Ed. Articles, 500 to 2,000 words, with photos, on dairy finance, production, and marketing. Pays on acceptance. Query.

DEALERSCOPE MERCHANDISING—North American Publishing Co., 401 N. Broad St., Philadelphia, PA 19108. Neil Spann, Ed. Articles, 750 to 3,000 words, for dealers and distributors of audio, video, personal computers for the home, office; satellite TV systems for the home; major appliances on sales, marketing, and finance. How-tos for retailers. Pays varying rates, on publication. Query with clips.

DELUXE—The Webb Company, 1999 Shepard St., St. Paul, MN 55116. George Bonneville, Ed. Distributed to employees of financial institutions. Articles, 1,000 to 1,400 words, on personal improvement, professional development/business interest; life style; foods, recipes, and activities. Pays $300 to $600, on acceptance. Query with SASE.

DENTAL ECONOMICS—P.O. Box 3408, Tulsa, OK 74101. Dick Hale, Ed. Articles, 1,200 to 3,500 words, on business side of dental practice, patient and staff communication, personal investments, etc. Pays $100 to $250, on acceptance.

DOMESTIC ENGINEERING—385 N. York Rd., Elmhurst, IL 60126. Stephen J. Shafer, Ed. Articles, to 3,000 words, on plumbing, heating, air conditioning, and process piping. Photos. Pays $20 to $35 per printed page, on publication.

DRAPERIES & WINDOW COVERINGS—P.O. Box 13079 , North Palm Beach, FL 33408. Katie Renckens, Ed. Articles, 1,000 to 2,000 words, for retailers, wholesalers, designers and manufacturers of draperies and window coverings. Profiles, with photos, of successful businesses in the industry. Pays $150 to $250, after acceptance. Query.

DRUG TOPICS—680 Kinderkamack Rd., Oradell, NJ 07649. Valentine A. Cardinale, Ed. News items, 500 words, with photos, on drug retailers and associations. Merchandising features, 1,000 to 1,500 words. Pays $100 to $150 for news, $200 to $400 for features, on acceptance. Query for features.

EARNSHAW'S INFANTS & CHILDREN'S REVIEW—393 Seventh Ave., New York, NY 10001. Christina Gruber, Ed. Articles on retailers, retail promotions, and statistics for children's wear industry. Pays $50 to $200, on publication. Query. Limited market.

ELECTRICAL CONTRACTOR—7315 Wisconsin Ave., Bethesda, MD

20814. Larry C. Osius, Ed. Articles, 1,000 to 1,500 words, with photos, on construction or management techniques for electrical contractors. Pays $100 per printed page, before publication. Query.

ELECTRONIC MANUFACTURING NEWS—1350 E. Touhy Ave., Des Plaines, IL 60018. Diane Pirocanac, Man. Ed. Articles, 500 to 750 words, on interest to engineers and managers in the electronic manufacturing industry. Payment varies, on acceptance. Query required.

EMERGENCY—P.O. Box 159, Carlsbad, CA 92008–0032. Laura Gilbert, Assoc. Ed. Features (to 3,000 words) and department pieces (to 1,000 words) of interest to paramedics, emergency medical technicians, and ambulance personnel: disaster management, advanced first-aid, and medical assessment. Pays $100 to $400 for features, $50 to $250 for department pieces. Photos are a plus. Guidelines available.

EMPLOYEE SERVICES MANAGEMENT—NESRA, 2400 S. Downing, Westchester, IL 60153. Pamela A. Tober, Ed. Articles, 800 to 2,500 words, for human resource, fitness, and employee service professionals.

ENGINEERED SYSTEMS—7314 Hart St., Mentor, OH 44060. Robert L. Schwed, Ed. Articles, case histories, on business management and legal issues related to hvac engineering systems in large systems in large buildings or industrial plants. Pays $4.75 per column inch, $12 per illustration, on publication. Query.

ENTREE—825 7th Ave., New York, NY 10019. Terence Murphy, Ed. Articles, 100 to 2,500 words, on trends and people in better housewares industry, both retailers and manufacturers. Pays from $400, on acceptance.

ENTREPRENEUR—2311 Pontius Ave., Los Angeles, CA 90064. Articles for established and aspiring independent business owners, on all aspects of running a business. Pays $100 to $400, on acceptance. Queries required.

EXECUTIVE REPORT—Riverview Publications, 3 Gateway Ctr., Pittsburgh, PA 15222. John R. McCarty, Ed. Articles, 600 to 2,500 words, on business news in western PA. Pays 10¢ a word, on publication.

EXPORT MAGAZINE—386 Park Ave. South, New York, NY 10016. Robert Weingarten, Ed. Articles, 1,000 to 1,500 words, on the business of agents and distributors who import products in foreign countries. Pays $300 to $350, with photos, on acceptance. Query preferred.

FARM JOURNAL—230 W. Washington Sq., Philadelphia, PA 19105. Practical business articles on growing crops and producing livestock. Pays $50 to $500, on acceptance. Query required.

FINANCIAL WORLD—1450 Broadway, New York, NY 10018. Douglas A. McIntyre, Pub. Features and profiles of large financial institutions and the people who run them. Pays varying rates, on publication. Queries are required.

THE FISH BOAT—P.O. Box 2400 , Covington, LA 70434. Robert A. Carpenter, Ed. Articles on commercial fishing, seafood marketing and processing. Short items on commercial fishing and boats. Pays varying rates.

FITNESS MANAGEMENT—P.O. Box 1198, Solana Beach, CA 92075. Edward H. Pitts, Ed. Authoritative features, 750 to 2,500 words, and news shorts, 100 to 750 words, for owners, managers, and program directors of fitness centers. Content must be in keeping with current medical practice; no fads. Pays 8¢ a word, on publication. Query.

FLORIST—29200 Northwestern Hwy., P.O. Box 2227, Southfield, MI 48037.

Susan Nicholas, Man. Ed. Articles, to 2,000 words, with photos, on retail florist business improvement. Photos. Pays 8¢ a word.

FLOWERS &—Teleflora Plaza, Suite 260, 12233 W. Olympic Blvd., Los Angeles, CA 90064. Marie Moneysmith, Exec. Ed. Articles, 1,000 to 3,500 words, with how-to information for retail florists. Pays from $400, on acceptance. Query with clips.

FOOD MANAGEMENT—747 Third Ave., New York, NY 10017. Donna Boss, Ed. Articles on foodservice in healthcare, schools, colleges, prisons, business and industry. Trends and how-to pieces, with management tie-in. Pays to $500. Query.

FOREIGN TRADE—8208 W. Franklin, Minneapolis, MN 55426. John Freivalds, Ed. Articles and interviews, 1,700 to 2,100 words, on topics related to international trade that examine problems managers have faced, and deal with how they solved them. Pays $400, on publication. Guidelines.

THE FOREMAN'S LETTER—24 Rope Ferry Rd., Waterford, CT 06386. Carl Thunberg, Ed. Interviews, with photos, with top-notch supervisors and foremen. Pays 8¢ to 12¢ a word, extra for photos, on acceptance.

FRANCHISE—747 Third Ave., New York, NY 10017. Michael J. McDermott, Ed. "The Business Magazine of Franchising": articles (1,200 to 1,500 words) on franchise-related business topics. Pays varying rates, on publication. Query required.

FREQUENT FLYER—888 Seventh Ave., New York, NY 10106. Jane Levere, Ed. Articles, 1,000 to 3,000 words, on all aspects of frequent business travel, international trade, aviation, etc. No pleasure travel or personal experience pieces. Pays up to $500, on acceptance. Query required.

GARDEN DESIGN—1733 Connecticut Ave. N.W., Washington, DC 20009. Duke Johns, Man. Ed. Association of American Landscape Architects. Articles, 1,500 to 2,000 words, on classic and contemporary examples of residential landscape, garden, art, history, and design. Interviews. Pays $300, on publication. Query.

GLASS DIGEST—310 Madison Ave., New York, NY 10017. Charles Cumpston, Ed. Articles, 1,200 to 1,500 words, on building projects and glass/metal dealers, distributors, storefront and glazing contractors. Pays varying rates, on publication.

GLASS NEWS—P.O. Box 7138, Pittsburgh, PA 15213. Liz Scott, Man. Ed. Articles, to 1,500 words, on developments in glass manufacturing, glass factories, types of glass. Personality profiles. Pays 5¢ to 10¢ a word, on publication. Query with SASE.

GOLF SHOP OPERATIONS—5520 Park Ave., Box 395, Trumbull, CT 06611–0395. Dave Gould, Ed. Articles, 200 to 800 words, with photos, on successful golf shop operations; new ideas for merchandising, display, bookkeeping. Short pieces on golf professionals and retailers. Pays $250 to $350, on publication. Query with outline.

GOVERNMENT EXECUTIVE—1730 M St. N.W., 11th fl., Washington, DC 20036. Timothy Clark, Ed. Articles, 1,500 to 3,000 words, for civilian and military government workers at the management level.

GREENHOUSE MANAGER—P.O. Box 1868, Fort Worth, TX 76101. Jim Batts, Man. Ed. How-to articles, success stories, 500 to 1,800 words, accompanied by color slides, of interest to professional greenhouse growers. Profiles. Pays $50 to $300, on acceptance. Query required.

HARDWARE AGE—Chilton Way, Radnor, PA 19089. Richard L. Carter, Man. Ed. Articles on merchandising methods in hardware outlets. Photos. Pays on acceptance.

HARDWARE TRADE (FORMERLY *NORTHERN HARDWARE*)—2965 Broadmoor Valley Rd., Suite B, Colorado Springs, CO 80906. Edward Gonzales, Ed. Articles, 800 to 1,000 words, on unusual hardware and home center stores and promotions in Northwest and Midwest. Photos. Pays 8¢ a word, extra for photos, on publication. Query.

HARVARD BUSINESS REVIEW—Harvard Graduate School of Business Administration, Boston, MA 02163. Query Editors on new ideas about business management of interest to senior executives. Pays on publication.

HEALTH FOODS BUSINESS—567 Morris Ave., Elizabeth , NJ 07208. Mary Jane Dittmar, Ed. Articles, 1,500 words, with photos, on managing health food stores. Shorter pieces on trends, research findings, preventive medicine, alternative therapies. Interviews with doctors and nutritionists. Brief items for "Quote/Unquote" (include source). Pays on publication. Query. Guidelines.

HEATING/PIPING/AIR CONDITIONING—2 Illinois Center, Chicago, IL 60601. Robert T. Korte, Ed. Articles, to 5,000 words, on heating, piping and air conditioning systems in industrial plants and large buildings; engineering information. Pays $60 per printed page, on publication. Query.

HOMEOWNERS—8520 Sweetwater, Suite F57, Houston, TX 77037. Theresa Seegers, Man. Ed. Articles, 200 to 500 words, on buying and selling real estate, mortgages, investments, home improvement, interior design, consumer and business trends: "material should emphasize the importance of consulting a real estate professional on any real estate matter." Pays 10¢ to 20¢ a word, on acceptance. Query.

HOSPITAL GIFT SHOP MANAGEMENT—7628 Densmore, Van Nuys, CA 91406. Barbara Feiner, Ed. Articles, 750 to 2,500 words, with managerial tips and sales pointers; hospital and merchandise profiles. Pays $10 to $100, on acceptance. Query required.

HOSPITAL SUPERVISOR'S BULLETIN—24 Rope Ferry Rd., Waterford, CT 06386. Michele Dunaj, Ed. Interviews, articles with non-medical hospital supervisors on departmental problem solving. Pays 12¢ a word. Query.

HOSPITALS—211 E. Chicago Ave., Suite 700, Chicago, IL 60611. Frank Sabatino, Ed. Articles, 500 to 800 words, for hospital administrators. Pays varying rates, on acceptance. Query.

HUMAN RESOURCE EXECUTIVE—Axon Group, 1035 Camphill Rd., Fort Washington, PA 19034. David Shadovitz, Ed. Profiles, case stories, and opinion pieces (1,800 to 2,200 words) of interest to people in the personnel profession. Pays varying rates, on acceptance. Queries required.

INC.—38 Commercial Wharf, Boston, MA 02110. George Gendron, Ed. Feature articles about how owners and managers of small companies solve common problems. Pays to $1,500, on acceptance. Query.

INCENTIVE MARKETING—633 Third Ave., New York, NY 10017. Mary Riordan, Man. Ed. Articles on marketing, incentive travel, and product categories; motivation and incentive sales and merchandising strategies. Pays $125 to $800, on acceptance.

INCOME OPPORTUNITIES—380 Lexington Ave., New York, NY 10017. Stephen Wagner, Ed. Helpful articles, 1,000 to 2,500 words, on how to make money full- or part-time; how to run a successful small business, improve sales, etc. Pays varying rates, on acceptance.

INDUSTRIAL DESIGN—330 W. 42nd St., New York, NY 10036. Annetta Hanna, Man. Ed. Articles to 2,000 words, on product development, design management, graphic design, design history, fashion, art, and environments for designers and marketing executives. Profiles of designers and corporations that use design effectively. Pays $250 to $600, on publication.

INFOSYSTEMS—25W550 Geneva Rd., Wheaton, IL 60188. Wayne L. Rhodes, Ed. How-to articles, 6 to 8 pages, for managers in the data processing field. Pays negotiable rates, on publication. Query.

INSTANT & SMALL COMMERCIAL PRINTER—P.O. Box 368, Northbrook, IL 60065. Lori Bateman, Ed. Articles, 3 to 5 typed pages, for owners and/or managers of printing businesses specializing in retail printing: case histories, how-tos, technical pieces, interesting ideas. Opinion pieces, 1 to 2 typed pages. Photos. Pays $150 to $200 ($25 to $50 for opinion pieces), extra for photos, on publication. Query.

INSTITUTIONAL RESEARCH—See *Research Magazine.*

INTV JOURNAL—80 Fifth Ave., Suite 501, New York, NY 10011. William Dunlap, Ed. Features and short pieces on trends in independent television. Pays to $500, after publication. Query.

JEMS, JOURNAL OF EMERGENCY MEDICAL SERVICES—P. O. Box 1026, Solana Beach, CA 92075. Rick Minerd, Man. Ed. "Articles (1,500 to 3,000 words) should address a wide audience (nurses, paramedics, EMTs, and physicians) exploring topics so that each group better understands the role and responsibilities of the others." Pays 10¢ a word. Guidelines available. Queries are required.

LOS ANGELES BUSINESS JOURNAL—3345 Wilshire, #207, Los Angeles, CA 90010. David Yochum, Ed. Feature articles on specific industries in Los Angeles, stressing the news, trends, and analysis. Pays after publication.

LOS ANGELES LAWYER—Box 55020, Los Angeles, CA 90055. Susan Pettit, Ed. Journalistic features, 12 to 16 pages, and consumer articles, 8 to 12 pages, on legal topics. Pays $200 to $600, on acceptance. Query required.

LOTUS—P.O. Box 9123, Cambridge, MA 02139. Chris Brown, Sr. Ed. Articles, 1,500 to 2,000 words, for business and professional people using Lotus software. Query with outline required. Pay varies, on acceptance.

LP-GAS MAGAZINE—131 W. First St., Duluth, MN 55802. Zane Chastain, Ed. Articles, 1,500 to 2,500 words, with photos, on LP-gas dealer operations: marketing, management, etc. Photos. Pays to 15¢ a word, extra for photos, on acceptance. Query.

MACHINE DESIGN—Penton Publications, 1100 Superior Blvd., Cleveland, OH 44114. Robert Aronson, Exec. Ed. Articles, to 10 typed pages, on design-related topics for engineers. Pays varying rates, on publication. Submit outline or brief description.

MAGAZINE DESIGN & PRODUCTION—4551 W. 107th St., Suite 343, Overland Park, KS 66207. Maureen Waters, Man. Ed. Articles, 6 to 10 typed pages, on magazine design and production: printing, typesetting, design, computers, layout, etc. Pays $100 to $200, on acceptance. Query required.

MAINTENANCE TECHNOLOGY—1300 S. Grove Ave., Barrington, IL

60010. Robert C. Baldwin, Ed. Articles with how-to information on maintenance of electrical and electronic systems, mechanical systems and equipment, and plant facilities. Payment varies, on acceptance. Query required.

MANAGE—2210 Arbor Blvd., Dayton, OH 45439. Doug Shaw, Ed. Articles, 1,500 to 2,200 words, on management and supervision for first-line and middle managers. Pays 5¢ a word.

MANUFACTURING SYSTEMS—Hitchcock Bldg., Wheaton, IL 60188. Tom Inglesby, Ed. Articles, 500 to 2,000 words, on computer and information systems for industry executives seeking to increase productivity in manufacturing firms. Pays 10¢ to 20¢ a word, on acceptance. Query required.

MANUFACTURING WEEK—600 Community Dr., Manhasset, NY 11030. Howard Roth, Ed. News stories and features, to 1,000 words, to be read by executives in "widely divergent manufacturing industries, from shoelaces to jumbo jets." Pays 30¢ a word, on acceptance.

MEDICENTER MANAGEMENT—1640 5th St., Santa Monica, CA 90401. Rebecca Morrow, Ed. Articles, 1,500 to 3,000 words, on the business of practicing medicine: in-office testing, quality controls, customer relations, equipment development, advertising and marketing, joint ventures, etc. Pay varies, on acceptance. Query required.

MEMPHIS BUSINESS JOURNAL—88 Union, Suite 102, Memphis, TN 38103. Barney DuBois, Ed. Articles, to 2,000 words, on business, industry trade, agri-business and finance in the Mid-South trade area. Pays $80 to $200, on acceptance.

MINIATURES DEALER—633 W. Wisconsin Ave., Suite 304, Milwaukee, WI 53203. Geraldine Willems, Ed. Articles, 1,000 to 1,500 words, on advertising, promotion, merchandising of miniatures and other small business concerns. Pays to $200, on publication.

MIX MAGAZINE—2608 Ninth St., Berkeley, CA 94710. David Schwartz, Ed. Articles, varying lengths, for professionals, on audio, video, and music entertainment technology. Pays 10¢ a word, on publication. Query required.

MODERN HEALTHCARE—740 N. Rush St., Chicago, IL 60611. Clark Bell, Ed. Features on management, finance, building design and construction, and new technology for hospitals, health maintenance organizations, nursing homes, and other health care institutions. Pays $7 per column inch, on publication. Query.

MODERN TIRE DEALER—P.O. Box 5417, 110 N. Miller Rd., Akron, OH 44313. Lloyd Stoyor, Ed. Merchandising management and service articles, 1,000 to 1,500 words, with photos, on independent tire dealers and retreaders. Pays $200 to $300, on publication.

NATIONAL FISHERMAN—21 Elm St., Camden, ME 04843. James W. Fullilove, Ed. Articles, 200 to 2,000 words, aimed at commercial fishermen and boat builders. Pays $3 per inch, extra for photos, on publication. Query preferred.

NATION'S BUSINESS—1615 H St. N.W., Washington, DC 20062. Articles on business-related topics, including management advice and success stories aimed at small- to medium-sized businesses. Pays negotiable rates, after acceptance. Guidelines available.

NEPHROLOGY NEWS & ISSUES—18582 Beach Blvd., Suite 201, Huntington Beach, CA 92648. David G. Anast, Ed. "We publish strictly news articles and opinion essays on dialysis, kidney transplantations, and kidney disease. We are not interested in patient testimonials, poems, humor, or any other 'soft' journalism." Pays varying rates, on publication. Photos a plus. Queries required.

NEW BUSINESS—P.O. Box 3312, Sarasota, FL 34230. Business-related articles of regional/general interest. Pays $75 to $225, on publication. Query.

NEW CAREER WAYS NEWSLETTER—67 Melrose Ave., Haverhill, MA 01830. William J. Bond, Ed. How-to articles, 1,500 to 2,000 words, on new ways to succeed in business careers. Pays varying rates, on publication. Query with outline.

NEW HAVEN BUSINESS DIGEST—375 Orange St., New Haven, CT 06510. Kim Hanson, Ed. Feature articles, 1,500 to 2,000 words, on successful New Haven-area businesses and owners. Pays $2.75 per published inch, on publication. Query required.

NORTHEAST INTERNATIONAL BUSINESS—401 Theodore Fremd Ave., Rye, NY 10580. David E. Moore, Exec. Ed. Articles, 1,000 to 1,500 words, on global marketing strategies, and short (500 words) pieces with tips on operating abroad. Profiles, 3,000 to 3,500 words, on individuals or companies. Pays $12 a column inch, on acceptance and on publication. Query required.

NORTHERN HARDWARE—See *Hardware Trade.*

NURSINGWORLD JOURNAL—470 Boston Post Rd., Weston, MA 02193. Shirley Copithorne, Ed. Articles, 500 to 1,000 words, for nurses and nurse educators, on all aspects of nursing. B & W photos. Pays from 25¢ per column inch, on publication.

OPPORTUNITY MAGAZINE—6 N. Michigan Ave., Suite 1405, Chicago, IL 60602. Jack Weissman, Ed. Articles, 900 words, on sales psychology, sales techniques, self-improvement. Pays $20 to $40, on publication.

OPTIONS—7628 Densmore Ave., Van Nuys, CA 91406. Barbara Feiner, Man. Ed. Articles (1,000 to 3,000 words) on practice management and related business topics for doctors in group practice. Pays $50 to $200, on acceptance. Queries required.

THE OWNER BUILDER—1516 Fifth St., Berkeley, CA 94710. Patrick Lynch, Ed. Articles of interest to people building or remodeling their own homes: how-tos, profiles of owner builders, materials and technique reviews. Pays varying rates, on publication. Limited free-lance market.

PC WEEK—800 Boylston St., Boston, MA 02119. Jennifer DeJong, Exec. Ed. Features, 1,500 to 2,500 words, for volume buyers of PCs and related equipment and software within large organizations; corporate strategy profiles; reviews of PC-related products. Pays $500 to $1,000, on acceptance. Query required.

PET BUSINESS—5400 N.W. 84th Ave., Miami, FL 33166. Amy Jordon Smith, Ed. Brief documented articles on animals and products found in pet stores; research findings; legislative/regulatory actions. Pays $4 per column inch, on publication. Photos, $10 to $20.

PETS/SUPPLIES/MARKETING—One E. First St., Duluth, MN 55802. David D. Kowalski, Ed. Articles, 1,000 to 1,200 words, with photos, on pet shops, and pet and product merchandising. Pays 10¢ a word, extra for photos. No fiction or news clips. Query.

PHOTO MARKETING—3000 Picture Pl., Jackson, MI 49201. Perry Washburn, Man. Ed. Business articles, 1,000 to 3,500 words, for owners and managers of camera stores or photo processing labs. Pays $150 to $500, extra for photos, on publication.

PHYSICAL THERAPY JOB NEWS—470 Boston Post Rd., Weston, MA 02193. Shirley Copithorne, Ed. Articles, case studies, and profiles (1,500 to 2,500 words) of interest to professional and student physical therapists. Guidelines available. Pays on publication.

PHYSICIANS FINANCIAL NEWS—McGraw-Hill Health Care Group, 800 Second Ave., New York, NY 10017. Joseph Lisanti, Sr. Ed. Articles (1,000 words) on investment and personal finance and non-clinical medical economic subjects. Pays $400, after acceptance.

PHYSICIAN'S MANAGEMENT—7500 Old Oak Blvd., Cleveland, OH 44130. Bob Feigenbaum, Ed. Articles, about 2,500 to 3,000 words, on finance, investments, malpractice, and office management for primary care physicians. No clinical pieces. Pays $125 per printed page, on acceptance. Query.

PNG REPORT—P.O. Box 337, 121 North Main, Iola, WI 54945. Deb Lengkeek, Ed. Professional Numismatists Guild publication, for coin and bullion dealers. Management advice and business articles (2,000 to 3,000 words) aimed at improving work-related issues. Payment varies, on publication. Query.

P.O.B.—5820 Lilley Rd., Suite 5, Canton, MI 48187. Victoria L. Dickinson, Assoc. Ed. Technical and business articles, 1,000 to 4,000 words, for professionals and technicians in the surveying and mapping fields. Technical tips on field and office procedures and equipment maintenance. Pays $150 to $400, on acceptance.

POLICE MAGAZINE—P.O. Box 847, Carlsbad, CA 92008–9970. F. McKeen Thompson, Ed. Articles and profiles (1,000 to 3,000 words) on specialized groups, equipment, issues and trends of interest to people in the law enforcement profession. Pays $100 to $400, on acceptance.

POOL & SPA NEWS—3923 W. Sixth St., Los Angeles, CA 90020. News articles for the swimming pool, spa, and hot tub industry. Pays from 8¢ to 12¢ a word, extra for photos, on publication. Query first.

THE PRESS—302 Grote St., Buffalo, NY 14207. Cory Ireland, Ed. Quarterly. Short profiles, 800 to 1,200 words, on cartoonists and industry and advertising personalities for advertising executives at newspapers and ad agencies. Pays 10¢ a word, on acceptance.

PRIVATE PRACTICE—Box 12489, Oklahoma City, OK 73157. Cindy Wickersham, Asst. Ed. Articles, 1,500 to 2,000 words, on state or local legislation affecting medical field. Pays $250 to $350, on publication.

PROFESSIONAL OFFICE DESIGN—111 Eighth Ave., New York, NY 10011. Muriel Chess, Ed. Articles, to 1,500 words, on space planning and design for offices in the fields of law, medicine, finance, accounting, advertising, and architecture/design. Pays competitive rates, on publication. Query required.

PROGRESSIVE GROCER—1351 Washington Blvd., Stamford, CT 06902. Michael J. Sansolo, Man. Ed. Articles related to retail food operations; ideas for successful merchandising, promotions, and displays. Short pieces preferred. Cartoons and photos. Pay varies, on acceptance.

RADIO-ELECTRONICS—500-B Bi-County Blvd., Farmingdale, NY 11735. Brian C. Fenton, Man. Ed. Technical articles, 1,500 to 3,000 words, on all areas related to electronics. Pays $50 to $500, on acceptance.

REAL ESTATE TODAY—National Association of Realtors, 430 N. Michigan Ave., Chicago, IL 60611. Articles on all aspects of residential, finance, commercial-investment, and brokerage-management real estate, to 2,000 words. Query required. Pays in copies.

REMODELING—Hanley-Wood, Inc., 655 15th St., Suite 475, Washington, DC 20005. Wendy A. Jordan, Ed. Articles, 250 to 1,700 words, on remodeling and industry news for residential and light commercial remodelers. Pays 20¢ a word, on acceptance. Query.

RESEARCH MAGAZINE—2201 Third St., P.O. Box 77905, San Francisco, CA 94107. Anne Evers, Ed. Articles of interest to stock brokers, 1,000 to 3,000 words, on financial products, selling, how-tos, and financial trends. Profiles of publicly held companies. Pays from $300 to $900, on publication. Same requirements for *Institutional Research,* for institutional investors. Query.

RESTAURANTS USA—311 First St. N.W., Washington, DC 20001. Sylvia Rivchun, Ed. Articles, 2,500 to 3,500 words, on the food service and restaurant business. Pays $350 to $750, on acceptance. Query.

ROOFER MAGAZINE—P.O. Box 06253, Ft. Myers, FL 33906. Mr. Shawn Holiday, Ed. Technical and non-technical articles, human-interest pieces, 500 to 1,500 words, on roofing-related topics: new roofing concepts, energy savings, pertinent issues, industry concern. No general business or computer articles. Pays negotiable rates, on publication. Guidelines.

RV BUSINESS—29901 Agoura Rd., Agoura, CA 91301. Katherine Sharman, Exec. Ed. Articles, 1,500 to 2,500 words, on manufacturing, financing, selling and servicing recreational vehicles. Articles on legislative matters affecting the industry. Pays varying rates.

THE SAFETY COMPLIANCE LETTER—24 Rope Ferry Rd., Waterford, CT 06386. Margot Levin, Ed. Interview-based articles, 800 to 1,250 words, for safety professionals, on solving OSHA-related safety and health problems. Pays to 15¢ a word, on acceptance. Query.

SALES & MARKETING MANAGEMENT—Bill Communications, Inc., 633 Third Ave., New York, NY 10017. A. J. Vogl, Ed. Short and feature articles of interest to sales and marketing executives of medium to large corporations. Pays varying rates, on acceptance. Queries preferred.

SALES MOTIVATION—1640 Fifth St., Santa Monica, CA 90401. Helene Kass, Ed. Articles (1,500 to 2,500 words) on methods of organizing and implementing employee motivational programs. Pays 10¢ a word, after acceptance. Queries preferred.

SALTWATER DEALER—One Bell Rd., Montgomery, AL 36117. Dave Ellison, Ed. Articles (300 to 1,250 words) for merchants who carry saltwater tackle and marine equipment; business focus is required, and writers should provide practical information for improving management and merchandising. Pays varying rates, on acceptance.

SECURITY MANAGEMENT—1655 N. Ft. Myer Dr., Suite 1200, Arlington, VA 22209. Mary Alice Crawford, Pub. Articles, 2,500 to 3,000 words, on legislative issues related to security; case studies of innovative security applications; management topics: employee relations, training programs, etc. Pays 10¢ a word, on publication. Query.

SELLING DIRECT—6255 Barfield Rd., Atlanta, GA 30328. Robert S. Rawls, Ed. Articles, 400 to 1,800 words, for independent salespersons selling to homes, stores, industries, and businesses. Pays 10¢ a word, on publication.

SIGN BUSINESS—P.O. Box 1416, Broomfield, CO 80020. Michele Crockett, Ed. Articles specifically targeted to the sign business. Pays $50 to $200, on acceptance.

SNACK FOOD MAGAZINE—131 W. First St., Duluth, MN 55802. Jerry Hess, Ed. Articles, 600 to 1,500 words, on trade news, personalities, promotions, production in snack food manufacturing industry. Short pieces; photos. Pays 12¢ to 15¢ a word, $15 for photos, on acceptance. Query.

SOFTWARE NEWS—1900 W. Park Dr., Westborough, MA 01581. Edward J. Bride, Ed. Technical features, 1,000 to 1,200 words, for computer-literate audience, on how software products can be used. Pays about $500 to $750, on publication. Query preferred.

SOUTHERN LUMBERMAN—P.O. Box 1627, Franklin, TN 37064. Nanci P. Gregg, Ed. Articles on pine and hardwood sawmill operations, interviews with industry leaders, how-to technical pieces with an emphasis on increasing production and efficiency. Pays $100 to $250 for articles with B&W photos. Queries preferred.

SOUVENIRS AND NOVELTIES—401 N. Broad St., Suite 226–27, Philadelphia, PA 19108. Articles, 1,500 words, quoting souvenir shop managers on items that sell, display ideas, problems in selling, industry trends. Photos. Pays from $1 per column inch, extra for photos, on publication.

SUCCESSFUL FARMING—1716 Locust St., Des Moines, IA 50336. Loren Kruse, Ed. Articles, to 2,000 words, for farming families, on all areas of business farming: money management, marketing, machinery, soils and crops, livestock, and buildings; profiles. Pays from $300, on acceptance. Query required.

TEXTILE WORLD—4170 Ashford-Dunwoody Rd., N.E., Suite 420, Atlanta, GA 30319. L. A. Christiansen, Ed. Articles, 500 to 2,000 words, with photos, on manufacturing and finishing textiles. Pays varying rates, on acceptance.

TILE WORLD/STONE WORLD—485 Kinderkamack Rd., Oradell, NJ 07649. Articles, 300 to 1,000 words, on new trends in installing and designing with tile and stone. For design professionals. Pays $80 per printed page, on publication. Query.

TOP SHELF—199 Ethan Allen Hwy., Ridgefield, CT 06877. Jane Tougas, Ed. Dir. Trade news and advice (1,000 to 2,500 words) for bar owners and managers. "The emphasis is on personalities; taboos include irresponsible marketing of alcohol and glorification of overconsumption." Pays $300 to $600, on acceptance. Query.

TOURIST ATTRACTIONS AND PARKS—Suite 226–27, 401 N. Broad St., Philadelphia, PA 19108. Chuck Tooley, Ed. Articles, 1,500 words, on successful management of parks and leisure attractions. News items, 250 and 500 words. Pays 7¢ a word, on publication. Query.

TRAILER/BODY BUILDERS—1602 Harold St., Houston, TX 77006. Paul Schenck, Ed. Articles on engineering, sales, and management ideas for truck body and truck trailer manufacturers. Pays from $100 per printed page, on acceptance.

TRAINING, THE MAGAZINE OF HUMAN RESOURCES DEVELOPMENT—50 S. Ninth St., Minneapolis, MN 55402. Jack Gordon, Ed. Articles, 1,000 to 2,500 words, for managers of training and development activities in corporations, government, etc. Pays to 15¢ a word, on acceptance. Query.

THE TRAVEL AGENT—825 Seventh Ave., New York, NY 10019. Richard Kahn, Ed. Articles, 1,500 words, with photos, on travel trade, for travel agents. Pays $50 to $75, on acceptance.

THE TRAVEL BUSINESS MANAGER—90 Montgomery Ave., Suite 184, Rockville, MD 20850. Eleanor Alexander, Ed. Articles and features, 1,000 to 1,800 words, on management and strategic issues in the travel industry. Pays $150 to $250, on publication. Query required. Send SASE for guidelines.

TRAVELAGE EAST/SOUTHEAST—555 N. Birch Rd., Ft. Lauderdale, FL 33304. Marylyn Springer, Ed. Articles, 1,500 to 2,000 words, for travel agents and other travel industry personnel. Pays $2 per column inch, on publication.

TRUCKER/USA—P.O. Box 2029, Tuscaloosa, AL 35403. Phil Willis, Ed. Features, 250 to 1,000 words, for heavy-duty truck drivers. Pays $10 to $50, on acceptance.

VENDING TIMES—545 Eighth Ave., New York, NY 10018. Arthur E. Yohalem, Ed. Feature and news articles, with photos, on vending machines. Pays varying rates, on acceptance. Query.

VIEW—80 Fifth Ave., Suite 501, New York, NY 10011. Peter Caranicas, Ed. Features and short pieces on trends in the business of television programming (network, syndication, cable and pay). Profiles. Pays to $400, after publication.

VIRGINIA BUSINESS—600 E. Broad St., Richmond, VA 23219. James Bacon, Ed. Articles, 1,000 to 2,500 words, related to the business scene in Virginia. Pays varying rates, on acceptance. Query required.

WESTERN INVESTOR—400 S.W. Sixth Ave., Suite 1115, Portland, OR 97204. Business and investment articles, 800 to 1,200 words, about companies and their leaders listed in the Western Investor data section. Pays from $50, on publication. Query first.

WINES & VINES—1800 Lincoln Ave., San Rafael, CA 94901. Philip E. Hiaring, Ed. Articles, 1,000 words, on grape and wine industry, emphasizing marketing and production. Pays 5¢ a word, on acceptance.

WOMEN IN BUSINESS—9100 Ward Parkway, Box 8728, Kansas City, MO 64114. Margaret E. Horan, Ed. Publication of the American Business Women's Association. Features, 1,000 to 2,000 words, for career women from 25 to 55 years old; no profiles. Pays 15¢ a word, on acceptance. Query.

WOOD 'N ENERGY—P.O. Box 2008, Laconia, NH 03247. Jason Perry, Ed. Profiles and interviews, 1,000 to 2,500 words, with retailers and manufacturers of alternative energy equipment. Pays $150 to $250, on acceptance.

WOODSHOP NEWS—Pratt St., Essex, CT 06426–1122. Ian C. Bowen, Ed. Features (1 to 3 typed pages) for and about people who work with wood: business stories, profiles, news. Pays $2 per column inch, on publication. Queries preferred.

WORLD OIL—Gulf Publishing Co., P.O. Box 2608, Houston, TX 77252. T. R. Wright, Jr., Ed. Engineering and operations articles, 3,000 to 4,000 words, on petroleum industry exploration, drilling or producing. Photos. Pays from $50 per printed page, on acceptance. Query.

WORLD SCREEN NEWS—80 Fifth Ave., Suite 501, New York, NY 10011. Peter Caranicas, Ed. Features and short pieces on trends in the business of international television programming (network, syndication, cable and pay). Pays to $500, after publication.

WORLD WASTES—6255 Barfield Rd., Atlanta, GA 30328. Bill Wolpin, Ed./Pub. Christi Baggett, Asst. Ed. Case studies, 1,000 to 2,000 words, with photos, of refuse haulers, landfill operators, resource recovery operations and transfer stations, with solutions to problems in field. Pays from $125 per printed page, on publication. Query preferred.

YOUNG FASHIONS—370 Lexington Ave., New York, NY 10017. Articles, 2,000 to 4,000 words, that help store owners and department store buyers of children's clothes with merchandising or operations; how-to pieces. Payment varies, on acceptance. Query required.

COMPANY PUBLICATIONS

Company publications (also called house magazines or house organs) are excellent, well-paying markets for writers at all levels of experience. Large corporations publish these magazines to promote good will, familiarize readers with the company's services and products, and interest customers in these products. Always read a house magazine before submitting an article; write to the editor for a sample copy (offering to pay for it) and the editorial guidelines. Stamped, self-addressed envelopes should be enclosed with any query or manuscript. The folowing list includes only a sampling of publications in this large market.

THE COMPASS—Mobil International Aviation and Marine Sales, Inc., 150 E. 42nd St., New York, NY 10017. T. F. Gerrety, Ed. Articles, to 3,500 words, on the sea and deep sea trade. Photos. Pays to $250, on acceptance. Query.

FORD NEW HOLLAND NEWS—Div. of Sperry Corp., New Holland, PA 17557. Gary Martin, Ed. Articles, to 1,000 words, with strong photo support, on production agriculture, research and rural human interest. Pays on acceptance. Query.

THE FURROW—Deere and Company, John Deere Rd., Moline, IL 61265. George R. Sollenberger, Ed. Articles and humor, to 1,500 words; researched agricultural-technical features; rural social- and economic-trend features. Pays to $1,000, on acceptance.

INLAND—Inland Steel Co., 18 South Home Ave, Park Ridge, IL 60068. Sheldon A. Mix, Man. Ed. Imaginative articles, essays, commentaries, any length, of special interest in Midwest. Pays varying rates, on acceptance.

THE MODERN WOODMEN—Modern Woodmen of America, Mississippi River at 17th St., Rock Island, IL 61201. Gloria Bergh, Manager, Public Relations. Family- and community-oriented, general-interest articles; some quality fiction. Photos. Pays from $50, on acceptance. Publication not copyrighted.

RAYTHEON MAGAZINE—141 Spring St., Lexington, MA 02173. Robert P. Suarez, Ed. Articles by assignment only. Pays $1,000 to $1,250, on acceptance, for articles 800 to 1,200 words. Query with writing sample.

ASSOCIATIONS, ORGANIZATIONS

CALIFORNIA HIGHWAY PATROLMAN—2030 V St., Sacramento, CA 95818. Carol Perri, Ed. Articles, on transportation safety, California history, travel, topical, consumerism, humor, general items, etc. Photos a plus. Pays 2 ½ ¢ a word, extra for B&W photos, on publication. Guidelines with SASE.

CATHOLIC FORESTER—425 W. Shuman Blvd., Naperville, IL 60566. Barbara Cunningham, Ed. Official publication of the Catholic Order of Forresters, a fraternal life insurance company for Catholics. Articles, to 2,000 words, of interest to Middle America. Fiction, to 3,000 words, that deals with contemporary issues; no sex or violence. Pays from 5¢ a word, on acceptance.

COLUMBIA—Box 1670, New Haven, CT 06507. Richard McMunn, Ed. Knights of Columbus. Articles, 1,500 words, for Catholic families. Must be accompanied by color photos or transparencies. No fiction. Pays to $500 for articles and photos, on acceptance.

THE ELKS MAGAZINE—425 W. Diversey Pkwy., Chicago, IL 60614. Fred D. Oakes, Exec. Ed. Articles, 3,000 words, on business, sports, and topics of current interest; for non-urban audience with above-average income. Informative or humorous pieces, to 2,500 words. Pays $150 to $500 for articles, on acceptance. Query.

FIREHOUSE—33 Irving Pl., New York, NY 10003. Janet Kimmerly, Exec. Ed. Articles, 500 to 2,000 words: on-the-scene accounts of fires, trends in firefighting equipment, controversial fire service issues, and life styles of firefighters. Humorous fillers, to 100 words. Pays $100 to $200 for features, to $25 for fillers, on publication. Query.

FOCUS—Turnkey Publications, 4807 Spicewood Springs Rd., Suite 3150, Austin, TX 78759. Greg Farman, Ed. Magazine of the North American Data General Users Group. Articles, 700 to 4,000 words, on Data General computers. Photos a plus. Pays to $100, on publication. Query required.

GEOBYTE—P.O. Box 979, Tulsa, OK 74101. Ken Milam, Man. Ed. Publication of the American Association of Petroleum Geologists. Articles, 20 typed pages, on computer applications in exploration and production of oil, gas, and energy minerals for geophysicists, geologists, and petroleum engineers. Pay varies, on acceptance. Queries preferred.

KIWANIS—3636 Woodview Trace, Indianapolis, IN 46268. Chuck Jonak, Exec. Ed. Articles, 2,500 words (sidebars, 250 to 350 words), on life style, relationships, world view, education, trends, small business, religion, health, etc. No travel pieces, interviews, profiles. Pays $400 to $1,000, on acceptance. Query.

THE LION—300 22nd St., Oak Brook, IL 60570. Robert Kleinfelder, Sr. Ed. Official publication of Lions Clubs International. Articles, 800 to 2,000 words, and photo essays, on Club activities. Pays from $50 to $400, including photos, on acceptance. Query.

OPTIMIST MAGAZINE—4494 Lindell Blvd., St. Louis, MO 63108. Patricia A. Gamma, Ed. Articles, to 1,500 words, on activities of local Optimist club, and techniques for personal and club success. Pays from $100, on acceptance. Query.

RESTAURANTS USA—311 First St. N.W., Washington, DC 20001. Sylvia Rivchun, Ed. Publication of the National Restaurant Association. Articles, 2,500 to 3,500 words, on the food service and restaurant business. Pays $350 to $750, on acceptance. Query.

THE ROTARIAN—1560 Sherman Ave., Evanston, IL 60201. Willmon L. White, Ed. Publication of Rotary International, world fellowship of business and professional men. Inspirational and art-of-living articles, education, environment, and business management and ethics pieces. Pays $350 to $1,000, on acceptance. Query.

WOODMEN OF THE WORLD MAGAZINE—1700 Farnam St., Omaha, NE 68102. Leland A. Larson, Ed. Articles on history, travel, sports, do-it-yourself projects, health, science, etc. Photos. Pays 5¢ a word, extra for photos, on acceptance.

RELIGIOUS AND DENOMINATIONAL

ADVANCE—1445 Boonville Ave., Springfield, MO 65802. Gwen Jones, Ed. Articles, 1,200 words, slanted to ministers, on preaching, doctrine, practice; how-to features. Pays 3¢ to 4¢ a word, on acceptance.

AGLOW MAGAZINE—P.O. Box 1548, Lynnwood, WA 98046–1557. Gwen Weising, Ed. First-person articles and testimonies, 1,000 to 2,000 words, that encourage, instruct, inform or entertain Christian women of all ages, and relate to the work of the Holy Spirit. Should deal with contemporary issues. Pays 8¢ to 10¢ a word, on acceptance. Queries required.

AMERICA—106 W. 56th St., New York, NY 10019. George W. Hunt, S.J., Ed. Articles, 1,000 to 2,500 words, on current affairs, family life, literary trends. Pays $75 to $150, on acceptance.

AMERICAN BIBLE SOCIETY RECORD—1865 Broadway, New York, NY 10023. Clifford P. MacDonald, Man. Ed. Material related to work of American Bible Society: translating, publishing, distributing. Pays on acceptance. Query.

AMIT WOMAN—817 Broadway, New York, NY 10003. Micheline Ratzerdorfer, Ed. Articles, 1,000 to 2,000 words, of interest to Jewish women: Middle East, Israel, history, holidays, travel. Pays to $75, on publication.

ANNALS OF ST. ANNE DE BEAUPRÉ—P.O. Box 1000, St. Anne de Beaupré, Quebec, Canada G0A 3C0. Roch Achard, C.Ss.R., Ed. Articles, 1,100 to 1,200 words, on Catholic subjects and on St. Anne. Pays 2¢ to 4¢ a word, on acceptance.

BAPTIST LEADER—American Baptist Churches, P.O. Box 851, Valley Forge, PA 19482–0851. L. Isham, Ed. Practical how-to or thought-provoking articles, 1,200 to 1,600 words, for local church education lay leaders and teachers.

THE B'NAI B'RITH INTERNATIONAL JEWISH MONTHLY—1640 Rhode Island Ave. N.W., Washington, DC 20036. Marc Silver, Ed. Original, lively articles, 500 to 3,000 words, on trends, politics, personalities, and culture of the Jewish community. Fiction, 1,000 to 4,000 words. Pays 10¢ to 25¢ a word, on publication. Query.

BREAD—6401 The Paseo, Kansas City, MO 64131. Karen De Sollar, Ed. Church of the Nazarene. Devotional, Bible study and Christian guidance articles, to 1,200 words, for teen-agers. Religious short stories, to 1,500 words. Pays from 3¢ a word for prose, on acceptance.

BRIGADE LEADER—Box 150, Wheaton, IL 60189. Steve Neideck, Ed. Inspirational articles, 1,000 to 1,800 words, for Christian men who work with boys. Pays $60 to $150. Query only.

CATECHIST—2451 E. River Rd., Dayton, OH 45439. Patricia Fischer, Ed. Informational and inspirational articles, 1,200 to 1,500 words, for Catholic teachers, coordinators, and administrators in religious education programs. Pays $25 to $75, on publication.

CATHOLIC DIGEST—P.O. Box 64090, St. Paul, MN 55164. Address Articles Ed. Articles, 2,000 to 2,500 words, on Catholic and general subjects. Fillers, to 300 words, on instances of kindness rewarded, for "Hearts Are Trumps"; accounts of good deeds, for "People Are Like That." Pays from $200 for original articles, $100 for reprints, on acceptance; $4 to $50 for fillers, on publication.

CATHOLIC LIFE—35750 Moravian Dr., Fraser, MI 48026. Robert C. Bayer, Ed. Articles, 600 to 1,200 words, on Catholic missionary work in Hong Kong, India, Latin America, Africa, etc. Photos. No fiction or poetry. Pays 4¢ a word, extra for photos, on publication.

CATHOLIC NEAR EAST MAGAZINE—1011 First Ave., New York, NY 10022. Michael Healy, Ed. Articles, 1,000 to 1,800 words, on the people of the Balkans, Near East, Middle East, and India —and their religious history, sacred rituals, artistic heritage, living culture, and faith traditions. Special interest in Eastern Catholic churches. Color photos illustrate all articles. Pays 10¢ a word, on publication. Query with SASE.

CATHOLIC TWIN CIRCLE—6404 Wilshire Blvd., Suite 900, Los Angeles, CA 90048. Mary Louise Frawley, Ed. Articles and interviews of interest to Catholics, 1,000 to 2,000 words, with photos. Strict attention to Catholic doctrine required. Enclose SASE. Pays 10¢ a word, on publication.

CHARISMA AND CHRISTIAN LIFE—190 N. Westmonte Dr., Altamonte Springs, FL 32714. Howard Earl, Senior Ed. Charismatic/Evangelical Christian articles, 1,000 to 2,000 words, for developing the spiritual life. Photos. Pays varying rates, on publication.

THE CHRISTIAN CENTURY—407 S. Dearborn St., Chicago, IL 60605. James M. Wall, Ed. Ecumenical. Articles, 1,500 to 2,500 words, with a religious angle, on political and social issues, international affairs, culture, the arts. Poetry, to 20 lines. Photos. Pays about $25 per printed page, extra for photos, on publication.

CHRISTIAN HERALD—40 Overlook Dr., Chappaqua, NY 10514. Dean Merrill, Ed. Interdenominational. Articles, personal-experience pieces, to 1,500 words, on biblically oriented topics. Short verse. Pays from 10¢ a word for full-length features, from $10 for short pieces, after acceptance. Query first.

CHRISTIAN SINGLE—127 Ninth Ave. N., Nashville, TN 37234. Cliff Allbritton, Ed. Articles, 600 to 1,200 words, on leisure activities, inspiring personal experiences, for Christian singles. Humor. Pays 5¢ a word, on acceptance. Query. Send SASE for guidelines.

CHRISTIAN SOCIAL ACTION (FORMERLY *ENGAGE/SOCIAL ACTION*)—100 Maryland Ave. NE, Washington, DC 20002. Lee Ranck, Ed. Articles, 1,500 to 2,000 words, on social issues for concerned persons of faith. Pays $75 to $100, on publication.

CHRISTIANITY TODAY—465 Gundersen Dr., Carol Stream, IL 60188. Harold Smith, Man. Ed. Doctrinal, social issues and interpretive essays, 1,500 to 3,000 words, from evangelical Protestant perspective. Pays $300 to $500, on acceptance. Query required.

CHURCH & STATE—8120 Fenton St., Silver Spring, MD 20910. Joseph L. Conn, Man. Ed. Articles, 600 to 2,600 words, on religious liberty and church-state relations issues. Pays varying rates, on acceptance. Query.

CHURCH ADMINISTRATION—127 Ninth Ave. N., Nashville, TN 37234. Gary Hardin, Ed. Southern Baptist. How-to articles, 1,500 to 1,800 words, on administrative planning, staffing, pastoral ministry, organization, and financing. Pays 5¢ a word, on acceptance. Query.

CHURCH EDUCATOR—Educational Ministries, 2861-C Saturn St., Brea, CA 92621. Robert G. Davidson, Ed. Articles, 200 to 3,000 words, with a personal approach to Christian education; articles on youth programs; Advent or Lenten material. How-tos for adult and juvenile Christian education. Pays 3¢ a word, on publication.

THE CHURCH HERALD—6157 28th St. S.E., Grand Rapids, MI 49506. John Stapert, Ed. Reformed Church in America. Articles, 500 to 1,500 words, on Christianity and culture, politics, marriage, and home. Pays $40 to $125, on acceptance.

THE CHURCH MUSICIAN—127 Ninth Ave. N., Nashville, TN 37234. W.

M. Anderson, Ed. Articles for spiritual enrichment, testimonials, human-interest pieces, and other subjects of interest to music directors, pastors, organists, pianists, choir coordinators, and members of the music council in local churches. No clippings. Pays to 5¢ a word, on acceptance. Same address and requirements for *Glory Songs* (for adults), and *Opus One* and *Opus Two* (for teen-agers).

THE CIRCUIT RIDER—P.O. Box 801, Nashville, TN 37202. Keith Pohl, Ed. Articles for United Methodist pastors, 800 to 1,600 words. Pays $25 to $100, on acceptance. Query with SASE preferred.

COLUMBIA—Box 1670, New Haven, CT 06507. Richard McMunn, Ed. Knights of Columbus. Articles, 1,500 words, for Catholic families. Must be accompanied by color photos or transparencies. No fiction. Pays to $500 for articles with photos, on acceptance.

COMMENTARY—165 E. 56th St., New York, NY 10022. Norman Podhoretz, Ed. Articles, 5,000 to 7,000 words, on contemporary issues, Jewish affairs, social sciences, religious thought, culture. Serious fiction; book reviews. Pays on publication.

COMMONWEAL—15 Dutch St., New York, NY 10038. Margaret O'Brien Steinfels, Ed. Catholic. Articles, to 3,000 words, on political, religious, social and literary subjects. Pays 3¢ a word, on acceptance.

CONFIDENT LIVING—Box 82808, Lincoln, NE 68501. Jan Reeser, Man. Ed. Articles, to 1,500 words, on relating biblical truths to daily living. Photos. Pays 4¢ to 10¢ a word, extra for photos, on acceptance. No simultaneous submissions or reprints. SASE required.

DAILY MEDITATION—Box 2710, San Antonio, TX 78299. Ruth S. Paterson, Ed. Inspirational nonsectarian articles, 650 to 2,000 words. Fillers, to 350 words; verse, to 20 lines. Pays ½¢ to 1 ½¢ a word for prose, 14¢ a line for verse, on acceptance.

DECISION—Billy Graham Evangelistic Association, 1300 Harmon Pl., Minneapolis, MN 55403. Roger C. Palms, Ed. Articles, Christian testimonials, 1,800 to 2,000 words. Poems, 4 to 20 lines, preferably free verse; narratives, 500 to 1,000 words. Pays varying rates, on publication.

THE DISCIPLE—Box 179, St. Louis, MO 63166. James L. Merrell, Ed. Articles on Christian living; devotionals, 150 words. Poetry; short humor. Pays $10 to $35 for articles, $2 to $10 for poetry, on publication.

DISCOVERIES—6401 The Paseo, Kansas City, MO 64131. Fiction for children, grades 3 to 6, 400 to 500 words, defining Christian experiences and demonstrating Christian values and beliefs. Pays 3 ½¢ a word for first rights, 2¢ a word for second rights, on acceptance. Query.

ENGAGE/SOCIAL ACTION MAGAZINE—See *Christian Social Action*.

THE EPISCOPALIAN—1201 Chestnut St., Philadelphia, PA 19107. Richard H. Schmidt, Man. Ed. Articles to 2,000 words that show Episcopalians solving problems; action stories; profiles. Pays $25 to $100, on publication.

THE EVANGEL—901 College Ave., Winona Lake, IN 46590. Vera Bethel, Ed. Free Methodist. Personal-experience articles, 1,000 words. Short, devotional items, 300 to 500 words. Fiction, 1,200 words, on Christian solutions to problems. Serious poetry, 8 to 12 lines. Pays $25 for articles, $45 for fiction, $5 for poetry, on publication. Return postage required.

EVANGELICAL BEACON—1515 E. 66th St., Minneapolis, MN 55423.

George Keck, Ed. Evangelical Free Church. Articles, 250 to 1,750 words, on religious topics; testimonials; pieces on current issues from an evangelical perspective; short inspirational and evangelistic devotionals. Pays 3¢ to 4¢ a word, on publication. Send SASE for writers' guidelines.

FAITH TODAY—Box 8800, Sta. B, Willowdale, Ontario, Canada M2K 2R6. Brian C. Stiller, Ed. Audrey Dorsch, Man. Ed. Articles, 1,500 words, on current issues relating to the church in Canada. Pays negotiable rates, on publication. Queries are preferred.

THE FUNDAMENTALIST JOURNAL—2220 Langhorne Rd., Lynchburg, VA 24514. Deborah Huff, Ed. Articles, 500 to 2,000 words, that examine matters of contemporary interest to all Fundamentalists: news articles, profiles, human-interest pieces; moral and religious issues; Bible studies. Payment varies, on publication.

THE GEM—Box 926, Findlay, OH 45839. Marilyn Rayle Kern, Ed. Articles, 300 to 1,600 words, and fiction, 1,000 to 1,600 words: true-to-life experiences of God's help, of healed relationships, and of growing maturity in faith. For adolescents through senior citizens. Pays $15 for articles and fiction, $7.50 to $10 for fillers, after publication.

GROUP, THE YOUTH MINISTRY MAGAZINE—Box 481, Loveland, CO 80539. Joani Schultz, Ed. Dir. Interdenominational magazine for leaders of high-school-age Christian youth groups. Articles, 500 to 1,700 words, about successful youth groups or youth group projects. Short how-to pieces, to 300 words, for "Try This One"; news items, to 500 words, for "News, Trends, and Tips." Pays to $150 for articles, $15 to $25 for department pieces, on acceptance. Guidelines available.

GUIDE—Review and Herald Publishing Co., 55 W. Oak Ridge Dr., Hagerstown, MD 21740. Stories and articles, to 1,800 words, for Christian youth, ages 10 to 14. Pays 3¢ to 4¢ a word, on acceptance.

GUIDEPOSTS—747 Third Ave., New York, NY 10017. True first-person stories, 250 to 1,500 words, stressing how faith in God helps people cope with life. Anecdotal fillers, to 250 words. Pays $100 to $400, $50 for fillers, on acceptance.

HOME LIFE—127 Ninth Ave. N., Nashville, TN 37234. Mary P. Darby, Asst. Ed. Southern Baptist. Articles, preferably personal-experience, and fiction, to 2,000 words, on Christian marriage, parenthood, and family relationships. Human-interest pieces, 200 to 500 words; cartoons and short verse. Pays to 5¢ a word, on acceptance.

INSIDE MAGAZINE—226 S. 16th St., Philadelphia, PA 19102. Jane Biberman, Ed. Articles, 1,500 to 3,000 words, and fiction, 2,000 to 3,000 words, of interest to Jewish men and women. Pays $100 to $500, on acceptance. Query.

INSIGHT—55 West Oak Ridge Dr., Hagerstown, MD 21740. Christopher Blake, Ed. Seventh-day Adventist. Personal-experience narratives, articles and humor, to 1,500 words, for high school students. Parables; shorts; poetry. Pays 10¢ to 15¢ a word, extra for photos, on acceptance. Same requirements for *Insight Out,* for Christian non-denominational readers. Query.

INTERACTION—See *Teachers Interaction.*

KEY TO CHRISTIAN EDUCATION—8121 Hamilton Ave., Cincinnati, OH 45231. Kim Jackson, Ed. Articles on teaching methods, and success stories for workers in Christian education. Pays varying rates, on acceptance.

LIGHT AND LIFE—901 College Ave., Winona Lake, IN 46590. Robert

Haslam, Ed. Fresh, lively articles about practical Christian living, and sound treatments of vital issues facing the Evangelical in contemporary society. Pays 4¢ a word, on publication. Query.

LIGUORIAN—Liguori, MO 63057. Rev. Norman J. Muckerman, Ed. Francine O'Connor, Man. Ed. Catholic. Articles and short stories, 1,500 to 2,000 words, on Christian values in modern life. Pays 10¢ to 12¢ a word, on acceptance.

LIVE—1445 Boonville Ave., Springfield, MO 65802. John T. Maempa, Adult Ed. Sunday school paper for adults. Fiction, 1,500 to 2,000 words, and articles, 1,000 to 1,500 words, on applying Bible principles to everyday living. Pays 2¢ to 3¢ a word, on acceptance. Send SASE for guidelines.

THE LIVING LIGHT—United States Catholic Conference, Dept. of Education, 1312 Massachusetts Ave. N.W., Washington, DC 20005. Berard L. Marthaler, Exec. Ed. Theoretical and practical articles, 1,500 to 4,000 words, on religious education, catechesis and pastoral ministry.

LIVING WITH CHILDREN—127 Ninth Ave. N., Nashville, TN 37234. Articles, 800, 1,450, or 2,000 words, on parent-child relationships, told from a Christian perspective. Pays 5¢ a word, after acceptance.

LIVING WITH PRESCHOOLERS—127 Ninth Ave. N., Nashville, TN 37234. Articles, 800, 1,450, or 2,000 words, and fillers, to 300 words, for Christian families. Pays 5¢ a word, on acceptance.

LIVING WITH TEENAGERS—127 Ninth Ave. N., Nashville, TN 37234. Articles told from a Christian perspective for parents of teenagers; first-person approach preferred. Poetry, 4 to 16 lines. Pays 5¢ a word, on acceptance.

THE LOOKOUT—8121 Hamilton Ave., Cincinnati, OH 45231. Mark A. Taylor, Ed. Articles, 1,000 to 1,500 words, on families and people overcoming problems by applying Christian principles. Inspirational or humorous shorts, 500 to 800 words; fiction. Pays 4¢ to 6¢ a word, on acceptance.

THE LUTHERAN—8765 W. Higgins Rd., Chicago, IL 60631. Edgar R. Trexler, Ed. Articles, to 2,000 words, on Christian ideology, personal religious experiences, family life, church, and community. Pays $100 to $400, on acceptance. Query.

MARRIAGE & FAMILY (FORMERLY *MARRIAGE & FAMILY LIVING***)**—Division of Abbey Press, St. Meinrad, IN 47577. Kass Dotterweich, Man. Ed. Expert advice, personal-experience articles with moral, religious, or spiritual slant, to 2,500 words, on marriage and family relationships. Pays 7¢ a word, on acceptance.

MARRIAGE PARTNERSHIP (FORMERLY *PARTNERSHIP***)**—Christianity Today, Inc. 465 Gundersen Dr., Carol Stream, IL 60188. Ron Lee, Man. Ed. Articles, 500 to 2,000 words, related to marriage, for men and women who wish to fortify their relationship. Cartoons, humor, fillers. Pays $50 to $300, on acceptance. Query and SASE required..

MATURE LIVING—127 Ninth Ave. N., Nashville, TN 37234. Jack Gulledge, Ed. General-interest and travel articles, nostalgia and fiction, 900 words, for Christians 60 years and older. Profiles, 25 lines; must include a B/W action photo. Brief, humorous items for "Cracker Barrel." Pays 5¢ a word, $25 for profile and photo, $5 for humor on acceptance. Buys all rights.

MATURE YEARS—201 Eighth Ave. S., Nashville, TN 37203. United Methodist. Articles on retirement or related subjects, 1,500 to 2,000 words. Humorous and serious fiction, 1,500 to 1,800 words, for adults. Poetry, to 14 lines. Include Social Security No. with manuscript. Buys all rights.

MESSENGER OF THE SACRED HEART—661 Greenwood Ave., Toronto, Ont., Canada M4J 4B3. Articles and short stories, about 1,500 words, for American and Canadian Catholics. Pays from 2¢ a word, on acceptance.

MIDSTREAM—515 Park Ave., New York, NY 10022. Murray Zuckoff, Ed. Jewish-interest articles and book reviews. Fiction, to 3,000 words, and poetry. Pays 5¢ a word, after publication.

THE MIRACULOUS MEDAL—475 E. Chelten Ave., Philadelphia, PA 19144. Robert P. Cawley, C.M. Ed. Dir. Catholic. Fiction, to 2,400 words. Religious verse, to 20 lines. Pays from 2¢ a word for fiction, from 50¢ a line for poetry, on acceptance.

MODERN LITURGY—160 E. Virginia St., #290, San Jose, CA 95112. Ken Guentert, Ed. Creative material for worship services; religious parables, to 1,000 words; how-tos, essays on worship, 750 to 1,600 words. Plays. Poetry. Pays in copies and subscription.

MOMENT—3000 Connecticut Ave., Suite 300, Washington, DC 20008. Charlotte Anker, Man. Ed. Sophisticated articles and some fiction, 2,500 to 5,000 words, on Jewish topics. Pays $150 to $400, on publication.

MOMENTUM—National Catholic Educational Assn., 1077 30th St. N.W., Suite 100, Washington, DC 20007–3852. Patricia Feistritzer, Ed. Articles, 500 to 1,500 words, on outstanding programs, issues, and research in education. Book reviews. Pays 2¢ a word, on publication. Query.

MOODY MONTHLY—820 N. La Salle Dr., Chicago, IL 60610. Mike Umlandt, Man. Ed. Articles, 1,200 to 1,800 words, on the Evangelical Christian experience in school, the home, and the workplace. Pays 10¢ to 15¢ a word, on acceptance. Query.

THE NATIONAL CHRISTIAN REPORTER—See *The United Methodist Reporter.*

NEW ERA—50 E. North Temple, Salt Lake City, UT 84150. Brian Kelly, Ed. Articles, 150 to 3,000 words, and fiction, to 3,000 words, for young Mormons. Poetry; photos. Pays 5¢ to 10¢ a word, 25¢ a line for poetry, on acceptance. Query.

NEW WORLD OUTLOOK—475 Riverside Dr., Rm. 1351, New York, NY 10115. George M. Daniels, Exec. Ed. Articles, 1,500 to 2,500 words, on Christian missions, religious issues, and public affairs. Pays on publication.

OBLATES MAGAZINE—15 S. 59th St., Belleville, IL 62222. Address Jacqueline Lowery Corn. Articles, 500 to 600 words, for mature Catholics, that inspire, uplift, and motivate through positive Christian values in everyday life. Inspirational poetry, to 16 lines. Pays $75 for articles, $25 for poems, on acceptance. Send complete manuscript only. Guidelines.

OPUS ONE AND OPUS TWO—See *The Church Musician.*

OUR FAMILY—Box 249, Battleford, Sask., Canada S0M 0E0. Nestor Gregoire, Ed. Articles, 1,000 to 3,000 words, for Catholic families, on modern society, family, marriage, current affairs. Fiction, 1,000 to 3,000 words. Humor; verse. Pays 7¢ to 10¢ a word for articles and fiction, 75¢ to $1 a line for poetry, on acceptance. SASE with international reply coupons required with all submissions. Guidelines.

OUR SUNDAY VISITOR—Huntington, IN 46750. Robert Lockwood, Ed.

In-depth featuures, 1,000 to 1,200 words, on the Catholic church in America today. Pays $150 to $250, on acceptance

PARISH FAMILY DIGEST—Noll Plaza, Huntington, IN 46750. George P. Foster, Ed. Articles, 750 to 900 words, fillers and humor, for Catholic families and parishes. Pays 5¢ a word, on acceptance.

PARTNERSHIP—See *Marriage Partnership.*

PENTACOSTAL EVANGEL—1445 Boonville Ave., Springfield, MO 65802. Richard Champion, Ed. Assemblies of God. Religious personal experience and devotional articles, 500 to 1,500 words. Verse, 12 to 30 lines. Pays 4¢ a word, on publication.

PRESBYTERIAN SURVEY—100 Witherspoon, Louisville, KY 40202. Vic Jameson, Ed. Articles, 1,500 words, of interest to members of the Presbyterian Church or ecumenical individuals. Pays to $200, on acceptance.

PRESENT TENSE—165 E. 56th St., New York, NY 10022. Murray Polner, Ed. Serious articles, 2,000 to 3,000 words, with photos, on news concerning Jews throughout the world; first person encounters and personal experience pieces. Literary-political reportage. Contemporary themes only. Pays $200 to $300, on publication. Query.

THE PRIEST—200 Noll Plaza, Huntington, IN 46750. Articles, to 2,500 words, on life and ministry of priests, current theological developments, etc., for priests, permanent deacons, and seminarians. Pays $35 to $100, on acceptance.

PURPOSE—616 Walnut Ave., Scottdale, PA 15683–1999. James E. Horsch, Ed. Articles, 350 to 1,200 words, on Christian discipleship themes, with good photos; pieces of history, biography, science, hobbies, from a Christian perspective. Fiction, to 1,200 words, on Christian problem solving. Poetry, 3 to 12 lines. Pays to 5¢ a word, to $1 a line for poetry, on acceptance.

QUEEN—25 S. Saxon Ave., Bay Shore, NY 11706. James McMillan, M.M.M., Ed. Publication of Montfort Missionaries. Articles and fiction, 1,000 to 2,000 words, related to the Virgin Mary. Poetry. Pay varies, on acceptance.

THE RECONSTRUCTIONIST—Church Road & Greenwood Ave., Wyncote, PA 19095. Dr. Jacob Staub, Ed. Articles and fiction, 2,000 to 3,000 words, relating to Judaism. Poetry. Pays $18 to $36, on publication.

ST. ANTHONY MESSENGER—1615 Republic St., Cincinnati, OH 45210. Norman Perry, O.F.M., Ed. Articles, 2,500 to 3,500 words, on personalities, major movements, education, family, and social issues. Human interest pieces. Humor; fiction (2,500 to 3,000 words). Pays 14¢ a word, on acceptance. Query for nonfiction.

ST. JOSEPH'S MESSENGER—P.O. Box 288, Jersey City, NJ 07303. Sister Ursula Maphet, Ed. Inspriational articles, 500 to 1,000 words, and fiction, 1,000 to 1,500 words. Verse, 4 to 40 lines. Query first.

SEEK—8121 Hamilton Ave., Cincinnti, OH 45231. Eileen H. Wilmoth, Ed. Articles and fiction, to 1,200 words, on inspirational and controversial topics and timely religious issues. Christian testimonials. Pays to 3¢ a word, on acceptance. Guidelines.

SHARING THE VICTORY—8701 Leeds Rd., Kansas City, MO 64129. Skip Stogsdill, Ed. Articles, interviews, and profiles, to 800 words, for co-ed Christian athletes and coaches in high school and college. Pays from $75, on publication. Query required.

SIGNS OF THE TIMES—P. O. Box 7000, Boise, ID 83707. Kenneth J. Holland, Ed. Seventh Day Adventist. Feature articles on Christians who have performed community services; current issues from a Biblical perspective; health, home, marriage, human-interest pieces; inspirational articles, 500 to 2,000 words. Pays 12¢ to15¢ a word, on acceptance.

SISTERS TODAY—The Liturgical Press, St. John's Abbey, Collegeville, MN 56321. Sister Mary Anthony Wagner, O.S.B., Ed. Articles, 500 to 3,500 words, on Roman Catholic theology, religious issues for women and the Church. Poetry, to 34 lines. Pays $5 per printed page, $10 per poem, on publication. Send articles to Editor at St. Benedict's Convent, St. Joseph's MN 56374. Send poetry to Sister Audrey Synnott, R.S.M., 1437 Blossom Rd., Rochester, NY 14610.

SOCIAL JUSTICE REVIEW—3835 Westminster Pl., St. Louis, MO 63108. Rev. John H. Miller, C.S.C., Ed. Articles 2,000 to 3,000 words, on social problems in light of Catholic teaching and current scientific studies. Pays 2¢ a word, on publication.

SPIRITUAL LIFE—2131 Lincoln Rd. N.E., Washington, DC 20002–1199. Steven Payne, O.C.D., Ed. Professional religious journal. Religious essays, 3,000 to 5,000 words, on spirituality in contemporary life. Pays from $50, on acceptance. Guidelines.

SPIRITUALITY TODAY—7200 W. Division St., River Forest, IL 60305. Richard Woods, O.P., Ed. Quarterly. Biblical, liturgical, theological, ecumenical, historical, and biographical articles, 4,000 words, about the challenges of contemporary Christian life. Pays from 1 ½¢ a word, on publication. Query preferred, with SASE. Guidelines.

STANDARD—6401 The Paseo, Kansas City, MO 64131. Articles, 300 to 1,500 words: true experiences; poetry, to 20 lines; fiction, 800 to 1,500 words, with Christian emphasis but not preachy; fillers, puzzles, cryptograms of Scripture verses or inspiriring quotes; cartoons in good taste. Pays 3 ½¢ a word, on acceptance.

SUNDAY DIGEST—850 N. Grove Ave., Elgin, IL 60120. Articles, 1,000 to 1,800 words, on Christian faith in contemporary life; inspirational and how-to articles; free-verse poetry. Anecdotes, 500 words. Pays $40 to $190 (less for reprints), on acceptance.

SUNDAY SCHOOL COUNSELOR—1445 Boonville Ave., Springfield, MO 65802–1894. Sylvia Lee, Ed. Articles, 1,000 to 1,500 words, on teaching and Sunday school people, for local Sunday school teachers. Pays 3¢ to 5¢ a word, on acceptance.

SUNSHINE MAGAZINE—Sunshine Press, Litchfield, IL 62056. Peggy Kuethe, Ed. Inspirational articles, to 600 words. Short stories, 1,000 words, and juveniles, 400 words. No heavily religious material or "born again" pieces. Pays varying rates, on acceptance.

TEACHERS INTERACTION—1333 S. Kirkwood Rd., St. Louis, MO 63122. Martha S. Jander, Ed. Articles, 800 to 1,200 words; how-to pieces, to 100 words, for Lutheran volunteer church school teachers. Pays $10 to $35, on publication. Limited free-lance market.

TEENS TODAY—Church of the Nazarene, 6401 The Paseo, Kansas City, MO 64131. Karen De Sollar, Ed. Short stories that deal with teens demonstrating Christian principles, 1,200 to 1,500 words. Pays 3¢ a word, on acceptance.

THEOLOGY TODAY—Box 29, Princeton, NJ 08542. Craig Dykstra, Ed.

Articles, 1,500 to 3,500 words, on theology, religion, and related social issues. Literary criticism. Pays $50 to $100, on publication.

THE UNITED CHURCH OBSERVER—85 St. Claire Ave. E., Toronto, Ont., Canada M4T 1M8. Factual articles, 1,500 to 2,500 words, on religious trends, human problems, social issues. No poetry. Pays after publication. Query.

UNITED EVANGELICAL ACTION—P. O. Box 28, Wheaton, IL 60189. Don Brown, Ed. National Assn. of Evangelicals. News-oriented expositions and editorials, 750 to 1,000 words, on current events of concern and consequence to the evangelical church. Pays about 7¢ to 10¢ a word, on publication. Query with writing samples required.

THE UNITED METHODIST REPORTER—P.O. Box 660275, Dallas, TX 75266–0275. Spurgeon M. Dunnam, III, Ed. John Lovelace, Man. Ed. United Methodist. Religious features, to 500 words. Religious verse, 4 to 12 lines. Photos. Pays 4¢ a word, on publication. Send for guidelines. Same address and requirements for *The National Christian Reporter* (interdenominational).

UNITED SYNAGOGUE REVIEW—155 Fifth Ave., New York, NY 10010. Rochel Berman, Ed. Articles, 1,000 to 1,200 words, on issues of interest to conservative Jewish community. Query.

UNITY MAGAZINE—Unity School of Christianity, Unity Village, MO 64065. Philip White, Ed. Inspirational and metaphysical articles, 500 to 1,500 words. Pays 5¢ to 9¢ a word, on acceptance.

VIRTUE—P. O. Box 850, Sisters, OR 97759. Articles and fiction for Christian women. Query only, except for "One Woman's Journal," "In My Opinion," and fiction.

VISTA MAGAZINE—P. O. Box 50434, Indianapolis, IN 46250–0434. Articles and adult fiction, on current Christian concerns and issues. First-person pieces, 750 to 1,500 words. Opinion pieces from an Evangelical perspective, 500 to 750 words. Pays from 2¢ to 4¢ a word.

YOUNG SALVATIONIST—The Salvation Army, 799 Bloomfield Ave., Verona, NJ 07044. Robert R. Hostetler, Ed. Articles, 600 to 1,200 words, teach the Christian view to everyday living, for teenagers. Short shorts, first-person testimonies, 600 to 800 words. Pays 4¢ to 5¢ a word, on acceptance. SASE required. Guidelines.

THE YOUNG SOLDIER—The Salvation Army, 799 Bloomfield Ave., Verona, NJ 07044. Robert R. Hostetler, Ed. For children 6 to 12. Must carry a definite Christian message or teach a Biblical truth. Fiction, 800 to 1,000 words. Some poetry. Fillers, puzzles, etc. Pays 4¢ a word, $3 to $5 for fillers, puzzles, on acceptance.

HEALTH

ACCENT ON LIVING—P. O. Box 700, Bloomington, IL 61702. Raymond C. Cheever, Pub./Ed. Articles, 250 to 1,000 words, about physically disabled people: their careers, recreation, sports, self-help devices, and ideas that can make daily routines easier. Good photos a plus. Pays 10¢ a word, on publication. Query.

AIM PLUS—Arthritis Information Magazine, 45 W. 34th St., New York, NY 10001. Tim Moriarty, Ed. Gayle Turim, Assoc. Ed. Well-researched articles, 800 to 1,200 words, about arthritis: how to cope with it emotionally; new treatments; exceptional people, etc. Also, articles on general health and general interest pieces. Pays $320 to $480, on acceptance. Query required. Guidelines.

AMERICAN BABY—475 Park Ave. S., New York, NY 10016. Judith Nolte, Ed. Articles, 1,000 to 2,000 words, for new or expectant parents on prenatal infant care. Pays varying rates, on acceptance.

AMERICAN FITNESS—15250 Ventura Blvd., Suite 310, Sherman Oaks, CA 91403. Peg Angsten, Ed. Brenda Sutton, Man. Ed. Articles, 500 to 1,500 words, on exercise, health, sports, nutrition, etc. Illustrations, photos, cartoons.

AMERICAN HEALTH: FITNESS OF BODY AND MIND—80 Fifth Ave., New York, NY 10011. Address Editorial Dept. Features, 1,000 to 3,000 words, on recent developments in nutrition, exercise, medicine, prevention and psychology. Shorter news items on similar topics: medical advances, consumer health, and life styles. Pays from $125 per manuscript page, on acceptance. Query required.

AMERICAN JOURNAL OF NURSING—555 W. 57th St., New York, NY 10019. Mary B. Mallison, R.N., Ed. Articles, 1,500 to 2,000 words, with photos, on nursing. Query.

ARTHRITIS TODAY—The Arthritis Foundation, 1314 Spring St. N.W., Atlanta, GA 30309. Cindy McDaniel, Ed. Self-help, how-to, general interest, and inspirational articles (1,000 to 2,500 words); "slice-of-life" fiction (750 to 2,500 words) and short fillers (100 to 250 words) to help people with arthritis live more productive, independent and pain-free lives. Pays from $350, on acceptance.

BESTWAYS—1501 S. Sutro Terrace, P.O. Box 2028, Carson City, NV 89701. Barbara Bassett, Ed. Articles, 1,000 to 1,500 words, on healthful cooking, natural food, general health, life styles, exercise, nutrition. Pays from $150, on publication. Query.

CHILDBIRTH EDUCATOR—475 Park Ave. S., New York, NY 10016. Marsha Rehns, Ed. Articles, 2,000 words, on maternal and fetal health, childcare, child development, and teaching techniques for teachers of childbirth and baby care classes. Pays $500, on acceptance. Query with detailed outline.

EAST WEST: THE JOURNAL OF NATURAL HEALTH & LIVING—17 Station St., Box 1200, Brookline, MA 02147. Features, 1,500 to 2,500 words, on holistic health, natural foods, gardening, etc. Material for "Body," "Healing," "In the Kitchen," and "Beauty and Fitness." Interviews. Photos. Pays 10¢ to 15¢ a word, extra for photos, on publication.

EXPECTING—685 Third Ave., New York, NY 10017. Evelyn A. Podsiadlo, Ed. Articles, 700 to 1,800 words, for expectant mothers. Pays $300 to $500, on acceptance.

HEALTH—3 Park Ave., New York, NY 10016. Articles, 800 to 2,500 words, on medicine, nutrition, fitness, emotional and psychological well-being. Pays up to $2,000, on acceptance. Query.

HEALTH PROGRESS—4455 Woodson Rd., St. Louis, MO 63134. Judy Cassidy, Ed. Journal of the Catholic Health Association. Features, 1,500 to 2,000 words, on hospital management and administration, medical-moral questions, public policy, technological developments and their impacts, nursing, and financial and human resource management. Pays by arrangement. Query.

HIPPOCRATES—475 Gate Five Rd., Suite 100, Sausalito, CA 94965. John Kiefer, Editorial Coordinator. Articles, 850 to 5,000 words, on health and medicine; pieces for "Food," "Sports," "Drugs," "Mind," "Family," and "Housecalls" departments. Pays 50¢ to 80¢ a word, on acceptance. Query required.

HOSPITALS—211 E. Chicago Ave., Chicago, IL 60611. Frank Sabatino, Ed. Articles, 800 to 1,500 words, for hospital administrators, on financing, staffing, coordinating, and providing facilities for health care services. Pays varying rates, on acceptance. Query.

IDEA TODAY—6190 Cornerstone Ct. East, Suite 204, San Diego, CA 92121–3773. Patricia Ryan, Ed. Practical articles, 1,000 to 3,000 words, on new exercise programs, business management, nutrition, sports medicine, and dance-exercise techniques. Payment negotiable, on acceptance. Query preferred.

LET'S LIVE—P.O. Box 74908, Los Angeles, CA 90004. Debra A. Jenkins, Ed. Articles, 1,000 to 1,500 words, on preventive medicine and nutrition, alternative medicine, diet, exercise, recipes, and natural beauty. Pays $150, on publication. Query.

MUSCULAR DEVELOPMENT—Strength and Health Publishing, P.O. Box 1707, York, PA 17405. Jan Dellinger, Ed. Articles, 5 to 10 typed pages, geared to serious weight training athletes, on any aspects of competitive body building and powerlifting. Photos. Pays $50 to $200, on publication. Query.

NEW BODY—888 Seventh Ave., New York, NY 10106. Constance Cardozo, Ed. Well-researched, service-oriented articles, 800 to 1,500 words, on exercise, nutrition, diet and health for women aged 18 to 35. Writers should have some background in or knowledge of the health field. Pays $100 to $300, on publication. Query.

NURSING 88—1111 Bethlehem Pike, Springhouse, PA 19477. Maryanne Wagner, Ed. Most articles are clinically oriented, and assigned to nursing experts. Covers legal, ethical, and management aspects of nursing. No poetry. Pays $25 to $250, on publication. Query.

NURSING HOMES—23860 Miles Rd., Cleveland, OH 44128. Neil Scott, Ed. Articles, 1,000 to 2,500 words, of interest to administrators, managers, and supervisory personnel in nursing homes; human-interest, academic and clinical pieces; book reviews, 250 to 300 words. Pays $50 for articles, $30 for reviews, on acceptance. Photos, graphics welcome.

NURSINGWORLD JOURNAL—470 Boston Post Rd., Weston, MA 02193. Eileen Devito, Man. Ed. Articles, 500 to 1,500 words, for and by nurses and nurse-educators, on aspects of current nursing issues. Pays from 25¢ per column inch, on publication.

PATIENT CARE—690 Kinderkamack Rd., Oradell, NJ 07649. Robert L. Edsall, Ed. Articles on medical care, for physicians; mostly staff written. Pays varying rates, on publication. Query; all articles assigned.

THE PHYSICIAN AND SPORTSMEDICINE—4530 W. 77th St., Minneapolis, MN 55435. Cindy Christian Rogers, Features Ed. News and feature articles, 500 to 3,000 words, on fitness, sport, and exercise. Medical angle necessary. Pays $150 to $900, on acceptance. Guidelines.

A POSITIVE APPROACH—1600 Malone, Municipal Airport, Millville, NJ 08332. Ann Miller, Ed. Articles, 500 words, on all aspects of the positive-thinking disabled/handicapped person's private and business life. Well-researched articles of interest to the visually and hearing impaired, veterans, the arthritic, and all categories of the disabled and handicapped, on interior design, barrier-free architecture, gardening, wardrobe, computers, and careers. Pays 10¢ a word, on publication.

RECOVERY LIFE (FORMERLY *RECOVERY*)—P.O. Box 31329, Seattle, WA 98103. Neil Scott, Ed. Articles, to 1,500 words, for recovering alcoholics, on how to meet the challenge of sobriety. First-person recovery stories, with helpful how-to's for others, 500 to 1,000 words. SASE for guidelines.

RN—Oradell, NJ 07649. Articles, to 2,000 words, preferably by R.N.s, on nursing, clinical care, etc. Pays 10¢ to 15¢ a word, on acceptance. Query.

RX HOME CARE—30 Vreeland Rd., Florham Park, NJ 07932. Cliff Henke, Sr. Ed. Articles, 1,500 to 2,000 words, on marketing aspects of home health care and rehabilitation equipment. Pays 12¢ a word, on acceptance. Query first.

VEGETARIAN TIMES—P.O. Box 570, Oak Park, IL 60603. Paul Obis, Pub. Articles, 750 to 2,500 words, on health, nutrition, exercise and fitness, meatless meals, etc. Personal-experience and historical pieces, profiles. Pays $25 to $300, on publication.

VIBRANT LIFE—55 W. Oak Ridge Dr., Hagerstown, MD 21740. Features, 1,000 to 2,800 words, on total health: physical, mental, and spiritual. No disease-related articles or manuscripts geared to people over 50. Seeks upbeat articles on how to live happier and healthier lives; Christian slant. Pays $150 to $400, on acceptance.

VIM & VIGOR—8805 N. 23rd Ave., Suite 11, Phoenix, AZ 85021. Leo Calderella, Ed. Positive articles, with accurate medical facts, on health and fitness, 1,200 words. Pays $250 to $350, on publication.

THE WALKING MAGAZINE—711 Boylston St., Boston, MA 02116. Bradford Ketchum, Ed. Articles, 1,500 to 2,500 words, on fitness, health, equipment, nutrition, travel and adventure, famous walkers, and other walking-related topics. Shorter pieces, 150 to 800 words, and essays for "Ramblings" page. Photos welcome. Pays $750 to $1,200 for features, $100 to $500 for department pieces. Guidelines.

YOGA JOURNAL—2054 University Ave., Berkeley, CA 94704. Stephan Bodian, Ed. Articles, 1,200 to 4,000 words, on holistic health, consciousness, spirituality, and yoga. Pays $50 to $250, on publication.

YOUR HEALTH—1720 Washington Blvd., Box 10010, Ogden, UT 84409. Libby Hyland, Ed. Articles, 1,200 words, on individual health care needs: prevention, treatment, fitness, nutrition, etc. Photos required. Pays 15¢ a word, after acceptance. Guidelines.

EDUCATION

AMERICAN SCHOOL & UNIVERSITY—401 N. Broad St., Philadelphia, PA 19108. Dorothy Wright, Ed. Articles and case studies, 1,200 to 1,500 words, on design, construction, operation, and management of school and college facilities. Payment varies.

THE BIG APPLE PARENTS' PAPER—One World Trade Center, Suite 8817, New York, NY 10048. Helen Rosengren Freedman, Ed. Articles (600 to 750 words) for NYC parents. Pays $50, on acceptance.

CAPSTONE JOURNAL OF EDUCATION—P.O. Box Q, Tuscaloosa, AL 35487. Alexia M. Kartis, Asst. Ed. Articles, to 5,000 words, on contemporary ideas in educational research.

CHANGE—4000 Albemarle St. N.W., Suite 500, Washington, DC 20016. Reports, 1,500 to 2,000 words, on programs, people, and institutions of higher education. Intellectual essays, 3,000 to 5,000 words, on higher education today. Payment varies.

CLASSROOM COMPUTER LEARNING—Peter Li, Inc., 2169 Francisco Blvd. E., Suite A-4, San Rafael, CA 94901. Holly Brady, Ed. Articles, to 3,000 words, for teachers of grades K-12, related to uses of computers in the classroom: human-interest and philosophical articles, how-to pieces, software reviews, and hands-on ideas. Pay varies, on acceptance.

ELECTRONIC EDUCATION—Electronic Communications, 1311 Executive Center Dr., Suite 220, Tallahassee, FL 32301. Sally Warner, Man. Ed. Articles, to 1,000 words, for K-12 administrators, on the uses of technology in education. Query.

FOUNDATION NEWS—1828 L St. N.W., Washington, DC 20036. Arlie W. Schardt, Ed. Articles, to 2,000 words, on national or regional activities supported by, or of interest to, grant makers. Pays to $1,500, on acceptance. Query.

GIFTED EDUCATION PRESS—P.O. Box 1586, 10201 Yuma Ct., Manassas, VA 22110. Maurice Fisher, Pub. Articles, to 1,200 words, written by educators, laypersons, and parents of gifted children, on the problems of identifying and teaching gifted children and adolescents. "Interested in incisive analyses of current programs for the gifted, and recommendations for improving the education of gifted students." Pays with subscription.

HOME EDUCATION MAGAZINE—P.O. Box 1083, Tonasket, WA 98855. Mark J. Hegener, Ed. Positive, informative articles, 2,500 words, on alternative education, including home schooling, alternative and community schools, cooperative learning, and other educational options. Pays on publication.

THE HORN BOOK MAGAZINE—Park Sq. Bldg., 31 St. James Ave., Boston, MA 02116. Anita Silvey, Ed. Articles, 600 to 2,800 words, on books for young readers, and related subjects, for librarians, teachers, parents, etc. Pays $25 per printed page, on publication. Query.

INDUSTRIAL EDUCATION—26011 Evergreen Rd., Suite 204, Southfield, MI 48076. Kelley Callaghan, Ed. Educational and instructional articles, 1,000 to 1,500 words, for secondary and post-secondary technical education classes. Photos and drawings. Pays $30, on publication.

INSTRUCTOR—7500 Old Oak Blvd., Cleveland, OH 44130. Elizabeth A. Compelio, Ed. How-to articles on elementary classroom teaching and computers in the classroom, with practical suggestions and project reports. Pays varying rates, on acceptance.

ITC COMMUNICATOR—International Training in Communication, 4249 Elzevir Rd., Woodland Hills, CA 91364. JoAnn Levy, Ed. Educational articles, 200 to 800 words, on leadership, language, speech presentation, meetings procedures, personal and professional development, written and spoken communication techniques. SASE required. Pays in copies.

JOURNAL OF CAREER PLANNING & EMPLOYMENT—62 Highland Ave., Bethlehem, PA 18017. Patricia A. Sinnott, Ed. Articles, 3,000 to 4,000 words, on topics related to college career planning, placement, and recruitment. Pays $200 to $400, on acceptance. Query first with clips. Guidelines available.

KEY TO CHRISTIAN EDUCATION—8121 Hamilton Ave., Cincinnati, OH 45231. Kim Jackson, Ed. Fillers, articles, to 1,500 words, on Christian education; tips for teachers in the local church. Pays varying rates, on acceptance.

LEARNING 88/89—1111 Bethlehem Pike, Springhouse, PA 19477. Charlene Gaynor, Ed. How-to, why-to, and personal-experience articles, to 3,000 words, for teachers of grades K-8. Tested classroom ideas for curriculum roundups, to 600 words. Pays to $300 for features, on acceptance.

614

MEDIA & METHODS—1429 Walnut St., Philadelphia, PA 19102. Robin Larsen, Ed. Articles, 800 to 1,500 words, on media, technologies, and methods used to enhance instruction and learning in high school and university classrooms. Pays $50 to $100, on publication. Query.

THE MINORITY ENGINEER—44 Broadway, Greenlawn, NY 11740. James Schneider, Ed. Articles, 1,000 to 3,000 words, for college students, on career opportunities in engineering, scientific and technological fields; techniques of job hunting; developments in and applications of new technologies. Interviews. Profiles. Pays 10¢ a word, on publication. Query. Same address and requirements for *The Woman Engineer.*

NATIONAL BEAUTY SCHOOL JOURNAL—3899 White Plains Rd., Bronx, NY 10467. Mary Jane Tenerelli, Ed. Articles, 1,500 to 2,000 words, on running a cosmetology school; teaching techniques, problems, new procedures, etc. "All articles must be relevant to schools, not to salons." Pays $150, on publication.

PHI DELTA KAPPAN—8th and Union St., Box 789, Bloomington, IN 47402. Pauline Gough, Ed. Articles, 1,000 to 4,000 words, on educational research, service, and leadership; issues, trends, and policy. Pays from $250, on publication.

SCHOOL ARTS MAGAZINE—50 Portland St., Worcester, MA 01608. David W. Baker, Ed. Articles, 800 to 1,000 words, on art education with special application to the classroom. Photos. Pays varying rates, on publication.

SCHOOL SHOP—Box 8623, Ann Arbor, MI 48107. Alan H. Jones, Pub./ Exec. Ed. Articles, to 10 double-spaced typed pages, for teachers and administrators in industrial, technical, and vocational educational fields, with particular interest in classroom projects and computer uses. Pays $25 to $150, on publication. Guidelines.

TEACHER UPDATE—P.O. Box 429, Belmont, MA 02178. Nick Roes, Ed. Original suggestions for classroom activities. Each page should have a unifying theme, preferably related to specific monthly issue. Pays $20 per published page, on acceptance. Readers are mostly preschool teachers.

TEACHING AND COMPUTERS—Scholastic, Inc., 730 Broadway, New York, NY 10003. Ms. Mickey Revenaugh, Ed. Articles, 300 to 500 words, for computer-using teachers in grades K-8. Payment varies, on acceptance.

TODAY'S CATHOLIC TEACHER—26 Reynolds Ave., Ormond Beach, FL 32074. Ruth A. Matheny, Ed. Articles, 600 to 800 words and 1,200 to 1,500 words, on Catholic education, parent-teacher relationships, innovative teaching, teaching techniques, etc. Pays $15 to $75, on publication. SASE required.

WILSON LIBRARY BULLETIN—950 University Ave., Bronx, NY 10452. Milo Nelson, Ed. Articles, 2,500 to 3,000 words, on libraries, communications, and information systems. News, reports, features. Pays from $250, extra for photos, on acceptance.

THE WOMAN ENGINEER—See *The Minority Engineer.*

FARMING AND AGRICULTURE

ACRES USA—10008 E. 60 Terrace, Kansas City, MO 64133. Articles on biological agriculture. Pays 6¢ a word, on publication. Query required.

AMERICAN BEE JOURNAL—51 N. Second St., Hamilton, IL 62341. Joe M. Graham, Ed. Articles on beekeeping, for professionals. Photos. Pays 75¢ a column inch, extra for photos, on publication.

BEEF—1999 Shepard Rd., St. Paul, MN 55116. Paul D. Andre, Ed. Articles on beef cattle feeding, cowherds, stocker operations, and related phases of the cattle industry. Pays to $300, on acceptance.

BUCKEYE FARM NEWS—Ohio Farm Bureau Federation, 35 E. Chestnut St., Columbus, OH 43216. George D. Robey, Man. Ed. Articles and humor, to 1,000 words, related to agriculture. Pays on publication. Query.

FARM & RANCH LIVING—5400 S. 60th St., Greendale, WI 53129. Bob Ottum, Ed. Articles, 2,000 words, on rural people and situations; nostalgia pieces; profiles of interesting farms and farmers, ranches and ranchers. Poetry. Pays $15 to $400, on acceptance and on publication.

FARM INDUSTRY NEWS—1999 Shepard Rd., St. Paul, MN 55116. Joe Degnan, Ed. Articles for farmers, on new products, buying, machinery, equipment, chemicals, and seeds. Pays $175 to $400, on acceptance. Query required.

FARM JOURNAL—230 W. Washington Sq., Philadelphia, PA 19105. Earl Ainsworth, Ed. Articles, 500 to 1,500 words, with photos, on the business of farming, for farmers. Pays 20¢ to 50¢ a word, on acceptance. Query.

FLORIDA GROWER & RANCHER—1331 N. Mills Ave., Orlando, FL 32803. Frank H. Abrahamson, Ed. Articles and case histories on farmers, growers and ranchers. Pays on publication. Query; buys little freelance material.

THE FURROW—Deere & Company, John Deere Rd., Moline, IL 61265. George Sollenberger, Exec. Ed. Specialized, illustrated articles on farming. Pays to $1,000, on acceptance.

HARROWSMITH—Camden House Publishing Ltd., Camden East, Ont., Canada K0K 1J0. Wayne Grady, Ed. Articles, 700 to 4,000 words, on country life, homesteading, husbandry, organic gardening and alternative energy with a Canadian slant. Pays $150 to $1,500, on acceptance. Query with SASE/international reply coupon.

HARROWSMITH/USA—The Creamery, Ferry Rd., Charlotte, VT 05445. Tom Rawls, Ed. Investigative pieces, 4,000 to 5,000 words, on ecology, energy, health, gardening, do-it-yourself projects, and the food chain. Short pieces for "Screed" (opinions) and "Gazette" (news briefs). Pays $500 to $1,500 for features, $50 to $600 for department pieces, on acceptance. Query required. Send SASE for guidelines.

NORDEN NEWS—601 W. Cornhusker Hwy., Lincoln, NE 68501. Gary Svatos, Ed. Technical articles, 1,200 to 1,500 words, and clinical features, 500 words, on veterinary medicine. Photos. Pays $200 to $250, $100 for shorter pieces, extra for photos, on publication.

THE OHIO FARMER—1350 W. Fifth Ave., Columbus, OH 43212. Andrew L. Stevens, Ed. Articles on farming, rural living, etc., in Ohio. Pays $20 per column, on publication.

PEANUT FARMER—P.O. Box 95075, Raleigh, NC 27625. Dayton Matlick, Ed./Pub. Articles, 500 to 1,500 words, on production and management practices in peanut farming. Pays $50 to $350, on publication.

PENNSYLVANIA FARMER—704 Lisburn Rd., Camp Hill, PA 17011. John R. Vogel, Ed. Articles on farmers in PA, NJ, DE, MD, and WV; timely business-of-farming concepts and successful farm management operations.

RURAL HERITAGE—P.O. Box 516, Albia, IA 52531. Allan Young, Ed./Pub. How-to and feature articles, 300 to 2,500 words, related to draft horses and rural living. Pays 3¢ to 10¢ a word, $5 to $25 for photos, on acceptance. Queries preferred.

SHEEP! MAGAZINE—Route 1, Helenville, WI 53137. Dave Thompson, Ed. Articles, to 1,500 words, on successful shepherds, woodcrafts, sheep raising and sheep dogs. Photos. Pays $80 to $250, extra for photos, on publication.

SMALL ACREAGE MANAGEMENT—Rt. 1, Box 146, Silex, MO 63377. Kelly Klober, Ed. Articles, 500 to 800 words, on land uses for small farm owners. Pays 1¢ to 3¢ a word, on publication. Query.

SMALL FARMER'S JOURNAL—P.O. Box 2805, Eugene, OR 97402. Address the Editors. How-tos, humor, practical work horse information, livestock and produce marketing, and articles appropriate to the independent family farm. Pays negotiable rates, on publication. Query first.

SUCCESSFUL FARMING—1716 Locust St., Des Moines, IA 50336. Loren Kruse, Man. Ed. Articles on farm production, business, and families; also farm personalities, health, leisure, and outdoor topics. Pays varying rates, on acceptance.

WALLACES FARMER—1501 42nd St., #501, W. Des Moines, IA 50265. Monte Sesker, Ed. Features, 600 to 700 words, on farming in IA, MN, NE, KS, ND, and SD; methods and equipment; interviews with farmers. Pays 4¢ to 5¢ a word, on acceptance. Query.

THE WESTERN PRODUCER—Box 2500, Saskatoon, Saskatchewan, Canada S7K 2C4. Address Man. Ed. Articles, to 1,000 words, on agricultural and rural subjects, preferably with a Canadian slant. Photos. Pays from 10¢ a word, $15 for b&w photos and cartoons, on acceptance.

ENVIRONMENT, CONSERVATION, WILDLIFE, NATURAL HISTORY

THE AMERICAN FIELD—222 W. Adams St., Chicago, IL 60606. William F. Brown, Ed. Yarns about hunting trips, bird-shooting; articles to 1,500 words, on dogs and field trials, emphasizing conservation of game resources. Pays varying rates, on acceptance.

AMERICAN FORESTS—1516 P St. N.W., Washington, DC 20005. Bill Rooney, Ed. Well-documented articles, to 2,000 words, with photos, on recreational and commercial uses and management of forests. Photos. Pays on acceptance.

THE AMICUS JOURNAL—Natural Resources Defense Council, 122 E. 42nd St., Rm. 4500, New York, NY 10168. Peter Borrelli, Ed. Investigative articles, book reviews, and poetry related to national and international environmental policy. Pays varying rates, on acceptance. Queries required.

ANIMAL KINGDOM—New York Zoological Society, Bronx, NY 10460. Nancy Christie, Assoc. Ed. First-person articles, 1,500 to 2,000 words, on "popular" natural history, "based on author's research and experience as opposed to textbook approach." Payment varies, on acceptance. Guidelines.

ANIMALS—Massachusetts Society for the Prevention of Cruelty to Animals, 350 S. Huntington Ave., Boston, MA 02130. Suzanne Satagaj, Ed. Asst. Informative, well-researched articles, to 3,000 words, on animal welfare and pet care, conservation and international wildlife; no personal accounts or favorite pet stories. Pays to $300, on publication. Query.

THE ATLANTIC SALMON JOURNAL—1435 St. Alexandre, Suite 1030, Montreal, Quebec, Canada H3A 2G4. Terry Davis, Ed. Articles, 1,500 to 3,000 words. Material related to Atlantic salmon: conservation, ecology, travel, politics, biology, how-tos, anecdotes, cuisine. Pays $100 to $350, on publication.

BIRD WATCHER'S DIGEST—P.O. Box 110, Marietta, OH 45750. Mary B. Bowers, Ed. Articles, 600 to 2,500 words, for bird watchers: first-person accounts; how-tos; pieces on endangered species; profiles. Cartoons. Pays to $5 to $50, on publication.

ENVIRONMENTAL ACTION—1525 New Hampshire Ave. N.W., Washington, DC 20036. News and features, varying lengths, on a broad range of political and/or environmental topics: energy, toxics, self-sufficiency, etc. Book reviews; environmentally-related consumer goods. Pays $75 to $125 for features, $25 for news items and book reviews, extra for photos, on publication. Query required.

EQUINOX—7 Queen Victoria Rd., Camden East., Ont., Canada K0K 1J0. Jody Morgan, Asst. Ed. Articles, 3,000 to 6,000 words, on popular geography, wildlife, astronomy, science, the arts, travel, and adventure. Department pieces, 300 to 500 words, for "Nexus" (science and medicine), and "Habitat" (man-made and natural environment). Pays $1,250 to $2,000, for features, $100 to $300 for short piecess, on acceptance.

HARROWSMITH/USA—The Creamery, Ferry Rd., Charlotte, VT 05445. Tom Rawls, Ed. Investigative articles, 4,000 to 5,000 words, on ecology, energy, health, gardening, and the food chain. Short pieces for "Screed" (opinions) and "Gazette" (news briefs). Do-it-yourself projects. Pays $500 to $1,500 for features, from $50 to $600 for department pieces, on acceptance. Query required; SASE. Guidelines.

THE LOOKOUT—Seamen's Church Institute, 50 Broadway, New York, NY 10004. Carlyle Windley, Ed. Factual articles on the sea. Features, 200 to 1,500 words, on the merchant marines, sea oddities, etc. Photos. Pays $25 to $100, on publication.

NATIONAL GEOGRAPHIC MAGAZINE—17th and M Sts. N.W., Washington, DC 20036. Wilbur E. Garrett, Ed. First-person, general-interest, heavily-illustrated articles on science, natural history, exploration, and geographical regions. Query required.

NATIONAL PARKS MAGAZINE—1015 31st St. N.W., Washington, DC 20007. Michele Strutin, Ed. Articles, 1,000 to 2,000 words, on natural history, wildlife, outdoors activities, travel and conservation as they relate to national parks: illustrated features on the natural, historic and cultural resources of the National Park System. Pieces about legislation and other issues and events related to the parks. Pays $100 to $400, on acceptance. Query. Send for guidelines.

NATIONAL WILDLIFE & INTERNATIONAL WILDLIFE—8925 Leesburg Pike, Vienna, VA 22184. Mark Wexler, Man. Ed., Nat. Wildlife. Jon Fisher, Man. Ed., Inter. Wildlife. Articles, 1,000 to 2,500 words, on wildlife, conservation, environment; outdoor how-to pieces. Photos. Pays on acceptance. Query.

NATURAL HISTORY—American Museum of Natural History, Central Park West at 79th St., New York, NY 10024. Alan Ternes, Ed.-in-Chief. Informative articles, to 3,000 words, by experts, on anthropology and natural sciences. Pays $1,000 for features, on acceptance. Query.

OCEANS—2001 W. Main St., Stamford, CT 06902. Michael Robbins, Ed. Articles, to 5,000 words, with photos, on marine life, oceanography, marine art, undersea exploration, seaports, conservation, fishing, diving, boating. Pays on acceptance. Query. Guidelines.

OUTDOOR AMERICA—1401 Wilson Blvd., Level B, Arlington, VA 22209. Quarterly publication of the Izaak Walton League of America. Articles, 1,500 to 2,000 words, on natural resource conservation issues and outdoor recreation; especially fishing, hunting, and camping. Pays from 20¢ a word for features, on publication. Query Articles Ed. with published clips.

SEA FRONTIERS—3979 Rickenbacker Causeway, Virginia Key, Miami 33149. Jean Bradfish, Exec. Ed. Illustrated articles, 500 to 3,000 words, on scientific advances related to the sea, biological, physical, chemical, or geological phenomena, ecology, conservation, etc., written in a popular style for lay readers. Send SASE for guidelines. Pays $50 to $450, on acceptance. Query.

SIERRA—730 Polk St., San Francisco, CA 94109. Jonathan F. King, Ed. Articles, 250 to 2,500 words, on environmental and conservation topics, politics, hiking, backpacking, skiing, rafting, cycling. Book reviews and children's departments. Photos. Pays from $75 to $1,000, extra for photos, on acceptance. Query.

SMITHSONIAN MAGAZINE—900 Jefferson Dr., Washington, DC 20560. Marlane A. Liddell, Articles Ed. Articles on history, art, natural history, physical science, profiles, etc. Query.

SPORTS AFIELD—250 W. 55th St., New York, NY 10019. Tom Paugh, Ed. Articles, 2,000 words, with quality photos, on hunting, fishing, natural history, conservation, personal experiences, new hunting/fishing spots. How-to pieces; humor, fiction. Pays top rates, on acceptance.

MEDIA AND THE ARTS

AHA! HISPANIC ARTS NEWS—Assoc. of Hispanic Arts, 173 E. 116th St., New York, NY 10029. Dolores Prida, Ed. Interviews and book reviews with Hispanic authors, to 500 words. Pays on publication. Query required.

AIRBRUSH ACTION—317 Cross St., Lakewood, NJ 08701. Address the Editors. Articles, 500 to 3,000 words, on airbrush and art-related topics. Pays $75 to $300, on publication. Query.

THE AMERICAN ART JOURNAL—40 W. 57th St., 5th fl., New York, NY 10019. Jane Van N. Turano, Ed. Quarterly. Scholarly articles, 2,000 to 10,000 words, on American art of the 17th through 20th centuries. Photos. Pays $200 to $400, on acceptance.

AMERICAN INDIAN ART MAGAZINE—7314 E. Osborn Dr., Scottsdale, AZ 85251. Roanne P. Goldfein, Man. Ed. Detailed articles, 10 typed pages, on American Indian arts: painting, carving, beadwork, basketry, textiles, ceramics, jewelry, etc. Pays varying rates, on publication. Query.

AMERICAN THEATRE—355 Lexington Ave., New York, NY 10017. Jim O'Quinn, Ed. Features, 500 to 4,000 words, on the theater and theater-related subjects. Payment negotiable, on publication. Query.

ART & ANTIQUES—89 Fifth Ave., New York, NY 10003. Jeffrey Schaire, Ed. Investigative pieces or personal narratives, 1,500 words, and news items, 300 to 500 words, on art or antiques. Pays 50¢ a word, on publication. Query first.

ART GALLERY INTERNATIONAL—P.O. Box 52940, Tulsa, OK 74152. Debra Carter Nelson, Ed. Articles, 1,500 to 2,500 words, on contemporary artists and their recent works; no restrictions on style, medium, or subject matter; a "gallery in print" for readers to view and collect art work. Query with clips, visual samples, and SASE. Pays 10¢ a word or $50 per printed page, after publication.

ARTS ATLANTIC—P.O. Box 848, Charlottetown, P.E.I., Canada C1A 7L9. Joseph Sherman, Ed. Articles and reviews, 800 to 2,500 words, on visual, performing and literary arts, crafts in Atlantic Canada. Also, "idea and concept" articles of universal appeal. Pays from 14¢ a word, on publication. Query.

BLUEGRASS UNLIMITED—Box 111, Broad Run, VA 22014. Peter V. Kuykendall, Ed. Articles, to 3,500 words, on bluegrass and traditional country music. Photos. Pays 6¢ to 8¢ a word, extra for photos.

BROADCASTER—7 Labatt Ave., Toronto, Ont., Canada M5A 3P2. Lynda Ashley, Ed. Articles, 500 to 2,000 words, on broadcasting, satellites, and the cable industry. Rates negotiable. Payment on publication.

CLAVIER MAGAZINE—200 Northfield Rd., Northfield, IL 60093. Olivia Wu, Man. Ed. Practical articles, interviews, master classes, and humor pieces, 2,000 words, for keyboard performers and teachers. Pays $35 to $45 per column inch, on publication.

DANCE MAGAZINE—33 W. 60th St., New York, NY 10023. William Como, Ed.-in-Chief. Features on dance, personalities, techniques, health issues, and trends. Photos. Query; limited free-lance market.

DANCE TEACHER NOW—3020 Beacon Blvd., West Sacramento, CA 95691. Laurie Davis, Asst. Ed. Articles, 1,500 to 2,500 words, for professional dance teachers and dancers, on practical aspects of a dance teacher's professional life, and political or economic issues related to the dance profession. Profiles on teachers or schools. Must be thoroughly researched. Pays $100 to $300, on publication.

DARKROOM PHOTOGRAPHY—9021 Melrose Ave., Suite 203, Los Angeles, CA 90069. Thom Harrop, Ed. Articles on post-camera photographic techniques, 1,000 to 2,500 words, with photos, for all levels of photographers. Pays $100 to $500. Query.

DESIGN GRAPHICS WORLD—Communications Channels, 6255 Barfield Rd., Atlanta, GA 30328. Eric Torrey, Ed. Articles, 1,500 to 2,000 words, on news, trends, and current methods of engineering and architecture, computer graphics, reprographics, and related design fields. Pays on publication. Query required.

THE DRAMA REVIEW—See *TDR: A Journal of Performance Studies.*

DRAMATICS—International Thespian Society, 3368 Central Pkwy., Cincinnati, OH 45225–2392. Don Corathers, Ed. Articles, interviews, how-tos, 750 to 4,000 words, for high school students on the performing arts: theater, puppetry, dance, mime, one-act plays, film, etc. Prefer articles that "could be used by a better than average high school teacher to teach students something about the performing arts. Pays $15 to $200. Manuscripts preferred; graphics and photos accepted.

DV-8 MAGAZINE—228 W. Broadway/Storefront, New York, NY 10013. Laurie Litchford, Ed. Unformulaic fiction (to 4,000 words) and articles (1,600 words) on new artists in music, art, and fashion; short profiles; all forms of experimental journalism. Poetry suitable for young, urban-oriented readers. Payment varies. Query preferred.

THE ENGRAVERS JOURNAL—26 Summit St., Box 318, Brighton, MI 48116. Michael J. Davis, Man. Ed. Articles, varying lengths, on topics related to the engraving industry and small business operations. Pays $60 to $175, on acceptance. Query first.

EXHIBIT—1776 Lake Worth Dr., Lake Worth, FL 33460. Address Editor.

Articles, to 1,000 words, with color transparencies, on fine arts, techniques, new movements, profiles of artists. Query.

FILM QUARTERLY—University of California Press, 2120 Berkeley Way, Berkeley, CA 94720. Ernest Callenbach, Ed. Film reviews, historical and critical articles, book reviews, to 5,000 words. Pays on publication. Query.

FLUTE TALK—Instrumentalist Publishing Co., 200 Northfield Rd., Northfield, IL 60093. Kathleen Goll-Wilson, Ed. Articles, 6 to 12 typed pages, on flute performance and pedagogy; flute-related poetry; fillers; photos and line drawings. Thorough knowledge of the instrument a must. Pays $45 per page, on publication. Queries preferred.

FRETS—20085 Stevens Creek, Cupertino, CA 95014. Phil Hood, Ed. Articles, 750 to 3,000 words, for musicians, on acoustic string instruments, instrument making and repair, music theory and technique. Covers jazz, folk, bluegrass, classical, etc. Profiles of musicians and instruments. Pays $150 to $350, on acceptance. Query.

FUNCTIONAL PHOTOGRAPHY—See *Pro Imaging Systems*.

GUITAR PLAYER MAGAZINE—20085 Stevens Creek, Cupertino, CA 95014. Tom Wheeler, Ed. Articles, 1,500 to 5,000 words, on guitarists, guitars, and related subjects. Pays $75 to $300, on acceptance. Buys one-time and reprint rights.

HIGH FIDELITY—825 Seventh Ave., New York, NY 10019. Michael Riggs, Ed. Articles, 2,000 to 3,000 words, on stereo equipment, video equipment, and classical and popular recorded music. Pays on acceptance. Query.

INDUSTRIAL PHOTOGRAPHY—50 W. 23rd St., New York, NY 10010–5292. Lynn Roher, Ed. Articles on techniques and trends in current professional photography; audio visuals, etc., for industrial photographers and executives. Query.

INTERNATIONAL MUSICIAN—Paramount Bldg., 1501 Broadway, Suite 600, New York, NY 10036. Articles, 1,500 to 2,000 words, for professional musicians. Pays varying rates, on acceptance. Query.

JAZZIZ—P. O. Box 8309, Gainesville, FL 32605. Michael Fagien, Ed. Feature articles on all aspects of jazz: interviews, profiles, concept pieces. Departments include "Reviews," "Video," and "Audio." Emphasis on new releases. Pays varying rates, on acceptance. Query.

KEYBOARD MAGAZINE—20085 Stevens Creek, Cupertino, CA 95014. Dominic Milano, Ed. Articles, 1,000 to 5,000 words, on keyboard instruments and players. Photos. Pays $125 to $500, on acceptance. Query.

MEDIA HISTORY DIGEST—c/o Editor & Publisher, 11 W. 19th St., New York, NY 10011. Hiley H. Ward, Ed. Articles, 1,500 to 2,000 words, on the history of the media, for wide consumer interest. Puzzles and humor related to media history. Pays varying rates, on publication. Query.

MODERN DRUMMER—870 Pompton Ave., Cedar Grove, NJ 07009. Ronald L. Spagnardi, Ed. Articles, 500 to 2,000 words, on drumming: how-tos, interviews. Pays $50 to $500, on publication.

MUSIC MAGAZINE—P. O. Box 96, Station R, Toronto, Ont., Canada M4G 3Z3. Articles, with photos, on musicians, conductors, and composers, for all classical music buffs. Pays $100 to $300, on publication. Query required. Guidelines.

MUSICAL AMERICA/OPUS—825 Seventh Ave., New York, NY 10019.

Shirley Fleming, Ed. Authoritative articles, 1,000 to 1,500 words, on classical music subjects. Pays around 15¢ a word, on acceptance.

NEW ENGLAND ENTERTAINMENT—43 Schoosett St., Rte. 139, Pembroke, MA 02359. Paul J. Reale, Ed. News features and reviews on arts and entertainment in New England. Light verse. Pays $10 to $25, $1 to $2 for verse, on publication.

OPERA NEWS—The Metropolitan Opera Guild, 1865 Broadway, New York, NY 10023. Patrick O'Connor, Ed. Articles, 600 to 2,500 words, on all aspects of opera. Pays 13¢ a word for articles, on publication. Query.

PERFORMANCE—1203 Lake St., Suite 200, Fort Worth, TX 76102–4504. Don Waitt, Pub./Ed.-in-Chief. Reports on the touring industry: concert promoters, booking agents, concert venues and clubs, as well as support services, such as lighting, sound and staging companies. Pays 35¢ per column line, on publication.

PETERSEN'S PHOTOGRAPHIC—8490 Sunset Blvd., Los Angeles, CA 90069. Bill Hurter, Ed. Articles and how-to pieces, with photos, on still, video, and darkroom photography, for beginners, advanced amateurs, and professionals. Pays $60 per printed page, on publication.

PHOTOMETHODS—1090 Executive Way, Des Plaines, IL 60018. Alfred DeBat, Ed. Articles, 1,500 to 3,000 words, on innovative techniques in imaging (still, film, video), working situations, and management. Pays from $75, on publication. Query.

PLAYBILL—71 Vanderbilt Ave., New York, NY 10169. Joan Alleman, Ed.-in-Chief. Sophisticated articles, 700 to 2,000 words, with photos, on theater and subjects of interest to theater-goers. Pays $100 to $500, on acceptance.

POPULAR PHOTOGRAPHY MAGAZINE—1515 Broadway, New York, NY 10036. Jason Schneider, Ed. Dir. How-to articles, 500 to 2,000 words, for amateur photographers. Query first with outline and photos.

PREVUE—P.O. Box 974, Reading, PA 19603. J. Steranko, Ed. Lively articles on films and film-makers; entertainment features and celebrity interviews. Length: 4 to 25 pages. Pays varying rates, on acceptance. Query with clips.

PRO IMAGING SYSTEMS (FORMERLY *TECHNICAL PHOTOGRA-PHY*)—210 Crossways Park Dr., Woodbury, NY 11797. David A. Silverman, Ed.-in-Chief. Incorporating *Functional Photography*. Features, 8 to 10 double-spaced pages, on applications and techniques of imaging for staff image producers. Some material on audio-visuals, film, and video. Pays varying rates, on publication. Query.

PROFESSIONAL STAINED GLASS—245 W. 29th St., 13th fl., New York, NY 10001–5208. Chris Peterson, Man. Ed. Practical articles of interest to stained glass professionals. No historical articles. Pays $100 to $150, on publication. Query required.

RIGHTING WORDS—P.O. Box 6811, F.D.R. Sta., New York, NY 10150. Jonathan S. Kaufman, Ed. Journal of Language and Editing. Articles (3,000 words) on topics of interest to professional editors. Pays from $100, on acceptance.

ROLLING STONE—745 Fifth Ave., New York, NY 10151. Articles on American culture, art, and politics. Query required. Rarely accepts free-lance material.

SHEET MUSIC MAGAZINE—223 Katonah Ave., Katonah, NY 10536. Josephine Sblendorio, Man. Ed. Pieces, 1,000 to 2,000 words, for pianists and organists, on musicians and composers, how-tos, and book reviews (to 500 words); no hard rock or heavy metal subjects. Pays $75 to $200, on publication.

SOAP OPERA DIGEST—254 W. 31st St., New York, NY 10001. Lynn Davey, Man. Ed. Features, to 1,500 words, for people interested in daytime and nighttime soaps. Pays from $225, on acceptance. Query with clips.

SPLASH—561 Broadway, 4B, New York, NY 10012. Lisa D. Black, Ed. Dir. Articles, 750 to 2,000 words, on arts and contemporary culture. Reviews, 500 to 750 words; interviews; editorials, 450 to 1,250 words. Sophisticated and black humor, 250 to 500 words. Pays $25 to $300, after publication.

SUN TRACKS—Box 2510, Phoenix, AZ 85002. Andy Van De Voorde, Music Ed. Music section of *New Times*. Long and short features, record reviews, and interviews. Pays $25 to $500, on publication. Query.

TDR: A JOURNAL OF PERFORMANCE STUDIES (FORMERLY *THE DRAMA REVIEW*)—721 Broadway, 6th fl., New York, NY 10003. Rebecca Schneider, Man. Ed. Eclectic articles on experimental performance and perform-ance theory; cross-cultural, examining the social, political, historical, and theatrical contexts in which performance happens. Submit query or manuscript with SASE. Pays 3¢ a word, on publication.

TECHNICAL PHOTOGRAPHY— *See Pro Imaging Systems.*

THEATRE CRAFTS MAGAZINE—135 Fifth Ave., New York, NY 10010. Patricia MacKay, Ed. Articles, 500 to 2,500 words, for professionals in the business, design, and production of theatre, film, video, and the performing arts. Pays on acceptance. Query.

TOTAL TELEVISION—Atlantic Cable Television Publishing, 3 Media Crossways, Woodbury, NY 11797. Maggie Melluso, Ed. Interviews and profiles, 800 words, of motion picture and TV celebrities. Payment varies, on acceptance. Query.

VIDEO CHOICE—Connell Communications, Inc., Rt. 202S, 331 Jaffrey Rd., Peterborough, NH 03458. Deborah Navas, Ed. Articles, 2,000 words, on special-interest, non-theatrical videos. Pays $400, on acceptance. Query required.

VIDEO MAGAZINE—460 W. 34th St., New York, NY 10001. Judith Hud-nutt Sawyer, Ed.-in-Chief. How-to and service articles on home video equipment, technology, and programming. Interviews and human-interest features related to non-broadcast television, from 800 to 2,500 words. Pays varying rates, on accept-ance. Query.

VIDEOMAKER—P.O. Box 4591, Chico, CA 95927. Bradley Kent, Ed. Au-thoritative, how-to articles geared at hobbyist and professional video camera/cam-corder users: instructionals, innovative applications, tools and tips, industry devel-opments, new products, etc. Pays varying rates, on publication. Queries preferred.

WASHINGTON JOURNALISM REVIEW—2233 Wisconsin Ave. N.W., Washington, DC 20007. Bill Monroe, Ed. Articles, 500 to 3,000 words, on print or electronic journalism. Pays 20¢ a word, on publication. Query.

HOBBIES, CRAFTS, COLLECTING

ANTIQUE MONTHLY—P.O. Drawer 2, Tuscaloosa, AL 35402. Elizabeth McKenzie, Sr. Ed. Articles, 750 to 1,200 words, on the exhibition and sales (auc-tions, antique shops, etc.) of decorative arts and antiques more than 100 years old, with photos or slides. Pays varying rates, on publication.

THE ANTIQUE TRADER WEEKLY—Box 1050, Dubuque, IA 52001. Kyle D. Husfloen, Ed. Articles, 1,000 to 2,000 words, on all types of antiques and collectors' items. Photos. Pays from $5 to $150, extra for photos, on publication. Query preferred. Buys all rights.

ANTIQUES & AUCTION NEWS—P.O. Box 500, Mount Joy, PA 17552. Weekly newspaper. Factual articles, 600 to 1,500 words, on antiques, collectors, and collections. Photos. Pays $5 to $20, after publication.

ANTIQUEWEEK—P.O. Box 90, Knightstown, IN 46148. Tom Hoepf, Ed. Articles, 500 to 1,500 words, on antiques, collectibles, restorations, genealogy. Auction and antique show reports. Photos. Pays from $1 per inch, $75 to $125 for in-depth articles, on publication. Query. Guidelines.

AOPA PILOT—421 Aviation Way, Frederick, MD 21701. Richard C. Collins, Ed. Magazine of the Aircraft Owners and Pilots Assn. Articles, to 2,500 words, with photos, on general aviation for beginning and experienced pilots. Pays to $750.

THE AUTOGRAPH COLLECTOR'S MAGAZINE—P.O. Box 55328, Stockton, CA 95205. Joe Kraus, Ed. Articles, 100 to 1,500 words, on all areas of autograph collecting: preservation, framing and storage, specialty collections, documents and letters, collectors and dealers. Queries preferred. Pays 5¢ a word, on publication.

BIRD WATCHER'S DIGEST—P.O. Box 110, Marietta, OH 45740. Mary B. Bowers, Ed. Articles, 600 to 3,000 words, on bird-watching experiences and expeditions: information about rare sightings; updates on endangered species. Pays to $50, on publication.

THE BLADE MAGAZINE—P.O. Box 22007, Chattanooga, TN 37422. J. Bruce Voyles, Ed. Articles, 500 to 3,000 words: historical pieces on knives and old knife factories, etc.; interviews with knifemakers; how-to pieces. Pays from 5¢ a word, on publication.

CHESS LIFE—186 Route 9W, New Windsor, NY 12550. Don Maddox, Ed. Articles, 500 to 3,000 words, for members of the U.S. Chess Federation, on news, profiles, technical aspects of chess. Features on all aspects of chess: history, humor, puzzles, etc. Fiction, 500 to 2,000 words, related to chess. Photos. Pays varying rates, on acceptance. Query; limited freelance market.

CLASSIC AMERICA—P.O. Box 2516, Westfield, NJ 07090. Richard O. Aichele, Ed. Articles, 600 to 2,000 words, related to America from 1800 to 1930. Topics include historical events, travel, antiques, collectibles, life styles. Pieces with "how it can still be enjoyed today" slant are of special interest. Pays 8¢ a word, on acceptance. Guidelines.

COLLECTOR EDITIONS—170 Fifth Ave., New York, NY 10010. Joan Muyskens Pursley, Man. Ed. Articles, 750 to 1,500 words, on collectibles, mainly glass and porcelain. Pays $150 to $350, within 30 days of acceptance. Query with photos.

CRAFTS 'N THINGS—14 Main St., Dept. W, Park Ridge, IL 60068. Nancy Tosh, Ed. How-to articles on all kinds of crafts projects, with instructions. Pays $35 to $200, on publication. Send manuscript with instructions and photograph of the finished item.

DOLLS, THE COLLECTOR'S MAGAZINE—170 Fifth Ave., New York, NY 10010. Krystyna Poray Goddu, Ed. Articles, 500 to 2,500 words, for knowledgeable doll collectors: sharply focused with a strong collecting angle, and concrete information: value, identification, restoration, etc. Pays $100 to $350, after acceptance. Query.

FINESCALE MODELER—1027 N. Seventh St., Milwaukee, WI 53233. Marcia Stern, Asst. Ed. How-to articles for people who make nonoperating scale models of aircraft, automobiles, boats, figures. Photos and drawings should accompany articles. One-page model-building hints and tips. Pays from $30 per published page, on acceptance. Query preferred.

GAMBLING TIMES—1018 N. Cole Ave., Hollywood, CA 90038. Len Miller, Ed. Gambling-related articles, 1,000 to 6,000 words. Pays $100 to $150, on publication.

GAMES—810 Seventh Ave., New York, NY 10019. R. Wayne Schmittberger, Ed. Articles on games and puzzles. Quizzes, tests, brainteasers, etc. Photos. Pays varying rates, on acceptance.

THE HOME SHOP MACHINIST—2779 Aero Park Dr., Box 1810, Traverse City, MI 49685. Joe D. Rice, Ed. How-to articles on precision metalworking and foundry work. Accuracy and attention to detail a must. Pays $40 per published page, extra for photos and illustrations, on publication. Send SASE for writer's guidelines.

KITPLANES—P.O. Box 6050, Mission Viejo, CA 92690. Dave Martin, Ed. Articles geared to the growing market of aircraft built from kits and plans by home craftsmen, on all aspects of design, construction and performance, 1,000 to 4,000 words. Pays $100 to $300, on publication.

THE LEATHER CRAFTSMAN—Box 1386, Fort Worth, TX 76101. Nancy Sawyer, Ed. Articles on leather crafters, helpful hints and projects of varying difficulty. Pays $50 to $200, on publication.

LOST TREASURE—P.O. Box 937, Bixby, OK 74008. Kathy Dyer, Man. Ed. Factual articles, 1,000 to 3,000 words, on treasure hunting, metal detecting, prospecting techniques, and legendary lost treasure. Profiles. Photos. Pays 3¢ a word; preference given to stories with photos.

MINIATURE COLLECTOR—170 Fifth Ave., New York, NY 10010. Joan Muyskens Pursley, Man. Ed. Articles, 800 to 1,200 words, with photos, on outstanding 1/12-scale (dollhouse) miniatures and the people who make and collect them. Original, illustrated how-to projects for making miniatures. Pays varying rates, within 30 days of acceptance. Query with photos.

MODEL RAILROADER—1027 N. Seventh St., Milwaukee, WI 53233. Russ Larson, Ed. Articles, with photos of layout and equipment, on model railroads. Pays $75 per printed page, on acceptance. Query.

NATIONAL DOLL WORLD—306 E. Parr Rd., Berne, IN 46711. Rebekah Montgomery, Ed. Informational articles about doll collecting.

NEW ENGLAND ANTIQUES JOURNAL—4 Church St., Ware, MA 01082. Bryan McMullin, Ed. Well-researched articles, to 2,500 words, on antiques of interest to collectors and/or dealers, auction and antiques show reviews, to 1,000 words, antiques market news, to 500 words; photos desired. Pays to $150, on publication. Query or send manuscript. Reports in 2 to 4 weeks.

THE NEW YORK ANTIQUE ALMANAC—Box 335, Lawrence, NY 11559. Carol Nadel, Ed. Articles on antiques, shows, shops, museums, art, investments, collectibles, collecting suggestions; related humor. Photos. Pays $5 to $75, extra for photos, on publication.

NOSTALGIA WORLD—Box 231, North Haven, CT 06473. Bonnie Roth, Ed. Articles, 500 to 3,000 words, on all kinds of collectibles: records, TV memorabilia (The Monkees, Dark Shadows, Elvira, etc.), comics, gum cards, toys, sheet music, monsters, magazines, dolls, movie posters, etc. Pays $10 to $50, on publication.

NUTSHELL NEWS—633 W. Wisconsin Ave., Suite 304, Milwaukee, WI 53203. Sybil Harp, Ed. Articles, 1,200 to 1,500 words, for architectural miniatures enthusiasts, collectors, craftspeople and hobbyists. Pays 10¢ a word, on publication. Query first.

PETERSEN'S PHOTOGRAPHIC—8490 Sunset Blvd., Los Angeles, CA 90069. Bill Hurter, Ed. How-to articles on all phases of still photography of interest to the amateur and advanced photographer. Pays $60 per printed page for article accompanied by photos, on publication.

PLATE WORLD—9200 N. Maryland Ave., Niles, IL 60648. Alyson Sulaski Wyckoff, Ed. Articles on artists, collectors, manufacturers, retailers of limited-edition (only) collector's plates. No antiques. Internationally oriented. Pays varying rates, on acceptance. Query first with writing samples.

POPULAR CERAMICS—3639 San Fernando Rd., Glendale, CA 91204-2989. Joel E. Edwards, Ed. Coord. Instructive, how-to pieces, 500 to 1,000 words, on ceramics projects and ceramics-related human-interest stories. Pays $25 to $100, on publication.

POPULAR MECHANICS—224 W. 57th St., New York, NY 10019. Bill Hartford, Man. Ed. Articles, 300 to 2,000 words, on latest developments in mechanics, industry, science; features on hobbies with a mechanical slant; how-tos on home, shop, and crafts projects. Photo sketches. Pays to $1,000, $25 to $100 for short pieces, on acceptance. Buys all rights.

POPULAR PHOTOGRAPHY—1515 Broadway, New York, NY 10036. Jason Schneider, Ed. Dir. How-to articles, 500 to 2,000 words, for amateur photographers. Payment varies. Query with outline.

THE PROFESSIONAL QUILTER—Oliver Press, Box 4096, St. Paul, MN 55104. Jeannie M. Spears, Ed. Articles, 500 to 1,500 words, for small businesses related to the quilting field: business and marketing skills, personality profiles. Graphics, if applicable; no how-to quilt articles. Pays $25 to $75, on publication.

RAILROAD MODEL CRAFTSMAN—P.O. Box 700, Newton, NJ 07860. William C. Schaumburg, Ed. How-to articles on scale model railroading; cars, operation, scenery, etc. Pays on publication.

R/C MODEL SHOPPER—544 Second St., San Francisco, CA 94107. Charlotte Kester, Ed. Articles, to 1,000 words, on radio-control model planes, boats, helicopters, and cars; photos helpful. Pays 10¢ a word, on publication. Query with clips preferred.

R/C MODELER MAGAZINE—P.O. Box 487, Sierra Madre, CA 91024. Patricia E. Crews, Ed. Technical and semi-technical how-to articles on radio-controlled model aircraft, boats, helicopters, and cars. Query.

RESTORATION—Box 50046, Tucson, AZ 85703. W.R. Haessner, Ed. Articles, 1,200 to 1,800 words, on restoring autos, trucks, planes, trains, etc. Pays $10 per page, on publication. Query.

THE ROBB REPORT—1 Acton Pl., Acton, MA 01720. Attn: Geoffrey Douglas. Feature articles on investment opportunities, classic and collectible autos, art and antiques, home interiors, boats, travel, etc. Pays on publication. Query with SASE and published clips.

73 AMATEUR RADIO—WGE Center, Peterborough, NH 03458. Larry Ledlow, Ed. Articles, 1,500 to 3,000 words, for electronics hobbyists and amateur radio operators. Pays $50 to $75 per printed page.

SEW NEWS—P.O. Box 1790, News Plaza, Peoria, IL 61656. Linda Turner Griepentrog, Ed. Articles, to 3,000 words, "that teach a specific technique, inspire a reader to try new sewing projects, or inform a reader about an interesting person, company, or project related to sewing, textiles, or fashion." Emphasis is on fashion sewing. Pays $25 to $400, on acceptance. Queries required.

TEDDY BEAR REVIEW—170 Fifth Ave., New York, NY 10010. Joan Muyskens Pursley, Man. Ed. Articles on antique and contemporary teddy bears for makers, collectors, and enthusiasts. Pays varying rates, within 30 days of acceptance. Query with photos.

TREASURE—6745 Adobe Rd., Twenty-Nine Palms, CA 92277. Jim Williams, Ed. Articles, to 2,500 words, and fillers, 300 words, of interest to treasure hunters: How-to (building projects and hunting techniques); Search (where to look for treasure); and Found (stories of discovered treasure). Photos and illustrations welcome. Pays from $30 for fillers, to $125 for features, on publication. Same address and requirements for Treasure Search and Treasure Found.

TROPICAL FISH HOBBYIST—211 W. Sylvania Ave., Neptune City, NJ 07753. Ray Hunziker, Ed. Articles, 500 to 3,000 words, for beginning and experienced tropical and marine fish enthusiasts. Photos. Pays $35 to $250, on acceptance. Query.

WEST ART—Box 6868, Auburn, CA 95604. Martha Garcia, Ed. Features, 350 to 700 words, on fine arts and crafts. No hobbies. Photos. Pays 50¢ per column inch, on publication. SASE required.

WESTERN & EASTERN TREASURES—P.O. Box 1095, Arcata, CA 95521. Rosemary Anderson, Man. Ed. Illustrated articles, to 1,500 words, on metal detecting, treasure-hunting, rocks, and gems. Pays 2¢ a word, extra for photos, on publication.

THE WINE SPECTATOR—Opera Plaza, Suite 2040, 601 Van Ness Ave., San Francisco, CA 94102. Jim Gordon, Man. Ed. Features, 600 to 2,000 words, preferably with photos, on news and people in the wine world. Pays from $100, extra for photos, on publication. Query required.

WOMEN'S CIRCLE COUNTED CROSS-STITCH—306 E. Parr Rd., Berne, IN 46711. Denise Lohr, Ed. How-to and instructional counted cross-stitch. Short stories, interviews and photos of top designers, book reviews, tips, humor. Pays varying rates, on publication.

WOMEN'S CIRCLE COUNTRY NEEDLECRAFT—306 E. Parr Rd., Berne, IN 46711. Jeanine Newer, Ed. How-to and instructional needlecrafts; related interviews, humor, book reviews tips, and short fiction. Photos. Pays varying rates, on publication.

WOODEN BOAT—P.O. Box 78, Brooklin, ME 04616. Jonathan Wilson, Ed. How-to and technical articles, 4,000 words, on construction, repair and maintenance of wooden boats; design, history and use of wooden boats; and profiles of outstanding wooden boat builders and designers. Pays $6 per column inch. Query preferred.

THE WOODWORKER'S JOURNAL—P.O. Box 1629, 517 Litchfield Rd., New Milford, CT 06776. Thomas G. Begnal, Man. Ed. Original plans for woodworking projects, with detailed written instructions and at least one B/W photo of finished product. Pays $80 to $120 per published page, on acceptance.

WORKBENCH—4251 Pennsylvania Ave., Kansas City, MO 64111. Robert N. Hoffman, Ed. Articles on do-it-yourself home improvement and maintenance projects and general woodworking articles for beginning and expert craftsmen. Complete working drawings with accurate dimensions, step-by-step instructions, lists of materials, and photos of the finished product must accompany submission. Queries welcome. Pays from $125 per published page, on acceptance.

YELLOWBACK LIBRARY—811 Boulder Ave., Des Moines, IA 50315. Gil O'Gara, Ed. Articles, 300 to 2,000 words, on boys/girls series literature (Hardy Boys, Nancy Drew, Tom Swift, etc.) for collectors, researchers, and dealers. "Especially welcome are interviews with, or articles by past and present writers of juvenile series fiction." Pays in copies.

YESTERYEAR—P.O. Box 2, Princeton, WI 54968. Michael Jacobi, Ed. Articles on antiques and collectibles, for readers in WI, IL, IA, MN, and surrounding states. Photos. Will consider regular columns on collecting or antiques. Pays from $10, on publication.

ZYMURGY—Box 287, Boulder, CO 80306. Charles N. Papazian, Ed. Articles, 750 to 2,000 words, appealing to beer lovers and homebrewers. Pays $25 to $75, for on publication. Query.

POPULAR & TECHNICAL SCIENCE; COMPUTERS

AIR & SPACE—National Air & Space Museum, Washington, DC 20560. George Larson, Ed. General-interest articles, 1,000 to 3,500 words, on aerospace experience, past, present, and future; travel, space, history, biographies, essays, commentary. Pays varying rates, on acceptance. Query first.

AMIGA WORLD—IDG Communications, 80 Elm St., Peterborough, NH 03458. Bob Ryan, Technical Ed. Articles, 1,000 to 3,000 words, on programming, products and other topics related to Amiga systems. Pays $350 to $800, on publication. Query first.

ANTIC, THE ATARI RESOURCE—544 Second St., San Francisco, CA 94107. Nat Friedland, Ed. Programs and information for the Atari computer user/owner. Reviews, 500 words, of hardware and software, original programs, etc. Game reviews, 400 words. Pays $50 per review, $60 per published page, on publication. Query.

APPLE APPLICATIONS—See *Compute!*

ASTRONOMY—1027 N. Seventh St., Milwaukee, WI 53233. Richard Berry, Ed.-in-Chief. Articles on astronomy, astrophysics, space programs, research. Hobby pieces on equipment; short news items. Pays varying rates, on acceptance.

BIOSCIENCE—American Institute of Biological Science, 730 11th St. N.W., Washington, DC 20001. Laura Tangley, Features Ed. Articles, 2 to 4 journal pages, on new developments in biology or on science policy, for professional biologists. Pays $200 per journal page, on publication. Query required.

BYTE MAGAZINE—One Phoenix Mill Ln., Peterborough, NH 03458. Frederic Langa, Ed. Features on new technology, how-to articles, and reviews of computers and software, varying lengths, for sophisticated users of personal computers. Payment is competitive. Query.

CBT DIRECTIONS—Weingarten Publications, 38 Chauncy St., Boston, MA 02111. Jane Stein, Ed. Articles (2,500 words) and news items (500 words and up) on computer-based training and interactive video for industry and government professionals in program development. Pays $100 to $600, on acceptance. Query.

COMMODORE MAGAZINE—1200 Wilson Dr., West Chester, PA 19380. Susan West, Ed. Software reviews, programs, do-it-yourself projects, buyers guides, etc., for Commodore computer users. Pays varying rates on publication. Query.

COMPUTE!—324 W. Wendover Ave., Suite 200, Greensboro, NC 27408. Gregg Keizer, Ed. In-depth feature articles on using the personal computer at home, work, and school. Industry news, interviews with leaders in the pc field, product information, hardware and software reviews. For users of Amiga, Apple, Atari ST, Commodore 64/128, IBM, Tandy, and compatibles. Also: *Apple Applications,* Gregg Keizer, Ed.; and *PC Magazine,* Lance Elko, Ed.

COMPUTE!'S GAZETTE—324 W. Wendover Ave., Suite 200, Greensboro, NC 27408. Kathleen Martinek, Man. Ed. Lance Elko, Ed. Articles, to 2,000 words, on Commodore 64/128, including home, education, and business applications, games, and programming. Original programs also accepted.

COMPUTER PRODUCT SELLING—425 Park Ave., New York, NY 10022. Betty J. Taylor, Ed. News and features for computer sales professionals. Pays 30¢ a word, on publication.

DIGITAL NEWS—33 West St., Boston, MA 02111. Corey Sandler, Ed. Newspaper articles of varying lengths, covering products, applications, and events related to Digital's VAX line of computers. Pay varies, on acceptance. Query required.

DISCOVER MAGAZINE—Family Media, Inc., 3 Park Ave., New York, NY 10016. Query.

ENVIRONMENT—4000 Albemarle St. N.W., Washington, DC 20016. Christine Mlor, Ed. Factual articles, 2,500 to 5,000 words, on scientific, technological and environmental policy and decision-making issues. Pays $100 to $300. Query.

FINAL FRONTIER—P.O. Box 11519, Washington, DC 20008. Tony Reichhardt, Ed. Articles (1,500 to 2,500 words), columns (800 words), and shorts (250 words) about people, events, and "exciting possibilities" of the world's space programs. Pays 25¢ a word, on acceptance. Query.

FOCUS—Turnkey Publications, 4807 Spicewood Springs Rd., Suite 3150, Austin, TX 78759. Greg Farman, Ed. Articles, 700 to 4,000 words, on Data General computers. Photos a plus. Pays to $100, on publication. Query required.

THE FUTURIST—World Future Society, 4916 Elmo Ave., Bethesda, MD 20814. Timothy Willard, Man. Ed. Features, 1,000 to 5,000 words, on subjects pertaining to the future: environment, education, science, technology, etc. Pays in copies.

GENETIC ENGINEERING NEWS—1651 Third Ave., New York, NY 10128. John Sterling, Man. Ed. Articles on all aspects of biotechnology; feature articles and news articles. Pays varying rates, on acceptance. Query.

GEOBYTE—American Association of Petroleum Geologists, P.O. Box 979, Tulsa, OK 74101. Ken Milam, Man. Ed. Articles, 20 typed pages, on computer applications in exploration and production of oil, gas, and energy minerals for geophysicists, geologists, and petroleum engineers. Pay varies, on acceptance. Queries preferred.

HAM RADIO—Main St., Greenville, NH 03048. Rich Rosen, Ed. Articles, to 2,500 words, on amateur radio theory and construction. Pays $40 per printed page, on publication. Query. Guidelines.

HANDS-ON ELECTRONICS—See *Popular Electronics.*

INCIDER—80 Elm St., Peterborough, NH 03458. Articles for Apple II computer users: applications-oriented, focuses on hardware and software solutions in the home, school, and small business. Software and hardware reviews. Pays on acceptance. Query preferred.

LINK-UP—143 Old Marlton Pike., Medford, NJ 08055. Joseph A. Webb, Ed. Dir. How-to pieces, hardware and software reviews, and current trends, 600 to 2,500 words, for business and education professionals who use computers and modems at work and at home. Pays $80 to $200, on publication. Photos a plus.

LOTUS—P. O. Box 9123, Cambridge, MA 02139. Chris Brown, Feature Ed. Articles, 1,500 to 3,000 words, on business and professional applications of Lotus software. Query with outline required. Pays $700 to $1500, on acceptance.

MACINTOSH BUSINESS REVIEW—VNU Business Publications, 1625 The Alameda, Suite 900, San Jose, CA 95126. Charles Rubin, Exec. Ed. Articles for business users of Apple Computer's Macintosh: 2,000 to 2,200 words on the latest developments in applications; product reviews, 2,000 to 2,500 words; product implementation and analysis, 2,000 to 2,500 words; product surveys. Submissions must be on disk or made electronically. Pays 50¢ a word, on acceptance. Guidelines.

MACWORLD—Editorial Proposals, 501 Second St., Ste. 600, San Francisco, CA 94107. Reviews, news, consumer, and how-to articles relating to Macintosh personal computers; varying lengths. Query or send outline with screenshots, if applicable. Pays from $300 to $3,000, on acceptance. Send SASE for writers guidelines.

MICROAGE QUARTERLY—2308 S. 55th St., Tempe, AZ 85282. Linnea Maxwell, Ed. Distributed through MicroAge stores. Articles on business uses of microcomputers; prefer writers with experience in microcomputer industry and knowledge of technology and products. Query first. Pays varing rates on publication.

MODERN ELECTRONICS—76 N. Broadway, Hicksville, NY 10081. Art Salsberg, Ed.-in-Chief. How-to features, technical tutorials, and construction projects related to latest consumer electronics circuits, products, and personal computer equipment. Lengths vary. Query with outline required. Pays $80 to $150 per published page, on acceptance.

NETWORK WORLD—Box 1971, Framingham, MA 01701. John Gallant, Ed. Articles, to 2,500 words, about applications of communications technology for management-level users of data, voice, and video communications systems, Pays varying rates, on acceptance.

NIBBLE—52 Domino Dr., Concord, MA 01742. David Krathwohl, Ed. Programs and programming methods, as well as short articles, reviews, and general-interest pieces for Apple Computer users. Send short cover letter and sample program runs with manuscript. Pays $50 to $500 for articles, $20 to $250 for shorter pieces. Send SASE for writers' guidelines.

NIBBLE MAC—52 Domino Dr., Concord, MA 01742. David Krathwohl, Ed. Articles using Macintosh programs; product reviews, tutorials, and general-interest articles for Macintosh users. Articles on use of Hyper Card stackware and publishable Hyper Card stacks. Pays $40 to $500, after acceptance. Programs must be submitted on disk. Send SASE for guidelines.

OMNI—1965 Broadway, New York, NY 10023. Patrice Adcroft, Ed. Articles, 1,000 to 3,500 words, on scientific aspects of the future: space colonies, cloning, machine intelligence, ESP, origin of life, future arts, life styles, etc. Pays $800 to $4,000, $150 for short items, on acceptance. Query.

PC MAGAZINE—See *Compute!*

PC TECH JOURNAL—10480 Little Patuxent Pkwy., Ste. 800, Parkview, Columbia, MD 21044. Julie Anderson, Ed. How-to pieces and reviews for technically sophisticated computer professionals. Pays $150 to $1,500, on acceptance. Query required. Guidelines.

PCM MAGAZINE—Falsoft, Inc., 9509 US Highway 42, P. O. Box 385, Prospect, KY 40059. Kevin Nichols, Ed. Articles and computer programs for Tandy portables and MS-DOS computers. Pays varying rates, on publication.

PERSONAL COMPUTING—Hayden Publishing, 10 Holland Dr., Hasbrouck Heights, NJ 07604. Fred Abatemarco, Ed.-in-Chief. Articles for managerial-level business audience and savvy personal computer users. Pays on acceptance.

PERSONAL PUBLISHING—25W550 Geneva Ave., Wheaton, IL 60188. Dan Brogan, Ed. Articles, 1,500 to 2,000 words, on desktop publishing technology. Pay varies, on publication. Queries required.

POPULAR ELECTRONICS (FORMERLY *HANDS-ON ELECTRONICS*)—500-B Bi County Blvd., Farmingdale, NY 11735. Julian S. Martin, Ed. Features, 1,500 to 2,500 words, for electronics hobbyists and experimenters. "Our readers are science oriented, understand computer theory and operation, and like to build projects. Fillers and cartoons. Pays $100 to $350, on acceptance.

POPULAR SCIENCE—380 Madison Ave., New York, NY 10017. C. P. Gilmore, Ed. Articles, with photos, on developments in applied science and technology. Short illustrated articles on new inventions and products; photo essays, to 4 pages. Pays from $150 per printed page, on acceptance.

PROFILES—Kaypro Corp., 533 Stevens Ave., Solana Beach, CA 92075. Gwyn Price, Pub. Tutorials, 2,500 to 3,000 words, geared to beginner and intermediate users of CP/M and MS-DOS computers. Pays $350, on acceptance. Query required.

THE RAINBOW—Falsoft, Inc., 9509 U. S Highway 42, P. O. Box 385, Prospect, KY 40059. Jutta Kaphammer, Submissions Ed. Articles and computer programs for Tandy color computers. Pays varying rates, on publication.

RUN—CW Communications, 80 Elm St., Peterborough, NH 03458. Dennis Brisson, Ed.-in-Chief. Articles, 6 to 10 typed pages, geared to Commodore home computer users: applications, program listings, hints, and tips to "help readers get the most out of their Commodore." Query first for technical subjects. Pays $100 per printed page.

SEA FRONTIERS—3979 Rickenbacker Causeway, Virginia Key, Miami, FL 33149. Jean Bradfisch, Exec. Ed. Illustrated articles, 500 to 3,000 words, on scientific advances related to the sea, biological, physical, chemical, or geological phenomena, ecology, conservation, etc., written in a popular style for lay readers. Send SASE for guidelines. Pays $50 to $450, on acceptance. Query.

SEXTANT—716 E St. S.E., Washington, DC 20003. Charles Floto, Ed. Articles related to Zenith computers, on hardware, software, and personal experience. Pays $50 to $100 a page, on publication. Query. Guidelines.

SHAREWARE MAGAZINE—1030D E. Duane Ave., Sunnyvale, CA 94086. M. Palmer Barnes, Man. Ed.-in-Chief. Software and hardware reviews, 2,500 words, and computer-oriented fiction. Payment varies, on acceptance. Query.

SPACE WORLD—National Space Society 922 Pennsylvania Ave. S.E., Washington, DC 20003. Lively, non-technical features on all aspects of international space program. Pays $150 to $250, on publication. Query; guidelines available.

START MAGAZINE—Antic Publishing, 544 Second St., San Francisco, CA 94107. Andrew Reese, Ed. Articles, to 4,000 words, and programming features, 1,500 to 2,500 words, for beginning and experienced users of Atari ST computers. Submit hard copy and disk. Pay varies, on publication. Guidelines.

TECHNOLOGY REVIEW—M.I.T., W59–200, Cambridge, MA 02139. Jonathan Schlefer, Ed. General-interest articles and more technical features, 1,500 to 5,000 words, on technology, the environment, and society. Pay varies, on publication. Query.

ANIMALS

ANIMAL KINGDOM—New York Zoological Society, Bronx, NY 10460. Nancy Christie, Assoc. Ed. First-person articles, 1,500 to 2,000 words, on "popular" natural history, "based on author's research and experience as opposed to textbook approach." Payment varies, on acceptance. Guidelines.

BIRD TALK—Box 6050, Mission Viejo, CA 02690. Karyn New, Ed. Articles for pet bird owners: care and feeding, history, outstanding personal adventures, humor. Pays from 5¢ a word, after publication. Query preferred.

CAT FANCY—P.O. Box 6050, Mission Viejo, CA 92690. Linda Lewis, Ed. Articles, from 1,500 to 3,000 words, on cat care, health, grooming, etc. Pays 5¢ a word, or $150 to $300 for photo story with quality color slides or black & white prints, on publication.

DOG FANCY—P. O. Box 6050, Mission Viejo, CA 92690. Linda Lewis, Ed. Articles, 1,500 to 3,000 words, on dog care, health, grooming, breeds, activities, events, etc. Photos. Pays from 5¢ a word, on publication.

EASTERN HORSE WORLD—See *Horseworld USA*.

HORSE & RIDER—941 Calle Negocio, San Clemente, CA 92672. Ray Rich, Ed. Articles, 500 to 3,000 words, with photos, on Western riding and general horse care: training, feeding, grooming, etc. Pays varying rates, on publication. Buys all rights. Guidelines.

HORSE ILLUSTRATED—P.O. Box 6050, Mission Viejo, CA 92690. Jill-Marie Jones, Ed. Articles, 1,500 to 2,500 words, on all aspects of owning and caring for horses. Photos. Pays 3¢ to 5¢ a word, on publication.

HORSEMAN—25025 I45N, Suite 390, Spring, TX 77380. David T. Gaines, Ed./Pub. Instructional articles, to 2,500 words, with photos, for Western trainers and riders. Pays from $50.

HORSEMEN'S YANKEE PEDLAR—785 Southbridge St., Auburn, MA 01501. Nancy L. Khoury, Pub. News and feature-length articles, about horses and horsemen in the Northeast. Photos. Pays $2 per published inch, on publication. Query.

HORSEPLAY—P.O. Box 130, Gaithersburg, MD 20877. Cordelia Doucet, Ed. Articles, to 3,000 words, on eventing, show jumping, horse shows, dressage, driving and fox hunting, for horse enthusiasts. Pays 10¢ a word, buys all rights, after publication.

HORSEWORLD USA (FORMERLY *EASTERN HORSE WORLD*)—P.O.

632

Box 249, Huntington, NY 11746. Diana DeRosa, Ed. Horse-related articles of varying lengths of interest to horse enthusiasts. Pays on publication. Query.

PURE BRED DOGS/AMERICAN KENNEL GAZETTE—51 Madison Ave., New York, NY 10010. Marion Lane, Exec. Ed. Judy Hartop, Sr. Ed. Articles, 1,000 to 2,500 words, relating to pure-bred dogs. Pays from $100 to $300, on publication. Query preferred.

SHEEP! MAGAZINE—Route 1, Helenville, WI 53137. Dave Thompson, Ed. Articles, to 1,500 words, on successful shepherds, woodcrafts, sheep raising and sheep dogs. Photos. Pays $80 to $250, extra for photos, on publication.

WILDBIRD—Box 6050, Mission Viejo, CA 92690. Tim Gallagher, Man. Ed. Features, 1,500 to 2,000 words, and columns, 700 to 1,000 words, for field birders and garden birders. "No pieces on taming wild birds." Pays from $100 for features, $25 for columns, extra for photos. Guidelines.

PARENTING, CHILD CARE, AND DEVELOPMENT

AMERICAN BABY—475 Park Ave. S., New York, NY 10016. Judith Nolte, Ed. Articles, about 2,000 words, for new or expectant parents; pieces on pregnancy and child care. No poetry. Pays on acceptance.

BABY TALK—185 Madison Ave., New York, NY 10016. Patricia Irons, Ed. Articles, 1,500 to 3,000 words, by parents or professionals, on babies, baby care, etc. Pays varying rates, on acceptance. SASE required.

CHILD MAGAZINE—477 Madison Ave., 22nd fl., New York, NY 10022. Jackie Leo, Ed. Nancy Clark, Features Ed. Articles, 1,500 to 2,500 words, for parents who want the best for their children: schools, health, books, travel, and childcare. Pays $500 to $1,000, on acceptance. Query preferred.

CHILDREN (FORMERLY *RODALE'S CHILDREN*)—33 E. Minor St., Emmaus, PA 18098. Eileen Nechas, Ed. Authoritative, informative articles, 1,000 to 3,000 words, on health, fitness, education, psychology, nutrition, and lifestyle, of interest to parents with children to age 15. Pays 30¢ a word, on acceptance. Query.

EXPECTING—685 Third Ave., New York, NY 10017. Evelyn A. Podsiadlo, Ed. Articles, 700 to 1,800 words, for expectant mothers. Pays $300 to $500, on acceptance.

GROWING CHILD/GROWING PARENT—22 N. Second St., Lafayette, IN 47902. Nancy Kleckner, Ed. Articles to 1,500 words on subjects of interest to parents of children under 6, with emphasis on the issues, problems, and choices of being a parent. No personal-experience pieces or poetry. Pays 8¢ to 15¢ a word, on acceptance. Query.

GROWING UP—See *Tender Years*.

LIVING WITH CHILDREN—127 Ninth Ave. N., Nashville, TN 37234. Articles, 800, 1,450, or 2,000 words, on parent-child relationships, told from a Christian perspective. Pays 5¢ a word, after acceptance.

LIVING WITH PRESCHOOLERS—127 Ninth Ave. N., Nashville, TN 37234. Articles, 800, 1,450, or 2,000 words, and fillers, to 300 words, for Christian families. Pays 5¢ a word, on acceptance.

LIVING WITH TEENAGERS—127 Ninth Ave. N., Nashville, TN 37234. Articles told from a Christian perspective for parents of teenagers; first-person approach preferred. Poetry, 4 to 16 lines. Pays 5¢ a word, on acceptance.

MARRIAGE & FAMILY (FORMERLY *MARRIAGE & FAMILY LIV-ING*)—Abbey Press Publishing Div., St. Meinrad, IN 47577. Kass Dotterweich, Man. Ed. Expert advice, personal-experience articles with moral, religious, or spiritual slant, to 2,500 words, on husband-wife and parent-child relationships. Pays 7¢ a word, on acceptance.

NEW YORK FAMILY—420 E. 79th St., New York, NY 10021. Felice Shapiro, Susan Ross, Eds. Articles related to family life in New York City. Pays $50 to $100, on publication.

PARENTING—501 Second St., San Francisco, CA 94107. Address the Editor. Articles, 150 to 3,500 words, for parents of children up to 10 yrs., especially under 6 yrs. Topics include education, health, fitness, nutrition, child development, psychology, and social issues. Pays up to $2,000. Query.

PARENTS—685 Third Ave., New York, NY 10017. Ann Pleshette Murphy, Ed.-in-Chief. Articles, 2,000 to 3,000 words, on growth and development of infants, children, teens; family; women's issues; community; current research. Informal style with quotes from experts. Pays from $750, on acceptance. Query.

TENDER YEARS (FORMERLY *GROWING UP*)—5127 Summit Ave., Greensboro, NC 27405. John A. Edwards, Man. Ed. Articles, 1,000 to 3,000 words, for families with infants, young children and adolescents. Technical articles, fiction, and poetry. Pays $25 to $50. Query required.

THINKING FAMILIES—605 Worcester Rd., Towson, MD 21204. Marjory Spraycar, Ed. Articles (1,500 to 2,500 words) on developmental and educational topics related to elementary school children. Pays $300 to $1,000, on publication. Query required.

WORKING PARENTS—18 E. 41st St., New York, NY 10017. Janet Spencer King, Ed. Articles, to 1,800 words, of interest to parents with children six years old or younger. Poetry, any length. Pays varying rates, on publication. Query preferred.

MILITARY

THE AMERICAN LEGION MAGAZINE—Box 1055, Indianapolis, IN 46206. Michael D. LaBonne, Ed. Articles, 750 to 1,800 words, on current world affairs, public policy, and subjects of contemporary interest. Pays $100 to $1,000, on acceptance. Query.

ARMY MAGAZINE—2425 Wilson Blvd., Arlington, VA 22201. L. James Binder, Ed-in-Chief, Features, to 5,000 words, on military subjects. Essays, humor, history, news reports, first-person anecdotes. Pays 10¢ to 17¢ a word, $10 to $25 for anecdotes, on publication.

LEATHERNECK—Box 1775, Quantico, VA 22134. William V.H. White, Ed. Articles, to 3,000 words, with photos, on U.S. Marines. Pays $50 per printed page, on acceptance. Query.

LIFE IN THE TIMES—The Times Journal Co., Springfield, VA 22159–0200. Barry Robinson, Ed. Articles, to 2,000 words, on current military family life. Pays $100 to $350, on acceptance.

MILITARY LIFESTYLE MAGAZINE—1732 Wisconsin Ave. N.W., Washington, DC 20007. Hope Daniels, Ed. Articles, 800 to 2,000 words, for military families in the U.S. and overseas, on lifestyles, travel, fashion, nutrition, and health; fiction. Pays $200 to $800, on publication. Query first.

OFF DUTY MAGAZINE—3303 Harbor Blvd., Suite C-2, Costa Mesa, CA

92626. Bruce Thorstad, U.S. Ed. Informative, entertaining and useful articles, 900 to 1,800 words, for military service personnel and their dependents, on making the most of off-duty time and getting the most out of service life: military living, travel, personal finance, sports, military people, American trends, etc. Military angle essential. Pays 13¢ to 16¢ a word, on publication. European and Pacific editions also. Query required. Guidelines.

THE RETIRED OFFICER MAGAZINE—201 N. Washington St., Alexandria, VA 22314. Address Manuscript Ed. Articles, 750 to 2,000 words, of interest to military retirees and their families. Current military/political affairs: recent military history (especially Vietnam and Korea), humor, travel, hobbies, military family life styles, and second-career job opportunities. Photos a plus. Pays to $500, extra for photos, on acceptance. Queries required, no unsolicited manuscripts; address Manuscript Ed. Guidelines.

VFW MAGAZINE—Broadway at 34th, Kansas City, MO 64111. James K. Anderson, Ed. Magazine for Veterans of Foreign Wars and their families. Articles, 1,000 words, on current issues and history, with veteran angle. Photos. Pays from $200, extra for photos, on acceptance.

WESTERN

AMERICAN WEST—7000 E. Tanque Verde Rd., Suite 30, Tucson, AZ 85715. Mae Reid-Bills, Man. Ed. Well-researched, illustrated articles, 1,000 to 2,500 words, linking the contemporary West with its historic past and emphasizing places to see and things to do for the Western traveler. Pays from $200, on acceptance. Query required.

OLD WEST—See *True West.*

PERSIMMON HILL—1700 N.E. 63rd St., Oklahoma City, OK 73111. Marcia Preston, Ed. Published by the National Cowboy Hall of Fame. Articles, 1,500 to 3,000 words, on Western history and art, cowboys, ranching, and nature. Pays from $100 to $250, on acceptance.

REAL WEST—Charlton Publications, Inc., Division St., Derby, CT 06418. Ed Doherty, Ed. True stories of the Old West, 1,000 to 4,000 words. Photos. Pays from 4¢ a word, on acceptance.

TRUE WEST—P.O. Box 2107, Stillwater, OK 74076. John Joerschke, Ed. True stories, 500 to 4,500 words, with photos, about the Old West to 1930. Some contemporary stories with historical slant. Source list required. Pays 3¢ to 5¢ a word, extra for B&W photos, on publication. Same address and requirements for *Old West.*

WILD WEST—105 Loudoun St. S.W., Leesburg, VA 22075. William M. Vogt, Ed. Features, 4,000 words, with 500-word sidebars, and department pieces, 2,000 words, on Western history from the earliest North American settlements to the end of the 19th century. Pays $150 to $300, on publication. Query.

HISTORICAL

AMERICAN HERITAGE—60 Fifth Ave., New York, NY 10011. Byron Dobell, Ed. Articles, 750 to 5,000 words, on U.S. history and background of American life and culture. No fiction. Pays from $300 to $1,500, on acceptance. Query. SASE.

AMERICAN HERITAGE OF INVENTION &TECHNOLOGY—60 Fifth

Ave., New York, NY 10011. Frederick Allen, Ed. Articles, 2,000 to 5,000 words, on history of technology in America, for the sophisticated general reader. Query. Pays on acceptance.

AMERICAN HISTORY ILLUSTRATED—2245 Kohn Road, P.O. Box 8200, Harrisburg, PA 17105. Articles, 3,000 to 5,000 words, soundly researched. Style should be popular, not scholarly. No travelogues, no fiction. Pays $300 to $600, on acceptance. Query with SASE required.

AMERICANA—29 W. 38th St., New York, NY 10018. Sandra J. Wilmot, Ed. Articles, 1,000 to 2,500 words, with historical slant: restoration, crafts, food, collecting, travel, etc. Pays $600 to $800, on acceptance. Query.

CHICAGO HISTORY—Clark St. at North Ave., Chicago, IL 60614. Russell Lewis, Ed. Articles, to 4,500 words, on urban political, social and cultural history. Pays to $250, on publication. Query.

CLASSIC AMERICA—P.O. Box 2516, Westfield, NJ 07090. Richard W. Aichele, Ed. Articles, 600 to 2,000 words, related to America from 1800 to 1930. Topics include historical events, travel, antiques, collectibles, lifestyles. Pieces with "how it can still be enjoyed today" slant are of special interest. Pays 8¢ to 16¢ a word, on acceptance. Guidelines.

EARLY AMERICAN LIFE—Box 8200, Harrisburg, PA 17105. Frances Carnahan, Ed. Illustrated articles, 1,000 to 3,000 words, on early American life: arts, crafts, furnishings, architecture; travel features about historic sites and country inns. Pays $50 to $500, on acceptance. Query.

HEARTLAND JOURNAL—4114 N. Sunset Ct., Madison, WI 53705. Jeri McCormick and Lenore Coberly, Eds. Articles, 100 to 4,000 words, "on times and places that are gone." Writers must be over 60 years old. Pays in copies.

HISTORIC PRESERVATION—1785 Massachusetts Ave. N.W., Washington, DC 20036. Thomas J. Colin, Ed. Lively feature articles from published writers, 1,500 to 4,000 words, on residential restoration, preservation issues, and people involved in saving America's built environment. High-quality photos. Pays $300 to $1,000, extra for photos, on acceptance. Query required.

COLLEGE, CAREERS

AMPERSAND—303 N. Glenoaks Blvd., Suite 600, Burbank, CA 91502. Stewart Weiner, Exec. Ed. Articles, 1,000 to 2,000 words, of interest to college students. Focus on films and popular entertainment. Pays $750 to $1,000, on acceptance. Query required.

THE BLACK COLLEGIAN—1240 S. Broad St., New Orleans, LA 70125. K. Kazi-Ferrouillet, Man. Ed. Articles, to 2,000 words, on experiences of black students, careers and how-to subjects. Pays on publication. Query.

CAMPUS LIFE—465 Gundersen Dr., Carol Stream, IL 60188. Jim Long, Sr. Ed. Articles reflecting Christian values and world view, for high school and college students. Humor and general fiction. Photo essays, cartoons. Pays from $150, on acceptance. Limited free-lance market.

CAMPUS USA—1801 Rockville Pike, Suite 216, Rockville, MD 20852. Gerald S. Snyder, Ed. Articles (500 to 1,500 words) on the tastes, feelings, and moods of today's college students: careers, college financing, travel, movies, fashion, autos, and sports. Pays $250 to $750, on publication. Query required.

CAMPUS VOICE—505 Market St., Knoxville, TN 37902. Lively, in-depth articles, 2,000 to 3,500 words, of interest to college students. Department pieces,

1,000 to 2,000 words. Pays $300 to $2,000, on acceptance. Query required. Send SASE for guidelines.

CAREER WORLD—General Learning Corp., 60 Revere Dr., Northbrook, IL 60062–1563. Bonnie Bekken, Ed. Educational articles on careers and occupations for students in grades 6 through 12. Queries preferred. Pays varying rates, on publication.

CIRCLE K—3636 Woodview Trace, Indianapolis, IN 46268. Karen J. Pyle, Exec. Ed. Serious and light articles, 2,000 to 2,500 words, on community service and involvement, self-help, leadership development, youth issues, and careers. Pays $100 to $250, on acceptance. Queries required.

COLLEGE WOMAN—303 N. Glenoaks Blvd., Suite 600, Burbank, CA 91502. Stewart Weiner, Exec. Ed. Articles, 2,500 words, of interest to college women, on topics from controversial, on-campus issues to fashion and sports. Fillers, to 500 words. Pays $750 to $1,000, on acceptance. Query required.

MOVING UP—303 N. Glenoaks Blvd., Suite 600, Burbank, CA 91502. Stewart Weiner, Exec. Ed. Articles, 500 to 2,500 words, of interest to college men, concerning careers, relationships, fitness, personal style, and self-awareness; profiles; opinion pieces; humor. Pays on acceptance. Query required.

PANACHE—76–05 51st Ave., Elmhurst, NY 11373. Michael Weiss, Ed. Fiction, 500 to 2,000 words; personality profiles; articles on events and landmarks relating to college life, 500 to 2,000. East Coast: address Robin Clark; West Coast: address Catie Lott. Pays $30 to $100, on publication. Query required.

U MAGAZINE—5206 Maine St., Downers Grove, IL 60515. Verne Becker, Ed. Articles and fiction (to 2,000 words), poetry, for college students. All material should reflect a Christian world view. Queries required.

WHAT'S NEW MAGAZINE—Multicom, Inc., 11 Allen Rd., Boston, MA 02135. Bob Leja, Ed. General-interest articles, 150 to 300 words, on music, movies, books, cars, travel, sports, food, wine, consumer electronics, computers, arts and entertainment. Pays $25 to $250, on publication. Query required.

ALTERNATIVE MAGAZINES

EAST WEST: THE JOURNAL OF NATURAL NEALTH & LIVING—17 Station St., Box 1200, Brookline, MA 02147. Features, 1,500 to 2,500 words, on holistic health, natural foods, gardening, etc. Material for "Body," "Healing," "In the Kitchen," and "Beauty and Fitness." Interviews. Photos. Pays 10¢ to 15¢ a word, extra for photos, on publication.

FATE—Clark Publishing Co., 3510 Western Ave., Highland Park, IL 60035. Jerome Clark, Ed. Documented articles, to 3,000 words, on strange happenings. First-person accounts, to 300 words, of true psychic or unexplained experiences. Pays from 5¢ a word for articles, $10 for short pieces, on publication.

NEW AGE—342 Western Ave., Brighton, MA 02135. Address Manuscript Ed. Articles for readers who take an active interest in social change and personal growth, health and contemporary issues. Features, 2,000 to 4,000 words; columns, 750 to 1,500 words; short news items, 50 words; and first-person narratives, 750 to 1,500 words. Pays varying rates. Query.

NEW REALITIES—4000 Albermarle St. N.W., Washington, DC 20016. Neal Vahle, Ed. Articles on holistic health, personal growth, parapsychology, alternative lifestyles, new spirituality. Query required.

WILDFIRE—Bear Tribe Publishing, Box 148, Tum Tum, WA 99034. Matthew Ryan, Man. Ed. Articles (1,000 to 2,500 words) with strong Native American focus on personal development, alternative life styles, natural healing, spirituality, and ecology. Fiction (900 to 4,500 words) and poetry (20 lines). Pays to $125, on publication.

YOGA JOURNAL—2054 University Ave., Berkeley, CA 94704. Stephan Bodian, Ed. Articles, 1,200 to 3,000 words, on holistic health, spirituality, yoga, and transpersonal psychology; "new age" profiles; interviews. Pays $75 to $200, on publication.

OP-ED MARKETS

Op-ed pages in newspapers (those that run opposite the editorials) offer writers an excellent opportunity to air their opinions, views, ideas, and insights on a wide spectrum of subjects and in styles, from the highly personal and informal essay to the more serious commentary on politics, foreign affairs, and news events. Humor and nostalgia often find a place here.

THE ANCHORAGE DAILY NEWS—Pouch 6616, Anchorage, AK 99502. Seeks articles, 800 to 900 words, that "balance the national and international orientation of the editorial page," on natural resources, local issues, humor, seasonal topics, oil, etc. Preference for local writers. Pays $50, on publication. Submit manuscript with SAS postcard.

THE ATLANTA CONSTITUTION—P.O. Box 4689, Atlanta, GA 30302. Patricia Carr, Op-Ed Ed. Articles related to the Southeast, Georgia or the Atlanta metropolitan area, 200 to 800 words, on a variety of topics: law, economics, politics, science, environment, performing and manipulative arts, humor, education; religious and seasonal topics. Pays $50 to $150, on publication.

THE BALTIMORE SUN—501 N. Calvert St., Baltimore, MD 21278. Harold Piper, Op-Ed Ed. Articles, 750 to 1,000 words, for Opinion Commentary page, on a wide range of topics: politics, education, foreign affairs, life styles, etc. Humor. Pays $75 to $125, on publication.

BOSTON HERALD—One Herald Sq., Boston, MA 02106. Shelly Cohen, Editorial Page Ed. Pieces, 600 to 800 words, on human-interest, political, regional, life style, and seasonal topics. Pays $50 to $75, on publication. Prefer submissions from regional writers.

THE CHICAGO TRIBUNE—435 N. Michigan Ave., Chicago, IL 60611. Richard Liefer, Op-Ed Ed. Pieces, 500 to 800 words, on politics, government, economics, education, environment, foreign and domestic affairs. Writers must have experience in their fields. Pays $100 to $250, on publication.

THE CHRISTIAN SCIENCE MONITOR—One Norway St., Boston, MA 02115. Cynthia Hanson, Op. Page Coord. Pieces, 600 to 700 words, for "Opinion and Commentary" page, on politics, domestic and foreign affairs. Humor. Payment varies. Query preferred.

THE CHRONICLE—901 Mission St., San Francisco, CA 94103. Ms. Lyle York, "This World" Ed. Articles, 1,500 to 2,500 words, on a wide range of subjects. Pays $75 to $150, on publication. SASE required.

THE CLEVELAND PLAIN DEALER—1801 Superior Ave., Cleveland, OH 44114. Dennis R. Ryerson, Ed. Dir. Pieces, 800 to 1,000 words, on politics, economics, foreign affairs, and regional issues. Pays $50 to $100, on publication.

DALLAS MORNING NEWS—Communications Center, Dallas, TX 75265. Carolyn Darta, "Viewpoints" Ed. Pieces, 750 words (1,000 words for Sunday issue), on politics, education, foreign and domestic affairs, seasonal and regional issues. Pays $75 to $100, on publication. SASE required.

DES MOINES REGISTER—Box 957, Des Moines, IA 50304. James Flansburg, "Opinion" Page Ed. Articles, 600 to 800 words, on all topics. Humor. Pays $25 to $250, on publication.

THE DETROIT FREE PRESS—321 W. Lafayette St., Detroit, MI 48231. Address Op-Ed Editor. Articles, 750 to 800 words, on topics of local interest, and opinion pieces. Pays varying rates, on publication.

THE DETROIT NEWS—615 Lafayette Blvd., Detroit, MI 48231. Richard Burr, Ed. Pieces, 500 to 900 words, on science, economics, foreign and domestic affairs, education, environment, regional topics, religion and politics. Humor. Priority to local writers and local issues. Pays varying rates, on publication.

THE LOS ANGELES HERALD EXAMINER—Box 2416, Terminal Annex, Los Angeles, CA 90051–0416. Editorial Page Ed. Articles, to 800 words, on local topics not covered by syndicated columnists. Humor. Pays $50, on publication.

LOS ANGELES TIMES—Times Mirror Sq., Los Angeles, CA 90053. Janice Jones, Op. Ed. Ed. Commentary pieces, to 800 words, on many subjects. Pays $150 to $250, on publication. SASE required.

LOUISVILLE COURIER-JOURNAL—525 W. Broadway, Louisville, KY 40202. Keith L. Runyon, Op-Ed. Ed. Pieces, 400 to 800 words, on politics, economics, regional topics, life styles, law, education, environment, humor, nostalgia, foreign and domestic affairs, poetry and seasonal topics. Pays varying rates, on publication.

THE MIAMI HERALD—One Herald Plaza, Miami, FL 33132–1693. Joanna Wragg, Op-Ed. Ed. Informed opinion pieces, to 800 words, on all subjects. Pays $35 to $50, on publication. SASE required.

MILWAUKEE JOURNAL—Box 661, Milwaukee, WI 53201. James P. Cattey, Op-Ed Ed. Occasional pieces, 600 to 700 words, on various subjects. Pays $30 to $35, on publication.

THE NEW YORK TIMES—229 W. 43rd St., New York, NY 10036. Leslie H. Gelb, Op-Ed Ed. Pieces, 750 words, on topics including public policy, science, lifestyles, and ideas. Pays $150, on publication.

NEWSDAY—Long Island, NY 11747. James Lynn, "Viewpoints" Ed. Pieces, 600 to 1,500 words, on foreign and domestic affairs, politics, economics, life styles, law, education, and the environment. Seasonal pieces. Prefer policy experts and local writers. Pays $100 to $300, on publication.

THE OAKLAND TRIBUNE—Box 24424, Oakland, CA 94623. Jonathan Marshall, Editorial Page Ed. Articles, 800 words, on a wide range of topics; no humor or life style materials. Pays $20 to $35, on publication.

THE ORANGE COUNTY REGISTER—P.O. Box 11626, Santa Ana, CA 92711. K.E. Grubbs, Jr., Ed. Articles on a wide range of local and national issues and topics. Pays $50 to $100, on publication.

PITTSBURGH POST GAZETTE—50 Blvd. of the Allies, Pittsburgh, PA 15222. Joe Plummer, Assoc. Ed. Articles, to 800 words, on politics, law, economics, life style, religion, foreign and domestic affairs. Pays varying rates, on publication. SASE required.

THE REGISTER GUARD—P.O. Box 10188, Eugene, OR 97440. Don Robinson, Editorial Page Ed. All subjects; regional angle preferred. Pays $10 to $25, on publication. Local writers preferred; limited free-lance market.

THE SACRAMENTO BEE—21st and Q, P.O. Box 15779, Sacramento, CA 95852. Peter Schrag, Editorial Page Ed. Op-ed pieces, to 750 words; topics of regional interest preferred. Pays $100 to $200, on publication. Query.

ST. LOUIS POST-DISPATCH—900 N. Tucker Blvd., St. Louis, MO 63101. Articles on economics, education, science, politics, foreign and domestic affairs, and the environment. Pays $50, on publication.

ST. PAUL PIONEER PRESS DISPATCH—345 Cedar St., St. Paul, MN 55101. Robert J.R. Johnson, Ed. Uses occasional pieces, to 750 words, on topics related to Minnesota and western Wisconsin. Pays $50, on publication. Query first.

ST. PETERSBURG TIMES—Box 1121, 490 First Ave. S., St. Petersburg, FL 33731. Jack Reed, "Perspective" Section Ed. Authoritative articles, to 2,000 words, on current political, economic, and social issues. Payment varies, on publication. Query first.

SEATTLE POST-INTELLIGENCER—101 Elliott Ave. W., Seattle, WA 98119. Charles J. Dunsire, Editorial Page Ed. Current events articles, 800 to 1,000 words, with Pacific Northwest themes. Pays $75 to $100, on publication.

THE WALL STREET JOURNAL—World Financial Center, 200 Liberty St., New York, NY 10281. Tim Ferguson, Editorial Features Ed. Articles, 850 to 1,100 words, on politics, economics, life styles, law, education, environment, humor, nostalgia, science, foreign and domestic affairs, religion, human-interest, and seasonal topics. Submit manuscript with SASE.

ADULT MAGAZINES

CAVALIER—2355 Salzedo St., Coral Gables, FL 33134. Nye Willden, Man. Ed. Articles with photos, and fiction, 1,500 to 3,000 words, for sophisticated young men. Pays to $400 for articles, to $250 for fiction, on publication. Query for articles.

CHIC—9171 Wilshire Blvd., Ste. 300, Beverly Hills, CA 90210. Doug Oliver, Exec. Ed. Articles, interviews, erotic fiction, 2,500 to 4,500 words. Pays $750 for articles, $500 for fiction, on acceptance.

FORUM, THE INTERNATIONAL JOURNAL OF HUMAN RELATIONS—1965 Broadway, New York, NY 10023–5965. John Heidenry, Ed. Articles, 2,500 words; especially interested in true, first-person sexual adventures. Pays $800, on acceptance. Query.

GALLERY—800 Second Ave., New York, NY 10017. Marc Lichter, Ed.-in-Chief. Articles, investigative pieces, interviews, profiles, to 3,500 words, for sophisticated men. Short humor, satire, service pieces. Photos. Pays varying rates, half on acceptance, half on publication. Query.

GEM—G&S Publications, 1472 Broadway, New York, NY 10036. Will Martin, Ed. Sex-related (not pornographic) articles and fiction, 500 to 2,500 words. Humor, satire, and spoofs of sexual subjects. Pays $50 to $100, after acceptance. All submissions must be accompanied by SASE.

GENESIS—22 West 27th St., 8th Fl., New York, NY 10001. J.J. Kelleher, Ed.-in-Chief. Articles, 2,500 words; celebrity interviews, 2,500 words. Sexually-explicit nonfiction features, 3,000 words. Photo essays. Pays 60 days after acceptance. Query.

HARVEY FOR LOVING PEOPLE—Suite 2305, 450 Seventh Ave., New York, NY 10001. Harvey Shapiro, Ed./Pub. Sexually-oriented articles and fiction, to 2,500 words. Pays to $200, on publication. Query for articles.

HUSTLER—2029 Century Park E., Suite 3800, Los Angeles, CA 90067. Tim Conaway, Exec. Ed. Investigative articles and profiles, 4,500 words. Pays from $1,500, on acceptance. Query.

PENTHOUSE—1965 Broadway, New York, NY 10023. Peter Bloch, Exec. Ed. General-interest or investigative articles, to 5,000 words. Interviews, 5,000 words, with introductions. Pays to 50¢ a word, on acceptance.

PLAYBOY—919 N. Michigan Ave., Chicago, IL 60611. John Rezek, Articles Ed. Alice K. Turner, Fiction Ed. Articles, 3,500 to 6,000 words, and sophisticated fiction, 1,000 to 8,000 words (6,000 preferred), for urban men. Humor; satire. Science fiction. Pays to $5,000 for articles, to $2,000 for fiction ($1,000 for short-shorts), on acceptance.

PLAYERS—8060 Melrose Ave., Los Angeles, CA 90046. H.L. Sorrell, Ed. Articles, 1,000 to 3,000 words, for black men: travel, fashion, grooming, entertainment, sports, interviews, fiction, humor, satire, health, and sex. Photos a plus. Pays on publication.

PLAYGIRL—801 Second Ave., New York, NY 10017. Nancie S. Martin, Ed. Articles, 2,000 to 2,500 words, for women age 18 to 34. Celebrity interviews, 1,500 to 2,000 words. Humor. Cartoons. Pays varying rates, on acceptance.

FICTION MARKETS

This list gives the fiction requirements of general- and special-interest magazines, including those that publish detective and mystery, science fiction and fantasy, romance and confession stories. Other good markets for short fiction are the *College, Literary and Little Magazines* where, though payment is modest (usually in copies only), publication can help a beginning writer achieve recognition by editors at the larger magazines. Juvenile fiction markets are listed under *Juvenile, Teenage, and Young Adult Magazines*. Publishers of book-length fiction manuscripts are listed under *Book Publishers*.

All manuscripts must be typed double-space and submitted with self-addressed envelopes bearing postage sufficient for the return of the material. Use good white paper; onion skin and erasable bond are not acceptable. *Always* keep a copy of the manuscript, since occasionally a manuscript is lost in the mail. Magazines may take several weeks (often longer) to read and report on submissions. If an editor has not reported on a manuscript after a reasonable amount of time, write a brief, courteous letter of inquiry.

ABORIGINAL SCIENCE FICTION—P.O. Box 2449, Woburn, MA 01888–0849. Charles C. Ryan, Ed. Stories, 2,500 to 4,500 words, with a unique scientific idea, human or alien character, plot, and theme of lasting value; "must be science fiction, no fantasy, horror, or sword and sorcery." Pays $250. Guidelines.

AIM MAGAZINE—P.O. Box 20554, Chicago, IL 60620. Ruth Apilado, Ed. Short stories, 800 to 1,000 words, geared to promoting racial harmony and peace. Pays from $15 to $25, on publication. Annual contest.

ALFRED HITCHCOCK'S MYSTERY MAGAZINE—380 Lexington Ave., New York, NY 10017. Cathleen Jordan, Ed. Well-plotted, plausible mystery, suspense, detection and crime stories, 1,000 to 14,000 words; "ghost stories, humor, private eye, atmospheric tales are all possible, as long as they include a crime." Pays 5¢ a word, on acceptance.

ALOHA, THE MAGAZINE OF HAWAII—828 Fort Street Mall, Honolulu, HI 96813. Cheryl Tsutsumi, Ed. Fiction, to 4,000 words, on Hawaii and its ethnic groups. Pays 10¢ a word, on publication. Query.

AMAZING STORIES—Box 110, Lake Geneva, WI 53147. Patrick L. Price, Ed. Science fiction and fantasy, to 25,000 words. Pays 6¢ to 8¢ a word, on acceptance.

ANALOG: SCIENCE FICTION/SCIENCE FACT—380 Lexington Ave., New York, NY 10017. Stanley Schmidt, Ed. Science fiction, with strong characters in believable future or alien setting: short stories, 2,000 to 7,500 words; novelettes, 10,000 to 20,000 words; serials, to 70,000 words. Pays 5¢ to 8¢ a word, on acceptance. Query for novels.

ARKANSAS TIMES—Box 34010, Little Rock, AR 72203. Mel White, Ed. Fiction, to 6,000 words: must have an Arkansas slant. Pays from $250, on acceptance.

THE ATLANTIC—8 Arlington St., Boston, MA 02116. William Whitworth, Ed. Short stories, 2,000 to 6,000 words, of highest literary quality, with "fully developed narratives, distinctive characterization, freshness in language, and a resolution of some kind." Pays $2,500, on acceptance.

THE ATLANTIC ADVOCATE—P.O. Box 3370, Fredericton, N.B., Canada E3B 5A2. H.P. Wood, Ed. Fiction, 1,000 to 1,500 words, with regional angle. Pays to 10¢ a word, on publication.

THE ATLANTIC SALMON JOURNAL—1435 St. Alexandre, Suite 1030, Montreal, Quebec, Canada H3A 2G4. Terry Davis, Ed. Fiction, 1,500 to 2,500 words, related to the conservation of Atlantic salmon. Pays $100 to $400, on publication.

THE BOSTON GLOBE MAGAZINE— *The Boston Globe*, Boston, MA 02107. Ande Zellman, Ed. Short stories, to 3,000 words. Include SASE. Pays on publication.

BOYS' LIFE—1325 Walnut Hill Ln., P.O. Box 152079, Irving, TX 75015–2079. W. E. Butterworth IV, Fiction Ed. Publication of the Boy Scouts of America. Humor, mystery, SF, adventure, 750 to 2,500 words, for 8- to 18-year-old boys; study back issues. Pays from $750, on acceptance.

BUFFALO SPREE MAGAZINE—Box 38, Buffalo, NY 14226. Johanna V. Shotell, Ed. Fiction and humor, to 1,800 words, for readers in the western New York region. Pays $75 to $100, on publication.

CAMPUS LIFE—465 Gundersen Dr., Carol Stream, IL 60188. James Long, Sr. Ed. Fiction and humor reflecting Christian values (no overtly religious material), 1,000 to 4,000 words, for high school and college students. Pays from $150 to $400, on acceptance. Limited free-lance market. Queries only; SASE.

CAPPER'S—616 Jefferson Ave., Topeka, KS 66607. Nancy Peavler, Ed.

Novel-length family-oriented or romance stories: no short stories. Pays $150 to $200. Submit complete manuscript.

CAT FANCY—P.O. Box 6050, Mission Viejo, CA 92690. Linda W. Lewis, Ed. Fiction, to 3,000 words, about cats. Pays 5¢ a word, on publication.

CATHOLIC FORESTER—425 W. Shuman Blvd., Naperville, IL 60566. Barbara A. Cunningham, Ed. Official publication of the Catholic Order of Foresters. Fiction, to 3,000 words (prefer shorter); "looking for more contemporary, meaningful stories dealing with life today." No sex or violence or "preachy" stories; religious angle not essential. Pays from 5¢ a word, on acceptance.

CAVALIER—2355 Salzedo St., Coral Gables, FL 33134. Maurice DeWalt, Fiction Ed. Sexually oriented fiction, to 3,000 words, for sophisticated young men. Pays to $300, on publication.

CHESAPEAKE BAY MAGAZINE—1819 Bay Ridge Ave., Annapolis, MD 21403. Betty Rigoli, Ed. Short stories, to 15 pages; must be related to Chesapeake Bay area. Pays $85 to $125, on publication.

CLINTON STREET QUARTERLY—P.O. Box 3588, Portland, OR 97208. David Milholland, Ed. Short stories, 2 to 20 pages: "First-person accounts, thought-provoking, non-rhetorical essays and idea pieces." Pays varying rates, on publication.

COBBLESTONE—20 Grove St., Peterborough, NH 03458. Carolyn P. Yoder, Ed. Fiction related to monthly theme, 500 to 1,200 words, for children aged 8 to 14 years. Pays 10¢ to 15¢ a word, on publication. Send SASE for editorial guidelines.

COMMENTARY—165 E. 56th St., New York, NY 10022. Marion Magid, Ed. Fiction, of high literary quality, on contemporary social or Jewish issues. Pays on publication.

THE COMPASS—Mobil International Aviation and Marine Sales, Inc., 150 E. 42nd St., New York, NY 10017. J. A. Randall, Ed. Short stories, to 2,500 words, on the sea, sea trades, and aviation. Pays to $500, on acceptance. Query.

CORVETTE FEVER—Box 44620, Ft. Washington, MD 20744. Pat Stivers, Ed. Corvette-related fiction, about 300 lines. Pays 10¢ a word, on publication.

COSMOPOLITAN—224 W. 57th St., New York, NY 10019. Betty Kelly, Fiction and Books Ed. Short shorts, 1,500 to 3,000 words, and short stories, 4,000 to 6,000 words, focusing on contemporary man-woman relationships. Solid, upbeat plots, sharp characterization; female protagonists preferred. Pays $300 to $600 for short shorts, from $1,000 for short stories. Payment negotiable.

COUNTRY WOMAN—P.O. Box 643, Milwaukee, WI 53201. Kathy Pohl, Man. Ed. Fiction, 750 to 1,000 words, of interest to rural women; protagonist must be a country woman. "Stories should focus on life in the country, its problems and joys, as experienced by country women; must be upbeat and positive." Pays $90 to $125, on acceptance.

CRICKET—Box 300, Peru, IL 61354. Marianne Carus, Ed.-in-Chief. Fiction, 200 to 1,500 words, for 6- to 12-year-olds. Pays to 25¢ a word, on publication. Return postage required.

DISCOVERIES—6401 The Paseo, Kansas City, MO 64131. Address Middler Ed. Fiction, 600 to 800 words, for children grades 3 to 6, defining Christian experiences and values. Pays 3 ½¢ a word, on acceptance.

643

DOG FANCY—P.O. Box 6050, Mission Viejo, CA 92690. Linda W. Lewis, Ed. Fiction, to 2,500 words: dog must be central element of the story; no "talking dog" stories. Pays 5¢ a word, on publication.

EASYRIDERS MAGAZINE—P. O. Box 3000, Agoura Hills, CA 91301–0800. Lou Kimzey, Ed. Fiction, 3,000 to 5,000 words. Pays from 10¢ a word, on acceptance.

ELLERY QUEEN'S MYSTERY MAGAZINE—380 Lexington Ave., New York, NY 10017. Eleanor Sullivan, Ed. High-quality detective, crime, and mystery stories, 4,000 to 6,000 words; "we like a mix of classic detection and suspenseful crime." 'First Stories" by unpublished writers. Pays 3¢ to 8¢ a word, on acceptance.

ENTERTAINER MAGAZINE—9420 Towne Sq. Ave., Suite 15, Cincinnati, OH 45242. John Tymoski, Ed. General comedy, 750 words. Pays $15 and copies, on publication.

ESQUIRE—1790 Broadway, New York, NY 10019. Lee Eisenberg, Ed.-in-Chief. "We do not accept unsolicited manuscripts."

ESSENCE—1500 Broadway, New York, NY 10036. Susan L. Taylor, Ed.-in-Chief. Fiction, 800 to 2,500 words, for largely black, female readership, ages 18 to 49; "uplifting stories of triumph that reflect a slice of life." Pays $500 to $1,300, on acceptance.

FAMILY CIRCLE—110 Fifth Ave., New York, NY 10011. Kathy Sagan, Travel & Fiction Ed. Limited market: seeks quality short stories that reflect real-life situations. No unsolicited manuscripts.

FAMILY MAGAZINE—P.O. Box 4993, Walnut Creek, CA 94596. Address Editors. Short stories, to 2,000 words, of interest to high school-educated military wives between 20 and 35. Pays from $100 to $300, on publication.

FICTION INTERNATIONAL—English Dept., San Diego State Univ., San Diego, CA 92182. Harold Jaffe and Larry McCaffery, Eds. Post-modernist and politically committed fiction and theory. Submit between Sept. and Jan. 15th.

GALLERY—401 Park Ave. S., New York, NY 10152. Marc Lichter, Ed. Dir. Fiction, to 4,000 words, for sophisticated men. Pays varying rates, half on acceptance, half on publication.

GENTLEMEN'S QUARTERLY—350 Madison Ave., New York, NY 10017. Tom Jenks, Literary Ed. Fiction, to 3,000 words. Pays on acceptance. No unsolicited manuscripts.

GOLF DIGEST—5520 Park Ave., Trumbull, CT 06611. Jerry Tarde, Ed. Unusual or humorous stories, to 2,000 words, about golf; golf "fables," to 1,000 words. Pays 50¢ a word, on acceptance.

GOOD HOUSEKEEPING—959 Eighth Ave., New York, NY 10019. Naome Lewis, Fiction Ed. Short stories, 1,000 to 3,000 words, with strong identification figures for women, by published writers and "beginners with demonstrable talent." Novel condensations or excerpts. Pays top rates, on acceptance.

GUN DOG—1901 Bell Ave., Des Moines, IA 50315. Bob Wilbanks, Man. Ed. Occasional fiction, humor related to gun dogs and bird hunting. Pays $100 to $350, on acceptance.

HARPER'S MAGAZINE—666 Broadway, New York, NY 10012. General fiction, 2,000 to 5,000 words. No unsolicited poetry. Address Man. Ed.

HICALL—1445 Boonville Ave., Springfield, MO 65802. Sinda Zinn, Ed. Fiction, to 1,800 words, for 15- to 19-year-olds. Strong evangelical emphasis a must:

believable characters working out their problems according to biblical principles. Pays 3¢ a word for first rights, on acceptance.

HIGHLIGHTS FOR CHILDREN—803 Church St., Honesdale, PA 18431. Kent L. Brown Jr., Ed. Fiction on sports, humor, adventure, mystery, etc., 900 words, for 9- to 12-year-olds. Easy rebus form, 200 to 250 words, and easy-to-read stories, to 600 words, for beginning readers. "We are partial to stories in which the protagonist solves a dilemma through his own resources, rather than through luck or magic." Pays on acceptance. Buys all rights.

HOMETOWN PRESS—2007 Gallatin St., Huntsville, AL 35801. Rusty Bynum, Ed.-in-Chief. Fiction, 800 to 2,500 words, well-crafted and tightly written, suitable for family reading. New and unpublished writers welcome. Pays 12¢ a word, on acceptance. SASE for guidelines.

ISAAC ASIMOV'S SCIENCE FICTION MAGAZINE—380 Lexington Ave., New York, NY 10017. Gardner Dozios, Ed. Short science fiction and fantasies, to 15,000 words. Pays 6¢ to 8¢ a word, on acceptance.

LADIES' HOME JOURNAL—100 Park Ave., New York, NY 10017. Fiction with strong identification for women. Short stories and full-length manuscripts accepted through agents only.

LIVE—1445 Boonville Ave., Springfield, MO 65802. John T. Maempa, Adult Ed. Fiction, 1,100 to 2,000 words, on applying Bible principles to everyday living; include Social Security number. Send SASE for guidelines. Pays 2¢ to 3¢ a word, on acceptance.

LOLLIPOPS—Good Apple, Inc., P. O. Box 299, Carthage, IL 62321–0299. Jerry Aten, Ed. Teaching ideas and activities covering all areas of the curriculum for preschool to second-grade children. Rates vary.

THE LOOKOUT—8121 Hamilton Ave., Cincinnati, OH 45231. Mark Taylor, Fiction Ed. Inspirational short-shorts, 1,000 to 1,800 words. Pays to 5¢ a word, on acceptance.

MCCALL'S—230 Park Ave., New York, NY 10169. Helen Delmonte, Fiction Ed. Short stories, to 2,500 words; short-shorts, 1,000 words: contemporary themes with strong identification for intelligent women. Family stories, love stories, humor, suspense; must have strong plots. Pays from $2,000 for stories, $1,500 for short-shorts, on acceptance.

MADEMOISELLE—350 Madison Ave., New York, NY 10017. Eileen Schnurr, Fiction Ed. Short stories, 1,500 to 5,000 words, of interest to young single women. Looking for strong voices, fresh insights, generally classic form; no genre fiction. Male point-of-view about personal relationships welcome. Pays $1,000 for short shorts, to $2,000 for stories, on acceptance.

THE MAGAZINE OF FANTASY AND SCIENCE FICTION—Box 56, Cornwall, CT 06753. Edward Ferman, Ed. Fantasy and science fiction stories, to 10,000 words. Pays 5¢ to 7¢ a word, on acceptance.

MATURE LIVING—127 Ninth Ave. N., Nashville, TN 37234. Jack Gulledge, Ed. Judy Pregel, Asst. Ed. Fiction, 900 to 1,475 words, for senior adults. Must be consistent with Christian principles. Pays 5¢ a word, on acceptance.

MEMPHIS—460 Tennessee St., P.O. Box 256, Memphis, TN 38101. Ed Weathers, Manuscripts Ed. Traditional stories, 3,000 to 5,000 words; preference given to fiction set within 300 miles of Memphis, and Memphis writers ("but we're flexible").

MICHIGAN, THE MAGAZINE OF THE DETROIT NEWS—615 W. Lafayette Blvd., Detroit, MI 48231. Beaufort Cranford, Ed. Fiction with a Michigan slant, to 3,000 words. Pays $200 to $500, on publication.

MIDSTREAM—515 Park Ave., New York, NY 10022. Murray Zuckoff, Ed. Fiction on Jewish themes, to 3,000 words. Pays 5¢a word, after publication.

MILITARY LIFESTYLE MAGAZINE—1732 Wisconsin Ave. N.W., Washington, DC 20007. Hope Daniels, Ed. Fiction, to 2,000 words, for military families in the U.S. and overseas. Pays from $200 to $350, on publication.

MS.—1 Times Square, New York, NY 10036. No unsolicited fiction.

NA'AMAT WOMAN—200 Madison Ave., 18th fl., New York, NY 10016. Judith A. Sokoloff, Ed. Short stories, approx. 2,500 words, with Jewish theme. Pays 8¢ a word, on publication.

NATIONAL RACQUETBALL—400 Douglas Ave., Suite B, Dunedin, FL 34698. Helen Quinn, Pub./Man. Ed. Fiction, related to racquetball. Pays $1.65 per column inch, $50 per printed page, on publication.

NETWORK WORLD—Box 9171, Framingham, MA 01701. John Gallant, Ed. Computer related stories, 1,000 to 2,000 words. Payment varies, on publication.

THE NEW YORKER—25 W. 43rd St., New York, NY 10036. Pat Strachan, Fiction Ed. Short stories, humor, and satire. Pays varying rates, on acceptance. Include SASE.

NORTHEAST MAGAZINE— *The Hartford Courant,* 285 Broad St., Hartford, CT 06115. Lary Bloom, Ed. Short stories, to 4,000 words; must have Connecticut tie-in, or be universal in theme and have non-specific setting. Pays $300 to $600, on acceptance.

OMNI—1965 Broadway, New York, NY 10023–5965. Ellen Datlow, Fiction Ed. Strong, realistic science fiction, to 12,000 words. Some contemporary hard-edged fantasy. Pays to $2,000, on acceptance.

OUR FAMILY—Box 249, Battleford, Sask., Canada S0M 0E0. N. Gregoire, O.M.I., Ed. Fiction, 1,000 to 3,000 words, on the struggle to live the Christian life in the face of modern-day problems. Pays 7¢ to 10¢ a word, on acceptance. Write for guidelines. Enclose international postal reply coupons with SAE.

PENTHOUSE—1965 Broadway, New York, NY 10023. No unsolicited manuscripts.

PLAYBOY—919 N. Michigan Ave., Chicago, IL 60611. Alice K. Turner, Fiction Ed. Quality fiction, 1,000 to 10,000 words (average 6,000): suspense, mystery, adventure and sports short stories; stories about contemporary relationships; science fiction. Active plots, masterful pacing, and strong characterization. Pays from $1,000 to $3,000, on acceptance.

PLAYGIRL—801 Second Ave., New York, NY 10017. Mary Ellen Strote, Fiction Ed. Contemporary, romantic fiction, 1,000 to 4,000 words. Pays from $500, after acceptance.

PLOUGHSHARES—Box 529, Cambridge, MA 02139. Address Fiction or Poetry Ed. Serious fiction, to 7,000 words. Poetry. Pays $10 to $50, on publication.

PRIME TIMES—2802 International Ln., Suite 210, Madison, WI 53704. Joan Donovan, Exec. Ed. Circulates to approx. 300,000 mid-life readers. Excellent fiction, to 4,000 words, shorter lengths preferred; general themes. Pays varying rates, on publication. Query first.

PULPSMITH—5 Beekman St., New York, NY 10038. Harry Smith, General Ed. Tom Tolnay, Man. Ed. Nancy Hallinan, Fiction Ed. Literary genre fiction; mainstream, mystery, SF, westerns, and fantasy. Short lyric poems, sonnets, ballads. Essays and articles. Pays $35 to $100 for fiction, $20 to $35 for poetry, on acceptance. Annual; submit from Oct. 15 to May 15 only. SASE.

PURPOSE—616 Walnut Ave., Scottdale, PA 15683–1999. James E. Horsch, Ed. Fiction, 1,200 words, on problem solving from a Christian point of view. Poetry, 3 to 12 lines. Pays up to 5¢ a word, to $1 per line for poetry, on acceptance.

RANGER RICK MAGAZINE—8925 Leesburg Pike, Vienna, VA 22184–0001. Betty Blair, Fiction Ed. Nature- and conservation-related fiction, for 7- to 12-year-olds. Maximum: 900 words. Pays to $550, on acceptance. Buys all rights.

REDBOOK—224 W. 57th St., New York, NY 10019. Deborah Purcell, Fiction Ed. Fresh, distinctive short stories, of interest to women, about love and relationships, friendship, careers, parenting, family dilemmas, confronting basic problems of contemporary life and women's issues. Pays $850 for short-shorts (up to 9 manuscript pages), from $1,000 for short stories (to 20 pages). Allow 8 to 10 weeks for reply. Manuscripts without SASE will not be returned. No unsolicited novellas or novels accepted.

ROAD KING—P.O. Box 250, Park Forest, IL 60466. George Friend, Ed. Short stories, 1,200 to 1,500 words, for and/or about truck drivers. Pays to $400, on acceptance.

ROD SERLING'S THE TWILIGHT ZONE MAGAZINE—401 Park Ave. S., 3rd fl., New York, NY 10016–8802. Tappan King, Ed.-in-Chief. Fiction, to 7,500 words: human-centered fantasies, horror, and science fiction involving "ordinary people in extraordinary events." Avoid genre clichés. Pays 6¢ to 10¢ a word, half on acceptance, half on publication.

ST. ANTHONY MESSENGER—1615 Republic St., Cincinnati, OH 45210. Norman Perry, Ed. Fiction that makes readers think about issues, lifestyles and values. Pays 14¢ a word, on acceptance. Query first.

THE SATURDAY EVENING POST—1100 Waterway Blvd., Indianapolis, IN 46202. Glenn Carter, Fiction Ed. Upbeat short stories, 500 to 4,000 words, that lend themselves to illustration. Humor. Rarely publishes unsolicited fiction. SASE required for reply.

SCHOLASTIC SCOPE—Scholastic, Inc., 730 Broadway, New York, NY 10003. Fran Claro, Ed. Fiction for 15- to 18-year-olds, with 4th to 6th grade reading ability. Short stories, 500 to 1,000 words, on teen-age interests and relationships; family, job and school situations. Pays good rates, on acceptance.

SEA KAYAKER—1670 Duranleau St., Vancouver, B. C., Canada V6H 3S4. John Dowd, Ed. Short stories exclusively related to ocean kayaking, 1,500 words. Pays on publication. Include international reply coupons and SAE.

SEVENTEEN—850 Third Ave., New York, NY 10022. Sara London, Fiction Ed. High-quality, literary short fiction focusing on the teenage experience. Pays on acceptance.

SPORTS AFIELD—250 W. 55th St., New York, NY 10019. Tom Paugh, Ed. Fiction on hunting, fishing, and related topics. Outdoor adventure stories. Humor. Pays top rates, on acceptance.

STRAIGHT—8121 Hamilton Ave., Cincinnati, OH 45231. Carla Crane, Ed. Well-constructed fiction, 1,000 to 1,500 words, showing Christian teens using Bible principles in everyday life. Contemporary, realistic teen characters a must. Most interested in school, church, dating, and family life stories. Pays about 3¢ a word, on acceptance. Send SASE for guidelines.

SUNDAY DIGEST—850 N. Grove Ave., Elgin, IL 60120. Janette L. Pearson, Ed. Short stories, 1,000 to 1,500 words, with evangelical religious slant. Pays 10¢ a word, on acceptance. Query.

SUNSHINE MAGAZINE—Sunshine Press, Litchfield, IL 62056. Peggy Kuethe, Ed. Wholesome fiction, 900 to 1,200 words; short stories for youths, 400 to 700 words. Pays to $100, on acceptance. Guidelines.

SWANK—888 Seventh Ave., New York, NY 10106. Bob Rosen, Fiction Ed. Graphic erotic short stories, to 2,500 words. Study recent issue before submitting material. Pays on publication. Limited market.

'TEEN—8490 Sunset Blvd., Los Angeles, CA 90069. Address Fiction Dept. Short stories, 2,500 to 4,000 words: mystery, travel, adventure, romance, humor for teens. Pays from $100, on acceptance.

TEENS TODAY—Nazarene Publishing House, 6401 The Paseo, Kansas City, MO 64131. Karen De Sollar, Ed. Short stories, 1,200 to 1,500 words, that deal with teens demonstrating Christian principles in real-life situations; adventure stories. Pays 3 ½¢ a word, on acceptance.

TQ/TEEN QUEST—Box 82808, Lincoln, NE 68501. Barbara Comito, Man. Ed. Fiction, to 2,000 words, for Christian teens. Pays 4¢ to 10¢ a word, on acceptance.

VANITY FAIR—350 Madison Ave., New York, NY 10017. Address Fiction Ed. Fiction of high literary quality. Very limited market.

VIRTUE—P.O. Box 850, Sisters, OR 97759. Becky Durost Fish, Ed. Fiction with a Christian slant. Pays 10¢ a word, on publication.

WESTERN PEOPLE—Box 2500, Saskatoon, Sask., Canada S7K 2C4. Short stories, 1,000 to 2,500 words, on subjects or themes of interest to rural readers in Western Canada. Pays $40 to $150, on acceptance. Enclose international reply coupons and SAE.

WILDFOWL—1901 Bell Ave., Suite #4, Des Moines, IA 50315. B. Wilbanks, Man. Ed. Occasional fiction, humor, related to duck hunters and wildfowl. Pays $200 to $350, on acceptance.

WOMAN'S DAY—1515 Broadway, New York, NY 10036. Eileen Herbert Jordan, Fiction Ed. Short fiction, humorous or serious, geared to women. Pays top rates, on acceptance.

WOMAN'S WORLD—P.O. Box 6700, Englewood, NJ 07631. Mary McHugh, Fiction Ed. Fast-moving short stories, about 4,500 words, with light romantic theme. Mini-mysteries, 1,600 to 1,700 words, with "whodunit" or "how-dunit" theme. No science fiction, fantasy, or historical romance. Pays $1,000 for short stories, $500 for mini-mysteries, on acceptance. Submit manuscript with SASE.

WOODMEN OF THE WORLD MAGAZINE—1700 Farnam St., Omaha, NE 68102. Leland A. Larson, Ed. Family-oriented fiction. Pays 5¢ a word, on acceptance.

YANKEE—Yankee Publishing Co., Dublin, NH 03444. Judson Hale, Ed. Edie Clark, Fiction Ed. High-quality, literary short fiction, to 4,000 words, with setting

in or compatible with New England. "No sap buckets or lobster pot stereotypes."
Pays $1,000, on acceptance.

DETECTIVE AND MYSTERY

ALFRED HITCHCOCK'S MYSTERY MAGAZINE—380 Lexington Ave.,
New York, NY 10017. Cathleen Jordan, Ed. Well-plotted mystery, detective, suspense and crime fiction, 1,000 to 14,000 words. Submissions by new writers strongly
encouraged. Pays 5¢ a word, on acceptance.

ARMCHAIR DETECTIVE—129 W. 56th St., New York, NY 10019. Michael
Seidman, Ed. Articles on mystery and detective fiction; biographical sketches, reviews, etc. Pays $10 a printed page, except for reviews.

ELLERY QUEEN'S MYSTERY MAGAZINE—380 Lexington Ave., New
York, NY 10017. Eleanor Sullivan, Ed. Detective, crime, and mystery fiction,
approximately 4,000 to 6,000 words. No sex, sadism, or sensationalism. Particularly
interested in new writers and "first stories." Pays 3¢ to 8¢ a word, on acceptance.

FRONT PAGE DETECTIVE—See *Inside Detective.*

INSIDE DETECTIVE—Reese Communications, Inc., 460 W. 34th St., New
York, NY 10001. Rose Mandelsberg, Ed. Timely, true detective stories, 5,000 to
6,000 words, or 10,000 words. No fiction. Pays $250 to $500, extra for photos, on
acceptance. Query. Same address and requirements for *Front Page Detective.*

MASTER DETECTIVE—460 W. 34th St., New York, NY 10001. Art Crockett, Ed. Detailed articles, 5,000 to 6,000 words, with photos, on current cases,
emphasizing human motivation and detective work. Pays to $250, on acceptance.
Query.

OFFICIAL DETECTIVE STORIES—460 W. 34th St., New York, NY
10001. Art Crockett, Ed. True detective stories, 5,000 to 6,000 words, on current
investigations, strictly from the investigator's point of view. No fiction. Photos. Pays
$250, extra for photos, on acceptance. Query.

TRUE DETECTIVE—460 W. 34th St., New York, NY 10001. Art Crockett,
Ed. Articles, from 5,000 words, with photos, on current police cases, emphasizing
detective work and human motivation. No fiction. Pays $250, extra for photos, on
acceptance. Query.

SCIENCE FICTION AND FANTASY

ABORIGINAL SF—P.O. Box 2449, Woburn, MA 01888–0849. Charles C.
Ryan, Ed. Short stories, 2,500 to 4,500 words, and poetry, 1 to 2 typed pages, with
strong science content, lively, unique characters, and well-designed plots. No sword
and sorcery or fantasy. Pays $250 for fiction, $20 to $25 for poetry, $4 for SF jokes,
and $15 for cartoons, on publication.

AMAZING STORIES—Box 110, Lake Geneva, WI 53147. Patrick L. Price,
Ed. Science fiction and fantasy, to 15,000 words. Also general-interest science
articles; query first on nonfiction. Pays 6¢ to 8¢ a word, on acceptance.

ANALOG SCIENCE FICTION/SCIENCE FACT—380 Lexington Ave.,
New York, NY 10017. Stanley Schmidt, Ed. Science fiction, with strong characters
in believable future or alien setting: short stories, 2,000 to 7,500 words; novelettes,
10,000 to 20,000 words; serials, to 80,000 words. Also uses future-related articles.
Pays to 7¢ a word, on acceptance. Query on serials and articles.

THE ASYMPTOTICAL WORLD—P.O. Box 1372, Williamsport, PA 17703.

Michael H. Gerardi, Ed. Psychodramas, fantasy, experimental fiction, 1,500 to 2,500 words. Illustrations, photographs. Pays 2¢ a word, on acceptance.

BEYOND: SCIENCE FICTION & FANTASY—P.O. Box 1124, Fair Lawn, NJ 07410. Roberta Rogow, Ed. Science fiction and fantasy: original, exciting, thought-provoking fiction (3,000 to 5,000 words) and poems (10 to 20 lines). Pays ¼¢ a word, on publication.

DIFFERENT WORLDS—2814–29th St., San Francisco, CA 94110. Tadashi Ehara, Ed. Articles, to 5,000 words, on role-playing games: reviews, variants, source materials, etc. Pays 1¢ a word, on publication. Query preferred.

DRAGON MAGAZINE—P.O. Box 110, Lake Geneva, WI 53147. Roger E. Moore, Ed.-in-Chief; Patrick L. Price, Fiction Ed. Articles, 1,500 to 10,000 words, on fantasy and SF role-playing games. Fiction, 1,500 to 8,000 words. Pays 6¢ to 8¢ a word for fiction, slightly lower for articles, on publication. Query.

EMPIRE/WAYSTATION FOR THE SF WRITER—1025 55th St., Oakland, CA 94608. Millea Kenin, Ed. Articles, 2,000 words preferred, on the craft of writing science fiction and fantasy. Cartoons, illustrations, poetry. Pays negotiable rates, on publication. Query. Send 45¢ SASE for guidelines.

FANTASY MACABRE—P.O. Box 20610, Seattle, WA 98120. Jessica Salmonson, Ed. Fiction, to 3,000 words, including translations. "We look for a tale that is strong in atmosphere, with menace that is suggested and threatening rather than the result of dripping blood and gore." Pays 1¢ a word, to $30 per story, on publication.

FOOTSTEPS—Box 75, Round Top, NY 12473. Bill Munster, Ed. Material related to horror, supernatural, or the weird tale: essays, reviews, profiles, fiction, to 3,500 words. Poetry to 40 lines. Pays 1¢ a word.

GRUE MAGAZINE—Box 370, Times Square Sta., New York, NY 10108. Peggy Nadramia, Ed. Fiction, 3,500 words, and macabre/surreal poetry of any length. "We seek very visceral, original horror stories with an emphasis on characterization and motivation." Pays ½¢ per word for fiction, $5 per poem, on publication.

HAUNTS—Nightshade Publications, Box 3342, Providence, RI 02906. Joseph K. Cherkes, Ed. Horror, science/fantasy, and supernatural short stories with strong characters, 1,500 to 8,000 words. No explicit sexual scenes or gratuitous violence. Pays ¼¢ to ⅓¢ a word, on publication. Submit June 1 to Dec. 1.

THE HORROR SHOW—Phantasm Press, 14848 Misty Springs Lane, Oak Run, CA 96069. David B. Silva, Ed. Contemporary horror fiction, to 4,000 words, "with a style that keeps the reader's hand trembling as he turns the pages." Pays ½¢ to 1¢ per word, on acceptance. Send SASE for guidelines.

ISAAC ASIMOV'S SCIENCE FICTION MAGAZINE—380 Lexington Ave., New York, NY 10017. Gardner Dozois, Ed. Short, character-oriented science fiction and fantasy, to 15,000 words. Pays 5¢ to 8¢ a word, on acceptance. Send SASE for requirements.

THE MAGAZINE OF FANTASY AND SCIENCE FICTION—Box 56, Cornwall, CT 06753. Edward Ferman, Ed. Fantasy and science fiction stories, to 10,000 words. Pays 5¢ to 7¢ a word, on acceptance.

MAGICAL BLEND—Box 11303, San Francisco, CA 94101. Silma Smith, Literary Ed. Positive, uplifting articles on spiritual exploration, lifestyles, occult, white magic and fantasy. Fiction and features to 5,000 words. Poetry, 4 to 40 lines. Pays in copies.

NEW BLOOD—540 W. Foothill Blvd., Suite 3730, Glendora, CA 91740. Chris Lacher, Ed. Fiction and poetry considered "too strong" for other periodicals. Interviews and reviews. Pays from 1¢ a word, on acceptance.

OMNI—1965 Broadway, New York, NY 10023–1965. Ellen Datlow, Ed. Strong, realistic science fiction, 2,000 to 10,000 words, with real people as characters. Some fantasy. No horror, ghost or sword and sorcery tales. Pays $1,250 to $2,000, on acceptance.

OWLFLIGHT—1025 55th St., Oakland, CA 94608. Millea Kenin, Ed. Science fiction and fantasy, 3,000 to 8,000 words. Science fiction/fantasy poetry, 8 to 100 lines. Photos, illustrations. Pays 1¢ a word, extra for illustrations, on publication. Send 45¢ SASE for guidelines.

PORTENTS—12 Fir Pl., Hazlet, NJ 07730. Deborah Rasmussen, Ed. Fiction, to 3,000 words: contemporary horror, dark fantasy, exceptional gothic, and supernatural horror. No werewolves, vampires, ghouls, religion, or sex. Pays ¼¢ a word, on publication.

SCIENCE FICTION CHRONICLE—P.O. Box 2730, Brooklyn, NY 11202. Andrew Porter, Ed. News items, 200 to 1,000 words, for SF and fantasy readers, professionals, and booksellers. Photos and short articles on authors' signing, events, conventions. Pays 3¢ to 5¢ a word, on publication.

ROD SERLING'S TWILIGHT ZONE MAGAZINE—800 Second Ave., New York, NY 10017. Tappan King, Ed.-in-Chief. Fiction, to 7,500 words: human-centered stories of horror, science fiction, suspense, and the supernatural involving "ordinary people in extraordinary events." Pays 7¢ to 10¢ a word, half on acceptance, half on publication. Reply time: 2 to 6 months. Simultaneous submissions accepted.

SPACE AND TIME—138 W. 70th St., #4B, New York, NY 10023. Fantasy fiction, to 12,000 words; science fiction, supernatural, sword and sorcery. Pays ½¢ a word, on acceptance.

THRUST: SCIENCE FICTION & FANTASY REVIEW—8217 Langport Terrace, Gaithersburg, MD 20877. D. Douglas Fratz, Ed. Articles, interviews, 2,000 to 6,000 words, for readers familiar with SF and related literary and scientific topics. Book reviews, 100 to 800 words. Pays 1¢ to 2¢ a word, on publication. Query preferred.

TWISTED—6331 N. Lakewood Ave., Chicago, IL 60660. Christine Hoard, Ed. Fiction and articles (to 5,000 words); poetry (to 1 page). "No sword and sorcery, or hard science fiction. We prefer horror and dark fantasy." Pays in copies.

2AM—P.O. Box 6754, Rockford, IL 61125–1754. Gretta M. Anderson, Ed. Fiction, of varying lengths. "We prefer dark fantasy/horror; great science fiction and sword and sorcery stories are welcome." Profiles and intelligent commentaries. Poetry, any length. Pays from ½¢ a word, on acceptance. Guidelines.

CONFESSION AND ROMANCE

INTIMACY—355 Lexington Ave., New York, NY 10017. Natasha Brooks, Ed. Fiction, 2,000 to 3,000 words, for women age 18 to 45; must have contemporary, glamorous plot and contain two romantic and intimate love scenes. Pays $75 to $100, on publication. Same address for *Jive,* geared toward younger women seeking adventure, glamour, and romance.

JIVE—See *Intimacy.*

MODERN ROMANCES—215 Lexington Ave., New York, NY 10016. Colleen Brennan, Ed. Confession stories with reader-identification and strong emotional tone, 1,500 to 7,500 words. Articles for blue-collar, family-oriented women, 300 to 1,500 words. Pays 5¢ a word, after publication. Buys all rights.

TRUE CONFESSIONS—215 Lexington Ave., New York, NY 10016. Helen Vincent, Ed. Timely, emotional, first-person stories, 2,000 to 10,000 words, on romance, family life, and problems of today's young blue-collar women. Pays 5¢ a word, after publication.

TRUE EXPERIENCE—215 Lexington Ave., New York, NY 10016. H.M. Atkocius, Ed. Realistic first-person stories, 4,000 to 8,000 words (short shorts, to 2,000 words), on family life, single life, love, romance, overcoming hardships, health, religion, etc. Short romantic and seasonal poetry. Pays 3¢ a word, after publication.

TRUE LOVE—215 Lexington Ave., New York, NY 10016. Jean Sharbel, Ed. Fresh, true first-person stories, on young love, marital problems, and topics of current interest. Pays 3¢ a word, a month after publication.

TRUE ROMANCE—215 Lexington Ave., New York, NY 10016. Patricia Byrdsong, Ed. True, romantic first-person stories, 2,000 to 12,000 words. Love poems. Articles, 300 to 700 words, for young wives and singles. Pays 3¢ a word, a month after publication.

POETRY MARKETS

The following list of magazines includes markets for both serious and light verse. Although major magazines pay good rates for poetry, the competition to break into print is very stiff, since editors use only a limited number of poems in each issue. On the other hand, college, little, and literary magazines use a great deal of poetry, and though payment is modest (usually in copies) publication in these journals can establish a beginning poet's reputation, and can lead to publication in the major magazines. Poets will also find a number of competitions offering cash awards for unpublished poems in the *Literary Prize Offers* list.

Poets should also consider local newspapers as possible verse markets. Although they may not specifically seek poetry from free lancers, newspaper editors often print verse submitted to them, especially on holidays and for special occasions.

The market for book-length collections of poetry at commercial publishers is extremely limited. There are a number of university presses that publish poetry collections, however (see *University Presses*), and many of them sponsor annual competitions. Consult the *Literary Prize Offers* list for more information.

ALCOHOLISM & ADDICTION MAGAZINE—P.O. Box 31329, Seattle, WA 31329. Jennifer Merrill, Poetry Ed. Verse on recovery from chemical or other addictions.

ALOHA—828 Fort St. Mall, Suite 640,, Honolulu, HI 96813. Cheryl Chee Tsutsumi, Ed. Poetry relating to Hawaii. Pays $25 per poem, on publication.

AMAZING STORIES—Box 110, Lake Geneva, WI 53147. Patrick Lucien

Price, Ed. Serious and light verse, with SF/fantasy tie-in. Pays $1 per line for short poems, somewhat less for longer ones, on acceptance.

AMERICA—106 W. 56th St., New York, NY 10019. Patrick Samway, S.J., Literary Ed. Serious poetry, preferably in contemporary prose idiom 10 to 25 lines. Occasional light verse. Submit 2 or 3 poems at a time. Pays $1.40 per line, on publication. Guidelines.

THE AMERICAN SCHOLAR—1811 Q St. N.W., Washington, DC 20009. Joseph Epstein, Ed. Highly original poetry, 10 to 32 lines, for college-educated, intellectual readers. Pays $50, on acceptance.

THE AMICUS JOURNAL—Natural Resources Defense Council, 122 E. 42nd St., New York, NY 10168. Peter Borrelli, Ed. Poetry related to national and international environmental policy. Pays on acceptance.

THE ATLANTIC—8 Arlington St., Boston, MA 02116. Peter Davison, Poetry Ed. Previously unpublished poetry of highest quality. Limited market; only 3 to 4 poems an issue. Interest in young poets. Occasionally uses light verse. Pays excellent rates, on acceptance.

CAPE COD LIFE—P.O. Box 222, Osterville, MA 02655. Mary Short-sleeve, Ed. Poetry, all kinds, with special interest in coastal themes. Pays after publication.

CAPPER'S—616 Jefferson St., Topeka, KS 66607. Nancy Peavler, Ed. Traditional poetry and free verse, 4 to 16 lines. Submit up to 6 poems at a time, with SASE. Pays $3 to $6, on acceptance.

CHILDREN'S PLAYMATE—P.O. Box 567, Indianapolis, IN 46206. Elizabeth A. Rinck, Ed. Poetry for children, 5 to 7 years old, on good health, nutrition, exercise, safety, seasonal and humorous subjects. Pays from $10, on publication. Buys all rights.

THE CHRISTIAN SCIENCE MONITOR—One Norway St., Boston, MA 02115. Davis Holmstrom, Ed., The Home Forum. Fresh, vigorous nonreligious poems of high quality, on various subjects. Short poems preferred. Pays varying rates, on acceptance. Submit no more than 3 poems at a time.

CLASS—27 Union Sq. West, New York, NY 10003. Jennifer Charles, Ed. Poetry, 8 to 10 lines, related to the Third World population in the U.S. Pays varying rates, after publication.

COBBLESTONE—20 Grove St., Peterborough, NH 03458. Carolyn P. Yoder, Ed. Poetry, to 100 lines, on monthly themes, for 8- to 14-year-olds. Pays varying rates, on publication. Send SASE for guidelines and themes.

COMMONWEAL—15 Dutch St., New York, NY 10038. Rosemary Deen, Ed. Catholic. Serious, witty poetry. Pays 50¢ a line, on publication.

COMPLETE WOMAN—1165 N. Clark St., Chicago, IL 60610. Address Assoc. Ed. Poetry. Pays $10, on publication. SASE necessary for return of material.

COSMOPOLITAN—224 W. 57th St., New York, NY 10019. Karen Burke, Poetry Ed. Poetry about relationships and other topics of interest to young, active women. Pays from $25, on acceptance.

COUNTRY WOMAN—P.O. Box 643, Milwaukee, WI 53201. Kathy Pohl, Man. Ed. Traditional rural poetry and light verse, 10 to 20 lines, on rural experiences and country living. Pays $35 to $40, on acceptance.

DECISION—Billy Graham Evangelistic Assn., 1300 Harmon Pl., Minneapolis, MN 55403. Roger C. Palms, Ed. Poems, 5 to 20 lines, on Christian themes; preference for free verse. Pays on publication.

THE DISCIPLE—Box 179, St. Louis, MO 63166. Journal of Disciples of Christ. Poetry, on religious, seasonal, and historical subjects. Pays $7.50, on publication.

EVANGEL—Dept. of Christian Education Free Methodist Hdqtrs., 901 College Ave., Winona Lake, IN 46590. Vera Bethel, Ed. Free Methodist. Devotional or nature poetry, 8 to 16 lines. Pays $5, on publication.

THE EVANGELICAL BEACON—1515 E. 66th St., Minneapolis, MN 55423. George Keck, Ed. Denominational publication of Evangelical Free Church of America. Some poetry related to Christian faith. Pays 4¢ a word, $2.50 minimum, on publication.

FAMILY CIRCLE—110 Fifth Ave., New York, NY 10011. No unsolicited poetry.

FARM AND RANCH LIVING—5400 S. 60th St., Greendale, WI 53129. Bob Ottum, Ed. Poetry, to 20 lines, on rural people and situations. Photos. Pays $35 to $75, extra for photos, on acceptance and on publication. Query.

GOLF DIGEST—5520 Park Ave., Trumbull, CT 06611–0395. Lois Hains, Asst. Ed. Humorous golf-related verse, 4 to 8 lines. Pays $20 to $25, on acceptance. Send SASE.

GOOD HOUSEKEEPING—959 Eighth Ave., New York, NY 10019. Rosemary Leonard, Ed. Light, humorous verses, quips, and poems. Pays $25 for four lines, $50 for eight lines, on acceptance.

LADIES' HOME JOURNAL—100 Park Ave., New York, NY 10017. No unsolicited poetry; submit through agent only.

LEATHERNECK—Box 1775, Quantico, VA 22134. W.V. H. White, Ed. Publication related to the U.S. Marine Corps. Marine-related poetry. Pays from $10, on acceptance. SASE required.

MARRIAGE & FAMILY (FORMERLY *MARRIAGE & FAMILY LIV-ING*)—Abbey Press Publishing Div., St. Meinrad, IN 47577. Kass Dotterweich, Man. Ed. Verse on marriage and family. Pays $15, on publication.

MATURE YEARS—201 Eighth Ave. S. , Nashville, TN 37202. John P. Gilbert, Ed. United Methodist. Poetry, to 14 lines, on pre-retirement, retirement, seasonal subjects, aging. No saccharine poetry. Pays 50¢ to $1 per line.

MCCALL'S MAGAZINE—230 Park Ave., New York, NY 10169. Overstocked.

MIDSTREAM—515 Park Ave., New York, NY 10022. Murray Zuckoff, Ed. Poetry of Jewish interest. Pays $25, on publication.

THE MIRACULOUS MEDAL—475 E. Chelten Ave., Philadelphia, PA 19144. Robert P. Cawley, C.M., Ed. Catholic. Religious verse, to 20 lines. Pays 50¢ a line, on acceptance.

MODERN BRIDE—One Park Ave., New York, NY 10016. Mary Ann Cavlin, Man. Ed. Short verse of interest to bride and groom. Pays $25 to $35, on acceptance.

MODERN MATURITY—3200 E. Carson St., Lakewood, CA 90712. Ian Ledgerwood, Ed. Short verse to 40 lines. Pays from $50, on acceptance.

THE NATION—72 Fifth Ave., New York, NY 10011. Grace Schulman, Poetry Ed. Poetry of high quality. Pays after publication.

NATIONAL ENQUIRER—Lantana, FL 33464. Jim Allan, Asst. Ed. Amusing or philosophical short poems. Submit seasonal/holiday material at least 2 months in advance. Pays from $20, after publication.

NEW ENGLAND ENTERTAINMENT DIGEST—P.O. Box 735, Marshfield, MA 02050. Paul J. Reale, Ed. Light verse, of any length, related to the entertainment field. Pays $3, on publication.

THE NEW REPUBLIC—1220 19th St. N.W., Washington, DC 20036. Richard Howard, Poetry Ed. Poetry for liberal, intellectual readers. Pays $75, after publication.

THE NEW YORKER—25 W. 43rd St., New York, NY 10036. First-rate poetry and light verse. Pays top rates, on acceptance. Include SASE.

PENTECOSTAL EVANGEL—1445 Boonville, Springfield, MO 65802. Richard G. Champion, Ed. Journal of Assemblies of God. Religious and inspirational verse, 12 to 30 lines. Pays to 40¢ a line, on publication.

PURPOSE—616 Walnut Ave., Scottdale, PA 15683–1999. James E. Horsch, Poetry Ed. Poetry, to 8 lines, with challenging Christian discipleship angle. Pays 50¢ to $1 a line, on acceptance.

ST. JOSEPH'S MESSENGER—P.O. Box 288, Jersey City, NJ 07303. Sister Ursula Marie Maphet, Ed. Light verse and traditional poetry, 4 to 40 lines. Pays $5 to $15, on publication.

THE SATURDAY EVENING POST—1100 Waterway Blvd., Indianapolis, IN 46202. Address Post Scripts Ed. Light verse and humor. Pays $15, on publication.

SCORE, CANADA'S GOLF MAGAZINE—287 MacPherson Ave., Toronto, Ontario, Canada M4V 1A4. Poetry, to 50 words, on the Canadian and U.S. golf scene. Pays to $20, on publication.

SEVENTEEN—850 Third Ave., New York, NY 10022. Poetry, to 40 lines, by teens. Submit up to 5 poems. Pays $15, after acceptance.

UNITED METHODIST REPORTER—P.O. Box 660275, Dallas, TX 75266–0275. Spurgeon M. Dunnam III, Ed. Religious verse, 4 to 16 lines. Pays $2, on acceptance.

WESTERN PEOPLE—P.O. Box 2500, Saskatoon, Sask., Canada S7K 2C4. Mary Gilchrist, Man. Ed. Short poetry, with Western Canadian themes. Pays on acceptance. Send International Reply Coupons.

POETRY SERIES

The following university presses publish book-length collections of poetry by writers who have never had a book of poems published. Each has specific rules for submission, so before submitting any material, be sure to write well ahead of the deadline dates for further information. Some organizations sponsor competitions in which prizes are offered for book-length collections of poetry; see *Literary Prize Offers.*

THE ALABAMA PRESS POETRY SERIES—Dept of English, Drawer A1, Univ. of Alabama, University, AL 35486. Address Thomas Rabbitt or Dara Wier. Considers unpublished book-length collections of poetry for publication as part of the Alabama Press Poetry Series. Submissions accepted during the months of September, October, and November only.

UNIVERSITY OF GEORGIA PRESS POETRY SERIES—Athens, GA 30602. Poets who have never had a book of poems published may submit book-length poetry manuscripts for possible publication. Open during the month of September each year. Manuscripts from poets who have published at least one volume of poetry (chapbooks excluded) are considered during the month of January.

WESLEYAN UNIVERSITY PRESS—110 Mt. Vernon St. Middletown, CT 06457. Considers unpublished book-length poetry manuscripts by poets who have never had a book published, for publication in the Wesleyan New Poets Series. There is no deadline. Submit manuscript and $15.00 reading fee.

GREETING CARD MARKETS

Greeting card companies often have their own specific requirements for submitting ideas, verse, and artwork. The National Association of Greeting Card Publishers, however, gives the following general guidelines for submitting material: Each verse or message should be typed, double-space, on a 3 × 5 or 4 × 6 card. Use only one side of the card, and be sure to put your name and address in the upper left-hand corner. Keep a copy of every verse or idea you send. (It's also advisable to keep a record of what you've submitted to each publisher.) Always enclose an SASE, and do not send out more than ten verses or ideas in a group to any one publisher.

The Greeting Card Association brings out a booklet for free lancers, *Artists and Writers Market List,* with the names, addresses, and editorial guidelines of greeting card companies. Send a self-addressed stamped envelope and $5.00 to The Greeting Card Association, 1350 New York Ave., NW, Suite 615, Washington, DC 20005.

AMBERLEY GREETING CARD COMPANY—11510 Goldcoast Dr., Cincinnati, OH 45249–1695. Ned Stern, Ed. Humorous ideas for birthday, illness, friendship, congratulations, "miss you," etc. Risqué and non-risqué humor. Pays $40. Buys all rights.

AMERICAN GREETINGS—10500 American Rd., Cleveland, OH 44144. Robert A. Lanning, Writing Mgr. Contemporary, humorous, and studio cards. Study current offerings and query before submitting.

BLUE MOUNTAIN ARTS, INC.—P.O. Box 1007, Boulder, CO 80306. Attn: Editorial Staff, Dept. TW. Poetry and prose about love, friendship, family, philosophies, etc. Also material for special occasions and holidays: birthdays, get well, Christmas, Valentine's Day, Easter, etc. No artwork or rhymed verse. Pays $200 per poem published on a notecard.

FRAVESSI-LAMONT, INC.—11 Edison Pl., Springfield, NJ 07081. Address Editor. Short verse, mostly humorous or sentimental; cards with witty prose. No Christmas material. Pays varying rates, on acceptance.

FREEDOM GREETING CARD COMPANY—P.O. Box 715, Briston, PA 19007. Submit to Jay Levitt. Verse, traditional, humorous, and love messages. Inspirational poetry for all occasions. Pays $1 a line, on acceptance. Query with SASE.

GALLANT GREETINGS CORPORATION—2654 West Medill, Chicago, IL 60647. Ideas for humorous and serious greeting cards. Pays $35 per idea, in 45 days.

HALLMARK CARDS, INC.—2501 McGee, Box 419580, Mail Drop 276, Kansas City, MO 64141. Query Carol King; no samples. Humor for everyday and seasonal greeting cards. Mostly staff-written; "freelancers must show high degree of skill and originality." Guidelines with SASE.

THE MAINE LINE COMPANY—P.O. Box 418, Rockport, ME 04856. Attn: Perri Ardman. Untraditional humorous cards. Send SASE with three first-class stamps for guidelines. Pays $50 per card.

OATMEAL STUDIOS—Box 138 TW, Rochester, VT 05767. Dawn Abraham, Ed. Humorous, clever, and new ideas needed for all occasions. Query with SASE or send samples.

OUTREACH PUBLICATIONS—P.O. Box 1010, Siloam Springs, AR 72761. Address Creative Ed. Christian greeting cards for most occasions. Pays varying rates, on acceptance.

RED FARM STUDIOS—P.O. Box 347, 334 Pleasant St., Pawtucket, RI 02862. Traditional cards, for graduations, weddings, birthdays, get-wells, anniversaries, friendship, new baby, sympathy, Christmas, and Valentines. No studio humor. Pays varying rates. SASE required.

VAGABOND CREATIONS, INC.—2560 Lance Dr., Dayton, OH 45409. George F. Stanley, Jr., Ed. Greeting cards with graphics only on cover (no copy) and short tie-in copy punch line on inside page: birthday, everyday, Valentine, Christmas, and graduation. Mildly risqué humor with double entendre acceptable. Ideas for humorous buttons and illustrated theme stationery. Pays $15, on acceptance.

WARNER PRESS PUBLISHERS—1200 E. Fifth St., Anderson, IN 46012. Cindy M. Grant, Product Ed. Sensitive prose and inspirational verse card ideas; religious themes. Submit everyday ideas in Jan. and Feb.; Christmas material in April and May. Pays $15 to $30, on acceptance. Guidelines with SASE.

WILLIAMHOUSE-REGENCY, INC.—28 W. 23rd St., New York, NY 10010. Query Nancy Boecker. Captions for wedding invitations. Payment varies, on acceptance. SASE required.

COLLEGE, LITERARY AND LITTLE MAGAZINES

FICTION, NONFICTION, POETRY

The thousands of literary journals, little magazines, and college quarterlies published today welcome work from novices and pros alike; editors are always interested in seeing traditional and experimental fiction, poetry, essays, reviews, short articles, criticism, and satire, and as long as the material is well-written, the fact that a writer is a beginner doesn't adversely affect his chances for acceptance.

Most of these smaller publications have small budgets and staffs, so they may be slow in their reporting time; several months is not unusual. In addition, they usually pay only in copies of the issue in which published work appears and some, particularly college magazines, do not read manuscripts during the summer.

Publication in the literary journals can, however, lead to recognition by editors of large-circulation magazines, who read the little magazines in their search for new talent. There is also the possibility of having one's work chosen for reprinting in one of the prestigious annual collections of work from the little magazines.

Because the requirements of these journals differ widely, it is always important to study recent issues before submitting work to one of them. Copies of magazines may be in large libraries, or a writer may send a postcard to the editor and ask the price of a sample copy. When submitting a manuscript, always enclose a self-addressed envelope, with sufficient postage for its return.

For a complete list of literary and college publications and little magazines, writers may consult such reference works as *The International Directory of Little Magazines and Small Presses,* published annually by Dustbooks (P.O. Box 100, Paradise, CA 95969).

THE AGNI REVIEW—Boston University, Creative Writing Program, 236 Bay State Rd., Boston, MA 02215. Askold Melnyozuk, Ed. Short stories and poetry. Pays in copies.

ALASKA QUARTERLY REVIEW—Dept. of English, Univ. of Alaska, 3211 Providence Dr., Anchorage, AK 99508. Address Eds. Short stories, novel excerpts, poetry (traditional and unconventional forms). Submit manuscripts between August 15 and May 15. Pays in copies.

ALBANY REVIEW—4 Central Ave., Albany, NY 12210. Short fiction (1,750 to 3,500 words), essays, interviews, and articles with a local focus (750 to 1,000 words); poetry and satire. Pays in copies.

ALBATROSS—4014 SW 21st Rd., Gainesville, FL 32607. Richard Smyth, Richard Brobst, Eds. High-quality poetry: especially interested in ecological and nature poetry written in narrative form. Interviews with well-known poets. Submit 3 to 5 poems at a time with brief bio. Pays in copies.

AMELIA—329 E St., Bakersfield, CA 93304. Poetry, to 100 lines; critical essays, to 2,000 words; reviews, to 500 words; belles lettres, to 1,000 words; fiction, to 3,500 words; fine pen and ink sketches; photos. Pays $35 for fiction and criticism, $10 to $25 for other nonfiction and artwork, $2 to $25 for poetry. Annual contest.

THE AMERICAN BOOK REVIEW—Publications Center, Univ. of Colorado, English Dept., Box 226, Boulder, CO 80309. Don Laing, Man. Ed. John Tytell, Ronald Sukenick, Eds. Book reviews, 700 to 1,200 words. Pays $50 honorarium and copies. Query first.

THE AMERICAN POETRY REVIEW—1616 Walnut St., Rm. 405, Philadelphia, PA 19103. Address Eds. Highest quality contemporary poetry. Responds in 8 weeks. SASE a must.

AMERICAN QUARTERLY—National Museum of American History, Smithsonian Institution, Washington, DC 20560. Gary Kulik, Ed. Scholarly essays, 5,000 to 10,000 words, on any aspect of U.S. culture. Pays in copies.

THE AMERICAN SCHOLAR—1811 Q St. N.W., Washington, DC 20009. Joseph Epstein, Ed. Articles, 3,500 to 4,000 words, on science, politics, literature, the arts, etc. Book reviews. Pays $450 for articles, $100 for reviews, on publication.

THE AMERICAN SCHOLAR—1811 Q St. N.W., Washington, DC 20009. Joseph Epstein, Ed. Non-technical articles and essays, 3,500 to 4,000 words, on current affairs, the American cultural scene, politics, arts, religion and science. Pays $450, on acceptance.

THE AMERICAN VOICE—Heyburn Bldg., Suite 1215, Broadway at 4th Ave., Louisville, KY 40202. Frederick Smock, Ed. Short stories and essays, to 10,000 words; free verse. "Looking for vigorously original work by new and established writers." Pays $400 for prose, $150 for poetry, on publication.

AMHERST REVIEW—Box 486, Sta. 2, Amherst, MA 01002. Elizabeth Bradburn, Ed. Fiction, to 8,000 words, and poetry, to 160 lines. Photos, paintings, and drawings. Pays in copies. Submit material September through March only.

ANOTHER CHICAGO MAGAZINE—Box 11223, Chicago, IL 60611. Fiction, essays on literature, and poetry. Pays $5 to $25, on acceptance.

ANTAEUS—26 W. 17th St., New York, NY 10011. Daniel Halpern, Ed. Short stories, essays, documents, parts-of-novels, poems. Pays on publication.

ANTIETAM REVIEW—Room 215, 33 W. Washington St., Hagerstown, MD 21740. Ann Knox, Ed.-in-Chief. Fiction, to 5,000 words; poetry. Submissions from regional artists only (MD, PA, WV, VA, DC), from Oct. through Feb. Pays from $25 to $100. annual Literary Award for fiction.

THE ANTIGONISH REVIEW—St. Francis Xavier Univ., Antigonish, N.S., Canada. George Sanderson, Ed. Poetry; short stories, essays, book reviews, 1,800 to 2,500 words. Pays in copies.

ANTIOCH REVIEW—P.O. Box 148, Yellow Springs, OH 45387. Robert S. Fogarty, Ed. Timely articles, 2,000 to 8,000 words, on social sciences, literature, and humanities. Quality fiction. Poetry. No inspirational poetry. Pays $10 per printed page, on publication.

THE ARCHER—Pro Poets, 2285 Rogers Ln. N.W., Salem, OR 97304. Winifred Layton, Ed. Contemporary poetry, to 30 lines. Pays in copies.

THE ATAVIST—P.O. Box 5643, Berkeley, CA 94705. Robert Dorsett, Loretta Ko, Eds. Poetry and poetry criticism, any length. Translations of original poetry. Pays in copies.

AURA LITERARY/ARTS REVIEW—P.O. Box 76, Univ. Center, UAB, Birmingham, AL 35294. Randy Blythe, Ed. Fiction and essays on literature, to 6,000 words; poetry; photos and drawings. Pays in copies.

BACKBONE—P.O. Box 95315, Seattle, WA 98145. Mildred Jesse, Ed. Essays, fiction, and poetry that "inspire poetic, feminist, and political dialogue." Send to 8 poems, 2 stories or essays, at a time. Pays in copies.

BALL STATE UNIVERSITY FORUM—Ball State Univ., Muncie, IN 47306. Bruce W. Hozeski, Ed.-in-Chief. Creative and imaginative fiction and poetry; scholarly articles of general interest. Pays in copies.

BELLES LETTRES—Box 987, Arlington, VA 22216. Janet Mullaney, Ed. Reviews and essays, 250 to 2,000 words, on literature by women. Literary puzzles. Query required. Pays in copies.

BELLOWING ARK—P.O. Box 45637, Seattle, WA 98145. Robert Ward, Ed. Poetry and fiction, varying lengths, that explore the processes of conflict and affirmation in a human context. B&W photos; line drawings. Pays in copies.

BELOIT POETRY JOURNAL—RFD 2, Box 154, Ellsworth, ME 04605.

First-rate contemporary poetry, of any length or mode. Pays in copies. Send SASE for guidelines.

BITTERROOT—P.O. Box 489, Spring Glen, NY 12483. Menke Katz, Ed.-in-Chief. Poetry, to 50 lines; B&W camera-ready drawings. Pays in copies. Annual contests. Send SASE for information.

BLACK MULLET REVIEW—P.O. Box 22814, Tampa, FL 33622. Gina Bergamino-Frey, Ed. High-quality short fiction and poetry (to 3 pages). Pays in copies.

BLACK RIVER REVIEW—855 Mildred Ave., Lorain, OH 44052. Kaye Coller, Ed. Poetry; short book reviews; essays; B&W artwork. Pays in copies. Contests. Guidelines.

THE BLACK WARRIOR REVIEW—P.O. Box 2936, Tuscaloosa, AL 35487. Amber Vogel, Ed. Fiction; poetry with intention; reviews and essays. Pays per printed page. Annual awards.

THE BLOOMSBURY REVIEW—1028 Bannock St., Denver, CO 80204. Tom Auer, Ed.; Ray Gonzalez, Poetry Ed. Book reviews, publishing features, interviews, essays, poetry, up to 800 words. Pays $5 to $25, on publication.

BLUELINE—English Dept., SUNY, Potsdam, NY 13676. Anthony Tyler, Ed. Essays, fiction, to 2,500 words, on Adirondack region or similar areas. Poetry, to 44 lines. No more than 5 poems per submission. Pays in copies.

BOSTON REVIEW—33 Harrison Ave., Boston, MA 02111. Margaret Ann Roth, Ed.-in-Chief. Reviews and essays, 800 to 3,000 words, on literature, art, music, film, photography. Original fiction, to 5,000 words. Poetry. Pays $40 to $150.

BOULEVARD—4 Washington Square Village, 9R, New York, NY 10012. David Brezovec and Richard Burgin, Eds. High-quality fiction and articles, to 30 pages; poetry. Published three times a year. Pays to $100, on publication.

BUCKNELL REVIEW—Bucknell Univ., Lewisburg, PA 17837. Interdisciplinary journal in book form. Scholarly articles on arts, science, and letters. Pays in copies.

CAESURA—English Dept., Auburn Univ., Auburn, AL 36849. R. T. Smith, Man. Ed. Short stories, to 3,000 words; narrative and lyric poetry, to 150 lines. Pays in copies.

CALLALOO—Dept. of English, Univ. of Virginia, Charlottesville, VA 22903. Charles H. Rowell, Ed. Fiction and poetry by, and critical studies on, Afro-American and African artists and writers. Payment varies, on publication.

CALLIOPE—Creative Writing Program, Roger Williams College, Bristol, RI 02809. Martha Christina, Ed. Short stories, to 2,500 words; poetry. Pays in copies. No submissions April through July.

CALYX, A JOURNAL OF ART & LITERATURE BY WOMEN—P.O. Box B, Corvallis, OR 97339. M. Donnelly, Man. Ed. Fiction, 5,000 words, reviews, 1,000 words; poetry, to 6 poems. Pays in copies. Include short bio and SASE. Send for guidelines.

CANADIAN FICTION MAGAZINE—Box 946, Sta. F, Toronto, Ontario, Canada M4Y 2N9. High-quality short stories, novel excerpts, and experimental fiction, to 5,000 words, by Canadians. Interviews with Canadian authors; translations. Pays $10 per page, on publication. Annual prize.

THE CAPILANO REVIEW—Capilano College, 2055 Purcell Way, North

Vancouver, B.C., Canada V7J 3H5. Dorothy Jantzen, Ed. Fiction; poetry; drama; visual arts. Pays $12 to $50.

CAROLINA QUARTERLY—Greenlaw Hall 066A, Univ. of North Carolina, Chapel Hill, NC 27514. Robert Rubin, Ed. Fiction, to 7,000 words, by new or established writers. Poetry (no restrictions on length, though limited space makes inclusion of works of more than 300 lines impractical). Pays $3 per printed page for fiction, $5 per poem, on acceptance.

THE CENTENNIAL REVIEW—110 Morrill Hall, Michigan State Univ., East Lansing, MI 48824–1036. Linda Wagner, Ed. Articles, 3,000 to 5,000 words, on sciences, humanities, and interdisciplinary topics. Poetry; reviews. Pays in copies.

THE CHARITON REVIEW—Northeast Missouri State Univ., Kirksville, MO 63501. Jim Barnes, Ed. Highest quality poetry and fiction, to 6,000 words. Modern and contemporary translations. Book reviews. Pays $5 per printed page for fiction and translations.

THE CHICAGO REVIEW—Univ. of Chicago, Faculty Exchange Box C, Chicago, IL 60637. Elizabeth Arnold, Jenny Mueller, Eds. Essays; interviews; reviews; fiction; translations; poetry. Pays in copies.

CHIMERA CONNECTIONS—3712 NW 16th Blvd., Gainesville, FL 32605. Jeff VanderMeer, Duane Bray, Eds. Fiction (to 8,000 words), essays, interviews, articles (to 3,000 words), poetry and humor. Pays $20 for interviews, in copies for fiction and poetry.

CICADA—329 "E" St., Bakersfield, CA 93304. Single haiku, sequences or garlands, essays about the forms, haibun and fiction related to haiku or Japan. Pays in copies.

CIMARRON REVIEW—205 Morrill Hall, Oklahoma State Univ., Stillwater, OK 74078–0135. Deborah Bransford, Man. Ed. Poetry, fiction, essays, graphics/artwork. Seeks an individual, innovative style that focuses on contemporary themes. Pays in copies.

CINCINNATI POETRY REVIEW—Dept. of English, 069, Cincinnati, OH 45221. Dallas Wiebe, Ed. Poetry of all types. Pays in copies.

COLORADO REVIEW—English Dept., 322 Eddy, Colorado State Univ., Fort Collins, CO 80523. Poetry, short fiction, translations, interviews, articles on contemporary themes. Submit from September through May 1.

COLUMBIA, A MAGAZINE OF POETRY & PROSE—404 Dodge, Columbia Univ., New York, NY 10027. Articles and fiction, to 25 typed pages. Poetry. Pays in copies. Annual award. SASE required.

COMPASSION MAGAZINE—P.O. Box 553, Northampton, MA 01061. "Our focus is on social responsibility." Articles on family, community, and nature; some short poetry. Pays in copies. Guidelines.

CONFRONTATION—Dept. of English, C. W. Post of L. I. U., Greenvale, NY 11548. Martin Tucker, Ed. Serious fiction, 750 to 6,000 words. Crafted poetry, 20 to 200 lines. Pays $5 to $40, on publication.

THE CONNECTICUT POETRY REVIEW—P.O. Box 3783, New Haven, CT 06525. J. Claire White and James Wm. Chichetto, Eds. Poetry, 5 to 20 lines, and reviews, 700 words. Pays $5 per poem, $10 for a review, on acceptance.

CONNECTICUT RIVER REVIEW—490 Sherwood Place, 1A, Stratford, CT 06497. Rebecca Thompson, Ed. Poetry, to 40 lines. Pays in copies.

COTTON BOLL/ATLANTA REVIEW—Sandy Springs P.O. Box 76757, Atlanta, GA 30358. Mary Hollingsworth, Ed. Literary short stories, to 3,500 words; poetry, to 2 pages. Payment varies. Send SASE for guidelines. Contests.

CRAZY QUILT—3341 Adams Ave., San Diego, CA 92116. Address the Editors. Fiction, to 4,000 words, short poetry, one-act plays, and literary criticism. Pays in copies.

THE CREAM CITY REVIEW—Box 413, Univ. of Wisconsin, Milwaukee, WI 53201. Ron Tanner, Ed. "We serve a national and regional audience that seeks the best in fiction, poetry, and nonfiction; and we publish work by established and emerging writers." Submit up to three poems. Payment varies.

CRITICAL INQUIRY—Univ. of Chicago Press, Wieboldt Hall, 1050 E. 59th St., Chicago, IL 60637. W. J. T. Mitchell, Ed. Critical essays that offer a theoretical perspective on literature, music, visual arts, popular culture, etc. Pays in copies.

A CRITIQUE OF AMERICA—405 W. Washington St., Suite 418, San Diego, CA 92103. Progressive fiction, poetry, and arts features (to 9,000 words). Nonfiction sketches of American people and/or regions (to 9,000 words). Pays $100 to $2,000 for fiction and commentary, $20 to $200 for poetry, on acceptance.

CROTON REVIEW—P.O. Box 277, Croton-on-Hudson, NY 10520. Quality poetry, essays, short-short fiction (to 10 pages). Submissions accepted from Aug. to Dec. 15 only. Send SASE for guidelines first. Pays in copies.

CUBE LITERARY MAGAZINE—P.O. Box 2637, Newport News, VA 23602. Eric Mathews, Ed. Veronica Aracri, Poetry Ed. Fiction, to 5,000 words, poetry, to 50 lines, and creative or humorous essays. Pays in copies.

CUMBERLAND POETRY REVIEW—P.O. Box 120128, Acklen Sta., Nashville, TN 37212. Address Eds. High-quality poetry and criticism; translations. No restrictions on form, style, or subject matter. Pays in copies.

DENVER QUARTERLY—Univ of Denver, Denver, CO 80208. David Milofsky, Ed. Literary, cultural essays and articles; poetry; book reviews; fiction. Pays $5 per printed page, after publication.

DESCANT—Texas Christian Univ., T.C.U. Sta., Fort Worth, TX 76129. Betsy Colquitt, Ed. Fiction, to 6,000 words. Poetry to 40 lines. No restriction on form or subject. Pays in copies. Submit Sept. through May only.

THE DEVIL'S MILLHOPPER—The Devil's Millhopper Press, Coll. of Humanities, U. of South Carolina/Aiken, 171 University Pkwy., Aiken, SC 29801. Stephen Gardner, Ed. Poetry. Send SASE for guidelines. Pays in copies.

DV-8 MAGAZINE—228 W. Broadway/Storefront, New York, NY 10013. Laurie Litchford, Ed. Unformulaic fiction (to 4,000 words) and articles (1,600 words) on new artists in music, art, and fashion; short profiles; all forms of experimental journalism. Poetry suitable for young, urban-oriented readers. Payment varies. Query preferred.

ELECTRUM MAGAZINE—2222 Silk Tree Rd., Tustin, CA 92680. Roger Suva, Ed. Poetry: traditional, avant-garde, and free verse. Submit to 5 poems at a time. Pays in copies.

EMBERS—Box 404, Guilford, CT 06437. Katrina Van Tassel, Mark Johnston, Charlotte Garrett, Eds. Poetry of all types and styles. Submit before March 15 or October 15. Guidelines available. Pays in copies.

FACET—P.O. Box 4950, Hualapai, AZ 86412. Judith Porter, Ed. Fiction, to

3,500 words, with "strong characters and plots." Poetry, to 75 lines. Pays $7 to $20 for short stories, $5 to $7 for poetry, on publication.

FARMER'S MARKET—P.O. Box 1272, Galesburg, IL 61402. Short stories and novel excerpts, to 20 pages, and poetry, related to the Midwest. Pays in copies.

FAT TUESDAY—419 N. Larchmont, Ste. 104, Los Angeles, CA 90004. F.M. Cotolo, Ed. Annual. Short fiction, poetry, parts-of-novels, paragraphs, crystal thoughts of any dimension, to 5 pages. Pays in copies.

FICTION INTERNATIONAL—English Dept., San Diego State Univ., San Diego, CA 92182. Harold Jaffe, Larry McCaffery, Eds. Post-modernist and politically committed fiction and theory. Payment varies.

THE FIDDLEHEAD—Dept. of English, Univ. of New Brunswick, Fredericton, N.B., Canada E3B 5A3. Serious fiction, 2,500 words, preferably by Canadians. Pays about $10 per printed page, on publication.

FIELD—Rice Hall, Oberlin College, Oberlin, OH 44074. Stuart Friebert, David Young, Eds. Serious poetry, any length, by established and unknown poets; essays on poetics by poets. Translations by qualified translators. Pays $20 to $30 per page, on publication.

FINE MADNESS—P.O. Box 15176, Seattle, WA 98115. Poetry, any length; occasional reviews. Pays varying rates.

FOOTWORK—Cultural Affairs Office, Passaic County Comm. College, College Blvd., Patterson, NJ 07509. Maria Gillan, Ed. High quality fiction, to 4 pages, and poetry, to 3 pages, any style. Pays in copies.

FREE INQUIRY—P.O. Box 5, Buffalo, NY 14215–0005. Paul Kurtz, Ed. Robert Basil, Exec. Ed. Articles, 500 to 5,000 words, for "literate and lively readership. Topics provide food for thought, ideas for action, issues for lively debate on religion, philosophy, and culture." Pays in copies.

THE GAMUT—1216 Rhodes Tower, Cleveland State Univ., Cleveland, OH 44115. Lively articles on general-interest topics preferably concerned with the region, 2,000 to 6,000 words. Quality fiction and poetry. Photos. Pays $25 to $250, on publication. Send SASE for guidelines.

GARGOYLE—P.O. Box 30906, Bethesda, MD 20814. Richard Peabody, Ed. Fiction, 3 to 30 typed pages; poetry, 5 to 25 lines. Photos. Pays in copies.

THE GEORGIA REVIEW—Univ. of Georgia, Athens, GA 30602. Stanley W. Lindberg, Ed., Stephen Corey, Assoc. Ed. Short fiction; interdisciplinary essays on arts, sciences, and the humanities; book reviews; poetry. No submissions in June, July, or August.

GOLD DUST—Box 1658, Nevada City, CA 95959. Poetry, 15 to 140 lines; previously published work only. Pays in copies.

GRAIN—Box 1154, Regina, Sask., Canada S4P 3B4. Mick Burrs, Ed. Short stories, to 30 typed pages. Songs, essays, and drama. Poems (send no more than 6). Pays $30 to $100 for prose; $30 per poem, on publication.

GREEN'S MAGAZINE—P.O. Box 3236, Regina, Sask., Canada S4P 3H1. David Green, Ed. Fiction for family reading, 1,500 to 4,000 words. Poetry, to 40 lines. Pays in copies.

THE GREENSBORO REVIEW—Univ. of North Carolina, Greensboro, NC 27412. Jim Clark, Ed. Semi-annual. Poetry and fiction. Submission deadlines: Sept. 15 and Feb. 15. Pays in copies.

THE HARBOR REVIEW—English Dept., UMass-Boston, Boston, MA 02125. Fiction, to 10 pages, and poetry, any length. Submissions accepted only from February to May, with SASE. Pays in copies.

HAUNTS—Nightshade Publications, Box 3342, Providence, RI 02906. Joseph K. Cherkes, Ed. Short stories, 1,500 to 8,000 words: horror, science-fantasy, and supernatural tales with strong characters. Pays ¼¢ to ⅓¢ a word, on publication.

THE HAVEN, NEW POETRY—5969 Avenida la Barranca NW, Albuquerque, NM 87114. Michael McDaniel, Ed. Poetry, to 20 lines. Contests. Pays $5 to $15, on acceptance.

HAWAII REVIEW—Dept. of English, Univ. of Hawaii, 1733 Donagho Rd., Honolulu, HI 96882. Quality fiction, poetry, interviews, and literary criticism reflecting both regional and universal concerns.

HEARTLAND JOURNAL—4114 N. Sunset Ct., Madison, WI 53705. Jeri McCormick, Lenore Coberly, Eds. Fiction, 500 to 3,000 words, and poetry about times and places that are gone. Writers must be over 60 years old. Pays in copies. Contest.

HELICON NINE, THE JOURNAL OF WOMEN'S ARTS AND LETTERS—P.O. Box 22412, Kansas City, MO 64113. Poetry and fiction about women. Include SASE.

HERESIES—Box 1306, Canal Street Sta., New York, NY 10013. Feminist art/political slant; thematic issues. Fiction, to 12 typed pages; nonfiction; poetry.

HIGH PLAINS LITERARY REVIEW—180 Adams St., Suite 250, Denver, CO 80206. Robert O. Greer, Ed. Fiction (3,000 to 6,000 words), essays, poetry (to 5 pages), reviews and interviews. Pays $5 a page for prose, $10 for poetry, on publication.

HURRICANE ALICE: A FEMINIST REVIEW—207 Lind Hall, 207 Church St. SE, Minneapolis, MN 55455. Articles, fiction, essays, interviews, and reviews, 500 to 3,000 words, with feminist perspective. Pays in copies.

INDIANA REVIEW—316 N. Jordan Ave., Bloomington, IN 47405. Elizabeth Dodd, Kim McKinney, Ed. Fiction with an emphasis on style. Poems that are well executed and ambitious. Pays $5 a page for poetry; $25 per story.

INLET—Dept. of English, Virginia Wesleyan Coll., Norfolk, VA 23502. Joseph Harkey, Ed. Short fiction, 1,000 to 3,000 words (short lengths preferred). Poems of 4 to 40 lines; all forms and themes. Submit between September and March 1st, each year. Pays in copies.

INVISIBLE CITY—P.O. Box 2853, San Francisco, CA 94126. John McBride, Paul Vangelisti, Eds. Reviews, translations: especially interested in contemporary European literature. Pays in copies.

THE IOWA REVIEW—EPB 308, Univ. of Iowa, Iowa City, IA 52242. David Hamilton, Ed. Essays, poems, stories, reviews. Pays $10 a page for fiction and nonfiction, $1 a line for poetry, on publication.

JAM TO-DAY—372 Dunstable Rd., Tyngsboro, MA 01879. Don Stanford and Judith Stanford, Eds. Quality poetry and fiction, particularly from little-known writers. Pays $5 per printed page for fiction, $5 per poem, on publication.

JAPANOPHILE—Box 223, Okemos, MI 48864. Earl R. Snodgrass, Ed. Fiction, to 10,000 words, with a Japanese setting. Each story should have at least one

Japanese character and at least one non-Japanese. Pays to $20, on publication. Annual contest in December.

KANSAS QUARTERLY—Dept. of English, Denison Hall 122, Kansas State Univ., Manhattan, KS 66506. Literary criticism, art, and history. Fiction and poetry. Pays in copies. Annual awards. Query for articles and special topics.

KARAMU—Dept. of English, Eastern Illinois Univ., Charleston, IL 61920. John Guzlowski, Ed. Contemporary or experimental fiction. Poetry. Pays in copies.

LIGHT YEAR—Bits Press, Dept. of English, Western Reserve Univ., Cleveland, OH 44106. Robert Wallace, Ed. Annual. "The best funny, witty, or merely levitating verse being written." No restrictions on style or length. Pays $2 per poem plus 10¢ per line, on publication. Material will not be returned unless accompanied by SASE.

LILITH—250 W. 57th St., New York, NY 10017. Susan Weidman Schneider, Ed. Fiction, 1,500 to 2,000 words, on issues of interest to Jewish women.

THE LION AND THE UNICORN—English Dept., Brooklyn College, Brooklyn, NY 11210. Geraldine DeLuca, Roni Natov, Eds. Articles, from 2,000 words, offering criticism of children's and young adult books, for teachers, scholars, artists, and parents. Query preferred. Pays in copies.

LITERARY MAGAZINE REVIEW—English Dept., Kansas State Univ., Manhattan, KS 66506. Reviews and articles concerning literary magazines, 1,000 to 1,500 words, for writers and readers of contemporary literature. Pays modest fees and copies. Query.

THE LITERARY REVIEW—Fairleigh Dickinson Univ., 285 Madison Ave., Madison, NJ 07940. Walter Cummins, Martin Green, Harry Keyishian, William Zander, Eds. Serious fiction; poetry; translations; reviews; essays on literature. Pays in copies.

THE LONG STORY—11 Kingston St., N. Andover, MA 01845. Stories, 8,000 to 20,000 words; prefer committed fiction. Pays $1 a page, on publication.

THE MALAHAT REVIEW—Univ. of Victoria, P.O. Box 1700, Victoria, B.C., Canada V8W 2Y2. Constance Rooke, Ed. Fiction and poetry, including translations, and occasional articles. Pays from $20 per page, on acceptance.

THE MANHATTAN REVIEW—304 Third Ave., Suite 4A, New York, NY 10010. Highest quality poetry. Pays in copies.

MASSACHUSETTS REVIEW—Memorial Hall, Univ. of Massachusetts, Amherst, MA 01003. Literary criticism; articles on public affairs, scholarly disciplines. Short fiction. Poetry. No submissions between June and October. Pays modest rates, on publication. SASE required.

MEMPHIS STATE REVIEW—Dept. of English, Memphis State Univ., Memphis, TN 38152. Short stories, novel excerpts, to 4,500 words; poetry, to one page. Pays in copies. Annual award.

MICHIGAN HISTORICAL REVIEW—Clark Historical Library, Central Michigan Univ., Mt. Pleasant, MI 48859. Address Ed. Articles related to Michigan's political, social, economic, and cultural history. SASE.

MICHIGAN QUARTERLY REVIEW—3032 Rackham Bldg., Univ. of Michigan, Ann Arbor, MI 48109. Laurence Goldstein, Ed. Scholarly essays on all subjects; fiction; poetry. Pays $8 a page, on publication. Annual contest.

THE MICKLE STREET REVIEW—328 Mickle St., Camden, NJ 08102. Articles, poems, and artwork related to Walt Whitman. Pays in copies.

MID-AMERICAN REVIEW—Dept. of English, Bowling Green State Univ., Bowling Green, OH 43403. Robert Early, Ed. High-quality fiction, poetry, articles, and reviews of contemporary writing. Fiction to 20,000 words. Reviews, articles, 500 to 2,500 words. Pays to $75, on publication.

MIDWEST QUARTERLY—Pittsburg State Univ., Pittsburg, KS 66762. James B. M. Schick, Ed. Scholarly articles, 2,500 to 5,000 words, on contemporary issues. Pays in copies.

MIND IN MOTION—P.O. Box 1118, Apple Valley, CA 92307. Celeste Goyer, Ed. Fiction, 500 to 2,500 words: allegory, fable, surrealism, parody; poetry, to 45 lines; emphasis on universal concerns artfully directed toward everyday and esoteric. Pays in copies.

THE MINNESOTA REVIEW—English Dept., SUNY-Stony Brook, Stony Brook, NY 11794. Address the Editors. "Politically committed fiction (3,000 to 6,000 words), nonfiction (5,000 to 7,500 words), and poetry (3 pages maximum), for socialist, marxist, or feminist audience." Pays in copies.

MISSISSIPPI REVIEW—Center for Writers, Univ. of Southern Mississippi, Southern Sta., Box 5144, Hattiesburg, MS 39406–5144. Frederick Barthelme, Ed. Serious fiction, poetry, criticism, interviews. Pays in copies and small honorarium, on publication.

THE MISSISSIPPI VALLEY REVIEW—Dept. of English, Western Illinois Univ., Macomb, IL 61455. Forrest Robinson, Ed. Short fiction, to 20 typed pages. Poetry; send 3 to 5 poems. Pays in copies.

THE MISSOURI REVIEW—Dept. of English, 231 Arts & Science, Univ. of Missouri-Columbia, Columbia, MO 65211. Greg Michalson, Man. Ed. Poems, of any length. Fiction and essays. Pays $10 per printed page, on publication.

MODERN HAIKU—P.O. Box 1752, Madison, WI 53701. Robert Spiess, Ed. Haiku and articles about haiku. Pays $1 per haiku, $5 a page for articles.

MONTHLY REVIEW—122 W. 27th St., New York, NY 10001. Paul M. Sweezy, Harry Magdoff, Eds. Analytic articles, 5,000 words, on politics and economics, from independent socialist viewpoint. Pays $50, on publication.

THE MOUNTAIN—P.O. Box 1010, Galax, VA 24333. Address the Editors. Fiction (3,000 to 8,000 words) and general-interest nonfiction (500 to 6,000 words) reflecting mountain region life. Humor, 10 to 150 words. Pays $10 to $750 words, on publication.

THE MOVEMENT—P.O. Box 19458, Los Angeles, CA 90019. Virginia Hopkins, Ed. Articles dedicated to spiritual/transformational interests, 1,000 words. Pays in copies. Must include SASE.

MOVING OUT—P.O. Box 21249, Detroit, MI 48221. Poetry, fiction, articles, and art by women; Submit 4 to 6 poems at a time. Pays in copies.

THE MUSE LETTER—P.O. Box 45, Burlington, NC 27216–0045. J. William Griffin, Ed. Poems (up to 36 lines preferred) on any subject, in any form or style. Send up to five poems, typed single spaced. Pays $5 per poem, on publication.

THE NATIONAL STORYTELLING JOURNAL—P.O. Box 309, Jonesborough, TN 37659. Greta Talton, Ed. Articles, 1,500 to 6,000 words, related to storytelling: "Articles can have folkloric, historical, personal, educational, travel bias, as long as it is related to storytelling." Poetry. Pays in copies.

NEBO—Dept. of English, Arkansas Tech. Univ., Russellville, AR 72801. Poetry; mainstream fiction to 20 pages; critical essays to 10 pages. Pays in copies.

NEGATIVE CAPABILITY—62 Ridgelawn Dr. E., Mobile, AL 36608. Sue Walker, Ed. Poetry, any length; fiction, essays, art. Pays in copies. Annual Eve of St. Agnes poetry competition and annual fiction and essay contest.

NEW LETTERS—5216 Rockhill Rd., Kansas City, MO 64110. James McKinley, Ed. Fiction, 10 to 25 pages; nonfiction, 20 to 30 pages. Poetry; submit 3 to 6 at a time.

NEW MEXICO HUMANITIES REVIEW—Box A, New Mexico Tech, Socorro, NM 87801. Poetry, any length, any theme; essays dealing with southwestern and native American themes. Pays with subscription.

NEW ORLEANS REVIEW—Loyola Univ., New Orleans, LA 70118. John Mosier, Ed. Literary or film criticism, to 6,000 words. Serious fiction and poetry.

NEXUS—Wright State Univ., 006 Univ. Center, Dayton, OH 45435. Rebecca J. Edgerton, Ed. Short fiction (800 to 2,500 words), poetry, and B&W artwork. Submit Oct. through May. Guidelines. Pays in copies.

NIMROD—2210 S. Main St., Tulsa, OK 74114. Quality poetry and fiction, experimental and traditional. Pays in copies. Annual awards for poetry and fiction. Send SASE for guidelines.

THE NORTH AMERICAN REVIEW—Univ. of Northern Iowa, Cedar Falls, IA 50614. Peter Cooley, Poetry Ed. Poetry of high quality. Pays 50¢ a line, on acceptance.

THE NORTH DAKOTA QUARTERLY—Univ. of North Dakota, Box 8237, Grand Forks, ND 58202. Nonfiction essays in the humanities; fiction, reviews, graphics, and poetry. Limited market. Pays in copies.

THE NORTHERN REVIEW—Dept. of English, Univ. of Wisconsin/Stevens Point, Stevens Point, WI 54481. Address Man. Ed. Essays, articles (1,200 to 4,000 words), and fiction on or exploring northern themes. Pays in copies.

THE NORTHLAND REVIEW—51 E. Fourth St., Suite 412, Winona, MN 55987. Paul Drake, Ed. Articles and fiction (1,500 to 3,500 words) on contemporary themes. Poetry, any length. Query for articles. Pays in copies.

NORTHWEST REVIEW—369 PLC, Univ. of Oregon, Eugene, OR 97403. John Witte, Ed. Serious fiction, commentary, and poetry. Reviews. Pays in copies. Send SASE for guidelines.

NYCTICORAX—P.O. Box 8444, Asheville, NC 28814. John A. Youril, Ed. Short-short fiction and poetry (submit 4 to 8 poems at a time). Query about essays on literary criticism. Pays in copies.

OAK SQUARE—Box 1238, Allston, MA 02134. Anne E. Pluto, Fiction Ed. Scott Getchell, Poetry Ed. Experimental and traditional stories, 2,500 to 4,000 words; some poetry; nonpolitical essays and interviews. Pays in copies.

THE OHIO REVIEW—Ellis Hall, Ohio Univ., Athens, OH 45701–2979. Short stories, poetry, essays, reviews. Pays from $5 per page, plus copies, on publication.

THE ONTARIO REVIEW—9 Honey Brook Dr., Princeton, NJ 08540. Raymond J. Smith, Ed. Poetry and fiction. No unsolicited manuscripts.

OREGON EAST—Hoke College Center, EOSC, La Grande, OR 97850. Short fiction, nonfiction (to 3,000 words), and poetry (to 60 lines). Regional angle preferred. Pays in copies. Submit fiction by March 1, nonfiction by June.

ORPHIC LUTE—1705B 16th St., Los Alamos, NM 87544. Patricia Doherty Hinnebusch, Ed. Lyric poetry, traditional and contemporary (submit up to 4 poems at a time). Pays in copies.

OTHER VOICES—820 Ridge Rd., Highland Park, IL 60035. Dolores Weinberg, Lois Hauselman, Eds. Semi-annual. Fresh, accessible short stories and novel excerpts, to 5,000 words. Pays in copies and modest honorarium.

OUROBOROS—3912 24th St., Rock Island, IL 61201. Erskine Carter, Ed. Short stories (to 3,500 words) and poetry (submit 7 to 10 poems at a time). Guidelines. Pays in copies.

PAINTED BRIDE QUARTERLY—230 Vine St., Philadelphia, PA 19106. Lois McKee, Louis Camp, and Joanne DiPaolo, Eds. Fiction, nonfiction, and poetry of varying lengths. Pays in copies.

PANDORA—609 E. 11 Mile, #2, Royal Oak, MI 48067. Meg MacDonald, Ed. Ruth Berman, Poetry Ed. Science fiction and speculative fantasy, to 5,000 words; poetry. Pays to 4¢ a word, on publication.

PARIS REVIEW—541 E. 72nd St., New York, NY 10021. Address Fiction and Poetry Eds. Fiction and poetry of high literary quality. Pays on publication.

PARNASSUS—41 Union Sq. W., Rm. 804, New York, NY 10003. Herbert Leibowitz, Ed. Critical essays and reviews on contemporary poetry. International in scope. Pays in cash and copies.

PARTISAN REVIEW—Boston Univ., 141 Bay State Rd., Boston, MA 02215. William Phillips, Ed. Serious fiction, poetry and essays. Payment varies. No simultaneous submissions.

PASSAGES NORTH—William Bonifas Fine Arts Ctr., Escanaba, MI 49829. Elinor Benedict, Ed. Quality short fiction and contemporary poetry. Pays in copies, frequent prizes and honoraria.

THE PENNSYLVANIA REVIEW—Univ. of Pittsburgh, Dept. of English, 526 Cathedral of Learning, Pittsburgh, PA 15260. Articles and fiction, to 5,000 words, and poetry (send as many as six at once). Pays $5 a page for prose, $5 for poetry.

PERMAFROST—English Dept., Univ. of Alaska, Fairbanks, AK 99775. Poetry, short fiction, essays, translations, and B&W photos and graphics. No manuscripts accepted between April 1 and Aug. 1. Pays in copies.

PIEDMONT LITERARY REVIEW—P.O. Box 3656, Danville, VA 24543. Fiction, to 4,000 words. Poems, of any length and style. Special interest in young poets. Pays in copies. Submit up to 5 poems.

PIG IRON—P.O. Box 237, Youngstown, OH 44501. Rose Sayre, Jim Villani, Eds. Fiction and nonfiction, to 8,000 words. Poetry, to 100 lines. Pays $2 per published page, on publication. Query for themes.

PINCHPENNY—4851 Q St., Sacramento, CA 95819. Tom Miner, Elisabeth Goossens, Eds. Prose poems, tiny poems, short-short stories, B&W art. New writers welcome. Pays in copies.

PLAINS POETRY JOURNAL—Box 2337, Bismarck, ND 58502. Jane Greer, Ed. Poetry using traditional conventions in vigorous, compelling ways; no "greeting card'-type verse. No subject is taboo. Pays in copies.

PLOUGHSHARES—Box 529, Dept. M, Cambridge, MA 02139. Address Poetry Ed. Poetry. Pays $10 to $50, on publication. Query. Fiction overstocked.

POEM—c/o English Dept., U.A.H., Huntsville, AL 35899. Nancy Frey Dillard, Ed. Serious lyric poetry, any length. Pays in copies.

POET AND CRITIC—203 Ross Hall, Iowa State Univ., Ames, IA 50011. Neal Bowers, Ed. Poetry, reviews, essays on contemporary poetry. Pays in copies.

POET LORE—7815 Old Georgetown Rd., Bethesda, MD 20814. Margaret Buckley, Man. Ed. Original poetry, all kinds. Translations, reviews. Pays in copies. Annual narrative contest.

POETRY—60 West Walton St., Chicago, IL 60610. Joseph Parisi, Ed. Poetry of highest quality. Pays $1 a line, on publication.

PORTENTS—12 Fir Pl., Hazlet, NJ 07730. Deborah Rasmussen, Ed. Short stories (contemporary horror, dark fantasy, exceptional gothic, and supernatural horror), to 3,000 words. No werewolves, vampires, ghouls, religion, or sex. Pays ¼¢ a word.

PRAIRIE SCHOONER—201 Andrews Hall, Univ. of Nebraska, Lincoln, NE 68588. Hilda Raz, Ed. Short stories, poetry, essays, book reviews, and translations, to 6,000 words. Pays in copies. Annual contests.

PRISM INTERNATIONAL—E459–1866 Main Mall, Dept. of Creative Writing, Univ. of British Columbia, Vancouver, B.C., Canada V6T 1W5. Mike Peddie, Ed.-in-Chief; Catherine Burke, Man. Ed. High-quality fiction, poetry, drama, and literature in translation, varying lengths. Include international reply coupons. Pays $25 per published page. Annual short fiction contest.

PROOF ROCK—P.O. Box 607, Halifax, VA 24558. Don Conner, Ed. Fiction, to 2,500 words. Poetry, to 32 lines. Reviews. Pays in copies.

PUDDING—60 N. Main St., Johnstown, OH 43031. Jennifer Welch Bosveld, Ed. Poems, especially free verse and experimental, with fresh language, concrete images, and specific detail. Short articles about poetry in human services.

PUERTO DEL SOL—New Mexico State Univ., Box 3E, Las Cruces, NM 88003. Kevin McIlvoy, Ed. Short stories, to 30 pages; novel excerpts, to 65 pages; articles, to 45 pages, related to the Southwest; and reviews, to 15 pages. Poetry, photos. Pays in copies.

PULPSMITH—5 Beekman St., New York, NY 10038. Harry Smith, General Ed. Tom Tolnay, Man. Ed. Literary genre fiction; mainstream, mystery, SF, westerns. Short lyric poems, sonnets, ballads. Essays and articles. Pays $35 to $100 for fiction, $15 to $35 for poetry, on acceptance. Annual: submit Oct. 15 to May 15.

QUEEN'S QUARTERLY—Queens Univ., Kingston, Ont., Canada K7L 3N6. Articles, to 6,000 words, on a wide range of topics, and fiction, to 5,000 words. Poetry: send no more than 6 poems. B&W art. Pays to $150, on publication.

RACCOON—Ion Books, Inc., 3387 Poplar Ave., #205, Memphis, TN 38111. David Spicer, Ed. Poetry and poetic criticism, varying lengths. Pays in copies for poetry, $50 for criticism.

RAMBUNCTIOUS REVIEW—1221 W. Pratt Blvd., Chicago, IL 60626.

Mary Dellutri, Richard Goldman, Eds. Fiction, poetry, short drama. Pays in copies. Submit material Sept.through May.

RED CEDAR REVIEW—Dept. of English, Morrill Hall, Michigan State Univ., East Lansing, MI 48825. Fiction, 10 to 15 pages; poetry; interviews; book reviews; graphics. Pays in copies.

RELIGION AND PUBLIC EDUCATION—N155 Lagomarcino Hall, Iowa State Univ., Ames, IA 50011. Charles R. Kniker, Ed.-in-Chief; Paul Blakeley, Poetry Ed. Poems with mythological or religious values or themes. Pays in copies.

RHINO—1040 Judson Ave., Evanston, IL 60202. Enid Baron and Carole Hayes, Eds. "Authentic emotion in well-crafted poetry and prose poems." January to June reading period.

RIVERSIDE QUARTERLY—P.O. Box 464, Waco, TX 76703. Science fiction and fantasy, to 3,500 words; criticism; poetry; reviews. Send fiction to Redd Boggs, Box 1111, Berkeley, CA 94701; poetry to Sheryl Smith, 515 Saratoga, Santa Clara, CA 95050. Pays in copies.

ROANOKE REVIEW—Roanoke College, Salem, VA 24153. Robert R. Walter, Ed. Quality short fiction, to 10,000 words, and poetry, to 100 lines. Pays in copies.

SAN FERNANDO POETRY JOURNAL—18301 Halstead St., Northridge, CA 91325. Richard Cloke, Ed. Quality poetry, 20 to 100 lines, with social content; scientific, philosophic, and historical themes. Pays in copies.

SAN JOSE STUDIES—San Jose State Univ., San Jose, CA 95192. Fauneil J. Rinn, Ed. Poetry, fiction, and essays on interdisciplinary topics. Pays in copies. Annual awards.

SANSKRIT LITERARY/ART PUBLICATION—Univ. of North Carolina/Charlotte, Charlotte, NC 28223. Leigh Coulter, Ed.-in-Chief. Poetry, short fiction, photos, and fine art. Published annually. Pays in copies. Contest.

SCANDINAVIAN REVIEW—127 E. 73rd St., New York, NY 10021. Essays on contemporary Scandinavia. Fiction and poetry, translated from Nordic languages. Pays from $100, on publication.

SCRIVENER—McGill Univ., 853 Sherbrooke St. W., Montreal, Quebec, Canada H3A 2T6. Andrew Burgess, Ed. Poetry, 5 to 25 lines; prose, to 25 pages; reviews, to 3 pages; essays, to 8 pages. Photography and graphics. Pays in copies.

THE SEATTLE REVIEW—Padelford Hall, GN-30, Univ. of Washington, Seattle, WA 98195. Donna Gerstenberger, Ed. Short stories (to 20 pages) and poetry. Payment varies.

SENECA REVIEW—Hobart & William Smith Colleges, Geneva, NY 14456. Poetry. Pays in copies.

SHENANDOAH—Washington and Lee Univ., P.O. Box 722, Lexington, VA 24450. James Boatwright, Ed. Richard Howard, Poetry Ed. Highest quality fiction, poetry, criticism, essays and interviews. Annual contests.

THE SHORT STORY REVIEW—P.O. Box 882108, San Francisco, CA 94188. Dwight Gabbard, Ed. Short stories, to 3,500 words; interviews; book reviews, to 800 words. Query required for interviews and reviews. Send SASE for guidelines. Pays in copies.

SIDEWINDER—Division of Arts and Humanities, College of the Mainland,

Texas City, TX 77591. Brett Jarrett, Ed. Fiction and poetry of any length: "Our main concern is with the originality and skill in presentation, so we are not interested in genre or formula stories." Manuscripts only. Pays $50 to $100.

SING HEAVENLY MUSE! WOMEN'S POETRY & PROSE—P.O. Box 13299, Minneapolis, MN 55414. Short stories and essays, to 5,000 words. Poetry. Pays in copies.

SLIPSTREAM—Box 2071, New Market Sta., Niagara Falls, NY 14301. Fiction, 2 to 18 pages, and contemporary poetry, any length. Pays in copies. Query for themes.

SMALL PRESS REVIEW—Box 100, Paradise, CA 95969. Len Fulton, Ed. News pieces and reviews, to 250 words, about small presses and little magazines. Pays in copies.

SNOWY EGRET—107 S. Eighth St., Williamsburg, KY 40769. Humphrey A. Olsen, Alan Seaburg, Eds. Poetry to 10,000 words, and fiction and nonfiction, about 3,000 words, related to natural history. Pays $2 per page for prose, $2 to $4 for poetry, on publication. Send fiction and poetry to Alan Seaburg, Ed., 67 Century St., W. Medford, MA 02155.

SONORA REVIEW—Dept. of English, Univ. of Arizona, Tucson, AZ 85721. Heather Aronson, Michael Magoolahan, Eds. Fiction, poetry, reviews, literary nonfiction. Pays in copies. Annual prizes for fiction and poetry.

SOUTH DAKOTA REVIEW—Box 111, Univ. Exchange, Vermillion, SD 57069. John R. Milton, Ed. Exceptional fiction, 3,000 to 5,000 words, and poetry, 10 to 25 lines. Critical articles, especially on American literature, Western American literature, theory and esthetics, 3,000 to 5,000 words. Pays in copies.

SOUTHERN HUMANITIES REVIEW—9088 Haley Center, Auburn Univ., AL 36849. Thomas L. Wright, Dan R. Latimer, Eds. Short stories, essays, and criticism, 3,500 to 5,000 words; poetry, to 2 pages.

SOUTHERN POETRY REVIEW—Dept. of English, Univ. of North Carolina, Charlotte, NC 28223. Robert W. Grey, Ed. Poems. No restrictions on style, length, or content.

SOUTHERN REVIEW—43 Allen Hall, Louisiana State Univ., Baton Rouge, LA 70803. Fred Hobson, James Olney, Eds. Fiction and essays, 4,000 to 8,000 words. Serious poetry of highest quality. Pays $12 a page for prose, $20 a page for poery, on publication.

SOUTHWEST REVIEW—Southern Methodist Univ., Dallas, TX 72575. Willard Spiegelman, Ed. Fiction and essays, 3,000 to 7,500 words; book reviews. Poetry. Pays varying rates.

SOU'WESTER—Dept. of English, Southern Illinois Univ at Edwardsville, Edwardsville, IL 62026–1438. Dickie Spurgeon, Ed. Fiction, to 10,000 words. Poetry, especially poems over 100 lines. Pays in copies.

SPECTRUM—Anna Maria College, Box 72-A, Paxton, MA 01612. Robert H. Goepfert, Ed. Scholarly articles (3,000 to 15,000 words); short stories (to 10 pages) and poetry (to two pages); book reviews, photos and artwork. Pays in copies.

THE SPIRIT THAT MOVES US—P.O. Box 1585 TW, Iowa City, IA 52244. Morty Sklar, Ed. Biannual. Fiction, poetry, that is expressive rather than formal or sensational. Each issue focuses on a specific theme. Query. Pays in copies.

SPSM&H—329 "E" St., Bakersfield, CA 93304. Frederick A. Raborg, Jr., Ed.

Single sonnets, sequences, essays about the form, short fiction in which the sonnet plays a part, books and anthologies. Pays in copies.

STAND MAGAZINE—Univ. of North Alabama, English Dept., Florence, AL 35632–0001. John E. Kingsbury, Ed. Fiction and poetry of any length. No formulaic verse. Pays varying rates, on publication.

STONE COUNTRY—P.O. Box 132, Menemsha, MA 02552. Judith Neeld, Ed. High-quality contemporary poetry in all genres. Pays in copies. Semi-annual award. SASE required. Guidelines.

STORY QUARTERLY—P.O. Box 1416, Northbrook, IL 60065. Anne Brashler, Diane Williams, Eds. Short stories and interviews. Pays in copies.

STUDIES IN AMERICAN FICTION—English Dept., Northeastern Univ., Boston, MA 02115. James Nagel, Ed. Reviews, 750 words; scholarly essays, 2,500 to 6,500 words, on American fiction. Pays in copies.

SUNRUST—P.O. Box 58, New Wilmington, PA 16142. James Ashbrook Perkins, Nancy Esther James, Eds. Nonfiction, to 2,000 words, and poetry, to 75 lines, about rural life, nature, memories of the past, and small communities. Pays in copies.

TAR RIVER POERY—Dept. of English, East Carolina Univ., Greenville, NC 27834. Peter Makuck, Ed. Poems, all styles. Submit between September and May. Pays in copies.

TESTIMONY—P.O. Box 495, Montclair, NJ 07042. Sandra West, Ed. Poetry related to the Afro-American experience: "creative, soul-stirring poetry; sonnets, haiku, and political poetry." Pays in copies.

THE TEXAS REVIEW—English Dept., Sam Houston State Univ., Huntsville, TX 77341. Paul Ruffin, Ed. Fiction, poetry, articles, to 20 types pages. Reviews. Pays in copies.

THE THREEPENNY REVIEW—P.O. Box 9131, Berkeley, CA 94709. Wendy Lesser, Ed. Fiction, to 5,000 words. Poetry, to 100 lines. Essays, on books, theater, film, dance, music, art, television, and politics, 1,500 to 3,000 words. Pays to $50, on acceptance. Limited market. Query first with SASE.

TOUCHSTONE—P.O. Box 42331, Houston, TX 77042. Bill Laufer, Pub. Quarterly. Fiction, 750 to 2,000 words: mainstream, experimental. Interviews, essays, reviews. Poetry, to 40 lines. Pays in copies.

TRANSLATION—The Translation Ctr., 307A Mathematics Bldg., Columbia Univ., New York, NY 10027. Frank MacShane, Dir. Diane G. H. Cook, Man. Ed. Semiannual. New translations of contemporary foreign poetry and prose.

TRIQUARTERLY—Northwestern Univ., 1735 Benson Ave., Evanston, IL 60201. Serious, aesthetically informed and inventive poetry and prose, for an international and literate audience. Pays $20 per page for prose, $1 per line for poetry.

2 AM—P.O. Box 50444, Chicago, IL 60650–0444. Gretta Anderson, Ed. Articles, reviews, and personality profiles (500 to 2,000 words), as well as fantasy, horror, and some science fiction/sword and sorcery short stories (500 to 5,000 words). Pays ½¢ a word, on acceptance.

THE UNCOMMON READER—1220 Taransay, Henderson, KY 42420. Louis B. Hatchett, Jr., Ed. Quarterly. Humorous fiction and nonfiction, humorous, to 4,000 words, and poetry of up to four rhymed stanzas; no experimental fiction.

Pays $100 for articles, $25 to $100 for fiction, $10 to $50 for poems. Query for articles only.

THE UNIVERSITY OF PORTLAND REVIEW—Univ. of Portland, Portland, OR 97203. Thompson H. Faller, Ed. Scholarly articles and contemporary fiction, 500 to 2,500 words. Poetry. Book reviews. Pays in copies.

UNIVERSITY OF WINDSOR REVIEW—Dept. of English, Univ. of Windsor, Windsor, Ont., Canada N9B 3P4. Joseph A. Quinn, Ed. Short stories, poetry, criticism, reviews. Pays $10 to $25, on publication.

THE VILLAGER—135 Midland Ave., Bronxville, NY 10708. Amy Murphy, Ed. Fiction, 900 to 1,500 words: mystery, adventure, humor, romance. Short, preferably seasonal poetry. Pays in copies.

VIRGINIA QUARTERLY REVIEW—One W. Range, Charlottesville, VA 22903. Quality fiction and poetry. Serious essays and articles, 3,000 to 6,000 words, on literature, science, politics, economics, etc. Pays $10 per page for prose, $1 per line for poetry, on publication.

WASCANA REVIEW—c/o Dept. of English, Univ. of Regina, Regina, Sask., Canada S4S OA2. Joan Givner, Ed. Short stories, 2,000 to 6,000 words; critical articles; poetry. Pays $3 per page for prose, $10 for poetry, after publication.

WASHINGTON REVIEW—P.O. Box 50132, Washington, DC 20004. Clarissa Wittenberg, Ed. Poetry; articles on literary, performing and fine arts in the Washington, D.C., area, 1,000 to 2,500 words. Fiction, to 1,000 words. Area writers preferred. Pays in copies.

WEBSTER REVIEW—Webster Univ., 470 E. Lockwood, Webster Groves, MO 63119. Nancy Schapiro, Ed. Fiction; poetry; interviews; essays; translations. Pays in copies.

WEST BRANCH—English Dept., Bucknell Univ., Lewisburg, PA 17837. Karl Patten, Robert Taylor, Eds. Poetry and fiction. Pays in copies and subscriptions.

WIDE OPEN MAGAZINE—326 I St., Eureka, CA 95501. Clif Simms, Ed. Nonfiction (to 2,500 words) that logically presents solutions to problems current in the world; fiction (to 2,500 words) with solid plots; and poetry in all styles and forms. Pays $5 to $25 for prose, on publication. Guidelines.

THE WINDLESS ORCHARD—Dept. of English, Indiana-Purdue Univ., Ft. Wayne, IN 46805. Robert Novak, Ed. Contemporary poetry. Pays in copies.

WITHOUT HALOS—Ocean County Poets Collective, P.O. Box 1342, Point Pleasant Beach, NJ 08742. Frank Finale, Ed. Submit poems (to 2 pages) between Jan. 1 and June 30. Pays in copies.

WOMAN OF POWER—Box 827, Cambridge, MA 02238–0827. Char McKee, Ed. Fiction and nonfiction, to 3,500 words. Poetry; submit up to 5 poems at a time. Pays in copies.

WRITERS FORUM—Univ. of Colorado, Colorado Springs, CO 80933–7150. Alex Blackburn, Ed. Annual. Mainstream and experimental fiction, 1,000 to 10,000 words. Poetry (1 to 5 poems per submission). Emphasis on Western themes and writers. Send material October through May. Pays in copies.

WYOMING, THE HUB OF THE WHEEL—The Willow Bee Publishing Co., Box 9, Saratoga, WY 82331. Lenore A. Senior, Man. Ed. Fiction and nonfiction, to 2,500 words; poetry, to 80 lines. "An international literary/art magazine

673

devoted to peace, the human race, positive relationships, and the human spirit and possibilities." Pays in copies.

XANADU—Box 773, Huntington, NY 11743. Pat Nesbitt, Mildred Jeffrey, Barbara Lucas, Eds. Poetry on a variety of topics; no length restrictions. Pays in copies.

YALE REVIEW—1902A Yale Sta., New Haven, CT 06520. Kai Erikson, Ed. Serious poery, to 200 lines, and fiction, 3,000 to 5,000 words. Pays nominal sum.

HUMOR, FILLERS, SHORT ITEMS

Magazines noted for their excellent filler departments, plus a cross-section of publications using humor, short items, jokes, quizzes, and cartoons, follow. However, almost all magazines use some type of filler material, and writers can find dozens of markets by studying copies of magazines at a library or newsstand.

ALCOHOLISM & ADDICTION MAGAZINE—P. O. Box 31329, Seattle, WA 98103. News briefs, program updates, and personnel changes of interest to professionals in the addictions field.

THE AMERICAN FIELD—222 W. Adams St., Chicago, IL 60606. W.F. Brown, Ed. Short fact items and anecdotes on hunting dogs, and field trials for bird dogs. Pays varying rates, on acceptance.

THE AMERICAN LEGION MAGAZINE—Box 1055, Indianapolis, IN 46206. Parting Shots Page: short humorous anecdotes, appealing to military veterans and their families. General humor: no sex, religion, ethnic humor or political satire. Pays $15 for definitions, anecdotes and gags, on acceptance. No poetry.

THE AMERICAN NEWSPAPER CARRIER—P.O. Box 15300, Winston-Salem, NC 27103. Short, humorous pieces, to 1,200 words, for pre-teen and teen-age newspaper carriers. Pays $25, on publication.

ARMY MAGAZINE—2425 Wilson Blvd., Arlington, VA 22201. L. James Binder, Ed.-in-Chief. True anecdotes on military subjects. Pays $10 to $35, on publication.

THE ATLANTIC—8 Arlington St., Boston, MA 02116. Sophisticated humorous or satirical pieces, 1,000 to 3,000 words. Some light poetry. Pays from $750 for prose, on acceptance.

ATLANTIC SALMON JOURNAL—1435 St. Alexandre, Suite 1030, Montreal, Quebec, Canada H3A 2G4. Terry Davis, Ed. Fillers, 50 to 100 words, on salmon politics, conservation, and nature. Cartoons. Pays $10 for fillers, $25 for cartoons, on publication.

BICYCLING—33 E. Minor St., Emmaus, PA 18098. Anecdotes, helpful cycling tips, and other items for "Paceline" section, 150 to 250 words. Pays $50, on publication.

674

BIKEREPORT—Bikecentennial, P.O. Box 8308, Missoula, MT 59807. Daniel D'Ambrosio, Ed. News shorts from the bicycling world for "In Bicycle Circles." Pays $5 to $10, on publication.

CAPPER'S—616 Jefferson St., Topeka, KS 66607. Nancy Peavler, Ed. Household hints, recipes, jokes. Pays varying rates, on publication.

CASCADES EAST—716 N. E. 4th St., P. O. Box 5784, Bend, OR 97708. Geoff Hill, Ed. Fillers, related to travel, history, and recreation in Central Oregon. Pays 3¢ to 10¢ a word, extra for photos, on publication.

CASHFLOW—6255 Barfield Rd., Atlanta, GA 30328. Dick Gamble, Ed. Fillers, to 1,000 words, on varied aspects of treasury financial management and corporate finance, for treasury managers in public and private institutions. Pays on publication. Query.

CATHOLIC DIGEST—P.O. Box 64090, St. Paul, MN 55164. Features, to 300 words, on instances of kindness rewarded, for "Hearts Are Trumps." Stories about conversions, for "Open Door." Reports of tactful remarks or actions, for "The Perfect Assist." Accounts of good deeds, for "People Are Like That." Humorous pieces on parish life, for "In Our Parish." Amusing signs, for "Signs of the Times." Jokes; fillers. Pays $4 to $50, on publication. Manuscripts cannot be acknowledged or returned.

CHEESE MARKET NEWS—Gorman Publishing Co., 8750 W. Bryn Mawr, Chicago, IL 60631. Jerry Dryer, Ed. Fillers, 25 to 150 words, on innovative dairies, dairy processing operations, marketing successes, for milk handlers and makers of dairy products. Pays $25, on publication.

CHIC—9171 Wilshire Blvd., Suite. 300, Beverly Hills, CA 90210. Visual fillers, short humor, with humors, 100 to 125 words, for "Odds and Ends." Pays on acceptance.

CHICKADEE—56 The Esplanade, Ste. 306, Toronto, Ont., Canada M5E 1A7. Humorous poetry, 10 to 15 lines, about animals and nature, for children. Pays on publication. Enclose international reply coupons.

CHILDREN'S PLAYMATE—1100 Waterway Blvd., P. O. Box 567, Indianapolis, IN 46206. Elizabeth Rinck, Ed. Puzzles, games, mazes for 5- to 7-year-olds, emphasizing health, safety and nutrition. Pays about 8¢ a word (varies on puzzles), on acceptance.

CHRISTIAN HERALD—40 Overlook Dr., Chappaqua, NY 10514. Dean Merrill, Ed. Poetry and true anecdotes, humorous or instructive, on Christian marriage and child rearing. Pays $20, on acceptance.

THE CHURCH MUSICIAN—127 Ninth Ave. N., Nashville, TN 37234. W. M. Anderson, Ed. For Southern Baptist music leaders. Humorous fillers with a music slant. No clippings. Pays around 5¢ a word, on acceptance. Same address and requirements for *Glory Songs* (for adults) and *Opus One* and *Opus Two* (for teenagers).

COLUMBIA—Box 1670, New Haven, CT 06507. Richard McMunn, Ed. Magazine of the Knights of Columbus. Catholic family magazine. Humor and satire, to 1,000 words; captionless cartoons. Pays $200, $50 for cartoons, on acceptance.

COLUMBIA JOURNALISM REVIEW—Columbia University, 700 Journalism Bldg., New York, NY 10027. Gloria Cooper, Man. Ed. Amusing mistakes in news stories, headlines, photos, etc. (original clippings required), for "Lower Case." Pays $10, on publication.

675

COUNTRY—5400 S. 60th St, Greendale, WI 53129. Fillers, 50 to 200 words, for rural audience. Pays on acceptance. Address Dan Johnson.

COUNTRY WOMAN—P.O. Box 643, Milwaukee, WI 53201. Kathy Pohl, Man. Ed. Short verse, 4 to 20 lines, and fillers, to 250 words, on the rural experience. Pays $10 to $50, on acceptance.

CYCLE WORLD—853 W 17th St., Costa Mesa, CA 92627. Paul Dean, Ed. News items on motorcycle industry, legislation, trends. Pays on acceptance.

CZESCHIN'S MUTUAL FUND OUTLOOK & RECOMMENDATIONS—824 E. Baltimore St., Baltimore, MD 21202. Robert W. Czeschin, Ed. Short features, to 1,000 words, on all aspects of mutual funds and mutual fund investing: IRAs, switching strategies, non-U.S. funds, taxes, etc. Pays $100, on acceptance.

DOWN EAST—Camden, ME 04843. Anecdotes about Maine, to 1,000 words, for "I Remember." Humorous anecdotes, to 300 words, for "It Happened Down East." Pays $25 to $75, on acceptance

EBONY—820 S. Michigan Ave., Chicago, IL 60605. Charles L. Saunders, Man. Ed. Cartoons. Pays $75, on publication.

THE ELKS MAGAZINE—425 W. Diversey Pkwy., Chicago, IL 60614. Fred D. Oakes, Exec. Ed. Informative or humorous pieces, to 2,500 words. Pays from $150, on acceptance. Query.

FACES—20 Grove St., Peterborough, NH 03458. Carolyn Yoder, Ed. Puzzles, mazes, crosswordss, and picture puzzles, related to monthly themes, for children. Send SASE for list of themes before submitting.

FAMILY CIRCLE—Box 2822, Grand Central Sta., New York, NY 10017. "Bright Ideas" or suggestions on homemaking and community betterment, for "Readers' Idea Exchange." Pays $50. Submit postcards only; unpublished entries cannot be acknowledged or returned.

FARM AND RANCH LIVING—5400 S. 60th St., Greendale, WI 53129. Bob Ottum, Ed. Fillers on rural people and living, 200 words. Pays from $15, on acceptance and publication.

FATE—500 Hyacinth Pl., Highland Park, IL 60035. Jerome Clark, Ed. Factual fillers, to 300 words, on strange or psychic happenings. True stories, to 300 words, on psychic or mystic personal experiences. Pays $2 to $15.

FIELD & STREAM—1515 Broadway, New York, NY 10036. Duncan Barnes, Ed. Fillers on hunting, fishing, camping, etc., to 1,000 words, for "How It's Done." Cartoons. Pays $250 to $750 for fillers, $100 for cartoons, on acceptance.

FLARE—777 Bay St., Toronto, Ont., Canada M5W 1A7. Patricia McGee, Assoc. Ed. Career-related items, profiles, 100 to 150 words, for young Canadian working women aged 18 to 34. Pays on acceptance. Query.

FLY FISHERMAN—Harrisburg, PA 17105. Jack Russell, Assoc. Ed. Fillers, 100 words, on equipment tackle tips, knots, and fly-tying tips. Pays from $35, on acceptance.

FORD TIMES—One Illinois Center, 111 E. Wacker Dr., Ste. 1700, Chicago, IL 60601. John Fink, Ed. Short vacation/travel/dining anecdotes, 150 words, for "Road Show." Pays $50, on publication.

GALLERY—401 Park Ave. S., New York, NY 10016–8802. Marc Lichter, Ed. Dir., Barry Janoff, Man. Ed. Short humor, satire, and short service features for men. Pays varying rates, on acceptance and publication. Query.

GAMES—810 Seventh Ave., New York, NY 10019. R. Wayne Schmittberger, Ed. Short articles on playful subjects and original games and puzzles. Pays varying rates, on acceptance. Query.

GLAMOUR—350 Madison Ave., New York, NY 10017. Articles, 1,000 words, for "Viewpoint" section: opinion pieces for women. Pays $500, on acceptance. Send SASE.

GOLF DIGEST—5520 Park Ave., Trumbull, CT 06611. Topsy Siderowf, Ed. Asst. Short fact items, anecdotes, quips, jokes, light verse related to golf. True humorous or odd incidents, to 200 words. Pays from $25, on acceptance.

GOLF ILLUSTRATED—3 Park Ave., New York, NY 10016. Golf-related fillers; one- to two-paragraph news or personal-experience snippets, preferably of humorous or offbeat nature. Pays $25 to $100, on acceptance.

GOLF MAGAZINE—380 Madison Ave., New York, NY 10017. James Frank, Exec. Ed. Shorts, to 500 words, on golf. Pays $75 to $150, on publication.

GOOD HOUSEKEEING—959 Eighth Ave., New York, NY 10019. Rosemary Leonard, Ed. Four to eight lines of witty poetry, light verse, and quips with universal appeal, easy to illustrate for "Light Housekeeping" page. Seasonal material welcome. Pays $25 to $50, on acceptance.

GUIDEPOSTS—747 Third Ave., New York, NY 10017. Rick Hamlin, Features Ed. Inspirational anecdotes, to 250 words. Pays $10 to $50, on acceptance.

HOME LIFE—127 Ninth Ave. N., Nashville, TN 37234. Charlie Warren, Ed. Southern Baptist. Personal-experience pieces, 100 to 500 words, on Christian marriage and family relationships. Pays to 5¢ a word, on acceptance.

HOME MECHANIX—1515 Broadway, New York, NY 10036. Joseph Provey, Ed. Time- or money-saving tips for the home, garage, or yard; seasonal reminders for homeowners. Pays $50 to $75, on acceptance.

THE INDEPENDENT ASSIGNMENT—201 E. 36th St., New York, NY 10016. Alison R. Lanier, Ed. Short pieces, 200 to 300 words, by writers who have lived abroad, with advice, suggestions, warnings, and information for Americans who are now overseas. No travel tips or stories of personal interest. Pays $35, on acceptance.

INDEPENDENT LIVING—44 Broadway, New York, NY 11740. Anne Kelly, Ed. Short humor, to 500 words, for magazine addressing life styles of "physically challeneged and disabled." Pays 10¢ a word, on publication. Query.

JACK & JILL—1100 Waterway Blvd., Box 567, Indianapolis, IN 46206. Steve Charles, Ed. Poems, puzzles, games, science and crafts projects for 6- to 8-year-olds, with health or holiday themes. Instructions for activities should be clearly written, accompanied by diagrams and a list of needed materials. Pays varying rates on publication.

LADIES' HOME JOURNAL—"Last Laughs," 100 Park Ave., New York, NY 10017. Brief anecdotes about the funny business of being a woman today. Pays $25. Submissions cannot be acknowledged or returned.

MCCALL'S—230 Park Ave., New York, NY 10169. Parenting tips and ideas, or words of wisdom on raising children. Pays $10. Include home phone and Social Security number with submission.

MAD MAGAZINE—485 Madison Ave., New York , NY 10022. Humorous pieces on a wide variety of topics. Two- to eight-panel cartoons; sketches not necessary. Query with proposal and SASE. Pays top rates, on acceptance.

MATURE LIVING—127 Ninth Ave. N., MSN 140, Nashville, TN 37234. Brief, humorous, original items; 25-line profiles with action photos; "Grandparents Brag Board" items; inspirational pieces for senior adults, 125 words. Pays $5 to $15.

MATURE YEARS—201 Eighth Ave. S, Nashville, TN 37202. Poems, cartoons, puzzles, jokes, anecdotes, to 300 words, for older adults. Pays 4¢ a word, on acceptance. Include name, address, Social Security number with all submissions.

MIAMI/SOUTH FLORIDA MAGAZINE—See *South Florida Magazine.*

MID-WEST OUTDOORS—111 Shore Dr., Hinsdale, IL 60521. Gene Laulunen, Man. Ed. Where to and how to fish in the Midwest, 400 to 1,500 words, with two photos. Pays $15 to $35, on acceptance.

MODERN BRIDE—475 Park Ave. S., New York, NY 10016. Mary Ann Cavlin, Man. Ed. Humorous pieces, 500 to 1,500 words, for brides. Pays on acceptance.

MODERN MATURITY—3200 E. Carson St., Lakewood, CA 90712. Ian Ledgerwood, Ed. Money-saving tips; jokes, cartoons; etc. Submit seasonal material 6 months in advance. Pays from $50, on acceptance. Query.

MODERN PHOTOGRAPHY—825 Seventh Ave., New York, NY 10019. Barry Tanenbaum, Ed. How-to pieces, 200 to 300 words, with photos, on acceptance. Pays $25 to $50, on acceptance.

NATIONAL ENQUIRER—Lantana , FL 33464. Jim Allan, Asst. Ed. Short, humorous or philosophical fillers, witticisms, anecdotes, jokes, tart comments. Orignal items preferred. Short poetry with traditional rhyming verse, of amusing, philosophical or inspirational nature. No obscure or "arty" poetry. Occasionally uses longer poems of a serious or humorous nature. Submit seasonal/holiday material at least two months in advance. SASE and Social Security number with all submissions. Pays from $20, after publication.

NATIONAL REVIEW—150 E. 35th St., New York, NY 10016. William F. Buckley, Ed. Satire, to 900 words. Short, satirical poems. Pays $35 to $150, on publication.

NEW ENGLAND MONTHLY—P.O. Box 466, Haydenville, MA 01039. Mike Grudowski, Asst. Ed. Shorts, 400 to 1,000 words, on various aspects of life and culture in the six New England states. Pays $75 to $250, on acceptance

NEW JERSEY MONTHLY—55 Park Pl., Morristown, NJ 07960. Larry Marscheck, Ed. Short pieces related to life in New Jersey. Pays 30¢ a word, on acceptance.

NEW YORK—755 Second Ave. , New York, NY 10017. Eric Pooley, Sr. Ed. Short, lively pieces, to 400 words, highlighting events and trends in New York City for "Fast Track." Profiles to 300 words for "Brief Lives." Pays $25 to $150, on publication. Include SASE.

THE NEW YORKER—25 W. 43rd St., New York, NY 10036. Amusing mistakes in newspapers, books, magzines, etc. Pays from $10, extra for headings and tags, on acceptance. Address Newsbreaks Dept. Material returned only with SASE.

NORTHWEST LIVING—130 Second St. S., Edmonds, WA 98020. Terry Sheedy, Ed. Shorts, 100 to 400 words, related to the natural resources of the Northwest. Query first with SASE. Pays on publication.

ORBEN'S CURRENT COMEDY—1200 N. Nash St. #1122, Arlington, VA 22209. Robert Orben, Ed. Original, funny, performable one-liners and brief jokes on news, fads, topical subjects, etc. Openings, jokes, roast material, etc., for speakers. Pays $8, after publication. SASE required.

OUTDOOR LIFE—380 Madison Ave., New York, NY 10017. Clare Conley, Ed. Short instructive items and one-pagers on hunting, fishing, camping gear, boats, outdoor equipment. Photos. Pays on acceptance.

PARENTS—685 Third Ave., New York, NY 10017. Ann Pleshette Murphy, Ed. Short items on solutions to child care-related problems for "Parents Exchange." Pays $20, on publication.

PARISH FAMILY DIGEST—200 Noll Plaza, Huntington, IN 46750. George P. Foster, Ed. Family- or Catholic parish-oriented humor. Anecdotes, 250 words, of unusual parish experiences. Pays $5 to $12.50, on acceptance.

PENNYWHISTLE PRESS—Box 500-P, Washington, DC 20044. Anita Sama, Ed. Puzzlers, word games, stories, for 6- to 12-year-olds. Pays varying rates, on acceptance.

PEOPLE IN ACTION—P.O. Box 10010, Ogden, UT 84409. Profiles of gourmet chefs, first-class restaurant managers, food or nutrition experts and celebrity cooks; 700 words, including recipe plus color photos of the finished dish, and the cook. Query with SASE to editor.

PGA MAGAZINE—100 Ave. of the Champions, Palm Beach Gardens, FL 33418. Humorous pieces related to golf, to 1,500 words. Pays to $300, on acceptance.

PHILIP MORRIS MAGAZINE—153 Waverly Pl., 3rd Floor, New York, NY 10014. Frank Gannon, Ed. Tobacco trivia, products, anecdotes, history. Pays on publication.

PLAYBOY—919 N. Michigan Ave., Chicago, IL 60611. Address Party Jokes Ed. or After Hours Ed. Jokes; short original material on new trends, lifestyles, personalities; humorous new items. Pays $50 for jokes, on acceptance; $50 to $350 for "After Hours" items, on publication.

PLAYGIRL—801 Second Ave., New York, NY 10017. Humorous looks at daily life and relationships from male or female perspective, to 1,000 words, for "The Men's Room" and "The Women's Room." Query Nonfiction Ed. Cartoons dealing with women and women's issues. Kevin G. Loud, Cartoon Ed. Pays varying rates.

POPULAR MECHANICS—224 W. 57th St., New York, NY 10019. Bill Hartford, Man. Ed. How-to pieces, from 300 words, with photos and sketches, on home improvement and shop and craft projects. Pays $25 to $200, on acceptance. Buys all rights.

POPULAR SCIENCE MONTHLY—380 Madison Ave., New York, NY 10017. A. W. Lees, Home & Shop Ed. One-column fillers, 350 words, with photo or sketch if demo necessary: general workshop ideas, small home improvement projects, maintenance tips for home and car. Pays from $100, on acceptance.

READER'S DIGEST—Pleasantville, NY 10570. Anecdotes for "Life in These United States," "Humor in Uniform," "Campus Comedy," and "All in a Day's Work." Pays $300, on publication. Short items for "Toward More Picturesque Speech." Pays $50. Anecdotes, fillers, for "Laughter, the Best Medicine," "Personal Glimpses," etc. Pays $20 per two-column line. No submissions acknowledged or returned. Consult anecdotes page for guidelines.

RECOVERY LIFE (FORMERLY *RECOVERY*)—P. O. Box 31329, Seattle,

WA 98103. Stories, poetry and fillers of interest to those recovering from alcohol and other addictions. SASE required.

RIVER RUNNER—P.O. Box 697, Fallbrook, CA 92028. Ken Hulick, Ed. Tips for whitewater boaters of all levels. Pays from 5¢ a word, on publication.

ROAD KING—P. O. Box 250, Park Forest, IL 60466. Address Features Ed. Trucking-related cartoons for "Loads of Laughs"; anecdotes to 200 words, for "Trucker's Life." Pays $25 for cartoons, $25 for anecdotes, on publication. SASE required.

THE ROTARIAN—1560 Sherman Ave., Evanston, IL 60201. Willmon L. White, Ed. Occasional humor and short poems of all types. Payment varies, on acceptance.

RURAL HERITAGE—P. O. Box 516, Albia, IL 52531. Anecdotes and news-breaks, 100 to 750 words, related to draft horses, rural history, antiques, or old-time crafts. Pays 3¢ to 10¢ a word, on publication.

SACRAMENTO—1021 Second St., Sacramento, CA 95814. "City Lights," interesting and unusual people, places, and behind-the-scenes news items, 75 to 250 words. All material must have Sacramento tie-in. Pays on acceptance.

THE SATURDAY EVENING POST—1100 Waterway Blvd., Indianapolis, IN 46202. Jack Gramling, Post Scripts Ed. Humor and satire, to 300 words; light verse, cartoons, jokes, for "Post Scripts." Pays $15, on publication.

SCHOOL SHOP—Prakken Publishing Box 8623, 416 Longshore Dr., Ann Arbor, MI 48107. Alan H. Jones, Pub. and Exec. Ed. Puzzles and cartoons of interest to technology and industrial education teachers and administrators. Pay varies, on publication.

SCORE, CANADA'S GOLF MAGAZINE—287 MacPherson Ave., Toronto, Ont., Canada M4V 1A4. John Gordon, Man. Ed. Fillers, 50 to 100 words, related to Canadian golf scene. Rarely uses humor or poems. Pays $10 to $25, on publication. Include international reply coupons.

SELECT HOMES—3835 W. 30th Ave., Vancouver, B.C., Canada V6S 1W9. Pam Withers, Ed. Humorous pieces, 650 words, on homeowning and home renovating, for "Back Porch." Pays from $150, on acceptance. Query regional editors: Pam Withers, Western Editor (address above); or Eastern Editor, 1450 Don Mills Rd., Don Mills, Ont., Canada M3B 2X7.

SKI MAGAZINE—380 Madison Ave., New York, NY 10017. Dick Needham, Ed. Short, 100- to 300-word items on events and people in skiing, for "Ski Life" department. Humor, to 2,000 words, related to skiing. Pays on acceptance.

SKIING MAGAZINE—1515 Broadway, New York, NY 10036. Bill Grout, Ed.-in-Chief. Articles, to 600 words, on skiing; humorous vignettes, fillers on skiing oddities. Pays from 15¢ a word, on acceptance.

SNOWMOBILE—319 Barry Ave., Suite 101, Wayzata, MN 55391. Dick Hendricks, Ed. Short humor and cartoons on snowmobiling and winter "Personality Plates" sighted. Pays varying rates, on publication.

SOUTH FLORIDA MAGAZINE (FORMERLY *MIAMI/SOUTH FLORIDA MAGAZINE*)—600 Brickell Ave., Suite 207, Miami, FL 33131. Joseph McQuay, Man. Ed. Short pieces, 200 to 400 words, on local attractions. Short profiles on South Florida personalities, 500 words maximum. Pays on publication.

SOUTHERN OUTDOORS—1 Bell Rd., Montgomery, AL 35117. Larry

Teague, Ed. Humor, 800 to 1,200 words, related to the outdoors. Pays 15¢ to 20¢ a word, on acceptance.

SPORTS AFIELD—2550 W. 55th St., New York, NY 10019. Unusual, useful tips, 100 to 500 words, for "Almanac" section: hunting, fishing, camping, boating, etc. Photos. Pays 10¢ per column inch, on publication.

STAR—660 White Plains Rd., Tarrytown, NY 10591. Topical articles, 50 to 800 words, on human-interest subjects, show business, life styles, the sciences, etc., for family audience. Pays varying rates.

TOUCH—Box 7259, Grand Rapids, MI 49510. Carol Smith, Man. Ed. Fillers, Bible puzzles on themes from NIV version, for Christian girls aged 8 to 14. Pays 2¢ a word, on acceptance. Send SASE for theme update.

TRAILER BOATS—Box 5427, Carson, CA 90749–5427. Jim Youngs, Ed. Fillers and humor, preferably with illustrations, on boating and related activities. Pays $5 per column inch, extra for photos, on publication.

TRAVEL SMART—Dobbs Ferry, NY 10522. Interesting, unusual or travel-related tips, vacation or business information. Query for over 250 words. Pays $5 to $15.

TRUE CONFESSIONS—215 Lexington Ave., New York, NY 10016. Helen Vincent, Ed. Warm, inspirational first-person fillers, 300 to 700 words, about love, marriage, family life, for "The Feminine Side of Things." Pays after publication. Buys all rights.

THE VIRGINIAN—P. O. Box 8, New Hope, VA 24469. Hunter S. Pierce, IV, Ed. Fillers related to Virginia and adjacent regions of the South. Anecdotes and nostalgia preferred. Pays on publication.

VOLKSWAGEN'S WORLD—P. O. Box 3951, 888 W. Big Beaver, Troy, MI 48007–3951. Marlene Goldsmith, Ed. Anecdotes, to 100 words, zbout Volkswagen owners' experiences; humorous photos of Volkswagens. Pays from $15 to $40, on acceptance.

WASHINGTON'S ALMANAC—901 Lenora, Seattle, WA 98121. David Fuller, Man. Ed. Fillers and short humor related to Washington state. Pays varing rates, on publication.

WISCONSIN TRAILS—P. O. Box 5650, Madison, WI 53705. Short fillers about Wisconsin: places to go, things to see, etc., 500 words. Pays $100, on publication.

WOMAN—1115 Broadway, New York, NY 10010. Sherry Amatenstein, Ed. Short newsbreaks on medical and legal advances for women, for "Let's Put Our Heads Together." Pays on acceptance. Query.

WOMAN'S DAY—1515 Broadway, New York, NY 10036. Heart-warming anecdotes about a "good neighbor"; creative solutions to community or family problems. For "Tips to Share": short pieces of personal, instructive or family experiences, practical suggestions for homemakers. Pays $75, on publication.

WOOD 'N ENERGY—P.O. Box 2008, Laconia, NH 03247. Jason Perry, Ed. Short pieces, 150 to 500 words, for columns: "Reports" (energy news); "Regulations" (safety and standards news); and "Retailers Corner" (tips on running a retail shop). Pays to $50, on publication.

WOODENBOAT MAGAZINE—Box 78, Brooklin, ME 04616. Jon Wilson, Ed. Wooden boat-related activities and projects. Pays $5 to $50, on publication.

WORKING WOMAN WEEKENDS—342 Madison Ave., New York, NY 10173. Louise Washer, Assoc. Ed. Fillers, 250 to 750 words, on weekend entertaining, travel, cooking, recreation.

JUVENILE, TEENAGE, AND YOUNG ADULT MAGAZINES

JUVENILE MAGAZINES

ACTION—Dept. of Christian Education, Free Methodist Headquarters, 901 College Ave., Winona Lake, IN 46590. Vera Bethel, Ed. Stories, 1,000 words, for 10- to 12-year-olds. How-to features, 200 to 500 words. Verse. Seasonal material. Pays $25 for stories, $15 for features with photos or sketch, $5 for poetry, on publication.

CHICKADEE—The Young Naturalist Foundation, 56 The Esplanade, Suite 306, Toronto, Ont., Canada M5E 1A7. Janis Nostbakken, Ed. Animal and adventure storeis, 200 to 800 words, for children aged 3 to 8. Also, puzzles, activities, and observation games, 50 to 100 words. Pays varying rates, on publication. Send complete manuscript and international postal coupons. No outlines.

CHILD LIFE—1100 Waterway Blvd., P.O. Box 567, Indianapolis, IN 46206. Steve Charles, Ed. Articles, 500 to 1,200 words, for 7- to 9-year-olds. Fiction and humor stories, to 1,200 words. Puzzles. Photos. Pays about 8¢ a word, extra for photos, on publication. Buys all rights.

CHILDREN'S ALBUM—P.O. Box 6086, Concord, CA 94524. Kathy Madsen, Ed. Fiction and poetry by children 8 to 14. Science and crafts projects, with step-by-step instructions. Pays $50 per page. Guidelines.

CHILDREN'S DIGEST—1100 Waterway Blvd., P.O. Box 567, Indianapolis, IN 46202. Elizabeth Rinck, Ed. Health publication for children aged 8 to 10. Informative articles, 500 to 1,200 words, and fiction (especially realistic, adventure, mystery, and humorous), 500 to 1,500 words, with health, safety, exercise, nutrition, or hygiene as theme. Historical and biographical articles. Poetry. Pays 8¢ a word, from $10 for poems, on publication.

CHILDREN'S MAGIC WINDOW—1008 W. 80th St., Bloomington, MN 55420. Mary Morse, Ed.-in-Chief. Short stories and articles, 350 to 800 words, on topics from science and sports to health and family. Poetry, games, puzzles, riddles. Pays $35 to $200, after publication. Query for articles. Guidelines available.

CHILDREN'S PLAYMATE—Editorial Office, 1100 Waterway Blvd., P.O. Box 567, Indianapolis, IN 46206. Elizabeth Rinck, Ed. Humorous and health-related short stories, 500 to 700 words, for 5- to 7-year-olds. Simple science articles and how-to crafts pieces with brief instructions. "All About" features, about 500 words, on health, nutrition, safety, and exercise. Poems. Pays about 8¢ a word, $10 minimum for poetry, on publication.

CLUBHOUSE—Berrien Springs, MI 49103. Elaine Meseraull, Ed. Action-oriented Christian stories: features, 1,000 to 1,200 words; "Story Cubes" and "Thinker Tales" (parables), about 800 words. Children in stories should be wise, brave, funny, kind, etc. Pays to $35 for lead stories, $30 for parables and other stories.

COBBLESTONE—20 Grove St., Peterborough, NH 03458. Carolyn Yoder, Ed. Theme-related biographies, fiction, poetry, and short accounts of historical events, to 1,200 words, for children aged 8 to 14 years. Pays 10¢ to 15¢ a word for prose, varying rates for poetry, on publication. Send SASE for editorial guidelines with monthly themes.

CRICKET—Box 300, Peru, IL 61354. Marianne Carus, Ed.-in-Chief. Articles and fiction, 200 to 1,500 words, for 6- to 12-year-olds. Poetry, to 30 lines. Pays to 25¢ a word, to $3 a line for poetry, on publication. Send SASE for guidelines.

DISCOVERIES—6401 The Paseo, Kansas City, MO 64131. Stories, 400 to 500 words, for 3rd to 6th graders, with Christian emphasis. Poetry, 4 to 20 lines. Cartoons. Pays 3 ½¢ a word (2¢ a word for reprints), 25¢ a line for potry (minimum of $2), on acceptance.

THE DOLPHIN LOG—The Cousteau Society, 8440 Santa Monica Blvd., Los Angeles, CA 90069. Pam Stacey, Ed. Articles, 500 to 1,200 words, on a variety of topics related to our global water system: marine biology, ecology, natural history, and water-related stories, for children aged 7 to 15. Pays $25 to $150, on publication. Query.

ELECTRIC COMPANY MAGAZINE—See *3–2–1 Contact.*

THE FRIEND—50 E. North Temple, 23rd Floor, Salt Lake City, UT 84150. Vivian Paulsen, Man. Ed. Stories and articles, 1,000 to 1,200 words. "Tiny Tot" stories, to 250 words. Pays from 8¢ a word, from $15 per poem, on acceptance.

HIGHLIGHTS FOR CHILDREN—803 Church St., Honesdale, PA 18431. Kent L. Brown, Ed. Fiction and articles, to 900 words, for 2- to 12-year-olds. Fiction should have strong plot, believable characters, story line that holds reader's interest from beginning to end. No crime or violence. For articles, cite references used and qualifications. Easy rebus-form stories. Easy-to-read stories, 400 to 600 words, with strong plots. Pays from 8¢ a word, on acceptance.

HUMPTY DUMPTY'S MAGAZINE—1100 Waterway Blvd., P.O. Box 567, Indianapolis, IN 46206. Christine French Clark, Ed. Health publication for children ages 4 to 6. Easy-to-read fiction, to 600 words, some with health and nutrition, safety, exercise, or hygiene as theme; humor and light approach preferred. Crafts with clear, brief instructions. Short verse, narrative poems. Pays about 8¢ a word, from $10 for poems, on publication. Buys all rights.

JACK AND JILL—Box 567, Indianapolis, IN 46206. Steve Charles, Ed. Articles, 500 to 1,000 words, for 6- to 8-year-olds, on sports, nature, science, health, safety, exercise. Features, 1,000 to 1,200 words, on history, biography, life in other countries, etc. Fiction, to 1,200 words. Short poems, games, puzzles, projects. Photos. Pays about 8¢ a word, extra for photos, varying rates for fillers, on publication.

JUNIOR TRAILS—1445 Boonville Ave., Springfield, MO 65802. Cathy Ketcher, Ed. Fiction (1,000 to 1,800 words) with a Christian focus; must have believable characters and moral emphasis. Articles (500 to 1,000 words) on science, nature, biography. Pays 2¢ or 3¢ a word, on acceptance.

KID CITY (FORMERLY *ELECTRIC COMPANY MAGAZINE*)—See *3–2–1 Contact.*

LOLLIPOPS MAGAZINE—Good Apple, Inc., P.O. Box 299, Carthage, IL 62321–0299. Learning games and activities covering all areas of the curriculum; arts and crafts ideas; stories for ages 4 to 7. Pays varying rates, on publication. Query first.

MY OWN MAGAZINE—3500 Western Ave., Highland Park, IL 60035. Carolyn Good Quattrocki, Ed. Fiction, 200 or 400 words; poetry, 50 to 100 words, for children ages three to six. Stories and activities should teach concepts in safety, language, science, math, social studies, and health. Pays $150 to $200 for fiction, $100 for poetry, on acceptance. Guidelines available.

NATIONAL GEOGRAPHIC WORLD—1145 17th St. N.W., Washington, DC 20036. Pat Robbins, Ed. Picture magazine for young readers, ages 8 and older. Games and puzzles; proposals for picture stories. Pays $25 for games. Queries required for stories.

ODYSSEY—1027 N. 7th St., Milwaukee, WI 53233. Nancy Mack, Ed. Features, 600 to 1,500 words, on astronomy and space science for 8- to 12-year-olds. Short experiments, projects, and games. Pays $100 to $350, on publication.

ON THE LINE—616 Walnut, Scottdale, PA 15683–1999. Virginia A. Hostetler, Ed. Nature and how-to articles, 500 to 750 words, for 10- to 14-year-olds. Fiction, 800 to 1,200 words. Poetry, puzzles, cartoons. Pays to 4¢ a word, on acceptance.

OWL—The Young Naturalist Foundation, 56 The Esplanade, Suite 306, Toronto, Ont., Canada M5E 1A7. Sylvia Funston, Ed. Articles, 500 to 1,000 words, for children aged 8 to 12, about animals, science, people, technology, new discoveries, activities. Pays varying rates, on publication. Send for guidelines.

PENNYWHISTLE PRESS—Box 500-P, Washington, DC 20044. Anita Sama, Ed. Short fiction, 850 words, for 8- to 12-year-old children, 400 words for 5- to 8-year-olds. Puzzles and word games. Payment varies, on publication.

PLAYS, THE DRAMA MAGAZINE FOR YOUNG PEOPLE—120 Boylston St., Boston, MA 02115. Elizabeth Preston, Man. Ed. Needs one-act plays, programs, skits, creative dramatic material, suitable for school productions at junior high, middle, and lower grade levels. Plays with one set preferred. Uses comedies, dramas, satires, farces, melodramas, dramatized classics, folktales and fairy tales, puppet plays. Pays good rates, on acceptance. Send SASE for manuscript specification sheet. Buys all rights.

POCKETS—1908 Grand Ave., Box 189, Nashville, TN 37202. Shirley Paris, Ed. Ecumenical magazine for children ages 6 to 12. Fiction and scripture stories, 600 to 1,500 words; short poems; and articles about the Bible, 400 to 600 words. Pays from 7¢ a word, $25 to $50 for poetry, on acceptance. Guidelines.

RADAR—8121 Hamilton Ave., Cincinnati, OH 45231. Margaret Williams, Ed. Articles, 400 to 650 words, on nature, hobbies, crafts. Short stories, 900 to 1,100 words: mystery, sports, school, family, with 12-year-old as main character; serials of 2,000 words. Christian emphasis. Poems to 12 lines. Pays to 3¢ a word, to 40¢ a line for poetry, on acceptance.

RANGER RICK—1412 16th St. N.W., Washington, DC 20036. Gerald Bishop, Ed. Articles, to 900 words, on wildlife, conservation, natural sciences, and kids in the outdoors, for 6- to 12-year-olds. Nature-related fiction and science fiction welcome. Games, crafts, poems, and puzzles. Pays to $350, on acceptance.

SESAME STREET MAGAZINE— *See 3-2-1 Contact.*

SHOFAR—43 Northcote Dr., Melville, NY 11747. Alan A. Kay, Exec. Ed. Short stories, 500 to 750 words; articles, 250 to 750 words; poetry, to 50 lines; short fillers, games, puzzles, and cartoons for Jewish children, 8 to 13. All material must have a Jewish theme. Pays 10¢ a word, on publication. Submit holiday pieces at least three months in advance.

STONE SOUP, THE MAGAZINE BY CHILDREN—Box 83, Santa Cruz, CA 95063. Gerry Mandel, Ed. Stories, poems, plays, book reviews by children under 14. Pays in copies.

STORY FRIENDS—Mennonite Publishing House, Scottdale, PA 15683. Marjorie Waybill, Ed. Stories, 350 to 800 words, for 4- to 9-year-olds, on Christian faith and values in everyday experiences. Quizzes, riddles. Poetry. Pays to 5¢ a word, to $5 per poem, on acceptance.

SURPRISES—P.O. Box 236, Chanhassen, MN 55317. Peggy Simenson, Jeanne Palmer, Eds. Educational activities, puzzles, games in reading, language, math, science, cooking, music, and art. Articles about history, animals, and geography. Pays $15 to $25, on publication.

3-2-1 CONTACT—Children's Television Workshop, 1 Lincoln Plaza, New York, NY 10023. Jonathan Rosenbloom, Ed. Entertaining and informative articles, 600 to 1,000 words, for 8- to 14-year-olds, on all aspects of science, computers, scientists, and children who are learning about or practicing science. Pays $75 to $400, on acceptance. No fiction. Also publishes *Kid City* (formerly *Electric Company Magazine*) and *Sesame Street Magazine.* Query.

TOUCH—Box 7259, Grand Rapids, MI 49510. Carol Smith, Man. Ed. Upbeat fiction and features, 1,000 to 1,500 words, for Christian girls age 8 to 14; personal life, nature, crafts. Poetry; fillers, puzzles. Pays 2¢ a word, extra for photos, on acceptance. Query for theme with SASE.

TURTLE MAGAZINE FOR PRESCHOOL KIDS—1100 Waterway Blvd., Box 567, Indianapolis, IN 46206. Beth Wood Thomas, Ed. Stories about safety, exercise, health, and nutrition, for preschoolers. Humorous, entertaining fiction, 600 words. Simple poems. Stories-in-rhyme; easy-to-read stories, to 500 words, for beginning readers. Pays about 8¢ a word, on publication. Buys all rights. Send SASE for guidelines.

U.S. KIDS—245 Long Hill Rd., Middletown, CT 06457. Lewis K. Parker, Ed. Articles, 250 to 400 words, and fiction, 250 to 350 words, on issues related to kids ages 5 to 10, true-life adventures, science and nature topics, shorts. Pays $250 to $600, on acceptance. Query. Guidelines.

WEE WISDOM—Unity Village, MO 64065. Verle Bell, Ed. Character-building stories, to 800 words, for children through age 12. Pays varying rates, on acceptance.

WONDER TIME—6401 The Paseo, Kansas City, MO 64131. Evelyn J. Beals, Ed. Stories, 200 to 600 words, for 6- to 8-year-olds, with Christian emphasis to correlate with Sunday School curriculum. Features, to 300 words, on nature, crafts, etc. Poetry, 4 to 12 lines. Pays 3 ½¢ a word, from 25¢ a line for verse, $2.50 minimum, on acceptance.

YABA WORLD—5301 S. 76th St., Greendale, WI 53129. Peggy Larson, Ed. Articles, 1,500 words, on Young American Bowling Alliance league or tournament bowling. Profiles; how-tos. Photos. Pays $25 to $50, extra for photos, on acceptance. Query preferred.

YOUNG AMERICAN, AMERICA'S NEWSPAPER FOR KIDS—P.O. Box

12409, Portland, OR 97212. Kristina T. Linden, Ed. Upbeat, positive, sophisticated material for children ages 4 to 15. Fiction, to 1,000 words; articles, to 350 words, on science, humor, history and newsworthy young people; poetry. Pays 7¢ a word, $5 for photos, on publication.

YOUNG JUDEAN—50 W. 58th St., New York, NY 10019. Mordecai Newman, Ed. Articles, 500 to 1,000 words, with photos, for 9- to 12-year-olds, on Israel, Jewish holidays, Jewish-American life, Jewish history. Fiction, 800 to 1,500 words, on Jewish themes. Poetry, from 8 lines. Fillers, humor, reviews. Pays 5¢ a word.

TEENAGE AND YOUNG ADULT

ALIVE NOW!—P.O. Box 189, Nashville, TN 37202. Mary Ruth Coffman, Ed. Short essays, 250 to 400 words, with Christian emphasis. Poetry, one page. Photos. Pays $5 to $20, on publication.

BOP—3500 W. Olive Ave., Suite 850, Burbank, CA 91505. Julie Laufer, Ed. Interviews and features, 500 to 1,000 words, for teen-age girls, on stars popular with teen-agers. Photos. Pays varying rates, on acceptance. Query preferred.

BOYS' LIFE—1325 Walnut Hill Ln., Irving, TX 75038–3096. William B. McMorris, Ed. Publication of Boy Scouts of America. Articles and fiction, 1,500 words, for 8- to 18-year-old boys. Photos. Fillers. Pays from $500 for major articles and fiction, on acceptance. Query first.

CHRISTIAN LIVING FOR SENIOR HIGH—850 N. Grove, Elgin, IL 60120. Anne E. Dinnan, Ed. Articles and fiction, 1,000 to 1,500 words, of interest to Christian teens. Don't preach. Pays 10¢ a word, on acceptance.

EXPLORING—1325 Walnut Hill Ln., Box 152079, Irving, TX 75015–2079. Scott Daniels, Exec. Ed. Publication of Boy Scouts of America. Articles, 500 to 1,800 words, for 14- to 21-year-olds, on education, careers, Explorer post activities (hiking, canoeing, camping), and program ideas for meetings. No controversial subjects. Pays $150 to $500, on acceptance. Query. Send SASE for guidelines.

FREEWAY—Box 632, Glen Ellyn, IL 60138. Billie Sue Thompson, Ed. First-person true stories, personal experience, how-tos, fillers, and humor, to 1,000 words, with photos, for 13- to 22-year-olds. Must have Christian emphasis. Pays to 8¢ a word.

GRIT—208 W. Third St., Williamsport, PA 17701. Joanne Decker, Assignment Ed. Articles, 300 to 500 words, with photos, on young people involved in unusual hobbies, occupations, athletic pursuits, and personal adventures. Pays 15¢ a word, extra for photos, on acceptance.

HICALL—1445 Boonville Ave., Springfield, MO 65802. Rick Knoth, Ed. Articles, 500 to 1,000 words, and fiction, to 1,800 words, for 12- to 19-year-olds; strong evangelical emphasis. Pays on acceptance.

IN TOUCH—Box 50434, Indianapolis, IN 46250–0434. Jim Watkins, Ed. Articles, 500 to 1,000 words, on contemporary issues, athletes, and singers from conservative Christian perspective, for 13- to 19-year-olds. Pays 2¢ to 4¢ a word. Send SASE for guidelines.

KEYNOTER—3636 Woodview Trace, Indianapolis, IN 46268. Jack Brockley, Exec. Ed. Articles, 1,500 to 2,500 words, for high school leaders: general-interest features; self-help; pieces on contemporary teen-age problems. Photos. Pays $75 to $250, extra for photos, on acceptance. Query preferred.

LIGHTED PATHWAY—922 Montgomery Ave., Cleveland, TN 37311. Marcus V. Hand, Ed. Human-interest and inspirational articles, 800 to 1,000 words, for teen-agers. Short pieces, 600 to 800 words. Fiction, 1,000 to 1,200 words. Pays 2 ½¢ to 5¢ a word, on acceptance.

LISTEN MAGAZINE—6830 Laural St. N.W., Washington, DC 20012. Gary B. Swanson, Ed. Articles (1,500 to 2,000 words) providing teens with "a vigorous, positive, educational approach to the problems arising out of the use of tobacco, alcohol, and other drugs." Pays 5¢ to 7¢ a word, on acceptance.

MERLYN'S PEN, THE NATIONAL MAGAZINE OF STUDENT WRITING—P.O. Box 1058, East Greenwich, RI 02818. R. James Stahl, Ed. Writing by students in grades 7 through 10 only. Short stories, to 2,500 words; reviews, travel pieces, to 1,000 words; and poetry, to 100 lines. Pays in copies. Guidelines available.

NEW ERA—50 E. North Temple, Salt Lake City, UT 84150. Brian Kelly, Ed. Articles, 150 to 3,000 words, and fiction, to 3,000 words, for young Mormons. Poetry. Photos. Pays 3¢ to 10¢ a word, 25¢ a line for poetry, on acceptance. Query.

PIONEER—1548 Poplar Ave., Memphis, TN 38104. Tim Bearden, Ed. Southern Baptist. Articles, to 1,500 words, for 12- and 14-year-old boys, on teen problems, current events. Photo essays on Baptist sports personalities. Pays 4¢ a word, extra for photos, on acceptance.

QUE PASA—1086 Teaneck Rd., Teaneck, NJ 07666. Celeste Gomes, Ed. Articles (two to four pages) in Spanish or English on popular music stars, actors and actresses, and life styles of Latin celebrities for Hispanic teens. Fillers and humor. Pays from $50, on publication.

SCHOLASTIC SCOPE—730 Broadway, New York, NY 10003. Fran Claro, Ed. For 15- to 18-year-olds with 4th to 6th grade reading ability. Realistic fiction, 400 to 1,200 words, and plays, to 6,000 words, on teen problems. Profiles, 400 to 800 words, of interesting teen-agers, with B&W photos. Pays $125 for 500- to 600-word articles, from $200 for plays and short stories, from $150 for longer pieces, on acceptance.

SEVENTEEN—850 Third Ave., New York, NY 10022. Katherine Russell Rich, Articles Ed. Articles, to 2,500 words, on subjects of interest to teens. Sophisticated, well-written fiction, 1,500 to 3,500 words, for young adults. Poetry, to 40 lines, by teens. Short news and features, to 750 words, for "Mini-Mag." Articles, 1,000 words, by teens, for "Your Words." Pays varying rates, on acceptance.

SPLICE—10 Columbus Circle, Suite 1300, New York, NY 10019. James A. Baggett, Ed. Articles and personality profiles, 1,000 words, relating to the young adult movie and entertainment scene. Music articles dealing with movies or music videos. Pays varying rates, on publication. Queries preferred.

STRAIGHT—8121 Hamilton Ave., Cincinnati, OH 45231. Carla J. Crane, Ed. Articles on current situations and issues, humor, for Christian teens. Well-constructed fiction, 1,000 to 1,200 words, showing teens using Christian principles. Poetry by teen-agers. Photos. Pays about 3¢ a word, on acceptance. Guidelines.

TEEN POWER—Box 632, Glen Ellyn, IL 60138. Mark Oestreicher, Ed. First person (as told to), true teen experience stories with Christian insights and conclusion, 700 to 1,000 words. Include photos. Pays 5¢ to 7¢ a word, extra for photos, on acceptance.

TEENAGE—4 E. 43rd St., New York, NY 10017. Lori Bernstein, Ed.-in-Chief. Articles, profiles, interviews, short news reports, essays, humor, and celebrity interviews, for sophisticated young women: 500 to 2,000 words. Pays $75, on publication.

TEENS TODAY—Nazarene Headquarters, 6401 The Paseo, Kansas City, MO 64131. Karen De Sollar, Ed. Short stories, 1,200 to 1,500 words, dealing with teens demonstrating Christian principles in real-life situations. Adventure stories; stories about relationships and ethics. Pays 3 ½¢ a word, on acceptance.

TIGER BEAT—1086 Teaneck Rd., Teaneck, NJ 07666. Diane Umansky, Ed. Articles, to 4 pages, on young people in show business and music industry. Pays varying rates, on acceptance. Query. Unsolicited manuscripts sent without SASE will not be returned.

TIGER BEAT STAR—1086 Teaneck Rd., Teaneck, NJ 07666. Nancy O'Connell, Ed. Light celebrity fan pieces and interviews (pop/rock, movies and TV); occasional serious articles on topics of interest to teens. For articles, 300 words, payment is $50 per published page. Query.

TQ MAGAZINE—Box 82808, Lincoln, NE 68501. Nancy Bayne, Ed. Articles, to 1,800 words, and well-crafted fiction, to 2,500 words, for conservative Christian teens. B/W photos and color slides. Pays 4¢ to 10¢ a word, extra for photos, on publication.

WRITING!—60 Revere Dr., Northbrook, IL 60062–1563. Alan Lenhoff, Ed. Interviews, 1,200 words, for "Writers at Work" department, for high school students. Pays $200, on publication. Query.

YM—685 Third Ave., New York, NY 10017. No unsolicited material.

YOUNG AND ALIVE—4444 S. 52nd St., Lincoln, NE 68506. Richard Kaiser, Ed. Feature articles, 800 to 1,400 words, for blind and visually impaired young adults, on adventure, biography, camping, health, hobbies, and travel. Photos. Pays 3¢ to 5¢ a word, extra for photos, on acceptance. Write for guidelines.

YOUNG SALVATIONIST—The Salvation Army, 799 Bloomfield Ave., Verona, NJ 07044. Capt. Robert R. Hostetler, Ed. Articles for teens, 800 to 1,200 words, with Christian perspective; fiction, 800 to 1,200 words; short fillers. Young Soldier Section: fiction, 600 to 800 words; games and puzzles for children. Pays 3¢ a word, on acceptance.

YOUTH!—P.O. Box 801, Nashville, TN 37202. Christopher B. Hughes, Ed. Articles and fiction, 700 to 2,000 words, that help teen-agers develop a Christian identity and faith in contemporary culture. Photos. Pays 4¢ a word, on acceptance.

THE DRAMA MARKET

REGIONAL AND UNIVERSITY THEATERS

Community, regional, and civic theaters and college dramatic groups offer the best opportunities today for playwrights to see their plays produced, whether for staged production or for dramatic readings. Indeed, aspiring playwrights who can get their work produced by any of these have taken an important step toward breaking into the competitive dramatic field—many well-known playwrights received their first recognition in the regional theaters. Payment is generally not large,

688

but regional and university theaters usually buy only the right to produce a play, and all further rights revert to the author. Since most directors like to work closely with the authors on any revisions necessary, theaters will often pay the playwright's expenses while in residence during rehearsals. The thrill of seeing your play come to life on the stage is one of the pleasures of being on hand for rehearsals and performances.

Aspiring playwrights should query college and community theaters in their region to find out which ones are interested in seeing original scripts. Dramatic associations of interest to playwrights include the Dramatists Guild (234 W. 44th St., New York, NY 10036), Theatre Communications Group, Inc. (355 Lexington Ave., New York, NY 10017), which publishes the annual *Dramatists Sourcebook*, and The International Society of Dramatists, publishers of *The Dramatist's Bible* (P.O. Box 1310, Miami, FL 33153). *The Playwright's Companion*, published by Feedback Theatrebooks, P.O. Box 5187, Bloomington, IN 47402–5187, is an annual directory of theatres and prize contests seeking scripts.

Some of the theaters on the following list require that playwrights submit all or some of the following with scripts—cast list, synopsis, resumé, recommendations, return postcard—and with scripts and queries, SASEs must always be enclosed. Playwrights may also wish to register their material with the U.S. Copyright Office. For additional information about this, write Register of Copyrights, Library of Congress, Washington, DC 20559.

ACADEMY THEATRE—P.O. Box 77070, Atlanta, GA 30357. Linda C. Anderson, Lit. Mgr. Plays "stretching the boundaries of imagination, with elements of surrealism, poetic language, and imagery in comedy and drama format." Prefers local playwrights for New Play Program. Payment $250. Considers regional and national playwrights for New Play Premieres. Royalty and advance.

ACTORS THEATRE OF LOUISVILLE—316 W. Main St., Louisville, KY 40202. Michael Bigelow Dixon, Lit Mgr. One-act comedies and dramas (to 60 pages); include cast list. Annual contest. Guidelines.

A. D. PLAYERS—2710 W. Alabama, Houston, TX 77098. Jeannette Clift George, Artistic Dir. Carol E. Anderson, Lit. Mgr. Full-length or one-act comedies, dramas, musicals, children's plays and adaptations with Christian world view. Submit script with SAS postcard, resumé, cast list, and synopsis (Christmas plays should be submitted before Oct.). Reports in 2 months. Pays negotiable rates.

ALASKA REPERTORY THEATRE—P.O. Box 104700, Anchorage, AK 99510–4700. Andrew Traister, Artistic Dir. Full-length dramas, comedies, and adaptations. Query with synopsis only.

ALLEY THEATRE—615 Texas Ave., Houston, TX 77002. Robert Strane, Lit. Mgr. Full-length comedies, dramas, musicals, children's plays, and adaptations with cast to 20. Query with synopsis, cast list, resumé, and recommendations before Feb. 1. Pay varies.

ALLIANCE THEATRE COMPANY—1280 Peachtree St. N.E., Atlanta, GA 30309. Sandra Deer, Lit. Mgr. Full-length comedies, dramas, musicals, and adaptations. Query with synopsis and cast list. Pay varies.

AMERICAN LIVING HISTORY THEATRE—P.O. Box 2677, Hollywood, CA 90078. Dorene Ludwig, Artistic Dir. One-act, historically accurate (primary source materials) dramas. Submit script with SASE. Reports in 1 to 6 months. Pays varying rates.

AMERICAN PLACE THEATRE—111 W. 46th St., New York, NY 10036.

Chris Breyer, Lit. Mgr. "No unsolicited manuscripts accepted. We welcome scripts from writers who have had full or workshop productions of their plays and professional theatres. Others may send a synopsis and the first 20 pages with SASE. We seek challenging, innovative works and do not favor obviously commercial material."

AMERICAN REPERTORY THEATRE—64 Brattle St., Cambridge, MA 02138. Arthur Holmberg, Lit. Mgr. No unsolicited manuscripts. Submit one-page description of play, 10-page sample; nothing returned without SASE; 3 to 4 months for response.

AMERICAN STAGE COMPANY—P.O. Box 1560, St. Petersburg, FL 33731. Victoria Holloway, Artistic Dir. Full-length comedies and dramas. Send synopsis with short description of cast and production requirements with SAS postcard. Pays negotiable rates. Submit Sept. to Jan.

AMERICAN STANISLAVSKI THEATRE—485 Park Ave., #6A, New York, NY 10022. Sonia Moore, Artistic Dir. Full-length or one-act drama with important message. No offensive language. For cast aged 16 to 45. Submit script with SAS postcard in April and May; reports in Sept. No payment.

THE APPLE CORPS.—336 W. 20th St., New York, NY 10011. Bob Del Pazzo, Coordinator. All types of one-act and full-length plays. Send bio, synopsis with SASE. Allow 4 to 6 months for response. Payment varies. No phone calls.

ARENA STAGE—Sixth and Maine Ave. S.W., Washington, DC 20024. Lloyd Rose, Lit. Mgr. Submit one-page synopsis, first 10 pages of dialogue, resumé, and professional recommendations. No unsolicited manuscripts. Pays varying rates. Workshops and readings offered. Allow 2 to 4 months for reply.

ARKANSAS ARTS CENTER CHILDREN'S THEATRE—Box 2137, Little Rock, AR 72203. Bradley Anderson, Artistic Dir. Seeks solid, professional (full-length or one-act) scripts. Original, and, particularly, adapted work from contemporary and classic literature. Pays flat rate.

ARKANSAS REPERTORY THEATRE COMPANY—712 E. 11th St., Little Rock, AR 72202. Cliff Fannin Baker, Artistic Dir. Full-length comedies, dramas, and musicals; prefer up to 10 characters. Send synopsis, cast list, resumé, and return postage. Reports in 5 to 6 months.

ARTREACH TOURING THEATRE—3074 Madison Rd., Cincinnati, OH 45209. Kathryn Schultz Miller, Artistic Dir. One-act dramas and adaptations for touring children's theater; cast to 3, simple sets. Submit script with synopsis, cast list, resumé, recommendations and SASE. Payment varies.

ASOLO STATE THEATRE—P.O. Drawer E, Sarasota, FL 33578. John Ulmer, Artistic Dir. Full-length dramas, comedies, musicals, and children's plays. Small stage. Pays royalty or varying rates. Readings and workshops offered. No unsolicited manuscripts. Query with synopsis.

AT THE FOOT OF THE MOUNTAIN—2000 S. Fifth St., Minneapolis, MN 55454. Jan Magrane, Bernadette Cha, Rebecca Rice, Artistic Co-Directors. Full-length, one-act and musical plays by and about women. Query with synopsis, SAS postcard. Reports in 6 weeks. Pays royalty.

BARTER THEATER—P.O. Box 867, Abingdon, VA 24210. Rex Partington, Producing Dir. Full-length dramas, comedies, adaptations, musicals and children's plays. Full workshop and reading productions. Allow 6 to 8 months for report. Payment rates negotiable.

690

BERKELEY REPERTORY THEATRE—2025 Addison St., Berkeley, CA 94704. Sharon Ott, Artistic Dir. No unsolicited manuscripts; agent submissions or professional recommendations only. Reporting time: 3 to 4 months.

BERKSHIRE THEATRE FESTIVAL—Box 797, Stockbridge, MA 02162. Richard Dunlap, Artistic Dir. Full-length comedies, musicals and dramas; cast to 8. Submit through agent only.

BEVERLY HILLS PLAYHOUSE/SKYLIGHT THEATRE—6525 Sunset Blvd., Garden Suite #2, Beverly Hills, CA 90028. No unsolicited material.

BOARSHEAD THEATER—425 S. Grand Ave., Lansing, MI 48933. John Peakes, Artistic Dir. Full-length and one-act comedies and dramas with simple sets. Send precis, 5 pages of dialogue, cast list to 12 with descriptions, and resumé. SASE for reply.

CENTER STAGE—700 N. Calvert St., Baltimore, MD 21202. Rick Davis, Resident Dramaturg. Full-length and one-act comedies, dramas, musicals, adaptations. No unsolicited manuscripts. Send synopsis, resume, cast list, recommendations and production history, with return postcard and SASE. Pays varying rates. Allow 4 to 8 weeks for reply.

CIRCLE REPERTORY COMPANY—161 Ave. of the Americas, New York, NY 10013. B. Rodney Marriott, Assoc. Artistic Dir. Send full-length and one-act comedies or dramas with cast list. Offers criticism "as often as possible." Pays $2,500. Reports in 5 months. Readings.

CITY THEATRE COMPANY—University of Pittsburgh, B39 CL, Pittsburgh, PA 15260. Lynne Conner, Lit. Mgr. Full-length comedies and dramas; query Sept. to May. Cast to 12; simple sets. Readings. Royalty.

CLASSIC STAGE COMPANY—136 E. 13th St., New York, NY 10003. Carol Ostrow, Producing Dir. Carey Perloff, Artistic Dir. Full-length adaptations and translations of existing classic literature. Submit synopsis with cast list and SASE, Sept. to May. Offers workshops and readings. Pays on royalty basis.

CREATIVE THEATRE—102 Witherspoon St., Princeton, NJ 08540. Laurie Huntsman, Artistic Director. One-act participatory plays for children, grades K-6, and one-act plays for children grades 7–12; cast of 5 to 7; arena or proscenium staging. Submit manuscript with synopsis and cast list Jan. through March. Pays $300; $300 for music and lyrics.

THE CRICKET THEATRE—9 W. 14th St., Minneapolis, MN 55403. William Partlan, Art. Dir. Send full-length comedies, dramas, musicals, with synopsis, resumé; "prefer contemporary plays." Cast to 11. Reports in 6 months.

CROSSROADS THEATRE CO.—320 Memorial Pkwy., New Brunswick, NJ 08901. Rick Khan, Art. Dir. Sydne Mahone, Lit. Mgr. Full-length and one-act dramas, comedies, musicals, and adaptations; experimental pieces; one man/one woman shows. Queries only, with synopsis, cast list, resumé, and SASE.

DELAWARE THEATRE COMPANY—P.O. Box 516, Wilmington, DE 19899. Cleveland Morris, Artistic Dir. Full-length comedies, dramas, musicals, and adaptations, with cast to 10; prefer single set. Send cast list, synopsis, and SASE. Reports in 6 months. Pays royalty.

DENVER CENTER THEATRE COMPANY—1050 13th St., Denver, CO 80204. Barbara Sellers, Producing Dir. Send full-length comedies and dramas (cast to 12): June through Dec. Include cast list, resumé. Pay varies.

DETROIT REPERTORY THEATRE—13103 Woodrow Wilson Ave., De-

691

troit, MI 48238. Barbara Busby, Lit. Mgr. Full-length comedies and dramas. Enclose SASE. Pays royalty.

DORSET THEATRE FESTIVAL—Box 519, Dorset, VT 05251. Jill Charles, Art. Dir. Full-length comedies, musicals, dramas, and adaptations; cast to 8; simple set preferred. Agent submissions and professional recommendations only. Pays varying rates. Residencies at Dorset Colony House for Writers available Sept. through May. Inquire.

EAST WEST PLAYERS—4424 Santa Monica Blvd., Los Angeles, CA 90029. Full-length comedies, dramas, and musicals dealing with Asian American issues and/or including important roles for Asian actors. Cast up to 10. Send manuscript with synopsis, cast list, resumé, and SASE. Pays varying rates. Offers workshops and readings. Allow 3 months for reply.

EMPIRE STATE INSTITUTE FOR THE PERFORMING ARTS—Empire State Plaza, Albany, NY 12223. Patricia B. Snyder, Prod. Dir. Query for new musicals and plays for family audiences, with synopsis, cast list. Submit between June and August. Payment varies.

THE EMPTY SPACE THEATRE—95 S. Jackson St., Seattle, WA 98104. Kurt Beattie, Lit. Mgr. Unsolicited scripts accepted only from WA, OR, WY, MT, and ID. Outside five-state N.W. region: scripts accepted through agents or established theater groups only.

ENSEMBLE STUDIO THEATRE—549 W. 52nd St., New York, NY 10019. Address Lit. Mgr. Send full-length or one-act comedies and dramas, with cast list, resumé, and SASE, Sept. through April. Pays varies. Readings.

THE FAMILY REPERTORY CO.—9 Second Ave., New York, NY 10003. J. J. Johnson, Art. Dir. Contemporary, social works on a variety of topics. Full-length dramas and musicals for young people and adults. Submit manuscript with synopsis, resumé, and return postcard. Pays small fee.

FLORIDA STUDIO THEATRE—1241 N. Palm Ave., Sarasota, FL 33577. Jack Fournier, New Play Development. Innovative smaller cast plays that are pertinent and contemporary. Query first with synopsis and SASE. Pays varying rates.

GEVA THEATRE—75 Woodbury Blvd., Rochester, NY 14607. Ann Patrice Carrigan, Lit. Dir. Query for comedies and dramas with synopsis and cast list. Readings.

WILL GEER THEATRICUM BOTANICUM—Box 1222, Topanga, CA 90290. All types of scripts for outdoor theater, with large playing area. Submit synopsis with SASE. Pays varing rates.

EMMY GIFFORD CHILDREN'S THEATRE—3504 Center St., Omaha, NE 68105. James Larson, Artistic Dir. Unsolicited scripts accepted with SASE.

THE GOODMAN THEATRE—200 S. Columbus Dr., Chicago, IL 60603. Tom Creamer, Dramaturg. Queries required for full-length comedies or dramas. Include synopsis, cast list, resumé, recommendations, and to 10 pages of dialogue. Reports in 3 months. Readings and workshops.

THE GROUP THEATRE—3940 Brooklyn Ave., NE, Seattle, WA 98105. Tim Bond, Lit. Mgr. Full-length comedies, dramas, adaptations, and translations, cast to 10; simple set. Special interest in plays suitable for multi-ethnic cast; serious plays on social/cultural issues; satires. Query with synopsis, sample dialogue and resumé required. Reporting time: 4 weeks.

THE GUTHRIE THEATER—725 Vineland Pl., Minneapolis, MN 55403. Mark Bly, Lit. Mgr. Full-length comedies and dramas, and adaptations. Manuscripts accepted only from recognized theatrical agents. Query with detailed synopsis, cast size, resumé, return postcard and recommendations. Pays negotiable rates, and travel/residency expenses. Offers readings. Reports in 1 to 2 months.

HARRISBURG COMMUNITY THEATRE—513 Hurlock St., Harrisburg, PA 17110. Thomas G. Hostetter, Artistic Dir. Full-length comedies, dramas, musicals, and adaptations with cast to 20; prefers simple set. Submit script with cast list, resumé, synopsis, and SAS postcard. Best time to submit: June to August. Reporting time: 6 months. Pays negotiable rates.

HARTFORD STAGE COMPANY—50 Church St., Hartford, CT 06103. Constance Congdon, Lit. Mgr. Full-length plays of all types, for cast up to 12. No unsolicited manuscripts; submit through agent or send synopsis. Pays varying rates.

HIPPODROME STATE THEATRE—25 S. E. Second Place, Gainesville, FL 32601. Gregory von Hausch, Artistic Dir. Full-length plays with unit sets and casts up to 15. Submit in summer and fall. Enclose return postcard and synopsis.

HONOLULU THEATRE FOR YOUTH—Box 3257, Honolulu, HI 96801. John Kauffman, Art. Dir. Plays, 60 to 90 minutes playing time, for young people/ family audiences. Adult casts. Contemporary issues, Pacific themes, etc. Unit sets, small cast. Query or send manuscript with synopsis, cast list and SASE. Royalties negotiable.

HORIZON THEATRE COMPANY—P. O. Box 5376, Station E, Atlanta, GA 30307. Jeffrey and Lisa Adler, Co-Artistic Directors. Full-length comedies, dramas, and satires that utilize "heightened" realism and other highly theatrical forms. Cast to 10. Submit synopsis with cast list, resumé, and recommendations. Pays percentage. Readings. Reports in 3 months.

HUNTINGTON THEATRE COMPANY—252 Huntington Ave., Boston, MA 02115. Gary Mitchell, Asst. to the Prod. Dir. Full-length comedies and dramas. Query with synopsis, cast list, resumé, recommendations, and return postcard.

ILLINOIS THEATRE CENTER—400 Lakewood Blvd., Park Forest, IL 60466. Steve S. Billig, Artistic Dir. Full-length comedies, dramas, musicals and adaptations, for unit/fragmentary sets, and cast to 8. Send manuscript with recommendations and return postcard. Pays negotiable rates. Workshops and readings offered.

INVISIBLE THEATRE—1400 N. First Ave, Tucson, AZ 85719. Deborah Dickey, Lit. Mgr. Reads queries for full-length comedies, dramas, musicals, adaptations, Jan. through May. Cast to 10; simple set. Pays royalty.

JACKSONVILLE UNIVERSITY THEATRE—Dept. of Theatre Arts, College of Fine Arts, Jacksonville Univ., Jacksonville, FL 32211. Davis Sikes, Art. Dir. Submit full-length comedies and dramas, Sept. through Jan.; include resumé.

JEWISH REPERTORY THEATRE—344 E. 14th St., New York, NY 10003. Ran Avni, Artistic Dir. Full-length comedies, dramas, musicals, children's plays and adaptations, with cast to 10, relating to the Jewish experience. Pays varying rates. Enclose return postcard.

THE JULIAN THEATRE—New College Center, 777 Valencia St., San Francisco, CA 94110. Address New Plays. Full-length comedies and dramas with a social statement. Send 5- to 10-page scene, synopsis, cast description, and SASE. Pays on contractual basis. Allow 2 to 9 months for reply. Readings offered.

LAMB'S PLAYERS THEATRE—500 Plaza Blvd., P.O. Box 26, National City, CA 92050. Kerry Cederberg, Lit. Mgr. Full-length dramas, translations, adaptations, musicals. Special interest in works with Christian world view. Query with synopsis required. Pays varying rates.

LITTLE BROADWAY PRODUCTIONS—c/o Jill Shawn, P. O. Box 15068, N. Hollywood, CA 91615. Musicals and other plays for children performed by adult actors; 55 minutes, no intermission. Cast of 5 to 10. Submit manuscript with synopsis, return postcard, resumé, and SASE. Pays negotiable rates.

LONG ISLAND STAGE—P.O. Box 9001, Rockville Centre, New York 11571–9001. Clinton J. Atkinson, Art. Dir. Full-length dramas and adaptations. Query with SASE in late spring/early summer. Pays varying rates.

LOS ANGELES DESIGNERS' THEATRE—P. O. Box 1883, Studio City, CA 91604–0883. Richard Niederberg, Artistic Dir. Full-length comedies, dramas, muscials, fantasies or adaptations. Religious, political, social, and controversial themes considered. Payment varies.

LOS ANGELES THEATRE UNIT—P.O. Box 429, Los Angeles, CA 90078. Steve Itkin, Man. Dir. Kate Ward, Lit. Dir. Full-length and one-act comedies and dramas. Submit script and SASE. Reports in 2 to 3 months. Pays varying rates.

MCCARTER THEATRE COMPANY—91 University Pl., Princeton, NJ 08540. Robert Lancaster, Assoc. Art. Dir. Full-length comedies, dramas, adaptations. Pays to $500 for readings; varying rates for production.

THE MAGIC THEATRE—Bldg. D, Fort Mason, San Francisco, CA 94123. Eugenie Chan, Lit. Mgr. Comedies and dramas, ethnic-American, workshop productions. Query with synopsis, resumé and 3–5 pages of sample dialogue. Pays varies.

MANHATTAN PUNCH LINE—410 W. 42nd St., New York, NY 10036. Steve Kaplan, Art. Dir. Comedies. Showcase contract. SASE required.

MANHATTAN THEATRE CLUB—453 W. 16th, New York, NY 10011. Address Tom Szentgyorgyi. Full-length and one-act comedies, dramas and musicals. No unsolicited manuscripts. Send synopsis with 10–15 pages of dialogue, cast list, resumé, recommendations and SASE. Pays negotiable rates. Allow 6 months for reply.

MIDWEST PLAYLABS—c/o The Playwrights' Center, 2301 Franklin Ave. E., Minneapolis, MN 55406. Full-length, previously unproduced scripts (no musicals). Query. Pays stipend, room and board, and travel for two-week August conference.

MILL MOUNTAIN THEATRE—Center in the Square, One Market Square, Roanoke, VA 24011. Jo Weinstein, Lit. Mgr. Full-length or one-act comedies, dramas, musicals (one-acts limited to 25–40 minutes); include publicity, resumé. Payment varies.

MISSOURI REPERTORY THEATRE—4949 Cherry St., Kansas City, MO 64110. Felicia Londre, Dramaturg. Full-length comedies and dramas. Query with synopsis, cast list, resumé, and return postcard. Pays standard royalty.

MUSIC THEATRE GROUP/LENOX ARTS CENTER—735 Washington St., New York, NY 10014. John Hart, Lit. Mgr. Innovative musicals, to 1 ½ hours; cast to 10. Query only, with synopsis and return postcard. Best submission time: Sept. through Dec.

MUSICAL THEATRE WORKS—440 Lafayette St., New York, NY 10003. Mark Herko, Assoc. Artistic Dir. Full-length musicals, cast to 10; simple sets. Submit manuscript with SASE and cassette score. No payment.

THE NEGRO ENSEMBLE COMPANY—165 W. 46th St., Ste. 409, New York, NY 10036. Douglas Turner Ward, Art. Dir. Full-length comedies, dramas, musicals and adaptations pertaining to the Black experience. Submit March through May. Pays on royalty basis. Enclose return postcard.

NEW DRAMATISTS—424 W. 44th St., New York, NY 10036. Mary Elizabeth Carlin, Literary Associate. Workshop for member playwrights. Write for membership information.

NEW EHRLICH THEATRE—Boston Center for the Arts, 539 Tremont St., Boston, MA 02116. New full-length scripts (no musicals) by Massachusetts playwrights, for readings and workshop productions. Include SASE.

NEW TUNERS/PERFORMANCE COMMUNITY—1225 W. Belmont Ave., Chicago, IL 60657. George H. Gorham, Dramaturg. Full-length musicals only, for cast to 15; no wing/fly space. Send manuscript with cassette of score, cast list, resumé, and return postcard. Pays on royalty basis.

NEW YORK SHAKESPEARE FESTIVAL/PUBLIC THEATER—425 Lafayette St., New York, NY 10003. Gail Merrifield, Dir. of Plays and Musicals. Plays and musical works for the theater, translations, and adaptations. Submit manuscript, cassette (with musicals), and SASE.

ODYSSEY THEATRE ENSEMBLE—12111 Ohio Ave., Los Angeles, CA 90025. Ron Sossi, Artistic Dir. Full-length comedies, dramas, musicals, and adaptations: provocative subject matter, or plays that stretch and explore the possibilities of theater. Query with synopsis and return postcard. Pays variable rates. Allow 2 to 6 months for reply. Workshops and readings.

OLD GLOBE THEATRE—Simon Edison Center for the Performing Arts, Box 2171, San Diego, CA 92112. Address Robert Berlinger. Full-length comedies and dramas. No unsolicited manuscripts. Submit query with synopsis, or through agent.

EUGENE O'NEILL THEATRE CENTER—234 W. 44th St., Suite 901, New York, NY 10036. Annual competition to select new stage and television plays for development at organization's Waterford, CT location. Submission deadline: Dec. 1. Send SASE for guidelines to National Playwright's Conference, c/o above address. Pays stipend, plus travel/living expenses during conference.

PAPER MILL PLAYHOUSE—Brookside Dr., Millburn, NJ 07041. Maryan F. Stephens, Lit. Advisor. Full-length musicals only. Submit synopsis, tape, and resumé; reporting time, 3 to 4 months.

PENNSYLVANIA STAGE COMPANY—837 Linden St., Allentown, PA 18101. David Scott, Lit. Mgr. Full-length plays with cast to 8; one set. Full-length musicals, with unit set cast to 12. Send synopsis, cast list, and return postage. Pays negotiable rates. Allow 6 months for reply. Readings.

PEOPLE'S LIGHT AND THEATRE COMPANY—39 Conestoga Rd., Malvern, PA 19355. Alda Cortese, Lit. Mgr. One-act or full-length comedies, dramas, adaptations. Query with synopsis, resumé, ten pages of script required. Reports in 6 months. Payment negotiable.

PHILADELPHIA FESTIVAL FOR NEW PLAYS—3900 Chestnut St., Philadelphia, PA 19104. Richard Wolcott, Lit. Mgr. Full-length and one-act comedies, dramas; must be unproduced. Submit script with return postcard, resumé, and SASE. Pays varying rates.

PLAYHOUSE ON THE SQUARE—51 S. Cooper in Overton Sq., Memphis, TN 38104. Jackie Nichols, Artistic Dir. Full-length comedies, dramas; cast to 15. Query. Pays $500.

PLAYWRIGHTS HORIZONS—416 W. 42nd St., New York, NY 10036. Address Literary Dept. Full-length, original comedies, dramas, and musicals. Send synopsis and SASE. Pays varying rates.

PLAYWRIGHTS' PLATFORM—164 Brayton Rd., Boston, MA 02135. B. A. Creasey, Pres. Script development workshops and public readings for New England playwrights only. Full-length and one-act plays of all kinds. Residents of New England send scripts with short synopsis, resumé, return postcard, and SASE.

PORTLAND STAGE COMPANY—Box 1458, Portland, ME 04104. Richard Hamburger, Artistic Dir. Full-length comedies, dramas, and musicals, for cast to 8. Send synopsis and sample dialogue with return postcard. Pays fee, travel, and living arrangements if play is produced on mainstage; travel and living arrangements only if produced as reading or workshop production.

THE PUERTO RICAN TRAVELING THEATRE—141 W. 94th St., New York, NY 10025. Miriam Colon Valle, Artistic Dir. Full-length and one-act comedies, dramas, and musicals; cast to 8; simple sets. Payment negotiable.

THE REPERTORY THEATRE OF ST. LOUIS—Box 28030, St. Louis, MO 63119. Agented submissions only.

THE ROAD COMPANY—Box 5278 EKS, John City, TN 37603. Robert H. Leonard, Artistic Dir. Full-length and one-act comedies, dramas with social/political relevance to small-town audiences. Send synopsis, cast list, and production history, if any. Pays negotiable rates. Reports in 6 to 12 months.

ROUND HOUSE THEATRE—12210 Bushey Dr., Silver Spring, MD 20902. Address Production Office Mgr. Full-length comedies, dramas, and adaptations; cast to 10; prefer simple set. No unsolicited manuscripts.

SOCIETY HILL PLAYHOUSE—507 S. 8th St., Philadelphia, PA 19147. Walter Vail, Dramaturg. Full-length dramas and comedies; cast to 6; simple set. Submit synopsis and SASE. Reports in 6 months. Nominal payment.

SOHO REPERTORY THEATRE—80 Varick St., New York, NY 10013. Rob Barron, Dir. of Play Development. Full-length dramas, musicals, adaptations and mixed media works. No unsolicited manuscripts. Send brief precis, cast list, resumé, and up to 10 pages of script. Musicals: tape and lead sheets. Guidelines. Pays from $400. Readings offered.

SOUTH COAST REPERTORY—P. O. Box 2197, Costa Mesa, CA 92628. John Glore, Lit. Mgr. Full-length comedies, dramas, musicals, juveniles. Query first with synopsis and resumé. Payment varies.

STAGE ONE: THE LOUISVILLE CHILDREN'S THEATRE—425 W. Market St., Louisville, KY 40202. Dramatized classics, and plays for children ages 5 to 18. Submit script with resumé. Reports in 4 months.

STAGES—3201 Allen Parkway, Suite 101, Houston, TX 77019. Ted Swindley, Artistic Dir. Full-length and one-act comedies, dramas, and children's scripts, especially from Texan playwrights; cast to 12; simple set. Submit script, synopsis, resumé, and SASE.

696

STUDIO ARENA THEATRE—710 Main St., Buffalo, NY 14202. Comedies, dramas, children's plays; cast to 12. Particular interest in plays by and about women or minorities. Include synopsis, resumé, cast list.

TAKOMA THEATRE—6833 Fourth St. N.W., Washington, DC 20012. Milton O. McGinty, Art. Dir. Realistic, full-length dramas, comedies and musicals. Submit manuscript with SASE; report in 3 months. Payment negotiable.

MARK TAPER FORUM—135 N. Grand Ave., Los Angeles, CA 90012. Jessica Teich, Lit. Mgr. Full-length comedies, dramas, musicals, children's plays, adaptations. Query first.

THEATRE AMERICANA—Box 245, Altadena, CA 91001. Full-length comedies and dramas, preferably with American theme. Send manuscript with cast list and SASE. No payment. Allow 3 to 6 months for reply.

THEATRE/TEATRO—Bilingual Foundation for the Arts, 421 N. Ave., #19, Los Angeles, CA 90031. Margarita Galban, Art. Dir. Full-length plays about Hispanic experience; small casts. Submit manuscript with return postcard. Pays negotiable rates.

THEATREWORKS/USA—890 Broadway, 7th Fl., New York, NY 10003. Barbara Pasternack, Lit. Mgr. Small-cast children's musicals only. Playwrights must be within commutable distance to New York City. Submit in spring, summer. Pays royalty.

WISDOM BRIDGE THEATRE—1559 W. Howard St., Chicago, IL 60626. Christina Sumption, Lit. Mgr. Plays dealing with contemporary social/political issues; cast to 12.

WOOLLY MAMMOTH THEATRE COMPANY—1401 Church St. N.W., Washington, DC 20005. Grover Gardner, Lit. Mgr. Looking for off-beat material, unusual writing. Unsolicited scripts accepted. Pay negotiable.

GARY YOUNG MIME THEATRE—23724 Park Madrid, Casabasas, CA 91302. Gary Young, Art. Dir. Comedy monologues and two-person vignettes for children and adults, 1 minute to 90 minutes in length; casts of 1 or 2, and portable set. Pays varying rates. Enclose return postcard, resumé, recommendations, cast list and synopsis.

PLAY PUBLISHERS

ART CRAFT PLAY COMPANY—Box 1058, Cedar Rapids, IA 52406. Three-act comedies, mysteries, musicals, and farces, and one-act comedies or dramas, with one set, for production by junior or senior high schools. Pays on royalty basis or by outright purchase.

WALTER H. BAKER COMPANY—100 Chauncey St., Boston, MA 02111. Scripts for amateur production: one-act plays for competition, children's plays, musicals, religious drama, full-length plays for high school production. Three- to four-month reading period. Include SASE.

CHILDREN'S PLAYMATE MAGAZINE—1100 Waterway Blvd., P. O. Box 567, Indianapolis, IN 46206. Elizabeth A. Rinck, Ed. Plays, 200 to 600 words, for children aged 5 to 7: special emphasis on health, nutrition, exercise, and safety. Pays about 8¢ a word, on publication.

CONTEMPORARY DRAMA SERVICE—Meriweather Publishing Co., Box 7710, 885 Elkton Dr., Colorado Springs, CO 80903. Arthur Zapel, Ed. Easy-to-stage comedies, skits, one-acts, musicals, puppet scripts, full-length plays for schools and churches. Adaptations of classics and improvised material for classroom use. Comedy monologues and duets. Chancel drama for Christmas and Easter church use. Enclose synopsis. Pays by fee arrangement or on royalty basis.

THE DRAMATIC PUBLISHING CO.—311 Washington St., P. O. Box 109, Woodstock, IL 60098. Full-length and one-act plays, musical comedies for amateur, children, and stock groups. Must run at least thirty minutes. Pays on royalty basis. Address Sally Fyfe. Reports within 10 to 14 weeks.

DRAMATICS—The International Thespian Society, 3368 Central Pkwy., Cincinnati, OH 45225–2392. Don Corathers, Ed. One-act and full-length plays for high school production. Pays $50 to $200, on acceptance.

ELDRIDGE PUBLISHING COMPANY—P. O. Drawer 216, Franklin, OH 45005. Nancy Vorhis, Ed. Dept. One-, two-, and three-act plays and operettas for school, churches, community groups, etc. Special interest in comedies and Christmas plays. Include cassette for operettas. Pays varying rates. Responds in 2 to 3 months.

SAMUEL FRENCH, INC.—45 W. 25th St., New York, NY 10010. Lawrence R. Harbinson, Ed. Full-length plays for dinner, commmunity, stock, college, and high school theatres. One-act plays (30 to 45 minutes). Children's plays, 45 to 60 minutes. Pays on royalty basis.

HEUER PUBLISHING COMPANY—Drawer 248, Cedar Rapids, IA 52406. C. Emmett McMullen, Ed. One-act comedies and dramas for contest work; three-act comedies, mysteries or farces and musicals, with one interior setting, for high school production. Pays royalty or flat fee.

PIONEER DRAMA SERVICE—P. O. Box 22555, Denver, CO 80222. Full-length and one-act plays for young audiences: musicals, melodramas, religious scripts. No unproduced plays, plays with largely male casts or multiple sets. Query. Pays royalty or outright purchase.

PLAYS, THE DRAMA MAGAZINE YOUNG PEOPLE—120 Boylston St., Boston, MA 02116. Elizabeth Preston, Man. Ed. One-act plays, with simple settings, for production by young people, 7 to 17; holiday plays, comedies, dramas, farces, skits, dramatized classics, puppet plays, melodramas, dramatized folktales, and creative dramatics. Maximum lengths: lower grades, 10 double-spaced pages; middle grades, 15 pages; junior and senior high, 20 pages. Casts may be mixed, all-male or all-female; plays with one act preferred. Manuscript specification sheet available on request. Queries suggested for adaptations. Pays good rates, on acceptance. Buys all rights.

SCHOLASTIC SCOPE—730 Broadway, New York, NY 10003. Fran Claro, Ed. For ages 15 to 18 with fourth-grade reading ability. Plays, 6,000 words, on problems of contemporary teenagers, relationships between people in family, job, and school situations. Some mysteries, comedies, and science fiction; plays about minorities. Pays good rates, on acceptance.

THE TELEVISION MARKET

The almost round-the-clock television offerings on commercial, educational, and cable TV stations may lead free-lance writers to believe that opportunities to sell scripts or program ideas are infinite. Unfortunately, this is not true. With few exceptions, producers and programmers do not consider scripts submitted directly to them, no matter how good they are. In general free lancers can achieve success in this almost-closed field by concentrating on getting their fiction (short and in novel form) and nonfiction published in magazines or books, combed diligently by television producers for possible adaptations. A large percentage of the material offered over all types of networks (in addition to the motion pictures made in Hollywood or especially for TV) is in the form of adaptations of what has appeared in print.

Writers who want to try their hand at writing directly for this very limited market should be prepared to learn the special techniques and acceptable format of script writing. Also, experience in playwriting and a knowledge of dramatic structure gained through working in amateur, community, or professional theatres can be helpful.

This section of the Handbook includes a sampling of TV shows scheduled for broadcast during the 1988–89 season, and names and addresses of the production companies responsible for these shows. The lists should not be considered either complete or permanent. A more complete list of shows and production companies may be found in *Ross Reports Television,* published monthly by Television Index, Inc., 40–29 27th St., Long Island City, NY 11101. The cost is $4.05 ($4.34 for New York residents) prepaid for each issue (including first-class postage).

Since virtually all TV producers will read scripts and queries submitted only through recognized agents, we've included a list of agents who have indicated to us that they are willing to read queries from writers with television scripts. Society of Authors' Representatives (39 ½ Washington Sq. S., New York, NY 10012) will send out a listing of agents upon receipt of an SASE, and *Literary Market Place* (Bowker), available in most libraries, also has list of agents. Before submitting scripts to producers or to agents, authors should query to learn whether they prefer to see the material in script form, or as an outline or summary.

Writers may wish to register their story, treatment, series format, or script with the Writers Guild of America. This registration does not confer statutory rights, but it does supply evidence of authorship that is effective for ten years (and is renewable after that). To register material a writer should send one copy of his work, along with a $15 fee ($10 for members), to the Writers Guild of America Registration Service East, Inc., 555 W. 57th St., New York, NY 10019. Dramatic material can also be registered with the U.S. Copyright Office; for further information, write Register of Copyrights, Library of Congress, Washington, DC 20559. Finally, those interested in writing for television may want to read such daily trade newspapers as *Daily Variety* (1400 N. Cahuenga Blvd., Hollywood, CA 90028) and *Hollywood Reporter* (6715 Sunset Blvd., Hollywood, CA 90028).

TELEVISION SHOWS

ALF (NBC)—Alien Prod.

ALL MY CHILDREN (ABC)—ABC Prod.

ALMOST GROWN (CBS)—Universal TV

AMEN (NBC)—Carson Prod.

ANGELS 89 (FBC)—Aaron Spelling Prod.

ANYTHING BUT LOVE (ABC)—20th Century-Fox TV with Adam Prod.

BABY BOOM (NBC)—MGM/UA TV

BEAUTY AND THE BEAST (CBS)—Witt/Thomas Prod. with Republic Pictures

THE BOLD AND THE BEAUTIFUL (CBS)—Bell-Phillip TV Prod., Inc.

CHEERS (NBC)—Paramount TV

CHINA BEACH (ABC)—Warner Bros. TV with Sacret, Inc.

CITY COURT (FOX NETWORK)—Stephen J. Cannell Prod.

COACH (ABC)—Universal TV

COMING OF AGE (CBS)—Universal TV

THE COSBY SHOW (NBC)—Carsey-Werner Co.

DAY BY DAY (NBC)—Paramount TV

THE DAYS & NIGHTS OF MOLLY DODD (SYND.)—You and Me Kid Prod.

DEAR JOHN (NBC)—Paramount TV

DESIGNING WOMEN (CBS)COLUMBIA TV

DIAMONDS (USA NETWORK)—Grosso-Jacobson Prod. with Alliance Entertainment

A DIFFERENT WORLD (NBC)— Carsey-Werner Co.

DOLPHIN'S BAY (CBS)—Paramount TV

DUET (FBC)—Paramount TV

DYNASTY (ABC)—Aaron Spelling Prod.

EMPTY NEST (NBC)—Witt/Thomas/Harris Prod. with Touchstone Pictures

THE EQUALIZER (CBS)—Universal TV

FAMILY TIES (NBC)—Paramount TV

FATHER DOWLING (NBC)—Viacom Prod., Inc. with Fred Silverman Co.

A FINE ROMANCE (ABC)—New World TV

FIRST IMPRESSIONS (CBS)—Orion TV

FRANK'S PLACE (CBS)—Viacom Prod., Inc.

FRIDAY THE 13TH (SYND.)—Goalline Prod.

GENERAL HOSPITAL (ABC)—ABC Entertainment

GOLDEN GIRLS (NBC)—Witt/Thomas/Harris Prod. with Touchstone Pictures

GOOD MORNING MISS BLISS (DISNEY CHAN.)—NBC Prod.

GROWING PAINS (ABC)—Warner Bros. TV

HAVE FAITH (ABC)—20th Century-Fox TV with Adam Prod.

HEAD OF THE CLASS (ABC)—Warner Bros. TV with Eustis Elias Prod.

HEARTBEAT (ABC)—Aaron Spelling Prod.

HIGHWAY TO HEAVEN (NBC)—Michael Landon Prod., Inc.

HITCHCOCK (USA NETWORK)—Universal TV

THE HITCHHIKER (SYND.)—Round Valley Prod.

HOOPERMAN (ABC)—20th Century-Fox TV

HUNTER (NBC)—Stephen J. Cannell Prod.

700

IN THE HEAT OF THE NIGHT (NBC)—MGM/UA TV with Fred Silverman Co.

IT'S A LIVING (SYND.)—Witt/Thomas Prod.

IT'S GARRY SHANDLING'S SHOW (SHOWTIME)—Our Production Co.

JAKE AND THE FAT MAN (CBS)—Viacom Prod., Inc.

JAKE'S JOURNEY (CBS)—20th Century-Fox TV

JUST THE TEN OF US (ABC)—Warner Bros. TV with GSM Prod.

KATE AND ALLIE (CBS)—Reeves Entertainment Group

KNIGHTWATCH (ABC)—MGM/UA TV

L.A. LAW (NBC)—20th Century-Fox TV

MACGYVER(ABC)—Paramount TV

THE MAGICAL WORLD OF DISNEY (NBC)—Walt Disney TV

MAMA'S FAMILY (SYND.)—Joe Hamilton Prod.

MARRIED . . . WITH CHILDREN (FBC)—Columbia TV

MARY TYLER MOORE (CBS)—MTM Prod.

MATLOCK (NBC)—Viacom Prod., Inc.

MIAMI VICE (NBC)—Universal TV

MISSION IMPOSSIBLE (ABC)—Paramount TV

MR. BELVEDERE (ABC)—20th Century-Fox TV

MONSTERS (SYND.)—Laurel EFX, Inc.

MOONLIGHTING (ABC)—ABC Circle Film

MURDER, SHE WROTE (CBS)—Universal TV

MURPHY BROWN (CBS)—Warner Bros. TV with Shukovsky/English Prod.

MURPHY'S LAW (ABC)—New World TV

MY SECRET IDENTITY (SYND.)—Universal TV

MY TWO DADS (NBC)—Columbia TV

THE NEW ADVENTURES OF WINNIE THE POOH (ABC)—Walt Disney TV

THE NEW LEAVE IT TO BEAVER (SYND.)—Universal TV

THE NEW MUNSTERS (SYND.)—The Arthur Co.

NEWHART (CBS)—MTM Prod.

NIGHT COURT (NBC)—Warner Bros. TV with Starry Night Prod.

NIGHT HEAT (CBS)—Grosso-Jacobson Prod. with Alliance Entertainment

OUT OF THIS WORLD (SYND.)—Bob Booker Prod.

RAISING MIRANDA (CBS)—GTG Entertainment, Inc.

THE ROBERT GUILLAUME SHOW (ABC)—New World TV

ROSEANNE (ABC)—Carsey-Werner Co.

701

RYAN'S HOPE (ABC)—ABC Prod.

SIMON AND SIMON (CBS)—Universal TV

SOMETHING IS OUT THERE (NBC)—Columbia TV

SONNY SPOON (NBC)—Stephen J. Cannell Prod.

STAR TREK: THE NEXT GENERATION (SYND.)—Paramount TV

SUPERBOY (SYND.)—Superboy Prod., Inc.

TATTINGERS (NBC)—MTM Prod.

THIRTYSOMETHING (ABC)—MGM/UA TV

TOUR OF DUTY (CBS)—New World TV

THE TRACY ULLMAN SHOW (FBC)—20th Century-Fox TV

TV 101 (CBS)—GTG Entertainment, Inc.

21 JUMP STREET (FBC)—Stephen J. Cannell Prod.

227 (NBC)—Columbia TV

THE VAN DYKE SHOW (CBS)—GTG Entertainment, Inc.

WAR OF THE WORLDS (SYND.)—Goalline Prod.

WEBSTER (SYND.)—Paramount TV

WHO'S THE BOSS (ABC)—Columbia TV

WISE GUY (CBS)—Stephen J. Cannell Prod.

THE WONDER YEARS (ABC)—New World TV

THE YOUNG AND THE RESTLESS (CBS)—Bell-Phillip TV Prod., Inc.

TELEVISION PRODUCERS

ABC CIRCLE FILMS—9911 W. Pico Blvd., Los Angeles, CA 90067.

ABC ENTERTAINMENT—4151 Prospect Ave., Los Angeles, CA 90027.

ABC PRODUCTIONS—101 W. 67th St., NewYork, NY 10023.

ALIEN PRODUCTIONS—8660 Hayden Pl., Culver City, CA 90230.

BELL-PHILLIP TELEVISION PRODUCTIONS INC.—CBS Television City, 7800 Beverly Blvd., Los Angeles, CA 90036.

BOB BOOKER PRODUCTIONS—Universal Studio, Universal City, CA 91608.

STEPHEN J. CANNELL PRODUCTIONS—7083 Hollywood Blvd., Los Angeles, CA 90028.

CARSEY-WERNER PRODUCTIONS—34–12 36th St., Astoria, NY 11106.

CARSON PRODUCTIONS—10045 Riverside Dr., Toluca Lake, CA 91602.

COLUMBIA PICTURES TELEVISION—Columbia Plaza, Burbank, CA 91505.

GROSSO-JACOBSON PRODUCTIONS—767 Third Ave., New York, NY 10017.

GTG ENTERTAINMENT—The Culver Studios, 9336 W. Washington Blvd., Culver City, CA 90230.

JOE HAMILTON PRODUCTIONS—5746 Sunset Blvd., Hollywood, CA 90028.

MICHAEL LANDON PRODUCTIONS—10202 West Washington Blvd., Culver City, CA 90230.

MGM-UA TELEVISION—10000 W. Washington Blvd., Culver City, CA 90232.

MTM ENTERPRISES—4024 Radford Ave., Studio City, CA 91604.

NBC PRODUCTIONS—NBC-TV, 3000 W. Alameda Ave., Burbank, CA 91523.

NEW WORLD TV—1440 South Sepulveda Blvd., Los Angeles, CA 90025.

ORION PICTURES CORP.—1999 Century Park East, Los Angeles, CA 90067.

PARAMOUNT TELEVISION—5555 Melrose, Los Angeles, CA 90038.

REEVES ENTERTAINMENT—3500 W. Olive Ave., Suite 500, Burbank, CA 91505.

FRED SILVERMAN CO.—12400 Wilshire Blvd., W. Los Angeles, CA 90025.

AARON SPELLING PRODUCTIONS—1041 N. Formosa Ave., Los Angeles, CA 91146.

20TH CENTURY FOX TELEVISION—10201 W. Pico Blvd., Los Angeles, CA 90064.

UNIVERSAL TELEVISION—100 Universal City Plaza, Universal City, CA 91608.

VIACOM ENTERPRISES—10900 Wilshire Blvd., Los Angeles, CA 90024.

WALT DISNEY TELEVISION—500 South Buena Vista St., Burbank, CA 91521.

WARNER BROTHERS TELEVISION—4000 Warner Blvd., Burbank, CA 91505.

WITT-THOMAS-HARRIS PRODUCTIONS—846 N. Cahuenga Blvd., Bldg. D, Los Angeles, CA 90038.

TELEVISION SCRIPT AGENTS

MARCIA AMSTERDAM AGENCY—41 W. 82nd St., #9A, New York, NY 10024. Query with SASE.

BILL COOPER ASSOCIATES—224 W. 49th St., New York, NY 10019. Will look at developed ideas for comedies, dramas, theater, and motion pictures.

THE BRODY AGENCY—P.O. Box 291423, Davie, FL 33329. Hank Twerl, Script Consultant. Reads queries and scripts with SASEs.

PEMA BROWNE LTD—185 E. 85th St., New York, NY 10028. No scripts for ongoing shows. Reads queries. Prefer writers with credits.

THE CALDER AGENCY—4150 Riverside Dr., Burbank, CA 91505. Reads queries and synopses for features only; no episode TV material.

HOLLYWOOD TALENT AGENCY—478 Brownridge Dr., Thornhill, Ont.,

Canada M6K 2L8. Reads queries, scripts, treatments, and manuscripts. Query required.

SCOTT C. HUDSON TALENT REPRESENTATION—215 E. 76th St., New York, NY 10021. Reads queries and treatments, with SASEs. Considers screenplays and plays. Send bio and resumé.

OTTO R. KOZAK LITERARY AGENCY—P.O. Box 152, Long Beach, NY 11561. Query.

L. HARRY LEE LITERARY AGENCY—Box 203, Rocky Point, NY 11778. Reads queries accompanied by SASE only. Episodic and sit-com for shows produced in NYC; movies-of-the-week and mini-series.

LONDON STAR PROMOTIONS—7131 Owensmouth Ave., #C116, Canoga Park, CA 91303. Reads queries and synopses.

SUZANNE SHELTON—CNA Associates, 8721 Sunset Blvd., #202, Los Angeles, CA 90069. Reads queries accompanied by SASEs only. No episodic scripts. New series ideas or made-for-TV scripts only.

JACK TANTLEFF—c/o the Tantleff Office, 360 W. 20th St., New York, NY 10011. Reads queries.

DAN WRIGHT—c/o Ann Wright Representatives, Inc., 136 E. 57th St., New York, NY 10022. Reads queries. Specializes in motion pictures and television properties.

BOOK PUBLISHERS

The following list includes the major publishers of trade books (adult and juvenile fiction and nonfiction) and a representative number of small publishers from across the country. All companies in the list publish both hardcover and paperback books, unless otherwise indicated.

Before sending a complete manuscript to an editor, it is advisable to send a brief query letter describing the proposed book. The letter should also include information about the author's special qualifications for dealing with a particular topic and any previous publication credits. An outline of the book (or a synopsis for fiction) and a sample chapter may also be included.

It is common practice to submit a book manuscript to only one publisher at a time, although it is becoming more and more acceptable for writers, even those without agents, to submit the same *query* or *proposal* to more than one editor at the same time.

Book manuscripts may be sent in typing paper boxes (available from a stationer) and sent by first-class mail, or, more common and less expensive, by "Special Fourth Class Rate, Manuscript." For rates, details of insurance, and so forth, inquire at your local post office. With any submission to a publisher, be sure to enclose sufficient postage for the manuscript's return.

Royalty rates for hardcover books usually start at 10% of the retail price of the book and increase after a certain number of copies have been sold. Paperbacks generally have a somewhat lower rate, about 5% to 8%. It is customary for the publishing company to pay the author a cash advance against royalties when the book contract is signed or when the finished manuscript is received. Some publishers pay on a flat fee basis.

ABBEY PRESS—St. Meinrad, IN 47577. Keith McLellan, O.S.B., Pub. Religious fiction and value-based children's books. Nonfiction Christian books on marriage and family living. Query with table of contents and writing sample.

ABINGDON PRESS—201 Eighth Ave. S., Nashville, TN 37202. Etta Wilson, Ed. Picture books, read-aloud books, and middle-grade fiction; biographies, fantasy, concept books, ethnic stories, and devotional titles. Christian focus necessary; submit complete manuscript. Guidelines.

ACADEMIC PRESS—Harcourt, Brace, Jovanovich, Inc., 1250 Sixth St., San Diego, CA 92101. Scientific books for professionals; college science texts. Query.

ACADEMY CHICAGO, PUBLISHERS—213 West Institute Pl., Chicago, IL 60610. Anita Miller, Ed. General quality fiction; mysteries. History; biographies, travel; books by and about women. Royalty. Query with four sample chapters. SASE required.

ACCENT BOOKS—Box 15337, 12100 W. 6th Ave., Denver, CO 80215. Mary Nelson, Exec. Ed. Fiction and nonfiction from evangelical Christian perspective. Query with sample chapters. Royalty. Paperback only.

ACE BOOKS (IMPRINT OF *BERKLEY PUBLISHING GROUP)*—200 Madison Ave., New York, NY 10016. Susan Allison, V.P., Ed.-in-Chief. Science fiction and fantasy. Royalty. Query with first three chapters and outline.

ACROPOLIS BOOKS—2400 17th St. N.W., Washington, DC 20009–9964. A. J. Hackl, Ed. Nonfiction titles. Query with outline and sample chapters. Length varies. Royalty.

ADAMA BOOKS—306 W. 38th St., New York, NY 10018. Esther Cohen, Ed. Adult nonfiction. Young-adult fiction and nonfiction. Children's picture books. Books with international focus or related to political or social issues. Query with outline and sample chapter.

ADDISON-WESLEY PUBLISHING CO.—Rt. 128, Reading, MA 01867. General Publishing Group: Adult nonfiction on current topics: education, health, psychology, computers, human resources, business, biography, child care, etc. Royalty.

ALASKA NORTHWEST PUBLISHING CO.—130 2nd Ave. S., Edmonds, WA 98020. Ethel Dassow, Sr. Book Ed. Nonfiction, 50,000 to 100,000 words, with an emphasis on natural resources and history of Alaska, Northwestern Canada, and Pacific Northwest: how-to books; biographies; cookbooks; field guides; guidebooks. Send query or sample chapters with outline. Limited market.

THE AMERICAN PSYCHIATRIC PRESS—1400 K St. N.W., Washington, DC 20005. Carol C. Nadelson, M.D., Ed.-in-Chief. Books that interpret scientific and medical aspects of psychiatry for a lay audience, and that address specific psychiatric problems. Authors must have appropriate credentials to write on medical topics. Query required. Royalty.

APPLE BOOKS—See *Scholastic, Inc.*.

ARCHWAY PAPERBACKS—Pocket Books, 1230 Ave. of the Americas, New York, NY 10020. Patricia MacDonald, Sr. Ed. Young-adult contemporary fiction (mystery, romance, fantasy, problems) and nonfiction (sports, biography), for ages 11 and up. Query and SASE required; include outline and sample chapter.

705

ARCO PUBLISHING (*PRENTICE HALL PRESS*/A DIV. OF *SIMON & SCHUSTER*)—Gulf & Western Bldg., One Gulf & Western Plaza, 16th fl., New York, NY 10023. Charles Wall, Exec. Ed. Nonfiction, originals and reprints, from 50,000 words. Career guides, test preparation. Royalty. Query with outline. Return postage required.

ARCSOFT PUBLISHERS—P.O. Box 132, Woodsboro, MD 21798. Anthony Curtis, Pres. Nonfiction hobby books for beginners, personal computing, space science, desktop publishing, journalism, and hobby electronics, for laymen, consumers, beginners and novices. Outright purchase and royalty basis. Query. Paper only.

ATHENEUM PUBLISHERS (SUBSIDIARY OF *MACMILLAN PUBLISHING CO.*)—115 Fifth Ave., New York, NY 10003. Susan Ginsburg, Ed.-in-Chief. General nonfiction, biography, history, current affairs, fiction, belles-lettres. Query with sample chapters and outline.

THE ATLANTIC MONTHLY PRESS—19 Union Square West, New York, NY 10003. Gary Fisketjon, Ed. Dir. Fiction, general nonfiction. Hardcover and trade paperback. Royalty.

AUGSBURG BOOKS—Box 1209, 426 S. Fifth St., Minneapolis, MN 55440. Religious books for children, youth, or intergenerational family use; devotional, inspirational, and self-help books for Christian market. Query first.

AVERY PUBLISHING GROUP—350 Thorens Ave., Garden City Park, NY 11040. Nonfiction, from 40,000 words, on health, childbirth, child care, health cooking. Query first. Royalty.

AVIATION PUBLISHERS—Ultralight Publications, Inc., One Aviation Way, Lock Box 234, Hummelstown, PA 17036. Michael A. Markowski, Ed. Nonfiction, from 30,000 words, on aviation, cars, model cars and planes, boats, trains, health, and self-help. Query with outline and sample chapters. Royalty.

AVON BOOKS—105 Madison Ave., New York, NY 10016. Linda Cunningham, Ed. Dir. Modern fiction, general nonfiction, historical romance, 60,000 to 200,000 words. Science fiction, 75,000 to 100,000 words. Query with synopsis and sample chapters. Ellen Edwards, Historical Romance; John Douglas, Science Fiction. *Camelot Books:* Ellen Krieger, Ed. Fiction and nonfiction for 7- to 10-year-olds. Query. *Flare Books:* Ellen Krieger, Ed. Fiction and nonfiction for 12-year-olds and up. Query. Royalty. Paperback only.

BACKCOUNTRY PUBLICATIONS, INC. (DIV. OF *THE COUNTRYMAN PRESS, INC.*)—P. O. Box 175, Woodstock, VT 05091. Carl Taylor, Ed. Regional guidebooks, 150 to 300 pages, on hiking, walking, canoeing, bicycling, cross-country skiing, and fishing. Royalty. Query first.

BAEN BOOKS—Baen Enterprises, 260 Fifth Ave., New York, NY 10001. Elizabeth Mitchell, Sr. Ed. Jim Baen, Pres. High-tech science fiction; innovative fantasy. Query with synopsis and sample chapters. Royalty.

BAKER BOOK HOUSE—P. O. Box 6287, Grand Rapids, MI 49516–6287. Dan Van't Kerkhoff, Allan Fisher, Eds. General trade and professional books; academic and reference books; religious nonfiction. Royalty.

BALLANTINE BOOKS—201 E. 50th St., New York, NY 10022. Robert Wyatt, Ed.-in-Chief. General fiction and nonfiction. Query.

BALLANTINE/EPIPHANY—201 E. 50th St., New York, NY 10022. Toni Simmons, Ed. Nonfiction (personal growth, self help, decision-making, relationships, biography) with Christian elements or spiritual themes. Will consider fiction with inspirational qualities. Query with outline and sample chapters; manuscripts 60,000 to 75,000 words. Royalty.

BALSAM PRESS—122 E. 25th St., New York, NY 10010. Barbara Krohn, Exec. Ed. General and illustrated adult nonfiction. Royalty. Query.

BANTAM BOOKS—666 Fifth Ave., New York, NY 10103. Linda Grey, Pub., Stephen Rubin, Ed.-in-Chief, Adult Fiction and Nonfiction. General and educational fiction and nonfiction, 75,000 to 100,000 words. Carolyn Nichols, *Loveswept.* Judy Gitenstein, Ed., Dir., Books for Young Readers; fiction and science fiction, ages 6 to 12. Beverly Horowitz, Ed. Dir., Books for Young Adults; fiction and non-formula romance for teens. Agent submissions only.

BARRON'S—250 Wireless Blvd., Hauppauge, NY 11788. Grace Freedson, Acquisitions Ed. Nonfiction for juveniles (science, nature, history, hobbies, and how-to) and picture books for ages 3 to 6. Queries required. Guidelines.

BEACH BOOKS—See *National Press.*

BEACON PRESS—25 Beacon St., Boston, MA 02108. Joanne Wykoff, Exec. Ed. Deborah Johnson, Sr. Ed. General nonfiction: world affairs, sociology, psychology, women's studies, political science, art, anthropology, literature, history, philosophy, religion. Series: *Asian Voices* (fiction and nonfiction); *Barnard New Women Poets; Black Women Writers* (fiction); *Men and Masculinity* (nonfiction); *Virago/ Beacon Travelers* (nonfiction); *Night Lights* (juveniles). Query first. SASE required.

BEAR & COMPANY, INC.—P.O. Drawer 2860, Santa Fe, NM 87504. Barbara Clow, Ed. Nonfiction "that will help transform our culture philosophically, environmentally, and spiritually." Query with outline and sample chapters. Royalty.

BEAUFORT BOOKS—9 E. 40th St, New York, NY 10016. Eric Kampmann, Pub. Fiction and nonfiction. Query with outlines and sample chapters for nonfiction, one sample chapter for fiction; include list of previous publications and SASE.

BEECH TREE BOOKS (IMPRINT OF *WILLIAM MORROW AND CO., INC.*)—105 Madison Ave., New York, NY 10016. James Landis, Pub. and Ed.-in-Chief. Adult fiction and nonfiction. No unsolicited manuscripts.

BERKLEY PUBLISHING GROUP—200 Madison Ave., New York, NY 10016. Roger Cooper, Pub. and Ed. Dir. Ed Breslin, Ed.-in-Chief. General-interest fiction and nonfiction: science fiction, suspense and espionage novels; romance. Submit through agent only. Publishes both reprints and originals. Paper only.

BETHANY HOUSE PUBLISHING—6820 Auto Club Rd., Minneapolis, MN 55438. Address Editorial Dept. Fiction, nonfiction. Religious. Royalty. Query required.

BETTER HOMES AND GARDENS BOOKS—See *Meredith Corporation.*

BINFORD & MORT PUBLISHING—1202 N.W. 17th Ave., Portland, OR 97209. J. F. Roberts, Ed. Books on subjects related to the Pacific Coast and the Northwest. Lengths vary. Royalty. Query first.

JOHN F. BLAIR, PUBLISHERS—1406 Plaza Dr., Winston-Salem, NC 27103. Stephen D. Kirk, Ed. Dept. Biography, history, fiction, travel, and guidebooks, with North Carolina tie-in. Length: at least 75,000 words. Royalty. Query.

BONUS BOOKS—160 E. Illinois St., Chicago, IL 60611. Mike Emmerich, Ass't. Ed. Nonfiction; topics vary widely. Query with sample chapters. Royalty.

BOOKS FOR PROFESSIONALS—See *Harcourt, Brace, Jovanovich.*

THOMAS BOUREGY & CO, INC. (*AVALON BOOKS*)—401 Lafayette St., New York, NY 10003. Barbara J. Brett, Ed. Hardcover library books. Wholesome contemporary romances, and mystery romances about young single (never married) women. Wholesome westerns and contemporary adventure novels. Length: 35,000 to 50,000 words. Query with first chapter and outline. SASE required.

BRADBURY PRESS—866 Third Ave., New York, NY 10022. Barbara Lalicki, Ed. Hardcover: fiction (general, humor, science fiction), grades 4–12; nonfiction (biography, sports, history) up to grade 6; picture books, to age 8. Query or submit complete manuscript. Royalty.

BRANDEN PRESS—17 Station St., Box 843, Brookline Village, MA 02147. Adolph Caso, Ed. Novels and biographies, 250 to 350 pages. Query with SASE. Royalty.

BRETHREN PRESS—1451 Dundee Ave., Elgin, IL 60120. David B. Eller, Ed. Dir. Quality nonfiction in areas of Bible study and theology, Church history, practical discipleship and life style issues, social concerns, and devotional life/personal growth. Query with outline and sample chapters for 150- to 250-word manuscripts. Pays royalties or flat fee.

BROADMAN PRESS—127 Ninth Ave., N., Nashville, TN 37234. Harold S. Smith, Manager. Religious and inspirational fiction and nonfiction. Royalty. Query

CAMELOT BOOKS—See *Avon Books.*

CAROLRHODA BOOKS—241 First Ave. N., Minneapolis, MN 55401. Rebecca Poole, Ed. Complete manuscripts for ages 7–12: biography, science, nature, history, mystery, humor; picture books for ages 3–9, 10 to 15 pages. Guidelines. Outright purchase. Hardcover.

CARROLL AND GRAF PUBLISHERS, INC.—260 Fifth Ave., New York, NY 10001. Kent E. Carroll, Exec. Ed. General fiction and nonfiction. Royalty. Query with SASE.

CBI PUBLISHING—See *Van Nostrand Reinhold.*

CHARTER BOOKS (IMPRINT OF *BERKLEY PUBLISHING CO.*)—200 Madison Ave., New York, NY 10012. Roger Cooper, Pub. Adventure, espionage and suspense fiction, women's contemporary fiction, family sagas, and historical novels. Westerns, male action/adventure, and cartoon books. No unsolicited manuscripts. Royalty or outright purchase. Paperback.

CHATHAM PRESS—P. O. Box A, Old Greenwich, CT 06807. Roger H. Lourie, Man. Dir. Books on the Northeast coast, New England maritime subjects, and the ocean. Royalty. Query with outline, sample chapters, illustrations, and SASE large enough for the return of material.

CHELSEA GREEN PUBLISHING CO.—Box 283, Chelsea, VT 05038. Ian Baldwin, Jr., Ed. Fiction and nonfiction on natural history, biography, history, politics, and travel. Query with outline and sample chapters. Royalty.

CHICAGO REVIEW PRESS—814 N. Franklin St., Chicago, IL 60610. Linda Matthews, Ed. Nonfiction: sports, medicine, anthropology, travel, nature, and regional topics. Query with outline and sample chapters.

CHILDRENS PRESS—1224 W. Van Buren St., Chicago, IL 60607. Fran Dyra, Ed. Dir. Juvenile nonfiction: science, biography, 10,000 to 25,000 words, for supplementary use in classrooms. Query first. Picture books, 50 to 1,000 words. Royalty or outright purchase.

708

CHILTON BOOK CO.—201 King of Prussia Rd., Radnor, PA 19089. Alan F. Turner, Ed. Dir. Business, crafts, hobbies, automotive. Royalty. Query with outline, sample chapter, and return postage.

CHRONICLE BOOKS—One Hallidie Plaza, Ste. 806, San Francisco, CA 94102. Topical nonfiction, history, biography, fiction, art, photography, architecture, nature, food, regional, and children's books. Query with SASE.

CITADEL PRESS—See *Lyle Stuart, Inc.*

CLARION BOOKS—Ticknor & Fields, 52 Vanderbilt Ave., New York, NY 10017. James C. Giblin, Ed. Fiction and picture books. Lively stories, ages 8–12 and 10–14; short novels (40 to 80 pages), ages 7–10. Mysteries, American historical fiction, and humor; picture books for preschool to age 3. Nonfiction: Query Ann Troy, Sr. Ed. Biography, word plays, nature, social studies, and holiday themes. Royalty. Hardcover.

CLIFFHANGER PRESS—P.O. Box 29527, Oakland, CA 94604–9527. Nancy Chirich, Ed. Mystery and suspense. Unagented manuscripts only. Query with first three chapters and outline; SASE. Royalty. Guidelines.

CLOVERDALE PRESS—133 Fifth Ave., New York, NY 10003.. Book packager. Contemporary romance, romantic suspense, generational sagas, historicals, inspirational romances, male action adventure, medical fiction, YA fiction, and middle-grade fiction. New series ideas and individual manuscripts welcome. Query with outline and resumé. Address YA to Marion Vaarn; adult to Lisa Howell.

COLLIER BOOKS—See *Macmillan Publishing Co.*

COMPCARE PUBLISHERS—18551 Von Karman Ave., Irvine, CA 92715. Bonnie Hesse, Man. Ed. Adult nonfiction; young-adult nonfiction: books on recovery from addictive/compulsive behavior; growth in personal, couple, and family relationships. Submit complete manuscript. Royalty.

COMPUTE! PUBLICATIONS, INC.—P. O. Box 5406, Greensboro, NC 27403. How-to computer books; specializes in machine-specific publications. Query preferred. Royalty.

CONCORDIA PUBLISHING HOUSE—3558 S. Jefferson Ave., St. Louis, MO 63118. Practical nonfiction with explicit religious content, conservative Lutheran doctrine. Very little fiction. No poetry. Royalty. Query.

CONTEMPORARY BOOKS, INC.—180 N. Michigan Ave., Chicago, IL 60601. Nancy Crossman, Ed. Dir. Trade nonfiction, 100 to 400 pages, on health, fitness, sports, cooking, humor, business, popular culture, biography, real estate, finance, women's issues. Query with outline and sample chapters. Royalty.

DAVID C. COOK PUBLISHING CO.—850 N. Grove Ave., Elgin, IL 60120. Paul Mouw, Man. Ed., General Titles. Catherine Davis, Man. Ed., Children's Books. Fiction that "helps children better understand themselves and their relationship with God"; nonfiction that illuminates the Bible; picture books, ages 1 to 7; fiction for ages 8 to 10, 10 to 12, and 12 to 14. Lengths and payment vary. Query required. Guidelines.

COUNCIL OAK BOOKS—1428 South St. Louis, Tulsa, OK 74120–9990. Sally Dennison, Ed. High-quality fiction, from 60,000 words, and nonfiction, from 50,000 words. Subjects are new age, how-to, biographies, history, and cookbooks; no romances or westerns. Royalty. Query.

COWARD, McCANN (DIV. OF *PUTNAM PUBLISHING GROUP*)—200 Madison Ave., New York, NY 10016. Fiction and nonfiction through agents only.

CRAFTSMAN BOOK COMPANY—6058 Corte del Cedro, P.O. Box 6500, Carlsbad, CA 92008. Laurence D. Jacobs, Ed. How-to construction and estimating manuals for builders, 450 pages. Royalty. Query. Softcover.

CREATIVE ARTS BOOK CO.—833 Bancroft Way, Berkeley, CA 94710. Peg O'Donnell, Ed. Adult and juvenile fiction and nonfiction; no photography, technical books, science fiction, poetry, drama, romance, or art. *Black Lizard Books:* mystery and suspense fiction. Query with outline and sample chapters. Royalty.

THE CROSSING PRESS—22-D Roache Rd., P.O. Box 1048, Freedom, CA 95019. Elaine Goldman Gill, John Gill, Pubs. Fiction, health, men's studies, feminist studies, gay topics, cookbooks. Royalty.

CROSSWINDS—300 E. 42nd St., New York, NY 10017. Nancy Jackson, Sr. Ed. Fiction (mysteries, romances, occult, and problem novels) for ages 11 to 16. Submit complete manuscript (45,000 words). Guidelines.

THOMAS Y. CROWELL—See *Harper Junior Books Group.*

CROWN PUBLISHERS—225 Park Ave. S., New York, NY 10003. David Allender, Ed. Dir./Children's Books. Fiction (including horror and science fiction), nonfiction (biography, science, sports, nature, music, and history), and picture books for ages 3 and up. Query with outline and sample chapter; send manuscript for picture books. Guidelines.

JONATHAN DAVID PUBLISHERS, INC.—68–22 Eliot Ave., Middle Village, NY 11379. Alfred J. Kolatch, Ed.-in-Chief. General nonfiction: how-to, sports, cooking and food, self-help, etc. (specializing in Judaica). Royalty or outright purchase. Query with outline, sample chapter, and resumé required. SASE.

DAW BOOKS, INC.—1633 Broadway, New York, NY 10019. Elizabeth R. Wollheim, Ed.-in-Chief. Science fiction and fantasy, 60,000 to 120,000 words. Royalty.

DEL REY BOOKS—201 E. 50th St., New York, NY 10022. Shelly Shapiro, SF Ed. Lester del Rey, Fantasy Ed. Science fiction and fantasy, first novelists welcome. Material must be well-paced with logical resolutions. Fantasy with magic basic to plotline. Length, 70,000 to 120,000 words. Complete manuscripts preferred, or outline with three sample chapters. Royalty.

DELACORTE PRESS—245 E. 47th St., New York, NY 10017. Jackie Farber, Robert Miller, Eds. Adult fiction and nonfiction. Juvenile and YA fiction (George Nicholson, Ed.). Accepts fiction (mystery, YA, romance, fantasy, etc.) from agents only.

DELL PUBLISHING—666 Fifth Ave., New York, NY 10103. Dell Books: family sagas, historical romances, war action, occult/horror/psychological suspense, true crime, men's adventure. *Delta:* General-interest nonfiction, psychology, feminism, health, nutrition, child care, science. Juvenile Books: *Yearling* (kindergarten through 6th grade; no unsolicited manuscripts); and *Laurel-Leaf* (grades 7 through 12; no unsolicited manuscripts). Submissions policy for *Dell Books:* Send four-page narrative synopsis for fiction, or an outline for nonfiction. Enclose SASE. Address submissions to the appropriate Dell division, Editorial Dept., Book Proposal.

DELTA BOOKS—See *Dell Publishing Co.*

DEMBNER BOOKS—80 Eighth Ave., New York, NY 10011. Therese Eiben, Ed. Popular reference books, mystery fiction. No first-person tragedy, no romance or pornography, no fads. Send synopsis or sample chapter with SASE. Modest advances against royalties.

DEVIN-ADAIR PUBLISHERS, INC.—6 N. Water St., Greenwich, CT 06830. C. de la Belle Issue, Pub. J. Andrassi, Ed. Books on conservative affairs, Irish topics, Americana, computers, self-help, health, ecology. Royalty. Send outline, sample chapters, and SASE.

DIAL BOOKS FOR YOUNG READERS—2 Park Ave., New York, NY 10016. Phyllis Fogelman, Pub./Ed.in-Chief. Picture books; Easy-to-Read Books; middle-grade readers; young-adult fiction and some nonfiction. Submit complete manuscript for fiction; outline and sample chapters for nonfiction. Enclose SASE. Royalty. Hardcover only.

DILLON PRESS—242 Portland Ave. S., Minneapolis, MN 55415. Tom Schneider, Nonfiction Ed. Karin Snelson, Fiction Ed. Juvenile nonfiction: American Indian tribes, world and U.S. geography, U.S. states and cities, contemporary and historical biographies for elementary and middle-grade levels, unusual or remarkable animals. Short historical fiction for ages 8–12 based on a single event, mystery, adventure, and science fiction. Length, 10 to 90 pages. Royalty and outright purchase. Guidelines.

DODD, MEAD & CO.—71 Fifth Ave., New York, NY 10003. Jonathan Dodd, Pres. Adult fiction and nonfiction. Royalty. Query with SASE.

THE DONNING COMPANY—5659 Virginia Beach Blvd., Norfolk, VA 23502. Tony Lillis, Ed. Metaphysical and general interest, regional, humor titles. Cookbooks. Science fiction and fantasy. Query with outline and sample chapters. Royalty.

DOUBLEDAY AND CO.—666 Fifth Ave., New York, NY 10103. Hardcover: mystery/suspense fiction, science fiction, 70,000 to 80,000 words. Send query and outline to appropriate editor: *Crime Club* or Science Fiction. Wendy Barish, Pub., Books for Young Readers: "Only special books, appropriate for gifts in the bookstore market." Paperback: Martha Levin, Pub., *Anchor Press.* Adult trade books: general fiction and nonfiction, sociology, psychology, philosophy, women's, etc. Herman Gollob, Ed.-in-Chief. Query. SASE required.

DOWN EAST BOOKS—Box 679, Camden, ME 04843. Books about Maine and New England. Query with sample chapters and outline. Royalty.

THOMAS DUNNE BOOKS (IMPRINT OF *ST. MARTIN'S PRESS*)—175 Fifth Ave., New York, NY 10010. Thomas L. Dunne, Ed. Adult fiction (mysteries, trade, SF, etc.) and nonfiction (history, biographies, how-to, etc.). Query with outline and sample chapters and SASE. Royalty.

E. P. DUTTON (DIV. OF *N.A.L./PENGUIN*)—2 Park Ave., New York, NY 10016. Lucia Monfried, Ed.-in-Chief, Children's Books. Picture books, easy-to-read books; fiction and nonfiction for preschoolers to young adults. Submit outline and sample chapters with query for fiction and nonfiction, complete manuscripts for picture books and easy-to-read books. *E.P. Dutton Adult Trade:* Richard Marek, Pub., Joyce Engelson, Ed.-in-Chief.

EAST WOODS PRESS (IMPRINT OF *THE GLOBE PEQUOT PRESS*)—429 East Kingston Ave., Charlotte, NC 28203. Sally McMillan, Consulting Ed. Nonfiction on travel, cooking, natural science, regional history, and home improvement. Length requirements and payment rates vary. Query with sample chapter required.

WM. B. EERDMANS PUBLISHING COMPANY, INC.—255 Jefferson Ave. S.E., Grand Rapids, MI 49503. Jon Pott, Ed.-in-Chief. Protestant theological nonfiction; American religious history; some fiction. Royalty.

EMC CORP.—300 York Ave., St. Paul, MN 55101. Eileen Slater, Ed. Vocational, career, and consumer education textbooks. Royalty. No unsolicited manuscripts.

ENSLOW PUBLISHERS—Bloy St. & Ramsey Ave., Box 777, Hillside, NJ 07205. R. M. Enslow, Jr., Ed./Pub. Nonfiction for young adults and children on social issues and science topics. Also reference and professional books in science, technology, medicine, and business. Royalty. Query first.

PAUL S. ERIKSSON, PUBLISHER—208 Battel Bldg., Middlebury, VT 05753. General nonfiction; some fiction. Royalty. Query first.

M. EVANS & CO., INC.—216 E. 49th St., New York, NY 10017. Books on travel, health, self-help, popular psychology, and cookbooks. Western fiction for adults and fiction and nonfiction for young adults. Query with outline, sample chapter, and SASE. Royalty.

FACTS ON FILE PUBLICATIONS—460 Park Ave. S., New York, NY 10016. Gerard Helferich, Exec. Ed. Reference and trade books on business, science, health, language, history, the performing arts, etc. Query with outline and sample chapter. Royalty. Hardcover.

FARRAR, STRAUS & GIROUX—19 Union Sq. West, New York, NY 10003. Fiction, YA novels, picture books, and nonfiction (history, nature, biography, and science). Query with sample chapter. Address Editorial Dept.

FREDERICK FELL PUBLISHERS, INC.—2131 Hollywood Blvd., #204, Hollywood, FL 33020. Kathryn Leth, Ed. Nonfiction: how-tos, especially business and health. Query with letter or outline and sample chapter; include SASE. Royalty.

THE FEMINIST PRESS AT THE CITY UNIVERSITY OF NEW YORK—311 E. 94th St., New York, NY 10128. Florence Howe, Pub. Reprints of significant "lost" fiction, autobiographies or other feminist work from the past; biography; original anthologies for classroom adoption; handbooks; bibliographies. Royalty.

DONALD I. FINE, INC.—128 E. 36th St., New York, NY 10016. Literary and commercial fiction. General nonfiction. No queries or unsolicited manuscripts. Submit through agent only.

FIREBRAND BOOKS—141 The Commons, Ithaca, NY 14850. Nancy K. Bereano, Ed. Feminist and lesbian fiction and nonfiction. Royalty. Softcover.

FIRESIDE BOOKS (IMPRINT OF *SIMON & SCHUSTER*)—1230 Ave. of the Americas, New York, NY 10020. General nonfiction; cultural and issue-oriented fiction. Royalty basis or outright purchase. Submit outline and one chapter. Softcover.

FLARE BOOKS—See *Avon Books.*

FLEET PRESS CORPORATION—160 Fifth Ave., New York, NY 10010. P. Scott, Ed. General nonfiction and young reader books. Royalty. Query; no unsolicited manuscripts.

FORTRESS PRESS—2900 Queen Lane, Philadelphia, PA 19129. Harold W. Rast, Th.D., Dir. Serious nonfiction works, from 100 pages, on theology and religion, for the academic or lay reader. Royalty. Query preferred.

FOUR WINDS PRESS (IMPRINT OF *MACMILLAN PUBLISHING CO.*)—866 Third Ave., New York, NY 10022. Judith R. Whipple, Pub. Cindy Kane, Ed.-in-Chief. Juveniles: picture books, fiction for all ages. Nonfiction for young children. Query with SASE required. Hardcover only.

THE FREE PRESS—See *Macmillan Publishing Co.*

FRIENDS UNITED PRESS—101 Quaker Hill Dr., Richmond, IN 47374. Barbara Mays, Ed. Nonfiction, 200 pages, on Quaker history, biography, and Quaker faith experience. Royalty. Query with outline and sample chapters.

GAMUT BOOKS (IMPRINT OF *DODD, MEAD & CO.*)—71 Fifth Ave., New York, NY 10003. Cynthia Vartan, Sr. Ed. Self-help on business; health; inspiration/motivation guides to success in work and life; popular psychology. Submit a prospectus, table of contents, brief outline of each chapter, and two sample chapters. Paperback only.

GARDEN WAY PUBLISHING COMPANY—Storey Communications, Schoolhouse Rd., Pownal, VT 05261. Deborah Burns, Ed. How-to books on gardening, cooking, building, animals, country living. Royalty or outright purchase. Query with outline and sample chapter.

THE K. S. GINIGER CO., INC.—1133 Broadway, Suite 1301, New York, NY 10010. General nonfiction; reference and religious. Royalty. Query with SASE; no unsolicited manuscripts.

THE GLOBE PEQUOT PRESS—138 W. Main St., Box Q, Chester, CT 06412. Bruce Markot, Man. Ed. Nonfiction with regional focus; gardening, how-tos, nature and outdoor guides, journalism and media. Travel guidebooks a specialty. Royalty. Query with sample chapter, contents, and one-page synopsis. SASE required.

GOLD EAGLE BOOKS—See *Worldwide Library.*

GOLDEN PRESS—See *Western Publishing Co., Inc.*

THE STEPHEN GREENE PRESS, INC. (DIV. OF *VIKING/PENGUIN*)—15 Muzzey St., Lexington, MA 02173. Tom Begner, Pres. General nonfiction; fitness, sports, and nature. Royalty.

GREENWILLOW BOOKS (IMPRINT OF *WILLIAM MORROW AND CO., INC.*)—105 Madison Ave., New York, NY 10016. Susan Hirschman, Ed.-in-Chief. Children's books for all ages. Picture books.

GROSSET AND DUNLAP, INC. (DIV. OF *PUTNAM PUBLISHING GROUP*)—51 Madison Ave., New York, NY 10010. Material accepted through agents only.

GROVE PRESS—920 Broadway, New York, NY 10010. Fred Jordan, Ed.-in-Chief. General fiction and nonfiction. Query first.

HAMMOND INC.—Maplewood, NY 07040. Charles Lees, Ed. Nonfiction: cartographic reference, travel. Payment varies. Query with outline and sample chapters. SASE required.

HANCOCK HOUSE—1431 Harrion Ave., Blaine, WA 98230. David Hancock, Ed. Nonfiction: cookbooks, gardening, outdoor guides, Western history, American Indians, real estate, and investing. Royalty.

HARCOURT BRACE JOVANOVICH—1250 Sixth Ave., San Diego, CA 92101. Adult trade nonfiction and fiction. *Books for Professionals:* test preparation guides and other student self-help materials. *Miller Accounting Publications, Inc.:* professional books for practitioners in accounting and finance; college accounting texts. Juvenile fiction and nonfiction for beginning readers through young adults under imprints: *HBJ Children's Books, Gulliver Books,* and *Voyager Paperbacks.* Adult books: no unsolicited manuscripts or queries. Children's books: unsolicited manuscripts accepted by *HBJ Children's Books* only. Send query or manuscript to Manuscript Submissions, Children's Book Division.

HARLEQUIN BOOKS/CANADA—225 Duuncan Mill Rd., Don Mills, Ont., Canada M3B 3K9. *Harlequin Romance:* Karin Stoecker, Sr. Ed. Contemporary romance novels, 50,000 to 55,000 words, any setting, ranging in plot from the traditional and gentle to the more sophisticated. Query first. *Harlequin Regency:* Marmie Charndoff, Ed. Short traditional novels set in 19th century Europe, 50,000 to 60,000 words. *Harlequin Superromance:* Marsha Zinberg, Sr. Ed. Contemporary romance, 85,000 words, with North American or foreign setting. New writers: query first. Published writers: send manuscript, synopsis, and copy of published work. *Harlequin Temptation:* Lisa Boyes, Sr. Ed. Sensually charged contemporary romantic fantasies, 60,000 to 65,000 words. Query first.

HARLEQUIN BOOKS/U.S.—300 E. 42nd St., 6th fl., New York, NY 10017. *Harlequin American Romance:* Debra Matteucci, Sr. Ed. Contemporary romances, 70,000 to 75,000 words, set against backdrop of suspense and adventure. Query. Send for tip sheets. Paperback.

HARPER & ROW—10 E. 53rd St., New York, NY 10022. Fiction, nonfiction, biography, economics, etc. Trade Dept.: Agents only, Lorraine Shanley, Ed. Dir. College texts: address College Dept. Nonfiction paperback originals: address Paperback Dept. Religion, theology, etc.: address Religious Books Dept., Ice House One, 151 Union St., San Francisco, CA 94111. No unsolicited manuscripts; query only.

HARPER JUNIOR BOOKS GROUP—10 E. 53rd St., New York, NY 10022. K. Magnusson, Admin. Coord., West Coast: P. O. Box 6549, San Pedro, CA 90734. Linda Zuckerman, Exec. Ed. (query one address only). Juvenile fiction, nonfiction, and picture books imprints include: *Thomas Y. Crowell Co., Publishers:* juveniles, etc.; *J. B. Lippincott Co.:* juveniles, picture books, etc.; *Harper & Row:* juveniles, picture books, etc.; *Trophy Books:* paperback juveniles. All publish from preschool to young adult titles. Query for nonfiction only. Send complete manuscript for fiction. Royalty.

HARVEST HOUSE PUBLISHERS—1075 Arrowsmith, Eugene, OR 97402. Eileen L. Mason, Ed. Nonfiction (how-tos, educational, health) with evangelical theme. No biographies, history or poetry. Query first. SASE required.

HEALTH PLUS PUBLISHERS—Box 22001, Phoenix, AZ 855028. Paula E. Clure, Ed. Books on health and fitness. Query with outline and sample chapters.

HEARST BOOKS AND HEARST MARINE BOOKS—See *William Morrow and Co.*

HEMINGWAY WESTERN STUDIES SERIES—Boise State University, 1910 University Dr., Boise, ID 83725. Tom Trusky, Ed. Nonfiction relating to the Inter-Mountain West (Rockies) in areas of history, political science, anthropology, natural sciences, film, fine arts, literary history or criticism. Publishes up to two books annually.

HERALD PRESS—616 Walnut Ave., Scottdale, PA 15683. Paul M. Schrock, General Book Ed. Christian books for adults and children (age 9 and up): inspiration, Bible study, self-helf, devotionals, current issues, peace studies, church history, missions and evangelism, family life. Send one-page summary and sample chapter. Royalty.

HOLIDAY HOUSE, INC.—18 E. 53rd St., New York, NY 10022. Margery S. Cuyler, Vice Pres. General juvenile and young adult fiction and nonfiction. Royalty. Query with outline and sample chapter. Hardcover only.

HENRY HOLT AND CO.—115 W. 18th St., New York, NY 10011. John Macrae, Ed.-in-Chief. Fiction and nonfiction (mysteries, history, autobiographies, natural history, travel, art, and how-to) of highest literary quality. Royalty. Query with SASE required.

HOUGHTON MIFFLIN COMPANY—2 Park St., Boston, MA 02108. Fiction: literary, mainstream, historical, suspense and science fiction. Nonfiction: history, biography. Query Submissions Dept. with SASE. Children's Book Division, address Mary Lee Donovan: picture books, fiction and nonfiction for all ages. Query. Royalty.

H. P. BOOKS (DIV. OF *PRICE STERN SLOAN*)—360 N. La Cienga Blvd., Los Angeles, CA 90048. Illustrated how-tos, 50,000 to 80,000 words, on cooking, gardening, photography, health and fitness, automotive, etc. Royalty. Query with SASE.

HUNTER PUBLISHING, INC.—300 Raritan Center Pkwy., Edison, NJ 08818. Michael Hunter, Ed. Travel guides. Query with outline.

INTIMATE MOMENTS—See *Silhouette Books.*

JAMESON BOOKS—722 Columbus St., Ottawa, IL 61350. J. G. Campaigne, Ed. American historical fiction for *Frontier Library.* Some nonfiction. Query with outline and sample chapters. Royalty.

JOHNSON BOOKS, INC.—1880 S. 57th Court, Boulder, CO 80301. Michael McNierney, Ed. Nonfiction: western history, archaeology, geology, natural history, astronomy, travel guides, outdoor guidebooks, fly fishing, regional. Royalty. Query.

JOVE BOOKS—200 Madison Ave., New York, NY 10016. Fiction and nonfiction. No unsolicited manuscripts.

JOY STREET BOOKS (IMPRINT OF *LITTLE, BROWN & CO.*)—34 Beacon St., Boston, MA 02108. Melanie Kroupa, Ed.-in-Chief.
Juvenile fiction and nonfiction. Query with outline and sample chapters for nonfiction; send complete manuscript for fiction. Royalty.

KEATS PUBLISHING, INC.—27 Pine St., Box 876, New Canaan, CT 06840. An Keats, Ed. Nonfiction: health, inspiration, how-to. Royalty. Query.

ALFRED A. KNOPF, INC.—201 E. 50th St., New York, NY 10022. Ashbel Green, V.P. and Sr. Ed. Distinguished fiction and general nonfiction; query. Frances Foster, Juvenile Ed. Sherry Gerstein, Paperback Ed., *Books for Young Readers.* Fiction and nonfiction for children and teens, to age 14; picture books, 3,000 to 5,000 words, ages 2–10; and humor/poetry. Query for nonfiction, send manuscript for fiction. Royalty. Guidelines.

JOHN KNOX PRESS—341 Ponce de Leon Ave. N.E., Atlanta, GA 30365. Walter Sutton, Ed. Dir. Books that inform, interpret, challenge and encourage Christian faith and living. Royalty. Send SASE for "Guidelines for a Book Proposal."

LAUREL-LEAF BOOKS—See *Dell Publishing.*

LEISURE BOOKS (DIV. OF *DORCHESTER PUBLISHING CO.*)—276 Fifth Ave., New York, NY 10001. Tracey Lubben, Ms. Ed. Historical romance novels, from 90,000 words; horror novels from 80,000 words; men's adventure series, Western series, from 50,000 words. Query with synopsis and sample chapters. Royalty.

HAL LEONARD BOOKS—Box 13819, 8112 W. Bluemound Rd., Milwaukee, WI 53213. Glenda Herro, Ed. Prefer subjects related to music and entertainment. Query first. Royalty or flat fee.

LEXINGTON BOOKS—See *D.C. Heath & Co.*

LIBERTY HOUSE (IMPRINT OF *TAB BOOKS*)—60 E. 42nd St., Suite 557, New York, NY 10165. David J. Conti, Ed. Dir. Personal finance, investing, real estate, small business books; approach should be practical, realistic, results-oriented. Query with outline, sample chapters if available. Royalty.

J.B. LIPPINCOTT COMPANY—See *Harper Junior Books Group.*

LITTLE, BROWN & CO.—34 Beacon St., Boston, MA 02106. Fiction, general nonfiction, sports books; divisions for law and medical texts. Royalty. Submissions only from authors who have previously published in professional or literary journals, newspapers or magazines. Query Ed. Dept., Trade Div. Juvenile fiction (from fantasy and romance to YA and mystery) and nonfiction (science, history, and nature), picture books (ages 3–8), and humor/poetry (ages 8–10). Prefer manuscripts with SASE. Address Maria Modugno, Ed.-in-Chief. Guidelines.

LODESTAR (DIV. OF *E.P. DUTTON*)—2 Park Ave., New York, NY 10016. Virginia Buckley, Ed. Dir. Fiction (YA, mystery, fantasy, science fiction, western) and nonfiction (science, sports, nature, history) for ages 9–11, 10–14, and 12-up. Send manuscript for fiction; query for nonfiction.

LONGMAN FINANCIAL SERVICES PUBLISHING (DIV. OF *LONGMAN GROUP U.S.A.*)—520 N. Dearborn, Chicago, IL 60610. Books for professionals on financial services, real estate, insurance, securities, banking, etc. Send query with outline and sample chapters to Anita A. Constant, V.P./Pub. Royalty and flat fee.

LOTHROP, LEE & SHEPARD BOOKS (IMPRINT OF *WILLIAM MORROW & CO., INC.*)—105 Madison Ave., New York, NY 10016. Dorothy Briley, Ed.-in-Chief. Juvenile, picture books, fiction and nonfiction. Royalty. Query.

LOVESWEPT (IMPRINT OF *BANTAM BOOKS*)—666 Fifth Ave., New York, NY 10103. Carolyn Nichols, Assoc. Pub. Highly sensual, adult contemporary romances, approx. 55,000 words. Study field before submitting. Query required. Paperback only.

LYNX BOOKS—41 Madison Ave., New York, NY 10010. Judith Stern, Sr. Ed. Manuscripts, 80,000 to 120,000 words, on romance, sagas, men's adventure, horror, and thrillers; 70,000 words on self-help, business, and health; 40,000-word series for boys and girls, age 12. Hardcover and paperback. Royalty.

MARGARET K. MCELDERRY BOOKS—Macmillan Publishers, 866 Third Ave., New York, NY 10022. Margaret K. McElderry, Ed. Original and quality fiction, including fantasy, science fiction, and YA; some nonfiction and humor. All geared for ages 8–12, 10–14, and 12-up. Picture books for ages 3 and up.

MCGRAW-HILL BOOKS CO.—11 W. 19th St., 3rd fl., New York, NY 10011. Fiction and nonfiction. No unsolicited manuscripts. Queries only.

DAVID MCKAY COMPANY—201 E. 50th St., New York, NY 10022. Nonfiction. Unsolicited manuscripts neither acknowledged nor returned.

MACMILLAN PUBLISHING CO., INC.—866 Third Ave., New York, NY 10022. General Books Division: religious, sports, science and reference books. No fiction. Paperbacks, *Collier Books.* College texts and professional books in social sciences, humanities, *The Free Press.* Royalty.

MADRONA PUBLISHERS, INC.—P. O. Box 22667, Seattle, WA 98122. Sara Levant, Acquisitions Ed. General-interest nonfiction trade books (no poetry, children's books or fiction). Special interests: alcoholism and small business. Royalty.

MEADOWBROOK PRESS—18318 Minnetonka Blvd., Deephaven, MN 55391. Ann Williams, Submissions Ed. Upbeat, useful books on pregnancy, child-birth, and parenting. Travel, humor, some fiction, 60,000 words. Query with outline, sample chapters, and qualifications. Royalty or payment.

MENTOR BOOKS—See *New American Library.*

MERCURY HOUSE—P. O. Box 640, Forest Knolls, CA 94933. Ms. Alev Lytle, Exec. Ed. Quality fiction and nonficiton, 250 to 350 pages. Query with outline and sample chapters.

MEREDITH CORP. BOOK GROUP (*BETTER HOMES AND GARDENS BOOKS*)—1716 Locust St., Des Moines, IA 50336. David A. Kitchner, Man. Ed. Address Editors. Books on gardening, crafts, health, decorating, etc., mostly staff written. Query.

JULIAN MESSNER (DIV. OF *SIMON & SCHUSTER*)—Prentice Hall Bldg., Rt. 9W, Englewood Cliffs, NJ 07632. Jane Steltenpohl, Exec. Ed. Curriculum-oriented nonfiction. General nonfiction, ages 8 to 14: science, nature, biography, history, and hobbies. Lengths vary. Royalty.

MILLER ACCOUNTING PUBLICATIONS, INC.—See *Harcourt, Brace, Jovanovich.*

MINSTREL BOOKS (IMPRINT OF *SIMON & SCHUSTER*)—1230 Ave. of the Americas, New York, NY 10020. Patricia MacDonald, Sr. Ed. Fiction for girls and boys ages 7 to 11. Query first with detailed plot outline, sample chapter, and SASE. No unsolicited manuscripts. Royalty.

MOREHOUSE-BARLOW CO., INC.—105 Madison Ave., New York, NY 10020. E. Allen Kelly, Pub. Theology, pastoral care, church administration, spirituality, Angelican studies, history of religion, books for children, youth, elders, etc. Royalty or outright purchase. Query with outline, contents, and sample chapter.

WILLIAM MORROW AND CO., INC.—105 Madison Ave., New York, NY 10016. James Landis, Pub./Ed.-in-Chief. Adult fiction and nonfiction: no unsolicited manuscripts. *Morrow Junior Books:* David Reuther, Ed.-in-Chief. Children's books for all ages. *Hearst Marine Books:* Connie Roosevelt, Ed. *Hearst Books:* Ann Bramson, Ed. General nonfiction. Submit through agent only.

MORROW QUILL PAPERBACKS (DIV. OF *WILLIAM MORROW*)—105 Madison Ave., New York, NY 10016. Andrew Ambraziejus, Man. Ed. Trade paperbacks. Adult nonfiction. No unsolicited manuscripts.

THE MOUNTAINEERS BOOKS—306 Second Ave. W., Seattle, WA 98119. Stephen Whitney, Man. Ed. Nonfiction on mountaineering, backpacking, canoeing, kayaking, bicycling, skiing. Field guides, regional histories, biographies of outdoor people; accounts of expeditions. Nature books. Royalty. Submit sample chapters and outline.

MULTNOMAH PRESS—10209 SE Division St., Portland, OR 97266. Liz Heaney, Sr. Ed. Conservative, evangelical nonfiction. Send outline and sample chapters. Royalty.

THE MYSTERIOUS PRESS—129 W. 56th St., New York, NY 10019. William Malloy, Man. Ed. Mystery/suspense novels. Query with synopsis. SASE.

717

NAIAD PRESS, INC.—Box 10543, Tallahassee, FL 32302. Barbara Grier, Ed. Adult fiction, 60,000 to 70,000 words, with lesbian themes and characters: mysteries, romances, gothics, ghost stories, westerns, regencies, spy novels, etc. Royalty. Query with outline only.

NAL BOOKS (DIV. OF *NEW AMERICAN LIBRARY*)—1633 Broadway, New York, NY 10019. Michaela Hamilton, Ed. Dir. Fiction and nonfiction books. Manuscripts accepted only from agents and upon personal recommendation.

NATIONAL PRESS—7201 Wisconsin Ave., Suite 720, Bethesda, MD 20814. Karen McComas, Ed. Fiction for *Beach Books*. Nonfiction: history, criminology, reference, and health (*Zenith Editions*); cookbooks; sports; children's books and parenting; business, management, and automotive titles (*Plain English Press*). Royalty. Query with outline and sample chapters.

NATUREGRAPH PUBLISHERS—P. O. Box 1075 , Happy Camp, CA 96039. Barbara Brown, Ed. Nonfiction: Native American culture, natural history, outdoor living, land and gardening, holistic learning and health, Indian lore, crafts, and how-to. Royalty. Query.

THE NAVAL INSTITUTE PRESS—Annapolis, MD 21402. Nonfiction (60,-000 to 100,000 words): How-tos on boating and navigation; battle histories; biography; ship guides. Occasional fiction (75,000 to 110,000 words). Royalty. Query with outline and sample chapters.

THOMAS NELSON, INC.—Nelson Place at Elm Hill Pike, P. O. Box 141000, Nashville, TN 37214. William D. Watkins, Man. Ed. Religious adult nonfiction. Query with outline and sample chapter.

NEW AMERICAN LIBRARY—1633 Broadway, New York, NY 10019. Pat Taylor, Ed. Signet Books: Commercial fiction (historicals, sagas, thrillers, action/adventure novels, westerns, horror, science fiction and fantasy) and nonfiction (self-help, how-to, etc.). *Plume Books:* hobbies, business, health, cooking, child care, psychology, etc. *Mentor Books:* Nonfiction originals for the college and high school market. No unsolicited manuscripts.

NEW REPUBLIC BOOKS (IMPRINT OF *BASIC BOOKS*)—10 E. 53rd St., New York, NY 10022. Bill Newlin, Ed.-in-Chief. Books on politics, contemporary affairs, history, biography. Royalty. Query.

NEW YORK GRAPHIC SOCIETY BOOKS/LITTLE, BROWN AND CO.—34 Beacon St., Boston, MA 02108. Books on fine arts and photography. Query with outline or proposal and vita.

NEWMARKET PRESS—18 E. 48th St., New York, NY 10017. Theresa Burns, Man. Ed., Clifford Crouch, Asst. Ed. Nonfiction on health, self-help, child care, parenting, biography, and history. Some fiction. Query first. Royalty.

W.W. NORTON AND CO., INC.—500 Fifth Ave., New York, NY 10110. Liz Malcolm, Ed. Fiction and nonfiction. No occult, paranormal, religious, genre fiction (formula romance, SF, westerns), cookbooks, arts and crafts, YA or children's books. Royalty. Query with synopsis, 2–3 chapters, and resumé. Return postage and packaging required.

OAK TREE PUBLICATIONS—9601 Aero Dr., #202, San Francisco, CA 94123. Juvenile books for ages preschool to 12: picture books, pop-ups, unique crafts, activity and adventure books for children. Royalty. Query with synopsis, outline, illustrations and credentials. SASE required.

OPEN COURT PUBLISHING COMPANY—Box 599, Peru, IL 61354.

Scholarly books on philosophy, psychology, religion, oriental thought, history, public policy, and related topics. Send complete manuscript with outline and resumé. Royalty.

ORCHARD BOOKS (IMPRINT OF *FRANKLIN WATTS*)—387 Park Ave., New York, NY 10016. Sandra Jordan, Ed.-in-Chief. Hardcover picture books and fiction for juveniles; fiction for young adults. Submit complete manuscript. Royalty.

OSBORNE/MCGRAW HILL—2600 Tenth St., Berkeley, CA 94710. Cynthia Hudson, Ed.-in-Chief. Micro computer books for a general audience. Query. Royalty.

OXFORD UNIVERSITY PRESS—200 Madison Ave., New York, NY 10016. Authoritative books on literature, history, philosophy, etc.; college textbooks, medical, and reference books. Royalty. Query.

OXMOOR HOUSE, INC.—Box 2262, Birmingham, AL 35201. John Logue, Ed. Nonfiction: art, photography, gardening, decorating, cooking, and crafts. Royalty.

PACER BOOKS FOR YOUNG ADULTS (IMPRINT *BERKLEY PUBLISHING GROUP*)—200 Madison Ave., New York, NY 10016. Fiction: adventure, fantasy, and role-playing fantasy gamebooks. No unsolicited manuscripts; queries only. Address Geanine Thompson. Paper only.

PAGEANT BOOKS—225 Park Ave. S., New York, NY 10003. Arlene Friedman, Ed. Dir. Books on romance (historical, contemporary, regency), horror/occult, science fiction and fantasy, men's adventure, westerns, espionage/thriller, mystery, and young adult. Query with outline and sample chapters, or send completed manuscripts to Karen Haas or Carrie Feron. Royalty.

PANTHEON BOOKS (DIV. OF *RANDOM HOUSE*)—201 E. 50th St., New York, NY 10022. Address Iris Bromberg. Nonfiction: academic level for general readers on history, political science, sociology, etc.; picture books; folklore. Some fiction. Royalty. Query; no unsolicited manuscripts.

PARAGON HOUSE—90 Fifth Ave., New York, NY 10011. Ken Stuart, Ed.-in-Chief. Serious nonfiction, including biography and history. Query or send manuscript. Royalty.

PARKER PUBLISHING COMPANY, INC.—West Nyack, NY 10994. James Bradler, Pres. Self-help and how-to books, 65,000 words: health, money opportunities, business, etc. Royalty.

PEACHTREE PUBLISHERS, LTD.—494 Armour Circle, N.E., Atlanta, GA 30324. Wide variety of fiction and nonfiction. No religious material, SF/fantasy, romance, mystery/detective, historical fiction; no business, scientific, or technical books. Send complete manuscript for fiction; outline and sample chapters for nonfiction. Royalty.

PELICAN PUBLISHING CO., INC.—1101 Monroe St., Gretna, LA 70053. James L. Calhoun, Exec. Ed. General nonfiction: Americana, regional, architecture, how-to, travel, cookbooks, inspirational, motivational, music, parenting, etc. Juvenile fiction. Royalty.

PELION PRESS—See *The Rosen Publishing Group.*

PENGUIN BOOKS (DIV. OF *VIKING/PENGUIN, INC.*)—40 W. 23rd St., New York, NY 10010. Christine Pevitt, Ed.-in-Chief. Adult fiction and nonfiction. Royalty. No unsolicited material.

THE PERMANENT PRESS—R.D. 2, Noyac Rd., Sag Harbor, NY 11963. Judith Shepard, Ed. Seeks original and arresting novels. Trade books, biographies, political commentary. Query. Royalty.

PHILOMEL BOOKS (DIV. OF *THE PUTNAM & GROSSET GROUP*)—200 Madison Ave., New York, NY 10016. Patricia Lee Gauch and Paula Wiseman, Eds. Fiction, picture books, and some biographies. Fresh, original work with compelling characters and "a truly childlike spirit." Query required.

THE PILGRIM PRESS/UNITED CHURCH PRESS—132 W. 31 St., New York, NY 10001. Larry E. Kalp, Pub. Religious and general-interest nonfiction. Royalty. Query with outline and sample chapters.

PINEAPPLE PRESS—P.O. Drawer 16008, Sarasota, FL 34239. June Cussen, Ed. Serious fiction and nonfiction, 60,000 to 125,000 words. Query with outline and sample chapters. Royalty.

PIPPIN PRESS—229 E. 85th St., Gracie Sta., Box 92, New York, NY 10028. Barbara Francis, Pub. High-quality picture books for pre-schoolers; middle-group, humor and mystery fiction; imaginative fiction for children of all ages. Royalty. Query with outline.

PLAIN ENGLISH PRESS—See *National Press.*

PLENUM PUBLISHING CORP.—233 Spring St., New York, NY 10013. Linda Greenspan Regan, Sr. Ed. Nonfiction, approximately 300 pages, on science, social science, and humanities. Royalty. Query required. Hardcover.

POCKET BOOKS (DIV. OF *SIMON AND SCHUSTER*)—1230 Ave. of the Americas, New York, NY 10020. William R. Grose, Ed. Dir. Some original fiction and nonfiction. Mystery line: police procedurals, private eye and amateur sleuth novels; query with outline and sample chapters to Jane Chelius, Sr. Ed. Royalty.

POSEIDON PRESS (IMPRINT OF *POCKET BOOKS*)—1230 Ave. of the Americas, New York, NY 10020. William A. Grose, Ed. Dir. Ann Patty, V.P./Pub. General fiction and nonfiction. Royalty. No unsolicited material.

CLARKSON N. POTTER, INC.—225 Park Ave. S., New York, NY 10003. Carol Southern, Assoc. Pub./Ed. Dir. General trade books. Submissions accepted through agents.

PRAEGER PUBLISHERS (DIV. OF *GREENWOOD PRESS*)—1 Madison Ave., New York, NY 10010. Ron Chambers, Pub. General nonfiction; scholarly and reference books. Royalty. Query with outline.

PRENTICE HALL PRESS (DIV. OF *SIMON & SCHUSTER*)—Gulf & Western Bldg., New York, NY 10023. General nonfiction. Queries only. Address Editorial Dept. Royalty.

PRESIDIO PRESS—31 Pamaron Way, Novato, CA 94949. Nonfiction: contemporary military history, from 50,000 words. Selected fiction with military background. Royalty. Query.

PRICE STERN SLOAN PUBLISHERS, INC.—360 N. La Cienega Blvd., Los Angeles, CA 90048. Short, humorous children's books; adult trade nonfiction; home improvement, automotive, and photography. Royalty. Query with SASE required.

PRUETT PUBLISHING COMPANY—2928 Pearl, Boulder, CO 80301. Gerald Keenan, Man. Ed. Nonfiction: outdoors and recreation, western U.S. history and travel, adventure travel and railroadiana. Royalty. Query.

PUFFIN BOOKS—See *Viking/Penguin.*

G. P. PUTNAM'S SONS (DIV. OF *PUTNAM PUBLISHING CO.*)—200 Madison Ave., New York, NY 10016. General fiction and nonfiction. No unsolicited manuscripts or queries.

QUEST BOOKS (IMPRINT OF *THE THEOSOPHICAL PUBLISHING HOUSE*)—306 W. Geneva Rd., P. O. Box 270, Wheaton, IL 60189–0270. Shirley Nicholson, Sr. Ed. Nonfiction books on Eastern and Western religion and philosophy, holism, healing, meditation, yoga, astrology. Royalty. Query.

RAND MCNALLY & COMPANY—Publishing Group, Editorial Department, 8255 N. Central Park Ave., Skokie, IL 60076. World and U.S. atlases and maps; road atlases; custom publications. Royalty or outright purchase. Query with SASE required.

RANDOM HOUSE, INC.—201 E. 50th St., New York, NY 10022. Joni Evans, Pub. Jason Epstein, Ed. Dir. J. Shulman, Ed.-in-Chief, Juvenile Books. Stuart Flexner, Ed.-in-Chief, Reference Books. General fiction and nonfiction; reference and college textbooks. Fiction and nonfiction for beginning readers; paperback fiction line for 7- to 9-year-olds; 35 pages maximum. Royalty. Query with three chapters and outline for nonfiction; complete manuscript for fiction and SASE.

REGNERY GATEWAY—1130 17th St. N.W., Suite 620, Washington, DC 20036. Hardcover and trade paperback nonfiction on public policy, politics and international issues. Royalty. Query

RENAISSANCE HOUSE—541 Oak St., P. O. Box 177, Frederick, CO 80530. Eleanor H. Ayer, Ed. Western Americana, World War II, and Rocky Mountain West; biographies and historical books. Submit outline, two sample chapters, and short bio. Royalty.

REWARD BOOKS (DIV. OF *SIMON & SCHUSTER*)—Prentice Hall Press, Englewood Cliffs, NJ 07632. Ted Nardin, V.P. Nonfiction, how-to, and reference books on business, self-improvement, education, and technical subjects. Hardcover and paperback. Royalty.

RODALE PRESS—33 E. Minor St., Emmaus, PA 18098. Pat Corpora, Pub. Books on health, gardening, homeowner projects, cookbooks, inspirational topics, pop psychology, woodworking, natural history. Query with outline and sample chapter. Royalty and outright purchase.

ROSEN PUBLISHING GROUP—29 E. 21st St., New York, NY 10010. Roger Rosen, Pres. Ruth C. Rosen, Ed. Young adult books, to 40,000 words, on career and personal guidance, journalism, theater, self-help, etc. Pelion Press: music, art, history. Pays varying rates.

ROSSET & CO.—333 Park Ave. S., New York, NY 10010. Barney Rosset, Pub. Fiction and nonfiction on a variety of topics. Send complete manuscript or sample chapters and SASE.

RUTLEDGE HILL PRESS—513 Third Ave. S., Nashville, TN 37210. Ronald E. Pitkin, Pub. Southern interest fiction and nonfiction. Query with outline and sample chapters. Royalty.

ST. ANTHONY MESSENGER PRESS—1615 Republic St., Cincinnati, OH 45210. Karen Hurley, Man. Ed. Inspirational nonfiction for Catholics, supporting a Christian lifestyle in our culture; prayer aids, education, practical spirituality. Query with 500-word summary. Royalty.

721

ST. MARTIN'S PRESS—175 Fifth Ave., New York, NY 10010. General adult fiction and nonfiction. Royalty. Query first.

SANDLAPPER PUBLISHING, INC.—P.O. Box 1932, Orangeburg, SC 29116–1932. Frank N. Handal, Pub. Books on South Carolina history, culture, cuisine. Submit query with outline and sample chapters.

SCHOCKEN BOOKS (DIV. OF *PANTHEON BOOKS*)—201 E. 20th St., New York, NY 10022. General nonfiction: Judaica, women's studies, education, art history. Query with outline and sample chapter. Royalty.

SCHOLASTIC, INC.—730 Broadway, New York, NY 10003. *Point:* Brenda Bowen, Ed. Young adult fiction for readers 12 and up. *Apple Books:* Brenda Bowen, Ed. Fiction for readers ages 9 to 12. Submit complete manuscript with cover letter and SASE. Royalty. *Sunfire:* Ann Reit, Ed. American historical romances, for girls 12 and up, 55,000 words. Query with outline and three sample chapters. Write for tip sheets.

SCOTT, FORESMAN AND CO.—1900 E. Lake Ave., Glenview, IL 60025. Richard T. Morgan, Pres. Elementary, secondary, and college textbooks and material. Royalty.

CHARLES SCRIBNER'S SONS—866 Third Ave., New York, NY 10022. Robert Stewart, Ed.-in-Chief. Fiction, general nonfiction, science, history and biography; query first. Clare Costello, Ed., Books for Young Readers: fantasy, mystery, YA, SF, and problem novels, picture books, ages 5 and up, and nonfiction (science and how-tos). Query with outline and sample chapter.

SEVEN SEAS PRESS—International Marine Route 1, Box 220, Camden, ME 04843. Jonathan Eaton, Man. Ed. Books on boating (both sailing and power), other marine topics.

SHAPOLSKY PUBLISHERS—136 W. 22nd St., New York, NY 10011. Nonfiction manuscripts on current affairs, judaica, history, biography, how-to, and self-help; educational picture books, folk tales for young adults. Payment on royalty and flat fee basis.

HAROLD SHAW PUBLISHERS—388 Gunderson Dr., Box 567, Wheaton, IL 60189. Ramona Cramer Tucker, Dir. of Ed. Services. Nonfiction, 120 to 180 pages, with an evangelical Christian perspective. Query. Pays flat fee.

SIERRA CLUB BOOKS—730 Polk St., San Francisco, CA 94109. Nonfiction: environment, natural history, the sciences, outdoors and regional guidebooks; juvenile fiction and nonfiction. Royalty. Query with SASE.

ELISABETH SIFTON BOOKS/VIKING AND ELISABETH SIFTON BOOKS/PENGUIN—See *Viking Penguin Inc.*

SIGNET BOOKS—See *New American Library.*

SILHOUETTE BOOKS—300 E. 42nd St., New York, NY 10017. Karen Solem, Ed.-in-Chief. *Silhouette Romances:* Mary Tara Hughes, Sr. Ed. Contemporary romances, 53,000 to 58,000 words. *Special Edition:* Leslie Kazanjian, Sr. Ed. Sophisticated contemporary romances, 70,000 to 80,000 words. *Silhouete Desire:* Isabel Swift, Sr. Ed. Sensuous contemporary romances, 53,000 to 58,000 words. *Intimate Moments:* Leslie Wainger, Sr. Ed. Sensuous, sophisticated contemporary romances, 80,000 to 85,000 words. Historical romance: 95,000 to 105,000 words, set in England, France, and North America between 1700 and 1900; query with synopsis and three sample chapters to Eliza Shallcross/Tracy Farrell, Assoc. Eds. Query with synopsis and SASE to appropriate editor.

SIMON & SCHUSTER—1230 Ave. of the Americas, New York, NY 10020. No unsolicited material.

GIBBS SMITH, PUBLISHER/PEREGRINE SMITH BOOKS—P. O. Box 667, Layton, UT 84401. Madge Baird, Ed. Adult and juvenile fiction and nonfiction. Query. Royalty.

SOHO PRESS—One Union Sq., New York, NY 10003. Juris Jurjevics, Ed. Adult fiction mysteries, thrillers, and nonfiction, from 75,000 words. Send query with outline and sample chapters or complete manuscript. Royalty.

SPARKLER BOOKS—Pharos Books, 200 Park Ave., New York, NY 10166. Eileen Schlesinger, Ed. Picture books and nonfiction books for children, ages 6 and up. Query with outline. Royalty.

SPECTRA BOOKS (IMPRINT OF *BANTAM BOOKS*)—666 Fifth Ave., New York, NY 10103. Lou Aronica, Pub. Science fiction and fantasy, with emphasis on storytelling and characterization. Query; no unsolicited manuscripts. Royalty.

STANDARD PUBLISHING—8121 Hamilton Ave. , Cincinnati, OH 45231. Address Mark Plunkett. Fiction: juveniles, based on Bible or with moral tone. Nonfiction: biblical, Christian education. Conservative evangelical. Query preferred.

STEMMER HOUSE PUBLISHERS, INC.—2627 Caves Rd., Owings Mills, MD 21117. Barbara Boldridge, Ed. Juvenle fiction and adult fiction and nonfiction. Royalty. Query with SASE.

STERLING PUBLISHING CO., INC.—Two Park Ave., New York, NY 10016. Burton Hobson, Pres./Ed. Dir. How-to, self-help, hobby, woodworking, health, craft, and sports books. Royalty and outright purchase. Query with outline, sample chapter, and sample illustrations,

STONE WALL PRESS—1241 30th St. N.W., Washington, D.C. 20007. Nonfiction on fishing, outdoors, conservation, 200 to 300 manuscript pages. Royalty. Query first.

STRAWBERRY HILL PRESS—2594 15th Ave., San Francisco, CA 94127. Carolyn Soto, Ed. Nonfiction: biography, autobiography, history, cooking, health, how-to, philosophy, performance arts, and Third World. Query first with sample chapters, outline, and SASE. Royalty.

LYLE STUART, INC.—120 Enterprise Ave., Secaucus, NJ 07094. Allan J. Wilson, Ed. General fiction and nonfiction. *Citadel Press:* biography, film, history, limited fiction. Royalty. Query; no unsolicited manuscripts.

LYLE STUART/IRMA HELDMAN BOOKS—275 Central Park W., New York, NY 10024. Irma Heldman, Ed. Mystery and suspense, mainstream fiction, 65,000 words; query for nonfiction. Advance and royalty. Include return postage.

SUMMIT BOOKS—1230 Ave. of the Americas, New York, NY 10020. General-interest fiction and nonfiction of high literary quality. No category books. Royalty. query through agents only.

SUNFIRE—See *Scholastic, Inc.*

SWALLOW PRESS—P. O. Box 2080, Chicago, IL 60690. Self-help, history, biography. Western Americana. No unsolicited poetry or fiction. Royalty.

TAB BOOKS, INC.—Blue Ridge Summit, PA 17294. Raymond A. Collins, Vice-Pres., Editorial Dept. Nonfiction: electronics, computers, how-to, aviation, business, solar and energy, science and technology, back-to-basics, automotive, marine and outdoor life. Fiction: military. Royalty or outright purchase.

TAPLINGER PUBLISHING CO.—132 W. 22nd St., New York, NY 10011. Roy Thomas, Ed. Serious literary fiction. General nonfiction: history, art, etc. Royalty.

JEREMY P. TARCHER, INC.—9100 Sunset Blvd., Los Angeles, CA 90069. Jeremy P. Tarcher, Ed.-in-Chief. General nonfiction: psychology, personal development, health and fitness, women's concerns, science for the layperson, etc. Royalty. Query with outline, sample chapter, and SASE.

TAYLOR PUBLISHING CO.—1550 W. Mockingbird Ln., Dallas, TX 75235. Nonfiction: fine arts, biography, cooking, gardening, sports and recreation, true crime, humor/trivia, lifestyles. Query with outline and sample chapters. Royalty.

TEN SPEED PRESS—P.O. Box 7123, Berkeley, CA 94707. Mariah Bear, Ed. Self-help and how-to on careers, recreation, etc.; natural science, history, cookbooks. Query with outline and sample chapters. Royalty. Softcover.

TEXAS MONTHLY PRESS—Box 1569, Austin, TX 78767. Scott Lubeck, Dir. Fiction, nonfiction, related to Texas or the Southwest, 60,000 words. Royalty.

THUNDER'S MOUTH PRESS—93-99 Greene St., New York, NY 10012. Neil Ortenberg, Ed. Literary fiction and poetry collections; books on historical and political topics. Query first. Length requirement: poetry, 96 pages; fiction, to 200 pages. Royalty.

TICKNOR & FIELDS (SUBSIDIARY OF *HOUGHTON MIFFLIN COMPANY*)—52 Vanderbilt Ave., New York, NY 10017. General nonfiction and fiction. Royalty.

TIMES BOOKS (DIV. OF *RANDOM HOUSE, INC.*)—201 E. 50th St., New York, NY 10022. Jonathan B. Segal, Ed. Dir. General nonfiction. No unsolicited manuscripts or queries accepted.

TOR BOOKS—49 W. 24th St., New York, NY 10010. Beth Meacham, Ed.-in-Chief: Science fiction and fantasy. Michael Seidman, Exec. Ed.: Thrillers, espionage, and mysteries. Melissa Ann Singer, Ed.: Horror and dark fantasy. Wanda June Alexander, Assoc. Ed.: Historicals. Length: from 60,000 words. Query with outline and sample chapters. Royalty.

TROLL ASSOCIATES—100 Corporate Dr., Mahwah, NJ 07430. M. Francis, Ed. Juvenile fiction and nonfiction. Royalty or outright purchase. Query preferred.

TROPHY BOOKS—See *Harper Junior Books Group.*

TROUBADOR PRESS—360 N. Cienega Blvd., Los Angeles, CA 90048. Juvenile illustrated games, activity, paper doll, coloring, and cut-out books. Royalty or outright purchase. Query with outline and SASE.

TYNDALE HOUSE—336 Gundersen Dr., Box 80, Wheaton, IL 60189. Wendell Hawley, Ed.-in-Chief. Christian. Juvenile and adult fiction and nonfiction on subjects of concern to Christians. Picture books with religious focus for third-grade readers. Submit complete manuscripts. Guidelines.

UNION OF AMERICAN HEBREW CONGREGATIONS—838 Fifth Ave., New York, NY 10021. Bruce Black, Marketing Dir. Fiction and nonfiction from pre-school to adult. No poetry. Material that deals with traditional and controversial themes in Judaism that appeal to Jewish and non-Jewish readers. Query with detailed table of contents, outline, and sample chapter or complete manuscript.

UNIVERSE BOOKS—381 Park Ave. S., New York, NY 10016. Louis Barron, V.P./Ed.-in-Chief. Fine arts and art history, photography, design, social science, contemporary politics, music. Royalty. Query with SASE.

VAN NOSTRAND REINHOLD—115 Fifth Ave., New York, NY 10003. Chester C. Lucido, Jr., Pres./C.E.O. Business, professional, scientific, and technical publishers of applied reference works. *CBI Publishing Co.:* Food service and hospitality books. Royalty.

VIKING PENGUIN, INC.—40 W. 23rd St., New York, NY 10010. *Kestral Books:* Fiction and nonfiction, including biography, history, and sports, for ages 7–14; humor; and picture books for ages 2–6. Query Children's Books Dept. with outline and sample chapter. SASE required. Adult fiction and nonfiction. *Elisabeth Sifton Books/Viking:* Elisabeth Sifton, Pub. Adult hardcovers. *Frederick Warne:* Children's hardcovers and paperbacks. *Penguin Books:* Adult fiction and nonfiction paperbacks. *Elisabeth Sifton Books/Penguin:* Adult paperbacks. *Puffin Books:* Children's fiction and nonfiction paperbacks. Royalty. No unsolicited material.

WALKER AND COMPANY—720 Fifth Ave., New York, NY 10019. Fiction: mysteries, men's action, westerns, regency romance and espionage, horror, and science fiction. Nonfiction: Americana, biography, history, science, natural history, medicine, psychology, parenting, sports, outdoors, reference, popular science, self-help, business, music, and graphic arts. Juvenile nonfiction, including biography, science, history, music, and nature. Fiction and problem novels for YA. Royalty. Query with synopsis.

WALLACE-HOMESTEAD—580 Waters Edge, Lombard, IL 60148. William N. Topaz, General Man. Books on quilting, antiques and collectibles, crafts and hobbies. Submit query with outline. Royalty. Send for tip sheet.

FREDERICK WARNE—See *Viking Penguin, Inc.*

WARNER BOOKS—666 Fifth Ave., New York, NY 10103. Mel Parker, Ed.-in-Chief. Fiction: historical romance, contemporary women's fiction, unusual big-scale horror and suspense. Nonfiction: business books, health and nutrition, self-help and how-to books. Query with sample chapters. Also publishes trade paperbacks and hardcover titles.

FRANKLIN WATTS, INC.—387 Park Ave. S., New York, NY 10016. Nonfiction for grades 3–10, including science, history, and biography; query Margie Leather, Ed. Adult trade fiction and nonfiction; query Kent Oswald, Ed. Royalty. SASE required.

PETER WEED BOOKS—Beaufort Books, 9 E. 40th St., New York, NY 10016. Peter Weed, Ed. Fiction and nonfiction. No unsolicited manuscripts. Query first. Royalty.

WEIDENFELD & NICOLSON—841 Broadway, New York, NY 10003–4793. John Herman, Ed.-in-Chief. Query with sample chapter; no unsolicited manuscripts. Royalty.

WESTERN PUBLISHING CO., INC.—850 Third Ave., New York, NY 10022. Doris Duenewald, Pub., Children's Books; Eric Suben, Ed.-in-Chief, Children's Books. Adult nonfiction: field guides, cookbooks, etc. Children's books, fiction and nonfiction: picture books, storybooks, concept books, novelty books. Royalty and outright purchase. Query required. Same address and requirements for *Golden Press.*

ALBERT WHITMAN—5747 W. Howard St., Niles, IL 60648. Kathleen Tucker, Ed. Picture books; novels, biographies, mysteries, and general nonfiction for middle-grade readers. Submit complete manuscript for picture books, three chapters and outline for longer fiction, query for nonfiction. Royalty.

WILDERNESS PRESS—2440 Bancroft Way, Berkeley, CA 94704. Thomas Winnett, Ed. Nonfiction: sports, recreation, and travel in the western U.S. Royalty.

WILSHIRE BOOK COMPANY—12015 Sherman Rd., North Hollywood, CA 91605. Melvin Powers, Ed. Dir. Inspirational fiction. Nonfiction including health, hobbies, how-to, psychology, recreation, self-help, entrepreneurship, money making, and mail order. Query or send synopsis. Royalty.

WINDSWEPT HOUSE PUBLISHERS—Mt. Desert, ME 04660. Jane Weinberger, Ed. Children's picture books, 150 words, with black-and-white illustrations. Query first for how-to and teenage novels.

WINGBOW PRESS—2929 Fifth St., Berkeley, CA 94710. Randy Fingland, Ed. Nonfiction: women's interests, health, psychology, how-to. Query or sample chapter and outline preferred. Royalty.

WOODBINE HOUSE—10400 Connecticut Ave., Suite 512, Kensington, MD 20895. Terry Rosenberg, Ed. Nonfiction. Query with outline, sample chapter, and short biography. Royalty or outright purchase.

WORKMAN PUBLISHING CO., INC.—708 Broadway, New York, NY 10003. Address the Editors. General nonfiction. Normal contractual terms based on agreement.

WORLDWIDE LIBRARY (DIV. OF _HARLEQUIN BOOKS_)—225 Duncan Mill Rd., Don Mills, Ont., Canada M3B 3K9. Randall Toye, Ed. Dir. Espionage, thrillers and crime/suspense fiction; action adventure series and future fiction for _Gold Eagle;_ mystery fiction. Query. Paper only.

YANKEE BOOKS—Main St., Dublin, NH 03444. Sandra Taylor, Sr. Ed. Books relating specifically to New England: cooking, crafts, photography, maritime subjects, travel, gardening, nature, nostalgia, humor, folklore and popular history. No scholarly history, highly technical work, or off-color humor. Regional New England fiction considered. Royalty. Query or send proposal.

YEARLING BOOKS—See _Dell Publishing._

ZEBRA BOOKS—475 Park Ave. S., New York, NY 10016. Leslie Gelbman, Fiction Ed. Wendy McCurdy, Nonfiction Ed. Biography, how-to, humor, self-help. Fiction: adventure, regency, mainstream fiction, historical romance, gothic, historical, horror, etc. Query required.

ZENITH EDITIONS—See _National Press._

CHARLOTTE ZOLOTOW BOOKS (IMPRINT OF _HARPER & ROW_)—10 E. 53rd St., New York, NY 10022. Address the Editors. Juvenile fiction and nonfiction "with integrity of purpose, beauty of language, and an out-of-ordinary look at ordinary things." Royalty.

ZONDERVAN PUBLISHING HOUSE—1415 Lake Dr. S.E., Grand Rapids, MI 49506. Jean Bloom, Manuscript Review Ed. Religious. General fiction and nonfiction; academic and professional books. Query with outline, sample chapter, and SASE. Royalty. Guidelines.

UNIVERSITY PRESSES

University presses generally publish books of a scholarly nature or of specialized interest by authorities in a given field. A few publish fiction and poetry. Many publish only a handful of titles a year. Always query first. Do not send a manuscript until you have been invited to do so by the editor.

BRIGHAM YOUNG UNIVERSITY PRESS—209 University Press Bldg., Provo, UT 84602.

BUCKNELL UNIVERSITY PRESS—Bucknell University, Lewisburg, PA 17837.

CAMBRIDGE UNIVERSITY PRESS—32 East 57th St., New York, NY 10022.

THE CATHOLIC UNIVERSITY OF AMERICA PRESS—620 Michigan Ave. N.E., Washington, DC 20064.

COLORADO ASSOCIATED UNIVERSITY PRESS—University of Colorado, 1344 Grandview Ave., Boulder, CO 80309.

COLUMBIA UNIVERSITY PRESS—562 West 113th St., New York, NY 10025.

DUKE UNIVERSITY PRESS—Box 6679, College Station, Durham, NC 27708.

DUQUESNE UNIVERSITY PRESS—600 Forbes Ave., Pittsburgh, PA 15282.

FORDHAM UNIVERSITY PRESS—University Box L, Bronx, New York 10458–5172.

GEORGIA STATE UNIVERSITY—College of Business Administration, Business Publishing Division, University Plaza, Atlanta, GA 30303–3093.

HARVARD UNIVERSITY PRESS—79 Garden St., Cambridge, MA 02138.

INDIANA UNIVERSITY PRESS—10th and Morton Sts., Bloomington, IN 47404.

THE JOHNS HOPKINS UNIVERSITY PRESS—701 W. 40th St., Suite 275, Baltimore, MD 21211.

KENT STATE UNIVERSITY PRESS—Kent State Univ., Kent, OH 44242.

LOUISIANA STATE UNIVERSITY PRESS—LSU, Baton Rogue, LA 70893.

LOYOLA UNIVERSITY PRESS—3441 N. Ashland Ave., Chicago, IL 60657.

MEMPHIS STATE UNIVERSITY PRESS—Memphis State Univ., Memphis, TN 38152.

MICHIGAN STATE UNIVERSITY PRESS—1405 S. Harrison Rd., East Lansing, MI 48823–5202.

THE MIT PRESS—55 Hayward St., Cambridge, MA 02142.

NEW YORK UNIVERSITY PRESS—Washington Sq., New York, NY 10003.

OHIO STATE UNIVERSITY PRESS—175 Mount Hall, 1050 Carmack Rd., Columbus, OH 43210.

OHIO UNIVERSITY PRESS—Scott Quadrangle, Athens, OH 45701.

OREGON STATE UNIVERSITY PRESS—101 Waldo Hall, Corvallis, OR 97331.

THE PENNSYLVANIA STATE UNIVERSITY PRESS—215 Wagner Bldg., University Park, PA 16802.

PRINCETON UNIVERSITY PRESS—41 William St., Princeton, NJ 08540.

RUTGERS UNIVERSITY PRESS—109 Church St., New Brunswick, NJ 08901.

SOUTHERN ILLINOIS UNIVERSITY PRESS—Box 3697, Carbondale, IL 62901.

SOUTHERN METHODIST UNIVERSITY PRESS—Box 415, Dallas, TX 75275.

STANFORD UNIVERSITY PRESS—Stanford University, Stanford, CA 94305.

STATE UNIVERSITY OF NEW YORK PRESS—State University Plaza, Albany, NY 12246.

SYRACUSE UNIVERSITY PRESS—1600 Jamesville Ave., Syracuse, NY 13244–5160.

TEMPLE UNIVERSITY PRESS—Broad and Oxford Sts., Philadelphia, PA 19122.

UNIVERSITY OF ALABAMA PRESS—P.O. Box 2877, Tuscaloosa, AL 35487.

UNIVERSITY OF ARIZONA PRESS—1230 N. Park Ave., Suite 102, Tucson, AZ 85719.

UNIVERSITY OF CALIFORNIA PRESS—2120 Berkeley Way, Berkeley, CA 94720.

UNIVERSITY OF CHICAGO PRESS—5801 Ellis Ave., Chicago, IL 60637.

UNIVERSITY OF GEORGIA PRESS—University of Georgia, Athens, GA 30602.

UNIVERSITY OF ILLINOIS PRESS—54 E. Gregory Dr. , Champaign, IL 61820.

UNIVERSITY OF MASSACHUSETTS PRESS—Box 429, Amherst, MA 01004.

UNIVERSITY OF MICHIGAN PRESS—P.O. Box 1104, Ann Arbor, MI 48109.

UNIVERSITY OF MINNESOTA PRESS—2037 University Ave. S.E., Minneapolis, MN 55414.

UNIVERSITY OF MISSOURI PRESS—200 Lewis Hall, Columbia, MO 65211.

UNIVERSITY OF NEBRASKA PRESS—901 North 17th St., Lincoln, NE 68588–0520.

UNIVERSITY OF NEW MEXICO PRESS—UNM, Albuquerque, NM 87131.

UNIVERSITY OF NOTRE DAME PRESS—University of Norte Dame, Notre Dame, IN 46556.

UNIVERSITY OF OKLAHOMA PRESS—1005 Asp Ave., Norman, OK 73019.

UNIVERSITY OF PITTSBURGH PRESS—127 North Bellefield Ave., Pittsburgh, PA 15260.

UNIVERSITY OF SOUTH CAROLINA PRESS—USC Campus, Columbia, SC 29208.

UNIVERSITY OF TENNESSEE PRESS—293 Communications Bldg., Knoxville, TN 37996–0325.

UNIVERSITY OF UTAH PRESS—101 U.S.B., Salt Lake City, UT 84112.

UNIVERSITY OF WASHINGTON PRESS—P.O. Box 50096, Seattle, WA 98145–5096.

UNIVERSITY OF WISCONSIN PRESS—114 S. Murray St., Madison, WI 53715–1199.

THE UNIVERSITY PRESS OF KENTUCKY—663 S. Limestone St., Lexington, KY 40506–0336.

UNIVERSITY PRESS OF MISSISSIPPI—3825 Ridgewood Rd., Jackson, MS 39211.

UNIVERSITY PRESS OF NEW ENGLAND—17 ½ Lebanon St., Hanover, NH 03755.

THE UNIVERSITY PRESS OF VIRGINIA—Box 3608, University Sta., Charlottesville, VA 22903.

UNIVERSITY PRESSES OF FLORIDA—15 N.W. 15th St., Gainesville, FL 32603.

WAYNE STATE UNIVERSITY PRESS—5959 Woodward Ave., Detroit, MI 48202.

WESLEYAN UNIVERSITY PRESS—110 Mt.Vernon St., Middletown, CT 06457–6050.

YALE UNIVERSITY PRESS—92A Yale Sta., New Haven, CT 06520.

SYNDICATES

Syndicates are business organizations that buy material from writers and artists to sell to newspapers all over the country and the world. Authors are paid either a percentage of the gross proceeds or an outright fee.

Of course, features by people well known in their fields have the best chance of being syndicated. In general, syndicates want columns that have been popular in a local newspaper, perhaps, or magazine. Since most syndicated fiction has been published previously in magazines or books, beginning fiction writers should try to sell their stories to magazines before submitting them to syndicates.

Always query syndicates before sending manuscripts, since their needs change frequently, and be sure to enclose SASEs with queries and manuscripts.

ARKIN MAGAZINE SYNDICATE—761 N.E. 180th St., N. Miami Beach, FL 33162. Joseph Arkin, Ed. Dir. Articles, 750 to 2,200 words, for trade and professional magazines. Must have small-business slant, written in layman's language, and offer solutions to business problems. Pays 3¢ to 10¢ a word, on acceptance. Query preferred.

BUSINESS FEATURES SYNDICATE—P.O. Box 9844, Ft. Lauderdale, FL 33310. Dana K. Cassell, Ed. Articles, 1,500 to 2,000 words, for the independent retailer or small service business owner, on marketing, security, personnel, merchandising, general management. Pays 50% of sales.

CANADA WIDE FEATURES SYNDICATE—Box 345, Station A, Toronto, Ont., Canada M5W 1C2. Glenn-Stewart Garnett, Ed. Interviews with celebrities and international political figures, 1,500 to 2,000 words, with photos. Pays 50% of gross, on publication.

CONTEMPORARY FEATURES SYNDICATE—P. O. Box 1258, Jackson, TN 38301. Lloyd Russell, Ed. Articles, 1,000 to 10,000 words: how-to, money savers, business, etc. Self-help pieces for small business. Pays from $25, on acceptance.

FICTION NETWORK—Box 5651, San Francisco , CA 94101. Short stories, one submission per author; submit manuscript unfolded. SASE required. Pays on royalty basis. Allow 15 weeks for reply.

HARRIS & ASSOCIATES FEATURES—12084 Caminito Campana, San Diego, CA 92128. Dick Harris, Ed. Sports and family-oriented features, to 1,200 words; fillers and short humor, 500 to 800 words. Queries preferred. Pays varying rates.

HERITAGE FEATURES SYNDICATE—214 Massachusetts Ave. N.E., Washington, DC 20002. Andy Seamans, Man. Ed. Public policy news features; syndicates weekly by-lined columns and editorial cartoons. Query with SASE a must.

HISPANIC LINK NEWS SERVICE—1420 N St. N.W., Washington, DC 20005. Charles A. Ericksen, Ed. Trend articles and general features with Hispanic focus, 650 to 700 words; editorial cartoons. Pays $25 for op-ed column and cartoons, on acceptance. Send SASE for guidelines.

THE HOLLYWOOD INSIDE SYNDICATE—Box 49957, Los Angeles, CA 90049. John Austin, Dir. Feature material, 750 to 1,000 words, on TV and film personalities. Story suggestions for 3-part series. Pieces on unusual medical and scientific breakthroughs. Pays on percentage basis for features, negotiated rates for ideas, on acceptance.

KING FEATURES SYNDICATE—235 E. 45th St., New York, NY 10017. Dennis R. Allen, VP/Creative Dir. Columns, comics; most contributions on contract for regular columns.

LOS ANGELES TIMES SYNDICATE—Times Mirror Sq., Los Angeles, CA 90053. Commentary, features, columns, editorial cartoons, comics, puzzles and games; news services. Query for articles.

NATIONAL NEWS BUREAU—1318 Chancellor St., Philadelphia, PA 19107. Articles, 500 to 800 words, interviews, consumer news, how-tos, travel pieces, reviews, entertainment pieces, features, etc. Pays on publication.

NEW YORK TIMES SYNDICATION SALES—130 Fifth Ave., New York, NY 10011. Paula Reichler, Sr. V.P./Ed. Dir. Previously published articles only, to 2,000 words. Query with published article or tear sheet. Pays varying rates, on publication.

NEWSPAPER ENTERPRISE ASSOCIATION, INC.—200 Park Ave., New York, NY 10166. Diana L. Drake, Exec. Ed. Ideas for new concepts in syndicated columns. No single stories or stringers. Payment by contractual arrangement.

NORTH AMERICA SYNDICATE—1703 Kaiser Ave., Irvine, CA 92714. Rod Deacey, Sr. Ed. Columns, comic strips, and editorial cartoons.

OCEANIC PRESS SERVICE—P. O. Box 6538, Buena Park, CA 90622–6538. Nat Carlton, General Mgr. Buys reprint rights for foreign markets, on previously published novels, self-help, and how-to books; interviews with celebrities; illustrated features on celebrities, family, health, beauty, personal relations, etc.; cartoons, comic strips. Pays on acceptance. Query.

SELECT FEATURES OF NORTH AMERICA SYNDICATE—235 E. 45th St., New York, NY 10017. Susan Jarzyk, Acquisitions Ed., Select Features. Articles, 1,500 to 2,000 words, and series dealing with lifestyle trends, psychology, health, beauty, fashion; finance, jobs; business personality profiles. Query.

SINGER MEDIA CORPORATION—3164 W. Tyler Ave., Anaheim, CA 92801. Kurt D. Singer, Pres. Reprint rights to business management titles for Japan and Germany; Gothics, mysteries, and romances for Germany and Scandinavia; fantasies for Germany and France. Excerpts of nonfiction books, psychological quizzes, and family relations features. Pays on percentage basis or by outright purchase.

TRANSWORLD FEATURE SYNDICATE, INC.—2 Lexington Ave., Suite 1021, New York, NY 10010. Thelma Brown, Syndication Mgr. Feature material for North American and overseas markets. Query required.

TRIBUNE MEDIA SERVICES—64 E. Concord St., Orlando, FL 32801. Michael Argirion, Ed. Continuing columns, comic strips, features, electronic data bases.

UNITED FEATURE SYNDICATE—200 Park Ave., New York, NY 10166. Diana L. Drake, Exec. Ed. Syndicated columns; no one-shots or series. Payment by contractual arrangement. Send samples with SASE.

UNITED PRESS INTERNATIONAL—1400 Eye St. N.W., Washington, DC 20005. Bill G. Ferguson, Man. Ed. Seldom accepts free-lance material.

LITERARY PRIZE OFFERS

Each year many important prize contests are open to free-lance writers. The short summaries given below are intended merely as guides. Closing dates, requirements, and rules are tentative. No manuscript should be submitted to any competition unless the writer has first checked with the Contest Editor and received complete information about a particular contest.

Send an SASE with all requests for contest rules and application forms.

ACADEMY OF AMERICAN POETS—177 E. 87th St., New York, NY 10128. Offers Walt Whitman Award: Publication and $1,000 cash prize for a book-length poetry manuscript by a poet who has not yet published a volume of poetry. Closes in November.

ACTORS THEATRE OF LOUISVILLE—316 W. Main St., Louisville, KY 40202. Conducts One-Act Play Contest. Offers $1,000 for previously unproduced one-act script. Closes in April.

THE AMERICAN ACADEMY AND INSTITUTE OF ARTS AND LETTERS—633 W. 155th St., New York, NY 10032. Offers Richard Rogers Production Award, which consists of subsidized production in New York City by a non-profit theater for a musical, play with music, thematic review, or any comparable work other than opera. Closes in November.

AMERICAN HEALTH MAGAZINE—80 Fifth Ave., New York, NY 10011. Offers prize of $2,000 for short story about intense physical experience. Closes in April.

THE ASSOCIATED WRITING PROGRAMS ANNUAL AWARDS SERIES—Old Dominion University, Norfolk, VA 23508. Conducts Annual Awards Series in Short Fiction, the Novel, and Nonfiction. In each category the prize is book publication and a $1,000 honorarium. Closes in December. Offers the Edith Shiffert Prize in Poetry: $1,000 cash prize and publication by the University Press of Virginia for an unpublished book-length collection of poetry. Closes in December.

ASSOCIATION OF JEWISH LIBRARIES—15 Goldsmith St., Providence, RI 02906. Address Lillian Schwartz, Secretary. Conducts Sydney Taylor Manuscript Competition for best fiction manuscript for readers age 8 to 12. Prize is $1,000. Closes in December.

BEVERLY HILLS THEATRE GUILD/JULIE HARRIS PLAYWRIGHT AWARD—2815 N. Beachwood Dr., Los Angeles, CA 90068. Address Marcella Meharg. Offers prize of $5,000, plus possible $2,000 for productions in Los Angeles area, for previously unproduced and unpublished full-length play. Closes in November.

THE CHICAGO TRIBUNE/NELSON ALGREN AWARDS FOR SHORT FICTION—435 N. Michigan Ave., Chicago, IL 60611. Sponsors Nelson Algren Awards for Short Fiction, with a first Prize of $5,000 and three runners-up prizes of $1,000 for outstanding unpublished short stories of 10,000 words or less, by American writers. Closes in February.

COURT THEATRE—The University of Chicago, 5706 S. University Ave., Chicago, IL 60637. Offers Sergal Drama Prize: $1,500 for full-length unpublished and unproduced play. Closes in June of odd-numbered years.

EUEGENE V. DEBS FOUNDATION—Dept. of History, Indiana State Univ., Terre Haute, IN 47809. Offers Bryant Spann Memorial Prize of $750 for published or unpublished article or essay on themes relating to social protest or human equality. Closes in April.

DELACORTE PRESS—Dept. BFYR, 1 Dag Hammarskjold Plaza, New York, NY 10017. Sponsors Delacorte Press Prize for outstanding first young adult novel. The prize consists on one Delacorte hardcover and one Dell paperback contract, an advance of $4,000 on royalties, and a $1,000 cash prize. Closes in December.

FICTION NETWORK—P. O. Box 5651, San Francisco, CA 94101. Sponsors Fiction Competition, with a first prize of up to $1,500, for a short story to 2,500 words (no children's or young adult fiction). Closes in July.

FOREST A. ROBERTS-SHIRAS INSTITUTE—Forest Roberts Theatre, Northern Michigan Univ., Marquette, MI 49855. Dr. James Panowski, Dir. Conducts annual Playwriting Competition, with prize of $1,000, plus production, for original, full-length, previously unproduced and unpublished play. Closes in November.

FULCRUM, INC.—350 Indiana St., Ste. 510, Golden, CO 80401. Offers Fulcrum American Writing Award for a book of nonfiction by an American writer on topic chosen annually. The prize is $2,500, plus publication. Closes in November.

HIGHLIGHTS FOR CHILDREN—803 Church St., Honesdale, PA 18431. Conducts Contest for Juvenile Fiction, with cash prizes and publication for short stories. Closes in March.

HONOLULU MAGAZINE—36 Merchant St., Honolulu, HI 96813. Sponsors annual fiction contest, with cash prize of $500, plus publication in *Honolulu,* for unpublished short story with Hawaiian theme, setting, and/or characters. Closes in September.

HOUGHTON MIFFLIN COMPANY—2 Park St., Boston, MA 02108. Offers Literary Fellowship for fiction or nonfiction project of exceptional literary merit written by an American author. Work under consideration must be unpublished and in English. Fellowship consists of $10,000, of which $2,500 is an outright grant and $7,500 is an advance against royalties. There is no deadline.

HUMBOLDT STATE UNIVERSITY—English Dept., Arcata, CA 95521. Sponsors Raymond Carver Short Story Contest, with a prize of $500, plus publication in the literary journal *Toyon,* for an unpublished short story by a writer living in the U.S. Closes in November.

INDIANAPOLIS UNIVERSITY/PURDUE UNIVERSITY AT INDIANAPOLIS—IUPUI Univ. Theatre, 525 N. Blackford St., Indianapolis, IN 46202. Conducts National Children's Theatre Playwriting Competition, with a prize of $2,000 for an original, previously unpublished one-act children's play. Closes in November.

INTERNATIONAL SOCIETY OF DRAMATISTS—Fulfillment Center, P. O. Box 1310, Miami, FL 33153. Sponsors Adriatic Award: a prize of $250 for a full-length play. Closes in November.

JACKSONVILLE UNIVERSITY—Annual Playwriting Contest, Dept. of Theatre Arts., College of Fine Arts, Jacksonville Univ., Jacksonville, FL 32211. Davies Sikes, Dir. Conducts playwriting contest, with prize of $1,000 and production, for original previously unproduced script (full-length or one-act). Closes in January.

JEWISH COMMUNITY CENTER THEATRE IN CLEVELAND—3505 Mayfield Rd., Cleveland Heights, OH 44118. Dorothy Silver, Dir. of Cultural Arts. Offers cash award of $1,000 and a staged reading for an original, previously unproduced full-length play, on some aspect of the Jewish experience. Closes in December.

CHESTER H. JONES FOUNDATION—P. O. Box 498, Chardon, Oh 44143. Conducts the National Poetry Competition, with more than $1,800 in cash prizes (including a $1,000 first prize) for original, unpublished poems. Closes in March.

LINCOLN COLLEGE—Lincoln, IL 62656. Address Janet Overton. Offers the Billee Murray Denny Poetry Award for original poem by poet who has not previously published a volume of poetry. First prize of $1,000, 2nd prize of $450, and 3rd prize $200 are offered. Closes in May.

MADEMOISELLE MAGAZINE—350 Madison Ave., New York, NY

10017. Sponsors Fiction Writers Contest, with first prize of $1,000, plus publication, and second prize of $500, for short fiction by a writer aged 24 to 30. Closes in March.

MS. MAGAZINE—One Times Sq., New York, NY 10036. Sponsors annual fiction contest for short story. Prize is publication and an electronic typewriter. Closes in August.

NATIONAL ENDOWMENT FOR THE ARTS—Washington, DC 20506. Address Director, Literature Program. The National Endowment for the Arts offers fellowships to writers of poetry, fiction, scripts, and other creative prose. Deadlines vary; write for guidelines.

NATIONAL PLAY AWARD—P. O. Box 71011, Los Angeles, CA 90071. National Play Award consists of $7,500 cash prize, plus $5,000 for production, for an original, previously unproduced play. Sponsored by National Repertory Theatre Foundation. Closes in October of odd-numbered years.

THE NATIONAL POETRY SERIES—26 W. 17th St., New York, NY 10001. Sponsors annual Open Competition for unpublished book-length poetry manuscript. The prize is publication. Closes in January.

THE NEW ENGLAND THEATRE CONFERENCE—50 Exchange St., Waltham, MA 02154. First prize of $500 and second prize of $250 are offered for unpublished and unproduced one-act plays in the John Gassner Memorial Playwriting Award Competition. Closes in April.

NEW VOICES—551 Tremont St., Boston, MA 02116. Conducts Clauder Competition for a full-length play by a New England writer. The prize is $3,000 and workshop production. Closes in June of odd-numbered years.

NORTHEASTERN UNIVERSITY PRESS—English Dept., 406 Holmes, Northeastern Univ., Boston, MA 02115. Guy Rotella, Chairman. Offers Samuel French Morse Poetry Prize: publication of full-length poetry manuscript by U.S. poet who has published no more than one book of poems. Closes in September.

O'NEILL THEATER CENTER—234 W. 44th St., Suite 901, New York, NY 10036. Offers stipend, staged readings, and room and board at the National Playwrights Conference, for new stage and television plays. Closes in December.

THE PARIS REVIEW—541 E. 72nd St., New York, NY 10021. Sponsors the Aga Khan Prize for Ficiton: $1,000, plus publication, for previously unpublished short story. Closes in Junes. Offers Bernard F. Connors Prize: $1,000, plus publication, for previously unpublished poem. Closes in May. Offers John Train Humor Prize: $1,500, plus publication, for unpublished work of humorous fiction, nonfiction, or poetry. Closes in March.

PEN/NELSON ALGREN FICTION AWARD—568 Broadway, New York, NY 10012. Sponsor PEN/Nelson Algren Award: stipend of $1,000, plus one month residency on Long Island, for uncompleted novel or collection of short stories by an American writer who needs assistance to complete the work. Closes in November. Sponsors Renato Poggioli Translation Award: $3,000 grant for a translator working on his or her first book-length translation from Italian into English. Closes in Februray. Sponsors the Pen/Jerard Fund Award: $3,000 for a beginning women writer at an early point in her career for a work in progress of general nonfiction. Closes in May.

PLAYBOY MAGAZINE—919 N. Michigan Ave., Chicago, IL 60611. Sponsors College Fction Contest, with first prize of $3,000 and publication in *Playboy,* for a short story by a college student. Closes in January.

734

THE POETRY SOCIETY OF AMERICA—15 Gramercy Park, New York, NY 10003. Conducts annual contests, The Celia B. Wagner Memorial Award, the John Masefield Memorial Award, and the Elias Lieberman Student Poetry Award; all offer cash prizes for unpublished poems. Closes in December.

RADIO DRAMA AWARDS—3319 W. Beltline Hwy., Madison, WI 53713. Norman Michie, Exec. Producer. Wisconsin Public Radio conducts annual Radio Drama Awards competition for original scripts by writers in Illinois, Iowa, Michigan, and Wisconsin. Prizes for thirty-minute radio scripts and professional production and cash awards of $500 (first prize), $300 (second), and $200 (third). Closes in January.

REDBOOK MAGAZINE—224 W. 57th St., New York, NY 10019. Conducts Short Story Contest for original fiction. First prize is $2,000, plus publication. Second prize of $1,000 and third prize of $500 are also offered. Closes in May.

SAN JOSE STATE UNIVERSITY—One Washington Sq., San Jose, CA 95192. Address Dr. Howard Burman, Theatre Arts Dept. Sponsors Harold C. Crain Playwriting Contest, with prize of $500, plus production, for a previously unproduced full-length play. Closes in November.

SEVENTEEN—850 Third Ave., New York, NY 10022. Conducts *Seventeen/* Dell Fiction Contest for original unpublished fiction by writers aged 13 to 20. A first prize of $2,000, a second prize of $1,200, and third prize of $700 will be awarded. Winning entries will be considered for publication in *Seventeen* and future publications of Dell Publishing. Closes in January.

SIERRA REPERTORY THEATRE—P. O. Box 3030, Sonora, CA 95370. Offers Cummings/Taylor Award of $400, plus production, for original, previously unpublished, unproduced full-length play or musical. Closes in May.

SUNSET CENTER—P. O. Box 5066, Carmel, CA 93921. Richard Tyler, Dir. Offers prize of up to $2,000 for an original, unproduced full-length play in its annual Festival of Firsts Playwriting Competition. Closes in August.

SYRACUSE UNIVERSITY PRESS—1600 Jamesville Ave., Syracuse, NY 13244–5160. Address Director. Sponsors John Ben Snow Prize: $1,500, plus publication, for an unpublished book-length nonfiction manuscript about New York State, especially upstate or central New York. Closes in December.

THEATRE MEMPHIS—630 Perkins Extended, Memphis, TN 38117. Conducts New Play Competition for a full-length play or related one-acts. The prize is $3,000 and production. Closes in September. Biennial.

THE U. S. NAVAL INSTITUTE—Annapolis, MD 21402. Conducts the Arleigh Burke Essay Contest, with prizes of $2,000, $1,000, and $750, plus publication. for essays on the advancement of professional, literary or scientific knowledge in the naval or maritime services, and the advancement of the knowledge of sea power. Closes in December.

UNIVERSITY OF ALABAMA AT BIRMINGHAM—Dept. of Theatre and Dance, Univ. Sta., Birmingham, AL 35294. Rick J. Plummer, Dir. Conducts Ruby Lloyd Apsey Playwriting Competition, with $500 cash prize, plus production and travel expenses, for previously unproduced full-length play. Closes in January.

UNIVERSITY OF GEORGIA PRESS—Athens, GA 30602. Offers Flannery O'Connor Award for Short Fiction: a prize of $500, plus publication, for a book-length collection of short fiction. Closes in July.

UNIVERSITY OF HAWAII—Kennedy Theatre, Univ. of Hawaii, 1770 East-

735

West Rd., Honolulu, HI 96822. Conducts annual Kumu Kahua Playwriting Contest with cash prizes for original plays dealing with some aspect of Hawaiian experience. Closes in January.

UNIVERSITY OF HAWAII PRESS—2840 Kolowalu St., Honolulu, HI 96822. Sponsors Pacific Poetry Series competition, with prize of publication and royalty contract, for a book-length poetry manuscript by a writer who has not previously published a volume of poetry. Closes in March of odd numbered years.

UNIVERSITY OF IOWA—Dept. of English, English-Philosophy Bldg., University of Iowa, Iowa City, IA 52242. Offers The John Simmons Short Fiction Award and The Iowa School of Letters Award, each offering $1,000, plus publication, for an unpublished full-length collection of short stories (150 pages or more). Closes in September.

UNIVERSITY OF MASSACHUSETTS PRESS—Juniper Prize, Univ. of Massachusetts Pres, c/o Mail Office, Amherst, MA 01003. Offers Juniper Prize of $1,000, plus publication, for a book-length manuscript of poetry. Closes in October.

UNIVERSITY OF PITTSBURGH PRESS—Pittsburgh, PA 15260. Sponsors Drue Heinz Literature Prize: $5,000, plus publication and royalty contract for unpublished collection of short stories. Closes in August. Also sponsors the Agnes Lynch Starrett Poetry Prize: $1,000, plus publication and royalty contract for book-length collection of poems by poet who has not yet published a volume of poetry.

UNIVERSITY OF WISCONSIN/PARKSIDE—Fine Arts Div., Univ. of Wisconsin Parkside, Box 2000, Kenosha, WI 53141. Address Judith Tucker Snider. Offers award of $1,000, plus production, for an unpublished, unproduced, full-length or original play or musical. Closes in December.

UNIVERSITY OF WISCONSIN PRESS—Poetry Series, 114 N. Murray St., Madison, WI 53715. Ronald Wallace, Administrator. Offers Brittingham Prize in Poetry: $500, plus publication, for an unpublished book-length poetry manuscript. Closes in September.

THE WALT WHITMAN CENTER FOR THE ARTS AND HUMANITIES—2nd and Cooper Sts., Camden, NJ 08102. Sponsors the annual Camden Poetry Award: $1,000, plus publication, for an unpublished book-length collection of poetry. Closes in November.

WORD WORKS—P. O. Box 42164, Washington, DC 20015. Offers the Washington Prize of $1,000 for unpublished poem by American poet. Closes in November.

YALE UNIVERSITY PRESS—Box 92A, Yale Sta., New Haven, CT 06520. Address Editor, Yale Series of Younger Poets. Conducts Yale Series of Younger Poets Competition, in which the prize is publication of a book-length manuscript of poetry, written by a poet under 40 who has not previously published a volume of poems. Closes in February.

WRITERS COLONIES

Writers colonies offer isolation and freedom from everyday distractions, and a quiet place for writers to concentrate on their work. Though some colonies are quite small, with space for just three or four writers at a time, others can provide accommodations for as many as thirty or forty. The length of a residency may vary, too, from a couple of weeks to five or six months. These programs have strict admissions policies, and writers must submit a formal application or letter of intent, a resumé, writing samples, and letters of recommendation. Write for application information first, enclosing a stamped, self-addressed envelope.

CENTRUM FOUNDATION—The Centrum Foundation sponsors month-long residencies at Fort Worden State Park, a Victorian fort on the Strait of Juan De Fuca in Washington. Nonfiction, fiction, and poetry writers may apply for residency awards, which include housing and a $100 a week stipend. Application deadlines: October 1 and April 1; send letter explaining the project, short biographical note, and sample of published work. Families are welcome, but no separate working space is provided. For details, send SASE to Carol Jane Bangs, Director of Literature Programs, Centrum Foundation, Fort Worden State Park, P.O. Box 1158, Port Townsend, WA 98368.

CUMMINGTON COMMUNITY OF THE ARTS—Residencies for artists of all disciplines. Living/studio space in individual cottages or in two main houses on 100 acres in the Berkshires. Scholarships and work exchange available. During July and August, artists with children are encouraged to apply; there is a children's program with supervised activities. Applications accepted up to three months prior to time requested. Contact Executive Director, Cummington Community of the Arts, RR#1, Box 145, Cummington, MA 01026.

DORLAND MOUNTAIN COLONY—Novelists, playwrights, poets, nonfiction writers, and artists are encouraged to apply for residencies. Dorland is a nature preserve located in the Palomar Mountains of Southern California. Fee of $150 a month includes cottage, fuel, and firewood. Application deadlines are March 1 and September 1. Send SASE to Admissions Committee, Dorland Mt. Colony, Box 6, Temecula, CA 92390.

DORSET COLONY HOUSE—Writers and playwrights are offered low-cost room with kitchen facilities at the Colony House in Dorset, Vermont. Periods of residency are 3 to 6 weeks, and are available between October 1 and June 1. Application deadlines are September 15, December 15, and February 15 for the periods immediately following the deadlines. For more information, send SASE to John Nassivera, Director, Dorset Colony House, Dorset, VT 05251.

FINE ARTS WORK CENTER IN PROVINCETOWN—Fellowships, including living and studio space and monthly stipends, are available at the Fine Arts Work Center on Cape Cod, for writers to work independently. Residencies are for 7 months only; apply before February 1 deadline. For details, send SASE to Director, Fine Arts Work Center, P.O. Box 565, 24 Pearl St., Provincetown, MA 02657.

THE HAMBIDGE CENTER—Two-week to two-month residencies are offered to writers, artists, composers, historians, humanists, and scientists at the Hambidge Center for Creative Arts and Sciences located on 600 acres of quiet woods in the north Georgia mountains. Send SASE for application form to Executive Director, The Hambidge Center, P.O. Box 339, Rabun Gap, GA 30568.

THE MACDOWELL COLONY—Studios, room and board at the MacDowell Colony of Peterborough, New Hampshire, for writers to work without interruption in semi-rural woodland setting. Selection is competitive. Apply at least 6 months in advance of season desired; residencies average 5 to 6 weeks. For details and admission forms, send SASE to Admissions Coordinator, The MacDowell Colony, 100 High St., Peterborough, NH 03458.

THE MILLAY COLONY FOR THE ARTS—At Steepletop in Austerlitz,

New York (former home of Edna St. Vincent Millay) studios, living quarters, and meals are provided to writers at no cost. Residencies are for one month. Application deadlines are February 1, May 1, and September 1. To apply, send SASE to the Millay Colony for the Arts, Inc., Steepletop, Austerlitz, NY 12017.

MONTALVO CENTER FOR THE ARTS—Three-month, low-cost residencies at the Villa Montalvo in the foothills of the Santa Cruz Mountains south of San Francisco, for writers working on specific projects. There are a few small fellowships available to writers with demonstrable financial need. Send self-addressed envelope and 85¢ stamp for application forms to Montalvo Residency Program, P.O. Box 158, Saratoga, CA 95071.

UCROSS FOUNDATION—Residencies, 2 weeks to 4 months, at the Ucross Foundation in the foothills of the Big Horn Mountains in Wyoming, for writers to concentrate on their work without interruptions. Residencies are available from August through May. Application deadlines are March 1 for fall session and October 1 for spring session. For more information, send SASE to Director, Residency Program, Ucross Foundation, 2836 US Hwy 14–16 East, Clearmont, WY 82835.

VIRGINIA CENTER FOR THE CREATIVE ARTS—Residencies of 1 to 3 months at the Mt. San Angelo Estate in Sweet Briar, Virginia, for writers to work without distraction. Apply at least three months in advance. A limited amount of financial assistance is available. For more information, send SASE to William Smart, Director, Virginia Center for the Creative Arts, Sweet Briar, VA 24595.

HELENE WURLITZER FOUNDATION OF NEW MEXICO—Rent-free and utility-free studios at the Helene Wurlitzer Foundation in Taos, New Mexico, are offered to creative writers and artists in all media. Length of residency varies from 3 to 6 months. The Foundation is closed from October 1 through March 31 annually. For details, send SASE to Henry A. Sauerwein, Jr., Exec. Dir., The Helene Wurlitzer Foundation of New Mexico, Box 545, Taos, NM 87571.

YADDO—Artist, writers, and composers are invited for stays from 2 weeks to 2 months at Yaddo in Saratoga Springs, New York. There is no charge for any guest artist, though contributions are gladly accepted in the years following a residency. Requests for applications should be sent with SASE before January 15 or August 1 to Myra Sklarew, President, Yaddo, Box 395, Saratoga Springs, New York 12866. An application fee of $10 is required.

WRITERS CONFERENCES

Each year, hundreds of writers conferences are held across the country. The following list, arranged geographically, represents a sampling of conferences; each listing includes the location of the conference, the month during which it is usually held, and the name of the person from whom specific information may be received. Additional conferences are listed annually in the May issue of *The Writer* Magazine.

ARKANSAS

ARKANSAS WRITER'S CONFERENCE—Little Rock, Ar. June. Write Clovita Rice, 1115 Gillette Dr., Little Rock, Ar 72207.

California

ANNUAL WRITERS CONFERENCE IN CHILDREN'S LITERATURE—University City, CA. August. Write Lin Oliver, Dir. SCBW, P.O. Box 296, Mar Vista Station, Los Angeles, CA 90066.

ANNUAL SAN DIEGO STATE UNIVERSITY WRITERS CONFERENCE—San Diego, CA. January. Write Diane Dunaway, 8465 Jane St., San Diego, CA 92129.

ANNUAL BLACK WRITERS WORKSHOP CONFERENCE—Los Angeles, CA. July. Write Hazel Clayton Harrison, IBWA Conference Committee, P.O. Box 43576, Los Angeles, CA 90043.

Colorado

ASPEN WRITERS CONFERENCE—Aspen, Co. august. Write Karen Chamberlain, Dir., P.O. Drawer 7726D, aspen, Co 81612.

ANNUAL SCBW CONFERENCE—Denver, Co. September. Write Carolyn Gard, Dir. 5021 S. Boston St., Englewood, Co 80111.

Connecticut

WESLEYAN WRITERS CONFERENCE—Middletown, CT. June. Write Anne Greene, Assoc. Dir., Wesleyan Writers Conf., Wesleyan University, Middletown, CT 06457.

Washington, D.C.

ANNUAL SPRING WRITERS CONFERENCE—St. Albans School, Washington, D.C. May. Write Howard Bray, Pres. WIW, Suite 220, 733 Fifteenth St. NW, Washington, D.C. 20005.

Florida

ANNUAL OUTDOOR WRITERS ASSOC. OF AMERICA CONFERENCE—Marco Island, Fl. May. Write Sylvia G. Bashline, Dir. 2017 Cato ave., Suite 101, State College, Pa 16801.

ANNUAL FLORIDA WRITERS CONFERENCE—Orlando, Fl. May. Write Dana K. Cassell, P.O. Box 9844, Fort Lauderdale, Fl 33310.

Georgia

DIXIE COUNCIL OF AUTHORS AND JOURNALISTS INC.—St. Simons Island, GA. June. Write Ann Ritter, Coord., 1214 Laurel Hill Dr., Decatur, GA 30033.

Illinois

ILLINOIS WESLEYAN UNIVERSITY WRITERS' CONFERENCE—Bloomington, Il. July. Write Bettie Wilson Story, Dir., Iwuwc, Illinois Wesleyan University, P.O. Box 2900, Bloomington, Il 61702.

MISSISSIPPI VALLEY WRITERS CONFERENCE—Rock Island, Il. June. Write David R. Collins, 3403 45th St., Moline, Il 61265.

739

ANNUAL CHRISTIAN WRITERS INSTITUTE CONFERENCE—Wheaton, Il. May. Write June Eaton, Christian Writers Inst., 388 E. Gundersen Dr., Wheaton, Il 60188.

INDIANA

INDIANA UNIVERSITY WRITERS' CONFERENCE—Bloomington, IN. June. Write Maura Stanton, Dir., IUWC, 464 Ballantine Hall, Bloomington, IN 47405.

IOWA

IOWA SUMMER WRITING PROGRAM—Iowa City, Ia. July. Write Peggy Houston, Iowa Summer Writing Prog., Div. Cont. Educ., Univ. of Iowa, Iowa City, Ia 52242.

KENTUCKY

CREATIVE WRITING CONFERENCE—Richmond, KY. June. Write William Sutton, Dept. of English, Eastern Kentucky Univ., Richmond, KY 40475.

WRITING WORKSHOP FOR PEOPLE OVER 57—Lexington, KY. July. Write Council on Aging, Univ. of Kentucky, Ligon House, Lexington, KY 40506–0442.

ANNUAL APPALACHIAN WRITERS WORKSHOP—Hindman, KY. July. Write Mike Mullins, Dir., Box 844, Hindman, KY 41822.

LOUISIANA

DEEP SOUTH WRITERS CONFERENCE—Univ. of Southwestern Louisiana, Lafayette, La. September. Write John Fiero, Dir., Usl Box 44691, Univ. of Southwestern Louisiana, Lafayette, La 70504.

MAINE

STATE OF MAINE WRITERS CONFERENCE—Ocean Park (Old Orchard Beach), ME. August. Write Richard F. Burns, Box 296, Ocean Park, ME 04063.

STONECOAST WRITERS' CONFERENCE—Univ. of Southern Maine, Gorham, ME. August. Write Kenneth Rosen, English Dept., Univ. of Southern Maine, Portland, ME 04103.

ANNUAL MAINE WRITERS WORKSHOP—Oceanville, ME. August. Write George F. Bush, Dir., P.O. Box 905W, Stoningham, ME 04681.

MASSACHUSETTS

EASTERN WRITERS CONFERENCE—Salem, Ma. June. Write Claire Keyes, Rod Kessler, English Dept., Salem State College, Salem, Ma 01970.

NEW ENGLAND WRITERS' CONFERENCE AT SIMMONS COLLEGE—Boston, Ma. June. Write Theodore Vrettos, Dir., Simmons College, 300 The Fenway, Boston, Ma 02115.

HARVARD SUMMER WRITING PROGRAM—Cambridge, Ma. Summer. Write Harvard Summer School, Dept. 457, 20 Garden St., Cambridge, Ma 02138.

CAPE COD WRITERS' CONFERENCE—Craigville, Ma. august. Write Marion Vuilleumier, Box 111, West Hyannisport, Ma 02672.

MICHIGAN

CLARION WORKSHOP OF SCIENCE FICTION AND FANTASY WRITING—E. Lansing, MI. Summer. Write Prof. Albert Drake, Dir., c/o Mary Sheridan, Holmes Hall, Lyman Briggs School, Michigan State Univ., East Lansing, MI 48825.

ANNUAL WRITER'S CONFERENCE—Oakland University, Rochester, MI. October. Write Katherine Z. Rowley, Div. of Cont. Educ., Oakland Univ., Rochester, MI 48309–4401.

MINNESOTA

MISSISSIPPI RIVER CREATIVE WRITING WORKSHOP—St. Cloud, Mn. June. Write Bill Meissner, Dept. of English, Scsu, St. Cloud, Mn 56301.

MISSOURI

AVILA COLLEGE WRITER'S CONFERENCE—Kansas City, MO. August. Write David Wissmann, Dir., Avila College, 11901 Wornall Rd., Kansas City, MO 64145.

MONTANA

WESTERN MONTANA WRITERS CONFERENCE—Dillon, Mt. July. Write Conference Coordinator, Office of Cont. Educ., Wmc, Dillon, Mt 59725.

NEW HAMPSHIRE

ANNUAL SEACOAST WRITERS CONFERENCE—Portsmouth, NH. September. Send SASE to Dawn Ronco, R.F.D., 1 Wadleigh Falls Rd., Newmarket, NH 03857.

MILDRED I. REID WRITERS CONFERENCE—Contoocook, NH. July. Write Mildred I. Reid, Writers Colony, Penacook Rd., Contoocook, NH 03229.

NEW JERSEY

ANNUAL FALL WRITERS CONFERENCE—Jamesburg, NJ. November. Write Linda Cajio, Dir. New Jersey Romance Writers, P.O. Box 107, Highstown, NJ 08520.

NEW MEXICO

SOUTHWEST WRITERS CONFERENCE—Albuquerque, NM. September. Write Eileen Stanton, 620 Arizona SE, Albuquerque, NM 87108.

741

New York

NYU SUMMER WRITERS CONFERENCE—New York University, Ny. July. Write Walter James Miller, Nyu School of Cont. Educ., 332 Shimkin Hall, New York, Ny 10003.

ANNUAL IWWG WOMEN'S SUMMER WRITING CONFERENCE—Skidmore College, Saratoga Springs, Ny. July. Write Hannelore Hahn, Exec. Dir., International Women's Writing Guide, P.O. Box 810, Gracie Station, Ny 10028.

CORNELL UNIVERSITY WRITERS PROGRAM—Ithaca, Ny. Summer. Write Dean Charles W. Jermy, Jr., Dir., B12L Ives Hall, Cornell Univ., Ithaca, Ny 14853.

HOFSTRA'S ANNUAL SUMMER WRITERS' CONFERENCE—Hofstra Univ., Ny. July. Write James J. Kolb, Hofstra Memorial Hall, Room 232, Hempstead, Ny 11550.

VASSAR INSTITUTE OF PUBLISHING AND WRITING—Vassar College, Ny. Write Barbara Lucas, Vassar College, Box 300, Poughkeepsie, Ny 12601.

SOUTHAMPTON WRITERS' CONFERENCE—Southampton, Ny. July. Write Frank Taylor, Summer Office, Southampton Campus, L.I.U., Southampton, Ny 11968.

CHAUTAUQUA INSTITUTION ANNUAL WRITER'S WORKSHOP—Chautauqua, New York. July and august. Write Christopher McMillan, Dir., Schools Office, Box 1098, Chautauqua Institution, Chautauqua, Ny 14722.

North Carolina

BLUE RIDGE CHRISTIAN WRITERS CONFERENCE—Black Mountain, NC. July. Write Yvonne Lehman, P.O. Box 188, Black Mountain, NC 28711.

DUKE UNIVERSITY WRITERS' CONFERENCE—Durham, NC. June. Write Joe Ashby Porter, Dir., The Bishop's House, Duke University, Durham, NC 27708.

Ohio

ANTIOCH WRITERS WORKSHOP—Yellow Springs, OH. July. Write Sandra Love, Dir., Antioch University, Yellow Springs, OH 45387.

ANNUAL SKYLINE WRITERS' CONFERENCE AND WORKSHOP—N. Royalton, OH. August. Write Lizabeth Braskey, P.O. Box 33343, North Royalton, OH 44133.

Oklahoma

ANNUAL WRITERS OF CHILDREN'S LITERATURE CONFERENCE—Lawton, Ok. June. Write Dr. G. E. Stanley, P.O. Box 16355, Cameron Univ. Station, Lawton, Ok 73505.

Oregon

HAYSTACK PROGRAM IN THE ARTS—Cannon Beach, OR. Summer. Write Steve Reischman, P.O. Box 1491, Portland State Univ., Portland, OR 97207.

PHILADELPHIA WRITERS' CONFERENCE—Philadelphia, Pa. June. Send Sase to Kitty T. Baker, Pennswood Village, C205, Newtown, Pa 18940.

ST. DAVIDS CHRISTIAN WRITERS' CONFERENCE—Eastern College, St. Davids, Pa. June. Write S. Eaby, Registrar, 1775 Eden Road, Lancaster, Pa 17601–3523.

TENNESSEE

CHRISTIAN WRITERS' GRAND OLE WORKSHOP—Belmont College, Nashville, TN. June. Write Dr. John W. Steen, 6511 Currywood Dr., Nashville, TN 37205.

TEXAS

SOUTHWEST WRITER'S CONFERENCE—Galveston, TX. September. Write Patricia Robinson, Coord., Univ. of Houston, Cont. Educ., 4800 Calhoun Rd., Houston, TX 77004.

ANNUAL WRITERS' CONFERENCE—Dallas, TX. September. Write Janet Harris, P.O. Box 830688, C.N.1.1., Richardson, TX 75083–0688

VERMONT

BENNINGTON WRITING WORKSHOPS—Bennington, Vt. July. Write Brian Swann, Bennington Writing Workshops, Box W, Bennington College, Bennington, Vt 05201.

ANNUAL BREAD LOAF WRITERS' CONFERENCE—Ripton, Vt. august. Write Bread Loaf Writers' Conference, Middlebury College, W. Middlebury, Vt 05753.

VIRGINIA

ANNUAL HIGHLAND SUMMER CONFERENCE—Radford, VA. June. Write Dr. Grace Toney Edwards, Dir., Box 5917, Radford Univ., Radford, VA 24142.

VIRGINIA COMMONWEALTH UNIVERSITY'S WRITERS' WORKSHOP—Richmond, VA. July. Write Susan Robbins, English Dept. VCU, Richmond, VA 23284–2005.

WASHINGTON

PORT TOWNSEND WRITERS' CONFERENCE—Fort Worden State Park, WA. July. Write Carol Jane Bangs, CENTRUM, Box 1158, Port Townsend, WA 98368.

PACIFIC NORTHWEST WRITERS CONFERENCE—Tacoma, WA. July. Write Carol McQuinn, Exec. Sec., PNWC, 17345 Sylvester Rd. S.W., Seattle, WA 98119.

SEATTLE PACIFIC CHRISTIAN WRITERS' CONFERENCE—Seattle, WA. June. Write Rose Reynoldson, Humanities Dept., Seattle, Pacific Univ., Seattle, WA 98119.

WISCONSIN

SCHOOL OF ARTS AT RHINELANDER—Rhinelander, Wi. July. Write Genevieve Lewis, admin. Coord., School of arts at Rhinelander, 610 Langdon St., Rm. 727, Madison, Wi 53703.

ANNUAL MIDWEST WRITERS' CONFERENCE—River Falls, Wi. June. Write Michael Norman, 310 North Hall, Univ. of Wisconsin, River Falls, Wi 54022.

WYOMING

WYOMING WRITERS WORKSHOP—Riverton, WY. June. Write Florence Burgess, 533 No. 3rd East, Riverton, WY 82501.

CANADA

MARITIME WRITERS' WORKSHOP—Fredericton, New Brunswick. July. Write Steven Peacock, c/o Dept. of Extension, Univ. of New Brunswick, P.O. Box 4400, Fredericton, Nb E3B 5A3, Canada.

SASKATCHEWAN SCHOOL OF ARTS—Fort Sam, Sask. Summer. Write Nik Burton, Writing School Dir., 2550 Broad St., Regina., Sask., Canada S4P 3V7.

INTERNATIONAL

FOR TELEVISION: A WORKSHOP IN LONDON—London, England. July. Write Lynn Kaufman, Marketing Dept., UC Extension, 2223 Fulton St., Berkeley, CA 94720.

STATE ARTS COUNCILS

State arts councils sponsor grants, fellowships, and other programs for writers. To be eligible for funding, a writer *must* be a resident of the state in which he is applying. For more information, write to the addresses below.

ALABAMA STATE COUNCIL ON THE ARTS
Albert B. Head, Exec. Director
One Dexter Ave.
Montgomery, AL 36130

ALASKA STATE COUNCIL ON THE ARTS
Christine D'Arcy, Director
619 Warehouse Ave., Suite 220
Anchorage, AK 99501–1682

ARIZONA COMMISSION ON THE ARTS
Shelley Cohn, Exec. Director
417 W. Roosevelt
Phoenix, AZ 85003

OFFICE OF ARKANSAS STATE ARTS AND HUMANITIES
Bev Lindsey, Exec. Director
The Heritage Center, Suite 200
225 E. Markham
Little Rock, AR 72201

CALIFORNIA ARTS COUNCIL
JoAnn Anglin, Public Information Officer
1901 Broadway, Suite A
Sacramento, CA 95818–2492

COLORADO COUNCIL ON THE ARTS AND HUMANITIES
Barbara Neal, Exec. Director
770 Pennsylvania St.
Denver, CO 80203

COMPAS: WRITERS IN THE SCHOOLS
Molly LaBerge, Exec. Director
Randolph Jennings, Director, Arts Education Programs
308 Landmark Center
75 W. 5th St.
St. Paul, MN 55102

CONNECTICUT COMMISSION ON THE ARTS
John Ostrout, Deputy Director
227 Lawrence St.
Hartford, CT 06106

DELAWARE STATE ARTS COUNCIL
Cecelia Fitzgibbon, Exec. Administrator
Carvel State Building
820 N. French St.
Wilmington, DE 19801

FLORIDA ARTS COUNCIL
Chris Doolin
Dept. of State
Div. of Cultural Affairs
The Capitol
Tallahassee, FL 32399–0250

GEORGIA COUNCIL FOR THE ARTS
2082 E. Exchange Place, Suite 100
Tucker, GA 30084

HAWAII STATE FOUNDATION ON CULTURE AND THE ARTS
Sarah M. Richards, Exec. Director
335 Merchant St., Rm. 202
Honolulu, HI 96813

IDAHO COMMISSION ON THE ARTS
304 W. State St.
Boise, ID 83720

ILLINOIS ARTS COUNCIL
Eliud Hernandez, Coordinator of Literature Program
State of Illinois Center
100 W. Randolph, Suite 10–500
Chicago, IL 60601

INDIANA ARTS COMMISSION
47 South Pennsylvania St.
Indianapolis, IN 46204

IOWA STATE ARTS COUNCIL
Julie Baily, Grants Officer
State Capitol Complex
Des Moines, IA 50319

KANSAS ARTS COMMISSION
700 Jackson, Suite 1004
Topeka, KS 66603–3714

KENTUCKY ARTS COUNCIL
Roger L. Paige, Director
Berry Hill, Louisville Rd.
Frankfort, KY 40601

LOUISIANA COUNCIL FOR MUSIC AND PERFORMING ARTS, INC.
Literature Program Associate
7524 St. Charles Ave.
New Orleans, LA 70118

MAINE ARTS COMMISSION
David Cadigan
State House, Station 25
Augusta, ME 04333

MARYLAND STATE ARTS COUNCIL
Linda Vlasak, Program Director
Artists-in-Education
15 W. Mulberry St.
Baltimore, MD 21201

MASSACHUSETTS COUNCIL ON THE ARTS AND HUMANITIES
Pat Dixon, Literature Coordinator
80 Boylston St., 10th Fl.
Boston, MA 02116

MICHIGAN COUNCIL FOR THE ARTS
Barbara K. Goldman, Exec. Director
1200 Sixth Ave.
Detroit, MI 48226–2461

MINNESOTA STATE ARTS BOARD
Karen Mueller
Artist Assistance Program Associate
432 Summit Ave.
St. Paul, MN 55102

MISSISSIPPI ARTS COMMISSION
Stephen Young, Program Administrator
301 N. Lamar St., Suite 400
Jackson, MS 39201

MISSOURI ARTS COUNCIL
Teresa Goettsch, Program Administrator for Literature
Wainwright Office Complex
111 N. 7th St., Suite 105
St. Louis, MO 63101–2188

MONTANA ARTS COUNCIL
Julia A. Cook, Director, Artist Services
New York Block
48 North Last Chance Gulch
Helena, MT 059620

NEBRASKA ARTS COUNCIL
Douglas D. Elliot, Assistant Director
1313 Farnam On-the-Mall
Omaha, NE 68102–1873

NEVADA STATE COUNCIL ON THE ARTS
William L. Fox, Exec. Director
329 Flint St.
Reno, NV 89501

NEW HAMPSHIRE STATE COUNCIL ON THE ARTS
Phenix Hall, 40 N. Main St.
Concord, NH 03301–4974

NEW JERSEY STATE COUNCIL ON THE ARTS
Ronnie B. Weyl, Publications Coordinator
4 North Broad Street CN-306
Trenton, NJ 08625

NEW MEXICO ARTS DIVISION
Artist-in-Residence Program
224 E. Palace Ave.
Santa Fe, NM 87501

NEW YORK STATE COUNCIL ON THE ARTS
Gregory Kolovakos, Director, Literature Program
915 Broadway
New York, NY 10010

NORTH CAROLINA ARTS COUNCIL
Don Linder, Literature Coordinator
Dept. of Cultural Resources
Raleigh, NC 27611

NORTH DAKOTA COUNCIL ON THE ARTS
Donna Evenson, Exec. Director
Black Building, Suite 606
Fargo, ND 58102

OHIO ARTS COUNCIL
727 E. Main St.
Columbus, OH 43205–1796

STATE ARTS COUNCIL OF OKLAHOMA
Ellen Jonsson, Assistant Director
Jim Thorpe Bldg., Rm. 640
Oklahoma City, OK 73105

OREGON ARTS COMMISSION
835 Summer St., NE
Salem, OR 97301

PENNSYLVANIA COUNCIL ON THE ARTS
Peter Carnahan, Literature and Theatre Programs

Kimberly Camp, Artists-in-Education Program
Room 216, Finance Bldg.
Harrisburg, PA 17120

RHODE ISLAND STATE COUNCIL ON THE ARTS
Iona B. Dobbins, Exec. Director
95 Cedar St., Suite 103
Providence, RI 02903

SOUTH CAROLINA ARTS COMMISSION
Steve Lewis, Director, Literary Arts Program
1800 Gervais St.
Columbus, SC 29201

SOUTH DAKOTA ARTS COUNCIL
108 W. 11th St.
Sioux Falls, SD 57102

TENNESSEE ARTS COMMISSION
320 Sixth Ave., N., Suite 100
Nashville, TN 37219

TEXAS COMMISSION ON THE ARTS
P.O. Box 13406, Capitol Station
Austin, TX 78711

UTAH ARTS COUNCIL
G. Barnes, Literary Arts Coordinator
617 East South Temple
Salt Lake City, UT 84102

VERMONT COUNCIL ON THE ARTS
Janet Ressler, Grants Coordinator
136 State St.
Montpelier, VT 05602

VIRGINIA COMMISSION FOR THE ARTS
Peggy J. Baggett, Exec. Director
James Monroe Bldg., 17th Floor
101 N. 14th St.
Richmond, VA 23219

WASHINGTON STATE ARTS COMMISSION
110 9th and Columbia Bldg., MS GH-11
Olympia, WA 98504–4111

WEST VIRGINIA DEPT. OF CULTURE AND HISTORY
Arts and Humanities Division
The Cultural Center, Capitol Complex
Charleston, WV 25305

WISCONSIN ARTS BOARD
Mr. Arley Curtz, Exec. Director
131 W. Wilson St., Suite 301
Madison, WI 53702

WYOMING COUNCIL ON THE ARTS
Joy Thompson, Exec. Director
2320 Capitol Ave.
Cheyenne, WY 82002

748

ORGANIZATIONS FOR WRITERS

THE ACADEMY OF AMERICAN POETS
117 E. 87th St.
New York, NY 10128
Mrs. Edward Chase, *President*

Founded in 1934 to "encourage, stimulate, and foster the art of poetry," the AAP sponsors a series of poetry readings in New York City and numerous annual awards. Membership is open to all: $45 annual fee includes subscription to the monthly newsletter, admission to sponsored readings, and free copies of prize book selection.

AMERICAN MEDICAL WRITERS ASSOCIATION
9650 Rockville Pike
Bethesda, MD 20814
Lillian Sablack, *Executive Director*

Members of this association are engaged in communication about medicine and its allied professions. Any person actively interested in or professionally associated with any medium of medical communication is eligible for membership. The annual dues are $55.

AMERICAN SOCIETY OF JOURNALISTS AND AUTHORS, INC.
1501 Broadway, Suite 1907
New York, NY 10036
Alexandria Cantor, *Executive Director*

A nationwide organization dedicated to promoting high standards of nonfiction writing through monthly meetings, annual writers' conferences, etc, ASJA offers extensive benefits and services including referral service, numerous discount services, and the opportunity to explore professional issues and concerns with other writers. Members also receive a monthly newsletter. Membership is open to professional free-lance writers of nonfiction; qualifications are judged by Membership Committee. Call or write for application details. Initiation fee: $50; annual dues $120. Phone number: (212)997-0947.

THE AUTHORS LEAGUE OF AMERICA, INC.
(The Authors Guild and The Dramatists Guild)
234 W. 44th St.
New York, NY 10036

The Authors League of America is a national organization of over 14,000 authors and dramatists, representing them on matters of joint concern, such as copyright, taxes, and freedom of expression. Membership in the league is restricted to authors and dramatists who are members of The Author Guild and The Dramatists Guild. Matters such as contract terms and subsidiary rights are in the province of the two guilds.

A writer who has published a book in the last seven years with an established publisher, or one who has published several magazine pieces with periodicals of general circulation within the last eighteen months, may be eligible for active voting membership in The Authors Guild. A new writer may be eligible for associate membership on application to the Membership Committee. Dues: $75 a year.

The Dramatists Guild is a professional association of playwrights, composers, and lyricists, established to protect dramatists' rights and to improve working conditions. Services include use of the Guild's contracts, business counseling, publications, and symposia in major cities. All theater writers (produced or not) are eligible for membership.

THE INTERNATIONAL SOCIETY OF DRAMATISTS
Box 1310
Miami, FL 33153

Open to playwrights, agents, producers, screenwriters, and others involved in the theater. Publishes *Dramatist's Bible,* a directory of script opportunities, and *The Globe,* a newsletter, with information and news of theaters across the country. Also provides free referral service for playwrights.

MYSTERY WRITERS OF AMERICA, INC.
236 W. 27th St.
New York, NY 10001
Priscilla Ridgway, *Executive Secretary*

The MWA exists for the purpose of raising the prestige of mystery and detective writing, and of defending the rights and increasing the income of all writers in the field of mystery, detection, and fact crime writing. Each year, the MWA presents the Edgar Allan Poe Awards for the best mystery writing in a variety of fields. The four classifications of membership are: *active* (open to any writer who has made a sale in the field of mystery, suspense, or crime writing); *associate* (for nonwriters allied to the mystery field); *corresponding* (writers living outside the U.S.); *affiliate* (for unpublished writers and mystery enthusiasts). Annual dues: $50; $25 for corresponding members.

NATIONAL ASSOCIATION OF SCIENCE WRITERS, INC.
P.O. Box 294
Greenlawn, NY 11740

The NASW promotes the dissemination of accurate information regarding science through all media, and conducts a varied program to increase the flow of news from scientists, to improve the quality of its presentation, and to communicate its meaning to the reading public.

Anyone who has been actively engaged in the dissemination of science information is eligible to apply for membership. Active members must be principally involved in reporting on science through newspapers, magazines, TV, or other media that reach the public directly. Associate members report on science through limited-circulation publications and other media. Annual dues: $45.

THE NATIONAL WRITERS CLUB
1450 S. Havana, Suite 620
Aurora, CO 80012
James Lee Young, *Executive Director*

New and established writers, poets, and playwrights throughout the U.S. and Canada may become members of The National Writers Club, a nonprofit representative organization. Membership includes bimonthly newsletter, *Authorship.* Dues: $50 annually, ($40 Associates), plus a $15 one-time initiation fee. Add $20 outside the USA for annual membership fee.

NATIONAL WRITERS UNION
13 Astor Pl. 7th Fl.
New York, NY 10003

The National Writers Union, a new labor organization dedicated to bringing about equitable payment and fair treatment of free-lance writers through collective action, has 2,600 members, including book authors, poets, free-lance journalists, and technical writers in eleven locals nationwide. The NWU offers its members contract and agent information, health insurance plans, press credentials, grievance handling, a union newspaper, and sponsors events across the country. Membership is open to writers who have published a book, play, three articles, five poems, one short story or an equivalent amount of newsletter, publicity, technical, commerical, government or institutional copy, or have written an equivalent amount of unpublished material and are actively seeking publication. Dues range from $50 to $120.

OUTDOOR WRITERS ASSOCIATION OF AMERICA, INC.
2017 Cato Ave., Suite 101
State College, PA 16801
Sylvia G. Bashline, *Executive Director*
The OWAA is a non-profit, international organization representing professional communicators who report and reflect upon America's diverse interests in the outdoors. Membership (by nomination only) includes a monthly publication, Outdoors Unlimited; annual conference, annual membership directory; contests. OWAA also provides scholarships to qualified students.

PEN AMERICAN CENTER
568 Broadway
New York, NY 10012
PEN American Center is one of 86 centers that comprise International PEN, a worldwide association of literary writers, offering conferences, writing programs, and financial and educational assistance. Membership is open to writers who have published two books of literary merit, as well as editors, agents, playwrights, and translators who meet specific standards. (Apply to nomination committee.) PEN sponsors annual awards and grants and publishes the quarterly *Pen Newsletter;* and the biennial directory, *Grants and Awards Available to American Writers.*

POETS AND WRITERS, INC.
201 W. 54th St.
New York, NY 10019
Elliot Figman, *Executive Director*
Poets & Writers, Inc. was founded in 1970 to foster the development of poets and fiction writers and to promote communication throughout the literary community. A non-membership organization, it offers a nationwide information center for writers; *Poets & Writers Magazine* and other publications; as well as sponsored readings and workshops.

THE POETRY SOCIETY OF AMERICA
15 Gramercy Park
New York, NY 10003
Elise Paschen, *Administrative Director*
Founded in 1910, The Poetry Society of America seeks through a variety of programs to gain a wider audience for American poetry. The Society offers 17 annual prizes for poetry (with many contests open to non-members as well as members), and sponsors workshops, free public poetry readings, and publications. Maintains the Van Vooris Library of American Poetry. Dues: $30 annually.

ROMANCE WRITERS OF AMERICA
5206 FM 1960 West, #208
Houston, TX 77069
Bobbie Stinson, *Staff Secretary*
The RWA is an international organization with over 80 local chapters

751

across the U.S. and Canada, open to any writer, published or unpublished, interested in the field of romantic fiction. Annual dues of $45, plus $15 application fee for new members; benefits include annual conference, contest, market information, and bimonthly newsmagazine, *Romance Writers' Report.*

SCIENCE FICTION WRITERS OF AMERICA
P.O. Box 4236
West Columbia, SC 29171
Peter D. Pautz, *Executive Secretary*

The purpose of the SFWA, a professional organization of science fiction and fantasy writers, is to foster and further the interests of writers of fantasy and science fiction. SFWA presents the Nebula Award annually for excellence in the field and publishes the *Bulletin* for its members.

Any writer who has sold a work of science fiction or fantasy is eligible for membership. Dues: $50 per year for active members, $35 for affiliates, plus $10 installation fee; send for application and information. The *Bulletin* is available to nonmembers for $12.50 (four issues).

SOCIETY FOR TECHNICAL COMMUNICATION
815 15th St., NW
Washington, D.C. 20005
William C. Stolgitis, *Executive Director*

The Society for Technical Communication is a professional organization dedicated to the advancement of the theory and practice of technical communication in all media. The almost 14,000 members in the U.S. and other countries include technical writers and editors, publishers, artists and draftsmen, researchers, educators, and audiovisual specialists.

SOCIETY OF AMERICAN TRAVEL WRITERS
1100 17th St., Suite 1000
Washington, D.C. 20036
Ken Fischer, *Administrative Coordinator*

The Society of American Travel Writers represents writers and other professionals who strive to provide travelers with accurate reports on destinations, facilities, and services.

Membership is by invitation. Active membership is limited to salaried travel writers and others employed as freelancers, who have a steady volume of published or distributed work about travel. Initiation fee for active members is $150, for associate members $300. Annual dues: $90 (active); $170 (associate).

SOCIETY OF CHILDREN'S BOOK WRITERS
P.O. Box 296
Mar Vista Station
Los Angeles, CA 90066
Lin Oliver, *Executive Director*

This national organization of authors, editors, publishers, illustrators, filmmakers, librarians, and educators offers a variety of services to people who write, illustrate for or share an interest in children's literature. Full memberships are open to those who have had at least one children's book or story published. Associate memberships are open to all those with an interest in children's literature. Yearly dues are $35.

WESTERN WRITERS OF AMERICA
1753 Victoria
Sheridan, WY 82801
Barbara Ketcham, *Secretary/Treasurer*

Writers of fiction, nonfiction, and poetry pertaining to the traditions, legends, development, and history of the American West may join the nonprofit Western Writers of America. Its chief purpose is to promote a more widespread distribution, readership, and appreciation of the West and its literature. Dues are $60 a year. Sponsors annual Spur Awards, Saddleman Award, and Medicine Pipe Bearer's Award.

WRITERS GUILD OF AMERICA, EAST, INC.
555 W. 57th St.
New York, NY 10019
Mona Mangan, *Executive Director*

WRITERS GUILD OF AMERICA, WEST, INC.
8455 Beverly Blvd.
Los Angeles, CA 90048
Brian Walton, *Executive Director*

The Writers Guild of America (East and West) represents writers in the fields of radio, television, and motion pictures.

In order to qualify for membership, a writer must fulfill current requirements for employment or sale of material in one the these three fields.

The basic dues are $25 a quarter for the Writers Guild West and $12.50 a quarter in the case of Writers Guild East. In addition, there are quarterly dues based on percentage of the member's earnings in any one of the fields over which the Guild has jurisdiction. The initiation fee is $1,000 for Writers Guild East and $1,500 for Writers Guild West. (Writers living east of the Mississippi join Writers Guild East, and those living west of the Mississippi, Writers Guild West.)

AMERICAN LITERARY AGENTS

Most literary agents do not usually accept new writers as clients. Since the agent's only income is a percentage (10% to 20%) of the amount he receives from the sales he makes for his clients, he must have as clients writers who are selling fairly regularly to good markets. Always query an agent first. Do not send any manuscripts until the agent has asked you to do so. The following list is only a partial selection of representative agents. Addresses that include zip codes in parentheses are located in New York City (the majority of agents in this list are in New York). More extensive lists of agents can be obtained by sending a self-addressed, stamped envelope to Society of Authors' Representatives, 39½ Washington Square S., New York, NY 10012 or Independent Literary Agents Assn., Inc., c/o Sanford J. Greenburger Associates, 55 Fifth Ave., New York, NY 10003.

BRET ADAMS, LTD. 448 W. 44th St. (10036)

JULIAN BACH LITERARY AGENCY, INC. 747 Third Ave. (10017)

LOUIS BERMAN The Little Theatre Bldg., 240 W. 44th St. (10036)

GEORGES BORCHARDT, INC. 136 E. 57th St. (10022)

BRANDT & BRANDT, LITERARY AGENTS, INC. 1501 Broadway (10036)

THE HELEN BRANN AGENCY, INC. 157 W. 57th St. (10019)

CURTIS BROWN, LTD. 10 Astor Pl. (10003)

COLLIER ASSOCIATES 2000 Flat Run Rd., Seaman, OH 45679

DON CONGDON ASSOCIATES, INC. 156 Fifth Ave., Suite 625 (10010)

JOAN DAVES 21 W. 26th St. (10010–1083)

ANITA DIAMANT 310 Madison Ave., #1508 (10017)

CANDIDA DONADIO & ASSOCIATES, INC. 231 W. 22nd St. (10011)

ANN ELMO AGENCY, INC. 60 E. 42nd St. (10165)

JOHN FARQUHARSON, LTD. 250 W. 57th St., Suite 1914 (10107)

THE FOX CHASE AGENCY, INC. Public Ledger Bldg. #930, Independence Square, Philadelphia, PA 19106

ROBERT A. FREEDMAN DRAMATIC AGENCY, INC. 1501 Broadway, #2310 (10036)

SAMUEL FRENCH, INC. 45 W. 25th St. (10010)

GRAHAM AGENCY 311 W. 43rd St. (10036)

BLANCHE C. GREGORY, INC. 2 Tudor City Place (10017)

JOHN W. HAWKINS & ASSOCIATES, INC. (FORMERLY *PAUL R. REYNOLDS, INC.*) 71 W. 23rd St. (10010)

INTERNATIONAL CREATIVE MANAGEMENT, INC. 40 W. 57th St. (10019)

JCA LITERARY AGENCY, INC. 242 W. 27th St., #4A (10001)

KIDDE, HOYT & PICARD 335 E. 51st St. (10022)

KNOX BURGER ASSOCIATES, LTD. 39½ Washington Square S. (10012)

LUCY KROLL AGENCY 390 West End Ave. (10024)

THE LANTZ OFFICE 888 Seventh Ave. (10106)

LESCHER & LESCHER, LTD. 67 Irving Pl. (10003)

ELLEN LEVINE LITERARY AGENCY 432 Park Ave. S., #1205 (10016)

ELIZABETH MARTON 96 Fifth Ave. (10011)

HAROLD MATSON COMPANY, INC. 276 Fifth Ave. (10001)

GERARD MCCAULEY AGENCY, INC. P.O. Box AE, Katonah, NY 10536

MCINTOSH & OTIS, INC. 310 Madison Ave. (10017)

HELEN MERRILL, LTD. 435 W. 23rd St., #1A (10011)

WILLIAM MORRIS AGENCY, INC. 1350 Avenue of the Americas (10019)

HAROLD OBER ASSOCIATES, INC. 40 E. 49th St. (10017)

754

FIFI OSCARD ASSOCIATES, INC. 19 W. 44th St. (10036)

PINDER LANE PRODUCTIONS, LTD. 159 W. 53rd St. (10019)

RAINES & RAINES 71 Park Ave. (10016)

FLORA ROBERTS, INC. Penthouse A, 157 W. 57th St. (10019)

MARIE RODELL/FRANCES COLLIN LITERARY AGENCY 110 W. 40th St., Suite 2004 (10018)

ROSENSTONE/WENDER 3 E. 48th St. (10017)

RUSSEL & VOLKENING, INC. 50 W. 29th St. (10001)

JOHN SCHAFFNER ASSOCIATES, INC. 264 Fifth Ave. (10001)

SUSAN SCHULMAN AGENCY 454 W. 44th St. (10036)

THE SHUKAT COMPANY, LTD. 340 W. 55th St., #1A (10019)

PHILIP G. SPITZER LITERARY AGENCY 788 Ninth Ave. (10019)

STERLING LORD LITERISTIC, INC. 1 Madison Ave. (10010)

ROSLYN TARG LITERARY AGENCY, INC. 105 W. 13th St., #15E (10011)

WALLACE & SHEIL AGENCY, INC. 177 E. 70th St. (10021)

THE WENDY WEIL AGENCY, INC. 747 Third Ave. (10017)

MARY YOST ASSOCIATES, INC. 59 E. 54th St., #72 (10022)

INDEX TO MARKETS